ROSE ELLIOT'S
New Complete Vegetarian

ROSE ELLIOT'S
New Complete Vegetarian

STERLING

New York / London
www.sterlingpublishing.com

Cook's notes

IMPORTANT NOTE ABOUT OVEN TEMPERATURES Ovens need to be preheated to the specified temperature. All the temperatures in this book are based on a conventional oven. If you're using a fan-assisted oven, follow the manufacturer's instructions for adjusting the temperature — this usually means reducing it by 65°F (20°C).

Butter The type of butter is specified only where it is critical, otherwise use salted or unsalted.

Cheese More and more cheeses are vegetarian, but there are some important ones that are not as they contain rennet (an animal product). When buying cheese, always check that it's vegetarian or choose a vegetarian alternative — try Pecorino instead of Parmesan, Emmental instead of Gruyère, Danish Blue (or other blue cheeses marked "vegetarian") instead of Roquefort.

Eggs They are medium size unless specified otherwise. I always use free-range organic eggs. Pregnant women, the elderly or frail, and very young children need to avoid eating recipes containing raw eggs.

Stock powder, cubes, and concentrate There are some good ones available. Check the label and choose one containing natural ingredients.

Soy sauce Choose the most natural type you can find; traditionally brewed, without additives such as coloring or caramel. Dark Kikkoman (with the red top) is a reliable brand that's widely available, but try *shoyu* and wheat-free *tamari*; both are available from large supermarkets and health shops.

Wine and fortified wine As with cheese, wine is often not vegetarian or vegan so check the label (or ask the wine merchant for advice) when buying. When choosing sherry, pick the "fino" variety, as this is vegetarian, and with port, buy the "crusted" variety, named because of the sediment or "crust" that forms in the bottle.

The Vegetarian Society, the Vegan Society, and VIVA! (Vegetarian International Voice for Animals) are all excellent sources for information on products and ethical issues.

www.roseelliot.com

STERLING and the distinctive Sterling logo are registered trademarks of Sterling Publishing Co., Inc.

10 9 8 7 6 5 4 3 2 1

Published 2010 by Sterling Publishing Co., Inc. 387 Park Avenue South, New York, NY 10016 by arrangement with HarperCollins Publishers Ltd.
Text © Rose Elliot, 1985 and 2010
Photographs © Kate Whitaker, 2010
Illustrations © Vana Haggerty and Ken Lewis, 1985
Distributed in Canada by Sterling Publishing, c/o Canadian Manda Group, 165 Dufferin Street, Toronto, Canada M6K 3H6

Printed in China
All rights reserved

Rose Elliot asserts her moral right to be identified as the author of this work.

Sterling ISBN 978-1-4027-7895-7

For information about custom editions, special sales, premium and corporate purchases, please contact Sterling Special Sales Department at 800-805-5489 or specialsales@sterlingpublishing.com

Contents

Introduction

When I wrote my *Complete Vegetarian Cookbook* back in 1985, vegetarian and vegan food were not as popular or as mainstream as they are today. Nowadays, I look around my local supermarket and there is a wealth of fabulous fresh produce available. I can enjoy ingredients from around the world and if I am cooking for someone with a dietary requirement, there are loads of alternatives to pick from. In fact, following a healthy, nutritious, and varied diet has never been easier. So, I hope my *New Complete Vegetarian* recipe book will help you make the most of the glorious range of ingredients we can all enjoy.

In this book you'll find hundreds of delicious, easy-to-make vegetarian and vegan recipes. Here you'll find my classic recipes that I turn to again and again, and often get asked for, plus many new ones to enjoy. You'll also find information on cooking and preparing vegetables, fruits, beans and nuts, plus symbols for those recipes that are vegan and those that can be frozen. Many dishes include variations, so if you don't like a particular ingredient, you can often replace it with something else. In fact, I would always encourage you to try out new dishes and have fun making the recipes your own.

So, if you're one of my dear loyal readers from the past, I hope you will love this new edition as much as you did the first one; and if this is your first encounter with my *Complete Vegetarian Cookbook*, it's so good to have you here and I hope you will find it an inspiring and practical friend in the kitchen. Whether you're an old friend or a new one, I wish you many wonderful meals and health and happiness in your life and on your vegetarian journey.

Rose x

Soups

Soup is one of the most satisfying things to make and eat, and it's so varied and adaptable. It can be hot or chilled, smooth or chunky, thick or delicately light. Truly, there is a soup for all tastes and seasons.

In this chapter you'll find a mouth-watering variety of soups, from broths such as miso soup to thick and chunky soups like lentil with garlic and cumin (see pages 24 and 21). There are plenty of quick-to-make soups, plus elegant ones for entertaining. You'll also find a recipe for vegetarian stock. While using your own stock can give a beautiful flavor, it's also fine to use bouillon powder, concentrate, or cubes. You can also get excellent results using just water; I often do this when I want the pure taste of a particular vegetable to really sing through.

Many homemade soups freeze excellently, and you'll find the freezer symbol ❄ against those suitable for this; just remember to allow time — several hours at room temperature or overnight — for the soup to defrost.

Easy vegetable stock v

Although you can now buy very acceptable vegetarian stock powder, which I often use for speed, nothing beats a good home-made stock. It's easy to make — 10 minutes of simple preparation followed by an hour of slow simmering and you're done. It keeps perfectly for a week in the fridge or for 3–6 months in the freezer. This is a good basic stock but you can also jazz it up by adding a few cloves of garlic, some peppercorns and any other herbs you fancy, such as bay leaves or thyme.

MAKES ABOUT 1 QUART (1.2 LITERS) ❄
1 onion, roughly sliced
1 stalk of celery, roughly chopped
1 large carrot, roughly chopped
1 potato, roughly chopped
a few sprigs of parsley
2 quarts water

Put the vegetables and parsley into a large saucepan and add the water.

Bring to the boil, then turn the heat down, cover and leave to simmer for 40 minutes.

Strain through a sieve. Cool, then keep in the fridge or freezer in suitable-sized containers.

Tip
Toss the vegetables in 1–2 tablespoons of olive oil and roast for 20–30 minutes at 400°F (200°C) before proceeding, for a fuller flavor.

Artichoke soup

Smooth and creamy, this slips down your throat like velvet. Jerusalem artichokes are quite easy to peel if you use a potato peeler and are fairly ruthless about cutting off the little lumps. Put them into a bowl of cold water as they're done, to preserve their color.

SERVES 6 ❄
2 tbsp butter
1 onion, chopped
2lb (900g) Jerusalem artichokes, peeled and cut into even-sized chunks
1 quart light vegetable stock or water
5fl oz (150ml) ½ and ½ (optional)
1¼ cups milk
sea salt
freshly ground black pepper
freshly grated nutmeg
2 tbsp chopped fresh chives or flat-leaf parsley, to garnish

Melt the butter in a large saucepan and add the onion. Cover the pan and fry gently for 5–7 minutes or until fairly soft but not browned, then add the artichokes, cover the pan again and cook for a further 2–3 minutes, stirring often.

Pour in the stock or water, bring to the boil, then turn the heat down, cover and leave to simmer for about 20 minutes or until the artichokes are soft.

Blend the soup very well, and pass it through a sieve if you want it really smooth, then add the ½ and ½ if you're using it, and enough milk to make the soup the consistency you like.

Season to taste with salt, pepper and freshly grated nutmeg. Reheat, and serve with some chopped chives or parsley sprinkled on top.

VARIATION
Artichoke soup with truffle oil

Truffle oil adds a deep, earthy flavor to this beautiful soup. Make as described and season with salt and pepper, but omitting the nutmeg and herbs. Pour into warm bowls and swirl each with a good teaspoon of truffle oil.

Asparagus soup

One of my favorite summer soups, this makes a wonderful starter for a special occasion and can also be served chilled in hot weather.

SERVES 4 ❄

1 onion, chopped
1 potato (about 5oz (150g), peeled and cubed
1 tbsp olive oil
1lb 2oz (500g) asparagus, washed
about 3½ cups (1 liter) water
1 tsp vegetable bouillon powder or a stock cube
¼ cup ½ and ½
salt and freshly ground black pepper

In a large covered saucepan, fry the onion and potato cubes in the olive oil over a gentle heat. Fry for a few minutes, stirring periodically.

Break the tips off the asparagus stems by bending them until they snap. Place the tips to one side. Cut the stems into 1 in (2cm) pieces and add to the pan, along with half the water and the vegetable bouillon. Bring to the boil, then leave to simmer gently for about 30 minutes, until the asparagus is tender.

Meanwhile, heat the remaining water in another pan and cook the asparagus tips until tender, about 7 minutes. Drain, reserving the cooking water.

Purée the soup thoroughly and, for an extra-smooth texture, pour it through a sieve, back into the rinsed-out saucepan. Add the cooked asparagus tips together with their cooking water and the ½ and ½. Season well with salt and pepper.

Reheat gently before serving; don't let it boil.

Chilled avocado soup

This beautiful pale green, silky soup is very easy to make. Use avocados that are perfectly ripe but not overly so; they're just right when they feel slightly soft all over when you squeeze them gently in the palm of your hand. Avoid making this soup in advance; it just needs time to chill in the fridge so that it keeps its bright color.

SERVES 6

2 large ripe avocados
1 tbsp lemon juice
3 cups ice-cold skimmed milk
salt and freshly ground black pepper
2 tbsp chopped fresh chives, to garnish

Halve, stone and peel the avocados and cut them into rough chunks.

Put the chunks into a blender or food processor with the lemon juice and milk and blend very thoroughly until the mixture is silky smooth.

Taste and season well with salt and pepper. Chill in the fridge, with the serving bowls too, if there's room.

To serve, check the seasoning, as chilling can dull the flavor, then ladle the soup into the bowls and scatter some bright green chopped chives on top.

Red beet soup

One of my all-time favorite soups, this is a stunning deep ruby-red soup that looks mouth-watering with its white topping of yogurt or sour cream. It's wonderful hot, but I particularly like to make it from new-season red beet in the summer and serve it chilled. I think you'll have gathered by now that I'm rather partial to chilled soup!

SERVES 4 ❄

1 onion, chopped
1 tbsp olive oil
1 large potato peeled and diced
1 tbsp olive oil
1lb (450g) cooked fresh red beets (not in vinegar), peeled and diced
1 quart stock or water
1 tsp vegetable bouillon powder, stock cube or concentrate
salt and freshly ground black pepper
1 tbsp lemon juice
½ tsp grated lemon rind

TO GARNISH

thick natural Greek yogurt, sour cream or crème fraîche
coarsely ground black pepper

Fry the onion gently in the oil in a fairly large saucepan, with a lid on the pan, for about 5 minutes, being careful not to let it brown. Add the potato, stir, then cover and cook gently for about 5 minutes more.

Add the beets and stir in the stock or water and the bouillon powder, stock cube or concentrate.

Bring to a boil then cover and leave to simmer for about 20 minutes or until the potatoes are soft.

Blend the soup, then return it to the saucepan and flavor with salt, pepper and the lemon juice and just a touch of the grated rind. Reheat gently and serve topped with a spoonful of yogurt, sour cream or crème fraîche and a scattering of coarsely ground black pepper.

Borscht

You could serve this soup with the little curd cheese tarts on page 272 but it's also great accompanied by chunks of rye or wholegrain bread and goat cheese.

SERVES 4 ❄

2 tbsp olive oil
2 large onions, chopped
2 large carrots, diced
2 stalks of celery, sliced
4oz (125g) cabbage, chopped
2 tbsp olive oil
3½ cups water or vegetable stock
14oz can chopped tomatoes
1lb (450g) cooked red beets (not in vinegar), peeled and diced
salt and freshly ground black pepper
sugar

TO GARNISH
5fl oz (150ml) sour cream or thick natural yogurt (optional)
chopped fresh dill or chives (optional)

Heat the oil in a large saucepan, add the onions, carrots, celery and cabbage, stir them in the oil so they glisten, then fry over a gentle heat for about 10 minutes, with the occasional stir.

Pour in the water or vegetable stock and the tomatoes, bring to a boil, cover and leave to simmer for about 20 minutes or until all the vegetables are tender.

Add the beets to the soup and season well with salt, pepper and a little sugar. Bring to the boil again and simmer gently for 3–4 minutes.

Serve the borscht as it is or blend it a little. If you like, top with sour cream or yogurt and a scattering of **chopped dill or chives.**

Creamy butter bean soup with croûtons

This soup has a smooth, creamy texture that is complemented perfectly by its crunchy topping of golden-brown croûtons.

SERVES 4 ❄

4oz (125g) dried butter beans, soaked (see pages 176–7)
2 tbsp olive oil
1 large onion, chopped
1 potato, peeled and diced
2 carrots, diced
2 stalks of celery, chopped
1 quart water or unsalted stock
1 bouquet garni — a couple of sprigs of parsley, a sprig of thyme and a bay leaf tied together
5fl oz (150ml) ½ and ½ (optional)
salt and freshly ground black pepper
freshly grated nutmeg
a few croûtons or cubes of crispy wholegrain toast, to serve

Drain and rinse the beans.

Heat the oil in a large saucepan, add the vegetables and sauté for 7–8 minutes without browning, then add the butter beans, water or stock and the bouquet garni. Simmer gently, half covered, for about 1½ hours or until the butter beans are tender.

Remove the herbs and blend the soup (with the cream, if using). Season well with salt, pepper and nutmeg to taste.

Reheat gently — don't let the soup boil — and scatter over the crunchy golden croûtons or crisp wholegrain toast cubes at the last moment.

Butter bean and tomato soup v

I love to use dried butter beans for this, though I've given the option of canned, as dried beans are such a joy. You can buy them for practically nothing, keep them in the cupboard until you need them, then work some kitchen alchemy just by gently soaking and boiling, to produce a meal that's deeply satisfying and full of natural goodness. If you are cooking your own beans, use the cooking water for this soup, with some vegetable bouillon powder for extra flavor.

SERVES 4 ❄

2 tbsp olive oil
2 large onions, chopped
8oz (225g) dried butter beans, soaked, cooked until tender and drained, or 2 x 14oz can butter beans, drained and rinsed
3 cups water or unsalted vegetable stock (see page 11)
1 bay leaf
2 x 14oz cans chopped tomatoes
salt and freshly ground black pepper
sugar (optional)
chopped fresh flat-leaf parsley, to garnish

Heat the olive oil in a large pan, add the onions and fry over a gentle heat for about 10 minutes, until softened, but not browned.

Add the cooked butter beans, water or stock, bay leaf and tomatoes. Bring to a boil and simmer gently for 10—15 minutes.

Taste and season with salt, pepper and a little sugar if you think it needs it.

Blend a bit with a hand blender or leave the soup as it is. Serve sprinkled with the parsley.

Roasted butternut squash soup with chili oil v

This is so easy to make — it's pretty much a case of "roast and whiz". The butternut squash is cooked in the oven while you leisurely fry an onion and some garlic, then all you have to do is purée it with some vegetable stock, and there's your beautiful golden soup.

SERVES 4—6 ❄

1 butternut squash
2 tbsp olive oil, plus extra for brushing
1 onion, chopped
1 large garlic clove, crushed
5 cups (1.5 liters) vegetable stock
salt and freshly ground black pepper
4—6 tsp chili oil, to serve

Heat the oven to 375°F (190°C)

Cut the butternut squash in half lengthwise. You might find it easier to cut it in half widthways, then cut each of these pieces in half. It doesn't really matter how you do it, and there's no need to remove the seeds at this point.

Put the pieces of squash in a roasting pan, brush the cut surfaces with oil and bake for about 1 hour, or until the squash is soft.

While the squash is roasting, heat the olive oil in a saucepan over a gentle heat, add the onion, cover and cook gently for about 8 minutes. Add the garlic and cook for a further 2 minutes.

Scoop out the flesh of the butternut squash, discarding the seeds. Pull off and discard the skin — it will come away easily. Purée the flesh and their juices, along with the onion and garlic.

Put the purée into a pan and stir in enough vegetable stock to make a consistency that's pleasing to you. Season to taste with salt and pepper. Gently heat through, then serve with a swirl of chili oil on top of each bowl.

VARIATION

Roasted butternut squash with goat cheese toasts

Make the soup as described. While it's heating through, make the goat cheese toasts. Allow half a large slice of bread per serving. Toast the bread then top the toast with mashed soft-rind goat cheese and brown under a hot broiler. Cut each piece into small squares and put these on top of the soup just before serving.

Carrot and thyme soup v

This is a light and refreshing soup that's almost fat-free. It's thin and smooth, so you can sip it from a large mug as you warm your hands and eat a sandwich. If you think you might prefer it a bit thicker, start with less water; you can always add more. I like this soup so much that I often make double this amount! You really do need high-quality bouillon powder for this, both for the flavor and the extra body that it gives.

SERVES 4 ❄

1 onion, chopped
2 stalks of celery, sliced
3 carrots, sliced
1 small potato (about 4oz (125g)), peeled and diced
1 tsp dried thyme
1 quart water
4 tsp high-quality vegetable bouillon powder
salt and freshly ground black pepper
chopped fresh flat-leaf parsley (optional), to garnish

Put the onion, celery, carrots and potato into a large saucepan with the thyme, water and vegetable bouillon and bring to the boil.

Cover and simmer for 25–30 minutes or until the vegetables are very tender.

Blend or process until very smooth. Season with salt and pepper to taste (you won't need much salt because the bouillon powder is quite salty).

Serve in mugs, or in warm bowls, with some chopped parsley on top.

VARIATIONS

Carrot and coriander soup v

You can buy cartons of this everywhere but it's so easy and economical to make your own. Simply follow the main recipe but using 1 teaspoon of crushed coriander seeds instead of the thyme. Crush your own seeds with a pestle and mortar and enjoy their sweet orangey aroma, or use the ready-ground type for speed. Add a small bunch of chopped fresh coriander after blending.

Carrot and ginger soup v

Use 2–3 teaspoons of grated fresh root ginger instead of the thyme for this soup, which is warming, fragrant and uplifting, but not spicy hot.

Carrot and lemon soup v

For this refreshing soup, just add 1 teaspoon of finely grated lemon rind and 2 teaspoons of juice after cooking; taste and add a little more if you like.

Cauliflower soup with almonds

Cauliflower makes a beautiful creamy soup with a delicate flavor. Try it with the herb bread, quick and easy focaccia or hot garlic bread (see pages 377, 375 and 55).

SERVES 4 ❄

1 tbsp butter
1 tbsp olive oil
1 onion, chopped
1 potato (about 5oz (150g)
½ fairly small cauliflower (about 8oz (225g)), broken into florets
1 quart light vegetable stock or water
1 tsp vegetable bouillon powder
5fl oz (150ml) ½ and ½ (optional)
salt and freshly ground black pepper
a pinch or two of freshly grated nutmeg
2 tbsp sliced almonds, toasted (see page 139) to garnish

Melt the butter with the olive oil in a large saucepan. Add the onion and fry for 5–7 minutes, covered, until it is beginning to soften but not brown.

Add the potato and cauliflower to the pan and cook for an additional 2–3 minutes, stirring often. Be careful not to let them brown, as this will spoil the delicate flavor.

Pour in the stock or water and add the bouillon powder, bring to a boil, cover and leave to simmer over a gentle heat for about 20 minutes — until the vegetables are soft.

Blend until very smooth and velvety. Stir in the ½ and ½, if you're using it, and season well with salt and plenty of freshly ground pepper and grated nutmeg. Reheat, serve in warm bowls, and scatter some crunchy golden sliced almonds over.

Celery soup with lovage

The flavor of lovage is often likened to that of celery. It's more pungent and aromatic, but goes well with celery and together they make a lovely soup. In a perfect world, where the seasons are observed in cooking, this would be made with the first of the English celery and the last of the lovage from the garden — it's a perfect soup for a crisp autumn day. If you can't get hold of any lovage, use some finely chopped celery leaves instead.

SERVES 4 ❄

2 tbsp olive oil
1 onion, chopped
outside stalks from 1 head of celery (about 1 lb (450g) in total), sliced
8oz (225g) potatoes, peeled and cut into even-sized chunks
1 quart (1.2 liters) light vegetable stock or water and 1 tsp vegetable bouillon powder
2 tbsp chopped fresh lovage
5fl oz (150ml) ½ and ½ (optional)
salt and freshly ground black pepper

Heat the oil in a large saucepan, add the onion and fry for 5–7 minutes until soft but not browned. Add the celery and potatoes and cook for an additional 2–3 minutes, stirring often.

Pour in the stock or water and add the bouillon powder. Bring to a boil, cover and simmer for about 30 minutes until the vegetables are very soft.

Blend well, but stop when it's the consistency you like. Stir in the lovage, ½ and ½ (if using) and a good seasoning of salt and pepper. Reheat gently before serving.

Celery and tomato soup V

This is a quick soup with a refreshing flavor and a chunky texture. If you make it in a pressure cooker it can be on the table in less than 30 minutes from start to finish.

SERVES 4

3 onions, chopped
outside stalks from 1 head of celery, chopped
1 tbsp olive oil
2 garlic cloves, crushed
14oz can chopped tomatoes
2 cups (575ml) water or vegetable stock
salt, sugar and freshly ground black pepper
a squeeze of lemon juice

Fry the onions and celery together in the oil without browning for 5–10 minutes.

Add the garlic, tomatoes and water or stock, and simmer for a good 30 minutes or until the celery is meltingly tender.

Taste and season with salt, pepper, sugar and a squeeze of lemon juice to taste.

Chilled cherry soup

No one finds it odd to start a meal with melon and a fruit soup is simply taking this a stage further! This black cherry soup looks so delicious with its topping of sour cream or yogurt that I don't think you'll have much trouble persuading people to try it. Plump, perfectly ripe, deep-red fresh cherries are best eaten exactly as they are, without any adornment, so for this soup I use frozen, pitted black cherries.

SERVES 6

1lb (450g) frozen, pitted black cherries
3 cups water (850ml)
2 tbsp arrowroot or cornstarch
superfine sugar, to taste
5fl oz (150ml) dry red wine
a little lemon juice (optional)
5fl oz (150ml) sour cream, to garnish

Put the cherries into a saucepan with the water, bring to a boil and simmer gently until tender. This only takes a few minutes.

Mix the arrowroot with a little cold water to make a smooth paste, then stir a ladleful of the hot cherry liquid into the arrowroot mixture, mix and add it to the saucepan. Simmer for 2–3 minutes or until slightly thickened.

Remove from the heat and leave to cool, then add 3–4 tbsp of sugar to make it slightly sweet but refreshing. Chill in the fridge.

Before serving, taste and add a little more sugar if necessary or a drop or two of lemon juice to sharpen the flavor slightly. Top each bowlful with a spoonful of sour cream.

Spanish chickpea soup with garlic and mint v

I recommend using dried rather than canned chickpeas for this Spanish soup because the flavor depends on the quality of the few ingredients: chickpeas, fresh herbs, garlic, and olive oil. The oil is used both in the soup and to fry the crispy croûtons.

SERVES 4 ❄

8oz (225g) dried chickpeas (high-quality, Spanish variety if possible)
2 garlic cloves, crushed
a handful of fresh mint, stems removed
a small handful of parsley, stalks removed
6 tbsp olive oil
salt and freshly ground black pepper
2 large slices of bread, cut into cubes

Soak the chickpeas overnight in plenty of water, then drain, place in a large saucepan, cover generously with fresh water and simmer for about 1½ hours or until really tender. The time can vary, so go on cooking them until you can crush one easily between your fingers.

Drain the chickpeas and reserve the cooking liquid. Blend or process the chickpeas with 3 cups (850ml) of their liquid (made up with extra water if necessary), the garlic, mint, parsley and half the olive oil until very smooth.

Season with salt and freshly ground black pepper and reheat gently. While this is happening, fry the bread cubes in the remaining olive oil until golden brown.

Serve the croûtons in a bowl for people to add immediately before eating.

Chilled creamy cucumber soup

In contrast to the next recipe, this is a cooked cucumber soup. It's light, delicate and very refreshing.

SERVES 4 ❄

1 large cucumber, peeled and diced
1 small onion or shallot, chopped
3 cups (850ml) vegetable stock
2-3 sprigs of fresh mint
2 tsp arrowroot or cornstarch
¼ cup heavy cream
salt and freshly ground black pepper
sprigs of fresh mint, to garnish

Put the cucumber and chopped onion or shallot into a large saucepan with the stock and sprigs of mint. Bring to a boil and cover, simmering for 10–15 minutes.

Purée the soup thoroughly and return to the pan. Blend the arrowroot or cornstarch with the cream and stir into the soup.

Bring to a boil, stirring all the time, and cook for a few seconds until thickened slightly. (If you're using arrowroot, don't overcook it, because that will prevent the soup from thickening.) Season to taste.

Chill thoroughly, then serve in chilled bowls with a sprig of mint on top of each.

Bulgarian chilled cucumber soup with walnuts

Yogurt, cucumber, walnuts and dill may sound like rather a strange mixture but it works, I promise you. The choice of yogurt is up to you; thick strained Greek yogurt gives the richest result but you could use whole milk or low-fat yogurt if you want a lighter soup.

SERVES 4

1 large cucumber, peeled and cut into rough chunks
1 garlic clove, crushed
15fl oz (425ml) natural yogurt
1oz (25g) shelled walnut pieces
salt and freshly ground black pepper
2 tbsp chopped fresh dill, to garnish

Blend the cucumber with the garlic, yogurt, walnuts, about half a teaspoon of salt and a grinding of pepper, to a fairly smooth purée.

Taste and add some more salt and pepper if you think it needs it, then pour into a bowl and chill thoroughly.

Serve in chilled bowls sprinkled with the chopped dill.

Dal soup v

This light, refreshing soup is perfect for serving before a rice and curry meal. You can use either yellow split peas or split red lentils.

SERVES 4 ❄

6oz (175g) yellow split peas or split red lentils
1 large onion, chopped
2 tbsp rapeseed oil
1 garlic clove, crushed
1 tsp turmeric
2 tsp grated fresh root ginger
1 bay leaf
3½ cups (1 liter) water
juice of ½ lemon
salt and freshly ground black pepper
4 slices of lemon, to garnish

Cover the split peas or split red lentils with water and leave them to soak for a few hours, then drain and rinse.

Fry the onion in the oil in a large saucepan for 5 minutes, then add the garlic, turmeric, ginger and bay leaf and fry for an additional 5 minutes.

Stir in the split peas or lentils and the water. Bring to a boil, then cover and simmer gently for about 30 minutes or until the lentils or split peas are soft.

Remove the bay leaf and blend the soup. Add enough of the lemon juice to sharpen the soup and bring out the flavor. Season with salt and pepper.

Reheat gently and serve each bowl with a slice of lemon floating on top.

Fasolada v

This Greek bean soup is very filling and comforting, especially if you serve it with some country-style bread.

SERVES 4 ❄

6 tbsp olive oil
1 large onion, chopped
2 stalks of celery, sliced
2 carrots, chopped
1 garlic clove, crushed
8oz (225g) dried white beans, soaked (see pages 176—7), rinsed and drained
3½ cups (1 liter) unsalted vegetable stock (see page 11) or water
1 tbsp tomato purée
2 tbsp chopped fresh parsley
salt and freshly ground black pepper
squeeze of lemon juice

Heat the oil in a large saucepan and fry the onion, celery, carrots and garlic for 5 minutes, stirring from time to time to prevent them from sticking.

Add the drained beans, stock or water, tomato purée and parsley, and bring to a boil. Cover, reduce the heat and leave to simmer gently for about 1¼ hours or until the beans are tender. Season with salt and pepper to taste, and a little lemon juice.

Serve with lots of country-style bread. If there's any soup left over, it's even better the next day.

Flageolet soup

This soup makes the most of the delicate flavor of pale green flageolet beans, and the green leek helps to accentuate their natural green color. Use dried not canned beans for this soup, to get the best results.

SERVES 4 ❄

4oz (125g) flageolet or navy beans, soaked overnight
1 small onion, chopped
1 leek, sliced
2 tbsp (25g) butter
3 cups (850ml) unsalted vegetable stock (see page 11) or water
¼ cup heavy cream
1 tbsp chopped fresh parsley, plus extra to garnish
salt and freshly ground black pepper
fresh flat-leaf parsley, to garnish

Rinse and drain the beans.

Fry the onion and leek gently in the butter in a large saucepan, covered, for about 10 minutes.

Add the beans to the onion and leek, together with the stock or water. Simmer gently for about 1 hour or until the beans are tender.

Blend the soup thoroughly, with the cream and parsley, until very smooth. Season with salt and freshly ground black pepper.

Reheat gently without boiling, then scatter some fresh parsley over each bowlful before serving.

Gazpacho v

This unashamedly easy version of gazpacho is perfect for hot, lazy days. If you keep a can of tomatoes in the fridge in the summer you can rustle it up in a matter of minutes. It's nice served with some country-style bread or crunchy croûtons.

SERVES 6

1 large onion, cut into rough chunks
2 large garlic cloves, crushed
2 x 14oz cans chopped tomatoes in juice
¼ cup olive oil
2 tsp red wine vinegar
salt and freshly ground black pepper

TO SERVE

about 4in (10cm) cucumber, diced
1 small green or red pepper, seeded and finely chopped
1 tbsp chopped fresh chives
1 tbsp chopped fresh mint
croûtons (made by frying cubes of 3 slices of bread in olive oil and cutting into small dice)

Purée the onion, garlic and tomatoes in a blender or food processor. Stir in the olive oil, vinegar, some salt and a grinding of pepper and blend again.

Pour into a bowl or pitcher and chill.

Just before serving, stir the cucumber, pepper and herbs into the soup, then pour into individual bowls and pass the croûtons separately.

Hot and sour soup v

I've experimented with many versions of this soup to get it just right, and this one, with its mixture of fresh ingredients and spices preserved in sunflower oil, is my favorite. I love it; it's light, but the heat of the chili and the balance of flavors make it very satisfying and uplifting. It's perfect before an Asian meal, such as chili-braised tofu steaks or salt and pepper tofu (see pages 202 and 204). Don't be put off by the ingredients list; everything can be bought at a large super-market and the soup is quick and easy to make.

SERVES 4

FOR THE STOCK

stems from a large bunch of coriander
5 cups (1.5 liters) water
1 onion, quartered
2 stalks of lemon grass, split in half
4 garlic cloves, halved, no need to peel
4 kaffir lime leaves
3 slices of dried galangal
3 dried red chilies

FOR THE SOUP

1 tbsp mild-flavored olive oil
5oz (150g) enoki mushrooms, trimmed from their base
4 kaffir lime leaves, roughly torn
1–2 tsp lemon grass in sunflower oil
1–2 tsp galangal in sunflower oil
2 tsp tamarind in sunflower oil
1 tbsp tamari or shoyu soy sauce
salt
¼ cup chopped fresh coriander leaves

Put all the stock ingredients into a large saucepan, bring to a boil, then turn the heat down, cover and simmer gently for 15–20 minutes.

Remove from the heat and strain through a sieve into a large bowl, pressing to extract as much liquid as possible. Set aside for the moment, discarding the debris in the sieve. Rinse out and dry the saucepan.

Heat the oil in the saucepan, add the enoki mushrooms and lime leaves and cook for 1–2 minutes. Pour in the stock and stir in the lemon grass, galangal, tamarind, soy sauce and a little salt to taste. Bring the soup just to the boil, then remove from the heat, stir in the chopped coriander and serve.

Leek soup

Leek, potatoes, stock — this soup couldn't be simpler but it hits the spot every time. You can blend it, keep it as it is or blend half of it and leave the rest to give some texture.

SERVES 4 ❄

1 tbsp olive oil
1lb (450g) potatoes, peeled and diced
2 leeks, sliced
3 cups (850ml) water or light vegetable stock
5fl oz (150ml) ½ and ½ (optional)
salt and freshly ground black pepper
2 tbsp chopped fresh flat-leaf parsley, to garnish

Heat the oil in a large saucepan, add the potatoes and leeks and fry gently for about 5 minutes, stirring often and being careful not to let them brown.

Pour in the water or stock, bring to a boil then simmer, with a lid on the saucepan, for about 20 minutes or until the vegetables are tender.

Blend the soup, making it smooth or chunky, depending on your taste. Stir in the ½ and ½, if using, and season with salt and pepper.

Reheat gently without letting it boil. Ladle into warmed bowls and sprinkle over some chopped parsley.

Leek and carrot soup v

This pretty soup is pale golden and flecked with pieces of green leek, orange carrot and chopped fresh green herbs. It's very cheering and uplifting on a winter's day.

SERVES 4 ❄

2 large carrots, sliced
4 leeks, sliced
1 tbsp olive oil
3 cups (850ml) vegetable stock or water
a pinch or two of freshly grated nutmeg
salt and freshly ground black pepper
¼ cup chopped fresh chervil or flat-leaf parsley

In a large saucepan fry the carrots and leeks together in the oil for 10 minutes without browning.

Add the stock or water and cook gently for 30–40 minutes or until the vegetables are tender.

Blend, leaving some texture to the soup. Season with nutmeg, salt and pepper and stir in the chopped chervil or parsley just before serving.

Chunky leek and potato soup

This is comfort food, and it's quick and easy to make. I like it as it is or with some hot, buttery, crunchy garlic bread. It's also delicious with a soft mound of grated, sharp-tasting cheese melted into it.

SERVES 4 ❄

1 tbsp (15g) butter
1 tbsp olive oil
1 large onion, chopped
2lb (900g) potatoes, peeled and cut into chunky pieces
1½lb (700g) leeks, sliced
2 cups (575ml) water
1 tsp vegetable bouillon powder
salt and freshly ground black pepper
chopped parsley (optional)

Heat the butter and oil in a large saucepan, add the onion and fry gently for 5 minutes, without browning.

Add the potatoes and leeks, stir and fry gently for an additional 5 minutes, stirring often.

Pour in the water, stir in the bouillon powder and bring to a boil. Cover and simmer gently for about 15 minutes, until the vegetables are just tender.

Mash some of the potatoes roughly, to thicken the soup. Check the seasoning, then serve with some chopped parsley sprinkled over, if you like.

VARIATION

Chunky mushroom and potato soup

For this version, leave out the leeks and use 225g (8oz) sliced cremini mushrooms.

Classic lentil soup v

I think this smooth, golden soup is the most comforting of all soups and it couldn't be easier to make. It was the first solid food I gave my youngest daughter when she was six months old and she still adores it — in fact, it's a great favorite with all the family.

SERVES 4 ❄
1 large onion, chopped
1 tbsp olive oil
8oz (225g) split red lentils
3½ cups (1 liter) vegetable stock or
    water
1–2 tbsp lemon juice
salt and freshly ground black pepper

Heat the oil in a large saucepan and fry the onion for about 5 minutes or until it's lightly browned.

Add the lentils and stock or water and bring to a boil, then simmer for about 20 minutes or until the lentils are soft and golden.

Blend the soup, adding water to thin it if you wish. Add lemon juice to taste and season with salt and plenty of pepper. Reheat gently and serve.

VARIATIONS

Lentil soup with garlic and cumin v

Make as described, but shortly before serving, fry a chopped onion in a little olive oil with 2 crushed garlic cloves and 2 teaspoons of ground cumin. Stir into the soup just before serving.

Lentil soup with caramelized onions v

Make as described, and while the soup is cooking, slowly fry 2 finely sliced onions in a tablespoon of olive oil until deep golden brown and very soft. This will take at least 20 minutes. Serve each portion of soup with a glossy pile of caramelized onions on top, or stir through the soup before serving.

Lentil and mushroom soup

The lentils and mushrooms in this soup blend beautifully to make a deep, dark soup with a rich, earthy flavor. If they don't know, people sometimes think they're just eating mushroom soup, but of course the lentils give it extra body and are full of nourishment.

SERTVES 4 ❄
1 large onion, chopped
1 large garlic clove, crushed
1 tbsp olive oil
1 tbsp (15g) butter
4oz (125g) mushrooms, chopped
4oz (125g) green or Puy lentils
3 cups (850ml) water or unsalted
    vegetable stock
salt and freshly ground black pepper
chopped fresh flat-leaf parsley or
    flakes of Parmesan-style cheese,
    to garnish

Fry the onion and garlic in the olive oil and butter in a large saucepan for 5 minutes. Add the mushrooms and cook for an additional 4–5 minutes.

Add the lentils and the water or stock. Simmer gently, with a lid on the saucepan, for an additional 45 minutes or until the lentils are tender.

Blend the soup if you want a smoother texture and thin it with a bit more water if you wish. Season with salt and freshly ground black pepper.

Reheat the soup and serve it in warm bowls topped with some chopped parsley or flakes of Parmesan-style cheese.

Lentil, tomato and basil soup v

Although it's generally best to avoid cooking beans with tomatoes because the acidity can prevent them from softening properly, split red lentils are an exception as they are so quick to cook. The result is a lovely tasty soup.

SERVES 4 ❄
2 tbsp olive oil
1 large onion, chopped
1 stalk of celery, chopped
4oz (125g) split red lentils, washed
14oz can tomatoes
3 cups (850ml) unsalted stock or
    water
salt and freshly ground black pepper
squeeze of lemon juice
a few torn or shredded fresh basil
    leaves, to garnish

Heat the oil in a large saucepan, add the onion and celery and cook gently, covered, for 7–10 minutes without browning.

Add the lentils, tomatoes and stock or water, bring to a boil and simmer gently, with the pan half covered, for 25–30 minutes or until the lentils are tender. Blend to the consistency you like, then season with salt, freshly ground black pepper and perhaps a squeeze of lemon juice to brighten the flavor.

Serve very hot, in warm bowls, with a scattering of basil.

Lentil and vegetable soup v

Is there anything as satisfying, soothing and warming as a homemade lentil and vegetable soup filling the house with the scent of herbs? Plus, it's so cheap and easy to make. It's great as it is, or you could offer some flaked or grated strong cheese to stir into it and some chunks of country-style bread to mop up the juices.

SERVES 4 ❄
2 tbsp olive oil
1 onion, chopped
1 large garlic clove, crushed
2 large carrots, cut into small dice
2 stalks of celery, thinly sliced
2 tomatoes, chopped
2oz (50g) mushrooms, chopped
3-4oz (75–125g) cabbage, shredded
4oz (125g) dried green or Puy lentils,
    or a 14oz can
3½ cups (1 liter) unsalted stock
1 bouquet garni — a couple of sprigs
    of parsley, a sprig of thyme and a
    bay leaf tied together
2 tbsp chopped fresh flat-leaf
    parsley
salt and freshly ground black pepper

Heat the oil in a large saucepan, add the onion and cook, covered, for 5 minutes, then stir in the garlic and all the other vegetables, cover and cook gently for another 5 minutes, stirring occasionally to prevent sticking.

Add the lentils, stock and the bouquet garni and bring to a boil, then cover and leave to simmer for about 1 hour or until the lentils are tender.

Remove the bouquet garni, stir in the chopped parsley and season with salt and pepper.

Lettuce soup

Why throw away the outer leaves of a lettuce that you've so carefully grown just because they're too coarse for a salad? Make them into this fresh and summery soup instead.

SERVES 4 ❄
1 tbsp olive oil
1 tbsp (15g) butter
1 onion, chopped
1lb (450g) potatoes, peeled and
    diced
outside leaves of 2—3 lettuces,
    chopped
3½ cups (1 liter) water
5fl oz (150ml) ½ and ½
salt, freshly ground black pepper
freshly grated nutmeg
2 tbsp chopped fresh chives

Heat the olive oil and butter in a large saucepan and cook the onion and potato gently for 5 minutes with a lid on the pan, but don't brown them.

Add the lettuce leaves and stir them for a minute or two until they're glossy with the oil, then pour in the water or stock and bring to a boil. Simmer the soup gently, with a lid on the pan, for 15—20 minutes or until the potato is very tender.

Blend the soup and stir in the cream. Season with salt, pepper and a grating of nutmeg and stir in the chopped chives.

Reheat and serve in warm bowls.

Cream of mushroom soup

My father was brilliant at finding field mushrooms — probably due to years of practice growing up on a farm in the Yorkshire Dales — and this is the soup that my mother used to make with his precious finds. It works very well with other types of mushrooms too.

SERVES 4 ❄
8oz (225g) mushrooms
1 small onion, quartered
1 bay leaf
1 garlic clove, sliced
a few parsley stems
2 cups (575ml) vegetable stock
½ stick (50g) butter
3 tbsp (40g) flour
about 2 cups (575ml) milk
salt and freshly ground black pepper
freshly grated nutmeg
a pinch of cayenne pepper
1 tbsp sherry (optional)

Wash the mushrooms and remove the stems. If you're using field mushrooms take off the skins too, but this isn't necessary with cultivated mushrooms. Put the stems (and skins if you've removed them) into a medium-sized saucepan together with the onion, bay leaf, garlic, parsley stems and stock and bring to a boil, then leave to simmer for 10 minutes to extract the flavors. Strain the liquid into a measuring cup (discarding the stems) and fill with milk until it measures 3 cups.

Melt 3 tbsp (40g) of butter in the saucepan and stir in the flour. When it froths, pour in a quarter of the milk mixture and stir over a fairly high heat until it has thickened. Add the remaining milk in 3 batches, bringing to a gentle simmer to thicken before adding more liquid.

Chop or slice the mushrooms, fry them lightly in the remaining butter and add to the thickened milk.

Season with salt, pepper, a grating of nutmeg, a pinch of cayenne and the sherry if you're using it. Cook gently for 3–4 minutes to give the flavors a chance to blend, then serve.

Vegetarian-style minestrone soup

A filling, main course soup that's always great for feeding a crowd.

SERVES 4 ❄
2 tbsp olive oil
3 onions, chopped
1 large carrot, diced
2 stalks of celery, sliced
2 large garlic cloves, crushed
1 large potato, peeled and cut into
  ½ in (1cm) dice
a few leaves of cabbage, chopped
14oz can chopped tomatoes
3½ cups (1 liter) stock or water
bouquet garni
8oz (225g) dried haricot, borlotti or
  cannellini beans, cooked,
  or 2 x 14oz cans
2oz (50g) macaroni or small pasta
  shapes
salt and freshly ground black pepper
2 tbsp torn fresh basil leaves,
  to garnish
handful of grated strongly flavored
  cheese such as pecorino or
  Parmesan-style, to serve

Heat the oil in a large saucepan, add the onions, carrot and celery, cover and cook gently for 5 minutes, then add the garlic and the other vegetables and cook for an additional 5 minutes.

Add the tomatoes, stock or water and the bouquet garni. Bring to a boil, then boil for 10 minutes.

Add the drained cooked beans and the macaroni or pasta shapes and cook until the pasta is just tender, about 8—10 minutes.

Season with salt and pepper, and serve in warm bowls with torn fresh basil leaves sprinkled over the top. Serve the cheese separately for people to help themselves.

Miso soup v

This soup is so quick and easy and also very soothing and nourishing. You can buy dried wakame seaweed from any good health-food store and many supermarkets. You only need a little and what is left over will keep perfectly in a dry place for months. Good-quality, unpasterized miso is also widely available; you'll find it a useful flavoring for many savory dishes, but always remember to add it at the end of cooking to preserve the health-giving enzymes it contains.

SERVES 4
2in (5cm) piece of wakame seaweed
2 dried shiitake mushrooms, if
    available
1 quart (1.2 liters) water
4 scallions, chopped
4 tsp brown rice miso

Soak the wakame and shiitake mushrooms in a cupful of the water for about 10 minutes, then drain, reserving the liquid.

Cut the wakame into shreds, discarding any hard bits, and slice the mushrooms. Put these into a large saucepan, along with their soaking water, the quart (1.2 liters) of water, and the scallions and simmer for 5–10 minutes.

Put the miso into a small bowl, add a ladleful of the soup and stir until blended, then pour the mixture back into the pan. Leave the pan over heat for 2–3 minutes, without letting it boil, then serve.

French onion soup

You don't need beef stock to make a delectable French onion soup. This vegetarian version fills the house with its aroma as it cooks and keeps everyone satisfied, I promise you.

SERVES 4 ❄
1 tbsp olive oil
1lb (450g) onion, sliced
1 tbsp flour
3 cups (850ml) water
1 tbsp high-quality bouillon powder
3 tbsp sherry
1 large garlic clove, crushed
4 tsp Dijon mustard
salt and freshly ground black pepper
4 slices of baguette
3–4oz (75–125g) Gruyère cheese,
    grated

Heat the oil in a large saucepan and fry the onions slowly for 15–20 minutes until they're golden, stirring from time to time.

Add the flour and cook for a few seconds before stirring in the water, bouillon powder, sherry, garlic, mustard and some salt and pepper.

Bring to a boil, then leave to simmer gently, covered, for 30 minutes.

Just before the soup is ready, warm four heatproof soup bowls and lightly toast the baguette. Heat the broiler to medium-high.

Check the consistency of the soup, adding a splash of boiling water if it needs to be a bit thinner, and adjust the seasoning to taste.

Put a slice of toasted baguette into each bowl and ladle the soup on top. Scatter the grated cheese over and place the bowls under the broiler for a few minutes. Serve the soup immediately, bubbling and oozing with molten cheese.

Parsnip soup

This is one of the soups that I grew up with, and one I often made for guests when working at a retreat center. It's a beautiful soup that costs next to nothing to make.

SERVES 4 ❄
1 tbsp olive oil
1 tbsp (15g) butter
8oz (225g) parsnips, peeled and
    diced
1 carrot, sliced
1 potato, peeled and diced
1 onion, chopped
1 bay leaf
15fl oz (425ml) water
15fl oz (425ml) milk
salt and freshly ground black pepper
1—2 pinches of ground mace
dusting of paprika, to garnish

Heat the oil and butter in a large saucepan, add the parsnips, carrot, potato and onion and fry over a gentle heat, with a lid on the pan, for 10 minutes.

Add the bay leaf, water and milk. Bring to a boil, then simmer for 30 minutes. Remove the bay leaf, then blend the soup.

Season with salt, pepper and mace. Serve with a dusting of paprika on top.

Soupe au pistou v

This delicious soup from southern France makes a filling main course with warm crusty bread.

SERVES 4 ❋
2 onions, chopped
½ cup (100ml) olive oil
2 carrots, chopped
2 potatoes, peeled and diced
8oz (225g) zucchini, sliced
4oz (125g) green beans, sliced
1lb (450g) tomatoes, skinned and chopped
8oz (225g) dried haricot beans, soaked, cooked (see pages 176–7) and drained, or 2 x 14oz cans
6 cups (1.7 liters) vegetable stock or water plus 4 tsp bouillon powder
2oz (50g) vermicelli
salt and freshly ground black pepper
5 garlic cloves, crushed
leaves from a bunch of basil

Fry the onions in 3 tablespoons of the oil in a large saucepan for 5 minutes. Add the carrots and potatoes and cook for 5 minutes.

Add the zucchini, green beans, tomatoes, haricot beans and the stock. Bring to a boil, cover and simmer for 20–30 minutes.

Add the vermicelli and cook for 8–10 minutes or until it's tender. Season well.

While the soup is cooking, whisk together the remaining oil with the garlic and basil. Stir this fragrant purée into the soup and serve in warmed bowls.

Green pea soup with mint and cream

Frozen peas make a vivid green soup with a very smooth texture. It looks lovely swirled with cream and flecked with dark green chopped mint, and is good either hot or chilled.

SERVES 4
1 tbsp olive oil
1 tbsp (15g) butter
1 onion, chopped
2lb (900g) frozen peas
1 quart (1.2 liters) light vegetable stock or water
a few sprigs of thyme
salt and freshly ground black pepper

TO GARNISH
5fl oz (150ml) ½ and ½
2 tbsp chopped fresh mint

Heat the oil and butter in a large saucepan, add the onion and fry gently for 5–7 minutes, with a lid on the pan, until fairly soft but not browned.

Add the peas, the stock or water and the thyme. Bring to a boil, then simmer for about 15 minutes or until the vegetables are soft.

Blend, and if you want it silky soft, make sure you do this thoroughly. For perfection, you could then pass it through a sieve, pushing through as much of the pea purée as you can, but this isn't by any means essential — you'll still have a great soup without this extra effort.

Season the soup and gently reheat, then ladle into bowls and top each with a good splash of cream and a scattering of mint.

Potato soup with fresh herbs

Although this is a simple soup, it always tastes good, with its smooth creamy texture and topping of fresh green herbs.

SERVES 4 ❋
1 tbsp olive oil
1 tbsp (15g) butter
1 onion, chopped
1lb (450g) potatoes, peeled and diced
3 cups (850ml) water
salt and freshly ground black pepper
5fl oz (150ml) ½ and ½
2 tbsp chopped fresh herbs (such as chives, parsley or tarragon), to garnish

Heat the oil and butter in a large saucepan. Add the onion and fry gently, with a lid on the pan, for 3–4 minutes. Add the potatoes, stir, then cover and cook gently for an additional 5 minutes, without browning.

Pour in the water, bring to a boil, then simmer for about 15 minutes or until the potatoes are tender.

Blend the soup, stir in the ½ and ½, then season with salt and pepper.

Reheat and serve sprinkled with the fresh herbs.

Pumpkin soup

Pumpkin makes a very delicious soup, golden in color with a delicate yet distinctive flavor. It's lovely sprinkled with chopped parsley and served with garlic bread (see page 55).

SERVES 6 ❉
2¼lb (1kg) pumpkin (weight
    includes skin and seeds)
1 tbsp (15g) butter
1 tbsp olive oil
2 large onions, chopped
2 large garlic cloves, crushed
3½ cups (1 liter) vegetable stock
salt and freshly ground black pepper
5fl oz (150ml) heavy cream or crème
    fraîche

Cut the skin off the pumpkin, scoop out the seeds and cut the flesh into even-sized pieces.

Heat the butter and oil in a large saucepan, add the onions and cook, covered, for an additional 5 minutes, then add the garlic and pumpkin and cook for an additional 5 minutes.

Pour in the stock, season and bring to the boil. Cover and simmer until the pumpkin is tender (about 20 minutes).

Blend to a glorious golden purée, then add the cream and a splash more water to thin it if necessary.

Reheat gently then ladle into bowls and serve.

Spinach soup

Spinach makes a beautiful deep green soup with a sharp, iron-y flavor that's sweetened by a spoonful of cream.

SERVES 4 ❉
1 tbsp olive oil
1 onion, chopped
1 potato, peeled and chopped
1lb (450g) spinach leaves
3 cups (850ml) vegetable stock or
    water
salt and freshly ground black pepper
a pinch of freshly grated nutmeg
squeeze of lemon juice
¼ cup heavy cream or crème fraîche,
    to garnish

Heat the oil in a large pan, add the onion and potato and fry gently without browning, with a lid on the pan, for 5–10 minutes.

Push the spinach into the pan and pour in the stock or water. Bring to a boil, then simmer for 15–20 minutes or until the potato is tender.

Blend well, then adjust the consistency of the soup with a little water if necessary and season with salt, pepper, grated nutmeg and a squeeze of lemon juice.

Reheat, then serve in warmed bowls with a spoonful of cream or crème fraîche on top of each.

Spinach and lentil soup V

Green lentils and spinach are natural companions and this soup is earthy, warming and satisfying.

SERVES 4 ❉
1 tbsp olive oil
1 large onion, chopped
1 large garlic clove, crushed
4oz (125g) green lentils
8oz (225g) spinach leaves, washed
3½ cups (1 liter) unsalted vegetable
    stock or water
salt and freshly ground black pepper
2—3 tsp lemon juice
croûtons or thick yogurt, to serve
    (optional)

Heat the oil in a large saucepan, add the onion and fry for 10 minutes, with a lid on the pan, until the onion is almost tender and flecked with brown.

Stir in the garlic, lentils and spinach, then pour in the stock or water and bring to a boil. Simmer gently, with a lid on the pan, for about 45 minutes, until the lentils are soft.

Blend the soup, then reheat, season it with salt, freshly ground black pepper and lemon juice.

Serve just as it is, in deep, warm bowls, or top with a spoonful of crisp golden croûtons or thick Greek yogurt.

Green split pea soup v

These green split peas, which you can get at health-food stores, make a pleasant change from the more usual yellow ones, or indeed from the color of most dried beans, and they taste good too. As it's a winter soup, I use dried herbs here; both marjoram and savory are useful to have in the cupboard for adding depth of flavor, particularly to beans.

SERVES 4 ❄

6oz (175g) green split peas
1 quart (1.2 liters) water
1 onion, chopped
2 potatoes, peeled and sliced
2 stalks of celery, chopped
2 small leeks, sliced
½ tsp dried savory or marjoram
salt and freshly ground black pepper
garlic butter, to serve (optional)

Put the split peas into a large saucepan with the water, all the vegetables and the savory or marjoram and bring to the boil.

Simmer gently until the split peas are tender — about 50 minutes. This soup can be served as it is, with chunky pieces of vegetables in it, or blended until completely smooth, or part-blended, the choice is yours. If necessary, add a little more water to bring it to the consistency you like.

Season with salt and pepper, reheat and serve in warmed bowls, topped with a piece of garlic butter (a little softened butter mashed with a crushed garlic clove) for extra flavor. Or you could go the whole hog and serve it with crisp, buttery garlic bread (see page 55).

Chilled green split pea soup with mint

Here's another way to use dried green split peas, and it couldn't be more different from the previous one. I love this soup because it shows beans in a different light altogether — all spruced up and elegant.

SERVES 4 ❄

2 tbsp olive oil
1 large onion, chopped
1 stalk of celery, chopped
8 sprigs of fresh mint
4oz (125g) green split peas
3½ cups (1 liter) unsalted stock
a pinch of ground cloves
1 bay leaf
salt and freshly ground black pepper
heavy cream or crème fraîche, or
    mint sprigs, to garnish

Heat the oil in a large saucepan, add the onion and celery and fry gently, without browning, for about 10 minutes.

Meanwhile remove the leaves from the stems of the mint and set aside. Add the stems to the saucepan, together with the split peas, stock, ground cloves and bay leaf.

Bring to a boil, half covered with a lid, and simmer for about 40 minutes or until the split peas are tender.

Remove the bay leaf and mint stems, add the mint leaves and blend until smooth and creamy, then season with salt and pepper.

Cool then chill the soup in the fridge. Check the seasoning again before serving, then ladle into individual bowls and top with a spoonful of crème fraîche or cream, or a fresh mint sprig, or both.

Yellow split pea soup v

Normally I don't add any thickening to a lentil or split pea soup; they have enough body without. However, this soup is an exception. The split peas are cooked, puréed, then stirred into a roux of butter and flour, just like making a sauce. The result is a particularly smooth and creamy texture and buttery flavor.

SERVES 4—6 ❄

8oz (225g) yellow split peas
6 cups (1.7 liters) water or unsalted
    vegetable stock
2 tbsp (25g) butter or pure vegetable
    margarine
1 large onion, chopped
1 garlic clove, crushed
2 tbsp (25g) flour
salt and freshly ground black pepper

Put the split peas into a large saucepan with the liquid, bring to a boil and simmer gently for 40–50 minutes or until tender. You need a large pan for this because of the bubbling water. If this is a problem, try adding a little oil to the cooking water, or cook the peas using only 1 quart (1.2 liters) of water and add the rest when you blend the soup.

Blend the split peas until smooth and transfer to a bowl.

Melt the butter in the rinsed-out saucepan and fry the onion until golden. Stir in the garlic and flour, cook for a minute or two, then gradually pour in the split pea purée, stirring until you have a smooth mixture.

Let the soup simmer for 5–10 minutes to cook the flour, then season and serve.

Sweetcorn soup

A pretty, pale golden soup with a hint of sweetness. You can blend it until it's smooth, and then strain it too if you want it really delicate and silky; or half-blend it, leaving some pieces of sweetcorn for texture. You will need 2—3 sweetcorn cobs for this quantity of kernels, or you could use frozen kernels, which work well too.

SERVES 4 ❄

1 onion, chopped
1 tbsp of olive oil
1 tbsp (15g) butter
8oz(225g) sweetcorn kernels, frozen
    or cut from the cob
2½ cups (700ml) water
5fl oz (150ml) ½ and ½
a pinch or two of paprika, to taste,
    plus extra for garnishing
a squeeze of lemon juice
salt and freshly ground black pepper

In a large saucepan, fry the onion in the oil and butter, covered, for 10 minutes. Don't let the onion brown.

Add the sweetcorn and water, bring to the boil, then reduce the heat and simmer for 10–15 minutes.

Blend the soup until it is the texture you want, then stir in the cream, paprika and a little lemon juice, plus salt and pepper to taste.

Reheat gently, without boiling, and sprinkle a dusting of paprika pepper on top.

Tomato and fresh basil soup with cream

When it's made in the summer with just-picked tomatoes and fragrant fresh basil, this has to be one of the best soups of all, but even canned tomatoes give a very acceptable result as long as you a choose good-quality brands.

SERVES 4—6 ❄

1 tbsp olive oil
1 tbsp (25g) butter
1 onion, chopped
12oz (350g) potatoes, peeled and
    cut into even-sized chunks
1lb (450g) tomatoes, chopped
1 quart (1.2 liters) light vegetable
    stock or water
salt and freshly ground black pepper
sugar (optional)

TO GARNISH

5fl oz (150ml) heavy cream
2 tbsp torn fresh basil leaves

Heat the butter and oil in a large saucepan and add the onion. Fry for 5–7 minutes, covered, until fairly soft but not browned.

Add the potatoes, stir, cover and cook for an additional 5–10 minutes. Cover the pan but stir often to prevent sticking.

Add the tomatoes and the stock or water. Bring to a boil, then simmer, covered, for about 15 minutes or until the potatoes are very tender.

Blend thoroughly then pour the soup through a sieve into a clean saucepan to remove the seeds and skins of the tomatoes.

Taste and season with salt, pepper and a pinch or two of sugar if you think it needs it. Reheat and serve each bowl topped with a generous spoonful of cream and some basil.

Clear vegetable broth v

The better the stock, the better this soup will be. Homemade stock is great, if you have it (see page 11), but if not, good-quality vegetable bouillon powder or stock concentrate will also work well.

SERVES 4

2 stalks of celery, chopped
2 onions, chopped
2 carrots, diced
other vegetables as available
    (e.g. a few French beans or a little
    cabbage)
2 tsp olive oil
1 tsp yeast extract
1 tsp tomato purée
1 bay leaf
3 cups (850ml) vegetable stock
salt and freshly ground black pepper
2 tbsp chopped fresh chives, to
    garnish

Fry the celery, onion and carrot together in the oil without browning for 5 minutes.

Add the beans, broken into short lengths, and the cabbage, shredded. Cook over a gentle heat for an additional 5 minutes. Cover the pan but stir often.

Add the yeast extract, tomato purée, bay leaf and stock, bring to a boil and simmer for 20–30 minutes.

Season with salt and freshly ground black pepper. Sprinkle with the chopped chives before serving.

Clear mushroom broth v

Mushrooms make a delightful broth. You can use any type — field, portobello, shiitake or delicate little button mushrooms. Leave out the carrots and other vegetables, and add 8oz (225g) sliced or chopped mushrooms to the onions and celery after they have been frying for 5 minutes. Pour in the stock, bring to a boil and simmer for 10–15 minutes, then stir in 2 heaped tablespoons of chopped flat-leaf parsley before serving.

Creamy white bean soup with truffle oil

v

This silky-smooth soup is very easy to prepare and a sure-fire hit with everyone. The swirl of truffle oil on the top makes it luxurious enough for a special occasion.

SERVES 4
2 x 14oz cans haricot or cannellini beans or 7oz (200g) soaked and cooked until very tender
2 tbsp olive oil
1 onion, chopped
2 garlic cloves, crushed
1 tsp vegetable bouillon powder or a stock cube
salt and freshly ground black pepper

TO GARNISH
a little chopped fresh parsley
4 tsp truffle oil

Drain the beans, reserving the liquid if you are using ones you have cooked yourself.

Heat the olive oil in a large saucepan, add the onion, cover with a lid and cook gently, stirring occasionally, for 10 minutes or until the onion is soft but not brown.

Stir in the garlic and cook for a few seconds, then add the drained beans. Add enough water to the reserved bean liquid to equal 3 cups (850ml), or just use water and add to the pan, along with the bouillon powder or stock cube. Bring to a boil, then simmer, uncovered, for 10 minutes.

Blend the soup thoroughly until it is really smooth and creamy. Season to taste with salt and pepper.

Serve in bowls with a little finely chopped parsley, a grinding of pepper and a swirl of truffle oil.

Winter vegetable soup

A pale golden soup, full of flavor, and it couldn't be easier to make. Try a big, steaming bowl of it on a winter's day, with chunks of crusty bread.

SERVES 4 ❄
1 quart (1.2 liters) water
2 fairly large carrots
2 onions
2 potatoes
1 rutabaga (about 8oz (225g)
1 turnip (about 8oz (225g)
4 stalks of celery
1 tbsp (15g) butter
salt and freshly ground black pepper

Pour the water into a large saucepan and bring to a boil while you prepare the vegetables. Peel and cut them into fairly small chunks, then add them to the water, together with some salt, and simmer gently, covered, for about 30 minutes or until they're tender.

Blend the soup to the smoothness you want, and stir in the butter. Season to taste, then reheat and serve.

Vichyssoise

This classic chilled summer soup is always popular.

SERVES 6 ❄

1 onion, chopped
1 tbsp olive oil
1 tbsp (15g) butter
8oz (225g) potatoes, peeled and diced
1½lb (700g) leeks, sliced
2 cups (575ml) water
salt
2 cups (575ml) milk
freshly ground black pepper
5fl oz (150ml) heavy cream
2 tbsp chopped chives, to garnish

Fry the onion in the oil and butter for about 5 minutes in a large, covered saucepan but don't let it brown.

Add the potatoes and leeks and stir until they're coated glossy with the oil. Put the lid back on the pan, turn the heat right down and cook gently for an additional 15 minutes, stirring from time to time and being careful not to let it brown.

Stir in the water and a little salt and bring to a boil, then cover and leave to simmer for 20–30 minutes or until the vegetables are tender.

Purée the soup very thoroughly, adding some of the milk if you like, to make the process easier. Pour the soup into a bowl or pitcher — pouring it in through a sieve if you want the soup really velvety — and add the remaining milk. Taste and season the soup, then chill it.

Taste the soup again before serving, then spoon some cream over the top of each bowlful. Sprinkle with the chopped chives and serve.

Watercress soup

This is my family's favorite soup and the one I get the most requests to make.

SERVES 4—6 ❄

2lb (900g) potatoes, peeled
3 tbsp olive oil
salt
6 cups (2 liters) light vegetable stock or water
vegetable bouillon powder or a stock cube
3-4 oz fresh watercress
freshly ground black pepper

Slice the potatoes as thinly as you can; this helps them soften quickly in the oil.

Heat the oil in a large saucepan and add the potato slices with a sprinkling of salt, which also helps the softening process by drawing the water out of the potatoes. Cook very gently, covered, for 5–15 minutes, stirring often. The longer you can let them "sweat" like this, the better the soup. They can get flecked with some gold, but don't let them brown because that will spoil the flavor. Add 1–2 tablespoons of water if they start to stick.

Add three-quarters of the stock or water and the bouillon powder or stock cube. Bring to a boil, cover and simmer gently for 5–15 minutes or until the potatoes are soft. The timing will depend on how long you sweated the potato

for. If you got it very tender, this stage will take hardly any time.

Reserve some small sprigs of watercress for garnishing (one for each bowl), and add the rest to the soup. Blend thoroughly to a smooth, bright green cream. Adjust the consistency with the remaining water to get it to the consistency you like.

Season with salt and pepper (you may not need much salt, if any). Reheat and serve with watercress leaves and a grinding of black pepper on each bowlful.

Opposite: Watercress soup

First courses,
snacks, and drinks

Quick meals to eat on the move, snacks to rustle up in an instant and light dishes to whet the appetite in anticipation of the main course — that's what this chapter is about.

You'll find some stunning first courses that are perfect for a special occasion meal or weekend dinner, followed by deliciously simple bruschetta and crostini, then plenty of lunch-box sandwiches and wraps for kids and adults alike. If you're short on time, try these tasty savories on toast and super-quick ciabatta or pita pizzas (see pages 43–4 and 56). Finally, wash it all down with fresh peppermint tea or a nutritious smoothie (see pages 57–9).

First courses

Antipasto salad

A colorful Italian-style first course.

SERVES 6

8 oz (225g) button mushrooms
2 tbsp olive oil
1 small red pepper
2 tsp wine or cider vinegar
salt and freshly ground black pepper
1 bunch of radishes
½ bunch of scallions
2 heads of endive
½ cucumber
6 tomatoes
4 hardboiled eggs
6 oz chargrilled or marinated
    artichokes, from the deli
6 oz of sliced roasted peppers, from
    the deli
12 black olives, or your favorite
    olives, to garnish
vinaigrette (see page 78), to serve

Wash and slice the mushrooms; fry lightly in 1 tablespoon of the oil for 5 minutes, then leave to cool.

Slice the red pepper very thinly, discarding the seeds. Place on a flat dish and sprinkle with the remaining oil and wine or cider vinegar. Season with salt and pepper. If possible, leave for 1–2 hours to soften.

Wash and trim the radishes and scallions; slice the endive lengthways into quarters, and the cucumber, tomatoes and eggs into circles.

Arrange all the ingredients attractively on individual dishes or a large platter, garnish with olives and serve with vinaigrette.

Globe artichoke hollandaise

This is a delightful starter: cooked globe artichokes filled with hollandaise sauce. You pull off the leaves and dip the bases in the sauce, then enjoy the delicious heart. You'll need finger bowls, and bowls to put the discarded leaves after you've sucked the flesh from them. It's best to cook the artichokes ahead of time then gently reheat them just before serving.

SERVES 4

4 globe artichokes, stems removed
a squeeze of lemon juice
blender hollandaise (see page 67),
    to serve

Cut the stalks off the artichokes so that they will sit level, then wash them thoroughly under cold running water. You might like to trim the points off the leaves using scissors, so that they are less sharp; or you could leave them as they are.

Cook the artichokes in a large saucepan of boiling water, with a good squeeze of lemon juice added, for about 45 minutes, or until a leaf will pull off easily. Drain and rinse under cold water to cool quickly.

Open out the leaves to get to the center of the artichoke, like opening out the petals of a flower. Pull off and discard the central purple cluster of tender leaves. Underneath you will find the fluffy "choke", which is inedible, so you'll need to scoop this out with a knife or pointed teaspoon, then rinse the artichoke under cold running water.

Just before you want to serve the artichokes, reheat them in the microwave in a covered container on high for 4–6 minutes, or until heated through, or stand them in a shallow roasting pan or ovenproof dish, cover with foil and reheat in the oven preheated to 350° (180°C), for about 15 minutes or until heated through.

Place each artichoke on a warm plate. Spoon the hollandaise sauce into the center and serve at once.

Eggplant fritters with tomato sauce v

This is one of the simplest ways of preparing eggplant, but one of my favorites, and I think it's tasty enough to serve as an extra course or light meal on its own.

SERVES 6

1lb (450g) eggplant
plain flour for coating
salt and freshly ground black pepper
olive oil, for shallow-frying
grated Parmesan-style cheese
lemon wedges
watercress
15fl oz (425ml) homemade tomato
    sauce, sour cream and herb sauce
    or tartar sauce (see pages 70–1),
    to serve

Wash the eggplants and remove the stems, then cut them into ¼in (6mm) slices and dip them in flour that has been seasoned with salt and pepper.

Just before you want to serve the eggplant, heat a little oil in a frying pan and fry the slices, a few at a time, on both sides, until the outside is crisp and the inside feels tender when pierced with the point of a sharp knife.

As the fritters are ready, put them in a roasting pan lined with crumpled paper towels and keep them warm in a low oven until they are all ready.

Serve the fritters sprinkled with a little grated Parmesan-style cheese and garnished with wedges of lemon and sprigs of watercress. Serve the sauce separately.

Eggplant and tapenade rolls v

These rolls are easy to make and are wonderful as part of a selection of canapés or tapas, or arranged on individual plates with some yogurt and green herb dressing (see page 78), for a starter.

MAKES 24 OR 48 ROLLS

3 large eggplant
6–8 tbsp olive oil
1 quantity of tapenade (see page 48)
a sprig of flat-leaf parsley, to garnish

Heat the broiler.

Cut the stem ends from the eggplant, then cut them lengthways into slices about ¼in (6mm) thick. (You will probably get 8–10 slices from each eggplant.)

Brush the slices lightly on both sides with oil and place side by side in a single layer on a broiler; you may have to do them in batches. Broil for about 5 minutes or until pale brown on top, then turn them over and broil the other side until lightly browned and tender when pierced with a sharp knife. Leave to cool.

To make the rolls, spread one of the eggplant slices quite thinly with tapenade, then roll it up firmly like a Swiss roll. Place seam-side down on a serving plate. Continue in this way until you have done all of them. Serve them whole like this or cut each one in half, which makes them easier to eat if you're serving them as canapés. Garnish parsley sprigs.

VARIATIONS

Eggplant and hummus rolls v

Use 9oz (250g) bought or homemade hummus (see page 46) instead of the tapenade and include a little chopped coriander in each roll. Garnish with extra coriander.

Eggplant and garlic cheese rolls v

Use 9oz (250g) dairy or vegan cream cheese with garlic and herbs instead of the tapenade. Garnish with parsley.

Avocado and grapefruit salad v

I love this combination of sharp citrus fruit and buttery avocado. The colors are very pretty and fresh-looking, too.

SERVES 6
2 grapefruit
2 oranges
2 avocado
6 whole butter lettuce or iceberg lettuce leaves, for serving
1 tbsp chopped mint

Using a serrated knife, and holding the fruit over a bowl, cut, peel and pith the grapefruit and oranges and slice out the segments.

Thinly peel, stone and slice the avocados, and add to the grapefruit and oranges. Pile onto lettuce leaves and serve chilled and sprinkled with chopped mint.

Melon with ginger v

Adding ginger works magic on melons that are not sweet and fragrant enough to be eaten on their own.

SERVES 6
1 honeydew melon
3-4 tbsp chopped stem ginger
6 tbsp of the syrup from the preserved ginger

If the melon is really tender (it can be sliced into with a spoon), cut it into six wedges, remove the seeds, spoon the chopped ginger and the syrup over each piece of melon, and serve.

For less-than-perfect melon, slice off the skin, remove the seeds, and cut the flesh into small pieces. Place in a mixing bowl, add the chopped ginger and syrup and stir together. Serve in individual bowls.

VARIATION
Melon with crème de menthe v

A speciality of a friend of mine and, I must admit, I'd never have thought of this combination, but it's wonderful. Use a melon with white or pale green flesh — again, it's a fantastic way of cheering up a melon that's lacking in flavor. Cut the melon into wedges, pour 1–2 tablespoons of crème de menthe over each and garnish with a sprig of fresh mint if you have some.

Marinated mushrooms v

Serve these spicy, piquant mushrooms well chilled, with some bread to mop up the spicy juices.

SERVES 4
1lb (450g) baby button mushrooms
2 tbsp olive oil
2 tsp ground coriander
1 bay leaf
2 garlic cloves, crushed
salt and freshly ground black pepper
2 tbsp lemon juice
chopped fresh flat-leaf parsley, to serve

Wash the mushrooms, halving or quartering any larger ones, then fry them in the olive oil with the coriander, bay leaf and garlic for about 2 minutes, stirring all the time.

Put the mushrooms straight into a large bowl to prevent further cooking, then add the lemon juice and a grinding of black pepper. Cool, then chill the mixture.

Check the seasoning before serving the mushrooms on individual plates with a scattering of chopped parsley on top.

Pears with blue cheese and walnuts

The secret to this dish is using really ripe, sweet pears. I find it's safest to buy hard pears up to a week in advance and let them ripen gently at room temperature. Small pears with a rounded shape work best — Comice are perfect.

SERVES 4

4 ripe sweet pears
juice of 1 lemon
1 tbsp extra-virgin olive oil
salt and freshly ground black pepper
2oz (50g) shelled walnuts pieces
4oz (125g) watercress
4–6oz (125–175g) Stilton or Danish
   Blue cheese, broken into pieces

Preheat the broiler if you are toasting the walnuts. Peel the pears and cut into even-sized pieces, removing the core. Put into a bowl with the lemon juice, oil, some salt and a generous grinding of pepper, and mix together.

Spread the walnuts on a broiler pan and toast for a few minutes until they smell wonderful, but be careful not to burn them. Or use them untoasted if you prefer.

Arrange the watercress on four plates. Spoon the pears on top and divide the dressing between the plates.

Tuck pieces of cheese among the pears and watercress, and scatter with the walnuts, breaking them up a bit in your fingers as you do so. If they're still warm from the grill when you serve them, that's even better.

Salsify with butter, parsley and lemon

Salsify — and their close relative, scorzonera — look like long, rather dirty dark roots when you see them in the stores, but when they're peeled and cooked they have a delicious, delicate flavor.

SERVES 4

2¼lb (1kg) salsify or scorzonera
   (unpeeled weight)
2 tbsp lemon juice
salt
2 tbsp butter
freshly ground black pepper
2 tbsp chopped fresh flat-leaf
   parsley

Peel the roots, keeping them under cold water to preserve the color. Cut them into 1in (2.5cm) pieces and put them straight into a bowl of cold water with 1 tablespoon of lemon juice.

Bring 1in (2.5cm) of salted water to a boil in a large saucepan, add the roots and cook for about 10 minutes or until just tender.

Drain and add butter, the remaining lemon juice, the parsley and salt and pepper to taste. Heat gently to melt the butter, then serve at once.

Salsify fritters

These delicate fritters make a perfect first course.

SERVES 4

1½lb (700g) salsify or scorzonera
3 tbsp red wine vinegar
1–2 tbsp chopped fresh herbs (e.g.
   parsley or dill)
salt and freshly ground pepper
4oz (125g) all-purpose flour
1 tbsp olive oil
2 eggs, separated
5fl oz (150ml) water
vegetable oil, for deep-frying
lemon slices, to serve

Prepare and cook the salsify as described in the first two paragraphs of the previous recipe. Drain well, then sprinkle with the vinegar, herbs and some salt and pepper.

Mix the flour, oil, seasoning, egg yolks and water together to form a batter. Whisk the egg whites, then fold into the batter.

Heat enough oil to fill half of a medium-sized saucepan to 375°F (190°C) (or when a little batter sizzles if dropped into the oil). Coat the salsify pieces in batter, then fry for about 4 minutes or until browned. Drain and serve with the lemon slices.

Salsify mayonnaise

Cooked and mixed with mayonnaise, salsify makes a lovely dish that I think of as the vegetarian equivalent to a light fish dish, though I can't swear to this as I haven't eaten fish since I was three years old!

SERVES 4

2¼ lb (1kg) salsify or scorzonera
2 tbsp lemon juice
3 tbsp mayonnaise
3 tbsp natural yogurt

TO GARNISH

1 tbsp chopped fresh flat-leaf parsley
lemon slices

Peel and cook the salsify until tender. While still hot, add the lemon juice, mayonnaise and yogurt. Leave to cool.

Serve on individual plates, garnished with the parsley and lemon slices.

Easy spring rolls v

These may seem fussy, but actually they're easy to make and delicious served with a sweet chili dipping sauce.

MAKES 24 SPRING ROLLS

1 onion, chopped
1 tbsp olive oil
11 oz beansprouts
1 small pointed red pepper, seeded and sliced
1 garlic clove, crushed
a thumb-sized piece of fresh ginger root, peeled and grated or finely chopped
½ head of Napa cabbage, shredded
3 tbsp dark soy sauce
salt
9½ packet filo pastry (6 sheets, approximately 20in x 9½in (500mm x 240mm))
rapeseed or groundnut oil, for brushing
sweet chili sauce, to serve

Fry the onion in the oil in a large saucepan for 5 minutes or until beginning to soften. Add the bean sprouts, red pepper, garlic, ginger and cabbage, stir-fry for a further 5 minutes or until the vegetables are tender. Add the soy sauce and some salt to taste, then leave to cool.

Preheat the oven to 400°F (200°C). Cut each sheet of filo pastry in half right down the middle, and across, making 24 rectangles.

Take one rectangle of filo pastry and turn it so the corner is facing you. Put about a tablespoon of the vegetable mixture across the center of the filo, about ½in (1cm) from the top. Fold the top over, and fold the sides inward over the filling, then roll the pastry to make a spring roll shape.

Brush the spring roll with oil, or put some oil on a plate and dip the spring roll in this, to coat lightly. Place the spring roll on a baking sheet and repeat with the rest of the mixture until all the filo and (probably) all of the vegetable mixture is used.

Bake the spring rolls for about 10 minutes or until crisp and golden brown. Serve with a chili dipping sauce.

Sweet potato bhajis v

These crisp tasty fritters make a tempting starter or nibble. They're great with mango chutney, tomato salsa or cucumber and coriander raita (see pages 69 and 66); or add some hot cooked rice to make a light main course.

MAKES 8 / SERVES 4 AS A
STARTER, 2 AS A MAIN COURSE
12oz (350g) sweet potato
1 onion, very finely chopped
4oz (125g) chickpea flour
1 tsp dried red chili flakes
1 tsp baking powder
1 tsp salt
3 tbsp chopped fresh coriander
vegetable oil, for deep-frying

Peel and grate the sweet potatoes, then put into a bowl and add the onion, chickpea flour, chili flakes, baking powder, salt and coriander. Mix well; as you mix, the moisture from the vegetables will be drawn out and will bind everything together. Add a tablespoonful or so of water only if the chickpea flour remains dry.

Heat enough oil in a medium-sized saucepan for deep-frying. (The pan needs to be half full of oil.) When the oil reaches 350°F (180°C), or a cube of bread rises to the surface and turns golden brown in under 1 minute, put in 3–4 heaping teaspoons of the mixture, depending on the size of your pan. Don't make the bhajis too big — they're best when light and crisp — and don't crowd the pan, otherwise the oil will cool and the bhajis will stick together. Deep-fry the bhajis for about 4 minutes or until crisp, brown and cooked right through, then remove them with a slotted spoon and drain on paper towels. Keep the bhajis warm in a low oven or while you cook the rest of the mixture.

VARIATIONS
Cabbage bhajis v

These are delicious; use 12oz (350g) shredded green cabbage instead of the sweet potatoes.

Onion bhajis v

Use 1lb (450g) red onions instead of the sweet potatoes, and omit the extra onion in the main recipe.

Tomatoes with horseradish cream

This is simple but delicious — sliced tomatoes topped with a piquant creamy horseradish dressing. The better the tomatoes, the better this dish will be.

SERVES 4
6 large firm tomatoes
salt and freshly ground black pepper
4oz (125g) ricotta cheese
2 tbsp natural yogurt
2 tsp extra-virgin olive oil
½ tsp red wine vinegar
2 tsp horseradish sauce or 1 tsp
    grated horseradish
chopped fresh chives, to garnish

You could skin the tomatoes if you wish: cover with boiling water for a minute, then drain and slip off the skins. Slice the tomatoes, with skins or without, into bite-sized pieces, divide between four plates and season with salt and pepper.

To make the topping, mix together the ricotta cheese, yogurt, oil, vinegar and horseradish sauce until creamy. You could use a blender for this if you want it really smooth.

Season, then pour this mixture over the tomatoes and sprinkle with chopped chives.

Stuffed grape leaves
V

These are fun to make and delicious served as part of a selection of tapas, or arranged attractively on individual plates with some tzatziki or hummus (see pages 46 and 49) and a few juicy black olives.

SERVES 4–6
36 fresh grape leaves (if available) or preserved grape leaves
8oz (225g) brown basmati rice
1 large onion, chopped
2 tbsp chopped fresh parsley
2 fresh tomatoes, skinned and chopped
2oz (50g) pine nuts
2oz (50g) raisins
½ tsp cinnamon
2 garlic cloves, crushed
salt and freshly ground black pepper
6 tbsp olive oil
5fl oz (150ml) water
1–2 tbsp lemon juice
lemon wedges, to garnish

If you're using fresh grape leaves, fill a large saucepan halfway with water and bring it to a boil. Trim the leaves and put into the boiling water, cover and simmer for 2 minutes. Then drain and run under cold water to refresh them. Drain well. With preserved grape leaves, simply drain and rinse well under the cold tap.

Half fill the saucepan with water; add the rice and boil for 10 minutes, then drain.

Mix the rice, onion, parsley, tomatoes, pine kernels, raisins, cinnamon, garlic and seasoning together. Place a spoonful of this filling on each leaf, fold the edges over and place the little bundles side by side in a frying pan. Mix the oil and water together and pour over the vine leaves. Sprinkle the lemon juice on top.

Cook, covered, over a very gentle heat for 2–2½ hours or until the rice and leaves are tender. Keep an eye on the water level and add a little more from time to time if necessary. Serve garnished with lemon wedges.

Dips and snacks
Aïoli with crudités

This garlic-flavored mayonnaise from Provence, served with a gloriously colorful selection of whatever fresh vegetables are available, makes a wonderful first course or even a light meal. You need a blender or food processor to make this recipe.

SERVES 4–6
FOR THE CRUDITÉS
A selection of raw vegetables in bite-sized pieces; aim for maybe 4–5 different types of contrasting colors, such as: crunchy red radishes served whole with some of the green parts still attached; bright orange carrot cut into matchsticks; strips of seeded red pepper; cauliflower florets; small very fresh mushrooms; scallions, trimmed; pieces of crunchy fennel bulb; juicy cucumber in chunks; crisp leaves of endive or stalks of celery; quarters of firm tomatoes, or cherry tomatoes.

FOR THE AÏOLI
1 egg
2–4 garlic cloves, peeled and crushed
¼ tsp salt
¼ tsp mustard powder
¼ tsp pepper
2 tsp red wine vinegar
2 tsp lemon juice
7fl oz (200ml) extra-virgin olive oil

Break the egg into the blender and add the garlic, salt, mustard, pepper, vinegar and lemon juice.

continued next page

Avocado and cream cheese dip v

Baba ganoush v

Blend at a medium speed for about 1 minute. Then turn the speed to high and gradually add the oil, drop by drop, through the top of the lid.

When about half the oil has been added and you hear the sound of the mixture change, you can add the oil more quickly in a thin stream.

If the mixture is very thick you can thin it by stirring in a little hot water. Serve the aïoli in a bowl with the crudités on the side.

VARIATIONS
Quick and easy aïoli

Nothing beats the real thing, but you can make a good quick aïoli using high-quality bought mayonnaise with crushed garlic mixed into it. Start with 1 crushed clove of garlic and add more to taste.

Light aïoli

If you want to serve aïoli but hesitate on account of all the calories it contains, you might like to use half mayonnaise and half natural yogurt; or add some garlic to the ricotta mayonnaise (see page 77) and use that instead of full-fat mayonnaise.

While classic guacamole (see page 45) contains only avocado, tomatoes, coriander and chili, this dip has a base of cream cheese — full fat or low fat, whichever you choose — and a hint of garlic, Tabasco, lemon juice and wine vinegar. Both dips are delectable. Use vegan cream cheese if you prefer.

SERVES 4–6
9oz (250g) cream cheese
1 garlic clove, crushed
salt and freshly ground black pepper
Tabasco sauce
2 large, ripe avocados
1 tbsp lemon juice
dash of red wine vinegar
sprinkling of paprika, to garnish
tortilla chips or melba toast (see
    page 54), to serve

Mix together the cream cheese, garlic, some salt, pepper and a few drops of Tabasco.

Just before serving, peel and mash the avocados with the lemon juice. Mix with the ricotta. Check the seasoning, adding a dash of wine vinegar.

Spoon the dip onto a plate and sprinkle with paprika to give a nice touch of scarlet against the pale green. Serve with tortilla chips or crisp melba toast.

In this Middle Eastern dip the intense, subtle flavor of the eggplant blends with the rich, earthy taste of the tahini (sesame cream) and the texture is substantial without being heavy. I love it, especially the smoky version (see opposite). It looks beautiful in a shallow bowl, its pale surface swirled with golden-green olive oil. Serve with warm pita bread, thin crisp flatbread and colorful raw vegetables and olives.

SERVES 4 ❄
2 eggplant (about 1lb (450g))
2–3 tbsp extra-virgin olive oil
2 heaped tbsp tahini
2 tbsp lemon juice
1 large garlic clove, crushed
salt and freshly ground black pepper

TO GARNISH
extra olive oil, to swirl
a scattering of toasted sesame seeds
a little chopped flat-leaf parsley

Halve the eggplants lengthwise, removing the stems. Rub them lightly with a little of the olive oil and place on a baking sheet.

Bake at 400°F (200°C) for about 25 minutes or until they can be pierced easily with the point of a sharp knife. Cool.

Chop the eggplant flesh as finely as you can, then mix it with all the other ingredients. Alternatively, blend the eggplant, remaining oil, the tahini, lemon juice and garlic together until fairly smooth. Season with salt and pepper, then chill in the fridge.

To serve, spoon the baba ganoush onto a plate or shallow

Butter bean dip with sesame toast v

dish, swirl some olive oil over the top, and sprinkle with sesame seeds and chopped parsley.

VARIATIONS

Smoky baba ganoush v

Prick the eggplant in several places, then place under a very broiler, or on an oven rack placed on top of a gas burner, and char all over until black on the outside and soft inside. This takes about 25–30 minutes (remember to open the kitchen windows!). Cool slightly then scrape off the skin and discard. Blend the eggplant flesh to a pale cream with 2 tablespoons of olive oil, the tahini, lemon juice and garlic, a seasoning with salt and pepper to taste. Chill in the fridge until required, then serve garnished as described.

Baba ganoush with cumin and pine nuts v

For a spicier version add a large pinch — or more, to taste — of ground cumin to the mixture, either the smoked or unsmoked version, and scatter with some toasted pine nuts along with the chopped parsley.

Baba ganoush with pomegranate v

Make as described, either smoked or unsmoked, and scatter the top with some fresh pomegrate seeds (you won't need the whole pomegranate) and the chopped parsley.

Eggplant and yogurt dip

For this rather different, light and creamy version, instead of the tahini and lemon juice, mix the eggplant with 5fl oz (150ml) thick Greek yogurt and stir in a small bunch of fresh chopped herbs (chives, mint, coriander or dill). You can make this lighter by using low-fat yogurt or you can increase the richness by adding sour cream.

This is a creamy dip with a tangy flavor. If you use canned beans it's very quick to make, so it's a great standby. The dip is excellent served with hot crunchy sesame toast, which is very easy to make.

SERVES 4 ❄

4oz (125g) dried butter beans, soaked and cooked until tender (see page 176–7) or 400g can
1 small garlic clove, crushed (optional)
2 tbsp olive oil
2–3 tsp lemon juice or wine vinegar
salt and freshly ground black pepper
Tabasco sauce
lemon wedges, to garnish

FOR THE SESAME TOASTS

6 slices wholegrain bread
a little butter or vegan spread
a small handful of sesame seeds

Drain the butter beans, reserving the liquid. Purée the beans in a food processor or blender, adding enough of the reserved liquid to make a thick creamy purée; or mash them with a fork and beat in the liquid.

Stir in the garlic (if using), oil and enough lemon juice or wine vinegar to sharpen the mixture. Season well with salt and pepper and add a few drops of Tabasco. Chill the mixture in the fridge.

Just before you want to serve the dip, make the sesame toasts. Preheat the oven to 400°F (200°C). Cut the crusts off the bread and roll each slice with a rolling pin to flatten it a bit.

continued next page

Spread the bread with butter or vegan spread and sprinkle a good layer of sesame seeds on top, pressing them in with a knife. Cut the bread into fingers and place on a baking sheet. Bake for 10–15 minutes or until crisp and golden brown.

Meanwhile, spoon the dip on to small plates or into individual ramekin dishes and garnish each with a wedge of lemon. Serve with the hot sesame toasts.

VARIATIONS

Butter bean and black olive dip v

Make exactly as in the main recipe, but add 12 black olives, finely chopped, to the finished mixture or add them to the beans before blending.

Butter bean and black olive dip with hardboiled eggs

For this variation, cut four hardboiled eggs into wedges and arrange on six small plates. Spoon the bean and black olive dip on top and sprinkle with a little paprika. Garnish each plate with a few sprigs of watercress and a wedge of lemon.

Cannellini bean, black olive, sun-dried tomato and basil dip v

The flavors of the Mediterranean are in this simple dip, which is quick to whip up from a can of beans. It's great served with pieces of raw vegetables or chips for dipping, spooned on top of some lettuce as a starter, or spread on crackers, pita bread or crostini.

SERVES 4–6
1 small garlic clove, crushed
14oz can cannellini beans, drained and rinsed
juice of ½ lemon
3–4 sun-dried tomatoes, drained if in oil, or soaked in hot water for 30 minutes if dry
8 black olives, pitted
salt and freshly ground black pepper
1–2 sprigs of basil

Put the garlic, beans, lemon juice, tomatoes and olives into a food processor and blend to a thick purée. Alternatively, put them into a deep container and use an electric hand blender. Season to taste with salt and pepper, pour into a serving bowl and then tear the basil leaves over the top.

Serve with crisp pita strips and a chunky salad of Little Gem or Romaine hearts, firm tomatoes and batons of cucumber.

Cream cheese and sour cream dip

An American friend gave me this recipe, which she serves on Thanksgiving Day as a first course. Like the aïoli (see page 41), it's superb with a colorful selection of crisp fresh vegetables for dipping into the creamy mixture.

SERVES 6
FOR THE DIP
8oz (225g) low-fat fromage frais or quark
10fl oz (275ml) sour cream
1 garlic clove, crushed
2 tbsp finely chopped fresh chives
salt and freshly ground black pepper

FOR THE CRUDITÉS
A selection of about 5 different vegetables of contrasting colors, like those described for the aïoli on page 41.

Put the fromage frais or quark into a bowl, beat lightly with a fork, then stir in the sour cream, garlic and chives and mix to a smooth consistency.

Season with salt and pepper. Spoon the dip into a serving dish and chill in the fridge until required.

Arrange the colorful vegetables around the dip and serve.

Feta cheese and herb spread

This spread looks attractive in the center of a serving dish and surrounded by shiny black olives, whole red radishes, crunchy green scallions and quartered tomatoes.

SERVES 4 ❋

7oz (200g) feta cheese
4oz (125g) unsalted butter, softened
1 tbsp chopped fresh chives
1 tbsp chopped fresh dill
1 tbsp chopped fresh flat-leaf parsley
a pinch each of paprika and caraway
    seeds

Drain the feta cheese of any liquid from the packet, and blot with kitchen paper, then mash.

Put the butter into a bowl and beat with a spoon until creamy, then gradually beat in the mashed feta and the herbs and spices.

Chill the spread in the fridge, then serve it as suggested above or use it as a sandwich filling or a topping for savory biscuits.

Field bean pâté v

This wonderful coarse-textured pâté has a delicious earthy flavor. It's very economical and good served with fingers of hot wholegrain toast and a tomato salad. You do need a food processor or good blender to chop the beans.

SERVES 4 ❋

8oz (225g) dried field beans, soaked
    and cooked (see pages 176–7)
2 garlic cloves, chopped
a bunch of flat-leaf parsley
4 tsp red wine vinegar
2 tbsp extra-virgin olive oil
salt and freshly ground black pepper

Drain the beans, reserving the cooking liquid. Put the beans, garlic, parsley, vinegar and oil into a food processor or blender and blend thoroughly to break down the skins and make a coarse-textured purée.

Add a little of the bean cooking liquid if necessary to make a consistency like thick whipped cream.

Add salt and pepper to taste, then spoon the mixture into a shallow bowl or pâté dish.

Guacamole v

This is an authentic guacamole, just avocados, tomatos, coriander leaves, chili and seasoning, and I love it. It's great for entertaining; you can prepare the tomatoes, coriander and chilies in advance then mash in the avocados at the last minute to preserve their color. The quantity of chili is up to you — start with a little piece and gradually add more until it's hot enough for you.

SERVES 4

4 tomatoes, finely chopped
½ bunch of coriander, finely chopped
1–3 fresh green chilies (jalepenos),
    finely chopped
2 large avocados
salt and freshly ground black pepper
tortilla chips, to serve

Mix the tomatoes and coriander together in a bowl. Add a little of the chopped chilies.

Just before serving, remove the peel and stone from each avocado, cut the flesh into rough chunks and add to the bowl. Mash the avocado pieces with the tomato mixture to make a creamy, chunky dip.

Taste and add more chili gradually, until it's as you like it, then season to taste with salt and pepper. Serve within 30–60 minutes.

Haricot bean and garlic spread

This is great in sandwiches or on savory biscuits. The basic mixture can be varied in a number of ways (see below).

SERVES 4 ❄

4oz (125g) dried haricot or navy beans, soaked and cooked until tender (see pages 176–7), then cooled, or 14oz can, rinsed and drained
2 tbsp (25g) butter, softened
1 garlic clove, crushed
a few drops of lemon juice
salt and freshly ground black pepper

Mash the beans to a smooth paste with a fork, then gradually blend in the butter, garlic and lemon juice. Season well with salt and pepper.

VARIATIONS

Haricot bean and fresh herb spread

Instead of the garlic add 2 tablespoons of chopped fresh herbs, such as parsley.

Haricot bean and olive spread

Make as described, adding six black olives, pitted and finely chopped or mashed, or 2–3 teaspoons of vegetarian tapenade (see page 48).

Haricot bean and sundried tomato and basil spread

Make as described and stir in six sun-dried tomatoes, drained and finely chopped, or 2–3 teaspoons sun-dried tomato purée, and 2 tablespoons of chopped fresh basil.

Hazelnut and cream cheese pâté loaf

This easy-to-make loaf may sound unusual but guests who try it always ask for the recipe. Serve it with fresh salad, or in slices as a first course.

SERVES 4–6 ❄

2oz (50g) dried breadcrumbs (see page 183), for coating
9oz (250g) ricotta
4oz (125g) hazelnuts roasted (see page 139)
juice and grated rind of ½ lemon
2 tbsp chopped flat-leaf parsley
salt and freshly ground black pepper
a pinch of paprika
crisp lettuce leaves, slices of tomato or cucumber, grated carrot, sprigs of watercress, to serve

Cut a large square of wax or parchment paper and sprinkle the breadcrumbs over.

Put the ricotta, hazelnuts, lemon juice and rind and parsley into a bowl and mix until well combined. Add salt and pepper to taste and 1 or 2 pinches of paprika.

Turn the cream cheese mixture onto the paper on top of the breadcrumbs. Use the paper to form it into a roll, coating it completely with the crumbs.

Leave the roll in the paper and place in the fridge to chill for several hours.

To serve, unwrap the roll and discard the paper. Place on a bed of lettuce and surround with sliced tomato, cucumber, grated carrot, watercress or anything else you fancy. Alternatively, serve in slices on individual plates, on a pool of chilled tomato sauce (see page 71).

Hummus v

Homemade hummus is much better than the store-bought versions. You can make it exactly to your taste and if you keep the ingredients in stock, you can whip some up in moments any time you fancy it.

SERVES 4–6 ❄

7oz (200g) dried chickpeas, soaked and cooked or 2 x 14oz cans
2 garlic cloves, crushed
2 tbsp extra-virgin olive oil
1–3 tbsp tahini
2 tbsp lemon juice
salt and freshly ground black pepper

TO GARNISH

extra olive oil, for drizzling
sprinkling of paprika
lemon wedges
handful of black olives

Drain the chickpeas, reserving the liquid. Blend the chickpeas with the garlic, oil and tahini, starting with 1 tablespoon of the lemon juice and 8–9fl oz (250ml) of the liquid, to make a purée roughly the consistency of lightly whipped cream.

Taste, adding more tahini if you want a more intense flavor. Season with salt and pepper.

Put the hummus into a large shallow dish, drizzle some olive oil over, sprinkle with paprika and garnish with lemon wedges and black olives.

Lentil and mushroom pâté

The earthy flavor of both lentils and mushrooms combines to make this satisfying pâté. It can be served piled up on salad leaves or packed into a pâté dish, with some crackers or melba toast (see page 54).

SERVES 2 AS A MAIN MEAL, 4 AS A STARTER ❄
4oz (125g) dried green lentils or 14oz can
2oz (50g) button mushrooms
3 tbsp extra-virgin olive oil
1 garlic clove, crushed
1 tbsp chopped fresh parsley
salt and freshly ground black pepper
2–4 tsp lemon juice

If you're using dried lentils, cook them in plenty of water until they're very tender, about 45–50 minutes, then drain. If using canned lentils, simply drain and rinse.

Wipe the mushrooms and chop them up fairly finely.

Heat the oil in a small saucepan and fry the mushrooms and garlic for 2–3 minutes, then remove them from the heat and mix in the lentils and parsley.

Season with salt, pepper and lemon juice. Chill before serving.

Lentil and tomato spread

Quick-cooking split red lentils are used for this spread. It tastes great in sandwiches with some raw onion, chutney or sliced tomato.

SERVES 4 ❄
4oz (125g) split red lentils
7fl oz (200ml) water
2tbsp (25g) butter, softened
1 tbsp tomato purée
a few drops of lemon juice
salt and freshly ground black pepper

Cook the lentils in the water for 20–30 minutes or until they're tender and there's no water left. Leave to cool.

Mash the butter, tomato purée, lemon juice and some salt and black pepper into the cooked lentils. Beat well with a spoon to make a smooth pâté.

VARIATIONS
Lentil and chive spread

Make this as described but leaving out the tomato purée and adding 1–2 tablespoons of chopped chives instead.

Lentil and parsley spread

Make as described, leaving out the tomato purée and adding 2 tablespoons of chopped fresh parsley. One or two finely chopped scallions go well in this, too.

Red pepper hummus

Make as described, using 1 tablespoon of tahini and 2–4 roasted red peppers from a jar. Blend everything together before adding any liquid, because the red peppers add moisture to the mixture. Flavor with 1–2 pinches of paprika and a drop of Tabasco sauce if you want to make it hotter.

Mushroom pâté

This flavorsome pâté makes an excellent starter. Try it with some crackers or breadsticks.

SERVES 4
½oz (15g) dried porcini mushrooms
1lb (450g) mushrooms
1 garlic clove, peeled
2–4 tbsp chopped fresh parsley
2 tbsp (25g) butter or 2 tbsp olive oil
salt and freshly ground black pepper
a squeeze of lemon juice

TO SERVE
a little sour cream or crème fraîche
a sprinkling of paprika
sprigs of flat-leaf parsley

Rinse the porcini mushrooms thoroughly to get rid of any grit. Put them in a small bowl, cover with boiling water and leave to soak for 1 hour. Drain and reserve the liquid.

Put the soaked mushrooms and their liquid into a food processor with the ordinary mushrooms, the garlic and the parsley and whip until everything is finely chopped. Alternatively, roughly slice the mushrooms, then put all the ingredients into a deep bowl and use an electric hand blender.

Heat the butter or oil in a large saucepan and add the mushroom mixture. Stir, then cook, uncovered, for 15–20 minutes or until all liquid has boiled away. Remove the pan from the heat and season with salt, pepper and lemon juice. Leave to cool. Serve on individual plates with a heaped teaspoon of sour cream or crème fraîche, a sprinkling of paprika and a sprig of parsley on each.

Stilton pâté with walnuts and port

This easy-to-make recipe is perfect at Christmas. Serve it as a starter on individual plates with watercress and a few fresh walnuts, or pile it into a bowl and serve with crackers. Note that the only type of port that is vegetarian is "crusted", a very small category, named because of the "crust" of sediment that forms in the bottle. It is intended to be a more economical alternative to Vintage or Late-bottled Vintage and is made from a blend of several harvests. The date on the label refers to when it was bottled.

SERVES 6 ❄
8oz (225g) Stilton cheese
12oz (350g) cream cheese
3oz (75g) butter, softened
3 tbsp "crusted" port
2oz (50g) shelled walnuts, chopped
watercress, to garnish (optional)
crackers or breadsticks, to serve

Grate or crumble the Stilton, place in a bowl with the cream cheese and butter and mix well to a creamy consistency. Stir in the walnuts.

Either spoon the mixture into a small dish and smooth the top, or press it into a fat sausage shape and wrap it in a piece of foil, twisting the two ends like a cracker. Chill in the fridge for at least 2 hours.

Cut the roll into slices to serve, garnished with watercress, or serve from the bowl, with crackers or breadsticks.

Tapenade v

This can be served as part of a selection of starters or dips, or as part of a tapas platter, perhaps with some crunchy salted almonds, celery sticks, radishes and scallions. The better the olives, the better the flavor. You can use pitted ones if they look good, or buy them intact and pit them yourself (if you don't have an olive pitter this is an arduous task, however).

SERVES 4–6
11oz (300g) green or black whole
    olives, or 8oz (225g) pitted olives
3 tbsp capers, drained, or rinsed and
    drained if preserved in salt
3 garlic cloves, crushed
3 sprigs of flat-leaf parsley, stems
    removed
3 tbsp extra-virgin olive oil
a squeeze of lemon juice, to taste
a dash of Tabasco sauce (optional)

If using whole olives, remove the pits then purée with capers, garlic and parsley together with an electric hand blender or in a food processor.

Add the oil and blend well again to make a beautiful, thick mixture. Sharpen with a squeeze or two of lemon juice and perhaps a little dash of Tabasco for an extra kick, if you like.

Tzatziki

Creamy yet light and refreshing, this is great as a dip with pieces of pita bread as part of a tapas selection, along with juicy black olives, stuffed grape leaves (see page 41), some cherry tomatoes and any anything else you fancy.

SERVES 2–4
½ cucumber
salt
9oz (250g) thick full-fat Greek yogurt
1 small garlic clove, crushed
freshly ground black pepper
½ tsp red or white wine vinegar
1 tbsp chopped fresh mint or chives

Peel the cucumber and grate it coarsely. Put the grated cucumber into a sieve, mix with a pinch or two of salt, then cover with a small plate with a weight on top and leave over a bowl to drain for 30 minutes to draw out the extra liquid. Pat dry on paper towels.

Mix the yogurt, cucumber and garlic together in a bowl, then season to taste with salt and pepper. Put into a serving bowl and scatter with chopped mint or chives. Serve chilled.

Spicy vegetable and nut pâté with yogurt sauce

Another easy one to make, this pâté consists of crunchy vegetables and nuts, flavored with curry and garlic.

SERVES 6
2 tbsp (25g) butter
1 onion, finely chopped
1 carrot (about 2oz (50g), finely chopped
1 stalk of celery, chopped
½ green pepper (about 2oz (50g), seeded and chopped
½ red pepper (about 2oz (50g), seeded and chopped
1 garlic clove, crushed
1 tbsp mild curry powder
4oz (125g) hazelnuts, roasted (see page 139) and chopped
8oz (225g) ricotta cheese
salt and freshly ground black pepper

FOR THE SAUCE
2in (5cm) cucumber
7fl oz (200ml) natural yogurt
3 tbsp finely chopped fresh mint

Line a 1lb (450g) loaf pan with a strip of non-stick baking parchment to cover the base and come up the two narrow sides.

Melt the butter in a large saucepan and fry all the vegetables for 2–3 minutes; they should soften a little, but still be very crunchy.

Add the garlic and curry powder and cook for 1 further minute. Remove from the heat and stir in the rest of the ingredients. Season with salt and pepper.

Spoon the mixture into the prepared loaf tin — it won't fill it — and smooth the top. Cover with foil and chill in the fridge for several hours.

Meanwhile make the sauce. Peel and finely chop the cucumber and mix with the yogurt and mint. Season with salt and pepper.

To serve, slip a knife round the edges of the pâté to loosen it, then turn it out of the tin and cut into slices. Place one slice on each plate with some of the sauce on the side.

Bruschetta v

Bruschetta is easy to do and make a great snack, starter or canapé. The bases can be made in advance — they will keep for a week wrapped in foil or in an airtight container — and topped just before serving, so that they stay crisp. Choose up to four of the suggested toppings opposite.

FOR THE BASES

1 baguette, cut diagonally into 1cm (½in) slices
olive oil, for brushing

Pre-heat the oven to 300°F (150°C). Brush the bread on each side with olive oil, place on a baking sheet and bake for about 20 minutes or until crisp. Alternatively, you can grill the bread on both sides, or toast it in a toaster first and then brush it with the oil.

Unless I'm just making one or two for a quick snack, I prefer to do them in the oven because it's easier and they become really crisp and dry. This also means that you can make them in advance as described above.

VARIATIONS

Garlic bruschetta v

Rub both sides of the grilled or toasted bread with the cut surface of a garlic clove.

Herb bruschetta v

Use rosemary (or other herb) bread to make the bruschetta; or, if you're using a plain baguette, sprinkle each piece on both sides with a good pinch of crushed rosemary or dried thyme. Cook as described.

Barbecue bruschetta v

Bruschetta is great cooked over the barbecue: lay the bread on the grate, cook until crisp and striped with black, then turn the slices over and cook the other side. Have toppings and garnishes laid out ready for people to help themselves.

Crostini v

These are really just smaller, thinner versions of bruschetta with more delicate toppings. Use the slimmest baguette you can find. I usually cut this straight, into circles, rather than diagonally.

Toppings for bruschetta and crostini

Remember that people will be eating these with their fingers, so make sure that the toppings aren't too runny, and that there is something on top of the base for the pieces to stick to, so they don't fall off.

Butter bean dip v (see page 43) or drained cannellini beans mashed with garlic and vinaigrette and garnished with black olives.

Tapenade v, bought or homemade (see page 48) garnished with flat-leaf parsley.

Hummus v, bought or homemade (see page 46), cooked asparagus tips and sesame seeds.

Eggplant and sesame pâté v or baba ganoush (see page 42) garnished with black olives.

Smooth goat cheese topped with red onion marmalade (see page 68).

Mashed blue cheese, cubes of red beet and sprigs of dill.

Cooked chestnuts (canned or vacuum-packed) mashed to a coarse paste with butter, garlic, lemon juice and salt and pepper, then topped with caperberries.

Finely chopped tomato and torn basil leaves v mixed with olive oil, crushed garlic, salt and pepper.

Garlic and herb cream cheese with chargrilled or marinated artichoke hearts (from the deli or a jar).

Lentil and mushroom pâté v (see page 47) topped with grilled red and yellow pepper strips and thyme leaves.

Hummus, bought or homemade (see page 46), arugula, small cubes of feta cheese, sun-dried tomatoes and a few pine nuts.

Opposite: Bruschetta with assorted toppings

Sandwiches and wraps

Avocado salad v

This is nice on lightly toasted Granary or walnut bread. Mash a medium avocado, adding a squeeze of lemon juice to preserve the color, and salt and pepper to taste. Spread it over the bread. Add any salad leaves or fresh herbs you fancy — tender lettuce, fresh coriander, arugula, chopped scallions — and press the slices of bread together gently but firmly.

Brie and peach chutney

Make this as described for stilton and cranberry (see opposite) for a lighter, more summery sandwich. It's good made in a baguette which has had some of the middle scooped out.

Falafels in pita v

Fill a pita bread with chopped lettuce, add some whole or sliced falafels (see page 189) and any other salad you fancy, such as sliced cucumber, scallions, tomatoes and a few sprigs of coriander. Drizzle with a tablespoonful of tahini that you've mixed with water and a dash of lemon juice until smooth and creamy, or with tzatziki (see page 49), yogurt dip or mayonnaise thinned with water.

Goat cheese and red onion

This is made with the smooth, creamy goat cheese that looks like cream cheese. Spread it on your bread — whatever type you fancy (I like raisin and rosemary) top with some very thin slices of red onion, and press the slices together.

Greek salad in pita bread

Make a Greek salad as described on page 90, or just quickly put together some chopped cucumber, tomato and onion, with some feta cheese, a squeeze of lemon juice, a few black olives, a drop or two of olive oil, and pile into a pita pocket. So good!

Grilled Mediterranean vegetables and pesto v

Slice a selection of vegetables, such as zucchini, eggplant, red onion and red pepper, into bite-sized pieces, brush with olive oil and put under the broiler for about 10 minutes on each side or until tender and lightly browned, or save some from a previous meal. Mix with pesto and pile into a scooped-out baguette or roll them up in a wrap. You could also add some chickpeas, cubes of feta or some bought or homemade hummus (see page 46), to increase the protein content.

Hummus, coriander and black olive v

You can use pita bread for this, or slices of whatever type of bread you like. The most important thing is to put in a generous filling of creamy bought or homemade hummus (see page 46) with sliced, pitted olives and some chopped fresh coriander.

Mexican wrap v

Use leftover refried red beans (see page 200), if you have them; otherwise fry an onion in olive oil for 10 minutes, then mash into it the drained contents of a 14oz can of red kidney beans, a chopped tomato and chili powder to taste. Spread onto a tortilla wrap, top with any of the following: chopped avocado or guacamole (see page 45), vegan or dairy sour cream, grated vegan or dairy cheese and chopped coriander. Roll up neatly, making sure everything is enclosed.

Ploughman's

On the same theme as the two previous suggestions, but use your choice of British hard cheese — a good strong Cheddar or a crumbly Wensleydale, for instance — and a sweet-and-sour pickle.

Stilton and cranberry

For a luxurious winter sandwich, butter two slices of granary or walnut bread. Place a round lettuce on one slice, top with slices of Stilton and cranberry sauce, finish with another lettuce leaf, and press together with the second slice.

Tomato, mozzarella and olive

Brush a panini or half-size ciabatta with olive oil and fill with sliced tomato and mozzarella, then add **some lovely green basil leaves and pitted black olives. This is good with sliced avocado, too.**

Parsley pinwheels

I love making and eating these! They look irresistible, like slices from miniature savory Swiss rolls, and are an attractive addition to a sandwich selection. Fresh springy bread that's not too thin works best, such as an ordinary, medium-sliced white or wholegrain loaf.

MAKES 25 PINWHEELS ❄
5 tbsp (60g) soft butter
2 tbsp finely chopped fresh flat-leaf parsley
1–2 tsp hot water
5 slices from a large sliced loaf of bread

Beat the butter, parsley and hot water together in a bowl to make a light, creamy mixture.

Cut the crusts off the bread and flatten each slice slightly with a rolling pin. Spread the bread generously with the green butter mixture, then roll the slices up like Swiss rolls and if possible chill them for an hour or so.

When ready to serve, cut each roll into about five fairly thin slices.

VARIATION
Pâté or hummus pinwheels

These are lovely made with Swiss vegetable pâté, which you can buy at health-food stores. Use white bread for these pinwheels, for a good color contrast. Alternatively, use bought or homemade hummus (see page 46); same color, different flavor.

Asparagus rolls

These are very retro, but I've always loved them: tender asparagus wrapped in buttery wholegrain bread; what's not to like?

MAKES ABOUT 40 ROLLS ❄
1 sliced wholegrain loaf
softened butter, for spreading
8oz (225g) asparagus, cooked and drained

Cut the crusts from the bread and roll each slice with a rolling pin to make it thinner and more flexible.

Butter the bread. Put one spear of asparagus on each slice and roll the bread around the asparagus. Cut each roll into pieces so that they are "bite-sized". Cover and keep in a cool place until needed.

Asparagus and cheese on toast

Asparagus from a can may be a pale shadow of fresh asparagus, but it has its own charms, including tasting great on toast.

SERVES 1–2
½ small (14oz) can asparagus
4oz (125g) grated cheese
2 pieces of hot toast

Drain the asparagus and place on the toast.

Pile the grated cheese on top and place under a hot broiler for 3–5 minutes or until the cheese is golden brown and bubbly. Serve at once.

Avocado toast v

My favorite! I love this combination of buttery, creamy avocado and crisp wholegrain toast.

SERVES 2
1 large avocado
juice of ½ lemon
salt and freshly ground black pepper
2–4 slices of hot wholegrain toast
a dusting of chili powder (optional)

Peel, stone and thinly slice (or mash) the avocado, then sprinkle with lemon juice and season with salt and pepper.

Place, or spread, the avocado slices on the toast, dust lightly with chili powder if you're using this, and serve at once while the toast is still warm and crisp.

Melba toast v

This sounds a bit retro — indeed, it is retro — but I enjoy both making and eating it, and often find it just the perfect thing to accompany creamy dips. It's best to use bought sliced bread to make it as it's easier to cut. People always eat more of this than you think they will, so make plenty!

1–2 slices of sliced bread, white or wholegrain, for each person

Preheat the oven to 400°F (200°C).

Toast the bread, then lay the pieces of toast flat on a board and, using a sharp knife and a sawing motion, cut the toast in half horizontally, so you end up with two very thin slices, each toasted on one side.

Place the toast halves, uncooked side up, on a baking sheet and bake for about 7–10 minutes, until they are crisp and brown all over, and curling up at the edges. Leave to cool. Store in an airtight container or foil for up to one week.

Mushrooms on toast

Always a winner, you can't go wrong with tender, buttery baby mushrooms on crisp toast.

SERVES 2
1lb (450g) button mushrooms
1 tbsp olive oil
2 tbsp (25g) butter
2–4 large slices toast, white or wholegrain
salt and freshly ground black pepper
chopped fresh flat-leaf parsley, to garnish

Wipe the mushrooms, then slice and fry lightly in the oil and butter.

Just before the mushrooms are done, toast the bread.

Season the mushrooms with salt and pepper, then spoon them directly on top of the toast (no need to butter it), together with all their lovely juices. Sprinkle with a little chopped parsley and serve at once.

VARIATIONS
Garlic mushrooms on toast

Make as described, cooking 1–2 crushed large garlic cloves with the mushrooms.

Hummus on toast with vine tomatoes v

Quick, easy and so good!

SERVES 2

4oz (125g) hummus, bought or
    homemade (see page 46) or
2–4 large slices of wholegrain toast
2–4 clusters of cherry tomatoes on
    the vine

Spread the hummus on the toast –
no need to butter it first – and heat
through under the broiler.

Put the clusters of cherry
tomatoes under the broiler too for a
few minutes until lightly roasted,
then place one cluster on each piece
of toast and serve.

VARIATION
Swiss vegetable pâté and tomato toast v

Swiss vegetable pâté is a smooth,
savory spread that you can buy in
health-food stores. My family have
always liked it in sandwiches and
on toast. Just spread it straight
onto the toast, instead of the
hummus, heat through under the
broiler and top with the tomatoes,
as described.

Tomato and cheese on toast

This couldn't be simpler, yet makes
a lovely hot snack, rather like a very
simple pizza.

SERVES 2

4 slices wholegrain bread
1–2 tbsp olive oil
4 tomatoes, skinned or not, as you
    wish
4oz (125g) grated cheese

Toast the bread and brush one side
(or both sides, if you like) with olive
oil.

Slice the tomatoes thinly and
arrange on top of the toast, then
scatter the cheese evenly on top of
that.

Put the toast under a hot broiler
for 4–5 minutes or until the cheese
is golden brown and bubbling and
the tomatoes are heated through
and slightly softened. Serve at once.

Garlic bread

Hot garlic bread is unfailingly
popular and really easy to make.
You can also prepare it, ready for
popping in the oven, ahead of time,
and even freeze it (before baking).

SERVES 4–6

1 baguette or 1 small wholegrain loaf
3–4 garlic cloves
salt
4oz (125g) butter, softened

Set the oven to 400°F (200°C). Slice
the baguette or wholegrain loaf
three-quarters of the way through
into chunky slices — they should
just hold together at the base. Cut
the wholegrain loaf right through
into thin slices.

Make the garlic butter by
crushing the peeled cloves in a little
salt, then mixing into the butter.
Spread this butter on both sides of
each slice of bread. Push the bread
back into the original shape, then
wrap in foil and place on a baking
sheet in the oven. Bake for about
20 minutes or until it's heated
through and crisp on the outside.
Serve at once.

VARIATION
Quick garlic bread for one or two

Spread some slices of bread with
garlic butter made using a small
clove of garlic (as described). Broil
them, without any foil covering
them, until the butter has melted
and the bread is crisp round the
edges.

Hot garlic chickpeas in pita bread v

These sizzling hot, garlicy chickpeas make a wonderful snack; it's hard to stop eating them straight out of the pan! They're great packed into a pita pocket, along with anything else you fancy — such as sliced tomato, onion, chopped mint, a spoonful of mayonnaise or yogurt, or some sweet chutney.

SERVES 4

2 x 14oz cans chickpeas, drained
a little self-raising wholemeal flour, to coat
salt and freshly ground black pepper
6 tbsp olive oil
2–4 garlic cloves, crushed

TO SERVE

4 warm wholegrain pita breads
any of the optional extras mentioned above

Spread the chickpeas out on a large plate and sprinkle with the flour and a little salt and pepper. Turn them gently so that each one is coated with flour.

Heat the oil in a large frying pan, then add the chickpeas and garlic. Fry the chickpeas gently until they are crisp and golden, turning often. You may need to do them in more than one batch.

Slit open the top of each pitta bread, fill with the hot chickpeas and any extras you are adding, and serve.

Quick pita bread pizza

These quick pizzas taste surprisingly like the "real thing", yet can be whipped up in moments.

SERVES 2

2 wholegrain pita breads
6 tbsp tomato purée
1–2 tbsp finely chopped onion
1 tsp dried oregano
1 tbsp olive oil
½–1 tsp sugar
salt and freshly ground black pepper
4 tomatoes, thinly sliced
a few button mushrooms (optional), thinly sliced
4oz (125g) shredded mozzarella or grated Cheddar cheese
a drizzle of olive oil, a sprinkling of dried oregano and a few olives (optional), to garnish

Cut the pita breads open and separate the two halves. Put these on a baking sheet that will fit under your broiler.

Mix together the tomato purée, chopped onion, oregano, oil and adding sugar, salt and pepper to taste.

Spread each pita bread half with the tomato purée mixture.

Arrange the tomato slices on top to cover the surface and add a few thin slices of raw mushroom (if using), or any other ingredients you want — such as sweetcorn, thin strips of red pepper, artichoke hearts and olives — and sprinkle the cheese all over the top.

Place under a hot broiler for 5–6 minutes or until the top is golden brown and bubbling. Serve at once.

Quick ciabatta pizza

Ciabatta bread, split in half, makes a wonderfully light and crispy base for a quick pizza. A half-sized ciabatta is best, making one pizza each for four people once the ciabattas have been split in half; alternatively, cut a normal-size ciabatta into four. Do use good-quality canned tomatoes — they reduce to a delicious thick sauce far quicker than economy versions. Keep some ciabattas in the freezer and some canned tomatoes in the cupboard and you'll never be stuck for a tasty quick meal again!

SERVES 4

1 large onion, peeled and chopped
2 tbsp olive oil
14oz can chopped tomatoes in juice
½ tsp dried oregano
2 half-size ciabatta breads, or 1 normal-size ciabatta
salt and freshly ground black pepper
4oz (125g) grated Cheddar cheese or shredded mozzarella
a handful of pitted green olives

Sauté the onion in 1 tablespoon of oil for 5 minutes, covered, then add the tomatoes and oregano. Simmer, without a lid on the pan, for about 10 minutes or until thick.

Meanwhile, slice the bread in half lengthways. Put the pieces on a broiler pan or baking sheet and broil on both sides until just crisp; don't let them get really brown.

Drinks

Iced banana smoothie v

Brush the toasted bread lightly all over with the rest of the olive oil and place, outside up, on the broiler pan or baking sheet.

Season the tomato sauce with salt and pepper, then spread it over the top of the ciabatta halves, dividing it between them. Scatter with the grated cheese and put the olives on top.

Place under the hot broiler for about 7 minutes or until the sides of the pizzas are crisp and the cheese is melted and golden brown. Serve at once.

If you freeze chunks of banana and then whip them with freshly squeezed orange juice, the result is a wonderful, thick smoothie, almost like a completely natural ice cream shake.

MAKES 1 X 250ML (10FL OZ) GLASS

1 banana, peeled
7fl oz (200ml) freshly squeezed orange juice (using about 3 oranges)

Peel the banana and cut into roughly 1in (2cm) chunks, then freeze until solid.

To make the smoothie, put the frozen banana chunks into a blender or food processor with the orange juice, and whip to a pale, thick cream. Serve at once.

Fruit cup with vermouth v

This lovely fruit cup, which a friend of mine serves as an aperitif, is beautifully refreshing and great for drinking in the garden in the summer. All you do is mix together equal quantities of well-chilled apple juice, orange juice and white vermouth. Then add a few sprigs of fresh mint and a few slices of orange, lemon and/or cucumber, as available. You can use either still apple juice or a sparkling one if you want some bubbles.

Fresh peppermint tea v

This is the most refreshing way to end a meal, and good for the digestion if you've overindulged. You can use real peppermint, or spearmint, the variety most commonly grown in gardens and available in stores. It's less intense than peppermint.

MAKES 1 POTFUL
a large bunch of peppermint or spearmint
boiling water

Cram the mint into a large tea pot or French Press and fill to the top with boiling water.

Leave to stand for 4–5 minutes, then pour. If you're using a French Press you can push down the handle, separating the mint leaves from the water, as you would with coffee, but a teapot works fine too. You can top it up again with more boiling water if you wish.

Lassi v

This drink from India is refreshing in hot weather, but also nourishing because of the protein and calcium in the yogurt. It can be made salty or sweet, according to taste.

SERVES 1
1 heaped tbsp natural yogurt or vegan yogurt (see page 340)
7fl oz (200ml) chilled water
a pinch of salt, or 1–2 tsp clear honey and a pinch of cinnamon, or a few drops of triple-strength rose water

Put the yogurt into a glass and gradually stir in the water. Add the salt or honey and cinnamon or rose water.

Strawberry bliss in a glass v

This is the most wonderful fruit smoothie, sweet and delectable. The more powerful your blender, the smoother and better this will be. If you really love smoothies, you may find it worth investing in a good-quality, high-speed machine.

MAKES 1–2 LARGE GLASSES
1 sweet orange, peeled and cut into rough chunks
1 banana, peeled and roughly sliced
1 thick slice of fresh pineapple, peeled and cut into chunks
8oz (225g) strawberries, hulled (or leave unhulled if organic)
a small bunch of sweet red grapes
a cup of ice

Put all the ingredients into a high-speed blender and process until thick and smooth. If adding everything at once is a bit too much for your blender to handle, start with the oranges and use chilled water instead of ice, to get things moving. Drink as soon as possible.

VARIATIONS
Blackberry bliss in a glass v

The flavor of late summer! Use 8oz (225g) juicy ripe blackberries instead of the strawberries.

Blueberry bliss in a glass v

Deep purple, delicious and wonderful (so they say) for keeping those brain cells lively and youthful, blueberries make a great smoothie. Add 8oz (225g) of them instead of the strawberries.

Pomegranate bliss in a glass v

Leave out the strawberries and instead pop the juicy red seeds out of 1 large pomegranate by cutting it in half then bending back each half to release the seeds, dislodging them with the aid of a small pointed knife. Add the pomegranate seeds to the blender along with the other fruit and blend until completely smooth.

Green bliss in a glass v

Try adding a good handful of baby spinach leaves to any of these smoothies. You won't taste the spinach — it will be just like a fruit smoothie — but you'll notice the extra, sustained energy that the green leaves give you. A green smoothie must be one of the most health-giving drinks on the planet. You can use other dark green leaves too; kale, for instance. Start with a few leaves and add more once you get used to the flavor.

Yogurt and orange smoothie v

This is calming, revitalizing and quick to make.

**MAKES ABOUT ONE 250ML
(9FL OZ) GLASS**
1 orange, peeled
5fl oz (150ml) natural yogurt or
    vegan yogurt (see page 340)
a little honey (optional)

Break the orange into segments and place in blender. Add the yogurt, then blend for 30–60 seconds or until fairly smooth, adding a little honey to taste, if you like. There will still be some chunky pieces of orange, but these give the drink "body" and provide extra fiber.

Sauces
and relishes

A sauce can provide the perfect finishing touch to a dish; it can make the difference between ordinary and exceptional and transform some of your favorite dishes into something really special.

In this chapter you'll find many easy sauces and relishes that can accompany a variety of dishes — try some tangy Béarnaise with crispy eggplant fritters (see pages 63 and 36) or creamy mushroom and Marsala sauce with tofu escalopes (see pages 68 and 202). You'll also find many reliable classics — tomato sauce for pizza and delicious hollandaise (see pages 71 and 66). The good news is that they are all simple to make. Plus, if you're in a hurry, my ultra-easy blender béchamel sauces (see page 64) will turn a simple dish of steamed vegetables into a main course with just a topping of breadcrumbs, a scattering of grated cheese, and a flash under a hot broiler.

Apple sauce

You can use cooking apples, which cook to a lovely, soft, fluffy purée, or sweet eating apples, which require less sugar. Either way, the result is a pleasant, fruity sauce that goes well with lentil loaf or pease pudding.

SERVES 4–6 ❄
1lb (450g) apples
¼ cup water
¼ cup sugar
1 tbsp butter
salt

Peel and core the apples, then cut them into smallish pieces.

Put the apple pieces, water, sugar and butter into a medium-sized heavy-based saucepan and cook gently, with a lid on the pan, until the apples are soft.

Season with a little salt, then mash the mixture slightly with a wooden spoon to break up the apple. (Or you can blend it if you prefer a smoother consistency.)

VARIATIONS
Apple and cranberry sauce

For this version, cook 4oz (125g) fresh cranberries, washed and picked over, with the apples. You'll need to add more sugar as cranberries are very sharp.

Apple and red currant sauce

Use red currants instead of the cranberries or just soften the apples in 2 rounded tablespoons of red currant (or cranberry) jelly and leave out the sugar.

Blender Béarnaise sauce

This is a quick version of the classic rich French sauce. First, you reduce the vinegar in a saucepan to concentrate the flavor, then add it to the egg yolks in a blender and pour in the melted butter. It only takes a few minutes to make and is superb with dishes such as lentil and mushroom burgers or cashew and dill fritters (see pages 195 and page 147). A pleasant variation is to stir 4oz (125g) of fromage frais or yogurt into the finished sauce — this lightens it and makes enough to serve eight people.

SERVES 6
1 stick (125g) butter
2 tbsp red wine vinegar
1 tbsp very finely chopped onion
8 peppercorns, lightly crushed
2 egg yolks
1 tbsp lemon juice
salt and freshly ground black pepper

Melt the butter in a small saucepan.

Simmer the vinegar, onion and peppercorns together in another small pan until the vinegar has reduced by half.

Put the egg yolks and lemon juice into a blender and purée until just creamy, then strain in the vinegar mixture and blend again.

With the blender still going, slowly pour the melted butter in. As you do so, the mixture will thicken to a beautiful creamy consistency.

Season with salt and pepper and serve while still warm. If you need to keep it warm, transfer it to a bowl and stand in a saucepan or roasting pan of simmering water.

Quick blender béchamel sauce

This is a labor-saving way to make béchamel sauce and tastes just as good as the traditional version (see the cheese sauce on page 65). Parsley sauce is particularly easy when made by this method because you don't have to chop the parsley; simply pop the sprigs into the blender with everything else.

SERVES 4 ❋
2 tbsp (25g) butter
2 tbsp (25g) all-purpose flour
10–15 fl oz (275–425ml) milk
salt and freshly ground black pepper

Put the butter, flour, and milk into the blender, then add about ½ teaspoon of salt and a good grinding of black pepper.

Blend at high speed for a few seconds to break up the butter and mix everything together. There will be some lumpy bits of butter, but that doesn't matter.

Pour the mixture into a medium-sized saucepan and place over a moderate heat. Stir the sauce until it has thickened, then turn down the heat and leave to simmer gently for 15 minutes.

Lengthy simmering, to avoid a raw, floury taste, is particularly important with this method because there has been no initial cooking of the flour, as in traditional sauce-making.

VARIATIONS

Celery sauce

3–4 tablespoons of very finely chopped celery and ½ teaspoon of celery salt can be added to the sauce after blending and simmered until tender.

Cheese sauce

Add 4oz (125g) grated cheese after the sauce has cooked.

Egg sauce

Add three very finely chopped hardboiled eggs and a pinch of mace to the basic sauce.

Fennel sauce

Add 2–3 tablespoons of very finely chopped fennel bulb to the sauce before simmering.

Green herb sauce

Use 1–2 tablespoons of very finely chopped fresh green herbs (whatever is available), and add just before serving.

Lemon sauce

Add some finely grated lemon rind and juice to the basic white sauce. You can intensify the color with a pinch of turmeric.

Mushroom sauce

This is good with vegetables and for serving with pasta and gnocchi. To make it, wash and finely slice 4oz (125g) button mushrooms, fry them in a little butter for a minute or two, then add them to the sauce.

Mustard sauce

Add 1 tablespoons of French mustard and a little lemon juice to the sauce after cooking.

Onion sauce

Another useful variation, good when you want to add more flavor to a dish. Peel and finely chop an onion, then fry it in the butter before blending with the other ingredients. Try flavoring with a pinch of ground cloves.

Parsley sauce

Add sprigs of parsley into the blender with the other ingredients at the beginning of the process.

Watercress sauce

Add ½–1 bunch of finely chopped watercress to the sauce, or add unchopped watercress to the sauce and blend it.

Vegan béchamel sauce v

Use vegan margarine instead of butter, and soy milk.

Bread sauce

One of the delights of Christmas dinner, and it's every bit as good with a vegetarian main course as it is with a meat one.

SERVES 4–6 ❄

1 onion
3 cloves
1¼ cups (275ml) milk or unsweetened soy milk
1 bay leaf
2 large slices of fresh white bread, crusts removed
1 tbsp (15g) butter
1–2 tbsp heavy cream
salt and freshly ground black pepper
a pinch of freshly grated nutmeg

Put the onion, studded with the cloves, into a saucepan and add the milk and the bay leaf.

Bring to a boil, then take off the heat, add the slices of bread, cover and let stand for 15–30 minutes for the flavors to infuse.

Remove the onion and bay leaf, beat the mixture to break up the bread and stir in the butter and cream, adding salt, pepper and nutmeg to taste.

If you are making the sauce in advance, you can put back the onion and bay leaf once you have beaten it smooth; they will continue to flavor the sauce until you're ready to reheat and serve it.

Cheese sauce

Cheese sauce is useful both for incorporating into other dishes before baking or grilling, and for serving with vegetables to make them into more of a meal. It's worth using a strongly flavored cheese, and you can boost the flavor with a good seasoning of mustard, cayenne and freshly ground black pepper. Unsweetened soy milk makes a particularly good, creamy sauce and Double Gloucester gives it a pretty color.

MAKES 275ML (10FL OZ) ❄

2 tbsp (25g) butter
2 tbsp (25g) all-purpose flour
1 bay leaf
10–15fl oz (275–425ml) milk or unsweetened soy milk
2oz (50g) grated cheese — Cheddar or Double Gloucester
1 tsp mustard powder
cayenne pepper
salt and freshly ground black pepper

Melt the butter in a medium-sized saucepan and stir in the flour. Cook for a few seconds or until the flour bubbles round the edges, then add the bay leaf, turn up the heat and pour in about one-third of the milk or soy milk.

Stir hard until the sauce is very thick and smooth, add the milk in two batches, stirring until smooth and thick before adding more milk so that you finish with a thick pouring consistency.

Take the pan off the heat and beat in the grated cheese, mustard, a tiny pinch of cayenne pepper, and salt and pepper to taste. Don't let the sauce get too hot once the cheese has been added or it may break.

Cranberry sauce v

This rich, thick red sauce with a tangy flavor is a delight. Although you can find jars of cranberry sauce and jelly in any supermarket, it's much nicer to make your own from lovely juicy cranberries. It's delicious with white nut roast with parsley stuffing or chestnut pâté en croûte as part of a Christmas dinner (see pages 171 and 150). It keeps well in the fridge for 3–4 weeks.

SERVES 8 ❄

8oz (225g) fresh cranberries
5fl oz (150ml) water
6oz (175g) sugar

Sort out the cranberries by removing any bruised ones and taking off any little stems. Wash the berries and put them into a saucepan with the water.

Cook gently until the berries begin to "pop" and are tender — 7–10 minutes on a high heat.

Add the sugar and simmer for 5 minutes or until the sauce is glossy.

VARIATION

Gooseberry sauce v

This, too, is delicious with many nut and pulse dishes. Make in the same way, using just 4 tablespoons of water, then blend. You probably won't need as much sugar.

Cucumber raita

This refreshing yogurt dish is perfect with curries, lentil croquettes and bhajis.

SERVES 4–6
½ cucumber, peeled and diced
salt
10fl oz (275ml) natural yogurt
½ jalepeno, seeded and chopped
    (optional)

Put the cucumber into a sieve set over a bow, sprinkle with salt, cover with a small plate with a weight on top and leave for 30 minutes to draw out excess water. Then rinse, squeeze and pat dry the cucumber with paper towels.

Mix the cucumber with the yogurt and chili.

VARIATIONS
Cucumber and mint raita

Make as described, adding 2–3 tablespoons chopped fresh mint.

Cucumber and coriander raita

Make as described, adding 2–3 tablespoons chopped fresh coriander.

Vegetarian gravy v

Easy to make and delicious. Try it with toad-in-the-hole (see page 305) and easy creamy mash or with lentil loaf (see pages 131 and 192).

MAKES ABOUT 15FL OZ (JUST OVER 425ML)
1 onion, chopped
1½ tbsp rapeseed or olive oil
2 tbsp (25g) all-purpose flour
1 garlic clove, crushed
15fl oz (425ml) water
vegetable bouillon, stock cube or
    powder (optional)
1 tsp yeast extract
1–2 tsp dark soy sauce
salt and freshly ground black pepper

Fry the onion in the oil for 10 minutes. Sprinkle in the flour and, stirring all the time, let it brown over the heat.

Add all the remaining ingredients. Bring to the boil and leave to simmer for 10 minutes. If you like a smooth gravy, strain or blend. Season to taste and serve.

Classic hollandaise sauce

A rich, special-occasion sauce that is wonderful with asparagus, artichokes or salsify. This is the traditional method of making it, with a whisk in a bowl over a pan of hot water. It can also be made quickly in a blender or food processor (see opposite).

SERVES 6
1–2 tsp lemon juice
1 tbsp cold water
salt and freshly ground black pepper
2 egg yolks
1 stick (125g) butter, diced

Mix together 1 teaspoon of the lemon juice, water and some salt and pepper in a double saucepan or a bowl set over a pan of hot water (don't let the water boil).

Beat in the egg yolks, then whisk in a quarter of the butter, beating until the butter has melted and is beginning to thicken.

Add the rest of the butter in three batches, beating well between each batch. Add a little more lemon juice if you wish.

Quick blender hollandaise

This gorgeous sauce is easy to make if you use a blender. Make it just before you want to eat it.

SERVES 4
1 stick (125g) butter, diced
1 tbsp lemon juice
2 egg yolks
salt and freshly ground black pepper

Melt the butter in a small saucepan then bring to a boil.

Blend the lemon juice and egg yolks in a blender until pale and thick, then, with the machine still running, pour in the boiling melted butter and blend for a further minute. Season with salt and a pinch of pepper and serve at once.

Lemon lentil sauce v

This creamy, smooth lentil sauce that turn a plate of steamed or roasted vegetables into a complete meal. For spicier lentil sauces see the lentil dals on page 194.

SERVES 4 ❄
4oz (125g) red lentils
2 cups (575ml) water
1 onion
1 tbsp olive oil
2 tsp curry powder
juice and grated rind of 1 lemon
salt and freshly ground black pepper

Simmer the lentils in the water until tender — about 20 minutes.

Meanwhile, peel and chop the onion and sauté gently in the oil with the curry powder for 10 minutes.

Add the lemon juice and grated rind a little at a time, until it tastes right to you.

Puree or blend the sauce, season well with salt and pepper and serve.

Mint sauce v

Sharp-tasting yet sweet as well, mint sauce complements many lentil and bean dishes such as field bean burgers, lentil croquettes or white nut roast (see pages 190 and 192).

SERVES 4–6
1oz (25g) chopped fresh mint
1 tbsp sugar
1 tbsp boiling water
¼ cup cider vinegar or white wine
   vinegar

If you've got a liquidizer or hand blender, just wash the mint leaves and take off any stems, then blend with the other ingredients until the mint is finely chopped. Pour into a pitcher to serve.

If you'd rather make the sauce by hand, finely chop the mint leaves, then put them into a bowl. Add the sugar, water and vinegar and mix well.

Mushroom and Marsala sauce

Rich, creamy and luxurious, this adds a gourmet touch to any meal. Try it with cashew nut and parsley fritters, tofu escalopes or lentil croquettes (see pages 147, 202 and 192).

SERVES 4
2 tbsp (25g) butter
1 tbsp olive oil
2 tbsp finely chopped onion
9oz (250g) cremini mushrooms, sliced
1 tsp all-purpose flour
4fl oz (125ml) Marsala
7fl oz (200ml) crème fraîche
salt and freshly ground black pepper

Heat the butter and oil in a large saucepan. Add the onion, cover and cook gently for 2–3 minutes. Add the mushrooms and cook for 4–5 minutes, until they are tender.

Add the flour and stir over the heat for a minute or two, then pour in the Marsala and let the mixture bubble away over the heat for 3–4 minutes, or longer if you want to reduce it more. Stir in the crème fraîche, adding salt and pepper to taste. Reheat gently, then serve.

Mushroom and sour cream sauce

This is a creamy fresh-tasting sauce that's best served warm and is delicious with nut or pulse savories, burgers and also with plainly cooked vegetables.

SERVES 4–6
1 tbsp (15g) butter
4oz (125g) button mushrooms, chopped
5fl oz (150ml) sour cream
salt and freshly ground black pepper
a pinch of paprika

Melt the butter in a medium-sized saucepan and fry the mushrooms for about 5 minutes.

Stir in the sour cream and salt, pepper and a little paprika to taste.

Reheat gently, but don't let the sauce boil.

Red onion marmalade V

Sweet and tangy, this goes with so many things and is so good you can even eat it as it is. It makes a great topping for bruschetta (see page 50) and keeps well in the fridge for a week or so.

SERVES 4–8
2¼lb (1kg) red onions, thinly sliced
2 tbsp olive oil
2 tbsp light brown sugar
3 tbsp fino sherry
2 tbsp red wine vinegar
salt and freshly ground black pepper

Heat the oil in a large saucepan. Add the onions, cover and cook, stirring every 5 minutes, for about 15 minutes or until they're very tender. They must be really soft before you go on to the next stage.

Add the sugar, sherry and vinegar, then leave to simmer gently, without a lid, for about 30 minutes or until you have a thick, sticky mixture with hardly any liquid left. Remove from the heat, season to taste with salt and pepper and leave to cool. Store in a covered container in the fridge for about a week.

Red wine sauce

This sauce always makes a meal taste special. You can use either an inexpensive wine, or some extra of whatever you're having with the meal. Try this with the chestnut, sage and red wine loaf (see page 150).

SERVES 6 ❄

15fl oz (425ml) vegetable stock
15fl oz (425ml) red wine
1 bay leaf
a piece of onion
1 garlic clove, finely sliced
a pinch of dried thyme
½ tsp black peppercorns
2–3 parsley sprigs
1 tbsp redcurrant jelly
salt and freshly ground black pepper
3 tbsp (40g) butter, softened
3 tbsp (20g) all-purpose flour

Put the stock and red wine into a saucepan with the bay leaf, onion, garlic, thyme, peppercorns and parsley sprigs and bring to a boil. Let the mixture bubble away for 10–15 minutes so that the amount of liquid reduces to half. Strain into a clean saucepan and mix in the redcurrant jelly and some salt and pepper.

Next make a beurre manié: simply mash half the butter with the flour to make a paste and add this, in small pieces, to the still-warm sauce, mixing well after you've added each piece. This is an easy, foolproof way to thicken a sauce.

Put the sauce back over the heat and stir it until it has thickened slightly.

Let the sauce simmer gently for a few minutes to cook the flour. Check the seasoning again and beat the remaining butter into the sauce just before serving to make it look glossy and appetizing.

Tip
If you want to prepare the sauce in advance, after you've added the beurre manié and simmered the sauce for a few minutes, take it off the heat and dot the remaining butter over the top of the sauce to prevent a skin forming. When you're ready to eat, heat the sauce gently and stir the butter in.

Salsa v

Zingy and refreshing, this perks up so many dishes and can be made several hours in advance. Add the chili to taste — either cautiously if you're unsure or generously for hardened chili lovers.

SERVES 4–8

4 tomatoes, fairly finely chopped
1 garlic clove, crushed
4 scallions, chopped
2 tbsp chopped red onion
1 jalepeno, seeded and chopped
2 tbsp chopped fresh coriander
1 tbsp lime juice
½ tsp salt

Just mix everything together and set aside until you are ready to serve. If you have time, leave to stand for a while to bring out all the flavors.

Satay sauce v

This is a gorgeous tangy, creamy, protein-rich sauce that you can whip up in a moment. You can serve it with the deep-fried salt and pepper tofu (see page 204), or with cubes of fried smoked tofu; it's also fabulous in the cauliflower satay (see page 148). I like to use good-quality pure peanut butter, but you could also use cashew or almond butter if you like. You can find jars of tamarind and vegetarian Thai red curry paste (i.e. not containing fish) in large supermarkets.

SERVES 3–4
3 tbsp smooth peanut butter
5 tbsp coconut milk
1 tbsp tamarind paste
1 tbsp Thai red curry paste

Put the peanut butter into a small mixing bowl and gradually stir in the coconut milk, tamarind and curry paste to make a smooth cream. Transfer the sauce to a small serving bowl to serve.

Sour cream and herb sauce

This sauce is served cold, but can accompany both hot and cold dishes.

MAKES 1¼ CUPS (275ML)
5fl oz (150ml) sour cream
5fl oz (150ml) natural yogurt
2 tbsp chopped fresh herbs,
    (e.g.flat-leaf parsley, chives,
    tarragon, thyme)
salt and freshly ground black pepper

Simply mix everything together and season to taste.

VARIATION
Horseradish sauce

Make as described, leaving out the herbs and flavoring with 2–3 teaspoons of grated horseradish and 1–2 teaspoons of red wine vinegar. This is even nicer if you add a little mayonnaise, or replace 2 tablespoons of the yogurt with 2 tablespoons of mayonnaise. This is wonderful with walnut pâté en croûte (see page 283).

Tartar sauce

This tangy sauce can be made in moments and is a great way of livening up anything from lentil croquettes to grilled polenta or cheese fritters (see pages 192, 244 and 289).

SERVES 2–4
¼ cup mayonnaise
1–1½ tbsp small capers, rinsed
1–1½ tbsp small gherkins, drained
    and chopped
1 tsp finely chopped onion
1 tbsp chopped fresh flat-leaf parsley
a few drops of Tabasco sauce

Just put all the ingredients into a bowl and mix together. Keep in a covered container in the fridge until required.

VARIATION
Vegan tartar sauce v

This is delicious made with a good vegan mayonnaise; I like the egg-free one with garlic that is widely available in health-food stores.

Tomato sauce v

This sauce really couldn't be easier and is one of my standbys. I find it best not to let the tomatoes cook for very long this way the sauce has a much fresher flavor. It's worth buying good-quality canned tomatoes because they have a much richer flavor and produce a better sauce.

SERVES 4–6
1 onion
1 tbsp olive oil
1 garlic clove, crushed
1lb (450g) tomatoes, skinned or
    14oz can chopped tomatoes
1 tsp dried oregano (optional)
salt and freshly ground black pepper

Peel and chop the onion and fry it gently in the oil in a medium-sized saucepan, with a lid on the pan, until it's soft but not browned — about 10 minutes.

Add the garlic, along with the tomatoes and oregano (if using). Simmer, uncovered, for 10–15 minutes or until thick.

You can blend the sauce, or leave it chunky. Taste and season with salt and pepper.

Tip
The basic recipe can be varied in lots of ways. Try putting a bay leaf with the onion to draw out its lovely flavor while it softens; or add a little chopped fresh or dried basil, thyme or cinnamon to the finished sauce; or stir a couple of tablespoons of red wine into the blended mixture before you reheat it. It can be served chilled, too.

Onion relish with poppy seeds and paprika v

If you cover onion rings with an oil and vinegar dressing and leave them for an hour or so to marinate, they soften and become less hot. This relish is delicious as a side for spicy lentil and rice dishes.

SERVES 4
1 tbsp red wine vinegar
2 tbsp olive oil
salt and freshly ground black pepper
2 large mild onions, sliced into rings
1 tbsp poppy seeds
2 tsp paprika

Put the vinegar and oil into a shallow container with some salt and pepper and mix together.

Add the onion rings and mix again, so that they are all covered with the dressing.

Sprinkle with the poppy seeds and paprika.

Let stand for at least 1 hour, longer if possible, even overnight. Give it a stir every so often.

Quick no-cook chutney v

This is the easiest chutney recipe I know and it tastes delicious, just like a traditional one that's been bubbling over a hot stove for ages. To sterilize the jam jars, either run them through a hot dishwasher cycle, or wash them, stand them on a baking sheet and place in a cool oven, 275°F (140°C) for 10–15 minutes or until they are dry.

MAKES 3KG (7LB)
1lb (450g) pitted dates
1lb (450g) golden raisins
1lb (450g) apples, peeled
1lb (450g) onions
1lb (450g) dark muscovado sugar
2 cups (575ml) vinegar (I use cider
    vinegar)
1 tsp salt
freshly ground black pepper
dash of cayenne pepper, allspice and
    ground ginger

Finely chop the first four ingredients in a food processor or by hand, then stir in the sugar and vinegar.

Add the salt, some pepper, and a pinch each of cayenne, allspice and ground ginger.

Leave the mixture to stand for 24 hours, giving it a stir from time to time, then spoon into sterilized jars and seal. Store in a cool, dry place. It keeps very well, just like a traditional chutney.

Salads
and salad dressings

Salads are fantastically versatile and so easy to make. I love their vibrant colors, contrasting textures and delightful flavors. Plus, there's the added bonus of no slaving over a hot stove!

You can eat salads for almost any meal of the day and they can play various roles. Some, such as endive salad or fennel and cucumber salad (see pages 88 and 89), make great accompaniments; others, like the great veggie caesar (see page 86), can be wonderful starters or main courses, depending on portion size. You can complement any salad with whatever you fancy, such as fresh bread or potatoes.

Dressings are also quick and simple to make at home; I really don't know why anyone buys them. It's much better to spend your money on good-quality olive oil and various vinegars, starting with some red wine vinegar and adding others as you go, plus sea salt. Make the dressing straight into the salad bowl each time, or whisk up enough for several salads and keep in the fridge – as convenient as any bought dressing but a million times nicer!

Avocado dressing v

A luxurious and pretty dressing that I like on almost any salad. Try it on top of a red bean salad (see page 96) with a base of shredded lettuce.

SERVES 4–6
1 large ripe avocado
juice of ½ lemon
1 tbsp red wine or cider vinegar
1 tbsp best-quality extra-virgin olive oil
salt and freshly ground black pepper
Tabasco sauce or curry powder (optional)

Halve, pit and skin the avocado. Put the flesh into a blender or food processor with the rest of the ingredients and whip to a luscious pale green cream. Alternatively, put the ingredients into a deep bowl and use a hand blender.

You can perk up the flavor with a drop or two of Tabasco sauce or a pinch or two of curry powder.

Balsamic dressing with honey and mustard

This is a lovely sweet and tangy dressing, particularly good with slightly bitter salad leaves, though really it's delicious on almost anything. For a vegan version, use agave syrup or maple syrup instead of the honey.

MAKES ABOUT 5FL (150ML)
6 tbsp extra-virgin olive oil
2 tbsp balsamic vinegar
1 tbsp honey
1 tbsp wholegrain mustard

Either whisk the ingredients together in a bowl or put them into a screw-top jar and shake to combine. The latter is a handy way of making it because you can then keep the jar in the fridge.

Shake or whisk the dressing again before serving.

VARIATIONS
Balsamic dressing with garlic

Add a crushed garlic clove to the dressing and mix well.

Balsamic dressing with chili and soy

Make as described, adding 1 tablespoon of soy sauce such as tamari and 1 red jalepeno, seeded and finely sliced.

Feta dressing

This tangy dressing is made with feta cheese. It's a great way of adding protein as well as flavor to a salad.

SERVES 4
7oz (200g) feta cheese, drained and broken into pieces
5–6 tbsp milk
1 tbsp extra-virgin olive oil
1 garlic clove, crushed
salt and freshly ground black pepper

Simply whip everything together to a cream using an electric blender, or food processor.

Honey and cider vinegar dressing

A sweet dressing that's especially good on a shredded cabbage salad.

SERVES 2–4

1 tbsp honey
1 tbsp cider vinegar
3 tbsp extra-virgin olive oil
¼ tsp salt
freshly ground black pepper

Thoroughly combine all the ingredients in a bowl or screw-top jar.

VARIATION
Honey and mint dressing

Made by adding 1 tablespoon of chopped fresh mint or 1 teaspoon concentrated mint sauce (see page 67) to the main recipe.

Easy blender mayonnaise

Here, the use of a blender makes it easy to produce a creamy, delicious mayo every time. You could use entirely olive oil, or half peanut or grapeseed oil and half olive oil, as here, which gives a lighter flavor.

MAKES ABOUT 200ML (7FL OZ)

1 egg
¼ tsp salt
¼ tsp mustard powder
2–3 grindings of black pepper
2 tsp red wine vinegar
2 tsp lemon juice
3½fl oz (100ml) olive oil mixed with
   3½fl oz (100ml) peanut or
   grapeseed oil

Break the egg straight into the blender and add the salt, mustard, pepper, vinegar and lemon juice.

Blend for 1 minute at medium speed or until everything is well mixed, then turn the speed up to high and gradually add the oil, drop by drop, through the hole in the lid of the blender.

When you've added about half the oil, you will hear the motor change to a "glug-glug" noise and then you can add the rest of the oil more quickly, in a thin stream.

If the consistency of the mayonnaise seems a bit on the thick side, you can thin it with a little hot water.

Lemon mayonnaise

You can use homemade mayonnaise made by the traditional or the blender method, or you can use good-quality bought mayonnaise. I find this variation particularly lovely as a sauce for dishes, such as the new potato, pea and mint frittata or lentil croquettes (see pages 295 and 192); it adds a deliciously fresh yet rich note that complements them.

SERVES 4

heaping ¼ cup mayonnaise
1 tsp finely grated lemon rind
1–6 tsp freshly squeezed lemon juice
salt and freshly ground black pepper

Put the mayonnaise into a bowl and stir in the finely grated lemon rind. Add the lemon juice gradually, tasting as you go, to get the mixture the right degree of sharpness for you. I like to use the whole amount, but then I love lemon. Season to taste with salt and pepper.

Traditional-method mayonnaise

Making mayonnaise by hand is hard work, but you get a beautiful, creamy result and it's very satisfying to see the mixture gradually thicken as you whisk in the oil.

MAKES 7–10FL OZ (200–275ML)
2–3 egg yolks
¼ tsp salt
¼ tsp mustard powder
2 or 3 grindings of black pepper
2 tsp red wine vinegar
2 tsp lemon juice
7–10fl oz (200–275ml) olive oil and
    peanut oil, mixed

Put the egg yolks into a bowl and add the salt, mustard, pepper, vinegar and lemon juice.

Whisk for a minute or two until everything is well mixed and creamy, then start to add the oil, just a drop at a time, whisking hard after each addition.

When you have added about half the oil, the mixture will begin to thicken and look like mayonnaise, and then you can add the oil a little quicker, still whisking hard.

Go on whisking in the oil until the mixture is really thick — if you use three egg yolks you will probably be able to use 10fl oz (275ml) of oil, otherwise about 7fl oz (200ml) will be enough.

If the consistency of the mayonnaise seems a bit on the thick side, you can thin it with a little boiling water.

Mayonnaise and yogurt dressing

You can use either homemade mayonnaise or a good-quality store-bought one for this.

SERVES 4
2 tbsp mayonnaise
2 tbsp natural yogurt

Simply mix everything together.

Ricotta mayonnaise

My daughter Meg invented this dressing, which tastes very much like mayonnaise but contains only a fraction of the calories. You can vary the flavor by adding ½ teaspoon of Dijon mustard and you can also add a little skim milk if you want a thinner consistency.

SERVES 6–8
2 tbsp natural yogurt
4oz (125g) ricotta
2 tsp extra-virgin olive oil
½ tsp red wine vinegar
salt and freshly ground black pepper

Simply mix everything together to a smooth cream.

Sour cream dressing

Creamy and sweet and sour, this adds a touch of luxury to many green salads.

SERVES 6
10fl oz (275ml) sour cream
1 tsp Dijon mustard
1 tsp superfine sugar
1 tsp salt
½ tsp freshly ground white pepper

Just mix all the ingredients together until creamy. Keep in a covered container in the fridge for 4–5 days.

Tahini dressing v

The creamy texture and slightly bitter flavor of this dressing is addictive. It goes well with almost any vegetable or pulse salad. Try adding some chopped fresh herbs such as flat-leaf parsley or chives.

SERVES 2–4
1 heaped tbsp tahini
2 tbsp cold water
1 tbsp lemon juice
1 garlic clove, crushed (optional)
salt and freshly ground black pepper

Put the tahini into a bowl and gradually beat in the water and lemon juice. The mixture will be lumpy at first, but will gradually get light and fluffy as you beat in the liquid.

Add the garlic (if using) and season to taste.

Tofu dressing v

This dressing, made from tofu or bean curd (see page 203), is a bit like mayonnaise but considerably more nutritious and lower in oil. This is also nice with some chopped fresh herbs or scallions added.

MAKES ABOUT 12 FL OZ (350ML)
10½ oz silken tofu — from
  health-food stores
2 tsp red wine vinegar
1 tsp mustard powder
1 tsp muscovado sugar
2 tbsp extra-virgin olive oil
salt and freshly ground black pepper

If you've got a blender, simply whip all the ingredients together until combined. Or put the ingredients into a deep mixing bowl and use a hand blender.

Alternatively, put the tofu into a bowl and whisk until smooth, then add the vinegar, mustard and sugar and whisk again. Next beat in the oil, a little at a time. Season with salt and pepper.

Vinaigrette v

When I'm making this to dress a salad, I usually make it directly in the salad bowl, mix quickly and put the salad in on top. But if you need it for pouring over a salad, or for serving with avocados, for instance, it's easiest to make it by shaking all the ingredients together in a clean screw-top jar, and for this you may want to double the quantities given here. Store in the jar in the fridge for up to a week.

SERVES 4–6
1 tbsp wine vinegar (preferably red)
3–4 tbsp extra-virgin olive oil
salt and freshly ground black pepper

Mix everything together, adding plenty of seasoning. Some chopped fresh herbs, a crushed garlic clove, also a little mustard and a dash of sugar can be added to vary the flavor. You can also use different vinegars, such as cider or raspberry vinegar for a fruity flavor, balsamic vinegar for a rich, slightly sweet, mellow flavor, or rice vinegar, which is light and delicate.

VARIATION
Walnut vinaigrette v

Make as described, with 1–2 tablespoons of walnut oil replacing the same quantity of olive oil. Adding a crushed garlic clove also works well.

Yogurt and green herb dressing

This is a fresh-tasting, slightly sharp dressing that's good with most salad.

SERVES 4–6
10fl oz (275ml) natural yogurt
1–2 heaped tbsp finely chopped
  fresh herbs, especially flat-leaf
  parsley, also chives and mint
1 tbsp lemon juice
salt and freshly ground black pepper

Put the yogurt into a bowl and stir in the chopped herbs, lemon juice and salt and pepper to taste.

VARIATION
Yogurt and scallion dressing

Make as in the main recipe, using 3 tablespoons of chopped scallions instead of the chopped herbs.

Salads

How to sprout beans, grains and lentils v

Sprouted beans, grains and lentils may sound a bit "new age", but it's worth doing as they can add an interesting, crunchy element to salads and are highly nutritious, being rich in vitamins and minerals and containing high-quality protein.

Sprouting is easy to do. All you need is a jar (a big coffee jar is ideal), a piece of cheesecloth to go over the top, secured with an elastic band, and some beans or seeds. Most types are suitable, with the exception of red kidney beans and large beans like butter beans. Good ones to use are chickpeas, whole lentils, sunflower seeds, mung beans, aduki beans. Or you can buy some ready-made mixes of seeds and beans, which take the same amount of time to sprout.

Put half a cupful of your chosen beans or seeds into your jar, cover with cold water and leave to soak for 8–12 hours. Put the piece of cheesecloth over the top of the jar. Then drain off the water, fill the jar with fresh water, swish it round and then pour it all out again. All this can be done without removing the cheesecloth, which prevents the seeds or beans falling out. This rinsing has to be repeated twice a day, to keep the seeds damp (but they mustn't be left soaking in water or they'll rot rather than sprout). When I'm sprouting seeds, I keep them by the sink to remind me about the rinsing. They're ready when they've grown a little tail — usually in 2–4 days. They can be used right away, added to salads and sandwiches, or kept in the fridge for several days.

Aigroissade

I love this French chickpea and vegetable salad, but with its creamy mayonnaise dressing it's too high in fat and calories to enjoy very often. So I've gradually evolved ways of lightening it up. Char-grilled artichoke hearts can be bought from the deli section of any large supermarket.

SERVES 4–6
4oz (125g) chickpeas, soaked and cooked until tender (see pages 176–7) or 14oz can
12oz (350g) each of cooked carrots and cooked cut green beans
1 cup marinated or grilled artichoke hearts
⅔ cup natural yogurt
⅔ cup mayonnaise
2 large garlic cloves, crushed
1 tbsp wine vinegar
salt and freshly ground black pepper
crisp lettuce and watercress
chopped fresh flat-leaf parsley, to garnish

Drain the chickpeas and put them into a large bowl with the carrots and beans.

Halve the artichoke hearts and add them to the bowl.

To make the dressing, put the yogurt, mayonnaise, garlic and vinegar into a small bowl and mix well together until creamy. Season with salt and pepper.

Pour the dressing over the vegetables and mix carefully until everything is well coated.

Line a serving dish with lettuce leaves and watercress, spoon the vegetable mixture on top and sprinkle chopped parsley over it.

Alfalfa slaw v

SERVES 4–6
1lb (450g) grated cabbage
2 carrots, grated
4oz (125g) alfalfa sprouts
balsamic dressing (see page 75)

Mix all the vegetables together, then add enough vinaigrette to moisten.

Avocado and mushroom salad v

Made with fresh, tightly closed button mushrooms and ripe avocado, this is delicious.

SERVES 4
1lb (450g) baby button mushrooms
2 tbsp red wine vinegar
¼ cup extra-virgin olive oil
salt and freshly ground black pepper
2 avocados
2 tbsp lemon juice
1–2 tbsp chopped fresh chives

Wash the mushrooms, pat dry on paper towels and slice thinly. Put the slices into a bowl, add the vinegar, olive oil and some salt and pepper, and mix well. Let stand for 1 hour.

Just before you want to serve the salad, halve each avocado, remove the pit and peel. Cut the flesh into fairly large dice and sprinkle the lemon juice over it.

Add to the mushrooms, together with the chopped chives, and mix gently.

Sprouted bean salad with carrots and scallions v

In this salad, sprouted beans (see page 79) are combined with grated carrots, tomatoes, watercress and scallions. It's very vitalizing!

SERVES 4

2 handfuls of mixed sprouts such as mung, chickpea, aduki and sunflower
12oz (350g) carrots, coarsely grated
4 large tomatoes, sliced
small bunch of scallions, chopped
4oz packet mixed baby leaf salad
2oz packet watercress
vinaigrette dressing (see page 75)
salt and freshly ground black pepper

Put all the ingredients into a bowl and mix gently. Add enough vinaigrette to moisten the salad and make it glisten. Season with a little salt and pepper and serve.

VARIATION

Layered sprouted bean salad with tahini dressing v

This is particularly attractive arranged in layers in a glass bowl, with tahini dressing (see page 77) poured over the top.

Beansprout, mushroom and celery salad with coriander v

This is a bit like a salad stir-fry! You could even serve it with some hot cooked rice or noodles.

SERVES 4

1 stalk of celery, finely sliced
8oz (225g) beansprouts
6oz (175g) very fresh button mushrooms, finely sliced
a bunch of scallions, sliced
a small bunch of fresh coriander, roughly chopped
grated rind and juice of 1 lime
1 tbsp toasted sesame oil
1 tbsp extra-virgin olive oil
1 tbsp dark soy sauce
dash of honey, maple or agave syrup
salt and freshly ground black pepper

Put the celery, bean sprouts, sliced mushrooms, scallions and coriander in a bowl and mix gently.

Add the grated lime rind and juice, the sesame and olive oil and the soy sauce. Mix until everything is coated. Have a taste and add honey, maple or agave syrup, salt and pepper to taste.

Three-bean salad with mustard dressing v

Thin green French beans, tender broad beans and kidney beans in a tangy mustard dressing.

SERVES 4 ❄

8oz (225g) thin French beans, trimmed
8oz (225g) frozen broad (fava) beans
1 tbsp Dijon or wholegrain mild mustard
3 tbsp extra-virgin olive oil
1 tbsp red wine vinegar
salt and freshly ground black pepper
14oz can red kidney beans, drained and rinsed
2 tbsp chopped flat-leaf parsley

Cook the French beans in a little boiling water for 4–5 minutes, or until just tender. Thaw the broad beans by putting them in a sieve under the hot tap, then add to the same pan and cook for about 4 minutes. Drain all the beans, refresh by putting them under the cold tap to preserve the color, and drain again.

Mix the dressing directly in a large serving bowl, adding the mustard, oil, vinegar and some salt and pepper, and mixing together.

Add the kidney beans to the bowl, the cooked beans and the chopped parsley, and mix until all the beans are glossy with the dressing.

You can serve this salad straight away, but it's even better left to stand for an hour or so, to let the flavors blend.

Black and white bean salad with lemon thyme v

Bean salads are especially attractive when made from two or more contrasting beans and this is a particularly lovely combination.

SERVES 4–6 ❄

14oz can black beans
14oz can cannellini beans
½ tsp mustard powder
½ tsp soft dark brown sugar
4 tsp red wine vinegar
¼ cup extra-virgin olive oil
1 tbsp chopped lemon thyme (or other fresh herbs as available)
salt and freshly ground black pepper

Drain and rinse the beans.

Put the mustard, sugar and vinegar into a large bowl and mix together, then add the oil, herbs, beans and seasoning.

Mix gently, then, if there is time, leave for at least 30 minutes for the flavors to develop. Serve in a shallow bowl.

Red beet, apple and celery salad v

This is a pleasant mixture of contrasting tastes and textures: soft, earthy-flavored beets, crunchy sweet apple and salty celery.

SERVES 4–6

12oz (350g) cooked red beets — with or without skin, but with no added vinegar
2 sweet eating apples, such as Gala
1 heart of celery
cider vinegar vinaigrette (see page 78)
a few sprigs of watercress
2oz (50g) shelled walnuts, chopped

If the beets still have their skin on, peel it off and rinse the beets under the tap. Cut into chunky dice and place in a bowl.

Peel, core and dice the apples. Slice the celery and add both to the bowl.

Mix the salad, adding enough vinaigrette to make it glossy. Put into a salad bowl, serving dish or divide between individual plates, adding a few sprigs of watercress and sprinkling with chopped walnuts.

Red beet and horseradish salad v

A curiously pleasant mixture of flavors and textures, this salad makes a good accompaniment to cold savoury dishes.

SERVES 4

1½lb (700g) cooked red beets (with no added vinegar)
1 eating apple
1 tsp caraway seeds
1 tbsp sugar
2 tbsp red wine vinegar
1–2 tbsp horseradish sauce

Peel and dice the beets and the apple. Put them into a bowl with the caraway seeds, sugar, vinegar and horseradish sauce and mix them all together lightly. Chill in the fridge before serving.

Raw red beet salad v

Raw beets are said to contain enzymes that are particularly valuable for health, and features in many natural cancer cures. They are also said to contain a substance that helps to break up fat deposits in the body and thus aid slimming! In any case, I like the sweet, earthy flavor and vibrant ruby color of them; try them in this tasty main course salad.

SERVES 4

8–12oz (225–350g) raw red beets
4 eating apples
4 stalks of celery, finely sliced
¼ cup raisins
3 tbsp extra-virgin olive oil
1 tbsp red wine vinegar or cider vinegar
peel of ½ lemon
1 lettuce
1 tbsp chopped fresh chives, to garnish

Peel and coarsely grate the raw beets and apples, add the celery, raisins, oil and vinegar.

Remove the peel from the lemon using a potato peeler, then snip into ½in (1cm) slivers using scissors; add to the mixture. Allow to marinate for an hour or so if possible.

Serve on a bed of lettuce, top with a sprinkling of chopped chives.

Roasted red beet and goat cheese salad

This salad is a great combination of contrasting flavors and textures. I love to use baby beets if they're available, but if not, just cut normal-size ones down through their stems into quarters.

SERVES 4–6

1lb (450g) raw baby beets, preferably no bigger than plums
olive oil, for brushing
4oz bag of mixed salad leaves, including some frisée and baby lettuce leaves
a few sprigs of fresh dill or lovage, if available
7oz (200g) soft goat cheese
freshly black pepper
balsamic dressing (see page 75)

Preheat the oven to 375°F (190°C). If the beets still have leaves attached, cut these off about 2in (5cm) from the root. Put the beets in a roasting pan, brush with oil and roast in the oven for 30–45 minutes or until tender when pierced with the point of a sharp knife.

Divide the beets between individual plates, along with the salad leaves, dill or lovage and the goat cheese. Coarsely grind a little black pepper over the goat cheese if you wish. Drizzle some balsamic dressing over the salad leaves and serve.

Broad bean, pea and feta salad with mint

This dish is the taste of summer on a plate and works equally well with fresh or frozen broad beans, also known as favas, and peas. If the broad beans are much bigger than hazel nuts you could pop them out of their grey skins after cooking — a labor of love, but worth it for the brilliant color and delicate texture of the skinned beans.

SERVES 4

9oz (250g) frozen or podded broad beans 1lb 2oz (500g) in their pods
12oz (350g) frozen baby peas or podded peas (1½lb (700g) in their pods)
2 tbsp extra-virgin olive oil
1½ tsp white or red wine vinegar
salt and freshly ground black pepper
superfine sugar, to taste
7oz (200g) feta cheese, cut into 1cm (½in) cubes
about 8 good sprigs of mint, chopped

Cook the broad beans in half a panful of boiling water for 2 minutes, until beginning to soften or then add the peas, bring back to a boil and cook for a further minute or so, until tender.

Drain the peas and beans and return them to the pan. Mix in the oil, vinegar, salt, a grinding of pepper and perhaps a pinch or two of sugar to taste, if necessary. Add the feta and chopped mint and stir gently. Serve immediately, still warm, or eat it when it's cold. It's lovely either way.

Butter beans and mushrooms with coriander v

This succulent and spicy salad makes an excellent starter. Serve it with some bread to mop up the delicious juices.

SERVES 4 AS A STARTER,
2 AS A MAINS SALAD DISH
8oz (225g) baby button mushrooms
3 tbsp vegetable oil
3–4 tsp ground coriander
2 garlic cloves, crushed
4oz (125g) dried butter beans, soaked, cooked (see pages 176–7) and drained; or 14oz can drained and rinsed
1–2 tbsp freshly squeezed lemon juice
salt and freshly ground black pepper

TO SERVE
2 handfuls of salad leaves
2 tbsp chopped fresh flat-leaf parsley

Wash the mushrooms and halve or quarter them if necessary.

Heat the oil in a skillet and add the mushrooms. Fry for 2–3 minutes, just to soften them, then add the coriander and garlic, and fry for a minute or two more.

Remove the pan from the heat and add the butter beans and lemon juice, seasoning with salt and pepper to taste.

You can serve this salad straight away, warm and juicy from the pan, or let it cool. Pile it up on a base of pretty salad leaves and scatter with chopped parsley.

Butter bean, tomato and olive salad v

This succulent mixture of flavors is delicious as a first course for four people, or as a light lunch or supper for two, served with some bread and something green and leafy to make the meal complete.

SERVES 2–4
3 tbsp extra-virgin olive oil
1 tbsp wine vinegar
salt and freshly ground black pepper
1 mild onion, sliced
1lb (450g) tomatoes, sliced
14oz can butter beans, drained and rinsed or 4oz (125g) dried butter beans, soaked, cooked (see pages 176–7) and drained
a handful of black olives

Put the oil and vinegar into a mixing bowl, or straight into a salad bowl, and add a little salt and pepper.

Add the onion, tomatoes, butter beans and olives and turn everything gently to mix the ingredients.

Serve from the bowl, or on individual plates.

Greek butter bean salad v

This tastes like the bean salads you get all over Greece, which I love, but without all the hours of slow cooking. In fact, it's almost instant, though it does benefit from sitting for an hour or so. Enjoy it with Greek salad (see page 90), kalamata olives and ciabatta.

SERVES 4 ❀
¼ cup extra-virgin olive oil
2 garlic cloves, crushed
2 tbsp tomato purée
2 tbsp freshly squeezed lemon juice
2 x 14oz cans butter beans
Salt and freshly ground black pepper
chopped fresh flat-leaf parsley, to garnish

In a large bowl mix together the olive oil, garlic, tomato purée and lemon juice.

Drain and rinse the beans, and add to the bowl. Mix well and season with salt and pepper to taste.

If possible, let the salad sit for an hour or so for the flavors to develop.

Serve at room temperature, sprinkled with chopped parsley.

Roasted butternut squash salad with balsamic dressing v

A fabulous salad: meltingly tender pieces of sweet butternut squash bathed in a glossy tamari and balsamic dressing with a hint of chili, a scattering of sizzling hot sesame seeds and some peppery green arugula.

SERVES 4–6
1 butternut squash
a little olive oil for brushing
4 scallions, sliced
2 tsp sesame seeds
5oz (150g) arugula leaves, to garnish

FOR THE DRESSING
2 tbsp balsamic vinegar
2 tbsp extra-virgin olive oil
2 tbsp freshly squeezed lime juice
2 tsp tamari or other soy sauce
½ tsp dried red chili flakes
salt and freshly ground black pepper

Pre-heat the oven to 375°F (190°C), Cut the butternut squash in half lengthways and brush the cut surfaces with oil. Put them, cut-side up, into a roasting pan and bake for about 1 hour or until the squash is soft.

Set the squash aside until it's cool enough to handle, then scoop out and discard the seeds. Peel off the papery skin — it will come away easily — and cut the flesh into 1in (2.5cm) chunks.

Put all the dressing ingredients into a large bowl, with salt and pepper to taste, and mix well.

Add the butternut squash to the bowl, along with the scallions, and mix gently, so that it is coated with the glossy dressing. Check the seasoning.

Toast the sesame seeds by stirring them for a minute or two in a dry saucepan until they smell toasty and start to jump around.

Put the butternut squash salad on to individual plates, top with a scattering of sizzling sesame seeds and garnish generously with arugula.

VARIATION
Roasted butternut squash salad with balsamic dressing and feta

A delicious variation is to add 7oz (200g) feta cheese, cut or broken into small cubes or pieces. The creamy saltiness of the feta contrasts well with the sweet tenderness of the balsamic-glazed butternut squash and the fresh peppery arugula.

Red cabbage and apple salad

A lovely salad for the autumn, sweet apples and golden raisins with crisp red cabbage and walnuts, and a honey dressing.

SERVES 4
1lb (450g) red cabbage
2 sweet eating apples
1 celery heart
2oz (50g) golden or black raisins (optional)
small handful of chopped walnuts
honey and cider dressing (see page 76)

Wash and finely shred the cabbage. Wash the apples and chop, without peeling if the skins look good, and slice the celery. Place all these in a salad bowl.

If you're using the sultanas or raisins, cover them with boiling water and leave for 10 minutes, to plump them; drain, and mix with salad, along with the walnuts and enough honey dressing to make the mixture moist and shiny.

VARIATIONS
Green cabbage and apple salad

Make as described, but using tender fresh green cabbage instead of red cabbage. The walnuts are optional in this version.

Cauliflower and apple salad

Make as described, but use 1lb (450g) cauliflower (1 medium-sized cauliflower) instead of cabbage, and pine nuts instead of walnuts.

Cabbage salad with red pepper and raisins v

This colorful salad is excellent with baked potatoes, onion quiche or quick cheese and tomato flan (see pages 267 and 263).

SERVES 4

3 tbsp extra-virgin olive oil
1 tbsp wine vinegar
salt and freshly ground black pepper
12oz (350g) white cabbage, shredded
6oz (175g) carrots, chopped or coarsely grated
6oz (175g) red pepper, seeded and chopped
2 heaped tbsp chopped fresh flat-leaf parsley, chives or scallions
2oz (50g) raisins
2oz (50g) roasted unsalted peanuts or cashews, or pine nuts or chopped walnuts

Put the oil and vinegar into the base of a salad bowl, add some salt and pepper and mix together.

Add the cabbage, carrots, red peppers, parsley, chives or scallions and raisins, and turn everything over a few times with a spoon so that it all gets covered in the dressing.

If possible leave for an hour or so; this softens the cabbage and gives the flavors a chance to blend. Stir in the nuts just before serving.

Cabbage salad with mint and pomegranate

This salad is so pretty: pale cabbage with shiny ruby pomegranate seeds glinting among the bright green mint.

SERVES 4

1 tbsp chopped fresh mint
1 tbsp honey
1 tbsp red wine vinegar
3 tbsp extra-virgin olive oil
salt and freshly ground black pepper
1lb (450g) white cabbage, coarsely grated or finely shredded
1 pomegranate
3–4 sprigs of mint, to garnish

Put the chopped mint, honey, vinegar, oil and some salt and pepper into a large bowl and mix together to form a dressing.

Add the cabbage and mix thoroughly, so that it gets well coated with the sweet herb dressing.

Leave for at least 1 hour, so that the cabbage softens a little and absorbs all the flavors.

Just before you want to serve the salad, cut the pomegranate in two and, holding one half over a plate to catch the juice, bend the fruit backwards to make the seeds pop out, helped as necessary with the point of a sharp knife.

Add the pomegranate juice to the salad, and stir in some of the seeds. Then tip the salad out on to a large flat plate and decorate with the mint sprigs and remaining pomegranate seeds. Serve as soon as possible, while the pomegranate is bright and sparkling.

VARIATION

Sweet cabbage salad with lovage

Make as described, using chopped fresh lovage instead of mint. The pungent, aromatic flavor of lovage along with the sweet dressing makes this salad deliciously different. Lovage is not easy to find in the stores, but if you have the space to grow it, it's easy because it comes up every year.

A great veggie Caesar

Caesar salad, with its sweet, crisp leaves, creamy mayonnaise dressing, cheese and croûtons, seems like a great vegetarian salad, except that often it isn't. The mayonnaise may have Worcestershire sauce in it; there may be anchovies in the salad, and Parmesan cheese is not vegetarian. But it is possible to make a great veggie Caesar with Tabasco, capers and gherkins to pep up the mayonnaise, and Parmesan-style cheese or hard vegetarian pecorino to take the place of Parmesan.

SERVES 4
1 head Romaine, torn into large
   bite-sized pieces

FOR THE DRESSING
6 tbsp mayonnaise
1 tbsp freshly squeezed lemon juice
1 garlic clove, crushed
a few drops of Tabasco or hot chili
   sauce
4oz (125g) pecorino or Parmesan-
   style cheese, shaved with a potato
   peeler or coarsely grated
2 tbsp capers, drained and rinsed (or
   rinsed and drained if preserved in
   salt)
1–2 small gherkins, chopped
salt and freshly ground black pepper

FOR THE CROÛTONS
2–4 slices of bread
olive oil, for frying

Put the lettuce into a salad bowl.
   Mix the mayonnaise with the lemon juice, garlic and enough Tabasco or hot chili sauce to give it a pleasant kick. Add half the cheese, the capers and the gherkins, and add to the bowl with the lettuce. Scatter the rest of the cheese on top and season to taste with pepper and a little salt if necessary.
   To make the croûtons, fry the slices of bread in olive oil in a frying pan, until they are crisp and golden, turning them to fry the each side. Cut the fried bread into pieces and add to the salad bowl. Toss the salad and eat at once.

Celeriac remoulade

Celeriac, that knobbly root with the delicious celery flavor, makes a classic, creamy salad. I like it with some lovely bright green watercress. It's also delicious in a lighter, vinaigrette dressing (see the variation).

SERVES 4
1lb (450g) celeriac
6 tbsp mayonnaise: homemade or
   good-quality bought
1 tbsp freshly squeezed lemon juice
1 tsp Dijon mustard
1 tsp sugar
½ tsp salt
freshly ground black pepper

Peel the celeriac and cut into quarters, then coarsely grate .
   Put the grated celeriac into a bowl with the mayonnaise, lemon juice, mustard, sugar, salt and a good grinding of black pepper, and mix well.
   If possible, let sit for 30 minutes or so to give the celeriac a chance to soak up the flavor of the dressing, then serve.

VARIATION
Celeriac vinaigrette v

Grate the celeriac as described, then mix with vinaigrette (see page 78), so that it is all coated and glossy with the dressing. This is good with plenty of pepper added; you could grind it in, or add ½–1 teaspoon of coarsely ground black pepper from a jar, or crushed using a pestle and mortar.

Endive and walnut salad v

If you can get red endive, this salad is lovely made with half red and half white; otherwise just use white endive. Either way, it's crisp and refreshing.

SERVES 4–6

12oz (350g) white endive
12oz (350g) red endive
3 tbsp extra-virgin olive oil or half walnut oil and half olive oil
1 tbsp red wine vinegar
salt and freshly ground black pepper
2oz (50g) shelled walnut pieces, roughly chopped

Wash the endive, dry carefully, then slice, or pull the leaves apart.

Put the oil and vinegar into a salad bowl, add some salt and pepper and mix together, then add the endive and walnuts and toss in the oil until everything is shiny with the dressing. Serve at once.

VARIATION
Salad of Chinese leaves with scallions v

This salad is made in the same way as the previous one, using 1½lb (700g) Napa cabbage or bok choy leaves and adding a bunch of chopped scallions instead of (or, if you prefer, as well as) the walnuts. I also rather like it with some raisins added too; they give a pleasant touch of sweetness.

Chinese leaf and beansprout salad

In this recipe, I have emphasised the Chinese theme by mixing Napa cabbage with crunchy beansprouts and a sweet and sour soy sauce and sesame oil dressing. It's rather like a salad version of Chinese stir-fry.

SERVES 4

6oz (175g) fresh beansprouts
1 tbsp honey
3 tbsp sesame oil or olive oil
2 tbsp dark soy sauce
freshly ground black pepper
1in (2.5cm) fresh root ginger, finely grated
12oz (350g) Napa cabbage, shredded
2 carrots, coarsely grated

Cover the beansprouts with cold water and leave them to soak and become crisp while you make the dressing and prepare the other ingredients.

Put the honey, oil and soy sauce into the base of a large bowl with a grating of pepper and the ginger, and mix together.

Add the Napa cabbage and carrots, mix well, then drain the beansprouts and add these. Mix again and serve.

Coleslaw

Homemade coleslaw is better than any you can buy, and it's very quick and easy to make. You can control the richness — using mayonnaise gives the creamiest, most delicious result but for lighter versions you can replace some of this with natural yogurt.

SERVES 4

12oz (350g) white cabbage, shredded
1 large carrot, coarsely grated
1 small onion, finely sliced
2oz (50g) golden raisins (optional)
3 rounded tbsp mayonnaise
salt and freshly ground black pepper

Put the cabbage, carrot and onion into a large bowl with the sultanas, (if using).

Add the mayonnaise and some salt and pepper to taste and mix well.

Cover and leave for 2–3 hours before serving, if possible. This allows the vegetables to soften and the flavors to blend.

Endive salad v

Curly endive makes a lovely salad.
I wish that we could buy it as easily
in the UK as one can in France.
The lovely round, untidy green and
yellow heads taste wonderful with
a simple walnut vinaigrette.

SERVES 4
½ head curly endive
walnut vinaigrette (see page 78)
2oz (50g) shelled walnut pieces,
    lightly chopped

Wash the endive, discarding any
discolored or damaged leaves.
Break up or roughly chop.
    Put the endive into a salad bowl
with the vinaigrette, add the fresh
walnuts, and toss together. Serve
immediately.

Fatoush v

This Lebanese dish contains the
usual ingredients of Middle Eastern
salads — cucumber, tomato, green
pepper, onion, parsley and mint —
but also toasted pita bread. Sumac
is a traditional Lebanese spice that
can be bought from Middle Eastern
stores or, increasingly, many
supermarkets.

SERVES 2–4
1 head Romaine, roughly chopped
a small bunch of flat-leaf parsley,
    roughly chopped
leaves from a small bunch of mint,
    roughly chopped
3 tomatoes, diced
1 avocado, peeled and diced
1 cucumber, diced
1 green pepper, seeded and chopped
1 bunch of scallions, chopped
1 pita bread

FOR THE DRESSING
juice of 1 lemon
¼ cup extra-virgin olive oil
1 garlic clove, crushed
1–3 tsp sumac (if available)
salt and freshly ground black pepper

Put all the prepared vegetables into
a salad bowl and mix.
    Make the dressing in a small
bowl by combining the lemon juice,
oil, garlic, sumac — start with the
smaller quantity and add more to
taste — plenty of salt and a
grinding of pepper.
    Open the pita bread and toast
under a hot broiler or in a toaster
until crisp, then break into bite-
sized pieces and add to the salad.
    Give the dressing a final stir, then
add to the salad. Toss the salad to
combine everything, then serve.

Fennel, carrot and scallions salad v

A refreshing salad that's quick
to make, especially if you have
a food processor.

SERVES 4
2 tbsp lemon juice
2 tbsp extra-virgin olive oil
salt and freshly ground pepper
1 large fennel bulb
8oz (225g) carrots, coarsely grated
4 scallions, chopped

Put the lemon juice and oil into
a large bowl with a little salt and
pepper and mix to make a simple
dressing.
    Wash and slice the fennel,
trimming off any tough outer layers
but keeping any feathery green
tops; chop these green bits and add
to the bowl.
    Add the grated carrots and
scallions. Mix well together.
    If possible, leave for an hour or
so before serving — this salad
improves with standing.

Fennel and cucumber salad v

The mixture of fennel and cucumber is refreshing and clean-tasting, and this salad is excellent for when you're in a hurry because it's very simple to make. It goes well with many pasta dishes.

SERVES 4

1 tbsp red wine vinegar
2 tbsp olive oil
salt and freshly ground black pepper
1 cucumber
1 large fennel bulb
a little sugar (optional)

Put the vinegar, oil, salt and a grinding of pepper into a salad bowl and mix together.

Peel the cucumber and cut into medium-sized dice. Wash, trim and slice the fennel, discarding any coarse leaves but including any tender feathery fronds.

Add the cucumber and fennel to the dressing mixture in the bowl and stir well.

Check the seasoning — just a touch of sugar can be pleasant in this salad — then serve.

Flageolet and avocado salad v

I'm particularly fond of this tasty, colorful salad.

SERVES 2 AS A SALAD MEAL,
4 AS A STARTER

4oz (125g) dried flageolet beans, soaked, cooked and drained, or 14oz can, drained and rinsed
3 tbsp extra-virgin olive oil
1 tbsp white wine vinegar
¼ tsp mustard powder
salt and freshly ground black pepper
1 ripe avocado
a few crisp lettuce leaves, to serve
2 tbsp chopped chives, to garnish

Put the beans into a salad bowl.

Mix the oil with the vinegar, mustard and some salt and pepper and add to the beans.

Halve the avocado and gently remove the skin and the stone, then slice the flesh and add it to the beans. Turn the mixture gently, so that everything gets coated with the dressing. Serve on top of the lettuce leaves and sprinkled with chopped chives.

VARIATIONS

Flageolet and button mushroom salad v

Use 6oz (175g) sliced button mushrooms instead of the avocado.

Flageolet and scallion salad v

Use 6–8 large scallions, trimmed and chopped, instead of the avocado.

French bean salad with a coriander seed dressing v

French beans and button mushrooms are marinated in a spicy dressing of crushed coriander seeds, lemon juice and olive oil.

SERVES 4–6

¼ cup extra-virgin olive oil
1lb (450g) button mushrooms, halved or quartered
1 small bay leaf
1 tbsp coriander seed, crushed
juice of 1 small lemon
1lb (450g) French green beans, cooked and drained
1 tbsp chopped fresh flat-leaf parsley
salt and freshly ground black pepper

Heat the oil in a large saucepan and fry the mushrooms, bay leaf and coriander seeds for 2–3 minutes or until the mushrooms are beginning to soften.

Remove from the heat and pour in the lemon juice; add the beans, parsley and some salt and pepper.

Let stand until room temperature, then transfer to a bowl and chill in the fridge before serving.

Fusilli salad with arugula and avocado

V

Pasta spirals with buttery avocado make a good first course or summer lunch.

SERVES 4–6

8oz (225g) fusilli
salt and freshly ground black pepper
3 tbsp extra-virgin olive oil
1 tbsp red wine vinegar
1–2 garlic cloves, crushed
freshly ground black pepper
a large handful of arugula
2–4 scallions, finely chopped
2 avocados
2 tbsp freshly squeezed lemon juice

Cook the pasta in plenty of boiling salted water until just tender, then drain thoroughly.

Mix the oil, vinegar, garlic and some salt and pepper in a large bowl, add the hot pasta, turning it until well coated.

Cool slightly — it doesn't have to be completely cold — and add the arugula and scallions.

Halve each avocado, removing the skin and stone, and dice the flesh. Sprinkle with lemon juice to preserve the color.

Fold the avocado into the pasta mix, together with the scallions. Season to taste and serve.

Greek salad

Instant nostalgia to anyone who loves Greece and has happy holiday memories of being there. Sometimes when I'm in that mood, I'll go whole hog and serve this with spanikopita and some tzatziki too (see pages 282 and 49).

SERVES 4–6

2 green peppers
1 cucumber
1lb (450g) firm tomatoes
1 medium-sized sweet onion
¼ cup extra-virgin olive oil
1 tbsp freshly squeezed lemon juice
1 tbsp red wine vinegar
salt and freshly ground pepper
a handful of kalamata olives
7oz (200g) feta cheese, cut into ½in
   (1cm) dice
½–1 tsp dried oregano

Seed the peppers and cut them into chunky pieces; peel the cucumber and cut that into chunks, too; slice the tomatoes and the onion. Put them all into a bowl.

Drizzle in the oil, lemon juice and vinegar and mix gently, adding salt and pepper to taste, followed by the olives and cheese; mix again, gently.

Serve scattered with dried oregano.

VARIATION

Greek salad with roasted red peppers

Above is the traditional Greek salad we know and love, but recently I was served the salad with some embellishment in the form of the roasted red peppers. All you do is put 2 large red peppers on a baking sheet and broil them under a high heat for 20–25 minutes, turning until the skins are blistered and blackened in places, and when the peppers are cool enough to handle, peel off the skin, remove the core and seeds, rinse and cut into pieces. Add these to the salad, made as described but without the green peppers. You might like to snip some fresh oregano over the top instead of using dried.

Green salad v

A green salad can be adapted according to the season, and is perhaps the most useful basic salad of all. I think plenty of fresh herbs make all the difference and I personally like to make it quite pungent with garlic and onion rings, but leave these out if they're not to your taste.

SERVES 4

3 tbsp extra-virgin olive oil
1 tbsp red wine vinegar
salt and freshly ground black pepper
1 garlic clove, crushed (optional)
1 lettuce, shredded
other green salad as available (e.g.
    watercress, sliced endive, fennel
    or cucumber, finely shredded baby
    spinach)
2 heaped tbsp chopped fresh herbs
    (e.g. flat-leaf parsley, chives or
    scallions, mint, tarragon, basil)

First make the dressing by putting the oil and vinegar into the base of a salad bowl and mixing with a little pepper and the garlic (if using).

Add all the other ingredients and mix well, so that everything gets coated with the shiny dressing. Serve immediately.

VARIATIONS

Green salad with Gruyère cheese

This traditional French salad is a delicious variation on the classic green salad. Simply add 4–6oz (125–175g) diced Gruyère cheese. If you can't find a vegetarian Gruyère, you could use vegetarian Emmental or even Edam, which are much more widely available.

Haricot bean salad with green herb dressing v

This dish is best made well in advance to allow the flavors time to blend. You can dress the salad while the beans are still hot, leave it to cool, then chill before serving. It makes a good first course or addition to a salad selection, or can be served with hot garlic bread and a green salad or tomato salad (see pages 55, 91 and 103).

SERVES 4–6 ❉
8oz (225g) dried haricot beans, soaked and cooked (see pages 176–7) or use 2 x 14oz cans
1 tsp sugar
½ tsp mustard powder
1 garlic clove, crushed
salt and freshly ground black pepper
2 tbsp red wine vinegar
6 tbsp extra-virgin olive oil
2 heaped tbsp chopped fresh herbs (such as chives, parsley, chervil, tarragon and dill)

Drain the beans, rinsing the canned ones (if using).

Put the sugar, mustard and garlic into a bowl with a little salt and a grinding of pepper. Blend to a paste with the vinegar, then gradually stir in the oil to make a dressing.

Add the herbs and the beans and mix well. Allow to cool, then chill in the fridge before serving.

Insalata tricolore

So simple, so good; lovely as a first course or to accompany a simple pasta dish such as spaghetti with pesto (see page 225). Vegetarian mozzarella is available, but look for one made from cow's milk rather than the more traditional buffalo's milk, which usually contains animal rennet.

SERVES 2
2 large ripe tomatoes, sliced
1 ripe avocado, peeled and sliced
1 ball of mozzarella, sliced
2 tablespoons torn fresh basil leaves
extra-virgin olive oil and balsamic vinegar, for drizzling
salt and freshly ground black pepper

Arrange the slices of tomato, avocado and mozzarella attractively on a flat plate or two individual plates.

Scatter with the basil leaves, then drizzle with the olive oil and balsamic vinegar, sprinkle with a little salt and grind over some black pepper. Serve at once.

Puy lentil salad v

Combined with a good fruity olive oil, lemon juice and some crisp onion rings, Puy lentils make a delicious salad. Perfect accompanied by a crisp, herby green salad and a glass of wine on a summer's day.

SERVES 4 ❉
8oz (225g) Puy lentils (or small brown or green lentils)
1 tbsp lemon juice
3 tbsp extra-virgin olive oil
salt and freshly ground black pepper
1 onion
2–3 tbsp chopped fresh flat-leaf parsley

Soak the lentils in water for a couple of hours or so if possible — this speeds up the cooking process — then drain, rinse, put into a saucepan, cover with fresh water to come 2in (5cm) above the top of the lentils, and simmer them gently until tender but not mushy — about 45 minutes. For flavor and digestibility, it is important to get them (and indeed any pulse) really tender — "al dente" is for pasta, not beans.

Drain the lentils thoroughly (keep the cooking liquid, it makes good stock) and put them into a bowl with the lemon juice, oil and some salt and pepper.

Peel the onion and cut it into very thin rounds, then add these to the lentils, along with the chopped parsley, and mix everything gently together. Serve chilled or at room temperature.

Lentil salad with fresh ginger v

Serve this salad with a cucumber and sour cream salad and warm pita bread or flat bread.

SERVES 4

¼ cup extra-virgin olive oil
1 large garlic clove, crushed
2 tsp grated fresh root ginger
1 onion, chopped
8oz (225g) small whole brown lentils or green lentils
2 cups (575ml) water
1 small red pepper, seeded and finely chopped
1 tbsp freshly squeezed lemon juice
2–3 tbsp chopped fresh coriander or flat-leaf parsley
salt and freshly ground black pepper

Heat 2 tablespoons of the oil in a medium-sized saucepan and fry the garlic, ginger and half the onion for 2–3 minutes.

Add the lentils, stir, then add the water. Bring to a boil, cover and leave to cook slowly until the lentils are tender and all the water is absorbed (about 15–20 minutes). Keep an eye on it and add a splash or two more water if necessary.

Remove from the heat, add the remaining oil and onion, the red pepper, lemon juice, coriander or parsley and some seasoning.

Serve warm or at room temperature.

Chunky lettuce salad with yogurt and green herb dressing

For this salad you need a firm-packed lettuce, such as iceberg or Webb's, with a very solid heart.

SERVES 4

1 iceberg lettuce
1 tbsp freshly squeezed lemon juice
salt
yogurt and green herb dressing (see page 78)

Wash the lettuce as well as you can and remove the outer leaves as necessary.

Cut the lettuce down into thick slices and cut these across, so that you have chunky pieces.

Put the lettuce chunks onto a flat serving dish, or individual plates, and sprinkle with the lemon juice and some salt, if desired.

Spoon some dressing over the lettuce chunks just before serving.

Tip

The Ricotta Mayonnaise (see page 77) is also good with this salad.

Lettuce salad with sweet dill dressing v

In contrast to the previous salad, this is a way of adding interest to the soft-leaf varieties of lettuce. A sweet dressing with a bit of dill — dried dill for economy in the winter, fresh dill when available — cheers up these lettuces no end.

SERVES 4

1 tsp sugar or honey
1 tbsp chopped fresh dill or 1 tsp dried dill
1 tbsp wine vinegar
2 tbsp extra-virgin olive oil
salt and freshly ground black pepper
1 large soft-leaf lettuce, torn into pieces
1 small onion, sliced into thin rings.

Put the sugar or honey, dill, vinegar and oil into a salad bowl with a little salt and pepper and mix well.

Add the lettuce and onion, turn the salad gently until all the leaves are coated with the dressing, then serve immediately.

If you want to make this salad ahead of time, prepare the dressing and onion rings and leave to one side; wash and dry the lettuce and put it into a plastic bag in the fridge. The salad can then be assembled in moments just before you want to eat.

Mexican-style salad

A quick and attractive salad. Serve it with the easy spelt flour tortillas on page 365, fajitas or tortilla chips.

SERVES 4

1 large ripe avocado
2 tbsp freshly squeezed lemon juice
1 garlic clove, crushed
1 tbsp extra-virgin olive oil
1 tsp wine vinegar
salt and freshly ground black pepper
chili powder
8 large crisp lettuce leaves
14oz can red kidney beans or pinto
    beans, rinsed and drained
1 small onion, sliced into thin rings
4 firm tomatoes, sliced
1 green or red pepper, seeded and
    thinly sliced
4oz (125g) grated cheddar cheese
a little paprika

Halve, stone, peel and mash the avocado; mix with the lemon juice, garlic, oil and vinegar and season with salt, pepper and chili powder to taste.

Lay lettuce leaves on four plates, then layer the beans, onion, tomatoes, pepper and cheese on top, ending with a big spoonful of avocado and a sprinkling of paprika. Serve at once.

Chunky mixed salad bowl v

It's best if you can find a really hearty lettuce for this salad — an iceberg or a firm Romaine — so that you can cut it into nice chunky pieces. The other ingredients are largely a matter of personal taste and can be varied according to what is available.

SERVES 4

3 tbsp extra-virgin olive oil
1 tbsp wine vinegar
1 garlic clove, crushed (optional)
salt and freshly ground black pepper
1 good-sized firm lettuce, cut into
    chunky pieces
4 firm tomatoes, cut into wedges
½ cucumber, cut into chunky dice
1 small head of celery or endive,
    sliced
1 tbsp chopped fresh chives or
    scallions
1 mild onion, sliced into rings
    (optional)

First make the dressing: put the oil and vinegar into the base of a salad bowl and mix with a little salt, pepper and garlic (if using).

Add all the other ingredients and mix well, so that everything gets coated with the shiny dressing. Serve immediately.

Mushroom, tomato and avocado salad bowl v

This salad goes well with some cooked pasta tossed in olive oil or pesto and sprinkled with grated Parmesan-style cheese.

SERVES 4

2 ripe avocados
juice of ½ lemon
3 tbsp extra-virgin olive oil
1 tbsp red wine vinegar
salt and freshly ground black pepper
8oz (225g) tomatoes, sliced
8oz (225g) baby button mushrooms,
    finely sliced
1 tbsp chopped fresh chives or
    scallions

Halve each avocado, removing the stone and skin. Cut into ½in (1cm) dice and sprinkle with the lemon juice.

Pour the oil and vinegar into the base of a salad bowl and add a little salt and pepper.

Add the tomatoes, mushrooms, avocados and chives and turn everything gently to mix the ingredients and make sure that all the flavors blend together. Serve immediately.

Orange, mint and cucumber salad

Sweet and simple.

SERVES 4

4 large juicy oranges
1 hearty head of lettuce
1 cucumber
4 sprigs of mint, roughly chopped
sour cream dressing (see page 77) or
    natural Greek yogurt

Using a serrated knife, and holding
the fruit over a bowl, cut the peel
and pith from the oranges and slice
out the segments into the bowl
    Tear the lettuce and slice the
cucumber (peeled or unpeeled).
Add these to the bowl, along with
the mint.
    Serve as it is, simple, fat-free and
refreshing, or with the sour cream
dressing or Greek yogurt.

Orange and radish salad v

Bright red radishes and golden
segments of orange make a
colorful salad.

SERVES 4

6 large oranges
2 bunches of radishes
1 bunch of watercress
1 tbsp extra-virgin olive oil (optional)
freshly ground black pepper

Using a serrated knife, and holding
the fruit over a bowl, cut the peel
and pith from the oranges and slice
out the segments.
    Wash and trim the radishes as
necessary, then slice and add to the
bowl, along with the watercress.
    You can stir 1 tablespoonful of
olive oil into this, to blend with the
orange juice and make a dressing,
or leave it as it is, fresh and light.
It's also nice with some pepper
ground over it.

Pasta salad with tomato and basil

Tender pasta, juicy tomatoes and
fresh basil make a fragrant summer
salad. Use any chunky pasta you
fancy: penne rigate, farfalle or
conchiglie, for instance. Eat it cold
on a hot day.

SERVES 4

8oz (225g) penne or farfalle pasta
salt
2 tbsp olive oil
1 tbsp red wine vinegar
freshly ground black pepper
4 tomatoes, roughly chopped
1 mild onion, finely chopped
a small handful of basil leaves, torn

TO SERVE

6oz (175g) grated Parmesan-style
    cheese
sour cream dressing (see page 77)
    (optional)

Cook the pasta in plenty of boiling
salted water until just tender, then
drain thoroughly.
    Put the oil and vinegar into a bowl
with some salt and pepper and mix
together.
    Add the drained pasta, turning it
gently until coated with the dressing.
    Stir in the tomatoes, onion and
basil, taste and season with salt and
plenty of pepper.
    Mix gently to combine the
ingredients. Serve the grated cheese
separately.

VARIATION

Pasta salad with tomatoes and avocado

Add 1 large or 2 medium avocados,
sliced and tossed in lemon juice.

Potato salad

Homemade potato salad is so delicious and quick and easy to make, why buy it?

SERVES 6, OR MORE IF SERVED WITH OTHER SALADS
1½lb (700g) small new potatoes
salt
2 rounded tbsp mayonnaise
2 rounded tbsp fromage frais or natural yogurt
freshly ground black pepper
1 tbsp chopped fresh chives or parsley, to garnish

If the potatoes are different sizes, halve or quarter larger ones to make them all roughly the same size.

Cook the potatoes in boiling salted water until they are just tender.

Drain the potatoes and put them into a bowl with the mayonnaise and fromage frais or yogurt, add some salt and pepper to taste, then stir gently until everything is mixed and the potatoes are coated in the creamy dressing.

Check the seasoning adding more salt and pepper if necessary.

Serve warm or at room temperature, with some chives or parsley snipped over the top.

VARIATION
Potato salad with herb vinaigrette

Use the vinaigrette dressing on page 78, instead of the mayonnaise and fromage frais, and increase the quantity of fresh herbs to ¼ cup of chopped chives or dill, stirring them into the mixture.

Red bean salad v

The secret of making a really good red bean salad is firstly to make it in advance, so that the beans have a chance to soak up the flavor of the dressing, and secondly to include some tomato ketchup in the dressing!

SERVES 4 ❄
8oz (225g) dried red kidney beans, soaked and cooked (see pages 176–7) or 2 x 14oz cans
2 tbsp red wine vinegar
1 tbsp tomato ketchup
¼ cup extra-virgin olive oil
1 garlic clove, crushed
salt and freshly ground black pepper
1 small onion, sliced into thin rings
chopped flat-leaf parsley, to garnish

Drain the cooked beans or, if you're using canned beans, drain and rinse under the cold tap (this is to get rid of any added salt or sugar).

In a large bowl combine the vinegar, ketchup, oil, garlic and seasoning. Add the drained beans and onion and mix well. Allow to cool.

Sprinkle with chopped parsley.

Red bean, carrot and walnut salad v

A red bean salad with lots of colors and contrasting texture.

SERVES 4
3 tbsp extra-virgin olive oil
1 tbsp wine vinegar
1 tsp superfine sugar
½ tsp mustard powder
1 small garlic clove, crushed (optional)
salt and freshly ground black pepper
4oz (125g) dried red kidney beans, soaked, cooked (see pages 176–7) and drained, or 14oz can, drained and rinsed
1 heaped tbsp chopped scallions
6oz (175g) carrots, coarsely grated
2oz (50g) fresh walnut pieces, chopped

Start by making the dressing: put the oil, vinegar, sugar, mustard and garlic, (if using), into a large bowl and mix with a little salt and pepper.

Add all the other ingredients, except the nuts, and mix well, so that everything gets coated with the shiny dressing.

Stir in the nuts just before serving so they stay crisp.

Mixed root salad v

A salad of grated roots looks very pretty and is so much more delicious than it sounds! I was brought up on such salads, and I still like them to this day — lots of chewing, lots of vitamins, lots of vitality, and for practically no cost. A food processor is advised, though.

SERVES 4
2 parsnips
1 turnip
2 carrots
1 small rutabaga
1 raw red beet
3 tbsp mayonnaise
3 tbsp vinaigrette (see page 78)
1 tsp chopped fresh flat-leaf parsley
juice of 1 orange
1 tbsp golden raisins
3 tbsp natural yogurt
4 dates, pitted and chopped
salt and freshly ground black pepper
½ lettuce or 2 heads of endive,
    to serve

TO GARNISH
1 small onion, sliced into thin rings
tomato slices
2oz packet of watercress

Peel the root vegetables and grate them into separate bowls.

Mix the parsnips with mayonnaise, the turnip with vinaigrette and parsley, the carrots with orange juice and golden raisins, and the rutabaga with yogurt and chopped dates. Season each mixture with salt and pepper.

Arrange the lettuce or endive on a serving platter or individual plates, spoon on piles of the root vegetables, then garnish with slices of onion, tomatoes and watercress.

VARIATION
Quick mixed root vinaigrette v

This is a simpler version of the main recipe. Just grate the five types of root vegetable: parsnips, turnip, carrots, rutabaga and beets. Place the little piles separately on a bed of lettuce, pour a generous amount of balsamic dressing (see page 75) over them, and scatter with chopped chives.

Arugula salad with balsamic dressing

The pungency of arugula is beautifully balanced by the sweetness of the dressing in this simple salad. It goes well with so many dishes — omelette, cheese soufflé, pizza or with many pasta dishes (see pages 294, 301, 383 and 208–29). If you're looking for a quick and delicious salad to accompany a main course, this is it!

SERVES 2–4
1½ tsp Dijon mustard
1½ tsp honey
1 tbsp balsamic vinegar
2–3 tbsp extra-virgin olive oil
salt and freshly ground black pepper
5oz (150g) arugula leaves

Put the mustard, honey and vinegar into a deep bowl and mix. You can use the bowl from which you're going to serve the salad. Gradually beat in the oil, using 2 or 3 tablespoons, depending on how oily you like your dressings, then season to taste with salt and pepper.

Put the arugula into the bowl on top of the dressing. Toss the salad just before serving, ensuring that every leaf is glossy.

Salad Niçoise

This is my vegetarian version of this classic salad, combining all the usual ingredients except the tuna fish and anchovies. It makes an excellent lunch dish with soft warm wholegrain rolls or crunchy French bread.

SERVES 4

1 large Romaine
1 onion
1lb (450g) firm tomatoes
5 hardboiled eggs
1lb (450g) cooked French green
    beans
a handful of black olives
1 heaped tbsp capers, rinsed well
2 tbsp chopped fresh flat-leaf
    parsley
2 tbsp best-quality extra-virgin olive
    oil
1 tbsp red wine vinegar
salt and freshly ground black pepper
a drop or two of Tabasco sauce

Line a flat serving dish with leaves from the lettuce.

Thinly slice the onion, quarter the tomatoes and eggs and cut the French beans into even-sized lengths. Put the vegetables and eggs into a bowl and add the olives, capers, parsley, oil and vinegar, a little salt and pepper and a drop or two of Tabasco.

Mix gently so that everything gets coated with the oil. Heap the salad up on top of the lettuce leaves and serve as soon as possible.

VARIATION

Salade Niçoise with white beans

Make as described, adding a 14oz can of white beans (cannellini, haricot or butter beans), drained and rinsed, instead of, or as well as, the eggs. Make sure the white beans get well mixed with the dressing, to make them shiny and well-flavored.

Salata

Based on a Bulgarian salad, this is an interesting, colorful mixture.

SERVES 4

1 garlic clove, crushed
3 tbsp extra-virgin olive oil
1 tbsp wine vinegar
salt and freshly ground black pepper
1 mild onion, finely sliced
1 cucumber, sliced
2 large red peppers, roasted or raw,
    seeded and sliced
2 carrots, coarsely grated
4 tomatoes, chopped
2 tbsp chopped fresh flat-leaf
    parsley
7oz (200g) feta cheese, crumbled,
    to serve

Put the garlic into a deep bowl, add the olive oil, vinegar and some salt and pepper, and mix well.

Add all the other ingredients to the bowl, mixing well so that they all get coated in the oil.

Chill in the fridge and leave for at least 1 hour, then serve with the crumbled feta cheese on top.

Soba noodle, edamame and seaweed salad v

Soba or buckwheat noodles are quite easy to find in supermarkets and make a delicious salad when mixed with edamame (green soy) beans. You can buy them frozen, either in their pods or already shelled. The seaweed salad makes a pretty and very tangy addition that I love. You can buy dried seaweed salad mix from health-food stores and Asian stores.

SERVES 2–4

2oz (50g) dried seaweed salad mix
9oz (250g) soba noodles
4oz (125g) frozen shelled green
    soy beans
4 scallions, cut into shreds
1 tbsp toasted sesame oil
1 tbsp mirin, honey or agave syrup
1 tbsp rice vinegar or red wine
    vinegar
1 tbsp soy sauce
4 tsp sesame seeds, to garnish

Put the seaweed into a bowl, cover with warm water and leave to soak while you prepare the other ingredients.

Bring a large saucepan of water to a boil, add the noodles and green soy beans and cook for about 4 minutes, until the noodles are just tender; or follow the directions on the packet.

Drain the noodles and beans well, and put them back into the empty pan. Add the scallions, sesame oil, mirin, honey or agave syrup, vinegar and soy sauce.

Drain the seaweed thoroughly then add to the noodles and mix gently.

Toast the sesame seeds by stirring them for a minute or two in a dry saucepan until they smell cooked and start to jump around.

Serve the salad in a pretty bowl, or on individual plates, sprinkled with the toasted sesame seeds.

Cooked spinach salad

This salad of cooked spinach is eaten all over the Middle East and I really love the mixture of soft, dark green leaves, fruity olive oil and sharp-tasting lemon juice. Yogurt can be included in the dressing or served with the salad, as in this recipe, or it can be served with tzatziki or feta dressing (see pages 49 and 75). Cooked chickpeas can be also added, providing a pleasant contrast of color and texture as well as protein. I also like it with a topping of pine nuts or slivered almonds, fried golden and crisp in butter (see variations).

SERVES 4

2¼lb (1kg) spinach leaves
1 garlic clove, crushed
1 tbsp freshly squeezed lemon juice
3 tbsp extra-virgin olive oil
salt and freshly ground black pepper

TO SERVE

lemon wedges
10 fl oz (275ml) Greek yogurt

Wash the spinach well then cook it in just the water clinging to it. When it's wilted, drain it thoroughly and leave to cool.

Chop the spinach and put it into a bowl with the garlic, lemon juice, olive oil and some salt and pepper and mix well.

Serve with lemon wedges and a generous spoonful of thick Greek yogurt and an extra grinding of black pepper.

continued next page

Wilted spinach salad v

I created this salad for a vegan cookery demonstration and it caused a sensation. I very rarely use mock "meat", but I included mock bacon, added sizzling from the pan, to wilt the spinach and give a smoky flavor and crunchy texture. As an alternative, you could use smoked tofu, sliced very thinly and fried in olive oil until crisp on both sides. In the original recipe I used vegan feta-style cheese in olive oil, which, like the bacon, can be bought from health stores, but you could use dairy feta cheese instead for a vegetarian version.

SERVES 4

4oz feta cheese
4oz (115g) "mock" bacon
1 garlic clove, crushed
3 tbsp extra-virgin olive oil
1 tbsp red wine vinegar
1 tsp English or Dijon mustard
salt and freshly ground black pepper
1lb (450g) baby leaf spinach

Drain the oil from the feta cheese — you could use some of this to oil the pan for frying the bacon and making the dressing.

Fry the bacon in a lightly oiled frying pan, as described on the packet, until browned and crisp. Drain on paper towels.

Put the garlic, oil, vinegar and mustard in a salad bowl along with some salt and pepper and mix to make a dressing. Place the baby spinach on top and mix gently until it is all coated with the dressing. It will seem like a lot of leaves, but they will shrink when coated with the dressing. Add the cheese.

With kitchen scissors, snip the bacon into bite-sized pieces. Put them back in the frying pan, with a little more oil if necessary, and reheat until sizzling, then add them, and their oil, into the salad, and toss gently until everything is mixed.

VARIATIONS

Cooked spinach salad with chickpeas

Add a 14oz can of chickpeas, drained and rinsed, to the spinach and increase the amount of lemon juice to 2 tablespoons and the oil to ¼ cup.

Cooked spinach salad with pine nuts

Top the salad with 2oz (50g) pine nuts, toasted for a minute or two (don't turn your back!) under a hot broiler or by stirring in a dry saucepan over a moderate heat. If you're feeling adventurous you could also stir a handful of raisins into the salad; sounds odd, but their plump sweetness goes well with the iron-y bitterness of the spinach and the crunchy pine nuts.

Cooked spinach salad with sizzling almonds

If you have the time, blanch your own almonds (see page 139), then cut them into pointed slivers. Otherwise, sliced almonds are fine. Either way, fry them in 1 tablespoon of olive oil and a pat of salted butter for a minute or two until they're golden. Pour them, still sizzling, over the top of the salad.

Opposite: Soba noodle, edamame and seaweed salad (see page 99)

Sweetcorn salad with lime and coriander v

Sweetcorn, cut straight off the cob, is so good raw that I really don't know why anyone cooks it for a salad. Enjoy its juicy sweetness in this bright, late-summer mix. It goes well with some simply cooked pasta, not too al dente, and a glass of chilled white wine.

SERVES 4

2 sweetcorn cobs
¼ cup finely chopped red onion
1 red pepper, seeded and finely
  chopped
a small bunch of fresh coriander,
  roughly chopped
2 tbsp extra-virgin olive oil
juice of 1 lime
salt and freshly ground black pepper
a pinch or two of chili powder

Remove the outer leaves and silky threads from the sweetcorn cobs and trim the stem level with the base.

Stand one upright on its base on a firm chopping board and, using a sharp knife, cut the sweetcorn from the cob, removing a few rows from top to bottom. Continue round each cob like this until you've cut all the sweetcorn away. This is much easier than it sounds.

Put the sweetcorn in a colander and rinse under the cold tap; shake dry and put into a salad bowl.

Add the onion, red pepper and coriander to the bowl; pour in the oil and lime juice and mix well.

Season with salt, pepper and a pinch or two of chili powder to give it a bit of a kick, but not too much.

VARIATIONS

Sweetcorn salad with radishes and scallions v

This is very attractive and the flavor of the radishes works well with the sweetcorn. Make as described but leave out the red pepper, red onion and coriander. Add a large bunch of radishes, sliced into rings, and a handful of chopped scallions to the sweetcorn.

Sweetcorn salad with tomatoes and basil v

The sweetness of the corn enhances another late-summer ingredient: tomatoes. Make as described, leaving out the coriander and red pepper, and adding 4 sliced tomatoes or a couple of handfuls of cherry tomatoes, halved, and several large sprigs of basil, torn. Dress with lemon juice instead of lime.

Tabbouleh v

In this Middle Eastern bulgur wheat salad, parsley is used rather like a vegetable to provide the basis of the dish, and it's surprising what a big bunch you'll need for the weight required. If you haven't got enough I find you can use a bunch of watercress or some tender young spinach leaves instead. Bulgur wheat is available from health-food food stores and supermarkets.

SERVES 4

8oz (225g) bulgur wheat
4oz (125g) fresh flat-leaf parsley
1oz (25g) fresh mint leaves
1 onion
3 tomatoes
2 tbsp extra-virgin olive oil
juice of 1 lemon
1 garlic clove, crushed with a
  little salt
salt and freshly ground black pepper
a few crisp lettuce leaves to serve
  (optional)

Cover the bulgar wheat with boiling water and leave it to soak for 15 minutes, then drain thoroughly and put into a bowl.

Meanwhile, wash the parsley and mint and chop them up fairly finely. Peel and chop the onion and tomatoes, then add to the wheat, together with the oil, lemon juice and garlic. Mix everything together well and season to taste.

Serve spooned onto a flat serving dish, in a salad bowl or heaped up on crisp lettuce leaves. I like this salad with some whole black olives added.

Tip
You can use couscous instead of bulgur wheat; no need to soak it first.

Tomato salad v

One of the joys of late summer — hopefully eaten outside in the sunshine — this simple salad is perfect with some pasta, cooked until just tender, then tossed in olive oil or pesto.

SERVES 4
1½lb (700g) tomatoes
balsamic vinegar or freshly squeezed lemon juice
extra-virgin olive oil
sea salt and freshly ground black pepper
a sprig or two of fresh basil, torn

Wash the tomatoes and cut them into thin slices, then arrange the tomato slices in a wide shallow serving dish.

Drizzle the balsamic vinegar or lemon juice all over the tomatoes, then do the same with the olive oil.

Scrunch some sea salt over the top with your fingers, then some black pepper and finally the basil.

This salad is best if you can leave it for at least 30 minutes, for the juices to run and the flavors to blend together.

VARIATIONS

Tomato and onion salad v

Layer some very thinly sliced mild onion with the tomatoes. One small onion is enough to add flavor and texture but not overpower the tomatoes.

Tomato and avocado salad v

Pale, buttery avocado goes really well with the tomato. It's best to prepare the tomatoes as described, putting them in a bowl rather than a serving dish. Let them stand for 30 minutes or so, then gently mix in the sliced flesh of 1 ripe avocado, season to taste, and serve.

Tomatoes and broad beans in basil dressing v

This salad is best if you have time to pop the fava beans out of their skins; beautiful vivid green looks very pretty with the tomato and chopped basil. Frozen broad beans are fine — lovely and tender. It's only worth using fresh fava beans if you can get them when they're very young.

SERVES 4
12oz (350g) frozen broad beans
1lb (450g) tomatoes
2 tbsp extra-virgin olive oil
1 tbsp red wine vinegar
1 tbsp chopped fresh basil
salt and freshly ground black pepper

Cook the broad beans in a little fast-boiling water for about 3 minutes or until just tender, then drain and cool.

When the beans are cool enough to handle, pop off the grey outer skins using your fingers. This is a bit tedious, but worth it if you've got time.

Skin (see page 40) and slice the tomatoes, removing any hard pieces from the center.

Put the oil, vinegar and basil into a large bowl and mix together, then add the tomatoes, broad beans and some salt and pepper.

Mix gently, so that everything gets coated with the dressing. Serve immediately, or let the salad stand for up to 2 hours for the flavors to mingle.

Tomato, feta and olive salad

Simple, delicious and great with some chunky bread, such as ciabatta.

SERVES 4 AS A SIDE SALAD, 2–3 AS A MAIN DISH

1½lb (700g) firm tomatoes
1 onion
handful of black olives, kalamata if you can get them
3 tbsp extra-virgin olive oil
1 tbsp red wine vinegar
salt and freshly ground black pepper
7oz (200g) feta cheese

Wash the tomatoes and cut them into fairly thin slices. Peel and finely slice the onion.

Put the tomatoes and onion into a bowl and add the olives, oil, vinegar and some salt and pepper, and mix them lightly together.

Drain the feta cheese if necessary and pat dry on paper towels, then cut into ½in (1cm) dice and add to the bowl.

Tomatoes stuffed with cannellini beans

In the summer, when tomatoes are cheap and firm and good, I do think stuffed tomatoes make a nice change, and if you choose big tomatoes, though not beefsteak ones, they're not really tricky to do. Try these and see what you think!

SERVES 2–4

4 good-sized tomatoes
salt
14oz can cannellini beans, drained and rinsed
2 tbsp mayonnaise
2 tbsp natural yogurt
6 scallions, chopped
freshly ground black pepper

TO SERVE

handful of mixed salad leaves
balsamic dressing (see page 75)

Cut the tomatoes in half horizontally (not down through the stem end). Scoop out the seeds without damaging the tomatoes and sprinkle the insides of the tomato halves with salt.

To make the filling, just mash together the beans, mayonnaise, yogurt and scallions, and season to taste.

Spoon the bean mixture into the tomatoes, dividing it between them.

Arrange the tomatoes on individual plates with some salad leaves and drizzle with a little balsamic dressing.

VARIATIONS

Tomatoes stuffed with chickpeas

Use chickpeas, drained, instead of cannellini beans. You could bind these with hummus instead of the mayonnaise and yogurt, and leave out the scallions adding a tablespoonful of chopped fresh coriander instead.

Tomatoes stuffed with flageolet beans

Pale green flageolet beans make a pretty color contrast with the tomatoes. Use instead of the cannellini beans.

Tomatoes stuffed with creamy cheese v

Replace the beans with 9oz (250g) ricotta, cottage or cream cheese and, along with the scallions, stir in 1 tablespoon each of chopped chives and parsley. Or, even easier, just use some (vegan if you wish) herb and garlic cream cheese.

Tomatoes stuffed with avocado v

Mash the flesh of two avocados with a squeeze or two of lime juice, a crushed garlic clove, a small handful of chopped coriander and some salt and pepper, and pile into the seasoned tomato halves. Serve immediately.

Turkish salad v

I love the simplicity and fresh flavors of Middle Eastern salads, and this one from Turkey is no exception.

SERVES 2–4
6 tomatoes, cut into bite-sized pieces
1 cucumber, diced
1 green pepper, seeded and diced
a small bunch of scallions, chopped
a small bunch of flat-leaf parsley, chopped
2 tbsp freshly squeezed lemon juice
1 tbsp extra-virgin olive oil
salt and freshly ground black pepper

Simply mix all the ingredients together in a large bowl. Season well with salt and pepper and serve.

Rainbow layered wheat salad

This salad consists of different ingredients, chosen to contrast as much as possible in color, flavor and texture. When I serve it at home everyone makes their own selection, layering up the salad in their bowl and ending with a dollop of one of the low-fat creamy dressings. The wheat makes a lovely chewy salad. You can buy it at health-food stores and it's best to cook the whole bag, divide into portions and store the surplus in the freezer, ready for another occasion.

SERVES 4–6
3–4oz (75–125g) wholegrain wheat — soaked overnight in cold water
14oz can red kidney beans, drained and rinsed
2 tbsp extra-virgin olive oil
2 tbsp red wine vinegar
salt and freshly ground black pepper
1 tsp tomato purée
a dash of honey
potato salad (see page 96)
1 small-medium lettuce, washed and shredded
3 carrots, grated and tossed in a little orange juice
2 raw red beets, peeled, grated and tossed in a little orange juice
4 tomatoes, sliced
½ cucumber, diced

FOR THE TOPPING
ricotta mayonnaise, mayonnaise or sour cream dressing (see pages 76–7)
1 small container of mustard or watercress sprouts, cut, or sprouted seeds (see page 79)

Simmer the soaked wheat in plenty of water for 1¼ hours, or pressure cook it for 25 minutes. If you've cooked a whole bag of wheat, remove a fifth of it and put into a small mixing bowl; freeze the rest for other occasions.

Put the beans into another bowl. Mix half the oil and vinegar with the beans and half with the wheat. Season both mixtures with salt and pepper, adding a dash of tomato purée and just a very little honey to the beans.

Serve all the other ingredients — shredded lettuce, grated carrots and beets, sliced tomatoes, diced cucumber — separately in little bowls (soup bowls, or small wooden bowls if you have them).

Alternatively, put layers of the different ingredients in individual bowls, one for each person.

Spoon a generous amount of your chosen dressing over the salad and scatter with mustard and cress or sprouted seeds.

Side dishes

These are light vegetable dishes for serving alongside a main dish rather than taking the starring role. Nowadays, there is a wonderful array of good-quality vegetables available and many of them only need simple cooking and flavoring to be enjoyed at their best. Over the next few pages you'll find a brief guide to vegetables: how to choose, prepare and cook them for the best results.

Many of the recipes in this chapter can become main courses if served with some cooked beans or chickpeas, grated cheese, cooked rice, buttery noodles or baked potatoes. Speaking of potatoes, forever popular as a side dish, you'll find delicious, easy recipes for these, too: how to make really good roast potatoes and perfect mashed potatoes, as well as the crowning glory of potato dishes, gratin Dauphinoise (see pages 131 and 129).

A brief guide to cooking and preparing vegetables

Basic preparation

Choose small, tender vegetables which are bright and firm and look vital and full of life. I like to use organic as much as possible.

Allow 6oz (175g) vegetables per person (weighed before preparation), or 8oz (225g) where there is a lot of waste, as in leafy leeks and also spinach (except the packaged type) and 1lb (450g) for peas and beans in their pods.

Store vegetables in a cool place (the bottom of the fridge is ideal), and use them as soon as you can.

When preparing vegetables, cut away as little as possible and when cooking vegetables together, make sure they're a similar size — cut larger ones if necessary.

Basic cooking

The basic method of cooking, and the one that's suitable for nearly all vegetables, is boiling (I have described other methods in the recipes and alphabetical guide, pages 109–12, where they apply).

Boiling means plunging the prepared vegetables into boiling water, letting them boil vigorously until just tender, then draining immediately.

It's important to make sure the water has reached a rolling boil before adding the vegetables. The exception to this is root vegetables, which can be started with either boiling or cold water. Root vegetables need to be boiled in enough water to cover them, with a lid on the pan.

Other vegetables can either be cooked conservatively; that is, put into just enough boiling water to prevent them from boiling dry (about ½in (1cm) for 1½–2lb (700–900g)), and cooked with a lid on the pan — this is how I do them; or plunged, briefly, into a large pan three-quarters full of boiling water, and cooked uncovered.

Whichever method you use, keep testing the vegetables by piercing them with a sharp pointed knife. The moment they feel tender but still a bit resistant, remove them from the heat and drain thoroughly.

A variation of boiling is steaming. Here the vegetables are set above the water in a perforated steamer saucepan, metal colander or steaming basket so that they cook in the steam without touching the water. This is a good method for root vegetables and delicate ones such as asparagus. It works best for small quantities of vegetables because if you have too many they will not cook evenly, unless you have a tiered steamer.

Artichoke, globe Allow one per person. Break off the stem level with the base and snip off the points of the leaves. Wash the artichokes well. Immerse in boiling water to cover (use an enamel or stainless steel saucepan) and boil for 30–45 minutes or until a leaf pulls off easily. Turn the artichokes upside-down to drain. Serve with melted butter.

Artichokes, Jerusalem Peel, then boil in an enamel or stainless steel pan for 20–40 minutes or until tender. Or cook in butter as described on page 112.

Asparagus Bend the spears to break off the hard stems at the base and discard these. Wash the asparagus gently. Cook in a deep pan of boiling water, or by laying flat and covered with water in a large frying pan, or in a steamer, until just tender (7–10 minutes). Drain well. Or, rub asparagus with olive oil and roast at 400°F (200°C) for 7–10 minutes or until tender and slightly charred.

Beansprouts Wash, drain and stir-fry in 1–2 tbsp oil for 1–2 minutes. Best included in a mixture of stir-fried vegetables, as on page 151.

Broad beans also known as **Fava beans** Prepare and cook tiny ones as for French beans. Remove older beans from the pod, then boil in a large pan of unsalted boiling water for 5–10 minutes. Drain and, for perfection, pop off the grey skins to reveal the tender bright green beans inside. Serve with butter and chopped herbs.

Broccoli There are two types: slender purple sprouting and the thicker, clumpy type called calabrese. Prepare purple sprouting like asparagus. Divide calabrese into florets, cutting off the tough stem. You can peel the stem, which is tender and tastes good, cut it into matchsticks and cook with the florets. Both types of broccoli need to cook in boiling water for 5–7 minutes until just tender. Drain and serve with melted butter or a sauce.

Brussels sprouts Choose small firm ones. Trim off outer leaves and stalk ends. Cook really tiny ones whole; halve or quarter larger ones. I always cut any type of Brussels sprouts in half because it's easier to cook them perfectly if they're less dense, and I prefer the look and flavor of them done like this. Boil quickly until just tender (2–5 minutes). Drain well.

Butternut squash Halve lengthways, brush with olive oil, put on a baking sheet and bake at 375°F (190°C) for about 1 hour or until you can pierce it easily with a sharp knife; the timing will depend on the size of squash. Discard the seeds; scoop the tender flesh out of the skin. Alternatively, cut squash into chunks and roast as described for zucchini, for about 45 minutes.

Cabbage Trim off outer leaves, cut into quarters, then shred, removing the central core. Boil for 5–7 minutes; drain well, swirl with melted butter, salt and freshly grated black pepper.

Carrots Scrub tender carrots; scrape or peel older ones. Leave small carrots whole; halve, quarter, slice or dice larger ones. Boil in water to cover for 10–20 minutes, or steam for 10-20 minutes, or until tender: the timing will depend on the size of the carrots or pieces of carrot, and how tender you want them.

Cauliflower Break into florets, trim off tough stems. Boil for 3–5 minutes and drain very well. Or steam for 8–10 minutes. Serve plainly or tossed in butter or sour cream; or coat in batter, as for salsify fritters (page 38); or cover with cheese sauce (see page 65), top with crumbs and bake until golden.

Celeriac Peel well and cut into even-sized chunks. Boil in a stainless steel or enamel pan for

30–40 minutes. Serve with butter or make into a purée (see page 119).

Celery Choose small compact hearts and wash them well. Trim to about 6in (15cm), halve or quarter lengthwise. Or use outer stalks of celery only; trim and cut into even-sized lengths. Best braised, as on page 120.

Chinese cabbage or Napa cabbage Trim, shred finely and stir-fry as described on page 116.

Cucumber Peel and cut into ½in (1cm) slices and cook as described on page 121. I think cooked cucumber is a real delicacy; I'm surprised it's not often done.

Eggplant Slice or cube, with or without peeling. Brush them very lightly with oil and microwave or bake; or fry in oil, being careful not to use too much; eggplants are like blotting paper and will take up whatever oil you give them. You can roast eggplants as described for zucchini, page 112.

Endive Remove any damaged leaves and trim base. Insert the point of a knife in the base and twist to remove a cone-shaped "core"; this is supposed to reduce bitterness and ensure even cooking, though I'm not convinced. Cook as described for artichokes (see page 112), omitting the sauce.

Fennel Trim off stalk ends, base and run a potato peeler down the outer leaves to remove toughness. Boil and serve with butter, or braise as described for celery on page 120, omitting the chestnuts.

French green beans Top and tail as necessary; leave whole or cut large ones into shorter lengths, then

boil for 2–10 minutes, depending on size.

Kale A delicious vegetable with an intense, slightly bitter flavor. Remove the stalks, pulling the leaves away from the stem. Boil for 5–7 minutes, drain well and swirl with butter.

Kohlrabi Looks and sounds more exciting than it tastes, though it has an appealing, delicate flavor. Prepare and cook as for rutabaga. Although I think it's better raw, when you can appreciate the flavor and juicy crunchiness.

Leeks Cut off roots and most of the green part; slit down one side and rinse out any grit. Leave whole or slice. Cook as described for artichokes on page 112 or boil until tender: 1–2 minutes for sliced leeks, 8–10 minutes for thin whole ones. Drain well. Or shred the leeks finely and add to stir-fries, or cook for just a few minutes in oil and butter.

Lettuce Prepare and cook firm, hearty lettuces as for endive, but with no need to "core".

Mushrooms Wash but don't peel. Leave small ones whole, slice large ones. Trim the stalks from flat open mushrooms. Fry in butter or oil until tender. If they give off a little liquid, increase the heat and cook rapidly until it disappears; if they give off a lot, drain the mushrooms, reserving the liquid for stock. Heat another batch of butter and oil in the pan, put in the mushrooms, and fry them again, to finish cooking. This time they will not be swamped in liquid. Flat mushrooms are good brushed with oil and grilled.

Okra Top and tail; cook gently in oil for about 20 minutes. Good fried with onions, tomatoes and spices (see page 123).

Onions Bake in their skins at 400°F (200°C) for about 1 hour, slit and serve with butter, salt and pepper. Or remove the skins, cut the onions into sixths or quarters, toss in oil and roast as described for zucchini. Or peel, cut into even-sized pieces and boil for 15–45 minutes; or fry in butter or oil for about 10 minutes. For crisp onion rings, dip raw onion rings in milk and flour then deep-fry for 1–2 minutes.

Pak choi Sometimes also known as pak choy, bok choi/choy, this is a type of Chinese cabbage with thick, firm white stalks and green leaves. It has a delicious mild, fresh, juicy flavor. You can shred it, but I prefer to cut it in half from the top of the leaves to the root. Steam it, or steam-boil it by cooking in a covered saucepan containing ½ in (1cm) of water for 2–4 minutes until just tender. It's also great added to stir-fries or Thai curries.

Parsnips Prepare as for rutabaga. Mash with butter and serve or make into croquettes or bake with breadcrumbs and butter until crisp; or roast in oil as for roast potatoes (see page 131).

Peas Shell; boil for 5–10 minutes or braise with lettuce (page 125).

Peppers Halve each pepper, remove the stalk, core and seeds. Slice, fry in oil for about 15 minutes or until softened. Or, place under a hot broiler until the skin blackens and blisters in places. Cover with a plate or plastic bag, then when cool enough to handle, peel off the skin and remove the core and seeds; rinse and cut the flesh into pieces.

Or halve or quarter each pepper and roast as described for zucchini. Or fill pepper halves with stuffing and bake (see pages 159–61).

Potatoes Scrape or peel potatoes, or scrub and leave the skins on. Boil in water to cover until tender and serve with butter and chopped herbs, or mash with butter and milk or cream until light and fluffy. Or cook slowly in butter as for artichokes on page 112. To bake potatoes, see page 128. For baby potatoes and new potatoes, boil in just enough water to cover for about 20 minutes, depending on the size, until they are tender when pierced with a knife, then drain and add butter or olive oil, sea salt, pepper and some chopped parsley, mint or chives. For fries, cut potatoes into sticks, put one of these into a deep-frying pan one-third full of fat. When it starts to sizzle add the rest and cook until golden. Or, remove the fries with a strainer once they're tender, reheat the oil until very hot, then put the fries back in it for a quick second fry. Drain and serve immediately.

Pumpkin Prepare as for butternut squash.

Red Beet Cut off the leaves, if still attached, 4in (10cm) above the beet. Do not peel or cut the beet or the color will come out. Boil in water to cover, with a lid on the pan, for 1–2 hours. Slip off the skins, slice or cube the beet, re-heat in butter or a sauce. Or, scrub them, rub with oil, wrap in foil and bake in a moderate oven until you can pierce them easily with a knife.

Red cabbage Prepare and cook as described on page 133.

Runner beans Top and tail; cut down the sides of the beans to remove any tough strings. Cut into 1in (2.5cm) pieces or slice very thinly lengthwise. Boil for 5–10 minutes or until just tender.

Rutabaga Peel thickly, cut into even-sized pieces, cover with water and boil for 15–20 minutes or until tender; or steam for 20 minutes. Mash with butter and seasoning. Delicious prepared like the parsnips on page 125 or the celeriac on page 119, and can be brushed with oil and roasted as described for zucchini (see page 110) for 45–60 minutes.

Salsify and scorzonera Scrape, keeping the roots submerged. Cut into even-sized lengths, boil in water to cover in a stainless steel or enamel saucepan for 5–15 minutes or until tender. Serve with butter and herbs, in a creamy sauce or as fritters (see page 38).

Spinach If from the garden or market, wash very thoroughly. Remove any really tough stalks; keep the rest on for added flavor and texture. Spinach in a bag from a supermarket just needs to be rinsed in cold water; the stems are tender and cook quickly with the leaves. Put spinach into a large saucepan with just the water clinging to it from the washing. You don't need to add any. As the spinach boils down, chop it with kitchen shears and turn it so that it cooks evenly. Drain and serve with butter, salt and black pepper. It takes about 4–7 minutes, depending on how tender it is. Best not to serve spinach more than once a week because its high oxalic content hinders the absorption of magnesium and calcium.

Snow Peas Prepare as for French beans. Stir-fry or boil for 2–3 minutes maximum: don't let them lose their crunchiness. Sometimes I cut them in half lengthways, for a more delicate look.

Sweet potatoes Scrub, cut into pieces and bake like potatoes (page 128), or peel, boil and purée. Or cut into even-sized chunks (no need to peel), rub with oil and roast as described for zucchini (see page 110), for about 30 minutes or until tender and browned round the edges.

Sweetcorn Remove the leaves and silky threads, trim off the stalk. Immerse in a large pan of boiling unsalted water, simmer for about 10 minutes, until the yellow kernels are tender. Drain and serve with melted butter. Or cook in the microwave: you can put the whole cob in, with the husk still around it. Microwave for 2–3 minutes per cob. Peel back the green husk and silky threads and eat the corn. You can also microwave it without the husk; just place the corn cobs in a suitable dish, add a cupful of water, cover and microwave for a couple of minutes. Another way is to butter and season the cob, wrap in greaseproof paper and microwave. When opened, it's all ready to eat.

Swiss chard A delicious vegetable. Strip the leaves from the stems and cook as for spinach. Cut stems into 4in (10cm) lengths, boil for 4–5 minutes or until just tender. Drain and serve with melted butter, hollandaise (see pages 66–7) or a creamy sauce.

Tomatoes Remove the stems, cut a cross in the top of the tomatoes and bake at 350°F (180°C), for 10–15 minutes. Or halve and fry on both sides; or halve, season, dot with butter and bake or broil for 10 minutes. Vine tomatoes are delicious just cooked under the broiler or in the oven for 5–10 minutes until they just begin to collapse; don't let them cook too much.

Turnips Peel; leave baby turnips whole; halve or quarter larger ones. Boil for 5–10 minutes, drain well, return to the pan and dry out over heat. Or steam for 10–15 minutes. Serve with butter or as a purée, or diced and mixed with diced carrots.

Zucchini Top and tail finger-sized zucchini, slice, dice or coarsely grate older ones. Fry in butter; or boil until barely tender, drain well and serve with butter and herbs. Or rub them with olive oil and roast at 400°F (200°C) for about 30 minutes or until tender and slightly charred. Or brush long slices of zucchini with oil and cook on a griddle pan on top of the stove for an attractive stripy look and chargrilled flavor.

Artichokes in fresh tomato sauce

This way of cooking Jerusalem artichokes — slowly in a heavy-based saucepan with butter and just a little water — is called "stoved artichokes" and it brings out all their flavor. I added the sauce to bring some cheerful color and a taste of summer to this wintery vegetable. This makes a lovely starter or side dish.

SERVES 4

1½lb (700g) Jerusalem artichokes
2 tbsp (25g) butter
2 tbsp olive oil
¼ cup water
salt
14oz can best-quality chopped tomatoes
1 garlic clove, crushed
freshly ground black pepper

Peel the artichokes and cut into even-sized chunks. Put into a heavy-based saucepan with the butter, 1 tablespoon of the oil, the water and some salt and cook over a very gentle heat until just tender (about 20 minutes).

Meanwhile, make the sauce. Heat the remaining oil in a medium-sized saucepan and add the tomatoes and garlic.

Stir, then cook gently, uncovered, until reduced to a fairly thick purée. This takes about 10 minutes with good-quality canned tomatoes.

Purée the sauce with a blender, or leave it chunky, and season with salt and pepper. Serve the sauce with the cooked artichokes.

Stir-fried beansprouts with ginger v

Sweet and simple, and couldn't be quicker.

SERVES 2–4

1lb (450g) beansprouts
3 tbsp rapeseed oil
1 onion, very finely chopped
1 garlic clove, crushed
2–3 tsp grated fresh root ginger
1 tbsp fino sherry
1 tbsp dark soy sauce
1 tsp sugar
1 tsp toasted sesame oil (optional)

Wash and drain the beansprouts.

Get the oil very hot in a wok or large frying pan, add the onion, garlic and ginger and sizzle for 1 minute, stirring all the time.

Add the beansprouts and stir-fry for about 2 minutes until they're well coated with the oil and flavorings.

Mix in the sherry, soy sauce, sugar and toasted sesame oil (if using), reduce the heat and cook for a further 2–3 minutes or until everything is heated through. Serve at once.

Two-bean vegetable dish v

I like the way the French serve dried beans with fresh green beans in such dishes as *soupe au pistou* and *aigroissade* (see pages 25 and 79). It's an idea that works well in a simple vegetable dish, too, and the contrasting shades of green look attractive together. If you can't find savory, use chives, tarragon or extra parsley instead.

SERVES 4

6oz (175g) dried flageolet beans
1lb (450g) French green beans
2 tbsp (25g) butter
salt and freshly ground black pepper
1 tbsp chopped fresh flat-leaf parsley
1 tbsp chopped fresh savory

Soak, drain and rinse the flageolets — you can soak them overnight or give them the quick hot soak. (For the latter, put them into a saucepan and boil for 2 minutes, then cover and leave for 1 hour.) Then drain and cook the beans in fresh cold water for about 1 hour or until they're tender.

Meanwhile, top and tail the French beans and cook in a little boiling, salted water for 5–7 minutes or until they're tender.

Drain both types of bean and mix together with the butter. Season with salt and pepper to taste. Add the fresh herbs just before serving.

Haricot beans with apples

In Germany and Scandinavia, beans are often served with apple. It sounds an unlikely combination, but it works well. The apples collapse, bathing the beans in a soft sweet-sour sauce. I like it also as a light main dish, with potato cakes or Swiss rösti (see pages 161 and 129).

SERVES 4

1lb (450g) cooking apples
2 tbsp (25g) butter
8oz (225g) haricot or small navy beans, soaked, cooked (see pages 176–7) and drained, or 2 x 14oz cans, drained
2 tbsp sugar
salt and freshly ground black pepper

Peel, core and dice the apples.

Melt the butter in a fairly large saucepan and fry the apples gently in it, without browning, until they're soft.

Add the beans and cook gently until they're heated through. Stir in the sugar and salt and pepper to taste.

Runner beans with paprika v

A late-summer dish for when runner beans are cheap and plentiful. Green beans in olive oil are served everywhere in Greece; I've reduced the amount of oil and cooking time. It's lovely served warm or chilled. You can use other kinds of green beans instead of runners.

SERVES 4
1½lb (700g) runner beans
2 tbsp olive oil
1 tbsp mild paprika
a pinch of cayenne pepper
1 small garlic clove, crushed
5fl oz (150ml) water
salt and freshly ground black pepper
lemon wedges, to serve (optional)

Wash and top and tail the beans. Cut into thin slices, either diagonally, or long and thin, down the length of the beans.

Gently heat the oil, paprika and cayenne pepper in a medium-sized saucepan, then stir in the beans and garlic.

Pour in the water, bring to a boil, cover and leave over a gentle heat for 15 minutes or until the beans are meltingly tender and very little liquid remains. If there's some left, bubble it away over a high heat.

Check the seasoning and serve hot, warm or cold, with lemon wedges (if using).

Hot spiced red beet in apple sauce v

I really love this dish. Use bought cooked beets without vinegar or buy it raw and cook it as described on page 109.

SERVES 4
1lb (450g) cooking apples
2 tbsp water
¼–½ tsp ground cloves
1–2 tbsp sugar
1lb (450g) cooked red beets
salt

Peel, core and slice the apples; put into a medium-sized saucepan with the water and cook over a gentle heat, with a lid on the saucepan, for about 10 minutes or until very soft.

Mash with a spoon and mix in the ground cloves — they've a strong flavor so start with just a pinch — and just enough sugar to take off the sharpness. This can be all done ahead of time, if convenient.

Peel the beets, then cut it into chunky pieces. Add these to the sauce, together with some salt, and reheat gently.

VARIATION

Hot spiced red beet with apples and cranberries v

For this variation, which is nice at Christmas, cook 4oz (125g) cranberries with the apples. You will need to add a bit more sugar.

Purple sprouting broccoli with lemon butter

Such a delicious vegetable, purple sprouting broccoli compliments so many dishes. Leave out the lemon rind if you want a less intense flavor or, for Asian dishes, try the lime and sesame variation. Broccoli is also divine served with hollandaise (see pages 66–7) and makes a perfect course on its own.

SERVES 4
14oz (400g) trimmed purple
    sprouting broccoli
2 tbsp (25g) butter
2 tbsp freshly squeezed lemon juice
a pinch or two of grated lemon rind
salt and freshly ground black pepper

Half fill a large saucepan with water and bring to a boil. Add the broccoli, cover and cook for 4–6 minutes or until just tender — timing will depend on the thickness of the stems. Drain the broccoli and return it to the empty pan.

Add the butter, lemon juice and rind, some salt and a good grinding of pepper, and swirl gently around so that the broccoli is coated with the buttery juices. Serve at once.

VARIATION

Purple sprouting broccoli with sesame and lime v

Make as described above but add 1 tablespoon of toasted sesame oil instead of the butter, and fresh lime juice instead of the lemon, with a little of the grated rind to taste if you like, and perhaps a pinch or two of toasted sesame seeds scattered over.

Stir-fried broccoli with fresh ginger and almonds v

This is an excellent way of preparing ordinary broccoli (but not purple sprouting, which is best cooked simply as opposite). Ordinary broccoli is a great everyday, good-value vegetable and it's nice to cook it in different ways. This recipe makes the most of its vivid green color, the ginger is warming and uplifting and the almonds add a pleasant crunch.

SERVES 4

1½lb (700g) broccoli
2 tbsp rapeseed oil
a walnut-sized piece of fresh root
    ginger, finely grated
salt and freshly ground black pepper
1oz (25g) sliced or slivered almonds

Wash the broccoli and cut off the thick stems. Cut into small pieces, trimming the stems diagonally.

Heat the oil in a large saucepan or wok. Add the broccoli, ginger and a little salt and pepper and stir-fry for 2–3 minutes or until the broccoli has heated through and softened a little.

Sprinkle with almonds and serve at once.

Purée of Brussels sprouts with butter and cream

Brussels sprouts are one of my favorite vegetables, believe it or not! But you have to prepare and cook them right, as I've described on page 110. If that doesn't convince you, try this buttery purée. It's rich, so for a lighter everyday version, use a little of the cooking liquid or some milk instead of some or all of the cream.

SERVES 4–6

1½lb (700g) Brussels sprouts
1 tbsp (15g) butter
5fl oz (150ml) ½ and ½
salt and freshly ground black pepper
pinch of freshly grated nutmeg

Wash and trim the sprouts, then cook them in a little fast-boiling salted water for about 10 minutes or until they are tender.

Drain the sprouts thoroughly, then purée with an electric hand blender or in a food processor.

Put the puréed sprouts back into the saucepan and add the butter, then beat in enough cream to make a soft purée.

Season with salt, pepper and grated nutmeg. Reheat gently before serving.

Buttered cabbage with garlic and coriander

This is a simple way of cheering up ordinary cabbage. I like to use aromatic whole coriander seeds rather than ground coriander, but you could use the ready-ground type if whole seeds aren't available.

SERVES 4

1½–2lb (700–900g) firm white
    cabbage, shredded
salt and freshly ground black pepper
freshly grated nutmeg
1–2 large garlic cloves, crushed
2 tsp coriander seeds, crushed
2 tbsp (25g) butter

Put about ½in (1cm) water into a large saucepan, bring to a boil, then add the cabbage. Let the cabbage simmer gently, with a lid on the pan, for about 7–10 minutes or until it is just tender.

Drain the cabbage well in a colander — there won't be much liquid left — then put it back in the saucepan and add salt, pepper and grated nutmeg to taste.

Mash the garlic, coriander and butter together, then add this to the cabbage, mixing well. Serve at once.

Cabbage with sour cream

If you cook cabbage until it's just tender, then drain it well and stir in some sour cream, you get a delicious mixture — simple, yet good enough for a special occasion.

SERVES 4
1½–2lb (700–900g) firm cabbage, shredded
5fl oz (150ml) sour cream
salt and freshly ground black pepper
a pinch or two of freshly grated nutmeg, or ½–1 tsp caraway seeds (optional)

Put about 1in (2.5cm) water into a large saucepan, bring to a boil, then add the cabbage.

Let the cabbage simmer gently, with a lid on the pan, for about 7–10 minutes or until it is just tender.

Drain the cabbage thoroughly and stir in the sour cream, season well with salt and a good grinding of pepper. Add the grated nutmeg or caraway seeds (if using). Reheat for a minute or two, just to warm through the cream, then serve.

Cabbage with turmeric, cashew nuts and raisins V

In this recipe, the cabbage is stir-fried with turmeric and the result is golden and spicy. Try scattering some fresh coriander over the top.

SERVES 4
1½lb (700g) firm white cabbage
2 tbsp rapeseed oil
1 tsp turmeric
2 tbsp dried coconut (make sure it's unsweetened)
½oz (15g) raisins
2oz (50g) cashew nuts, coarsely chopped
salt and freshly ground black pepper

Wash the cabbage and shred fairly finely, removing the coarse leaves and stems.

Just before you want to eat the meal, heat the oil and turmeric in a large saucepan or wok; add the cabbage and stir-fry for 2½–3 minutes or until the cabbage has softened and reduced but is still crisp.

Stir in the coconut, raisins and cashew nuts. Season to taste and serve immediately.

Stir-fried Chinese cabbage with scallions V

If you prepare the leaves, scallions and ginger in advance and keep them in the fridge, this can be made very quickly just before a meal. This is quite delicately flavored; for a gutsier version, see the variation.

SERVES 4–6
1 head Napa cabbage or bok choy (about 1½–2lb (700–900g))
large bunch scallions
1 tbsp grated fresh root ginger
2 tbsp rapeseed or sesame oil
small bunch of coriander, chopped
1–2 tbsp dark soy sauce
salt and freshly ground black pepper

Wash the cabbage leaves and shred — not too finely. Wash, trim and chop the scallions, keeping as much of the green part as is fresh and tender. All this can be done in advance.

Just before the meal, heat the oil in a fairly large saucepan and add the cabbage and scallions and ginger. Turn them in the oil, over a fairly high heat for about 3 minutes until the leaves have softened just a little but are still crisp.

Quickly chop the coriander or snip it straight over the pan, stir in, along with the soy sauce, and salt and pepper to taste. Serve at once.

VARIATION

Stir-fried Chinese cabbage with black bean sauce v

For this sweet and sticky version, omit the ginger, coriander and soy sauce. Before cooking the leaves, make a quick sauce by mixing together ¼ cup of black bean sauce (available from supermarkets), ¼ cup of tomato ketchup and 2 teaspoons of cornstarch. Add this to the cabbage after 1 minute of stir-frying, and stir-fry for a further 2 minutes or so, until the cabbage is cooked but crisp, and glistening in the slightly thickened sauce.

Carrots cooked in butter with lemon and parsley

Tender young carrots are best for this recipe, but it also works well with older carrots, cut into matchsticks.

SERVES 4

1½lb (700g) carrots, preferably
    baby ones
1 tbsp (15g) butter
1 tbsp olive oil
5fl oz (150ml) water
2–3 tsp sugar
salt
a squeeze of lemon juice (optional)
freshly ground black pepper
1 tbsp chopped fresh flat-leaf parsley

Trim and peel the carrots, halving or quartering larger ones.

Put the butter, olive oil, water, 2 teaspoons of sugar and ½ teaspoon of salt into a medium-sized saucepan and heat until the butter has melted, then add the carrots and bring to a boil.

Cover the saucepan, reduce the heat and leave for 25–30 minutes or until the carrots are tender. Keep an eye on the water level and add a splash or two more if it seems to be boiling too fast.

Equally, if there's any liquid left, take the lid off the saucepan, turn up the heat and let the liquid bubble away until there's just a couple of tablespoons left.

Add a squeeze of lemon juice if you think it needs it, and salt, pepper and sugar to taste. Sprinkle with chopped parsley.

Carrots in coconut cream sauce with fresh coriander v

In this recipe, tender carrots are bathed in a golden sauce of coconut cream and turmeric and garnished with fresh green coriander. The flavor is spicy without being hot, making it an ideal accompaniment to curries and spiced rice dishes.

SERVES 4

1½lb (700g) carrots, cut into discs
¼ cup canned coconut cream
5fl oz (150ml) water
1 tsp turmeric
salt and freshly ground black pepper
sugar
freshly squeezed lemon juice
1 tbsp chopped fresh coriander
    or flat-leaf parsley

Put the carrots into a medium-sized, heavy-based saucepan with the coconut cream, water and turmeric.

Bring to a boil, stir, then cover, reduce the heat and simmer for 25–30 minutes or until the carrots are meltingly tender. Keep an eye on the water level and add a splash or two more if it seems to be boiling too fast.

Equally, if there is any liquid left, take the lid off the saucepan, turn up the heat and let the liquid bubble away until there's just a couple of tablespoons left.

Add a touch of sugar, a drop or two of lemon juice and some seasoning to taste, and sprinkle with chopped coriander or parsley.

Carrot and lemon purée

A vegetable purée is useful because it can take the place of both a cooked vegetable and a sauce or gravy. It also contrasts well with crispy dishes.

SERVES 4
1lb (450g) carrots
8oz (225g) potatoes, peeled
small pat of butter
grated rind and juice of 1 lemon
salt and freshly ground black pepper

Cut the carrots and potatoes into even-sized pieces and cook them together in boiling water for about 20 minutes or until tender. Drain, saving the water.

Purée the vegetables in a food processor or with an electric hand blender, adding the butter and 5fl oz (150ml) of the reserved water.

Put the purée back into the saucepan and reheat. Just before serving, add enough of the lemon rind and juice to give a pleasant tang — start with a little and keep tasting. Don't let the mixture get too hot once the lemon has been added, because this might make the purée taste slightly bitter.

Season with salt and pepper, and serve.

Golden-spiced cauliflower v

The cauliflower in this recipe comes out a pretty shade of gold because of the turmeric, and it's lightly and delicately spiced.

SERVES 4
1 head cauliflower
2 tbsp olive oil
2 tsp turmeric
4 cardamom pods
4 cloves
1 bay leaf
a small piece of cinnamon stick
1 garlic clove, crushed
salt and freshly ground black pepper
5fl oz (150ml) water

Trim the cauliflower and divide into even-sized florets.

Heat the oil in a medium-sized saucepan and fry the spices and bay leaf for 1–2 minutes, stirring continuously.

Add the cauliflower, garlic, seasoning and the water.

Bring to a boil, then simmer very gently, with a lid on the pan, for about 7 minutes or until the cauliflower is just tender and most of the liquid has been absorbed.

Check the seasoning, remove the bay leaf, cinnamon stick and cardamom, then serve.

Cauliflower in sour cream and tarragon sauce

I like the aniseedy flavor of tarragon in this, but parsley also works well.

SERVES 4
1 firm head cauliflower
salt and freshly ground black pepper
1 tbsp (15g) butter
2 rounded tsp all-purpose flour
5fl oz (150ml) water
5fl oz (150ml) sour cream
1 tbsp chopped fresh tarragon

Trim the cauliflower and divide into florets. Cook in ½in (1cm) boiling water for about 5–6 minutes or until just tender when pierced with the point of a sharp knife. Drain well and season with salt and pepper.

Meanwhile make the sauce. Melt the butter in a small saucepan and add the flour. Stir over a gentle heat until the flour bubbles, then add the water and stir until thick.

Cook gently for 5 minutes, then remove from the heat; mix in the sour cream, tarragon and seasoning to taste, and reheat. Pour the sauce over the cauliflower, and serve.

Cauliflower in tomato sauce v

This is an easy and attractive way of cooking cauliflower.

SERVES 4

1 onion, chopped
2 tbsp olive oil
1 garlic clove, crushed
14oz can chopped tomatoes
1¼ cups (275ml) water
salt and freshly ground black pepper
1 head cauliflower, washed and
    broken into florets
chopped fresh flat-leaf parsley

Cook the onion gently in the oil for 10 minutes or until it's soft but not browned, add the garlic and cook for a few seconds, then add the tomatoes and remove from the heat.

Blend the mixture in a food processor, blender, or with an electric hand blender.

Put this purée into a fairly large saucepan, pour in the water and add some salt and pepper.

Bring to a boil then add the cauliflower. Simmer gently, with a lid on the saucepan, for 10–15 minutes or until the cauliflower is just tender.

Check the seasoning, sprinkle with the chopped parsley, and serve.

Celeriac mash

This is easier to make than mashed potatoes — if you try blending potatoes in a food processor or with a hand blender they turn to glue. Here, by contrast, although there is some potato in the recipe, the greater proportion of celeriac prevents that from happening, so you can whip away.

SERVES 4 ❄

1lb (450g) celeriac
8oz (225g) potatoes
1 tbsp (15g) butter
up to 5fl oz (150ml) ½ and ½ or milk
    (optional)
salt and freshly ground black pepper

Peel the celeriac and potatoes, cut them into even-sized pieces and boil them in enough water to cover for about 20 minutes or until tender. Drain thoroughly, keeping the water.

Blend to a purée using an electric hand blender or food processor; or do it by hand using a potato ricer or masher.

Put the mixture back into the saucepan, set over a low heat. Add the butter and gradually beat in enough ½ and ½, milk or reserved cooking water to make a light fluffy mixture, softer than mashed potatoes. Season with plenty of salt and pepper.

Celery with almonds

The important thing with celery is to cook it until it's buttery tender; if you do that, even the outer stalks (remove any tough fibers by running a potato peeler down them) taste good. However, for this recipe, the inner stalks are best.

SERVES 4

1 tbsp olive oil
1 tbsp (15g) butter
1 head of celery, chopped into
    bite-sized pieces
2 tbsp chopped onion
salt and freshly ground black pepper
1 tsp cornstarch
5fl oz (150ml) single cream
2oz (50g) flaked almonds, toasted
    (see page 139)

Heat the oil and butter in a large saucepan over a gentle heat. Add the celery, onion and some salt and pepper, and cook, covered, over a very low heat for about 25 minutes or until the celery is completely tender.

Give the pan a stir every so often, and if there's any sign of the vegetables sticking, add a splash or two of water.

When the celery is really tender, sprinkle in the cornstarch, stir, then add the cream and stir again, until thickened.

Check the seasoning and serve scattered with almonds.

Braised celery with chestnuts

Celery hearts are perfect for this recipe, though you could use two normal-sized heads of celery, sliced lengthways into quarters.

SERVES 4

4 celery hearts
1 tbsp olive oil
1 tbsp (15g) butter
1 small onion, sliced
1 bay leaf
7oz cooked chestnuts
½ cup (125ml) vegetable stock
salt and freshly ground black pepper
1–2 tbsp chopped fresh flat-leaf
    parsley, to garnish

Preheat the oven to 350°F (180°C).
    Wash and trim the celery hearts, and slice each in half lengthways.
    Heat the oil and butter in a flameproof casserole and add the onion, celery and bay leaf. Sizzle over the heat for 1–2 minutes, and stir so that all the celery is coated with oil and butter.
    Add the chestnuts, stock and some seasoning.
    Bring to a boil, cover and bake for 1–1¼ hours or until the celery is very tender.
    Sprinkle with chopped parsley and serve.

Zucchini with fresh herbs

This is a good way to serve zucchini early in the season when they're young and tender and you want to make the most of their delicate flavor.

SERVES 4–6

½lb (700g) young zucchini
salt
2 tbsp (25g) butter
1 tbsp finely chopped fresh flat-leaf
    parsley
1 tbsp finely chopped fresh chives
freshly ground black pepper

Wash the zucchini and trim the ends.
    Cut the zucchini into ¼in (6mm) slices then cook them in ½in (1cm) boiling salted water for 5–7 minutes or until they're just tender but not soggy.
    Drain the zucchini well and add the butter, parsley and chives. Season with pepper and a little more salt to taste, if necessary.

Griddled zucchini with pecorino

Pecorino cheese is often vegetarian, while real Parmesan never is. You can get good Parmesan-style cheese or use Pecorino instead, as in this recipe, for its sharp, tangy flavor. Zucchini are just about the best vegetable to cook in a grill pan because the black stripes show up dramatically. Be prepared for a smoky kitchen, however — open the windows and turn on the fan!

SERVES 4

8 zucchini
olive oil, for brushing
freshly ground black pepper
1–2 tbsp chopped fresh flat-leaf
    parsley
4oz (125g) Pecorino cheese, grated

Cut the zucchini lengthways into thin slices — about ¼in (6mm). Brush the pieces lightly all over with oil.
    Heat a grill pan until a drop of water sizzles instantly.
    Lay some zucchini slices in the pan, as many as will fit without overlapping. Cook for a few minutes or until there are black stripes on the pieces when you lift them up. Turn the pieces over with tongs and cook the other side.
    As the slices are done, transfer them from the pan to a plate and keep them warm. Continue to cook the remaining slices in the same way.
    Grind some pepper over the slices — you probably won't need any salt as the pecorino is salty — scatter with parsley and cheese, and serve.

Braised cucumber with walnuts

People are sometimes surprised at the idea of cooking cucumber, but it's delicious, tender and has a delicate flavor.

SERVES 6

2 large cucumbers
salt
2 tbsp (25g) butter
1¼ cup (275ml) water
1 tbsp freshly squeezed lemon juice
1 bay leaf
6 peppercorns
1oz (25g) shelled walnut pieces, coarsely chopped, to garnish

Peel the cucumbers, cut them into 2in (5cm) chunks, then cut each chunk down into quarters.

Put the chunks into a colander, sprinkle with salt, cover with a small plate with a weight on top, and leave for about 30 minutes to draw out the excess liquid. Drain.

Melt the butter in a fairly large saucepan, add the cucumber chunks, water and lemon juice, bay leaf and peppercorns.

Bring to a boil, then leave to simmer for 10–15 minutes or until the cucumber is tender and looks translucent and most of the liquid has evaporated, leaving the cucumber glistening in just a little buttery stock. If there is more than 2–3 tablespoons of liquid, turn up the heat and let it bubble away.

Put the cucumber and the liquid into a warmed, shallow casserole or serving dish and sprinkle with chopped walnuts.

Fennel baked with cheese

Fennel makes a lovely vegetable dish. It's delicious steamed and served simply with a little butter and black pepper, or you can boil it then bake it with cheese, as in this recipe, which gives a tasty golden result.

SERVES 4–6

2 large fennel bulbs (about 1½lb (700g))
1¼ cups (275ml) water
salt
2 tbsp (25g) butter, plus extra for greasing
freshly ground black pepper
2oz (50g) grated Parmesan-style cheese

Preheat the oven to 400°F (200°C).

Trim the fennel bulbs and slice lengthways into quarters or eighths.

Put the water and a little salt into a medium-sized saucepan, bring to a boil then add the fennel and simmer for 20–30 minutes or until tender.

Remove the fennel from the saucepan with a slotted spoon and put it into a shallow greased ovenproof dish.

While you're doing this, let the water in which the fennel was cooked boil away vigorously until it has reduced to just a couple of tablespoons or so of well-flavored liquid. Pour this over the fennel, then dot with the butter, grind some pepper over the top and finally sprinkle with grated cheese.

Bake the fennel, uncovered, for 20–30 minutes or until it's heated through and golden brown on top.

Fennel with egg sauce

I think this creamy egg and nutmeg sauce goes perfectly with the slightly liquorice flavor of fennel. This is excellent as an accompanying vegetable, but it also makes a very good course on its own, served in small, individual ovenproof dishes.

SERVES 4–6

3 large fennel bulbs (about 1½lb (700g))
salt
1¼ cups (275ml) water
1 hardboiled egg, finely chopped
2 tbsp sour cream
freshly ground black pepper
a pinch or two of freshly grated nutmeg

Trim the fennel bulbs and slice lengthways into quarters or eighths. Put the water and a little salt into a medium-sized saucepan, bring to a boil, then add the fennel and simmer for 20–30 minutes or until the fennel feels tender when pierced with a sharp knife.

Remove the fennel with a slotted spoon, put into a shallow, heatproof dish and keep warm in a low oven.

Let the cooking water from the fennel boil rapidly until reduced to just a couple of tablespoons. Then take the saucepan off the heat and stir in the egg and sour cream to make a simple sauce. Season with salt, pepper and grated nutmeg to taste.

Spoon the sauce over the fennel and serve as soon as possible.

Tip
Try this recipe with large, mild onions instead of the fennel.

Purée of flageolets

A pretty pale green purée that has a delicate flavor and color. Although you can get canned flageolets, for this recipe, in which they play the starring role, it's best to use dried ones and cook them yourself — easy, as long as you remember to soak them for a few hours beforehand, or give them a quick hot soak.

SERVES 4 ❄

8oz (225g) dried flageolet beans, soaked and cooked (see pages 176–7)
1 small onion, chopped
2 tbsp (25g) butter
4–6 tbsp ½ and ½
salt and freshly ground black pepper
a pinch or two of freshly grated nutmeg
1 tbsp finely chopped fresh flat-leaf parsley, to garnish

Drain the beans, reserving the cooking liquid.

While the beans are cooking, fry the onion gently in the butter for about 10 minutes or until it is soft but not browned.

Blend the beans, in a food processor or with an electric hand blender, adding the cream, fried onions and enough of the reserved cooking liquid (if necessary) to make a smooth purée.

Season with salt, pepper and grated nutmeg. Reheat gently (don't let the mixture boil) and serve garnished with chopped parsley.

Kale with garlic butter

Kale has such a wonderful earthy flavor; you can just feel it doing you good as you eat it! The main thing is to cook it long enough for it to be tender to eat, but not so long as to take all the life out of it. Sometimes you can buy the kale ready prepared, but if not, it's easy to remove any tough stems and shred the leaves coarsely.

SERVES 4

1½lb (700g) curly kale, shredded
1 garlic clove, crushed
2 tbsp (25g) butter, softened
salt and freshly ground black pepper

Bring ½in (1cm) of water to a boil in a large saucepan. Add the kale, bring back to a boil and cook until it's tender (about 7 minutes).

While the kale is cooking, make the garlic butter by mixing the crushed garlic into the soft butter.

Drain the kale thoroughly and add the garlic butter, and salt and pepper to taste.

Leeks with tomatoes and coriander seeds v

This mixture of leeks and tomatoes, flavored with aromatic coriander seeds, is really delicious. It's good cold as a starter or hot as a side dish.

SERVES 4

2lb (900g) leeks
2 tbsp olive oil
1 garlic clove, crushed
1lb (450g) tomatoes, skinned (see recipe for Tomatoes with horseradish cream, page 40) and chopped
2–3 tsp coriander seeds, coarsely crushed
salt and freshly ground black pepper

Trim the roots and most of the leafy green tops off the leeks, then slit down one side and wash carefully under cold water. Cut into 1in (2cm) pieces.

Heat the oil in a medium-sized saucepan and add the garlic, tomatoes, leeks, coriander, half a teaspoon of salt and a grinding of black pepper.

Stir so that everything is well mixed, then leave to cook gently, without a lid, for 20–30 minutes or until the leeks are very tender and the tomatoes have formed a sauce around them. Stir frequently during the cooking time.

Check the seasoning, adding a good amount of freshly ground pepper, and serve.

Buttered snow peas with mint

For a simple vegetable dish, this is hard to beat. Snow peas have such a lovely, delicate flavor and are easy to cook. Like ordinary shelled peas, I think they are enhanced with a little sugar and some chopped fresh mint.

SERVES 6

1½lb (700g) snow peas
1 tbsp (15g) butter
a pinch or two of superfine sugar
salt and freshly ground black pepper
1 tbsp chopped fresh mint

Top and tail the snow peas, pulling off any stringy bits from the sides. You can leave them whole, or cut them down the middle into two long thin pieces (I like them done like this).

Put about 1in (2.5cm) water into a fairly large saucepan and bring to a boil. Add the snow peas and let them cook gently for 2–4 minutes or until they are just tender.

Drain, then put them back in the hot saucepan and add the butter, sugar, salt and pepper to taste and the chopped mint. Mix gently, so that all the snow peas are coated with the butter and seasonings.

Wild mushrooms in sour cream

For this simple but luxurious dish you can use the mixes of fresh wild mushroom that are available from large supermarkets; they often contain oyster, shiitake and enoki mushrooms.

SERVES 2–4

1 lb packs mixed wild mushrooms
1 tbsp olive oil
2 tbsp (25g) butter
2 garlic cloves, crushed
5fl oz (150ml) sour cream
salt and freshly ground black pepper
chopped fresh flat-leaf parsley, to
    garnish

Clean the mushrooms as necessary (you can wipe them, but I like to dunk them quickly in water). Drain well and pat dry. Halve or quarter any larger ones so that they are all roughly the same size.

Heat the oil and butter in a large saucepan, fry the garlic for a moment or two, then add the mushrooms and fry over a fairly high heat for 5 minutes or so, or until they are tender.

If the mushrooms release a lot of liquid, boil them vigorously for a minute or two without a lid on the saucepan to evaporate the liquid, or drain it off (save as stock, it's delicious).

Stir in the sour cream and salt and pepper and heat through gently. Serve at once, sprinkled with chopped parsley.

Spicy okra v

Okra is a vegetable you either love or hate. I'm definitely in the former category but people who don't like it often say it's because of the glutinous texture. One way around this is to make sure you buy only tender baby okra and treat it gently so that it stays whole. This goes well with rice and Caribbean dishes such as Jamaican "rice and peas" (see page 248).

SERVES 2–4

8oz (225g) firm baby okra
1 onion, chopped
2 tbsp olive oil
14oz can chopped tomatoes
1 garlic clove, crushed
2 tsp ground coriander
3 tsp garam masala
salt and freshly ground black pepper
2 tsp freshly squeezed lemon juice
1–2 tbsp chopped fresh coriander,
    to garnish

If the okra is large, top and tail it as necessary, being careful not to cut too deep. Young, tender okra can be used as it is.

Fry the onion in the oil for about 10 minutes or until it's soft and golden, then add the tomatoes, garlic, coriander, garam masala and a little salt.

Bring to a boil, then add the okra and let it simmer gently for 15–20 minutes or until tender.

Check the seasoning, adding pepper and more salt if necessary, plus a little lemon juice to taste.

Sprinkle with chopped fresh coriander and serve.

Pearl onions in a cream and nutmeg sauce

If you can find pearl onions, usually sold as "pickling onions", they're ideal for this recipe. To make peeling them easier, cover them with boiling water and leave for 5 minutes; the skins will then pop off easily. You can also use larger onions cut into quarters or eighths.

SERVES 4

1½lb (700g) pearl onions
5fl oz (150ml) sour cream
salt and freshly ground black pepper
a pinch or two of freshly grated
    nutmeg

Peel the onions using a sharp, pointed knife, leaving them whole if they're tiny, or cutting them into smaller sections if larger.

Bring 1in (2cm) of lightly salted water to a boil in a fairly large saucepan, add the onions, cover with a lid and boil for 7–10 minutes or until the onions feel just tender when pierced with a sharp knife.

Drain well (save the water, it makes delicious stock), then put the onions back into the saucepan and stir in the sour cream and some salt, pepper and nutmeg to taste.

Heat gently for a minute or two, stirring all the time, but don't let the mixture get too near boiling point or the cream may separate. Serve at once.

Steamed bok choy with toasted sesame oil v

This is simple to make and particularly good with spicy or Asian main courses.

SERVES 4

4 heads of bok choy, cut in half
    lengthways
dark soy sauce
1 tbsp tamari
1 tbsp roasted sesame oil
1 tbsp sesame seeds, toasted (see
    page 140), to garnish

You can cook the bok choy in a steamer for a few minutes until it's just tender, or you can "water steam" it: bring ½in (1cm) of water to a boil in a large saucepan, add the bok choy, cover and cook for about 4 minutes or until just tender. Drain well and return to the pan.

Add the tamari and sesame oil and swirl around so that the bok choy is coated. Serve sprinkled with the sesame seeds.

Curried parsnip cream

My original idea for this recipe was to cook and mash the parsnips, then make them into a savory bake. However, they tasted so good when they'd been mashed with some curry powder and cream that I never got any further; they were perfect as they were.

SERVES 4

1½lb (700g) parsnips
1 tbsp (15g) butter
2 tsp mild curry powder
5fl oz (150ml) ½ and ½
salt and freshly ground pepper
2 tbsp roughly chopped walnuts
    (optional), to garnish

Peel the parsnips and cut them into even-sized chunks, removing any hard core.

Put the parsnips into a saucepan with enough boiling water to cover, then boil with a lid on the pan, until the parsnips are tender (about 15–20 minutes). Drain.

While the parsnips are cooking, fry the onion in the butter for 7–8 minutes or until nearly tender, then stir in the curry powder and cook for an additional couple of minutes.

Mix the parsnips with the onions and the cream and mash or blend in a food processor or using a hand blender until smooth and creamy. Season to taste, scatter with some chopped walnuts (if using) and serve.

Sugar-glazed parsnips

This method of gently cooking parsnips with butter, sugar and just a little liquid leaves them glistening in a sweet buttery syrup. You can cook other root vegetables in this way; try carrots, turnips, sweet potatoes and swedes.

SERVES 4

1½lb (700g) parsnips
¾ cup (175ml) water or vegetable stock
2 tbsp (25g) butter
1 tbsp soft dark brown sugar
¼–½ tsp salt
freshly ground black pepper

Peel the parsnips and cut them into small even-sized pieces, removing any hard core.

Put the parsnips into a heavy-based saucepan with the water or stock, butter, sugar, salt and a grinding of black pepper.

Cover with a lid and simmer over a gentle heat for about 20 minutes or until the pieces of parsnip are tender and the liquid has reduced to a syrupy glaze.

Peas with lettuce

This is my favorite method of cooking peas, perfect for adding flavor to frozen ones. It's a great way of making use of the outer leaves of lettuces you might have grown, or bought from a market.

SERVES 4

1lb (450g) outside leaves of lettuce, such as Romaine
1lb (450g) shelled weight of fresh or frozen peas (about 3lb 5oz (1.5kg) peas in their pods)
1 tbsp (15g) butter
½ tsp sugar
salt and freshly ground black pepper

Wash the lettuce leaves then shred quite coarsely with a sharp knife.

Put the leaves into a heavy-based saucepan with the peas, butter, sugar and seasoning.

Set the pan over a moderate heat and cook for 15–20 minutes, with the lid on the pan, until the peas are tender. Frozen peas only take about 7–10 minutes.

Drain off any excess liquid that the lettuce has produced and serve.

VARIATION
Purée of peas and lettuce

The above mixture, blended, makes a really lovely purée.

Peperonata v

This Italian mixed pepper stew is one of those versatile dishes that can take the place of a vegetable dish or a sauce, adding moisture to a meal. It is also good served hot with spaghetti or as a filling for pancakes, or cold as part of a salad selection.

SERVES 4 ❄

3 tbsp olive oil
1 large onion, chopped
1½lb (700g) peppers, seeded and chopped (use a mixture of red, yellow and green)
1 garlic clove, crushed
14oz can chopped tomatoes
salt and freshly ground black pepper

Heat the oil in a large saucepan and fry the onion for 5 minutes or until beginning to soften but not brown.

Add the peppers and garlic and continue to fry for a further 10 minutes.

Add the tomatoes and leave the mixture to cook gently for 10–15 minutes, uncovered, until all the vegetables are soft and the mixture is fairly thick. Stir frequently to prevent sticking.

Season to taste, and serve.

Pommes Anna

This delicious potato dish cooks slowly in the oven and won't spoil. It's rather like a gratin Dauphinoise (see page 129), except that it's turned out like a cake for serving. It goes well with ratatouille or peperonata (see pages 132 and 125) to make a complete meal. You could also serve it as a separate course with cooked spinach or a green salad with chicory and walnuts.

SERVES 4–6
1 tbsp (15g) butter
1½lb (700g) waxy potatoes such as Red Bliss
4–6oz (125–175g) grated Gruyère cheese or Emmental
salt and freshly ground black pepper
chopped fresh flat-leaf parsley, to garnish

Line an 8in (20cm) cake pan with baking parchment. Preheat the oven to 325°F (160°C).

Melt the butter in a small saucepan, and use some to brush the inside of the lined cake pan.

Peel the potatoes, then slice them into thin rounds using a mandolin, grater or electric food processor.

Put the slices into a colander and rinse them thoroughly under cold water, then drain them and pat them dry with a clean cloth.

Arrange a layer of potato in the base of the pan. Sprinkle with some of the grated cheese and a little salt and pepper; then add another layer of potato and continue in this way until it is all used up, ending with a layer of grated cheese. Pour the remaining butter over the top and cover with foil.

Bake in the oven for about 2 hours or until the potato can be pierced easily with the point of a sharp knife.

Pour off any excess butter, then slip a knife around the sides of the tin to loosen the potato. Invert the tin over a warmed plate and turn the potato out. Remove the paper.

Sprinkle a little chopped parsley over the top of the potato and serve.

Tip
If you'd like the potatoes slightly browned all over, turn them out onto an ovenproof plate (as described above), increase the oven temperature slightly and bake for a few more minutes.

You could also keep a little of the cheese back for scattering over the cooked potato.

Potato and almond croquettes

This mixture of creamy potato and crunchy almonds is delicious and these crisp little croquettes make a good accompaniment to many dishes. They are useful for entertaining because they can be made in advance and then baked in the oven. For a light meal, serve them with a herby green salad or tomato salad.

SERVES 6 AS A SIDE DISH, 4 AS A LIGHT MEAL ❄
1½lb (700g) potatoes
2 tbsp (25g) butter
approximately ¼ cup milk
1oz (25g) ground almonds, plus extra for coating
1oz (25g) sliced almonds
salt and freshly ground black pepper
olive oil, for brushing

Peel and boil the potatoes; when they're nearly done, set the oven to 400°F (200°C).

Mash the potatoes with the butter and enough milk to make a light but firm mixture. Add the ground and sliced almonds and season well with salt and pepper.

Form into about 12 little sausages. Roll the potato croquettes in ground almonds, so that they are completely coated.

Put the croquettes on an oiled baking sheet and bake for about 30 minutes, turning them halfway through, until they are crisp and golden brown. Serve immediately.

Opposite: Peas with lettuce (see page 125)

Baked potatoes v

There are two methods of cooking baked potatoes: you can rub them with fat or oil before you bake them, which makes the skins soft and flavorsome; or you can just bake them as they are (with the skins still wet), which will result in lovely crispy, crunchy skins. Decide which method you want to follow, depending on your personal preference.

SERVES 4

4 unblemished potatoes (about 8oz (225g) each)
a little olive oil or butter (optional)

Preheat the oven to 450°F (230°C), Scrub the potatoes and cut out any blemishes if necessary.

Make 2–3 small cuts or fork pricks into each potato to allow the steam to escape.

Rub each in a little oil or butter (if using), then put them on a baking sheet and place in the oven.

Bake the potatoes for 1–1¼ hours or until they feel tender when squeezed slightly. Serve at once, particularly if you want them crisp.

Bircher potatoes v

In this recipe, invented by Dr Bircher-Benner (who also invented muesli), potatoes are scrubbed, cut in half and baked, cut side down, on a baking sheet. This means that the cut sides get crisp and golden, like roast potatoes, while the tops are like jacket-baked potatoes.

SERVES 4

4 potatoes
olive oil
salt
½–1 tsp caraway seeds (optional)

Preheat the oven to 400°F (200°C). Scrub the potatoes then cut each in half lengthways.

Lightly oil a baking sheet, then place the potatoes on it, cut side down.

Sprinkle the potatoes with salt and the caraway seeds (if using).

Bake for 40–50 minutes or until the tops of the potatoes feel soft when squeezed and the cut sides are crisp and golden brown.

VARIATION

Chunky oven chips v

These are delicious, easy and so much healthier than the bought type. Make them like Bircher potatoes (peeling the potatoes or not, according to your taste) and cut into chunky chips or wedges. Rub the chips all over with olive oil but don't make them too greasy. Put them on an oiled baking sheet in a single layer and bake as described, for about 40 minutes, turning them 2–3 times so that they get evenly browned.

New potatoes baked in butter

This Norwegian way of cooking new potatoes is easy and really conserves their delicate flavor. Try to choose potatoes that are roughly the same size; the smaller the better.

SERVES 4

1½lb (700g) baby new potatoes
3 tbsp (40g) butter
1 tsp salt
freshly ground black pepper
2–3 tbsp chopped fresh dill or other fresh green herbs, such as parsley or chives, to garnish

Preheat the oven to 325°F (160°C). Wash the potatoes and cut any larger ones so that they are all roughly the same size.

Put the potatoes into an ovenproof dish with the butter, salt and a little grinding of black pepper.

Cover the dish and place it in the oven for about 45 minutes or until the potatoes are tender when pierced with a sharp knife. Serve sprinkled with chopped dill or other fresh herb.

Gratin dauphinoise

This is my version of the classic French dish, which is a great favorite with my family. I make a generous quantity in a large shallow 10in x 13in (25cm x 33cm) gratin dish and serve it as a main meal, with just a lovely big leafy green salad or some cooked green beans or spinach.

SERVES 6

3 tbsp (40g) butter, softened
4½lb (2kg) potatoes
6 garlic cloves, crushed
salt and freshly ground black pepper
a pinch or two of freshly grated nutmeg (optional)
1¼ cups (275ml) heavy cream

Grease a shallow ovenproof dish generously with half the butter. Preheat the oven to 350°F (180°C).

Peel the potatoes and slice very thinly. With this quantity, it really helps if you have an attachment to your food processor. Otherwise, slice by hand or use a mandolin.

Rinse the potato slices well in cold water to get rid of excess starch and pat dry with a clean cloth.

Mix the butter with the crushed garlic, and use two-thirds of this to grease the gratin dish very generously.

Arrange the potato slices in the dish in rough layers (no need to be too fussy about this), seasoning between the layers with salt, pepper and some grated nutmeg (if using).

Pour the cream evenly over the top, then add about 1 cup of water and pour that over too.

Dot the remaining butter over the top, and bake, uncovered, for 1½–2 hours or until you can insert a sharp knife easily into the potatoes, and the top is golden brown. If it seems to be browning too quickly during the cooking time, cover it with a piece of foil, removing this for the last 10 minutes or so of cooking to crisp the top.

Tip
If there's any left over, it reheats to a gorgeous creamy, crunchy delight.

Rösti v

This delicious crisp golden "cake" of grated potato is very easy to make. It helps if you have a food processor with a grating attachment, though you can also grate the potatoes by hand.

SERVES 4

2¼lb (1kg) potatoes, unpeeled
1 small onion
2 tbsp chopped fresh flat-leaf parsley
salt and freshly ground black pepper
¼ cup olive oil

Grate the potatoes and onion coarsely. Mix with the chopped parsley and season with salt and pepper.

Heat 2 tablespoons of the oil in a large frying pan (approximately 11in (28cm) and add all the potatoes, pressing down firmly.

Fry for about 8 minutes or until the underside is crisp and golden. Slide the rösti out onto a plate, then invert another plate on top and turn it over. Heat the remaining oil in the pan, then slide the rösti back into the pan; the cooked side will now be upright. Cook for another 8 minutes or until the other side is golden brown and crisp.

Turn the rösti out onto a hot plate and serve it in big chunky wedges.

Tip
You can vary the basic potato cake in a number of ways — try adding different herbs or chopped scallions, or even a few sunflower seeds, sesame seeds or chopped toasted hazelnuts.

Lemon roast potatoes

In this recipe, chunky pieces of potato are boiled until almost tender, then mixed with melted butter, lemon juice and grated rind and heated through in a fairly hot oven until they're sizzling and golden. This is a great dish because it's quick to prepare and you can get it done ahead of time (ready to pop in the oven later), and there are lots of variations.

SERVES 4

2¼lb (1kg) potatoes
3 tbsp (40g) butter, melted
grated rind of 1 small lemon
1½ tbsp freshly squeezed lemon juice
salt and freshly ground black pepper

Preheat the oven to 400°F (200°C). Peel the potatoes, cut them into fairly small even-sized chunks (about the size of large walnuts) and cook in boiling water for about 15 minutes or until they are tender — they need to be well cooked, but not breaking up.

Mix the potatoes with the melted butter, lemon rind and juice.

Spread the potatoes out in a shallow, ovenproof dish and season with some salt and pepper.

Bake the for 40–60 minutes, turning them several times, until they are golden. Serve at once.

VARIATIONS
Garlic potatoes

This variation on lemon potatoes is also wonderful. Prepare the potatoes as described, but leave out the lemon. Crush 1–2 large garlic cloves and mix with the melted butter before adding to the potatoes.

Rosemary potatoes

This is fragrant and delicious. Leave out the lemon rind and juice, and scatter the potatoes with 1–2 tablespoons of chopped fresh rosemary (2–3 teaspoons dried) before putting them in the oven.

Spicy potatoes

These make an easy side dish to serve with a curry. Omit the lemon rind and juice. Toss the potatoes in 4 teaspoons of curry powder and 1–2 teaspoons of cumin seed.

Sesame potatoes v

For this crunchy, nutty-tasting version, replace the lemon juice, rind and melted butter with 3 tablespoons of toasted sesame oil, 2 tablespoons of dark soy sauce and 3–4 tablespoons of sesame seeds.

Easy potato pancakes

These crispy little German pancakes make a good quick supper dish. It's conventional — and I think delicious — to serve them with a sharp-tasting apple or cranberry sauce, or haricot beans with apples (see page 113), but children usually prefer them with tomato ketchup or baked beans!

SERVES 4

1lb (450g) potatoes
1 onion
salt and freshly ground black pepper
2 eggs
3 tbsp all-purpose flour
olive oil, for shallow-frying
cranberry or apple sauce, to serve

Grate the potatoes coarsely, peeled or unpeeled according to taste, and grate the onion. Mix the potatoes and onion with salt and pepper, the eggs and flour, and stir to make a batter.

Heat a little oil in a frying pan and fry a tablespoon of the mixture until golden and crispy, turning over so that both sides are cooked. Repeat until the batter is used up.

Drain on paper towels and serve immediately with the sauce and a crunchy salad.

VARIATION
Really easy potato pancakes v

Simply fry grated raw potatoes, seasoned with salt and pepper, in olive oil. Press them down well in the pan to help them hold together, and don't make them too high or too big, so they cook easily. They're crisp, golden and gorgeous!

Easy creamy mashed potatoes

Beautifully made, perfectly smooth, creamy, buttery mashed potato is so soothing and comforting, like a warm cuddle. If you love mashed potatoes, my top tip is to buy a potato ricer. It looks like a giant garlic press, and pushing the potatoes through this makes all the difference — you'll get lump-free mash every time. Choose a potato that's good for mashing, such as Yukon Gold.

SERVES 4

2¼lb (1kg) potatoes, peeled and cut into even-sized pieces
3 tbsp (40g) butter
¼ cup heavy cream
salt and freshly ground black pepper

Put the potatoes into a large saucepan with enough water to cover. Bring to a boil, then turn the heat down and leave to simmer for 15–20 minutes or until the potatoes are tender. Remove from the heat and strain, reserving the cooking water.

Pass the potatoes through a ricer, or mash them really well with a potato masher. Add the butter and leave it to melt, then mix gently and stir in the cream. Add a little of the reserved cooking water if necessary to get the consistency right. This often isn't necessary, and at most you'll only need a tablespoonful or two. Season to taste with salt and pepper and serve.

VARIATION
Garlic mashed potatoes

This is a lovely variation for when you want your potatoes to have an extra kick to them. Cook the potatoes as described in the main recipe. While they are cooking, melt the butter in a saucepan over a gentle heat: don't let it get really hot. Add 3 crushed garlic cloves to the butter and let it warm through very gently for a few minutes. Add the garlic butter to the potatoes after you have mashed them, along with the cream and seasoning.

Roast potatoes v

Crisp golden roast potatoes are one of the joys of life, and being able to turn out good ones every time is a skill worth cultivating. It's not difficult: the first step to success is using the right type of potatoes, ones that aren't too waxy and yet won't fall to pieces — like Red Bliss. I generally use olive oil, although rapeseed gives good results. Coating the cooked potatoes with some flour before putting them into the hot fat helps to make them extra crispy. I know this quantity sounds like a lot of potatoes, but they always seem to go!

SERVES 4–6

3lb 5oz (1.5kg) wax potatoes, like Red Bliss or Yukon Gold
olive or rapeseed oil, for roasting
4–5 tbsp all-purpose flour
sea salt, preferably Maldon

Preheat the oven to 425°F (220°C). Peel the potatoes and cut them into small, even-sized chunks about 1½in (4cm) in size.

Put the potatoes into a pan with just enough water to cover, bring to the boil, then turn down the heat and let them cook gently until they're almost done (about 10–15 minutes). The trick is to get them very nearly cooked but stop before they start to break up.

When the potatoes are almost ready, pour enough oil into a roasting pan to just cover the surface — about ¼in (6mm) deep. Put the pan into the oven to heat.

continued next page

Drain the potatoes into a colander. Then put them back in the pan, sprinkle with the flour, put a lid on the pan, and shake the potatoes gently but firmly, so that they get coated in flour and the edges get roughened up.

Put the potatoes into the hot oil — stand back because it will spit. Don't bother to turn them at this stage. Bake for 20 minutes. Have a look at the potatoes and if they're golden brown underneath, turn them over, and give them another 15–20 minutes or until they're golden brown all over. Drain well on paper towels or in a metal colander, sprinkle with salt, then serve.

Pumpkin baked with butter and garlic

Here's what to do with all the orange flesh you scooped out from your Halloween pumpkin! This is buttery, garlicky and delicious.

SERVES 4

1½lb (700g) pumpkin (weighed after the skin and seeds have been removed)
1 large garlic clove or 2 small ones
salt
½ stick (50g) butter, softened
freshly ground black pepper

Preheat the oven to 350°F (180°C).

Cut the pumpkin into smallish, even-sized pieces.

Peel the garlic and crush it into a paste with a little salt, then mix it with the butter.

Use half this garlic butter to grease an ovenproof dish generously, then add the pumpkin and top with the remaining butter and a good grinding of pepper.

Cover with foil and bake in the oven for about 40 minutes or until the pumpkin is tender, stirring it once or twice during the cooking so that the butter coats all the pieces.

Tip

Try puréeing the pumpkin after cooking.

Perfect ratatouille v

I've always loved ratatouille, which I associate with long, lazy summer days on holiday in France. I've included several versions here, a quick-and-easy one, an oven-baked version and this one, which takes a little longer, because you cook each type of vegetable separately, but gives a superb result.

SERVES 4 ❄

6–8 tbsp olive oil
2 red onions, chopped
2–4 garlic cloves, crushed
1lb (450g) tomatoes, chopped
2–3 sprigs of thyme
2 large red peppers, deseeded and diced
2 large yellow peppers, deseeded and diced
2 large zucchini, cut into small chunks
1 eggplant, cut into small chunks
1–2 tsp coriander seeds, crushed
salt and freshly ground black pepper
chopped fresh flat-leaf parsley

Heat 2 tablespoons of the oil in a saucepan, add the onions, cover, and cook gently for 10 minutes, stirring from time to time.

Add the garlic, tomatoes and thyme and simmer, uncovered, for 15–20 minutes or until thickened.

Meanwhile, heat another 2 tablespoons of oil in a frying pan, add the peppers, and fry, stirring often, for about 5 minutes or until they are beginning to soften. Take them out of the pan with a slotted spoon and put them on a plate.

Fry the zucchini, and then the eggplant, in the same way, putting them on the plate with the peppers as they are done.

Add more oil to the frying pan if necessary, but be careful not to allow the eggplant to absorb too much oil. It may appear rather dry at first, but be patient because it will soften without the addition of a lot of oil if you give it time.

When all the vegetables are done, add them to the tomato mixture, along with the crushed coriander seeds and salt and pepper to taste.

Cook over a gentle heat, uncovered, for 10–15 minutes or until the vegetables are all tender. Check the seasoning, and serve sprinkled with chopped parsley.

VARIATIONS
Quick-and-easy ratatouille v

Fry the onions and garlic in a large saucepan as described, then add the tomatoes, thyme, peppers, zucchini, eggplant and crushed coriander. Cook over a moderate heat, uncovered, for 20–25 minutes or until all the vegetables are tender. Season with salt and pepper. Serve sprinkled with chopped parsley.

Oven-baked ratatouille v

This method is fantastically easy. Put all the ingredients in a roasting pan or large shallow ovenproof dish. Mix gently so that everything is glossy with oil. Bake at 350°F (180°C) for about 40 minutes or until the vegetables are tender and lightly browned at the edges. Check the seasoning, scatter over chopped parsley and serve.

Red cabbage casserole v

This is a fantastic vegetable dish because you can more or less forget it while it cooks. It doesn't need any last-minute attention, it turns out moist and juicy so you don't need gravy and it can also be reheated if necessary and still tastes delicious. There are recipes for red cabbage throughout Europe. In France, chestnuts are sometimes added. In Russia, the red cabbage might be served with sour cream, which is a lovely addition, while in Denmark red cabbage is part of the traditional Christmas feast. Altogether, a lovely warming dish for winter — and if there's any left over, it's also good cold.

SERVES 6 ❋

1½lb (700g) red cabbage
2 large onions
2 large cooking apples
3 tbsp olive oil
2oz (50g) raisins or golden raisins
1 tbsp salt
1 tbsp dark soft brown sugar
1–2 tbsp freshly squeezed lemon juice
½ tsp ground cinnamon or allspice (optional)
a pinch of ground cloves (optional)

Shred the cabbage fairly finely with a sharp knife, discarding the hard core.

Put the cabbage into a large saucepan, cover it with cold water and bring to the boil. Remove from the heat and drain in a colander.

Meanwhile, peel and chop the onions and apples and fry them lightly in the oil in a large saucepan for 5–10 minutes.

Add the cabbage, together with the raisins, salt, sugar, lemon juice and the spices (if using). Mix well, then put a lid on the saucepan and leave the cabbage to cook very gently for 1½ hours, stirring from time to time, until it's very tender.

Alternatively, you can put the cabbage into an ovenproof casserole dish, cover with a lid and bake in the oven at 325°F (160°C) for about 2 hours.

VARIATION
Red cabbage with apples and cider v

For this delicious variation, add 1¼ cup (275ml) cider to the above mixture along with the sugar and lemon juice.

Root vegetables in turmeric and coconut sauce v

This is a beautiful dish of golden root vegetables bathed in a creamy, delicately flavored sauce.

SERVES 6

8oz (225g) carrots
8oz (225g) rutabaga
8oz (225g) parsnips
2 tbsp olive oil
1 onion, chopped
1 garlic clove, crushed
1 tsp grated fresh root ginger
1 tsp turmeric
14oz can coconut milk
1 small green pepper, seeded and
    sliced
salt and freshly ground black pepper

Peel the carrots, rutabaga and parsnips and cut them into even-sized chunky pieces.

Heat the oil in a medium-sized saucepan and fry the onion for 7–10 minutes, then stir in the garlic, ginger and turmeric and cook for a further 2 minutes.

Add the root vegetables, turning them with a spoon so that they all get coated with the spicy onion mixture, then add the coconut milk, green pepper and some salt and pepper to taste.

Cook over a low heat, covered, for about 15–20 minutes or until the vegetables feel tender when pierced with the point of a sharp knife.

Creamed spinach

A friend told me about this dish and it sounded so good I had to try it. You can make it in advance; it reheats perfectly.

SERVES 4

10 oz spinach leaves
a pat of butter
3 tbsp heavy cream
3 heaped tbsp Parmesan-style
    cheese, finely grated
salt and freshly ground black pepper
a pinch of freshly grated nutmeg

Rinse the spinach, put into a large saucepan with just the water clinging to it and cook, with a lid on the pan, for about 7 minutes or until completely tender.

Drain the spinach very well — the easiest way is to transfer it to a colander and press it with a spoon to squeeze out all the liquid.

Blend the spinach, in a food processor or with an electric hand blender, adding the butter, cream and grated cheese. Continue until the spinach is completely smooth and light.

Season with salt, pepper and nutmeg. Reheat the mixture gently, stirring all the time.

Split green peas with cream and leeks

A substantial yet elegant vegetable dish.

SERVES 4

6oz (175g) dried split green peas
15fl oz (425ml) water
2 tbsp (25g) butter
salt and freshly ground black pepper
2¼lb (1kg) leeks
¼ cup heavy cream
1–2 tbsp chopped fresh mint, to
    garnish

Put the split green peas into a saucepan with the water and simmer gently until very tender, about 50–60 minutes.

Blend the cooked split peas in a food processor or with a hand blender, adding more water if necessary, to make a soft consistency (like lightly whipped cream). Then add half the butter and season to taste.

Meanwhile, trim and wash the leeks and cut them into 1in (2.5cm) lengths. Cook in a little boiling water until just tender. Drain very well and add the remaining butter and some seasoning.

Spoon the leeks into a warmed serving dish, pour the split green pea sauce on top, and the cream and chopped mint on top of that. Serve at once.

Baked creamed rutabagas

This is a lovely vegetable dish that you can make in advance and just heat through in the oven when you want it. The crunchy breadcrumb topping contrasts well with the soft creamy swede.

SERVES 4 ❄
2lb (900g) rutabagas
1 tbsp (15g) butter, plus extra for greasing
2 tbsp whole milk or ½ and ½
salt and freshly ground black pepper
a pinch of freshly grated nutmeg

FOR THE TOPPING
approximately ¼ cup fresh breadcrumbs
a few pieces of butter

Preheat the oven to 350°C (180°F). Peel the rutabagas and cut into even-sized pieces. Put into a large saucepan, almost cover with cold water and cook gently, with a lid on the pan, until tender.

Drain off all the water, then return the pan to the heat briefly to dry the rutabagas a little. Mash them until smooth, adding the butter, milk or ½ and ½ and seasoning and beating well.

Lightly grease a shallow oven-proof dish and spoon the rutabagas mixture into it, smoothing the surface.

Sprinkle the top fairly generously with breadcrumbs and dot with butter. All this can be done in advance. Bake the rutabagas for about 40 minutes or until heated through and golden brown and crisp on top.

Glazed sweet potatoes

Sweet potatoes are so versatile: you can prick them and bake them in the oven like a jacket potato (they take half as long to cook); you can boil them, mash them, grill them and roast them; or, as in this recipe, glaze them.

SERVES 4
2¼lb (1 kg) sweet potatoes
3 tbsp (40g) butter
1½oz (40g) dark soft brown sugar
3 tbsp lemon juice
salt

Scrub the unpeeled potatoes and cut into even-sized pieces. Place in a saucepan, cover with water and boil gently until tender (about 15–20 minutes).

Drain them and peel off the skins. Preheat the oven to 400°F (200°C).

Use half the butter to grease a shallow ovenproof dish generously, then arrange the sweet potato pieces in the dish and sprinkle the sugar, lemon juice and a little salt over. Dot the remaining butter over and place, uncovered, in the oven.

Bake for 40–50 minutes or until the sweet potatoes are golden brown and glazed, turning them over once or twice during cooking.

Sweetcorn fritters

These are great as a first course, lunch or light dinner.

SERVES 3
12oz can sweetcorn (without sugar added), drained, or 8oz (225g) frozen sweetcorn kernels, defrosted
1 egg, separated
1oz (25g) wholegrain flour
salt and freshly ground black pepper
olive oil, for shallow-frying

Place the sweetcorn in a bowl with the egg yolk, flour and some salt and pepper and mix well.

Whisk the egg white until it's standing in soft peaks, then gently fold it into the sweetcorn mixture.

Heat a little oil in a frying pan and fry the sweetcorn mixture, a tablespoon at a time, on both sides, until crisp. (Stand back as you do so because the corn tends to "pop".)

As soon as they're ready, drain the fritters on kitchen paper. Keep the cooked ones warm in a low oven while you fry the remainder. Serve them immediately.

Vegetables
and nuts

This chapter includes many satisfying, mouth-watering main course dishes that everyone will enjoy. Some contain nuts, others don't, but all the recipes are easy to cook and really make the most out of the vibrant, nourishing ingredients used.

You'll find quick after-work dishes such as stir-fries, slow-cooked dishes like casseroles and stews, and special-occasion dishes that are perfect for entertaining.

Stuffed vegetables feature strongly — well, when nature provides a container as perfect as, say, a red pepper or aubergine, it seems obvious to fill it with something delicious! Whatever your taste, this chapter includes so many scrumptious recipes that you'll never again be stuck on what to cook for dinner.

Guide to nuts and seeds

Almonds Oval-shaped, with a ridged brown skin and well-known, distinctive flavor, almonds are useful in both sweet and savoury dishes. Grind them up and make them into nut roasts and croquettes or add them to muesli mix; or buy the sliced kind and sprinkle them over vegetable or rice mixtures, salads or trifles and puddings. To remove the brown skins yourself, put the almonds into a small saucepan, cover with cold water, bring to the boil and simmer for 1 minute; then drain. Pop the skins off the nuts using your finger and thumb. Sliced or blanched almonds can be toasted by stirring in a dry saucepan, under a broiler, or as described for hazelnuts.

Brazil nuts Whitish-yellow in color, flecked with brown, these large sausage-shaped nuts have a rich creamy flavor. They're good in nut roasts and chopped in salads.

Cashew nuts Creamy white and crescent-shaped, cashew nuts are available whole and, cheaper, in pieces. They have a pleasantly bland flavor which makes them useful in all kinds of sweet and savory dishes. They're delicious roasted (see under hazelnuts) or whipped into creams.

Chestnuts These are different from the other nuts in that they are lower in oil and protein and higher in starch. They're a useful addition to stews, casseroles and savory loaves. You can buy them in various forms: fresh, dried, frozen or vacuum-packed. You can also buy chestnut purée in cans, but I find this too smooth for most savory cooking; I prefer roasted, vacuum-packed chestnuts and you can find them in 7oz packets in most supermarkets.

Skinning fresh chestnuts is a labor of love. I recommend doing only 1lb (450g) at a time and chilling them in the freezer for 30–60 minutes before starting. Then, using a strong knife, cut them completely in half from top to bottom. Put them into boiling water to cover, and boil for 7–8 minutes. Then drain and remove the nuts with a paring knife. Keep the nuts warm as you work as this will help the skins come off. Put the skinned chestnuts into a saucepan, cover with water and simmer for 20–30 minutes or until tender. 1lb (450g) of good-quality chestnuts in their skins will yield around 12oz (350g) when skinned.

Dried chestnuts can be found in some health-food stores. To use these, soak overnight, then simmer gently in water for 2–3 hours or until tender. They roughly double in weight after soaking and cooking — 6oz (175g) will yield about 12oz (350g).

Frozen chestnuts can be found in some large supermarkets, especially around Christmas. Just cook them according to the packet directions.

MY RULE-OF-THUMB GUIDE TO QUANTITIES AND EQUIVALENTS IS

7oz (200g) vacuum pack of chestnuts is approximately equivalent to:

14oz (400g) fresh chestnuts in their skins or

3½oz (100g) dried chestnuts weighed before soaking

That quantity is usually right for two people as a main course; double it for recipes serving four.

Flax seeds, also called linseeds; different names, same seed. These are small, about the size of a sesame seed, with a nutty flavor. They can be golden or reddish brown; the color doesn't affect the taste, although I prefer the golden ones. Important for vegetarians as they're a valuable source of omega 3. Add them to muesli or sprinkle over salads. These seeds become sticky when mixed with water, so can be used to bind other ingredients, especially in raw food cookery.

Hazelnuts These little round brown pointed nuts are often sold without their dark brown skins; which is convenient for many recipes. If you want them unskinned, you'll need to go to a health-food store. Their flavor is enhanced by roasting. To do this, spread the hazelnuts out on a dry baking sheet and bake for 20–30 minutes in a moderate oven (375°F (190°C)) or until the nuts under the skins are golden brown. When they have cooled, the outer brown skins will rub off easily.

Hemp seeds Rather similar to flax seeds, best used raw, in muesli, salads, etc. Said to be nature's most balanced seed becausee it has omega 3 and omega 6 in a 3:1 ratio, which is what is required for perfect nutrition. However, as the diet of most people, including vegetarians, is biased too far towards omega 6, I think we're better off eating flax seeds (or taking the oil), with its 4:1 ratio of omega 3 to omega 6.

Macadamia nuts These look like large, creamy-color hazelnuts but are much richer, with a creamy, buttery flavor. You can buy them raw or roasted and salted. I like them added to salads or vegetable dishes. They can be whipped to a gorgeous cream.

Peanuts These little reddish-brown nuts are familiar to most people. Buy raw ones at a health-food store. You can roast them in the same way as hazelnuts (see page 139).

Pecan nuts These look like a smaller, darker version of walnuts and have a rich, almost sweet flavor and a very pleasant oily texture.

Pine nuts Sometimes called pine kernels, these are small, slim, creamy-colored nuts. They have a soft texture and a delicious pine flavor. They can be toasted, as for sliced almonds (see page 139), and sprinkled over vegetable, rice or fruit mixtures; made into pesto; or added to nut roasts and croquettes.

Pistachio nuts You can buy these still in their shells, ready for you to crack them open and eat the delectable green nuts inside, or already shelled, which is more convenient for using in recipes. Mixed with other nuts, in say a nut croquette or stuffing mixture, they add their own delicious note. They also make an attractive garnish, crushed and sprinkled over smooth and creamy dishes like dips or hummus.

Pumpkin seeds These big flat green seeds make a crunchy addition to muesli and salads. They can be ground in a coffee grinder and added to nuts to make pâtés, burgers, stuffings and so on. Roasting (as for hazelnuts, page 139) brings out their delicious flavor, but reduces some of their

nutritional value.

Sesame seeds These little seeds are brownish in their natural state; the white ones that you so often see for sale have had their outer skin removed, and most of their calcium too. It's worth going to a health-food store for the unhulled variety. They taste very nutty with a pleasant slight bitterness. Great sprinkled over Asian vegetable dishes and stir-fries, or breads, or added to muesli. The 'butter' made from them is called tahini, and is used to make dips such as hummus and in richly flavored dressings.

Sunflower seeds Pale greyish seeds with quite a sweet, delicate flavor. (If they have a strong, 'paint-like' flavor, they're not fresh and it's best to discard them.) Can be ground and made into burgers, dips, etc, or sprinkled over salads, added to muesli and so on. They sprout well (see page 79).

Walnuts Golden brown and with their familiar undulating shape, walnuts can be bought in halves or pieces. Their slightly bitter flavor adds intensity to savory mixtures and they are also good in salads.

How to grate nuts

Grated nuts are often called for in vegetarian recipes. This can be done easily using a blender, electric coffee grinder or food processor; or in one of the little hand grinders, with a set of drums that grate with varying degrees of coarseness.

Freezing nut and vegetable dishes

Most savory nut dishes and roasts freeze excellently, either before or after cooking. My family love what we consider in our house to be a "traditional" nut roast, that is, the white stuffed nut roast on page 171, and always want me to make it for Christmas, Easter and any family celebrations in between. I generally make it beforehand and freeze it uncooked. Then I take it out of the freezer the night before I need it, and cook it the next day. Most vegetable stews and casseroles freeze well, too. You'll find the freezer ❄ symbol by the dishes that are suitable for freezing.

Asparagus in hot lemon sauce

This is a delicious main course for the early summer when you want to make the most of the short asparagus season. The hot asparagus is coated with a lemon sauce, sprinkled with breadcrumbs and heated through just enough to warm the sauce and make the crumbs go crispy. Serve it on its own or with buttered baby new potatoes.

SERVES 4
2¼lb (1kg) asparagus
6 rounded tbsp mayonnaise
8oz (225g) fromage frais or other smooth soft low-fat white cheese
freshly squeezed lemon juice
Dijon mustard
salt and freshly ground black pepper
2oz (50g) fine fresh breadcrumbs
2oz (50g) Gruyère or Parmesan-style cheese, grated

Bend the spears of asparagus to break off the hard stems at the base — the asparagus breaks at the point where it gets too tough to eat. Discard the broken-off ends. Wash the asparagus gently but thoroughly to remove any grit.

Cook the asparagus in a deep pan of boiling water, or by laying the spears flat and covered with water in a large frying pan, or in a steamer, until just tender (7–10 minutes). Drain well.

While the asparagus is cooking, make the sauce by mixing together the mayonnaise and fromage frais. Sharpen with a little lemon juice and mustard and season with salt and pepper.

Preheat the oven to 400°F (200°C). Put the asparagus into a large, shallow ovenproof dish and pour the sauce over the top. Cover completely with a thin layer of breadcrumbs and sprinkle the cheese over.

Bake in the oven for 30–40 minutes or until heated through and golden on top. Be careful not to overcook this dish or the sauce might spoil.

Malanzane alla Parmigiana

This baked eggplant dish is a favorite of mine. I like to serve it with a green vegetable or salad. Although I don't usually bother with the process of salting and rinsing eggplant, in this particular case I think it's worth it, because it does prevent the eggplant from absorbing too much oil when fried.

SERVES 4 ❋
1½lb (700g) eggplant
salt
a little all-purpose flour, for coating
olive oil, for shallow-frying
15oz can tomatoes
2 garlic cloves, crushed
6oz (175g) Parmesan-style cheese, grated
freshly ground black pepper

Cut the eggplant into thin strips, sprinkle with salt and leave in a colander, covered with a small plate with a weight on top, for 30 minutes. Then rinse the eggplant and squeeze as dry as possible.

Preheat the oven to 375°F (190°C).

Dip the eggplant in flour then shallow-fry them in the oil until crisp on both sides and soft in the middle. Drain on paper towels.

Blend the tomatoes and garlic. Season with salt and pepper.

Layer the eggplant slices and cheese in a shallow ovenproof dish, then pour the tomato mixture evenly over the top. Bake, uncovered, towards the top of the oven, for 50–60 minutes or until browned and bubbling.

Eggplant stuffed with mushrooms and almonds

I think stuffed eggplant make a delicious main course. Here, they're stuffed with a moist and savory filling of mushrooms, onion, soy sauce and parsley, with the crunch of sliced almonds and a crisp topping of cheesy breadcrumbs.

SERVES 4 ❄

2 eggplant
5 tbsp olive oil, plus extra for greasing
2 onions, chopped
4oz (125g) button mushrooms, sliced
1 garlic clove, crushed
2 tbsp chopped fresh flat-leaf parsley
4oz (125g) sliced almonds
salt and freshly ground black pepper
2oz (50g) fresh breadcrumbs
2oz (50g) grated cheese

Cut the eggplant in half lengthways. With a sharp, pointed knife carefully cut right round the edge of the eggplant, about ⅛in (2mm) in from the skin. Then make criss-cross cuts up and down and from side to side across the flesh; these will help you to remove it. Using a knife or pointed teaspoon, scoop out the flesh out of the eggplant, leaving just the skins, which will hold the stuffing.

Heat 3 tablespoons of the oil in a frying pan and fry the eggplant skins for about 5 minutes on each side to soften them; drain them, then blot well with paper towels.

Arrange the skins cut side up in a lightly greased shallow ovenproof dish.

Preheat the oven to 400°F (200°C).

Heat the remainder of the oil in a saucepan, add the onions, and fry gently, covered and without browning, for 5 minutes. Stir in the eggplant flesh, mushrooms and garlic, and fry for 10 minutes. Cover the pan but stir often.

Remove from the heat and mix in the parsley, almonds and salt and pepper to taste.

Divide the mixture between the eggplant skins, piling it up well. Scatter the tops of the eggplant with breadcrumbs and cheese, dividing it between them.

Bake the eggplant for 30–40 minutes or until they're golden brown.

VARIATIONS

Vegan version V

Make as described except use 4oz (125g) grated vegan cheese instead of the breadcrumbs and dairy cheese (vegan cheese gets crisp when cooked, so you don't need the breadcrumbs too). Alternatively, retain the breadcrumbs but mix them with 1–2 tablespoons of olive oil.

Eggplant stuffed with mushrooms and pine nuts

This recipe is lovely made with pine nuts instead of almonds.

Eggplant stuffed with mushrooms and cheese

Increase the amount of mushrooms to 6oz (175g). Leave out the almonds and add 4oz (125g) grated cheese to the mixture before putting into the eggplant skins. Top with breadcrumbs and grated cheese as described.

Eggplant stuffed with feta and red pepper

A quick and tasty recipe.

SERVES 4 ❄

2 eggplant
5 tbsp olive oil
4 roasted and skinned red peppers from a jar, well drained and cut into strips
7oz (200g) feta cheese, drained and diced
3oz (75g) pitted black olives
salt and freshly ground black pepper

Cut the eggplant in half lengthways. With a sharp, pointed knife carefully cut right round the edge of the eggplant, about ⅛in (2mm) in from the skin. Then make criss-cross cuts up and down and from side to side across the flesh — these will help you to remove it. Using a knife or pointed teaspoon, scoop the flesh out of the eggplant, leaving just the skins, which will hold the stuffing.

Heat 3 tablespoons of the oil in a frying pan and fry the eggplant skins for about 5 minutes on each side to soften them; drain them, then blot well with paper towels.

Arrange the skins cut side up in a lightly greased shallow ovenproof dish.

Preheat the oven to 400°F (200°C).

Heat the remainder of the oil in a saucepan, add the chopped eggplant flesh, and fry for 10 minutes. Cover the pan but stir often.

Remove from the heat and mix in the peppers, feta and black olives. Season with salt and pepper to taste.

Divide the mixture between the eggplant skins and bake for 30–40 minutes or until they're golden brown.

Stuffed eggplant in béchamel sauce

This dish is quite different from the previous ones and is my version of a traditional Greek recipe. The original used minced meat, which I've replaced with quick-cooking lentils, while a tasty béchamel sauce covers it all to make a satisfying dish that just needs some quickly cooked French beans or purple sprouting broccoli to accompany it.

SERVES 6 ❋

3 eggplant (about 1½lb (700g))
salt
¼ cup olive oil
2 onions, chopped
3 tbsp tomato purée
3 garlic cloves, crushed in a little salt
6oz (175g) split red lentils
1 cup (225ml) water
2 tbsp chopped fresh flat-leaf parsley
3oz (75g) grated cheese
salt and freshly ground black pepper

FOR THE BÉCHAMEL SAUCE

2 tbsp (25g) butter
2 tbsp (25g) all-purpose flour
15fl oz (425ml) milk
1 egg
1–2 pinches of freshly grated nutmeg
2oz (50g) grated cheese

Cut the eggplant in half lengthways. With a sharp, pointed knife carefully cut right round the edge of the eggplant, about ⅛in (2mm) in from the skin. Then make criss-cross cuts up and down and from side to side across the flesh — these will help you to remove it. Using a knife or pointed teaspoon, scoop the flesh out of the eggplant, leaving just the skins, which will hold the stuffing.

Heat 3 tablespoons of oil in a frying pan and fry the eggplant skins for about 5 minutes on each side to soften them. Drain them, blot well with paper towels and place, cut side up, in a shallow ovenproof dish.

Preheat the oven to 400°F (200°C).

Fry the onions in the remaining oil in a saucepan; when it is soft but not brown — about 10 minutes — add the chopped eggplant flesh, tomato purée, garlic, lentils and water and cook, covered, for 20–30 minutes or until the lentils are done.

Remove from the heat, add the parsley and grated cheese and season to taste. Divide the filling between the eggplant skins, piling it up well.

To make the béchamel sauce, melt the butter in another saucepan and stir in the flour, then add one-third of the milk and stir over a high heat until the mixture is smooth and thick. Repeat the process twice more using the rest of the milk.

Remove from the heat and beat in the egg and salt, pepper and grated nutmeg to taste.

Pour the sauce over and round the eggplant, sprinkle with the grated cheese and bake for 35 minutes or until they're tender and the sauce is bubbly and golden brown.

Eggplant stuffed with chickpeas v

This is a lovely mixture with Middle Eastern flavorings, equally good served hot or cold. Serve with couscous or rice and a green salad. *Ras al hanout* is a mixture of Moroccan spices that many large supermarkets stock. If you can't get it, use ground cumin and a pinch of chili powder instead.

SERVES 4 ❋

2 eggplant
5 tbsp olive oil
1 large onion, chopped
1 large garlic clove, crushed
3 tbsp olive oil
1 tbsp *ras al hanout*
14oz can chickpeas, drained
2–3 tsp freshly squeezed lemon juice
2 tbsp chopped fresh flat-leaf parsley
salt and freshly ground black pepper

FOR THE TOPPING

¼ cup fresh breadcrumbs
1 tbsp olive oil

Preheat the oven to 400°F (200°C).

Cut the eggplant in half lengthways. With a sharp, pointed knife carefully cut right round the edge of the eggplant, about ⅛in (2mm) in from the skin. Then make criss-cross cuts up and down and from side to side across the flesh — these will help you to remove it. Using a knife or pointed teaspoon, scoop the flesh out of the eggplant, leaving just the skins, which will hold the stuffing.

Heat 3 tablespoons of the oil in a frying pan and fry the eggplant skins for about 5 minutes on each

continued next page

side to soften them. Drain them, then blot well with paper towels. Arrange the skins cut side up in a lightly greased shallow ovenproof dish.

Heat the remainder of the oil in a saucepan, add the onion, and fry, covered, for 5 minutes.

Add the scooped-out chopped flesh, stir, and fry for 10 minutes. Cover the pan but stir often.

Sprinkle in the *ras al hanout* and cook for another few seconds, then remove from the heat and stir in the chickpeas, lemon juice, parsley and salt and pepper to taste.

Divide the mixture between the eggplant skins, piling it up well. Mix together the breadcrumbs and olive oil for the topping and divide between the eggplant.

Bake the eggplant for 30–40 minutes or until they're golden brown and piping hot.

VARIATION
Eggplant stuffed with Puy lentils v

Little Puy lentils, which you can buy canned or cook yourself (see page 177), make a lovely filling for eggplant. Use 3½oz (100g) lentils, cooked in a generous amount of water for about 40 minutes or until tender, or a 14oz can. Drain the lentils and add instead of the chickpeas. You can use either *ras al hanout* or 3 teaspoons of ground coriander to flavor the mixture.

Stuffed eggplant in tomato sauce

Rich-tasting and delicious, this is wonderful served with a full-bodied red wine. Creamy mashed potatoes and cooked green beans go well with it.

SERVES 6 ❄
3 eggplant
6 tbsp olive oil
2 onions, chopped
3 large garlic cloves, crushed
2 tbsp tomato purée
2 tbsp vermouth
4oz (125g) pine nuts
3 tsp chopped mixed fresh herbs or
  1½ tsp dried (such as thyme and
  oregano)
salt and freshly ground black pepper
2oz (50g) fresh breadcrumbs
2oz (50g) grated cheese

FOR THE SAUCE
6 tbsp tomato purée
2 tbsp vermouth
1 cup (300ml) vegetable stock

Preheat the oven to 400°F (200°C). Cut the eggplant in half lengthwise. With a sharp, pointed knife carefully cut right round the edge of the eggplant, about ⅛in (2mm) in from the skin. Then make criss-cross cuts up and down and from side to side across the flesh — these will help you to remove it. Using a knife or pointed teaspoon, scoop the flesh out of the eggplant, leaving just the skins, which will hold the stuffing.

Heat 3 tablespoons of the oil in a frying pan and fry the eggplant skins for about 5 minutes on each side to soften them. Drain them, then blot well with paper towels.

Arrange the skins cut side up in a

lightly greased shallow ovenproof dish.

Heat the remainder of the oil in a saucepan, add the onions and fry, covered, for 5 minutes.

Stir in the scooped-out chopped flesh and fry for 10 minutes. Cover the pan but stir often. Add the garlic a minute or two before the eggplant is done.

Remove from the heat and add the tomato purée, vermouth, pine nuts, herbs and salt and pepper to taste.

Divide the mixture between the eggplant skins, piling it up well. Sprinkle the breadcrumbs and grated cheese on top, dividing it between the eggplant.

Make the sauce by mixing the tomato purée with the vermouth and gradually stirring in the stock to make a smooth consistency.

Pour the sauce around the eggplant and bake for 30–40 minutes or until they're golden brown.

Hot avocado with sherry stuffing

Hot stuffed avocado is delicious, with three provisos: make sure that the avocados are perfectly ripe — they should just yield all over to fingertip pressure — and make sure you only just warm them through in the oven, rather than cook them, and eat them straight away. The flavor spoils if they get too hot. For this reason, it's important to leave the preparation of the avocados until the last minute, though the filling can be made in advance.

SERVES 6

4oz (125g) Brazil nuts, finely grated
4oz (125g) Gruyère cheese, grated
2oz (50g) fine, fresh wholegrain
  breadcrumbs
3 tomatoes, finely chopped
1 small garlic clove, crushed
1 tbsp tomato purée
2 tbsp chopped fresh chives
4–6 tbsp fino sherry
salt and freshly ground black pepper
a few drops of Tabasco sauce
3 ripe avocados
juice of 1 lemon

FOR THE TOPPING

6 tbsp grated Gruyère cheese
6 tbsp fine fresh breadcrumbs

First make the stuffing: put the nuts, cheese, breadcrumbs, tomatoes, garlic, tomato purée and chives into a bowl and mix together.

Stir in enough sherry to make a soft mixture which will just hold its shape, then season with plenty of salt and pepper and enough Tabasco to give the mixture a pleasant kick. Set aside until just before the meal — you can make the stuffing a few hours ahead if convenient.

Preheat the oven to 450°F (230°C).

Just before the meal, halve each avocado and remove the skin and stone. Mix the lemon juice with a good pinch of salt and a grinding of pepper and brush all over the avocados.

Place the avocados in a shallow ovenproof dish. Spoon the stuffing mixture on top, dividing it evenly between the avocados; sprinkle a little cheese and a few breadcrumbs over.

Put the avocados into the oven and turn the heat down to 400°F (200°C). Bake for 15 minutes, then serve immediately. (I find it best to put the avocados into the oven just as everyone sits down for their first course — it's important that they are not overcooked.)

They are delicious with puréed potatoes and a lightly cooked vegetable, such as baby carrots.

Chinese stir-fried beansprouts with omelette strips

If you serve this with boiled rice it makes a complete meal that's quick to cook. As with all Chinese-style recipes, the preparation of the vegetables is best done in advance; so the actual cooking takes only a few minutes. If you're going to serve brown rice with this dish, remember to allow time for it to cook — around 45 minutes.

SERVES 4

12oz (350g) beansprouts
12oz (350g) Napa cabbage or
  bok choy
8oz (225g) button mushrooms
2 onions
1 garlic clove
2 tbsp dark soy sauce
1 tsp sugar
1 tbsp fino sherry
6 tbsp ground nut or rapeseed oil,
  plus extra for frying
2 tsp grated fresh root ginger
a small bunch of fresh coriander,
  roughly chopped

FOR THE OMELETTE STRIPS

a pat of butter for frying (optional)
4 eggs
salt and freshly ground black pepper

Wash the beansprouts, cabbage leaves and mushrooms. Cut the leaves and mushrooms into even-sized slices. Peel and very finely chop the onions and crush the garlic.

Mix together the soy sauce, sugar and sherry.

Whisk the eggs with some salt and freshly ground black pepper. Have ready a small omelette pan or frying pan for making omelette strips and a wok, large frying pan

continued next page

or large saucepan in which to stir-fry the vegetables.

When you're ready to cook the dish, get the wok or pan very hot, add the oil and when it's smoking hot, add the onions, garlic and ginger and stir-fry for 1 minute.

Add the beansprouts, cabbage and mushrooms and stir-fry them for 2 minutes, turning them over so that everything gets coated with the oil, garlic and ginger.

Pour in the soy sauce mixture, reduce the heat and cook for a further 3 minutes.

While this final cooking is going on, quickly make the omelette strips. Heat a little oil or oil and butter in the omelette pan and pour in half the beaten eggs; make an omelette by cooking the egg over a brisk heat, gently pushing the eggs towards the center as they cook, tipping the pan so that the uncooked part runs towards the edges. Turn it out flat onto a plate and cut it into long strips. Make another omelette in the same way.

Taste the cooked vegetable mixture and correct the seasoning with a little salt and pepper if necessary, toss in the omelette strips and fresh coriander. Serve immediately.

VARIATIONS

Chinese stir-fried bean-sprouts with tofu v

Instead of the omelette strips, use 2 x 5oz packets of marinated tofu chunks (from health-food stores and large supermarkets) or make your own: dice a 9oz packet of plain tofu, put into a plastic bag with 1 tablespoon of grated fresh root ginger, 2 garlic cloves, crushed, 2 tablespoons of dark soy sauce, 1 tablespoon of toasted sesame oil and 1 tablespoon of balsamic vinegar. Squish it all around, and leave to marinate until you're ready to add it to the stir-fry in place of the omelette strips. Add the tofu along with all of its marinade.

Chinese stir-fried bean-sprouts with edamame v

Edamame, which are tender green soy beans, can be bought frozen from health-food stores and some supermarkets. (They can also be bought in their pods from Asian stores but for this stir-fry we need them podded.) Simply thaw 8oz (225g) of the beans and add to the stir-fry with the beansprouts. You won't need the eggs too, unless you want to include them.

Tomato and walnut-stuffed cabbage baked in a cheese sauce

This costs very little to make but is tasty and satisfying. Served with potatoes baked in their jackets (see page 128), it makes a warming and economical meal. You could use other nuts if you want to.

SERVES 4 ❄
8 outer leaves of cabbage (savoy, Primo or January King)
1 onion, chopped
2 tbsp olive oil, plus extra for greasing
4oz (125g) shelled walnuts, chopped
4oz (225g) fresh breadcrumbs
14oz can tomatoes
salt and freshly ground black pepper
2oz (50g) grated cheese, for topping

FOR THE QUICK CHEESE SAUCE
2 tbsp (25g) butter
2 tbsp (25g) all-purpose flour
1¼ cups (275ml) milk
2oz (50g) grated cheese

Preheat the oven to 375°F (190°C). Put the cabbage leaves into a saucepan of boiling water for about 3 minutes or until pliable. Drain well.

Fry the onion in the oil for 10 minutes, add the nuts, breadcrumbs, tomatoes and seasoning. Divide the mixture between the cabbage leaves, roll them up and place in a greased shallow ovenproof dish.

Make a quick cheese sauce by putting all the ingredients except the cheese into a saucepan and whisking over the heat until it comes to the boil and thickens. Remove from the heat, stir in the grated cheese and some salt and pepper to taste.

Pour the sauce over the cabbage rolls, sprinkle with cheese and bake for 40–45 minutes.

Cashew nut and dill fritters v

These are delicious; crisp and crunchy on the outside, light and moist within, with the fresh flavor of dill. Serve them with lemon wedges and a creamy sauce, such as parsley or lemon, blender Béarnaise, tartar sauce or vegan tartar sauce (see pages 63 and 70).

SERVES 4 ✽

2 onions
3 tbsp olive oil
2oz (50g) wholewheat flour
15fl oz (425ml) soy milk
4oz (125g) cashew nuts, finely grated
2 tsp freshly squeezed lemon juice
¼ cup chopped fresh dill
salt and freshly ground black pepper
olive oil, for shallow-frying
lemon wedges, to garnish

FOR COATING

6 tbsp cornstarch
6–7 tbsp cold water
½ cup dried breadcrumbs (see page 183)

Chop the onions finely. Heat the oil in a large pan over a gentle heat, add the onions and cook gently until they are soft but not brown (about 10 minutes).

Stir in the flour and milk. Mix well and cook very gently for 2 minutes or until thickened. Add the cashew nuts and cook, stirring, for 2–3 minutes, then remove from the heat and add the lemon juice, dill and seasoning. Leave to cool.

When completely cold, divide into eight portions and press them into flat ovals, about ½in (1cm) thick or slightly less.

To make the coating, mix together the cornstarch and water to make a thick, coating consistency. Dip each fritter first in the cornstarch mixture then into the dried bread-crumbs, so that they are completely coated in crumbs. Press them gently back into shape if necessary.

Fry them on both sides in olive oil until golden brown and crisp. Drain well on paper towels and serve garnished with lemon wedges and with a creamy sauce.

VARIATION

Cashew nut and parsley fritters v

You can use other herbs to flavor these instead of dill. Parsley is lovely, especially the flat-leaf type. Use a heaping ¼ cup, in place of the dill.

Quick celery, cashew nut and tomato ragout

This is one of my most popular early recipes. It's quick and easy.

SERVES 4 ✽

1 onion, chopped
1 bay leaf
½ stick (50g) butter
1 head of celery, chopped and boiled for about 20 minutes or until tender
1 tbsp flour
24oz tomato purée
juice and rind of 1½ lemons
6oz (175g) cashew nuts, grated
1 tbsp chopped fresh flat-leaf parsley
pinch of mace or nutmeg
salt and freshly ground black pepper
hot toast, homemade crostini or garlic bread (see page 55), to serve

Fry the onion with the bay leaf in the butter, with the lid on the pan, for 10 minutes or until tender but not browned.

Drain the celery, chop into bite-sized pieces and add to the onion.

Stir in the flour and tomato purée. Cook until slightly thickened, then stir in the lemon juice and rind, cashew nuts, parsley and mace, and season with salt and pepper.

Serve immediately with hot toast, homemade crostini or garlic bread.

Easy cauliflower cheese

This really is quick and easy!

SERVES 4
1 large cauliflower
salt
8oz (225g) grated cheese

TO SERVE
hot wholegrain toast or rolls
watercress or tomato salad

Preheat the broiler to moderately hot.

Wash and trim the cauliflower, dividing it into small florets as you do so.

Heat 1in (2cm) salted water in a saucepan, add the cauliflower and cook for 4–5 minutes or until just tender.

Drain well and place in a lightly greased, shallow ovenproof dish.

Cover with the grated cheese and place under the broiler until the cheese has melted and is beginning to brown.

Serve immediately, with hot wholegrain toast or rolls, and a salad of watercress or sliced tomatoes.

Cauliflower satay v

I love this. Although the recipe may look long and complicated, it's very easy and all the preparation can be done in advance. I like to use good-quality pure peanut butter, but you could also use cashew or almond butter. You can find jars of tamarind paste and vegetarian Thai red curry paste (i.e. not containing fish) in large supermarkets.

SERVES 3–4
1lb 2oz (500g) florets (from 1 large cauliflower)

FOR THE MARINADE
1 tbsp peanut butter
2 tbsp coconut milk
1 tbsp dark soy sauce
2 tbsp rice vinegar
2 tbsp toasted sesame oil
2 tsp grated fresh root ginger
2 garlic cloves, crushed
2 tsp hot curry powder

FOR THE SATAY SAUCE
3 tbsp peanut butter
5 tbsp coconut milk
1 tbsp tamarind paste
1 tbsp Thai red curry paste

FOR THE CUCUMBER PICKLE
5 tbsp water
5 tbsp rice vinegar
1 tbsp sugar
1 small onion, cut into thin rings
1 cucumber, peeled, quartered and thinly sliced
1 red jalepeno chili, seeded and sliced (optional)

Halve or quarter the cauliflower florets as necessary so they're all bite-sized.

Bring 2in (5cm) of water to the boil in a large saucepan, add the cauliflower and parboil for 3 minutes. Drain and rinse under cold water.

Make the marinade: put all the ingredients into a large bowl and stir until smooth. Add the cauliflower and mix so that the pieces are all coated. Set aside.

For the satay sauce, put the peanut butter into a small bowl and gradually stir in the remaining ingredients, to make a smooth cream. Set aside.

Make the cucumber pickle by mixing all the ingredients together. Set aside.

A few minutes before you want to eat, put the cauliflower in an even layer on a broiler pan or baking tray that will fit under your broiler, and broil on high for about 10 minutes or until the cauliflower is heated through and beginning to crisp at the edges.

Serve the cauliflower on a big plate, with a bowl of satay sauce in the center, and a bowl of cucumber pickle, for people to help themselves.

Tip
Freeze what's left of the can of coconut milk for future use. It separates slightly after freezing but smoothes out as you mix it with other ingredients.

Oven-baked chestnut and mushroom casserole v

You can use fresh, dried or vacuum-packed chestnuts for this autumnal casserole. Fresh chestnuts, yielding about 1lb (450g) chestnuts after shelling (that's about 1½lb (700g) chestnuts in their shells), are the nicest, if you can get them. Prepare these as described on page 139. Baked potatoes go well with this.

SERVES 4
2 tbsp olive oil
2 large onions, thinly sliced
1 head of celery, sliced
8oz (225g) baby button mushrooms
2 tbsp flour
2 x 7oz packets vacuum-packed
    chestnuts
14oz can chopped tomatoes
1 cup (225ml) vegetable stock
1 cup (225ml) red wine
1 bay leaf
salt and freshly ground black pepper

Preheat the oven to 350°F (180°C).

Heat the oil in a large flameproof casserole dish that can later go into the oven. Add the sliced onions and celery and sauté for 10 minutes, browning them a bit, then add the whole mushrooms and cook for further minute or so.

Sprinkle the flour over the top of the vegetables and stir in, then add the chestnuts, and stir in the tomatoes, stock, wine and bay leaf. Season with salt and pepper.

Bake for 45 minutes.

This does not need to be served immediately; it will keep warm until you're ready to eat it, and is also lovely the next day — in fact, it tastes even better.

Chestnut and red wine casserole v

Chestnuts are excellent in a casserole, and here they are again, this time with more vegetables, herbs and spices. I always used to make this with dried chestnuts, which you treat much like dried beans (see page 139). However, vacuum-packed chestnuts are much easier and very good, and these days I generally use them. I like to eat this around Christmas time, with some buttery baby Brussels sprouts and creamy mashed potatoes.

SERVES 4 ❄
7oz (200g) dried chestnuts or
    2 x 7oz packets vacuum-packed
    chestnuts
2 large onions, chopped
1lb (450g) carrots, sliced
2 tbsp olive oil
4 garlic cloves, crushed
4oz (125g) button mushrooms,
    sliced
10 each of allspice berries, juniper
    berries and black peppercorns,
    lightly crushed
1 tbsp paprika
1 tsp each of dried thyme and
    rosemary
2 cups (575ml) vegetable stock
1¾ cups (400ml) red wine
salt

If you're using dried chestnuts, soak them overnight. The next day, cover with plenty of water and simmer for 2–3 hours or until tender. Drain and reserve the liquid, which you can use as part of the stock.

In a large saucepan, fry the onions and carrots in the oil for 10 minutes until browned, then add the garlic, mushrooms, chestnuts (drained or vacuum-packed, whichever you're using), spices, herbs, stock, wine and salt.

Bring to a boil, put a lid on the pan and leave to cook gently for 30–40 minutes or until the vegetables are tender and the liquid much reduced and thickened. If it's not as thick as you'd like, turn up the heat and let it bubble away for a few minutes to reduce a bit more.

Season with salt to taste and serve.

Savory chestnut bake v

You can use dried, canned, fresh or vacuum-packed chestnuts for this simple but tasty bake. As with many savory chestnut dishes, Brussels sprouts go really well, as do red or green winter cabbage and some roast or Bircher potatoes (see pages 131 and 128).

SERVES 4 ❄

1 onion, sliced
1 stalk of celery, chopped
1 tbsp olive oil
2 garlic cloves, crushed
2 x 7oz packets vacuum-packed
    chestnuts
4oz (125g) shelled walnuts, grated
4oz (125g) cashew nuts, grated
grated rind and juice of ½ lemon
1 glass red wine (optional)
small cupful of vegetable stock
    (optional)
salt and freshly ground black pepper
3–4 tbsp fresh breadcrumbs and
    little pieces of butter, for topping

Preheat the oven to 375°F (190°C).
    Fry the onion and celery in the oil in a large saucepan for 10 minutes, browning them lightly. Then add the garlic and cook for a few seconds more, stirring.
    Remove from the heat and add the chestnuts, mashing them well so that the mixture will hold together.
    Add the walnuts, cashew nuts, grated lemon rind and juice and the wine (if using). Mix well, and if necessary stir in a little stock to desired consistency (if using).
    Put the mixture into a shallow ovenproof dish, dot with the breadcrumbs and butter, cover with foil and bake for about 30 minutes, removing the foil 15 minutes before the end of cooking time to brown the top.

Chestnut, sage and red wine loaf

This is a moist savory loaf that slices well either hot or cold. Served with baked red cabbage, baked potatoes and sour cream, it makes a wonderful winter meal.
It's also very good as a vegetarian alternative to Christmas turkey, with a wine sauce, bread sauce, roast potatoes and baby sprouts.

SERVES 6 ❄

butter and dried breadcrumbs (see
    page 183) for lining loaf pan
½ stick (50g) butter
1 large onion, chopped
2 stalks of celery, finely chopped
3 x 7oz packets vacuum-packed
    chestnuts
2 garlic cloves, crushed
2 tbsp chopped fresh sage or
    1 tsp dried
1 tbsp red wine, fino sherry
    or brandy
1 egg
salt and freshly ground black pepper
1 fresh sage leaf

Preheat the oven to 350°F (180°C). Prepare a 1lb (450g) loaf pan by lining the base and narrow sides with a long strip of baking parchment. Brush well with butter and sprinkle lightly with the dried breadcrumbs.
    Melt the butter in a large saucepan and fry the onion and celery for 10 minutes, browning lightly.

Chop suey v

Mash the chestnuts roughly and add to the pan, along with the garlic, sage, wine and egg, and mix together, seasoning with salt and pepper.

Lay the sage leaf (if using) in the base of the prepared loaf pan and spoon the chestnut mixture on top, smooth over the surface and cover with a piece of foil. Bake in the pre-heated oven for 1 hour.

To serve, slip a knife round the sides of the loaf and turn out on to a warm dish.

VARIATION
Vegan chestnut, sage and red wine loaf v

Instead of butter, use ¼ cup of olive oil to fry the onion and celery, and just leave out the egg, adding a tablespoonful or so of water, stock or extra red wine (make sure it's vegan) instead.
Slice the loaf carefully with a sharp knife.

Although the list of ingredients always makes this dish look rather daunting, it's actually very easy to make. Just prepare everything in advance so you only have to cook them quickly at the last minute. You can really add whatever you like to a chop suey, so feel free to experiment. Ready-marinated tofu pieces are used here for speed, but you could use a pack of plain tofu and marinate it yourself (see page 203).

SERVES 4
1 onion
1 small red pepper
1 leek, trimmed
1 garlic clove
1in (2.5cm) piece of fresh root ginger
8oz (225g) beansprouts
4oz (125g) button mushrooms
a small bunch of scallions, trimmed
8oz can water chestnuts, drained
8oz can bamboo shoots, drained
2 tbsp ground nut or rapeseed oil
5oz (150g) marinated tofu pieces
salt
hot cooked rice, to serve

FOR THE STIR-FRY SAUCE

2 tbsp dark soy sauce
1 tbsp tomato ketchup
1 tsp sugar
1 tbsp fino sherry
2 tbsp water

Peel and chop the onion and thinly slice the pepper, discarding the seeds. Wash and finely slice the leek. Crush the garlic and grate the ginger, no need to peel first. Set everything aside.

Wash the beansprouts, slice the mushrooms and chop the scallions. Put them on one side too.

In a cup, mix together the soy sauce, tomato ketchup, sugar, sherry and water, and set aside until you're ready to make the meal,

When you're ready, heat 2 tablespoons of oil in a wok or large saucepan; get it nice and hot, then put in the onion, red pepper and leek and fry for 5 minutes.

Stir in the garlic and ginger and cook for a few seconds before adding the beansprouts, mushrooms, spring onions, water chestnuts, bamboo shoots and tofu.

Stir-fry over quite a high heat for about 3 minutes, then add the mixture from the cup. Stir well for 2–3 minutes or until everything is piping hot and bathed in a glossy sauce. Add a little salt to taste if necessary, and serve immediately on hot cooked rice.

Stuffed zucchini with almonds

This is a very pleasant, simple dish. Originally I used cream cheese, but ricotta or a reduced-fat cream cheese work well too. You could also use one of the lovely vegan cream cheeses you can buy. White breadcrumbs give a delicate flavor, but wholegrain can be used instead if preferred. Serve with a lemon or parsley sauce (see page 164) and a baby leaf salad.

SERVES 4
4 large zucchini
olive oil, for greasing
4oz (125g) fresh white breadcrumbs
8oz (225g) cream cheese (full fat or reduced fat), ricotta cheese or vegan cream cheese
¼ cup sliced almonds
juice and rind of ½ lemon
salt and freshly ground black pepper

Preheat the oven to 375°F (190°C).

Parboil the zucchini for 5 minutes, then slice in half lengthways and scoop out the flesh. Mash the zucchini flesh. Place the zucchini shells side by side in an oiled ovenproof dish.

Mix together the breadcrumbs, cheese, sliced almonds, mashed zucchini flesh and lemon juice and rind to taste. Season with salt and pepper.

Pile the almond mixture into the zucchini shells and bake for 45 minutes. Serve hot with a lemon or parsley sauce and some salad.

Stuffed zucchini with mushrooms

Another quick and easy zucchini recipe; to make a more substantial meal, serve it with some couscous or a cheese sauce and some new potatoes.

SERVES 4
4 large zucchini
1 garlic clove
4 tomatoes
6oz (175g) button mushrooms
2 tbsp (25g) butter
4oz (125g) fresh breadcrumbs
1 tbsp freshly squeezed lemon juice
1 tsp grated lemon rind
2 tbsp chopped fresh parsley
salt and freshly ground black pepper
olive oil, for greasing
1–2oz (25–50g) grated Gruyère or Parmesan-style cheese

Preheat the oven to 350°F (180°C). Prepare the zucchini as in the previous recipe.

Crush the garlic, slice the tomatoes and mushrooms, and fry lightly in the butter until tender, then mix with half the breadcrumbs, the mashed zucchini centers, the lemon juice and rind, parsley and some salt and pepper.

Pile the mixture into the prepared zucchini, place in a shallow oiled ovenproof dish, sprinkle with the rest of the breadcrumbs and the grated cheese. Bake for about 20 minutes or until crisp and golden.

Zucchini à la polonaise

Tender slices of zucchini in a lemony béchamel sauce with a generous breadcrumb topping.

SERVES 4
1½lb (700g) zucchini
1 stick (125g) butter
1 heaped tbsp all-purpose flour
1¼ cups (275ml) milk
juice of ½ lemon
salt and freshly ground black pepper
4oz (125g) fresh breadcrumbs
6 hardboiled eggs
1 tbsp chopped fresh parsley
1 tsp grated lemon rind
lemon slices and chopped fresh flat-leaf parsley, to garnish

Wash, top and tail and slice the zucchini into ¼in (6mm) slices. Sauté in a quarter of the butter, turning frequently, until tender. Set aside.

Meanwhile use another quarter of the butter to make a sauce, melting it, stirring in the flour, cooking for a minute or two, then removing from the heat and gradually adding the milk.

Return to the heat to thicken, stirring all the time. Add the lemon juice and seasoning, then simmer gently over a low heat while you make the polonaise topping.

Fry the breadcrumbs in the rest of the butter until golden and crisp.

Finely chop the hardboiled eggs and add to the breadcrumbs with the parsley, lemon rind and salt and pepper to taste.

To assemble, gently reheat the zucchini and put on a warm plate. Cover with the sauce and top with the breadcrumb mixture. Garnish with the lemon slices and parsley.

Fennel with orange and olive stuffing v

If, like me, you enjoy the fresh, aniseed flavor of fennel, you might like to try stuffing and roasting it. It's lovely with a fresh tomato salad.

SERVES 4

4 large fennel bulbs (each about 10–12oz (300–350g))
8oz (225g) fresh breadcrumbs
6 tbsp olive oil
grated rind and juice of 1 large orange
4oz (125g) pitted black or green olives
2 tsp chopped fresh thyme or 1 tsp dried thyme
salt and freshly ground black pepper
lemon slices, to garnish

Preheat the oven to 350°F (180°C). Wash and trim the fennel, running a potato peeler down the outer parts of the bulb to remove any toughness. Cut the bulbs in half, right down from the leafy tops to the bottom.

Put the fennel into a saucepan with enough cold water to cover, and bring to a boil. Simmer for 10–15 minutes or until the fennel feels tender when you insert a sharp knife. Drain well (the water makes beautiful stock for a soup or risotto) and leave to cool.

Make the stuffing by mixing the breadcrumbs, ¼ cup of the oil, the orange rind and juice, olives and thyme. Season with a little salt and a good grinding of pepper.

Gently pull back the outer layers of the fennel and fill with stuffing, packing it in well. Brush the fennel with the remaining oil.

Place the fennel, stuffing up, side by side in a shallow ovenproof dish and bake for about 45 minutes or until they are completely tender and slightly browned on top.

VARIATIONS

Fennel with orange and pine nut stuffing v

Make as described, using 3½oz (100g) pine nuts instead of the olives, and a tablespoonful of chopped fresh parsley instead of the thyme.

Fennel with cream cheese and almond stuffing

Prepare the fennel as described. Use only 4oz (125g) breadcrumbs and leave out the orange and olives. Mix the breadcrumbs with 8oz (225g) cream cheese (full or reduced fat), ricotta cheese or vegan cream cheese, ¼ cup of sliced almonds, the rind and juice of ½ lemon. Flavor with the thyme, as described, and salt and ground pepper. Use just 2 tablespoons of the oil to brush the fennel, and bake as described.

Squash stuffed with butter beans, tomatoes and olives

Try and get a nice tender squash or large zucchini for this recipe, so that you don't have to peel off the skin. This is good with buttery new potatoes and a cooked green vegetable.

SERVES 4–6

1 squash or large zucchini
½oz (15g) butter, plus extra for greasing
1 large onion, chopped
2 garlic cloves, crushed
4 tomatoes, chopped (or use canned ones)
6oz (175g) butter beans, soaked, cooked, and drained (see pages 176–7) or use 2 x 14oz (400g) cans, drained
1 tbsp chopped fresh parsley
4oz (125g) grated cheese
handful of pitted black olives
salt and freshly ground black pepper

FOR THE TOPPING

about ¼ cup dried breadcrumbs
2 tbsp (25g) butter

Preheat the oven to 400°F (200°C). Wash the squash and cut off the stem. Cut in half lengthways and scoop out and discard the seeds. If the squash is a bit on the tough side, or if you want to speed up the cooking time, you can par-cook it in salted boiling water for 5 minutes, then drain it well. This is not necessary if the squash is young and tender.

Put the squash halves into a greased shallow baking dish.

continued next page

Melt the butter and fry the onion and garlic for 10 minutes, but don't brown them, then add the tomatoes and cook for a further 3–4 minutes. Stir in the butter beans, parsley, grated cheese, the olives (if using) and salt and pepper to taste.

Pile the mixture into the two marrow halves, sprinkle with breadcrumbs and dot with a little butter.

Bake in the oven for about 45 minutes or until the marrow halves are tender and the top golden brown.

Stuffed squash baked with butter and thyme

Try serving this with gravy, apple and redcurrant sauce, roast potatoes and spinach for a vegetarian-style roast dinner.

SERVES 4–6

1 fat squash or large zucchni (about 2¼lb (1kg))
12oz (350g) fresh breadcrumbs
4oz (125g) butter, softened
juice and grated rind of 1 small lemon
1 tsp dried marjoram
3–4oz (75–125g) fresh parsley, chopped
salt and freshly ground black pepper
2 tbsp (25g) butter
a small bunch of thyme, crushed, or 1 tbsp dried thyme

Preheat the oven to 400°F (200°C). Cut the stalk off the squash, then peel the squash, keeping it whole. Cut a slice off one end and scoop out the seeds to leave a cavity for stuffing.

Make the stuffing by mixing together the breadcrumbs, all except for 2 tbsp (25g) of the butter, the lemon juice and rind, and the marjoram and parsley. Season with salt and pepper.

Push the stuffing mixture into the cavity of the squash, then replace the sliced-off end and secure with a skewer. Spread the remaining butter all over the outside of the squash and sprinkle with the crushed thyme.

Put the squash in an ovenproof dish, sprinkle with any thyme that's left over, cover loosely with a piece of greaseproof paper and bake for about 1 hour or until the squash is tender and can be pierced easily with the point of a sharp knife.

Squash with crispy stuffing v

Tender squash topped with a crunchy nut and crumb stuffing.

SERVES 4–6

1 squash or large zucchini
4 tbsp olive oil, plus extra for greasing
6oz (175g) fresh wholegrain breadcrumbs
6oz (175g) finely grated nuts (such as almonds, hazelnuts, Brazil nuts, walnuts or a mixture)
8oz (225g) button mushrooms, sliced
4 tomatoes, skinned (see page 40) and sliced
1 small onion, grated
salt and freshly ground black pepper
a few sprigs of fresh flat-leaf parsley and tomato slices, to garnish

Preheat the oven to 400°F (200°C).

Prepare the squash as for squash stuffed with butter beans (see page 153).

Put the squash halves into a greased shallow baking dish.

Fry the breadcrumbs and nuts together in the oil until crisp and golden, then add the mushrooms, tomatoes, grated onion, salt and pepper.

Spoon the mixture into the squash halves, pressing it together as you do so and piling it up well.

Bake for about 45 minutes or until the squash is tender and the filling brown and crisp on top. Decorate with the parsley and sliced tomato.

Opposite: Fennel with orange and pine nut stuffing (see page 153)

Croustade of mushrooms

Here is a slightly updated version of one of my most popular recipes — I've lost count of the number of times I've been asked for it!

SERVES 6 ❄
FOR THE BASE
4oz (125g) fresh breadcrumbs
4oz (125g) ground almonds, cashew
    nuts, hazelnuts or Brazil nuts
½ stick (50g) butter, softened
4oz (125g) sliced almonds or pine nuts
1 garlic clove, crushed
½ tsp herbes de Provence

FOR THE TOPPING
1lb (450g) mushrooms
2 tbsp (25g) butter
2 heaped tsp cornstarch
2 x 10oz cartons sour cream
salt and freshly ground black pepper
freshly grated nutmeg
2 tomatoes, sliced
1 tbsp chopped fresh flat-leaf
    parsley, to garnish

Preheat the oven to 450°F (230°C). First make the croustade by mixing together the breadcrumbs and ground almonds or other milled nuts. Blend in the butter with a fork and stir in the sliced almonds or pine nuts, garlic and herbes de Provence.

Press the mixture down very firmly on a large, flat dish — a 12in (30cm) pizza plate is ideal. Bake for 15–17 minutes or until crisp and golden brown.

Meanwhile make the topping. Wash and slice mushrooms, then sauté in the butter until tender. If they make a lot of liquid, either turn up the heat and let it bubble away for a few minutes or drain it off.

Sprinkle the cornstarch over the mushrooms and stir, then pour in the sour cream and stir over the heat for a minute or two until thickened.

Remove from the heat, season well with salt, pepper and nutmeg. Spoon the mushroom mixture on top of the croustade, top with tomato slices and sprinkle with a little salt and pepper. Return to oven for 10–15 minutes to heat through, then serve sprinkled with parsley.

VARIATIONS
Croustade of asparagus

For this delicious variation, replace the mushrooms with 1½lb (700g) trimmed asparagus, cut into 1in (2.5cm) lengths. You could cook the asparagus in boiling water for 8–10 minutes or until tender; or you could rub the asparagus with olive oil and roast it in the oven while the croustade bakes; take it out when it's tender. Mix the sour cream with the cornstarch and heat gently in a saucepan, stirring all the time, until slightly thickened. Stir the asparagus into the sour cream, season with salt, pepper and a pinch or two of nutmeg, and spoon onto the croustade base.

Croustade of leeks

Make in exactly the same way, frying 1lb (450g) sliced leeks in the butter until tender, instead of the mushrooms.

Nut mince v

Quick, easy and tasty, this is one of the vegetarian recipes from my childhood, but still good today. The garnish of fried bread gives a delicious contrast of texture.

SERVES 4 ❄
1 large onion, chopped
½ tsp dried basil
2 tbsp olive oil
2 x 14oz cans chopped tomatoes
8oz (225g) finely ground walnuts,
    almonds or hazelnuts
125g (4oz) fresh wholegrain
    breadcrumbs
2 tbsp sweet pickle or tomato
    ketchup
salt and freshly ground black pepper
triangles of fried bread, to garnish

Fry the onion with the basil in the oil for about 10 minutes or until lightly browned.

Add the tomatoes and all the other ingredients. Cook gently for 20 minutes, stirring from time to time.

Taste, season and serve garnished with small triangles of fried bread or wholegrain toast and parsley.

VARIATIONS
Easy vegetarian shepherd's pie v

Make the nut mince as described, put it into a shallow ovenproof baking dish, top with creamy mashed potatoes (made from 2¼lb (1kg) potatoes), a few dots of butter or vegan margarine, and bake at 400°F (200°C) for 30–40 minutes or until golden brown and bubbling.

Hazelnut croquettes in tomato sauce

In this recipe, hazelnut croquettes are baked in a fresh-tasting tomato sauce. These are delicious served with buttery noodles, grated Pecorino cheese and a crisp green salad with an olive oil dressing.

SERVES 3–4 ❈
1 tbsp olive oil, plus extra for greasing
2 onions, chopped
1 garlic clove, crushed
14oz can chopped tomatoes
salt and freshly ground black pepper
4oz (125g) hazelnuts, toasted (see page 139) and grated
2oz (50g) fresh wholegrain breadcrumbs
2oz (50g) Cheddar cheese, finely grated
2 rounded tsp tomato purée
1 egg, beaten
½ tsp dried thyme

Heat the oil in a medium-sized saucepan and fry the onions for 10 minutes or until softened but not browned.

Remove half the onions to a bowl and set aside for the moment — this is for the croquettes.

Add the garlic and tomatoes to the onions in the pan, and cook for a further 15 minutes or until the tomatoes have collapsed and reduced to a purée. Purée with an electric hand blender or in a food processor. Season with salt and pepper.

Preheat the oven to 350°F (180°C).

Make the croquettes by adding the grated hazelnuts to the fried onions in the bowl that you set aside earlier, and mix in the breadcrumbs, cheese, tomato purée, beaten egg, dried thyme and salt and pepper to taste.

Form the mixture into eight croquettes and place in a greased shallow ovenproof baking dish. Pour the tomato sauce over and around the croquettes and bake them for 25–30 minutes or until they are puffy but firm to the touch.

VARIATION
Hazelnut croquettes in ratatouille

A delicious variation is to bake the nut croquettes in ratatouille. Prepare and cook the ratatouille, as described on page 132, and put it into a shallow ovenproof dish. Add the nut croquettes and bake as described. These go well with fluffy couscous or cooked rice and a green salad.

Onions stuffed with lentils, cheese and thyme

You need really large onions for this warming, winter dish. They go well with Bircher potatoes (see page 128), which you can cook in the oven at the same time.

SERVES 4
4 large onions
14oz can green lentils, drained and rinsed, or 3½oz (100g) green lentils, cooked (see page 177) and drained
1 garlic clove, crushed
1 tbsp tomato purée
1 tbsp grated Cheddar cheese
½ tsp dried thyme
salt and freshly ground black pepper
olive oil, for greasing

Peel the onions and cook them for 15 minutes in boiling salted water, drain and cool.

Preheat the oven to 400°F (200°C).

With a sharp knife scoop out the inside of the onions, leaving the outer layers intact. Chop up the scooped-out onion flesh and mix it with the lentils, garlic, tomato purée, cheese and thyme. Season with salt and pepper.

Divide the mixture between the onions, pushing it well down into the cavities.

Put the onions into an oiled oven-proof dish and, if there's any of the stuffing mixture left over, scatter that round the onions. Bake for 30–40 minutes or until the onions are tender and filling lightly browned.

Italian stuffed onions

This dish, with its slightly unusual combination of flavors may seem bizarre but try it. The mixture of sweet and savory works really well, like cheese and chutney or curry and bananas. I like to use big Spanish onions to make this — they come into the stores in early September.

SERVES 4

4 large Spanish onions (unpeeled)
1 tbsp (15g) butter, plus extra for greasing
4 French macaroons
3oz (75g) fresh wholegrain breadcrumbs
½ tsp ground cinnamon
½ tsp ground cloves
½ tsp freshly grated nutmeg
2 eggs, beaten
2oz (50g) Parmesan-style cheese, Pecorino or mature Cheddar, grated
1–2oz (25–50g) golden raisins
milk (optional)
salt and freshly ground black pepper
couscous and a green salad or some creamy cooked spinach (see page 134), to serve

Rinse the onions but don't peel them. Put them into a large saucepan of water and simmer for about 20 minutes or until they feel tender when pierced with the point of a sharp knife. (Don't let them cook completely at this stage.) Drain the onions.

When they are cool enough to handle, remove the skins and root ends and cut the onions in half horizontally. Scoop out the center of each half, making a nice cavity for the stuffing and leaving three or four layers of onion. Arrange the onion halves in a greased shallow ovenproof dish.

Preheat the oven to 350°F (180°C). To make the stuffing, chop the scooped-out onion flesh fairly finely and put it into a bowl.

Crush the macaroons with the back of a wooden spoon or a rolling pin, and add to the onions, along with the breadcrumbs, spices, eggs, cheese and raisins.

Stir until everything is well mixed to a softish consistency. You might need to add a drop or two of milk if the natural juiciness of the onions together with the eggs is not sufficient. Season with salt and a good grinding of pepper, then spoon the mixture into the onion cavities, piling them full.

Put a piece of butter on top of each and bake, uncovered, for 30 minutes or until golden brown and bubbling.

Serve with couscous and a green salad or some creamy cooked spinach.

Lesco v

This spicy Hungarian stew is rather similar to the Italian peperonata on page 125, but it's made with green peppers and has a generous seasoning of paprika. You can serve it Hungarian style with a fried egg on top, but I prefer it with some basmati rice or couscous.

SERVES 4

1lb (450g) green peppers
2 onions
3 tbsp olive oil
2 garlic cloves, crushed
2 tbsp paprika
14oz can tomatoes
salt and freshly ground black pepper

Slice the peppers into even-sized pieces, discarding the seeds and stem.

Peel and chop the onions, then fry them in the oil in a large saucepan for about 5 minutes or until golden brown.

Remove from the heat and stir in the garlic, paprika, peppers, tomatoes and a seasoning of salt and pepper.

Cover and cook gently for about 30 minutes or until all the vegetables are tender.

Check the seasoning and serve.

Roasted pointed red peppers with feta and cherry tomatoes

These peppers are quick and simple to do and everyone loves them. They go very well with warm, fluffy couscous and, strange though as it may sound, roasted baby parsnips, which are included in this recipe.

SERVES 4
2 pointed red Ramiro peppers
olive oil, for brushing
7oz (200g) feta cheese
20 cherry tomatoes, halved
2 tbsp pesto (see page 225)
2 tbsp water
freshly ground black pepper

FOR THE PARSNIPS
14oz (400g) baby parsnips
2 tbsp olive oil

Preheat the oven to 375°F (190°C). Halve the peppers lengthways using a sharp knife, and cut right through the stem as well if you can. Scoop out the cores, rinsing away any stray seeds under the cold tap.

Put the peppers, cut side up, in a roasting pan or shallow oven-proof dish that has been lightly brushed with oil.

Drain the feta cheese and pat dry with paper towels, then cut into small dice, about ⅓in (7mm). Put it into a bowl with the cherry tomatoes.

Mix the pesto with the water to loosen it a little, and add to the bowl along with a grinding of black pepper — you probably won't need to add salt because both the feta and the pesto are salty. Stir gently until the tomatoes and feta are coated with the fragrant herby green liquid.

Spoon the mixture on top of the pepper halves, dividing it between them. Bake in the oven for 15–20 minutes or until the peppers are tender, the filling flecked with brown and the kitchen smells gorgeous.

If you want to serve the parsnips, cut them into halves or quarters, depending on how big they are, then parboil them in boiling water, for 3–4 minutes, until they are just tender. Drain well.

Put the parsnips into a roasting pan with the oil and stir gently until they are all coated. Bake in the oven with the peppers. Serve the peppers with the parsnips.

Peppers with lentil and tomato stuffing

When I wrote this recipe, green peppers were the only variety available. In this revised version, I use red and yellow peppers, halved rather than stuffed whole.

SERVES 4
2 red peppers
2 yellow peppers
1 tbsp olive oil, plus extra for greasing
1 large onion, chopped
2 garlic cloves, crushed
4 tomatoes, chopped
14oz can green lentils, drained and rinsed
2 tbsp pesto
salt and freshly ground black pepper

FOR THE TOPPING
2oz (50g) fresh breadcrumbs
2oz (50g) Parmesan-style cheese, grated

Preheat the oven to 400°F (200°C).

Using a sharp knife, cut the peppers in half lengthways slicing right down through the stems. Remove the core and seeds, rinse and place, cut side up, in a lightly greased shallow baking dish.

Fry the onion in the oil for 10 minutes, stirring in the garlic a minute or two before the onion's done. Add the tomatoes, lentils and pesto. Season with salt and pepper to taste.

Divide the mixture between the four peppers, piling them up well.

Sprinkle the breadcrumbs and grated cheese over and bake in the oven for 30–40 minutes or until the peppers are tender and the topping golden brown and crisp.

Peppers with olive stuffing

Easy, frugal and tasty. Serve with a green salad.

SERVES 4

4 red peppers
¼ cup olive oil, plus extra for greasing
1 onion, chopped
2 garlic cloves, crushed
6oz (175g) fresh breadcrumbs
4 tomatoes, chopped
6oz (175g) grated cheese
4oz (125g) pitted olives, green or black
1 tbsp chopped fresh flat-leaf parsley
salt and freshly ground black pepper
a few drops of Tabasco sauce

Preheat the oven to 350°F (180°C). Using a sharp knife, cut the peppers in half lengthways, slicing right down through the stems. Remove the core and seeds, rinse the peppers and place, cut side up, in a lightly greased shallow baking dish.

Fry the onion lightly in the olive oil in a large saucepan, covered, for 10 minutes, until tender.

Remove the pan from the heat and add the breadcrumbs, tomatoes, grated cheese, olives, parsley, and salt, pepper and Tabasco to taste.

Fill the peppers with the olive stuffing and bake for 40 minutes or until the filling is golden brown and the peppers tender.

Peppers stuffed with pine nuts, apricots and raisins v

There's a Middle Eastern flavor to this fragrantly spiced dish. The list of ingredients may look long, but the method is easy.

SERVES 4

1 onion, chopped
1 tbsp olive oil
1 garlic clove, crushed
2 tsp ground coriander
2 tsp ground cinnamon
6oz (175g) couscous
1½oz (40g) raisins
1½oz (40g) dried apricots, chopped
4 red peppers
2 tomatoes, chopped
2oz (50g) pine nuts
3oz (75g) pitted black olives
1 tbsp chopped fresh mint
1 tbsp chopped fresh flat-leaf parsley
salt and freshly ground black pepper
1 tbsp tomato purée
5fl oz (150ml) water

Fry the onion in the oil, in a large, covered saucepan for 8 minutes. Add the garlic, coriander and cinnamon and cook for 1–2 minutes more. Take the pan off the heat.

Preheat the oven to 350°F (180°C). Put the couscous into a bowl with the raisins and chopped apricots, cover generously with boiling water and set aside for a few minutes for the couscous to swell.

Slice the tops off the peppers, retaining them, and scoop out the seeds. Stand the peppers in a deep baking dish.

Drain any excess water from the couscous and mix it with the fried onion mixture, the tomatoes, pine nuts, olives, mint and parsley. Season to taste with salt and pepper.

Fill the peppers with the couscous mixture and replace the tops as lids. If there is any mixture left over, put it in the dish around the peppers.

Mix the tomato purée with the water, season with salt and pepper and pour round the peppers. Bake for 1 hour or until the peppers are very tender.

Peppers stuffed with almonds and red wine

Here red peppers are stuffed with a tasty filling of mushrooms, wine, breadcrumbs, nuts, and tomatoes. Great with creamy mash and green beans or baby zucchini tossed in butter and chopped fresh tarragon.

SERVES 6
3 red peppers
olive oil, for greasing
4oz (125g) almonds, finely grated
4oz (125g) Emmental cheese, grated
2oz (50g) fresh wholewheat
   breadcrumbs
8oz can tomatoes
4oz (125g) mushrooms, chopped
½ cup red wine (or dry cider or good
   vegetable stock)
1 garlic clove, crushed
salt and freshly ground black pepper

FOR THE TOPPING
¼ cup dried breadcrumbs
¼ cup grated Gruyère cheese

Preheat the oven to 375°F (190°C). Using a sharp knife, cut the peppers in half, slicing right down through the stems. Remove the core and seeds, rinse the peppers and place, cup side up, in a lightly greased shallow baking dish.

Next make the stuffing: mix together the almonds, Emmental cheese, breadcrumbs, tomatoes, mushrooms, wine (or cider or stock) and garlic, adding plenty of salt and pepper to taste.

Spoon the stuffing into the peppers, dividing it between them. Sprinkle with dried breadcrumbs and grated Gruyère cheese.

Bake, uncovered, for about 40 minutes or until the peppers are tender and the stuffing golden brown.

Potato bake

Potatoes are a wonderful food: cheap, popular and nutritious, containing iron, vitamin C and protein, as well as fiber. I like dishes that make them into a main meal. This bake makes a simple, homey supper that children love. It's good with a tomato sauce and a green vegetable. You can leave the skins on the potatoes, but I think it's better if they're peeled.

SERVES 4
1lb (450g) potatoes, peeled
½oz (15g) butter
1 garlic clove, crushed
salt and freshly ground black pepper
4oz (125g) grated cheese
¼ cup milk

Preheat the oven to 325°F (160°C). Slice the potatoes thinly — this is quickly done with a mandolin or the slicing side of a grater, or cut them by hand.

Mix the butter and garlic and use half to grease a shallow ovenproof dish.

Put a layer of potatoes in the base of the dish, sprinkle with salt, pepper and some of the cheese. Continue like this until everything is in, ending with the cheese.

Pour the milk over the top, dot with the remaining butter. Cover with foil and bake for 1 hour. Remove foil and bake for an additional 30 minutes or until the potato is tender.

Potato cakes

Potato cakes are delicious — creamy on the inside, crisp on the outside. If you add a little protein, in the form of grated cheese, chopped nuts or sunflower seeds, they make a delicious main dish.

SERVES 4
1lb (450g) potatoes
about 5fl oz (150ml) milk
4oz (125g) grated cheese, or
   chopped nuts (any type) or
   sunflower seeds
2 tbsp chopped fresh flat-leaf
   parsley
salt and freshly ground black pepper
2oz (50g) wholewheat flour
2 tbsp olive oil

Scrub the potatoes, cover with water and boil until tender. Drain, cool slightly, then slip off the skins with a small sharp knife.

Mash the potatoes, adding enough milk to make a firm consistency.

Stir in the cheese, nuts or sunflower seeds, the parsley and seasoning. Add some more milk if necessary — the mixture must be manageable but not too dry.

Divide into eight pieces, coat in flour and fry in the oil until crisp on both sides.

Drain and serve immediately with salad or with a tomato or parsley sauce and cooked vegetables.

Jacket potato boats

A dish from my childhood, which my children loved too. Children often like it with a "finger salad" of lettuce, tomato, cucumber and carrot sticks.

SERVES 4
4 large potatoes
2 tbsp (25g) butter
6oz (175g) Cheddar cheese, grated
a pinch of cayenne pepper
5fl oz (150ml) milk
salt and freshly ground black pepper

Scrub the potatoes, score them horizontally round the middle and bake at 450°F (230°C for 1 hour or until tender.

Cut around the score marks and pull apart.

Scoop out the potato flesh, mash it well, add the butter, cheese, a pinch of cayenne, the milk, and salt and pepper.

Pile the mixture back into the skins and brown under a hot broiler, or put back into the oven for 20 minutes until browned.

Potato and mushroom stew with sour cream

Simple ingredients, but together they make a delicious stew. Serve with a cooked green vegetable or green salad.

SERVES 4
2lb (900g) potatoes
1 onion
1 garlic clove
6oz (175g) button mushrooms
3 tbsp olive oil
1 tbsp mild paprika (look for Hungarian "rose" paprika)
2 tbsp (25g) all-purpose flour
15fl oz (425ml) vegetable stock
5fl oz (150ml) sour cream or natural yogurt
salt and freshly ground black pepper

Peel the potatoes and cut them into even-sized chunks, peel and chop the onion, crush the garlic, wash the mushrooms and cut them into halves or quarters if necessary.

Heat the oil in a large saucepan and fry the onion for about 5 minutes until golden, then stir in the garlic, potatoes, paprika and flour and cook for an additional minute or two.

Add the stock and bring to the boil. Put a lid on the saucepan and leave it over a gentle heat for about 20 minutes until the potatoes are very nearly tender, then add the mushrooms and cook for another 3–4 minutes.

Put the sour cream or yogurt into a small bowl and gradually add to it a ladleful of the liquid from the saucepan; mix well, then pour this into the saucepan and heat gently until the mixture is very hot.

Season to taste and serve.

Sweet potatoes with pine nuts, arugula and goat cheese

The sweet potatoes take only moments to prepare and 30 minutes to cook while you calmly slice the goat cheese and wash and dress the greens; quicker than ordering a take-out, and much better.

SERVES 4
4 sweet potatoes (about 12oz (350g) each)
3oz (75g) arugula
a little olive oil for dressing
2 x 3½oz packs soft white goat cheese
2oz (50g) pine nuts, toasted (see page 140), to garnish

Preheat the oven to 350°F (180°C).

Wash the sweet potatoes — no need to peel — scoring them lengthways down the center, and place them in a roasting pan. Roast for 30 minutes or until they feel soft when squeezed.

Toss the arugula in a little olive oil, to make it glossy, and divide between four plates.

Put a baked sweet potato on each plate, next to the arugula. Squeeze each sweet potato to open the top a little, spoon on the goat cheese and sprinkle with the pine nuts. Serve at once.

Red cabbage and chestnut casserole v

This is real warming winter food, a rich burgundy-colored casserole of succulent red cabbage and sweet-tasting chestnuts cooked with butter, onions and red wine. It's lovely served as a main dish with jacket potatoes that have been split and filled with sour cream and chopped chives. If there's any left over, it's very good cold as a salad. I use vacuum-packed chestnuts for this but you could use fresh, frozen or dried (see page 139 for how to prepare these).

SERVES 3–4
1 large onion, chopped
½ stick (50g) butter or ¼ cup olive oil
1½lb (700g) red cabbage
2 x 7oz packets vacuum-packed chestnuts
1¼ cups (275ml) red wine
salt and freshly ground black pepper
sugar

Preheat the oven to 300°F (150°C). Fry the onion in the butter or oil for 10 minutes, in a large saucepan, covered, until tender.

Wash and shred the cabbage, then add this to the onion and mix well so that it gets coated with the butter or oil.

Stir in the chestnuts, wine and some salt and pepper.

Bring to the boil, then transfer it to an ovenproof casserole dish, cover with a lid and bake slowly for 2–3 hours or until the cabbage is very tender.

Check the seasoning — you'll probably need to add more salt and pepper and some sugar to bring out the flavor.

This dish can be made in advance and reheated (in fact, it actually improves the flavor). It can also be cooked at the bottom of a hotter oven if you want to bake jacket potatoes (see page 128) at the same time.

Red cabbage stuffed with chestnuts

The sweetness of chestnuts goes particularly well with red cabbage and if you add butter and red wine too you'll get a really rich-tasting, warming dish that's just right for the winter when chestnuts and cabbage are in season. It's delicious with creamy mashed potatoes. I use vacuum-packed roasted chestnuts for ease and speed, but you could use fresh, frozen or dried.

SERVES 6
1 small–medium red cabbage, about 3lb 5oz (1.5kg)
1 stick (125g) butter
2 large onions, chopped
2 x 7oz packets vacuum-packed chestnuts
2 tbsp freshly squeezed lemon juice
salt and freshly ground black pepper
2 carrots, sliced
1 tbsp redcurrant jelly
1¼ cups (275ml) red wine

Wash and trim the cabbage, removing any tough or damaged leaves and cutting the core end level so the cabbage will sit upright.

Slice a lid from the top of the cabbage, and using a small sharp knife and a spoon, scoop out as much of the inside of the cabbage as possible, leaving a neat, good-sized cavity for stuffing.

Chop the cabbage that you've scooped out fairly finely.

Heat half the butter in a large saucepan and fry half the onions for about 5 minutes, without browning, then stir in the chopped-up cabbage and cook for another

continued next page

5 minutes, with a lid on the saucepan, stirring occasionally.

Add the chestnuts and half the lemon juice and season with salt and pepper. Leave to one side.

Put the whole cabbage into another large saucepan half filled with cold water. Bring to a boil and simmer for 2 minutes with a lid on the saucepan. Drain and rinse the cabbage under cold water.

Melt the remaining butter in a saucepan that's large enough to hold the whole cabbage, and fry the remaining onion and the carrots for 5 minutes.

Mix the redcurrant jelly and the rest of the lemon juice with the onion and carrots, add some salt and pepper, then place the whole cabbage on top and fill the cavity with the chestnut mixture, piling it up high.

Pour the wine around the sides of the cabbage, put the saucepan over a low heat and cover with a lid. Leave it to cook very gently for about 3 hours or until the cabbage feels beautifully tender when pierced with the point of a sharp knife.

Serve straight from the cooking pot.

Salsify with white wine and mushrooms

Cooked like this, in a wine-flavored lemon mayonnaise sauce, with a topping of crisp crumbs and a garnish of fresh lemon, salsify is excellent as a main course or starter. If you're serving this as a main course, accompany with a simply cooked green vegetable or buttered new potatoes.

SERVES 4

2¼lb (1kg) salsify or scorzonera
3 tbsp freshly squeezed lemon juice
salt and freshly ground black pepper
6 rounded tbsp good-quality or homemade mayonnaise (see pages 76–7)
8oz (225g) fromage frais
¼ cup dry white wine or cider
Dijon mustard
8oz (225g) button mushrooms, trimmed
2oz (50g) fresh wholewheat breadcrumbs
2oz (50g) Gruyère cheese, grated

Peel the salsify or scorzonera roots and cut them into 1in (2.5cm) pieces. As they're prepared, put them into a saucepan containing 3½ cups (1 liter) cold water and 2 tablespoons of the lemon juice — this will help to preserve their color.

When the salsify is all prepared, put the saucepan over the heat, bring to a boil and cook for about 10 minutes or until the salsify feels tender when pierced with the point of a sharp knife. Drain, sprinkle with the remaining lemon juice and season with salt and pepper.

While the salsify is cooking, make the sauce by mixing together the mayonnaise, fromage frais, white wine or cider and a dash of mustard if necessary. Season with salt and pepper.

Preheat the oven to 400°F (200°C).

Put the salsify into a large, shallow, ovenproof dish and add the mushrooms; pour the sauce over the top.

Cover completely with the breadcrumbs and cheese and bake for 30–40 minutes or until heated through and golden on top. (Timing will depend partly on the depth of the dish you've used, but be careful not to overcook, or the sauce may separate.) If the top isn't crisp enough, finish it off quickly under a hot broiler. Serve at once.

Salsify baked in a lemon sauce

Here is another salsify dish that's quick to make, creamy and delicate.

SERVES 4–6

2¼lb (1kg) salsify or scorzonera
salt
3 tbsp (25g) butter, plus extra for greasing
2 tbsp all-purpose flour
1¼ cups (275ml) water
2 tbsp freshly squeezed lemon juice
10fl oz (275ml) sour cream
1 tsp Dijon mustard
freshly ground black pepper

FOR THE TOPPING

Heaping ¼ cup fresh breadcrumbs
2 tbsp (25g) butter, diced

Peel the salsify, cut into 2in (5cm) lengths and cook in enough boiling salted water to cover, until just tender. Drain and put into a lightly greased shallow gratin dish.

Set the oven to 350°F (180°C). Melt the butter in a small saucepan and stir in the flour; when it bubbles add the water and stir until smooth and thick.

Remove from the heat and mix in the lemon juice, sour cream and mustard, and salt and pepper to taste.

Spoon the sauce over the salsify, sprinkle with breadcrumbs, dot with butter and bake for 40–45 minutes or until heated through and crisp on top.

Spinach roulade

This classic dish isn't nearly as tricky to make as it may seem. It's very often served cold, as a first course — and it's easier to roll up when cold — but I also like it hot, as a light main course, along with some lemon roast potatoes (see page 130), tomato sauce and baby carrots.

SERVES 4

1lb (450g) fresh spinach or 6oz (175g) chopped frozen spinach
1 tbsp (15g) butter
4 eggs, separated
freshly grated nutmeg
¼ cup grated Parmesan-style cheese
salt and freshly ground black pepper

FOR THE FILLING

6oz (175g) button mushrooms
1 tbsp (15g) butter
1 heaped tbsp cornstarch
1¼cups (275ml) ½ and ½

Preheat the oven to 400°F (200°C). Line a shallow Jelly roll tin, 9in x 13in (23cm x 33cm), with baking parchment to cover the base of the pan and to extend 2in (5cm) up each side.

If you're using fresh spinach, wash, drain well, then cook for a few minutes until fully wilted in a dry saucepan with only the water that clings to the leaves. Frozen spinach just needs thawing. In either case, drain the spinach into a colander and press it very well to extract as much water as possible.

Chop the spinach and mix with the butter, egg yolks and a seasoning of salt, pepper and nutmeg to make a smooth, creamy-looking purée. This can be done in a food processor or with an electric hand blender if you prefer.

Whisk the egg whites until they form stiff peaks and fold them into the spinach mixture.

Pour the mixture into the prepared pan, level the top and sprinkle with 2 tablespoons of the Parmesan-style cheese. Bake for 10–12 minutes or until the top is springy.

While the roulade is cooking, make the filling. Wipe and slice the mushrooms and fry them in the butter for 5 minutes or until tender. Mix together the cornstarch and ½ and ½; add this to the mushrooms and stir over the heat briefly until slightly thickened. Season with salt, pepper and nutmeg. Keep the mixture warm, but don't let it boil.

Have ready a large piece of baking parchment sprinkled with the remaining cheese. Turn the roulade out on to this, peeling off the lining paper.

Spread the filling over the roulade, then roll it up like a Jelly roll, starting at one of the long ends. Slide the roulade onto a warmed serving dish. Return to the oven for 5 minutes to heat through, then serve immediately.

Sweetcorn pudding

This is often served as an accompaniment to meat, but I think it makes a good light main dish in its own right, and one that usually goes down well with children. It's economical and quick to make.

SERVES 3–4

1¼ cups (275ml) milk
2 tbps (25g) butter, plus extra for greasing
4oz (125g) bread, weighed with the crusts removed
12oz can no-sugar-added sweetcorn kernels, drained
1 egg or 2 egg yolks
1 tbsp chopped fresh flat-leaf parsley
½ tsp paprika
salt and freshly ground black pepper
a little grated cheese

Preheat the oven to 375°F (190°C). Put the milk and butter into a saucepan and heat gently until the butter has melted.

Remove from the heat and with your fingers crumble the bread into the milk — don't worry if there are some lumpy pieces.

Leave to one side for a few minutes to allow the bread to soften, then mash it a bit, and add the sweetcorn, egg, parsley, paprika and salt and pepper to taste.

Spoon the mixture into a greased ovenproof dish and sprinkle with grated cheese.

Bake the pudding for 35–40 minutes or until set and golden brown.

Tomato pie

A quick and easy supper dish.

SERVES 4

1lb (450g) creamy mashed potatoes
8oz (225g) grated cheese
1 small onion, grated
salt and freshly ground black pepper
freshly grated nutmeg
1lb (450g) tomatoes, skinned (see page 40)
a pinch of dried basil
1 tbsp (15g) butter

Preheat the oven to 400°F (200°C). Add the grated cheese and onion to the potatoes, mix well and season with salt, pepper and nutmeg.

Spread half the mixture in a shallow buttered baking dish; smooth well to form base of pie.

Slice the tomatoes, season with salt and pepper and basil, and spread over the potato base.

Spreading with the rest of the potato to cover.

Rough up the top with the prongs of a fork and dot with the butter. Bake for 30–40 minutes or until golden brown.

VARIATIONS

Mushroom pie

Use 8–12oz (225–350g) sliced and lightly fried button mushrooms instead of the tomatoes.

Sweetcorn pie

Use 8oz (225g) packet of frozen sweetcorn, cooked according to the directions on the packet, instead of the tomatoes.

Stuffed tomatoes à la provençale v

In late summer, when large heirloom or beefsteak tomatoes are cheap and plentiful, they're good prepared with this simple garlic and herb stuffing. Serve with couscous and a crisp green salad.

SERVES 4

8 large tomatoes (about 1½lb (700g))
salt
1 large onion, chopped
5fl oz (150ml) olive oil
4 garlic cloves, crushed
3oz (75g) fine fresh wholewheat breadcrumbs
¼ cup chopped fresh flat-leaf parsley
½ tsp dried thyme
freshly ground black pepper

Cut a thin slice off the top of each tomato and leave these slices to one side to use as lids later.

Using a teaspoon, scoop out the tomato pulp to leave a cavity for stuffing (you won't need the pulp for this recipe but it can be used to flavor sauces and soups).

Sprinkle the inside of each tomato with a little salt then turn them upside down on a large plate and leave them while you prepare the filling.

Heat the olive oil in a large saucepan and fry the onion until it's golden, then take it off the heat and add the garlic, breadcrumbs, herbs and a good seasoning of salt and pepper.

Set the oven to 200°C (400°F). Place the tomatoes in a lightly greased baking dish; fill each with some of the stuffing mixture and arrange the reserved lids on top.

Bake for 15–20 minutes to heat them through. Serve at once.

Tomatoes stuffed with rice v

Like the stuffed tomatoes in the previous recipe, this can be served either as a starter or as a main course. If you're making it a main course, it's a good idea to begin with a starter like hummus and finish with yogurt and fruit, all of which add protein to the meal and continue the Middle Eastern theme.

SERVES 4

4oz (125g) long-grain brown rice
1¼ cups (275ml) water
salt
8 large tomatoes (about 1½lb (700g))
2 tbsp olive oil, plus extra for greasing
1 onion, chopped
2 garlic cloves, crushed
6 tbsp tomato purée
6 tbsp chopped fresh flat-leaf parsley
2 tbsp chopped fresh mint
a pinch of oregano
freshly ground black pepper
5fl oz (150ml) vegetable stock or red wine

Put the rice into a heavy-based saucepan with the water and half a teaspoon of salt; bring it to a boil then turn the heat right down, put a lid on the pan and cook the rice very gently for about 40 minutes or until it's tender and all the water has been absorbed.

While the rice is cooking prepare the tomatoes. Cut a small piece off the top of each and hollow out the center, using a teaspoon — keep the sliced-off tomato tops to use as lids later and the pulp for the filling. Sprinkle some salt inside each tomato then leave them upside down to drain.

Preheat the oven to 350°F (180°C).

To make the stuffing, heat the oil in a fairly large saucepan and fry the onion until it begins to soften (about 5 minutes) then add the garlic, rice, scooped-out tomato pulp, half the purée, the herbs and seasoning. Cook over a brisk heat until the mixture is fairly dry.

Arrange the tomatoes in a greased ovenproof dish, fill with the stuffing and put the reserved tops back as lids. Mix the remaining tomato purée with the stock or red wine and a little salt and pepper and pour it round the tomatoes, then bake them for about 20 minutes until they're tender.

Vegetable casserole v

You can use all kinds of vegetables for this casserole. It's good served just as it is, or with an extra cooked green vegetable, such as sprouts, and with grated cheese served separately for people to add at the table if they wish.

SERVES 4

1 tbsp olive oil
3 onions, sliced
1lb (450g) carrots, sliced
450g (1lb) potatoes, peeled and cut into even-sized pieces
2 stalks of celery, sliced
4–6oz (125–175g) button mushrooms, sliced
2 tbsp all-purpose flour
2 cups (575ml) water
2 vegetable stock cubes
1 tbsp tomato paste
2 bay leaves
salt and freshly ground black pepper
a pinch of sugar (optional)

Preheat the oven to 375°F (190°C).

Heat the oil in a large saucepan and fry the onions for 5 minutes until golden.

Add the rest of the vegetables and fry for a further couple of minutes, stirring often.

Mix in the flour; when it is well distributed, add the water, stock cubes, tomato paste, bay leaves and a little salt and pepper — you won't need much because of the stock cubes.

Bring the mixture to a boil, then transfer to a casserole dish and bake for 1 hour.

Check the seasoning, adding a little sugar if you think it needs it.

Chinese vegetables with almonds

If you get all the basic preparation done in advance, the actual cooking takes only a few minutes.

SERVES 4

1lb (450g) Napa cabbage, shredded
1 large onion, finely sliced
1 large carrot, finely diced
1 turnip, peeled and finely diced
8oz (225g) button mushrooms, sliced
10oz (300g) beansprouts
1 garlic clove, crushed
2 tsp cornstarch
1 tbsp dark soy sauce
2 tsp clear honey
¼ cup fino sherry
salt
2 tbsp ground nut or rapeseed oil
4oz (125g) sliced almonds, toasted under a moderate broiler until crisp and golden
hot cooked rice, to serve

Have all the vegetables prepared, ready to cook. Put the cornstarch into a small bowl or cup and mix to a smooth paste with the soy sauce, honey, sherry and salt.

Heat the oil in a large saucepan (or a wok, if you have one) and add the cabbage, onion, carrot and turnip.

Fry, stirring often, for 3 minutes, then add the rest of the vegetables, including the garlic, and fry for a further 1–2 minutes.

Give the sherry mixture a quick stir, then pour it over the vegetables, stirring for a moment or two until thickened. Season to taste. Add the almonds then serve immediately, with the rice.

Mixed vegetable platter

I think a huge platter of different-colored vegetables makes a wonderful vegetarian meal and is easy to do; you just need enough saucepans or a stacking steamer.

SERVES 4

1lb (450g) zucchini
8oz (225g) French beans
8oz (225g) small carrots
8oz (225g) baby onions
8oz (225g) frozen sweetcorn kernels
6 tomatoes
8oz (225g) button mushrooms
2 tbsp (25g) butter
6 hardboiled eggs
juice of ½ lemon
fresh flat-leaf parsley sprigs

TO SERVE

2 cups (575ml) lemon mayonnaise, hollandaise sauce or soured cream and herb sauce (see pages 76, 66 and 70)

Wash and top and tail the zucchini and beans; peel the carrots, leaving them whole; peel the onions. Cook the vegetables in separate pans in a little boiling water until tender.

Cook the sweetcorn according to the directions on packet.

Halve the tomatoes horizontally; scoop out the pulp, and chop.

Wash and chop the mushrooms and fry gently in one-third of the butter with the tomato pulp for 5 minutes, then heap into the tomato halves. Place under a moderate broil for 5–10 minutes to cook the tomatoes until softened.

Slice the eggs and keep warm.

When ready to serve, arrange the vegetables and hardboiled eggs attractively on a large warmed platter or individual plates.

Melt rest of the butter, mix with the lemon juice and pour over the vegetables. Garnish each tomato half with a parsley sprig. Serve with the sauce of your choice.

Tip

Many other combinations of vegetables can of course be used, aiming for as colorful and varied a mixture as possible: eggplant or peppers, sliced and fried; small new potatoes or asparagus, steamed or boiled. Also any of the stuffed vegetables in this chapter can form the centerpiece and source of protein.

VARIATION

Mixed vegetable platter with cheese fondue

Omit the hardboiled eggs from the main recipe, and serve a bowl of cheese fondue in the center, for people to spoon over their vegetables. For the fondue, make half the quantity of the recipe on page 288.

Vegetable and halloumi skewers

Everyone loves these skewers. They're perfect for a vegetarian barbecue, but you can also cook them under the broil indoors if the weather turns, or you want to bring a sunshine mood inside.

MAKES 24 SKEWERS

2 x 9oz packets halloumi cheese, drained
2 firm slender zucchini, cut into ½in (1cm) thick discs
4oz (125g) button mushrooms
2 red peppers, seeded and cut into strips
fresh basil leaves, to garnish
warm pita breads, to serve

FOR THE MARINADE

¼ cup tomato ketchup
2 tbsp honey or maple syrup
4 garlic cloves, crushed
2 tbsp olive oil
2 tbsp dark soy sauce
1 tbsp red wine vinegar

You will need 24 skewers, either wooden or metal. If you are using wooden ones, soak them in cold water for 20 minutes before using to prevent burning.

Cut the cheese into 16 cubes of about ¾in (2cm). Do this carefully because halloumi breaks easily.

Make the marinade by mixing all the ingredients together in a small bowl.

Put the halloumi, zucchini and mushrooms into a shallow dish, spoon the marinade over and stir gently to make sure all the pieces are coated. Cover and leave for at least 1 hour at room temperature.

Thread the halloumi, zucchini, mushrooms and pepper strips onto the skewers, shaking any excess marinade back into the dish.

Put the skewers on the grid over hot coals or under a hot broiler and cook for 7–10 minutes or until brown around the edges, turning them once or twice to cook evenly, and brushing with extra marinade as necessary to prevent the vegetables and cheese drying out.

Transfer the cooked skewers to a serving plate, pour any remaining marinade over the skewers, garnish with basil leaves and serve them with warm pita bread.

VARIATION

Vegan vegetable skewers v

Use a 9oz packet of plain tofu instead of the halloumi.

Spiced vegetables with dal v

This is a lovely lightly spiced dish. Serve with spiced rice (see page 252), poppadums and mango chutney.

SERVES 4

3 tbsp olive oil
1 onion, chopped
1 large garlic clove, crushed
1 tsp turmeric
1 tsp ground coriander
1 tsp ground cumin
1 bay leaf
2 carrots (about 8oz (225g)), thinly sliced
1lb (450g) potatoes, peeled and cubed
2 leeks, sliced
5fl oz (150ml) water
salt and freshly ground black pepper
dal (see page 194)

Heat the oil in a fairly large saucepan and fry the onion for 5 minutes until golden, then stir in the garlic, spices and bay leaf.

Put in the remaining vegetables and stir over the heat for a further 1–2 minutes so that they are all coated with the oil and spices.

Add the water and a little salt and pepper. Cover and leave to simmer for 15–20 minutes or until the vegetables are all tender, stirring from time to time and checking towards the end to make sure they do not burn — there will be very little water left. Alternatively, the spiced vegetables can be put into a casserole dish and baked at 325°F (160°C) for about 1–1½ hours or until tender when pierced with the point of a sharp knife.

Serve the vegetables with the dal.

Veggie stack on herby couscous

I love this as it tastes wonderful and looks so pretty: a glossy heap of colorful roasted vegetables on a base of herby couscous, topped with chopped fresh herbs and pine nuts, and drizzled with sweet balsamic dressing.

SERVES 4

1 large or 2 medium-sized sweet potatoes
2 large red onions
2 eggplant
2 red peppers
6 tbsp olive oil
7oz (200g) hummus, bought or homemade (see page 46)
a few sprigs of flat-leaf parsley
a few pine nuts, toasted (see page 140)
balsamic dressing with honey and mustard (see page 75)

FOR THE COUSCOUS

9oz (250g) couscous
1¾ cups (400ml) boiling water
1 tbsp olive oil
1 tsp salt
6 tbsp chopped fresh flat-leaf parsley
½–1 tsp harissa paste (optional)

Preheat the oven to 400°F (200°C). Peel the sweet potatoes and cut into ½in (1cm) thick rounds, aiming to get at least 12. Peel the onions and cut each into sixths. Cut the eggplant into chunky batons, about 3in (8cm) long and about ⅝in (1.5cm) thick; halve and seed the peppers and cut each half length-ways into sixths.

Put all the vegetables into a large roasting pan with the oil, moving them around so that they are all coated in the oil, then roast in the oven for about 30 minutes or until the vegetables are tender.

Meanwhile, prepare the couscous. Put it into a bowl, pour in the boiling water, add the oil and salt, and stir. Set aside for 10 minutes for the couscous to absorb all the water, then stir in the chopped parsley and harissa paste to taste (if using).

To serve the dish, divide the couscous between four plates, making a flat mound of it in the center. Put three rounds of sweet potatoes, flat, on top, then pile a heaped tablespoonful of hummus on top of them, and arrange the rest of the vegetables in a pile, standing the eggplant batons upright. Don't worry about being too neat; just create a lovely, colorful stack, as high as you can.

Put a few sprigs of parsley and a scattering of pine nuts on top, and drizzle the balsamic dressing over and around the stack. Serve at once, though it's also lovely warm or cold.

Vegetable and sweetcorn stew v

SERVES 4

1 large onion, chopped
3 tbsp olive oil
2 garlic cloves, crushed
1 large eggplant, cut into small chunks
1 leek, sliced
12oz (350g) carrots, sliced
8oz (225g) button mushrooms, sliced
24oz tomato pureé
2 cups (575ml) water or vegetable stock
8oz (225g) fresh sweetcorn cut from 2 cobs
salt and freshly ground black pepper
1–2 tbsp chopped fresh flat-leaf parsley, to garnish

Cook the onion in 1 tablespoon of the oil for 10 minutes in a medium-sized saucepan over a gentle heat, with a lid on the pan, stirring from time to time.

Add the garlic, eggplant, leek, carrots and mushrooms and stir over the heat for a further 5–10 minutes to soften the vegetables a bit.

Pour in the tomato pureé and water or vegetable stock. Bring to a boil, then simmer, uncovered, for 20–25 minutes or until the vegetables are tender and the sauce thick.

Stir in the sweetcorn, cook for a few minutes longer, then check the seasoning, scatter with chopped parsley and serve.

Romanian vegetable stew v

This stew is a gloriously colorful mixture of every sort of vegetable available.

SERVES 4
2 tbsp olive oil
2 large onions, sliced
2 stalks of celery, chopped
8oz (225g) carrots, sliced
8oz (225g) parsnips, peeled and diced
8oz (225g) zucchini, sliced
1lb (450g) leeks, trimmed and cut into 1in (2.5cm) pieces
3 large tomatoes, skinned (see page 40) and quartered
1lb (450g) potatoes, peeled and cut into chunks
2 tbsp (25g) all-purpose flour
2 cups (575ml) water or vegetable stock
2 tbsp tomato purée
2 bay leaves
1 garlic clove, crushed
salt and freshly ground black pepper

Heat the oil in a large saucepan and fry the onion for 5 minutes, then add the celery, carrots, parsnips, zucchini, leeks, tomatoes and potatoes and cook for a further 4–5 minutes, browning slightly and turning them often to prevent sticking.

Sprinkle the flour over the vegetables and mix gently to distribute it. Pour in the water or stock, stirring, and add the tomato purée, bay leaves, garlic and a seasoning of salt and pepper.

Bring to a boil then turn the heat down and leave to simmer very gently, covered, for about 25–30 minutes or until the vegetables are tender. Taste the mixture and add more seasoning if necessary.

White nut roast with parsley stuffing v

People often ask me what I make for Christmas dinner, and this nut roast is the answer, served with a lovely gravy, roast potatoes, cranberry sauce and bread sauce. This roast freezes very well; I freeze it before baking, thaw it overnight, then cook it the next day. I generally make double the quantity given here and bake it in a narrow 2lb (900g) loaf pan. If there's any left over, it's good cold, cut into slices and served with pickles.

SERVES 6 ❄
FOR THE WHITE NUT LAYERS
2 tbsp (25g) butter or vegan margarine
1 tbsp olive oil
1 large onion, chopped
8oz (225g) cashew nuts, finely ground — an electric coffee mill is great for this
4oz (125g) fresh white breadcrumbs
juice of 1 lemon
2–6 tbsp water or vegetable stock
salt and freshly ground black pepper
freshly grated nutmeg, to taste
a sprig of fresh flat-leaf parsley, to garnish

FOR THE GREEN STUFFING LAYER IN THE MIDDLE
3oz (75g) fresh white breadcrumbs
grated rind and juice of 1 lemon
1½ tsp herbes de Provence
¼ cup chopped flat-leaf parsley
3 tbsp (40g) butter or vegan margarine

Preheat the oven to 350°F (180°C).

To make the white nut mixture, melt the butter or margarine in a saucepan with the oil. Add the onion, cover and cook gently for 10–15 minutes until soft but not browned. Remove from the heat and mix with all the remaining ingredients, seasoning to taste with salt, pepper and nutmeg.

For the stuffing, mix everything together by hand, making sure the butter or margarine is well blended in: it's easiest to put all the ingredients (including whole sprigs of parsley) into a food processor and whiz to a green paste. Season to taste with salt and pepper.

To assemble the roast, grease a 1lb (450g) loaf pan with butter or oil and line with a strip of baking parchment to cover the base and narrow sides. Put half of the white mixture into the tin. Put the stuffing on top of the white mixture, covering it completely in an even layer, and press lightly into place. Top with the rest of the white mixture.

Cover with a piece of baking parchment and a top covering of foil. Bake in the oven for 45 minutes, then take the coverings off and bake for 15 minutes more or until golden brown.

Turn out onto a serving dish, remove the baking parchment and garnish the top with a parsley sprig. Serve in thick slices with golden roast potatoes, a lovely vegetarian gravy, cranberry sauce and all the other trimmings.

Beans

Beans – peas and lentils – are one of our earliest-known foods. They are nutritious, healthy and low in fat; an excellent source of protein, low-glycaemic carbohydrate and fiber; and packed full of valuable vitamins and minerals. That's why dieticians encourage us to eat them often.

I like them — love them, actually — for all of these health reasons but also because they are cheap and keep for weeks in the cupboard, ready for cooking. I love all the gentle processes involved in cooking them: the serene soaking, the unhurried boiling, the transformation from hard, dry seed to plump, moist bean that is full of flavor. Plus, I love the fact that you can also buy good-quality cans of beans for when you don't have time for all that slow cooking.

You can do so much with beans once you know how to cook them properly, which I explain at the beginning of the chapter. Then you can enjoy the easy, delicious recipes that follow.

Types of beans available

Aduki or adzuki beans Small, reddish-brown beans, round with a little point at one end. Have a pleasant, slightly sweet flavor. Good in vegetable stews and stir-fries.

Black beans A type of kidney bean, a little larger than red kidney beans, shiny black in color. Have a rich flavor and pleasant, mealy texture. Delicious in vegetable casseroles and salads; can be used instead of red kidney beans in any recipe.

Black-eyed peas Sometimes called black-eyed beans or cowpeas. About the same size as haricot beans, beige-colored with a black spot or "eye". They cook quickly and have a pleasant, slightly sweet flavor.

Brown lentils One of the many varieties of lentil readily available, these are dark brown or reddish brown, smaller than green lentils, with a very pleasant flavor.

Cannellini beans White kidney-shaped beans, a little larger than red kidney beans and a member of the same family. Pleasant flavor and texture; can be used in place of haricot, lima or red kidney beans.

Chickpeas Look like small hazelnuts, beige in color, cooking to a darker gold. Have a particularly delicious flavor and are excellent in salads and casseroles, also in dips, such as hummus and in crispy croquettes.

Edamame beans These are green soy beans. In Japanese restaurants they are sometimes served in their pods and you just pick the pods up in your fingers and suck out the beans. You can buy frozen edamame in their pods from Asian stores; or podded and frozen, like frozen peas, from health-food stores; or in cans.

Field beans One of the cheapest beans, which can be grown in gardens and allotments in temperate climates. They have a tough outer skin and need chopping after cooking in a food processor or sturdy blender to break this down and release the pleasant, earthy flavor. Excellent in a dip and as veggie burgers.

Flageolet beans Have an attractive pale green color, slim shape and delicate flavor when cooked. They make an excellent salad, particularly when combined with other pale green ingredients such as avocado; they also make a pretty pale green soup.

Green lentils These are lens-shaped — in fact, that's where the word "lens" comes from — and vary in color from light greenish-beige to brown. They keep their shape well after cooking and are excellent with spices and warm bread or rice, or made into tasty non-meat burgers. They're bigger than the brown lentils.

Lima or Butter beans One of the largest beans. These are flattish, kidney-shaped and creamy white in color. They absorb flavors particularly well and are useful for making pâtés or combined with tasty vegetables and spices.

Mung beans The small, round green beans from which bean-sprouts are produced. Delicious cooked with rice and spices in the traditional Indian dish *khitchari*.

Navy or Haricot beans These small, oval white beans belong to the kidney bean family. Probably best known in the form of "baked beans", they have a delicious slightly sweet flavor and mealy texture. Try them as Boston baked beans or as a salad.

Peas These are whole dried peas and look like wizened versions of fresh peas. They cook to the familiar "mushy peas" and make a cheap and filling winter vegetable or soup: follow the method for lentil soup on page 21 and flavor with some chopped mint.

Pinto beans *Pinto* means "speckled" and these beans are creamy colored with brown specks. They are a type of kidney bean and can be used in any recipe calling for red kidney or navy beans. They have a delicate, slightly sweet flavor and can be used in place of red kidney beans in any recipe.

Puy lentils These small, slightly marbled slate-green lentils are considered by many to be the best of all because of their unique peppery flavor and the fact that they hold their shape during cooking. They're grown in Le Puy region of France and are the only lentil to be named after the area in which they are grown. They're widely available from good supermarkets.

Red kidney beans Rich red in color and with the characteristic kidney shape, these have a lovely mealy texture and a delicious flavor. They make an excellent salad, combine well with rice (see Jamaican "rice and peas" on page 248) and can be used in many tasty main-course dishes.

Split red lentils These are lentils that have had the outer skin removed and are bright orange-red in color. Easy to buy at any supermarket, they have a pleasant savory flavor and cook quickly to a purée. Excellent made into soup, rissoles, savory spread, spicy dal, croquettes or loaves.

Soy beans Small, round and yellowish in color. The most protein-rich pulse, but they take a long time to cook and need careful flavoring. They can be made into an excellent alternative to cow's milk and this, in turn, can be made into tofu, a firm (or firmish) creamy-colored curd. You can buy lovely tofu in Asian stores and various good organic brands in large health-food stores and supermarkets; I find firm silken vacuum-packed tofu sold in large supermarkets the nearest to fresh tofu, but try different brands to find the one you like best.

Split peas Bright green or yellow in color, these, like split red lentils, have had their outer skin removed. Mix them with dressing to make an unusual salad, or tasty split peas with fennel seeds.

Choosing beans

Although beans will keep for many years, they become harder and drier with time. So for best results buy fresh stock from a store with a rapid turnover and store carefully in a screw-top jar or airtight cannister, using up each batch before topping up with the next. There is a new season of beans every autumn.

Equipment

The equipment required for cooking beans is simple and basic. A large sieve or colander is useful for washing the beans and a large saucepan in which to soak and cook them. As most beans take quite a long time to cook, a pressure cooker saves time, and a slow cooker can also be used. A blender or food processor is needed for puréeing the beans to make soups and dips, and is essential for preparing field beans.

Preparation, cooking and using

Washing Whether this is necessary or not depends on where the beans have come from. If you buy them from a serve-yourself tub in a market, then they will need washing and might need going over carefully to remove grit. If they're sold in a clean-looking packet, they're probably fine. If in doubt, spread the beans out on a large white plate or tray and sort through them carefully, removing any foreign bodies. Then put them into a large colander or sieve and wash them under cold water, moving them around with your fingers as you do so.

Soaking Most beans need soaking before cooking. This is unnecessary for split red lentils and optional for the other types of lentils, small green mung beans, split peas and black-eyed peas, although soaking these does reduce their cooking time slightly and may help them to cook more evenly.

Put the beans into a large saucepan and cover them with their height again in cold water. Either leave them to soak for 6–8 hours, or give them a quick hot soak.

To do this, put the beans into a saucepan, cover with plenty of water, bring to a boil, boil for 2 minutes, then remove from heat and soak for 45–60 minutes. This is as good as an overnight soak.

Rinsing Next, whether you've done the long cold or the quick hot soak, it's best to tip the beans into a colander and rinse thoroughly under cold water. This helps to remove some of the sugars, called oligosaccharides, which can make beans indigestible.

Basic cooking Put the rinsed beans into a large saucepan with a generous covering of fresh water. A homemade unsalted stock (see page 11) can be used instead of water, but do not use a salty stock or add salt, as this can toughen the outside of the beans and prevent them from cooking properly. Bring the water to a boil and allow to boil rapidly for 10 minutes. This destroys any toxins that may be present in some types of beans (especially red kidney beans), making them perfectly safe to eat. After this initial boiling the beans can be incorporated with other ingredients and cooked slowly, or they can be gently simmered on their own until tender and then mixed with other ingredients. See the table for cooking times, but remember that these can vary a little from batch to batch (particularly chickpeas).

Using a pressure cooker

This reduces the cooking time by about two-thirds. Boil the beans for 10 minutes as usual, then cook at 15lb (6.7kg) pressure for a third of the usual time given in the chart. Some of the beans, particularly lentils, tend to "froth up" when they come to a boil, and this can clog the valve of the pressure cooker. You can prevent this by adding 2 tablespoons of oil to the cooking water.

Soaking and cooking times for dried beans

	COLD SOAK	HOT SOAK	AVERAGE COOKING TIME
Aduki beans	6–8 hours	45–60 minutes	1–1½ hours
Black beans	6–8 hours	45–60 minutes	1–1½ hours
Black-eyed peas	6–8 hours	45–60 minutes	25–30 minutes
	unsoaked	unsoaked	35–45 minutes
Cannellini beans	6–8 hours	45–60 minutes	1–1½ hours
Chickpeas	6–8 hours	45–60 minutes	1–2 hours
Field beans	6–8 hours	45–60 minutes	30–60 minutes
Flageolet beans	6–8 hours	45–60 minutes	30–60 minutes
Lentils Brown	6–8 hours	45–60 minutes	25–30 minutes
	unsoaked	unsoaked	40–60 minutes
Green	6–8 hours	45–60 minutes	25–30 minutes
	unsoaked	unsoaked	40–60 minutes
Puy	6–8 hours	45–60 minutes	25–30 minutes
	unsoaked	unsoaked	40–60 minutes
Split red	unsoaked	unsoaked	20–30 minutes
Lima beans	6–8 hours	45–60 minutes	45–60 minutes
Mung beans	6–8 hours	45–60 minutes	25–30 minutes
	unsoaked	unsoaked	30–40 minutes
Navy beans	6–8 hours	45–60 minutes	1–1½ hours
Peas, whole dried	6–8 hours	45–60 minutes	45–60 minutes
Pinto beans	6–8 hours	45–60 minutes	1–1½ hours
Red kidney beans	6–8 hours	45–60 minutes	1–1¼ hours
Soy beans	6–8 hours	45–60 minutes	1–3 hours
Split peas	6–8 hours	45–60 minutes	25–30 minutes
	unsoaked	unsoaked	45–60 minutes

Using a slow cooker

It is important to boil the beans vigorously for 10 minutes before transferring them to the slow cooker. Beans that normally take 1–1½ hours to cook need 2–3 hours in a slow cooker with the heat set at "low". The cooking times given here are approximate; I've found that the timing varies quite a bit, especially with whole lentils and chickpeas. The important thing is to make sure the beans or lentils are really tender — they need to be cooked *thoroughly* in order to be digestible.

Flavoring and serving

Beans are simple to cook, but it's the flavoring and presentation that make all the difference to the attractiveness of the finished dish. Butter and well-flavored vegetable oils — in particular olive oil — enhance them greatly, as do small quantities of cream. Strongly flavored vegetables, such as onions, garlic, celery, mushrooms and tomatoes, also go particularly well with beans, as do some fruits, particularly sharp apples, pineapple, dried apricots, raisins, and also lemon juice. Do not add acid fruits or tomatoes until after the beans have softened — the beans may toughen otherwise.

Perhaps more than anything else, herbs and spices make all the difference to the appeal of the finished dish. It is surprising what the addition of a bay leaf or bouquet garni to the cooking water of any of the beans will do for the flavor. The bouquet garni herbs are bay leaf, fresh thyme, parsley and marjoram, and these can be used together or individually. Other useful herbs are mint and oregano, while of the spices, fennel, cumin, coriander and cinnamon are particularly good, as are chili powder, paprika, cloves, curry powder or paste and turmeric. Grated fresh root ginger, with its delicious citrus-like flavor, also comes in handy.

Pulse dishes look attractive served simply, in chunky pottery, with garnishes such as triangles of crisp toast or fried bread, raw onion or tomato rings, lemon wedges or chopped fresh flat-leaf parsley.

Storing cooked beans

Drained, cooked beans will keep for several days in a covered container in the fridge and they also freeze well. It is often worth cooking a double batch, using half and freezing the rest.

Guide to quantities

If you cook a 1lb 2oz (500g) bag of beans or lentils, then divide them into five equal portions, each will be the equivalent of a 14oz can (i.e. 3½oz (100g) dried beans when cooked equal a 14oz can), and that's enough for 1–2 people as a main course.

Freezing

Many made-up pulse dishes also freeze well and these recipes are marked ❅. Freeze the dishes after cooking unless stated otherwise and thaw before reheating. Croquettes and fritters are best frozen uncovered on a baking sheet and packed in plastic bags. Then you can get out individual ones, and fry or bake them while still frozen.

Aduki bean, carrot and ginger stir-fry v

Accompany with a cooked grain such as quinoa, millet or couscous.

SERVES 2–3
1 onion, sliced
¼ cup olive oil
1½lb (700g) carrots, thinly sliced
1 tbsp grated fresh root ginger
3½oz (100g) dried aduki beans,
   soaked, cooked (see page 178)
   and drained, or a 14oz can,
   drained and rinsed
1¼ (275ml) water or vegetable stock
a bunch of scallions, chopped
salt and freshly ground black pepper
a pinch of sugar (optional)

Fry the onion in the oil in a large saucepan for 4–5 minutes or until beginning to soften, then add the carrots and ginger and stir-fry for a further 3–4 minutes.

Add the aduki beans and water or stock, cover and leave to simmer gently for 10–15 minutes or until the carrots are just tender.

Stir in the scallions. Season with salt and pepper and a pinch of sugar if necessary.

Bean and green pepper goulash v

Serve this with a dollop of thick natural yogurt or sour cream, some rice and a green salad. Incidentally, if you want the best-flavored paprika it's worth looking out for the "Hungarian rose" variety, and buying only a small quantity at a time.

SERVES 3–4 ❋
1lb (450g) onions, sliced
2 tbsp olive oil
4 garlic cloves, crushed
2 large green peppers, seeded and
   sliced
2 x 14oz cans chopped tomatoes
¼ cup tomato purée
7oz (200g) dried cannellini or navy
   beans, soaked, cooked (see pages
   176–7) and drained, or 2 x 14oz
   cans, drained and rinsed
2–4 tsp paprika
salt and freshly ground black pepper
a little sugar (optional)
5fl oz (150ml) thick natural yogurt or
   sour cream (optional)

Fry the onions in the oil in a large saucepan, covered, for about 10 minutes or until the onion is soft, then add the garlic and green peppers and fry for a further 4–5 minutes.

Mix in the tomatoes, tomato purée and beans, along with the paprika, salt and pepper and perhaps a little sugar to taste.

Simmer the mixture for about 15 minutes, without a lid on the saucepan, to heat everything through and to reduce the liquid a little.

Serve with the yogurt or sour cream (if using).

VARIATION
Bean and green pepper goulash with smoked paprika

Use smoked paprika, which you can buy in a little tin from large supermarkets and Spanish food stores, for a change. A smoky flavor is something that people sometimes miss in vegetarian food and smoked paprika is a way of adding that. Try it in this goulash and see how you like the combination of sweet vegetables, smoky paprika and cool, sharp yogurt or sour cream.

Beans with marrow and sweetcorn v

For this Latin American dish you can use any beans; I like it with black-eyed peas, but navy or cannellini beans are also good. Choose a marrow that's tender enough for the skin to be left on or use zucchini. Pumpkin can be used instead, but the skin needs removing.

SERVES 3–4
3 tbsp olive oil
1 large onion, chopped
1 large garlic clove, crushed
14oz can chopped tomatoes
1 tsp dried basil
1 tsp dried oregano
7oz (200g) dried black-eyed peas,
    cannellini beans, Lima beans
    or red kidney beans, soaked and
    cooked until very nearly tender
    (see pages 176–7), or 2 x 14oz cans
1lb (450g) marrow or zucchini, cut
    into largish dice
4oz (125g) frozen sweetcorn kernels
salt and freshly ground black pepper

Heat the oil in a large saucepan and fry the onion for 5 minutes or until beginning to soften.

Add the garlic, tomatoes, basil and oregano, and cook fairly fast for about 10 minutes, without a lid on the saucepan, to make a thickish sauce.

Drain the peas, stir into the sauce and simmer gently for about 10 minutes or until the marrow or zucchini are nearly cooked, then mix in the sweetcorn and continue to cook until everything is tender and the mixture piping hot. Season with salt and pepper and serve at once.

Shepherd's beany pie

It's not essential to purée the cooked peas, but personally I think it gives a better result. You need creamy mashed potatoes prepared in advance to complete this dish (see page 131). I find it very helpful to plan ahead, making extra mashed potato for a meal the day before and keeping in the fridge until needed.

SERVES 4 ❄
2 tbsp olive oil
1 large onion, chopped
1 garlic clove, crushed
2oz (50g) mushrooms, chopped
7oz (200g) dried black-eyed peas,
    soaked and cooked (see pages
    176–7), or 2 x 14oz cans
14oz canned chopped tomatoes
1 tbsp tomato purée
1 tbsp chopped fresh flat-leaf parsley
1 tsp herbes de Provence
salt and freshly ground black pepper

TO SERVE
1½lb (700g) creamy mashed
    potatoes (see page 131)
2oz (50g) grated cheese

Preheat the oven to 400°F (200°C). Heat the oil in a large saucepan and fry the onion and garlic, with a lid on the pan, for about 5 minutes, then add the mushrooms and go on cooking for another 4–5 minutes.

Drain the peas and mash or blend them, depending on the texture you want.

Add the peas to the pan, along with the tomatoes, tomato purée, parsley and herbes de Provence and cook over a gentle heat for 10 minutes. Then season with salt and pepper.

Spoon the mixture into a shallow ovenproof dish, spread the mashed potato evenly over the top, rough up the surface with a fork and sprinkle with grated cheese.

Bake in the oven for 35–40 minutes or until golden brown.

Beorijch v

An unusual mixture of black-eyed peas and nuts, this is an Armenian dish that's rich in protein and quick to make. It's also very tasty. You can use any type of nuts — I particularly like Brazils. Serve piping hot, with new potatoes or a cooked grain and a cooked green vegetable or crisp green salad.

SERVES 3–4 ❊
1 large onion, chopped
2 tbsp olive oil
1 garlic clove, crushed
2 tomatoes, skinned (see page 40) and chopped (canned are fine)
1 tbsp tomato purée
7oz (200g) black-eyed peas, soaked and cooked (see pages 176–7), or 2 x 14oz cans
4oz (125g) mixed nuts, roughly chopped
2 tbsp chopped fresh flat-leaf parsley
salt and freshly ground black pepper
a little sugar (optional)

Fry the onion in the olive oil in a large saucepan, with a lid on the pan, for 10 minutes, then stir in the garlic, tomatoes and tomato purée and cook for a further 10 minutes to make a thick purée.

Drain the peas thoroughly, mashing them slightly as you do so. Add to the pan, along with the nuts and parsley.

Taste the mixture and season with salt, pepper and a pinch of sugar if you think it's necessary.

Cook over a gentle heat for about 10 minutes, stirring often to prevent sticking.

Black-eyed pea bake

A simple dish that's popular with children. A spicy tomato sauce goes well with it, or a tasty vegetarian gravy (see page 66). Although you can buy black-eyed peas in cans, they are one of the faster-cooking beans, taking 35–40 minutes unsoaked. If you can plan ahead and soak them first, they cook in about 25–30 minutes.

SERVES 4 ❊
12oz (350g) dried black-eyed peas
2 large onions, sliced
3 garlic cloves, crushed
2 tbsp olive oil, plus extra for greasing
½ tsp dried thyme
1 tsp dried marjoram
salt and freshly ground black pepper

FOR THE TOPPING
2oz (50g) fresh wholewheat breadcrumbs
2oz (50g) grated cheese

Drain and rinse the peas.

Fry the onions and garlic in the oil for 10 minutes or until the onion is tender but not browned, then add the peas, herbs and water to cover.

Simmer gently, until the peas are tender (about 25–40 minutes).

Preheat the oven to 350°F (180°C).

Purée the pea mixture in a food processor or with an electric hand blender. Season to taste with salt and pepper.

Spoon the mixture into a greased, shallow ovenproof dish, sprinkle with the breadcrumbs and grated cheese and bake in the oven for about 30 minutes or until the top is golden and crunchy.

Black-eyed pea and vegetable stew v

This is a colorful stew, with black-eyed peas peeping out of a rich red tomato sauce and a garnish of fresh green parsley. It goes well with baked or creamy mashed potatoes and some buttery spinach or green beans.

SERVES 3–4 ❊
7oz (200g) dried black-eyed peas, soaked and cooked (see pages 176–7), or 2 x 14oz cans
1 large onion
3 stalks of celery
3 carrots
1 green pepper
2 garlic cloves
2 tbsp olive oil
14oz can tomatoes
1 tbsp tomato purée
2–3 tbsp red wine (optional)
salt and freshly ground black pepper
2 tbsp chopped fresh flat-leaf parsley, to garnish

Drain the peas. Peel and chop the onion. Slice the celery thinly, then peel and dice the carrots. Remove the seeds from the green pepper, then slice it fairly thinly. Peel and crush the garlic.

Heat the oil in a large saucepan, add all the prepared vegetables and fry gently, without browning, for about 10 minutes.

Mix in the peas, tomatoes, tomato purée and the wine (if using). Season with salt and pepper and leave to cook gently for 10–15 minutes or until all the vegetables are tender.

Check the seasoning. Serve sprinkled with the parsley.

Boston baked beans v

"Boston runs to brains as well as beans and brown bread," noted the 19th-century journalist William Cowper Brann in his essay "*Beans and Blood*". Well, here's a recipe for the beans, made in the traditional way. You could use a slow cooker if you have one (see page 177).

SERVES 4 ❇
12oz (350g) dried navy beans
1 large onion
1 tbsp olive oil
1 tsp mustard powder
2 tsp black molasses
5fl oz (150ml) tomato purée or
    tomato juice (you can use the
    liquid from a can of tomatoes)
2 tbsp tomato purée
1¼ cups (275ml) unsalted vegetable
    stock (see page 11)
salt and freshly ground black pepper

Soak, drain and rinse the beans, then cook them in fresh water until they're almost tender (see pages 176–7) and drain them again.

Preheat the oven to 275°F (140°C).

Peel and slice the onion. Heat the oil in a Dutch oven and fry the onion for about 5 minutes, then add the rest of the ingredients and bring the mixture to a boil.

Cover the dish and put it into the oven. Cook for about 4 hours, stirring occasionally. Season to taste.

These beans are lovely served with chunks of hot wholegrain bread or garlic bread (see page 55).

Lima beans with apricots, cinnamon and almonds v

An unusual sweet and sour mixture with a Middle Eastern flavor. Serve with some fluffy basmati rice.

SERVES 2–3 AS A MAIN DISH,
4–6 AS A SIDE DISH ❇
1 onion, chopped
2 tbsp olive oil
1½–2 tsp cinnamon
4oz (125g) dried Lima beans,
    soaked, cooked (see pages
    176–7), and drained, or a 14oz
    can, drained and rinsed
4oz (125g) dried apricots, sliced
1½oz (40g) raisins
15fl oz (425ml) water
1oz (25g) creamed coconut, or ½ cup
    canned coconut cream or milk
1 tbsp freshly squeezed lemon juice
salt and freshly ground black pepper
2oz (50g) sliced almonds, toasted
    (see page 139), to garnish

Fry the onion in the oil in a large saucepan for 10 minutes, then stir in the cinnamon and cook for a further moment or two.

Add the beans, apricots, raisins and water, bring to a boil, then turn the heat down and leave to simmer, covered, for 15–20 minutes or until the apricots are tender.

Add the coconut cream, lemon juice and seasoning. Sprinkle the almonds over before serving.

Lima bean and cider casserole v

A large, Dutch oven is ideal for making this; otherwise fry the vegetables in a saucepan first and then transfer them to an ovenproof dish to finish cooking. A variation is to add medium–large peeled potatoes, one for each person, into the pot with the Lima beans and vegetables and cook them together. The potatoes soak up the flavors and are delicious, but you do need a large dish.

SERVES 3–4 ❇
1 tbsp (15g) butter or 1 tbsp olive oil
3 large onions, sliced
2 garlic cloves, crushed
1lb (450g) carrots, sliced
7oz (200g) dried Lima beans,
    soaked, cooked (see pages 176–7)
    and drained, or 2 x 14oz cans,
    drained
1¼ cups (275ml) vegetable stock
5fl oz (150ml) cider
bouquet garni (see page 178)
    or ½ tsp herbes de Provence
1 tsp cornstarch (optional)
salt and freshly ground black pepper

Preheat the oven to 325°F (160°C). Heat the butter or oil in a large saucepan and add the onions and garlic. Fry for 5 minutes, browning them slightly, then stir in the carrots and cook for another 4–5 minutes, stirring frequently to prevent sticking.

Add the Lima beans, stock, cider, bouquet garni or herbes de Provence and a little salt and pepper.

Lima bean and tomato cutlets

Bring to a boil, then cover and transfer to the oven to cook for 1½–2 hours. If you want a slightly thicker sauce, stir in 1 teaspoon of cornstarch blended with a little stock and let the mixture boil for a minute or two to thicken. Remove the bouquet garni (if using) before serving.

Natural dried breadcrumbs not the very bright orange ones can be found in supermarkets or you can easily make your own by drying out slices of wholegrain bread on a baking sheet, then crushing with a rolling pin or in a food processor. They keep well in an airtight tin or in the freezer. Serve the cutlets with a tasty gravy (see page 66), tomato or yogurt sauce and crisp green salad.

SERVES 2 ❄

3½oz (100g) dried Lima beans or
   1 x 14oz can
1 onion, chopped
1 tbsp olive oil
2oz (50g) dried wholegrain
   breadcrumbs
2 tbsp tomato chutney
1 tsp freshly squeezed lemon juice
1 egg
salt and freshly ground black pepper
oil, for shallow frying

FOR COATING

6 tbsp cornstarch
6–7 tbsp cold water
8 tbsp dried wholegrain
   breadcrumbs

Soak and cook the dried Lima beans until they're tender (see pages 176–7), then drain. If using canned beans, simply drain and rinse. Mash the beans.

Fry the onion in the oil until tender but not browned.

Mix the onion with the Lima beans and all the other ingredients, season with salt and pepper. Divide the mixture into four and shape each piece into a burger shape.

To make the coating, mix together the cornstarch and water to make a thick, coating consistency.

Dip each cutlet first in the cornstarch mixture then into the dried breadcrumbs, so that it is completely coated in crumbs. Press it gently back into shape if necessary.

Fry the cutlets in hot shallow oil until crisp and browned, then drain them well on paper towels.

VARIATION

Vegan Lima bean and tomato cutlets v

Leave out the egg and use a few more dried breadcrumbs, as necessary, to bind. The coating is already vegan — it's crisp, golden and crunchy every time.

Creamy Lima beans and mushrooms

For a deliciously creamy dish, use crème fraîche; for a lighter version, use natural yogurt or low-fat fromage frais. For a vegan version, use plain unsweetened vegan yogurt, cream cheese or cream mixed with a teaspoon of corn-starch to thicken.

SERVES 3–4

7oz (200g) dried Lima beans or
    2 x 14oz cans
8oz (225g) young white button
    mushrooms
1 tbsp (15g) butter
1 tbsp freshly squeezed lemon juice
5fl oz (150ml) crème fraîche, thick
    natural yogurt or low-fat fromage
    frais
salt and freshly ground black pepper
freshly grated nutmeg
1 tbsp chopped fresh flat-leaf
    parsley, to garnish

If you're using dried Lima beans, soak and cook them in the usual way (see page 176–7). Keep the Lima beans warm; heat canned beans in their liquid.

Wash the mushrooms and halve or quarter them if necessary.

Fry the mushrooms gently in the butter in a medium-sized saucepan for 2–3 minutes or until they're just tender, then drain the Lima beans and add, together with the lemon juice, crème fraîche, yogurt or fromage frais. Season to taste with the salt, pepper and nutmeg.

Heat gently, but don't allow the mixture to become too hot or the yogurt will separate. Serve sprinkled with chopped parsley.

Lima beans with tomatoes, mint and olive oil v

This is a Greek recipe for Lima beans and the result is moist and flavorsome. The beans can be served as a vegetable or with fluffy brown rice. They're also very good cold. It will freeze, but add the garlic later.

SERVES 3–4 AS A MAIN PROTEIN
DISH, 6 AS A SIDE DISH ❄

7oz (200g) dried Lima beans or
    2 x 14oz cans
2 large onions
2 garlic cloves
4 tbsp olive oil
1lb (450g) tomatoes, skinned (see
    page 40) or 14oz can
2 tbsp chopped fresh mint
salt and freshly ground black pepper
a pinch or two of sugar (optional)

Cover the Lima beans with a good layer of cold water and leave them to soak for several hours. Then rinse and put them into a saucepan of fresh cold water. Bring to a boil and simmer until tender (1–1¼ hours).

Drain the cooked or canned beans.

Peel and chop the onions, then crush the garlic. Fry the onions in the olive oil in a large saucepan for 10 minutes, allowing them to brown lightly, then stir in the garlic.

Chop the tomatoes and add to the saucepan, together with the beans, mint and some salt and black pepper.

Let the mixture simmer gently, covered, for about 20 minutes, to allow all the flavors to blend.

Taste and add more salt and freshly ground black pepper and a pinch of sugar if needed.

Lima beans with tomatoes and red pepper v

This is a simple dish that's good served with a tossed green salad and some good bread. It's also delicious cold, particularly if you stir in a few black olives and some extra olive oil.

SERVES 3–4 ❄

7oz (200g) dried Lima beans or
    2 x 14oz cans
2 large onions
2 large garlic cloves
2 tbsp olive oil
2 green peppers
14oz can chopped tomatoes
1 tbsp tomato purée
½ tsp chili powder
salt and freshly ground black pepper
a pinch or two of sugar
2 tbsp chopped fresh flat-leaf
    parsley, to garnish

Soak and cook the Lima beans as usual (see pages 176–7), then drain them. Drain and rinse canned beans (if using).

Peel and slice the onions and crush the garlic. Fry them gently in the olive oil until they're tender and lightly browned (about 10 minutes).

Halve the green peppers and remove the seeds, then slice them thinly and add to the onions and garlic. Sauté for 5 minutes.

Stir in the tomatoes, tomato purée and chili powder and cook gently for 10 minutes. Add the Lima beans and heat through gently.

Season with salt, pepper and a little sugar to taste. Sprinkle some chopped parsley over and serve.

Lima bean and vegetable gratin

This warming winter dish, made with root vegetables, works equally well with tender early summer vegetables such as young carrots, zucchini and French green beans.

SERVES 4 ❄

7oz (200g) dried Lima beans or
  2 x 14oz cans
5–10fl oz (150–275ml) milk
8oz (225g) carrots
8oz (225g) rutabaga
8oz (225g) leeks
4 stalks of celery
4 onions
3 tbsp (40g) butter
3 tbsp (40g) all-purpose flour
4oz (125g) grated cheese
salt and freshly ground black pepper
¼ cup fresh wholewheat
  breadcrumbs, for topping

If you're using dried beans, soak and cook them as usual (see pages 176–7). Drain the beans, reserving the liquid. If using canned beans, drain, reserve the liquid and rinse. Add enough milk to the reserved cooking liquid to equal 15oz.

Peel and dice the carrots and rutabaga; clean and slice the leeks and celery; peel and slice the onions. Cook all the vegetables together in boiling water until they're just tender, then drain.

Melt the butter in a large saucepan and stir in the flour; when it "froths", take the saucepan off the heat and stir in the milk mixture, then return the saucepan to the heat and stir until the sauce thickens.

Let the sauce simmer gently for about 10 minutes, to cook the flour, then stir in half the cheese, the Lima beans and cooked vegetables. Season with salt and pepper.

Put the mixture into a shallow heatproof dish, sprinkle with the breadcrumbs and remaining cheese and brown under the broiler.

VARIATION

Lima bean, vegetable and tomato gratin v

Leave out the milk, butter, flour and cheese and use one 14oz can chopped tomatoes, whipped to a purée or mashed and seasoned, instead of the cheese sauce. Top with the breadcrumbs as described and scatter with a little grated cheese, then grill. For a dairy-free version, toss the breadcrumbs in a couple of tablespoons of olive oil before scattering over the top, then broil without the final sprinkling of cheese.

VARIATIONS

Chickpeas with tomatoes and green pepper v

This is equally delicious made exactly as in the main recipe but using chickpeas instead of Lima beans.

Navy beans with tomatoes and green pepper v

Navy beans, which have a natural sweetness, work really well too, in place of the Lima beans.

Lima bean and vegetable curry v

This is a mild curry with a lovely spicy flavor.

SERVES 4

7oz (200g) dried Lima beans
    or 2 x 14oz cans
3 tbsp olive oil
1 onion, chopped
1 garlic clove, crushed
2 tsp grated fresh root ginger
1 tsp ground cumin
1 tsp turmeric
½ tsp chili powder
2 tomatoes, roughly chopped
1lb (450g) potatoes, peeled and cut
    into chunky cubes
1½ tsp salt
2 bay leaves
4oz (125g) frozen peas
2 tbsp chopped fresh coriander,
    to garnish

If you're using dried Lima beans, soak and cook them as usual (see pages 176–7). Drain the Lima beans, reserving the liquid and adding water to equal 1¼ cups.

Heat the oil in a large saucepan and add the onion and garlic. Cook without browning for 5 minutes, then stir in the ginger and spices and cook for 1 minute further.

Stir in the tomatoes, cover and cook for about 5 minutes, then add the potatoes and mix well so that they are coated with the spice mixture. Stir in the reserved 1¼ cups of liquid and the salt and bay leaves. Bring to a boil, cover and simmer gently until the potatoes are nearly cooked, then add the beans and peas and cook for an additional 5 minutes or so, just to heat through. Serve sprinkled with chopped coriander.

Cannellini beans with mushrooms and sour cream

This is very simple and quick to make. Serve as a side dish or as a main course with buttered noodles, warm bread or rice. It also works well with thick natural yogurt instead of the sour cream. For an excellent vegan version, see the variation below.

SERVES 3–4

7oz (200g) dried cannellini beans,
    soaked and cooked (see pages
    176–7), or 2 x 14oz cans
6oz (175g) chestnut mushrooms,
    sliced
2 tbsp (25g) butter
½ tsp cornstarch
11fl oz (300ml) sour cream
salt and freshly ground black pepper
freshly grated nutmeg

Drain the beans.

Fry the mushrooms in the butter for 3–4 minutes without browning, then add the cornstarch.

Cook for a few seconds, stirring, then add the sour cream, beans and salt, pepper and nutmeg to taste.

Heat gently, stirring all the time. Check the seasoning and serve immediately.

VARIATION

Cannellini beans with mushrooms and vegan sour cream v

Nowadays you can buy excellent sour cream from health-food stores. For a luxurious vegan version, use this instead of the dairy sour cream and replace the butter with 2 tablespoons of olive oil.

Tuscan beans with garlic and sage v

This is a wonderful recipe, full of the flavors of Tuscany, and so easy to make. Serve it with some good country-style bread and a glass of red wine for a simple, satisfying meal.

SERVES 4–6

3 onions, chopped
2 tbsp olive oil
3–4 garlic cloves, crushed or
    finely chopped
3 x 14oz cans cannellini beans (don't
    drain them)
3 tbsp chopped fresh sage
salt and freshly ground black pepper
1–3 tbsp freshly squeezed lemon
    juice

Cook the onions in the oil in a large saucepan for about 8 minutes or until almost tender. Stir in the garlic and cook for a couple of minutes more. Add the beans and their liquid, and the sage. Stir, then cover and cook over a very gentle heat for about 1 hour. You could cook it for less time, but this long cooking really brings out and blends all the flavors.

Season with salt and pepper, and add lemon juice, tasting as you go, to give it a zing. This is delicious hot, warm, or cold.

Channna dal v

Simple and delicious, this is one of my favorite curries.

SERVES 3–4
7oz (200g) dried chickpeas or
  2 x 14oz cans
3 tbsp olive oil
1 tsp cumin seeds
1 small onion, finely chopped
1 tsp grated fresh root ginger
½ tsp turmeric
1 tsp ground cumin
1 tsp ground coriander
1 tsp garam masala
salt and freshly ground black pepper
1 tbsp chopped fresh coriander, to
  garnish

If you're using dried chickpeas, soak and cook them as usual (see pages 176–7). Drain the chickpeas (cooked or canned), keeping the liquid.

Heat the oil in a medium-sized saucepan and fry the cumin seeds for 1 minute, then add the onion, ginger, turmeric, ground cumin and ground coriander and fry for 2 minutes, stirring all the time.

Mix in the chickpeas and 1¼ cups (275ml) of the reserved cooking liquid and bring to a boil.

Put a lid on the saucepan and leave to simmer gently for 10–15 minutes.

Stir in the garam masala and salt and pepper to taste. Cook for a minute or two more, then serve sprinkled with chopped coriander.

Creamed chickpeas with garlic v

This is very easy to make, especially if you use canned chickpeas. Sliced tomatoes and chopped fresh coriander or basil goes well with it.

SERVES 3–4
7oz (200g) dried chickpeas or
  2x 14oz cans
3 large garlic cloves, crushed
2 tbsp freshly squeezed lemon juice
salt and freshly ground black pepper
2 tbsp olive oil
paprika
lemon wedges, to garnish
wholegrain toast, to serve

Soak and cook the dried chickpeas as usual (see pages 176–7); drain and reserve the cooking liquid.

Mash or purée the chickpeas, adding some of the liquid if necessary (or a little water), to make a smooth, fairly thick consistency.

Flavor this purée with the garlic, lemon juice, salt, pepper and the oil. Transfer to a saucepan and stir until heated through.

Sprinkle the chickpea purée with paprika and serve with lemon wedges and wholegrain toast.

VARIATION
Chickpea purée with tomatoes and onions v

For a delicious Greek variation, add 2 onions, fried in olive oil until tender, 8oz (225g) skinned (see page 40), chopped tomatoes (or 8oz can) and a good tablespoon each of chopped fresh parsley and mint.

Moroccan chickpea and eggplant casserole v

This colorful chickpea and eggplant casserole is good with couscous or rice and a green salad. If there's any left over, it's delicious cold with crusty bread and some salad.

SERVES 4 ❄
2 large onions, chopped
3 tbsp olive oil
2 tsp ground cumin
2 tsp ground coriander
1 tsp ground cinnamon
2 eggplant, cut into chunky pieces
2 x 14oz cans chickpeas, drained and
  rinsed
4oz (125g) raisins
2 x 14oz chopped tomatoes
3 cups (850ml) water or vegetable
  stock
salt and freshly ground black pepper

Fry the chopped onions in the oil in a large saucepan, covered, for 10 minutes or until tender but not browned.

Stir in the cumin, coriander and cinnamon; cook for a few seconds, then stir in the eggplant, chickpeas, raisins, tomatoes and water or stock. Bring to a boil, then simmer, half covered, for about 30 minutes or until the vegetables are tender and the mixture has thickened.

Season with salt and pepper, and serve.

Chickpea and potato croquettes v

These creamy croquettes are good served a number of ways: with a tomato sauce and a green vegetable; with yogurt sauce and some salad; or curry sauce and spiced rice.

SERVES 4 ❄

7oz (200g) dried chickpeas, soaked and cooked (see pages 176–7) or 2 x 14oz cans
1lb (450g) potatoes, cooked, drained and mashed (not too wet)
1 garlic clove, crushed
½ tsp paprika
2 tbsp chopped fresh flat-leaf parsley
salt and freshly ground black pepper
vegetable oil, for shallow-frying

FOR COATING

6 tbsp cornstarch
6–7 tbsp cold water
½ cup dried breadcrumbs (see page 183)

Drain the chickpeas, and mash roughly with a fork. Mix the mashed chickpeas with the mashed potato, garlic, paprika and parsley. Season with salt and pepper.

Form the mixture into eight small croquettes.

To make the coating, mix together the cornstarch and water to make a thick, coating consistency.

Dip each croquette first in the cornstarch mixture then into the dried breadcrumbs, so that it is completely coated in crumbs. Press it gently back into shape if necessary.

Fry the croquettes in hot, shallow oil, then drain well on paper towels.

Alternatively, place the croquettes on an oiled baking sheet and bake for 30–40 minutes at 400°F (200°C) turning them over after about 20 minutes, to brown all over.

Chickpeas in tomato sauce v

This spicy chickpea mixture is also good served as a main dish with cooked rice or pasta. It will add protein to any meal.

SERVES 4

8oz (225g) dried chickpeas or 2 x 14oz cans
1 small onion
1 tbsp olive oil
1 garlic clove, crushed
4oz (125g) button mushrooms, sliced
14oz can chopped tomatoes
1 bay leaf
salt and freshly ground black pepper
¼–½ tsp chili powder
a pinch or two of sugar

Soak and cook the dried chickpeas as usual (see pages 176–7), then drain. Drain canned chickpeas. Leave to one side while you make the sauce.

Peel and chop the onion and fry it gently in the butter in a medium-sized saucepan for 5 minutes; don't let it brown.

Then stir in the garlic and mushrooms and fry for 5 minutes more.

Add the tomatoes and bay leaf and let the mixture cook over a moderate heat for 10–15 minutes or until most of the liquid has boiled away, leaving a nice thick sauce.

Season with salt, pepper and chili powder, plus a dash of sugar if you think it needs it. Then mix in the chickpeas and cook for a further few minutes to heat them through. Check the seasoning before serving.

Spanish chickpea stew v

This Spanish stew, called *cocido*, traditionally contains meat. Here's a delicious version made without. Serve steaming bowlfuls of it with bread or topped with chunky croûtons.

SERVES 4

11oz (300g) dried chickpeas or 3 x 14oz cans
unsalted vegetable stock (see page 11)
3 potatoes
2 onions
2 carrots
1 turnip
2 leeks
1 small cabbage
2 garlic cloves
1 tbsp paprika
bouquet garni (a couple of sprigs of parsley, a sprig of thyme and a bay leaf tied together)
2 tbsp olive oil
2 tbsp finely chopped fresh flat-leaf parsley
salt and freshly ground black pepper

If you're using dried chickpeas, soak them for several hours, then drain, rinse, put into a large saucepan, cover generously with the stock and simmer until almost tender (about 1½ hours).

Alternatively, put the canned beans into a large saucepan and cover generously with the stock.

Peel the potatoes and cut into even-sized chunks. Peel and slice the onions, carrots and turnip.

Wash the leeks thoroughly and cut into slices. Wash and quarter the cabbage and peel and crush the garlic.

Falafel v

Add the vegetables and garlic to the chickpeas in the saucepan, together with the paprika, bouquet garni, oil and a little more stock if necessary.

Simmer gently for 30 minutes or so until all the vegetables are tender. Remove the bouquet garni, then stir in the chopped parsley and season with salt and plenty of pepper.

Although falafel are widely available, homemade ones are so easy to make and delicious that there's no need to buy them. I find these are popular with children. You need to use dried chickpeas for this, and to soak them for 24 hours. I often deep-fry the falafel in about 1½in (4cm) of rapeseed oil in a saucepan, rather than go to all the trouble of using a deep-fryer. Serve with warm pita bread, sliced tomatoes, olives and hummus, or a tahini dressing (see page 77).

SERVES 4 ❄

9oz (250g) dried chickpeas
1 small bunch of parsley, tough
    stems removed
1 small onion, roughly chopped
2 garlic cloves, roughly chopped
1½ tsp ground cumin
1½ tsp ground coriander
a good pinch of chili powder
½ tsp baking powder
1½ tsp salt
freshly ground black pepper
rapeseed or ground nut oil, for
    deep-frying

Soak the chickpeas in plenty of cold water for 24 hours. Drain well.

Put the parsley into a food processor and chop. Remove the chopped parsley onto a plate, and set aside.

Without washing the food processor, put in the drained chickpeas, chopped onion and garlic, along with the ground cumin, coriander, chili powder, baking powder and salt.

Process very well until you have a smooth-grained mixture that holds together.

Remove from the food processor and let the mixture rest for 30 minutes if possible, then gently but thoroughly mix in the chopped parsley; adding it at this stage makes the falafel light.

Form walnut-sized pieces of the mixture into flat rounds. If you have time, let them rest again for 15 minutes. They can be prepared up to this stage several hours before you want to fry them.

Heat the oil to 350°F (180°C) or until a 1in (2.5cm) cube of bread dropped into it sizzles immediately, rises to the surface and browns in 60 seconds. Fry the falafel, a few at a time, turning them as necessary, until both sides are golden brown and crisp.

Drain on paper towels and serve at once.

Field bean burgers v

These are made from the beans you can grow yourself in the garden. They cost practically nothing and are chewy, filling and delicious. But you do need a food processor or strong blender to break down the skins of the beans.

SERVES 4 ❋

1 onion, chopped
2 tbsp olive oil
2 garlic cloves, crushed
12oz (350g) dried field beans, soaked and cooked (see pages 176–7)
¼ cup chopped fresh flat-leaf parsley
1 tbsp freshly squeezed lemon juice
salt and freshly ground black pepper
all-purpose flour, to coat
olive oil, for shallow-frying

Fry the onion in the oil for 5 minutes, then add the garlic and fry for a further 5 minutes.

Chop the beans in a food processor or blender, or using an electric hand blender, until reduced to a coarse purée.

Mix the onion, parsley and lemon juice with the beans and season to taste with salt and pepper.

Form the mixture into burgers, coat with flour, then shallow-fry on both sides until crisp and browned. Drain on paper towels and serve immediately, sizzling and crisp.

Navy bean and vegetable pie

An economical family dish using dried beans, this consists of a tasty bean and vegetable mixture topped with mashed potatoes and cheese and baked until golden brown. Serve with a green vegetable like spinach or broccoli.

SERVES 4 ❋

7oz (200g) dried navy beans
1 tbsp olive oil
1 large onion, chopped
1 large garlic clove, crushed
15fl oz (425ml) water or unsalted vegetable stock (see page 11)
2 tbsp tomato purée
½ tsp dried basil
salt and freshly ground black pepper
a little sugar
1lb (450g) carrots, diced
1lb (450g) leeks, sliced

FOR THE MASHED POTATO TOPPING

½lb (700g) potatoes, peeled
a pat of butter
a few tbsp milk
4oz (125g) grated cheese

Soak the beans as usual (see pages 176–7), then drain and rinse them.

Heat the oil in a large saucepan and fry the onion for about 10 minutes, then add the drained beans, garlic and water or stock.

Bring to a boil, then let it simmer gently for about 1 hour or until the beans are soft and the liquid reduced to a thick sauce.

Stir in the tomato purée and season with basil, pepper and a little sugar if necessary.

Meanwhile, in another saucepan, cook the carrots and leeks in enough water to cover until tender. Drain.

Boil the potatoes in another pan until tender, then mash with the butter and enough milk to give a creamy consistency, and season with salt and pepper to taste.

Preheat the oven to 375°F (190°C).

Put the leeks and carrots into a shallow ovenproof dish, pour the bean mixture on top, sprinkle most of the grated cheese over, then spread the mashed potato on top. Press the top down with a fork and sprinkle with the remaining cheese. Bake for 30–40 minutes or until piping hot, crisp and golden on top.

Thai bean cakes with chili-roasted asparagus v

This is very easy to make and looks and tastes stunning.

SERVES 4

2 x 14oz cans navy beans

2 scallions, chopped

a bunch of coriander leaves, roughly chopped

4 tsp vegetarian red Thai paste

4 dried lime leaves, crumbled

salt and freshly ground black pepper

2 tbsp cornstarch

olive oil, for shallow-frying

2–4 tbsp sweet chili sauce

a little chopped fresh coriander to garnish

lime wedges, to serve

FOR THE ASPARAGUS

1lb 2oz (500g) asparagus, tough stalk ends broken off

2 tbsp light-flavored olive oil

Set the oven to 400°F (200°C). Drain the beans in a sieve, then rinse under the cold tap. Blot thoroughly with paper towels so they're fairly dry.

Put the beans into a bowl and add the scallions, chopped coriander, Thai paste, crumbled lime leaves and some salt and pepper. Mash the beans with a potato masher to make a lumpy mixture that holds together.
Form into eight flat cakes.

Spread the cornstarch out on a piece of greaseproof paper and coat the cakes lightly in the cornstarch.

Put the asparagus into a roasting pan, drizzle the oil over, moving the asparagus around with your fingers to make sure it's all coated. Roast for about 7 minutes or until it is the tenderness you like and slightly browned.

While the asparagus is cooking, shallow-fry the bean cakes in the oil in a frying pan until crisp on both sides; drain on paper towels.

Serve the bean cakes heaped up on a plate with the asparagus and drizzle the chili sauce over the top. Sprinkle with chopped coriander and serve with lime wedges.

Easy cheesy lentils

This is cheap, nourishing and very easy to make. Serve with ketchup, pickles or chutney and a salad of sliced tomatoes and onions.

SERVES 4 ❄

1 onion, chopped

2 tbsp olive oil

1 garlic clove, crushed

8oz (225g) split red lentils

2½ cups (700ml) water

4oz (125g) grated mature Cheddar or Parmesan-style cheese

salt and freshly ground black pepper

Fry the onion in the oil in a large saucepan for 10 minutes.

Add the garlic, lentils and water. Bring to a boil, then cover, turn down the heat and cook gently for 15–20 minutes or until the lentils are pale and soft.

Beat in the grated cheese and season with salt and pepper. Serve at once.

Lentil and cheese slice

A simple, quick-to-make supper dish that children enjoy. They're also good cold with pickles, chutney, such as the quick no-cook chutney (see page 71) and salad.

SERVES 4 ❄

8oz (225g) split red lentils
1 onion, sliced
1 bay leaf
2 cups (450ml) water
2oz (50g) grated cheese
salt and freshly ground black pepper
1 tomato, thinly sliced
a pat of butter

Put the lentils, onion and bay leaf into a saucepan with the water and cook gently, without a lid, for 20–25 minutes or until the lentils are tender. Remove the bay leaf.

Preheat the oven to 425°F (220°C).

Beat half the cheese into the cooked lentils and season.

Grease a 8in (20cm) square cake pan, spoon in the lentil mixture, spreading to the corners.

Top with the remaining cheese and the tomato slices, and dot with butter. Bake for 20–25 minutes until cooked through and golden on top.

Lentils with coriander and fresh ginger v

This spicy lentil mixture is lovely with basmati rice or pita bread and a tomato and onion side salad or cucumber raita (see page 66).

SERVES 2–3

7oz (200g) dried green lentils or
    2 x 14oz cans
2 large onions, chopped
2 garlic cloves, crushed
3 tbsp (40g) butter
2 tsp grated fresh root ginger
2 tsp ground coriander
2 tsp ground cumin
2 tbsp chopped fresh coriander or
    flat-leaf parsley
a few drops of freshly squeezed
    lemon juice
salt and freshly ground black pepper

Cover the lentils generously with water, bring to a boil and simmer gently for 35–40 minutes or until tender, then drain. Or, simply drain the canned lentils.

Fry the onions and garlic in the butter for about 5 minutes, then add the ginger, ground coriander and cumin and cook for an additional 5 minutes.

Stir the onion and spices into the cooked lentils.

Stir in the chopped fresh coriander or parsley and season with a dash of lemon juice and salt and pepper to taste.

Tip
This basic, simple curry can be jazzed up with other vegetables such as sliced peppers or mushrooms. Simply fry them with the onions.

Lentil croquettes v

These croquettes are made with split red lentils and were my favorite meal when I was growing up as a vegetarian. My mother used to make them about once a week and we had them with her delicious onion gravy, mashed potatoes and mint sauce. Mango chutney goes well with them, too, but that wasn't around in those days. Today, I'd be more likely to eat them with tartar sauce (see page 70) and a salad.

SERVES 4 ❄

8oz (225g) split red lentils
15fl oz (425ml) water
1 onion, finely chopped
2 tbsp olive oil
1 tbsp freshly squeezed lemon juice
salt and freshly ground black pepper
wholewheat flour, for coating
olive oil, for shallow-frying

Put the lentils and water into a medium-sized saucepan and cook them for 20–30 minutes or until the lentils are pale and soft and all the water has been absorbed. A non-stick saucepan is best, if possible, to avoid sticking.

Fry the onion in the oil for about 10 minutes or until it's soft, then add to the lentils, together with the lemon juice and seasoning to taste. Mix it all together well, then form it into eight croquettes and coat each one with wholewheat flour.

continued next page

Opposite: Lentil and cheese croquettes in a chili tomato sauce (see page 193)

Heat the oil in a frying pan and fry the croquettes until they're crisp, then drain them on paper towels and keep warm.

Alternatively, place the croquettes on an oiled baking sheet and bake for 30–40 minutes, at 400°F (200°C) turning them over halfway through to brown both sides evenly.

For a crisper coating, instead of using flour, dip the croquettes in the cornstarch coating given for chickpea and potato croquettes (see page 188).

VARIATION
Lentil and cheese croquettes in a chili tomato sauce

Add 4oz (125g) grated cheese and ½ teaspoon each of paprika and mustard powder to the lentil mixture. Add ¼–½ teaspoon chili powder to the tomato sauce on page 71 and serve with the croquettes.

Lentil dal with coconut cream v

Dal is a classic accompaniment to curries. It's also delicious poured over lightly cooked root vegetables, turning them into a complete winter meal.

SERVES 4 ❄
8oz (225g) split red lentils
3 cups (850ml) water
1 bay leaf
2in (5cm) stick of cinnamon
4 cardamom pods
2 tsp ground coriander
2 tsp ground cumin
¼ cup olive oil
2 onions, chopped
2 garlic cloves, crushed
1 tbsp freshly squeezed lemon juice
½ cup canned coconut cream
salt and freshly ground black pepper

Put the lentils, water, bay leaf and cinnamon into a saucepan. Cook gently until the lentils are tender (about 20–25 minutes).

Meanwhile fry the spices in the oil for 1–2 minutes, then add the onions and garlic and fry for 10 minutes or until tender. Add this mixture, including the oil, to the cooked lentils, then stir in lemon juice, coconut cream and seasoning.

Cook gently until the coconut cream has dissolved, then remove the cardamoms and serve. For a smoother, creamy texture, blend and reheat before serving.

VARIATION
Lentil dal with coconut cream and chili v

For a hotter version, halve, seed and finely chop a green chili and fry with the onions.

Dal with fresh coriander v

I love this dal. It's quite liquid, perfect for pouring over cooked basmati rice or for dipping warm naan bread or other flatbread.

SERVES 4
7oz (200g) split red lentils
5 cups (1.5 liters) water
2 level tsp salt
1 onion, chopped
6 garlic cloves, finely chopped
2–4 tbsp light olive oil
¼ tsp turmeric
1 tsp garam masala
1 tomato, chopped
chopped fresh coriander

Wash the lentils. Put them into a saucepan with the water and salt. Bring to a boil. (There will seem to be a lot of water, but this is correct.)

Turn down the heat and simmer uncovered, skimming off the froth from the top — this takes about 20 minutes. Then partially cover the pan and leave to simmer gently for 40 minutes.

Meanwhile, fry the onion and garlic in the oil for about 10 minutes until light brown.

Add the turmeric and garam masala to the onion and cook for a few seconds, then add the onion mixture to the lentils.

Top with the chopped tomato and coriander.

Tip
Garam masala spices (which are sold in a grinder jar) ground over this dal give a delicious flavor.

Lentil and mushroom gratin

This is another favorite according to the many letters and comments I have received over the years. It consists of mushrooms covered with a smooth lentil purée and topped with crunchy breadcrumbs and grated cheese.

SERVES 4 ❄

6oz (175g) split red lentils
1 cup each (575ml) milk and water
2 tbsp olive oil
1 large onion, sliced
1 tsp grated lemon rind
2 tbsp freshly squeezed lemon juice
salt and freshly ground black pepper
1 tsp yeast extract or 1–2 tsp soy sauce
8oz (225g) mushrooms

FOR THE TOPPING

1oz (25g) fresh breadcrumbs
1oz (25g) grated cheese or 2 tbsp olive oil

Put the lentils into a saucepan with the milk and water and simmer for 20–30 minutes or until the lentils are golden and tender.

Preheat the oven to 350°F (180°C).

Meanwhile, heat half the olive oil in another saucepan, add the onion, cover and cook for about 10 minutes or until tender but not brown. Add to the lentils with the lemon rind and juice, salt, pepper and yeast extract or soy sauce. Blend this mixture to make a smooth, thick purée.

Wash and slice the mushrooms and fry in the remaining tablespoonful of olive oil for about 5 minutes or until just tender.

Place the fried mushrooms in a shallow baking dish and pour the lentil mixture over the top to cover. Sprinkle the breadcrumbs and cheese evenly over the top, or mix the breadcrumbs with 2 tablespoons of olive oil and use these instead, for a vegan topping. Bake for 40–45 minutes or until golden and bubbly.

VARIATIONS

Lentil and celery gratin

Use the outside stalks of one large head of celery, chopped and cooked in enough boiling water to cover until tender (about 20 minutes) instead of the mushrooms.

Lentil and zucchini gratin

Use 1lb (450g) courgettes, sliced, instead of the mushrooms.

Lentil and tomato gratin

Use 6 tomatoes, skinned (see page 40) and sliced, and ½ teaspoon of dried basil, or 1 tablespoon of chopped fresh basil, instead of the mushrooms. No need to fry the tomatoes — put them straight into the dish.

Lentil and fennel gratin

Use 1lb (450g) fennel, sliced and cooked in boiling water for 15–20 minutes or until tender, instead of the mushrooms. Drain, and use the cooking water with the milk for the lentil sauce.

Lentil and mushroom burgers

The mushrooms make these burgers moist while the lentils add texture and protein. The burgers hold together well and can be cooked in the oven, fried or barbecued. I like them with a dollop of creamy Béarnaise sauce (see page 63) or mayonnaise and some fresh watercress; but they are also lovely when eaten in a soft roll with lots of mustard or chutney.

SERVES 4

2 tbsp olive oil
1 onion, chopped
1lb (450g) mushrooms, chopped
2 large garlic cloves, crushed
4oz (125g) dried green lentils, cooked (see page 177) or soaked and cooked (see pages 176–7), or 14oz can
2 tbsp chopped fresh flat-leaf parsley
salt and freshly ground black pepper
all-purpose flour, for coating
olive oil, for greasing or shallow-frying

If you're going to bake the burgers in the oven, preheat it to 400°F (200°C).

Heat the oil in a large saucepan and fry the onion for 5 minutes or until beginning to soften, then add the mushrooms and garlic.

Fry over a moderate heat for 20–25 minutes or until all the liquid has evaporated and the mushrooms are reduced to a thick purée. Stir them from time to time while they are cooking. Remove from the heat.

continued next page

Drain the lentils very well and add to the mushrooms, with the parsley and salt and pepper to taste.

Form into eight burger shapes and roll the burgers lightly in flour.

Place the burgers on a greased baking sheet and bake for about 30 minutes, turning them over half-way through the cooking time.

Alternatively, fry the burgers quickly in a little hot oil on both sides, or brush them with oil and barbecue them.

Lentil and red pepper stew v

One of the nicest things about this stew is its color — it comes out a heart-warming vivid red and is really welcoming on a chilly day.

SERVES 4 ❄

4oz (125g) split red lentils
4oz (125g) dried navy beans
2 large onions
1½lb (700g) red peppers (about 4 large ones)
2 tbsp olive oil
3½ cups (1 liter) unsalted vegetable stock (see page 11) or water
¼ tomato purée
salt
sugar

Put the lentils and beans into a bowl and cover generously with cold water. Leave them to soak for several hours or overnight, then drain and rinse them.

Peel and chop the onions; slice the peppers, discarding the cores and seeds.

Heat the olive oil in a large saucepan and fry the onions for about 10 minutes to soften them, then add the red peppers and cook for 4–5 minutes more before stirring in the drained lentils and beans and the stock or water.

Bring the mixture to a boil and let it simmer gently, with a lid half on the saucepan, until the beans are tender (1–1¼ hours).

Mix in the tomato purée (this is left to the end, after the beans are tender, because it can prevent them from softening properly if added earlier) and some salt and sugar to taste. Serve immediately.

Spicy root vegetable and lentil stew v

This is real warming winter food — very filling and satisfying. You can add whatever herb and spice you prefer.

SERVES 3–4 ❄

3 tbsp olive oil
1½lb (700g) mixed root vegetables (e.g. rutabaga, parsnip, carrot, turnip), peeled and diced
2 stalks of celery, sliced
3 large onions, chopped
6oz (175g) split red lentils
2 garlic cloves, crushed
8oz can diced tomatoes
2½ cups (700ml) unsalted vegetable stock (see page 11)
2–3 tsp ground coriander
2–3 tsp ground cumin
salt and freshly ground black pepper
2 tbsp freshly squeezed lemon juice
a little chopped fresh flat-leaf parsley, to garnish

Heat 2 tablespoons of the oil in a large saucepan and add the root vegetables, celery and two-thirds of the onions. Sauté for about 5 minutes, without browning, then stir in the lentils and garlic and cook for 1–2 minutes.

Mix in the tomatoes and stock, put a lid on the saucepan and leave it to simmer away gently for about 30 minutes or until all the vegetables are tender and the lentils pale golden and soft.

Meanwhile, fry the remaining onion in the remaining oil for 10 minutes without browning, then add the ground coriander and cumin and fry for a further minute or two to draw out the flavor of the spices. Stir this mixture into the cooked lentils and add salt and pepper to taste, and the lemon juice. Scatter with a little chopped parsley before serving.

Tip
If you prefer to bake this, it takes about an hour in a moderate oven, 350°F (180°C).

Shepherd's lentil pie

Green lentils make a tasty moist filling for a shepherd's pie. If you can prepare the mashed potatoes in advance, this is quick to make.

SERVES 4–6 ❄
6oz (175g) dried brown or green lentils
2 cups (575ml) water
1 bay leaf
1 onion, finely chopped
1 tbsp olive oil
1 small carrot, chopped
1 stalk of celery, finely chopped
1 garlic clove, crushed
¼ cup wine (optional)
14oz can tomatoes
salt and freshly ground black pepper

FOR THE TOPPING
1½lb (700g) mashed potato
1oz (25g) grated cheese (optional)

Put the lentils, water and bay leaf into a medium-sized saucepan and leave to simmer gently or until the lentils are tender (35–45 minutes).

Preheat the oven to 400°F (200°C).

Fry the onion in the oil for 10 minutes, then add the carrot, celery and garlic and cook for a further couple of minutes, stirring from time to time.

Remove from the heat and stir in the wine (if using) and tomatoes; season to taste with salt and pepper.

Spoon the mixture into a lightly greased, shallow ovenproof dish and cover with the mashed potato. Level the surface, then rough it up with the prongs of a fork and sprinkle with the grated cheese (if using).

Bake for 45 minutes or until golden brown.

Spicy lentils and potatoes v

This is quick, easy and cheap. It's good with slices of firm raw tomato and some mango chutney.

SERVES 4
1 onion, chopped
2 tbsp olive oil
1 garlic clove, crushed
2 tsp cumin seeds
walnut-sized piece of fresh root ginger, finely grated
3 potatoes, peeled and cut into 2cm (1in) cubes
8oz (225g) split red lentils
2½ cups (700ml) water
salt and freshly ground black pepper

Fry the onion in the oil for 10 minutes in a large saucepan or large, deep, frying pan.

Add the garlic, cumin and ginger; stir-fry for 1–2 minutes, then add the potatoes and stir for a further minute or two.

Add the lentils, water and a little seasoning, bring to a boil, then cover, turn down the heat and cook gently for 15–20 minutes or until lentils are pale and soft and potatoes just tender when pierced with a sharp knife.

Check the seasoning and serve at once.

Lentil and spinach gratin

The marriage of lentils and spinach is a particularly pleasing one, and this is a nice easy dish to make.

SERVES 4
8oz (225g) split red lentils
2 cups (575ml) water
2¼lb (1kg) spinach
salt and freshly ground black pepper
8oz (225g) tomatoes, skinned and
    sliced
3–4oz (75–125g) grated cheese

Cook the lentils in the water for about 20 minutes or until they're soft and pale in color.

Meanwhile, wash the spinach and cook it in a saucepan, without additional water, for 7–10 minutes or until wilted. Drain off the excess liquid and chop the spinach, then season it with salt and pepper.

Preheat the oven to 375°F (190°C).

Put the spinach into a lightly oiled shallow ovenproof dish and arrange the tomatoes on top. Sprinkle with salt and pepper.

Season the lentils and then pour them over the tomatoes, spreading to the edges of the dish. Top with a layer of grated cheese.

Bake in the oven for about 40 minutes or until golden on top.

Green lentils and spinach v

Simple, delicious and very soothing to eat. Add the spices according to your taste.

SERVES 3
1lb (450g) spinach
7oz (200g) dried green lentils,
    soaked and cooked until tender
    (see pages 176–7), then drained,
    or 2 x 14oz cans, drained
1 large onion, chopped
1 tbsp olive oil
2 garlic cloves, crushed
1–2 tsp each of ground cumin and
    ground coriander
salt and freshly ground black pepper
2–3 tsp freshly squeezed lemon juice

Wash the spinach and cook in a dry saucepan over a moderate heat, with a lid on the pan, until wilted (about 7 minutes). Drain.

Add the drained lentils to the spinach placing the saucepan over a gentle heat to keep the spinach hot and heat the lentils through.

Fry the onion in the oil for 10 minutes or until tender, then stir in the garlic and spices and cook for a minute or two longer.

Add this mixture to the spinach and lentils, together with salt, pepper and lemon juice to taste. Serve at once.

Pease pudding

This makes a very good main dish in its own right, with crisp roast potatoes, a vegetable, savory vegetarian gravy (see page 66) and some mint or apple sauce.

SERVES 4
8oz (225g) yellow split peas
1 large onion
2 tbsp (25g) butter
salt and freshly ground black pepper

If possible soak the peas in cold water for a couple of hours or so — this speeds up the cooking time — then drain and rinse them, put them into a large saucepan with a good covering of cold water and simmer them gently, with the lid half on the pan, until they're tender. I find the cooking time of split peas seems to vary quite a bit; sometimes they're done in 30 minutes, at other times they can take as long as 1 hour. Watch the water level and add more if necessary as they cook; when they're done — soft but not soggy — drain them.

While this is happening, peel and chop the onion and fry gently in the butter until soft and golden (10 minutes).

Add the onion to the split peas and season with salt and pepper.

Traditionally pease pudding was steamed in a pudding cloth at this point, but I just serve it right away, or keep it warm in a covered dish in a low oven.

Tip
You can vary pease pudding in quite a few ways. It's nice with some grated lemon rind added or some chopped fresh marjoram or sage.

Red bean moussaka

Caraway, cumin and fennel seeds also go well with it — add them to the onion when it's nearly done — and a pinch of ground cloves is nice, too.

Baked pease pudding v

Add an egg to the mixture and bake it in a greased baking dish in a moderate oven, 350°F (180°C) for 30–40 minutes. Alternatively, for a vegan version, just put the mixture as it is (with oil instead of butter and no egg) into a fairly shallow dish, level and press the top, and bake.

For a simpler version of this dish, leave out the eggplant, sprinkle the bean mixture with breadcrumbs and bake as it is. It's also good made with black kidney beans.

SERVES 6
2 eggplant (about 1lb (450g)) sliced into ¼in (6mm) discs
salt
1 large onion, chopped
5 tbsp olive oil
1 garlic clove, crushed
7oz (200g) dried red kidney beans, soaked and cooked (see pages 176–7), then drained or 2 x 14oz cans, drained and rinsed
4 tomatoes
1 tbsp tomato purée
3–4 tbsp red wine (optional)
½ tsp ground cumin or cinnamon
freshly ground black pepper
sugar
1 egg
15fl oz (425ml) cheese sauce (see page 65)
2oz (50g) grated cheese

Sprinkle the eggplant discs with salt, place in a colander with a plate and a weight on top and leave for 30 minutes. Then rinse under the cold tap and squeeze dry. You can omit this stage, but it does help them not to absorb too much oil when you fry them.

Preheat the oven to 350°F (180°C).

Fry the onion in 1 tablespoon of the oil for 10 minutes, then add the garlic, drained kidney beans, tomatoes, tomato purée and wine (if using), mashing the beans a little.

Add the cumin or cinnamon and season with salt, pepper and a dash of sugar if necessary.

Fry the eggplant slices in the remaining oil, patting on kitchen paper to remove any excess.

Beat the egg into the cheese sauce.

Grease a shallow ovenproof dish, put half the eggplant slices into the base, cover with half the kidney bean mixture and then half the sauce. Repeat the layers, ending with the sauce, then sprinkle the top with the grated cheese. Bake for 1 hour or until bubbling and golden.

Quick and easy red bean and tomato pie

A quick meal that children enjoy. Serve with a green vegetable.

SERVES 4

1½lb (750g) potatoes, peeled and cut into chunks
a pat of butter, plus extra for greasing
4oz (125g) grated cheese
a little milk
salt and freshly ground black pepper
1 onion, chopped
1 tbsp olive oil
14oz can tomatoes
14oz can red kidney beans, drained, or 4oz (125g) dried red kidney beans, soaked, cooked (see pages 176–7) and drained

Preheat the oven to 400°F (200°C) or prepare a hot grill.

Cook the potatoes in enough water to cover until tender, then drain and mash with the butter, half the cheese and enough milk to make a soft consistency. Season with salt and pepper.

While the potatoes are cooking, fry the onion in the oil in a covered saucepan for 7–10 minutes or until tender.

Add the tomatoes and kidney beans to the onion, mashing them a little or puréeing them smooth in a food processor or with an electric hand blender. Season to taste.

Spoon the kidney bean mixture into a shallow greased ovenproof dish, spread the potato on top, sprinkle with the remaining cheese and bake for 25–30 minutes. Alternatively, have the bean mixture and potatoes piping hot when you put them in the dish, then just brown the top under the broiler.

Frijoles refritos v

This is a quick version of the traditional South American dish, *frijoles refritos*, which actually means "twice cooked". This refers to the initial cooking of the beans after soaking and then a second cooking when the beans are added to a pan containing lard and cooked until they are thick and creamy. Needless to say, my version doesn't include lard, and I also prefer to speed up the process by using canned beans. The result is delicious; creamy and spicy. It makes a wonderful spread when served with sour cream, sliced avocado, chopped tomato, shredded lettuce, tortilla chips and some crisp lettuce leaves. Or warm some corn tortillas in the oven and have a fajitas feast: put some of the refried beans into the center of a warm tortilla, fold the bottom of the tortilla up and the sides in, and then spoon your choice of the other ingredients on top.

SERVES 4 ❊

2 onions, chopped
3 tbsp olive oil
2 garlic cloves, crushed
¼–½ tsp chili powder
2 tsp ground cumin
2 x 14oz cans red kidney or pinto beans (don't drain them)
salt and freshly ground black pepper
2 tbsp chopped fresh coriander, to garnish

TO SERVE
shredded lettuce
chopped tomato
sour cream, vegan or dairy
1 large ripe avocado, sliced
tortilla chips and/or corn tortillas

In a large frying pan, fry the onions in the oil for 8 minutes, then add the garlic, chili powder and cumin and fry for another minute.

Add the beans, together with their liquid, mashing them with a fork or potato masher and mixing them with the onions and spices.

Continue to cook the beans for 5–10 minutes or until they're thick and creamy.

Serve in a large shallow dish, surrounded by lettuce leaves, chopped tomato and avocado slices, with some sour cream and chopped fresh coriander on top. Accompany with a bowl of tortilla chips.

Russian red beans with damson sauce v

This Russian dish has an unusual, sweet flavor which goes well with a crunchy salad of white cabbage. If you haven't any damson jam, you could use plum jam or redcurrant jelly. You do need dried basil for this as it's partly what gives the dish its special flavor. This is best if there's time for it to stand for a couple of hours after cooking.

SERVES 3–4
7oz (200g) dried red kidney beans, soaked and cooked (see pages 176–7), or 2 x 14oz cans red kidney beans (without added sugar and salt if possible)
2 tbsp damson or plum jam
½ tsp red wine vinegar
1 garlic clove, crushed
salt
½ tsp dried basil
½ tsp ground coriander

Drain the beans.

Sieve the jam and put it into a small saucepan with the vinegar; cook them gently over a low heat until the jam has melted.

Add the crushed garlic, a little salt and the basil and coriander.

Remove from the heat and add to the beans, stirring well so that all the beans get coated.

If possible, leave to stand for 2–3 hours, so that the flavors can develop. It's supposed to be served cold, but I prefer it warm, or at room temperature.

Red kidney bean stew v

A quick and easy stew with a vibrant color. I like it with a cooked green vegetable or green salad.

SERVES 4 ❄
1lb (450g) onions, chopped
2 tbsp olive oil
2 x 14oz cans chopped tomatoes
7oz (200g) dried red kidney beans, soaked, cooked (see pages 176–7) and drained, or
2 x 14oz cans red kidney beans (without added sugar and salt if possible), drained
salt and freshly ground black pepper
dash of tomato ketchup

Fry the onions in the oil in a large saucepan, covered, for about 10 minutes until they're soft but not browned.

Add the tomatoes and beans and season with salt, pepper and a dash of tomato ketchup, to taste.

Let the mixture simmer gently for 10–15 minutes, then serve.

VARIATIONS
Chili red beans v

Make as described, adding ½–1 teaspoon of chili powder, to taste (depending on your taste and how hot the chili powder is).

Red kidney beans with tomatoes, onions and cumin v

For this spicier version, add 2 teaspoons of whole cumin seeds to the onions after about 5 minutes. Continue as described.

West Indian red beans v

This recipe was told to a friend of mine by a West Indian woman as she was buying vegetables in a market. The creamed coconut gives the touch of sweetness so characteristic of Caribbean cookery. It also thickens the sauce.

SERVES 4
8oz (225g) dried red kidney beans
1 large onion, sliced
1 large carrot, sliced
1 large garlic clove, crushed
1 tbsp dried thyme
3oz (75g) creamed coconut (from a block) or ½ cup canned coconut cream
salt and freshly ground black pepper
hot cooked rice, to serve

Soak the beans for several hours in cold water (see pages 176–7), then drain and rinse them.

Put the beans, onion, carrot and garlic into a large saucepan and cover them with cold water; bring to a boil and bubble away vigorously for 10 minutes, then turn the heat down and leave to simmer gently for 45 minutes or until the beans are nearly cooked.

Add the thyme and continue cooking for another 15–30 minutes to finish cooking the beans.

Cut the creamed coconut into pieces and add to the bean mixture. Heat gently, stirring occasionally, until all the coconut has melted or pour in the canned coconut cream.

Season with salt and pepper and serve.

Split pea dal with hardboiled eggs

Serve with fluffy brown rice.

SERVES 4

8oz (225g) yellow split peas
2 tbsp olive oil
2 large onions, chopped
2 large garlic cloves, crushed
3 tsp ground cumin
3 tsp turmeric
1 tbsp freshly squeezed lemon juice
salt and freshly ground black pepper
1–2 tbsp chopped fresh flat-leaf
    parsley, to garnish
4 hardboiled eggs, cut into quarters,
    to serve

Soak the split peas in cold water for several hours, then rinse them and cook them in fresh cold water until they're tender (30–45 minutes). Drain off any excess liquid.

Meanwhile, heat the olive oil in a large saucepan and fry the onions and garlic, with a lid on the pan, for 5 minutes, then add the ground cumin and turmeric and fry for a further 5 minutes.

Mix in the cooked split peas and heat gently, stirring to prevent sticking. Add the lemon juice and salt and pepper to taste. Sprinkle with chopped parsley and serve with the hardboiled eggs.

VARIATION

Split peas with fennel seeds and hardboiled eggs

Make as described, omitting the cumin and turmeric. Fry 1 tablespoon of fennel seed in 1 tbsp (15g) butter for 1–2 minutes until the seeds start to pop, then pour them over the split peas, add the eggs and serve. Omit the parsley.

Yellow split pea purée with vegetables v

This recipe from Germany is not unlike our pease pudding. Baked potatoes go well with it.

SERVES 4

8oz (225g) yellow split peas
2 cups (575ml) water
2 onions, sliced
1 carrot, sliced
1 small leek, sliced
1 stalk of celery, sliced
a good pinch of dried mint or
    marjoram
1 tbsp freshly squeezed lemon juice
salt and freshly ground black pepper
2 tbsp olive oil

Soak the split peas in the water for 1 hour, then drain and rinse them and put them into a saucepan with the water, half the sliced onions and all the other vegetables and herbs. Simmer gently until the split peas are soft and the vegetables tender (about 30 minutes).

Purée the mixture in a food processor or with a hand blender. Add lemon juice, salt and pepper.

Spoon the mixture into a shallow heatproof dish.

Fry the remaining onion in the olive oil until it's beginning to soften, then pour the mixture over the top of the purée.

Put under a fairly hot broiler until the top is slightly crusted-looking and the onion very crisp and brown.

Chili-braised tofu with bok choy v

Rich brown, sticky, glossy "steaks" of tofu, oozing with flavor served with tender bok choy. The best tofu to use for this is the firm "silken" type. You can buy this fresh at Chinese stores, or in vacuum packs. Ume plum vinegar can be found in Asian stores and in good health-food stores. It lasts for ages and is great for bringing the flavor out of many dishes.

SERVES 2

12oz block firm silken tofu
2–3 heads of bok choy, cut in half
    lengthways
sesame seeds, to garnish

FOR THE MARINADE

2 tbsp ume plum vinegar
2 tbsp mild-flavored olive oil
2 tbsp shoyu or dark soy sauce, such
    as Kikkoman
2 tsp finely grated fresh root ginger
2 garlic cloves, crushed
2 tbsp sweet chili sauce

Drain the tofu thoroughly and blot well with paper towels or a clean cloth. Slice the tofu across the narrow end so you have eight chunky "steaks" each about ½in (1cm) thick. Do this gently, but don't worry if a few bits break off; they will also get coated with the tasty marinade.

Put all the marinade ingredients into a shallow dish that is large enough to hold all the pieces of tofu in a single layer, and mix together. Put the tofu slices in the dish, gently turning each one to coat with the marinade and leave to marinate for 10–30 minutes.

Roasted marinated tofu v

Heat a frying pan. Add the tofu slices to the pan with just the marinade clinging to them and fry over a fairly high heat for 2–3 minutes until they are brown and sticky on one side, then turn them over and fry for a further 2–3 minutes or until well browned and sticky. Add the remaining marinade to the pan, just to heat it through.

While the tofu is frying, heat 1cm (½in) of water in a large saucepan, add the bok choy, cover with a lid and boil for about 4 minutes or until tender, then drain.

Divide the bok choy and the tofu along with its marinade between 2 warm plates, sprinkle a few sesame seeds over the top and serve at once.

Tofu has been made and eaten in China and Japan for many centuries and is full of protein and nutrients. In its natural form it tastes quite bland, but will absorb flavors really well. The secret lies in the marinating and there are plenty of flavorings you can use. Once you've marinated the tofu, you can use it in any recipe that calls for marinated tofu, or you can continue with this recipe and roast it. Serve the roasted tofu with a salad or cooked green vegetable.

SERVES 2
9oz block firm silken tofu

FOR THE MARINADE
1½ tsp grated fresh root ginger
1 garlic clove, crushed
2 tbsp shoyu dark soy sauce
1 tbsp dark sesame oil
1 tbsp honey or maple syrup

Drain the tofu and blot dry with kitchen paper.

Cut the tofu into cubes, about ½in (1 cm) or a shade smaller, or slice it in half through the middle then across, so that you end up with four thin rectangles. Or cut it across into long fingers about ¼in (6mm) thick.

Make the marinade by mixing together all the ingredients. If you do this in a shallow ovenproof dish, you can roast the tofu in the same dish once it has marinated. If possible, leave the tofu to marinate for an hour or so, or for several hours, although if you're in a hurry, you can roast it right away.

Roast the tofu in an oven preheated to 400°F (200°C) for 25–30 minutes or until the tofu is brown and crisp. Turn the pieces after about 15 minutes.

VARIATION
Sesame-toasted tofu v

Marinate the tofu as described. You can put the tofu into the dish or cut it into chunky pieces and thread them onto 2 skewers, turning them so that the tofu gets covered all over with the marinade. Roast as described, for 10 minutes, then sprinkle the tofu with 1–2 tablespoons of sesame seeds and roast for an additional 15–20 minutes, turning the pieces a couple of times. Serve in warm pita bread or with rice and the satay sauce on page 70.

Salt and pepper tofu with lettuce and capers v

I love this! Delicious crisp chunks of deep-fried tofu sprinkled with flakes of sea salt and coarsely ground black pepper served with crunchy lettuce and creamy, piquant mayonnaise. For the best tofu to use see chili-braised tofu with bok choy on page 202. This dish is vegan if you use one of the excellent no-egg mayonnaises available.

SERVES 4

3–4 tbsp cornstarch
12oz block firm silken tofu, drained and cut into 1in (2.5cm) cubes
rapeseed oil, for deep-frying
1 tsp sea salt
1 tsp coarsely ground black pepper

FOR THE SALAD

hearts of 2–3 Little Gem or Romaine lettuces
2 rounded tbsp good-quality mayonnaise
1 tbsp freshly squeezed lemon juice
a small handful of capers

Spread the cornstarch out on a piece of greaseproof paper and sprinkle the tofu with cornstarch to coat it all over; it will cling to the wet surfaces of the tofu.

Heat enough oil for deep-frying in a small, heavy-based saucepan. When the oil reaches 350°F (180°C), or a cube of bread dropped into it rises to the surface and turns golden brown in under 1 minute, drop in the tofu and deep-fry for about 5 minutes or until very crisp. Drain on paper towels and sprinkle with the salt and pepper.

While the tofu is cooking, arrange the lettuce on two plates. Mix the mayonnaise with the lemon juice and perhaps a drop of water to make a pouring consistency, like cream.

Put the hot cooked tofu on top of the lettuce, top with a few caperberries, and drizzle with the mayonnaise. Serve immediately.

Stir-fried tofu with carrots and miso v

When using tofu in a stir-fried mixture, flavoring is all-important. Here the flavor is supplied by the garlic, ginger, soy sauce, miso, sherry and stock. It's lovely to use Chinese mushrooms if you can get them — they're available dried from Chinese grocers — but if not, use ordinary mushrooms. Miso is available from health-food stores or large supermarkets.

SERVES 2–3

8oz (225g) carrots
6 dried Chinese mushrooms or 4oz (125g) fresh mushrooms
1 onion
2 garlic cloves
2 tbsp dark soy sauce
½–1 tsp miso
1 tsp sugar
a few drops of Tabasco sauce
¼ cup boiling water
1 tbsp fino sherry
8oz (225g) firm silken tofu, drained
2 tsp grated fresh root ginger
3 tbsp ground nut or rapeseed oil

Prepare the carrots by peeling them and then cutting them into thin diagonal slices. Boil them for 4–5 minutes or until they're almost tender, then drain.

Soak the dried mushrooms in enough water just to cover them, then drain them and cut into narrow strips. Or, if you're using ordinary mushrooms, wash and slice them.

Peel and very finely chop the onion; crush the garlic.

Mix together the soy sauce, miso, sugar, Tabasco, hot water and sherry. Cut the tofu into smallish dice.

Tofu and mushroom stir-fry v

Dried Chinese mushrooms give this dish an excellent flavor, but if you can't find them, use ordinary fresh mushrooms instead.

SERVES 2

6 dried Chinese mushrooms or 4oz (125g) fresh mushrooms
8oz (225g) firm silken tofu, drained
olive oil, for shallow-frying
1 onion, chopped
garlic clove, crushed
1 piece of fresh root ginger (about 1in (2.5cm) long), grated
1 tbsp dark soy sauce
½ tsp vegetarian bouillon powder or crumbled stock cube
2 tbsp water or liquid drained from the soaked dried mushrooms
2oz (50g) sliced almonds, to garnish

If you're using dried mushrooms, rinse them under the tap then put them into a small bowl, cover them with boiling water and leave them for 1 hour. Drain the mushrooms, reserving the liquid. Cut the mushrooms into pieces. If you're using fresh mushrooms, wash and slice them.

Drain the tofu and cut into smallish cubes, heat a little oil in a large saucepan and fry the tofu quickly until it is lightly browned on all sides. Take it out of the oil and keep it warm.

Heat a little more oil in the saucepan and fry the onions for about 7 minutes, then add the garlic, ginger and the soaked dried or fresh mushrooms and fry for about 2 minutes or until the mushrooms are just tender.

Stir in the soy sauce, stock powder and water or mushroom liquid. Let the mixture blend for a moment or two, then add the tofu and cook gently for about 2 minutes to reheat the tofu and give it a chance to absorb the flavors of the sauce.

Sprinkle the almonds over the mixture just before serving it. Serve this with fluffy cooked rice and Napa cabbage leaves.

When ready to cook, heat the oil in a wok or large frying pan and fry the garlic, ginger and onion for a few seconds, then stir in the mushrooms and carrots; cook for 30 seconds, then pour in the soy sauce mixture and cook for a couple of minutes, so that all the flavors have a chance to blend. Mix in the tofu and stir-fry for a further 2 minutes, so that everything is hot. Serve immediately.

Pasta

For quick, filling food that's popular with kids and adults alike, you really can't beat pasta. It's cheap to buy, stores well, easy to cook and there are hundreds of ways of serving it. Fortunately for vegetarians and vegans, many of these dishes do not involve meat or fish, though vegans do need to avoid egg pasta and vegetarians have to watch out for the type of cheese used (see page 4).

In this chapter you'll find many classic pasta recipes – spaghetti with fresh tomato sauce and basil, ravioli with ricotta and spinach and spaghetti with pesto (see pages 226, 222 and 225), to name but a few. You'll also find some lesser-known combinations, such as penne with asparagus and morels, and lentil, tomato and red wine lasagna (see pages 220 and 216). Try experimenting with different ingredients to create your own mouth-watering recipes.

Types of pasta

There are many different types of pasta; here's a list of some of the most popular and widely available:

Anelli pasta rings Especially good in salads and savory bakes. The wholemeal version is particularly tasty. These rings can be hard to find, however – look in Italian delis.

Cannelloni are large pasta tubes. Parboiled, then filled with stuffing, such as the ricotta stuffing on page 212 or the walnut and tomato stuffing on the same page and baked in a tasty sauce, these make a delicious dish.

Conchiglie shells Available in various shapes and sizes. Delicious with olive oil, garlic and fresh herbs, or mixed with colorful vegetables.

Farfalle or butterflies. Good with butter or olive oil and grated cheese or mixed with vegetables.

Fettucce A wide, ribbon-like egg noodle.

Fettuccine is a narrower version. Both are excellent with creamy sauces.

Fusilli Pasta spirals, like little corkscrews. Look pretty when mixed with colorful vegetables and in salads.

Lasagna Broad strips of pasta that are cooked and then rolled round tasty ingredients or layered with them in an ovenproof dish and baked.

Linguine is flat spaghetti, use like spaghetti.

Maccheroni or macaroni Can be bought in straight or curved "elbow" versions, and in varying thicknesses, some with ridges. Serve with tasty sauces.

Penne Straight macaroni with diagonally cut ends, like the nib of a pen. Use like macaroni.

Ravioli Little cushions of pasta containing a filling; they are cooked and served with butter and grated cheese, or with a sauce.

Rigatoni Large, ridged pasta tubes, generally served in a sauce or in baked dishes. The ridges help the sauce to cling to the pasta.

Ruote di carro Wagon wheels; good with a sauce, popular with children, especially when served with the tomato sauce on page 71 and sprinkled with grated cheese.

Spaghetti Probably the best known and most popular type of pasta. Makes an excellent quick meal when served with a tasty sauce.

Tagliatelle Ribbon-like egg noodles, usually coiled into bundles before packing. Can be used like spaghetti; particularly good with creamy sauces.

Vermicelli Thin spaghetti, usually packed in coils. Cooks very quickly.

Wholegrain pasta Many of the above shapes can be bought in a wholegrain version, and the range is expanding. Wholegrain pasta looks quite dark in the packet, but is lighter after cooking.

How to make your own pasta

If you enjoy pasta and eat a fair amount of it, you might find it worthwhile making your own at home. Using a pasta machine makes it a surprisingly quick and easy process; it's fun to do and the results are very good.

Equipment

You'll need a large bowl for mixing the dough, a pastry wheel if you want to make ravioli (see page 222) and a pasta-making machine. You can buy electric pasta machines, also attachments for some food processors, but I think the little hand machines are fine for normal domestic use. These consist of rollers which are turned by a handle, and are easy both to use and to clean.

Ingredients

TO MAKE 6OZ (175G) PASTA
YOU WILL NEED:

3½oz (100g) all-purpose flour: wholegrain, wholewheat, unbleached white or a mixture. Bread flour made from hard wheat is best

¼ tsp salt

1 large egg

Method

Put the flour and salt into a bowl and crack in the egg. Using your hands, mix the flour, little by little, into the egg, until you have a fairly smooth dough.

Set the smooth sided rollers of your pasta machine to their widest position. Take a piece of pasta dough about the size of an egg, flatten it roughly with your hands, then feed it through the rollers. Fold the piece of dough into thirds, then feed it through again.

Do this six or seven times, until the dough is smooth and pliable then lay it to the side and repeat the process with the rest of the dough, keeping the pieces in the right order.

Next, tighten the rollers a notch and feed the pieces of pasta through again, once only this time, and without folding. Repeat three times, tightening the rollers a notch each time. Cut the pieces of pasta in half if they become too long to handle, and support them as they come through the machine so that they don't fall in folds and stick together.

If you want to make a lasagna, cannelloni or ravioli, feed the pasta through the machine again with the rollers on the next to smallest setting. The pasta can then be cut to the required size and used right away in savory bakes, without further drying or cooking. For ravioli, see page 222. If you want to make spaghetti, tagliatelle or other thin noodle shapes, pass the sheets of pasta through one of the cutting rollers, then spread it out on a clean, lightly floured dish towel or drape it over the edge of a saucepan or broom handle, and leave it to dry for 1 hour. It can then be cooked as described opposite, allowing 2–3 minutes only.

Guide to quantities

Fresh pasta can replace the same quantity of dried pasta in any recipe. Like dried pasta, fresh pasta will swell and expand as it cooks.

How to cook pasta

Serving pasta

Allow 1–2oz (25–50g) uncooked pasta for each person for a first course; 3–4oz (75–125g) per person for a main course. The main thing to remember when cooking pasta is that it needs plenty of water to enable it to move around, so allow 1 quart (1.2 liters) of water for every 4oz (125g) pasta, or 1 gallon (4 liters) for 1lb (450g) and use your largest saucepan, or two smaller ones if necessary, and add 1 teaspoon of salt. You can also add 1 tablespoon of olive oil, if you like: this helps prevent the pasta from sticking together. Bring the water to a boil.

When the water reaches boiling point, add the pasta. Long types like spaghetti need to be eased into the water. Hold the spaghetti like a bunch of flowers, stand it upright in the water and gradually let it all down into the water as it softens and bends. Drop other types of pasta into the water a few at a time, then give them a stir once they're all in. Let the pasta boil gently, without a lid on the pan.

It's important not to overcook the pasta. It should be tender but not soggy. Most packets state a cooking time, but it's best to treat this as a guide only, and to start testing the pasta well before that time is up. To see if pasta is cooked, take a piece out of the water and bite it. It's done if it is tender yet still have a little resistance: al dente — "to the tooth" as Italians say. If it's not quite ready, cook it for a bit longer, but keep testing.

Here is a rough guide to the cooking times of various types of pasta:

very thin pasta, small shapes
5–9 minutes
larger shapes, long tubes
10–20 minutes
fresh pasta
2–3 minutes

As soon as the pasta is done, pour it into a colander to drain. Give it a shake, then put it back into the saucepan or into a heated serving dish with a pat of butter or some olive oil and salt and freshly ground black pepper to taste.

Cooked pasta can be served simply, just with butter or olive oil and seasoning, and perhaps the addition of some crushed garlic or chopped fresh herbs, or a sprinkling of grated Parmesan-style* cheese. Or swirl it in pesto, serve with a tasty sauce, mix with some delicious cooked vegetables, or make it into a tasty dish such as baked lasagna or macaroni cheese: there are so many possibilities and they're all easy and delicious.

*(Although traditional Parmesan is not vegetarian, there are "Parmesan-style" cheeses that are. Delicious hard Pecorino cheese is often vegetarian and another good alternative.)

Mushroom-stuffed cannelloni in sour cream

Succulent mushroom cannelloni nestling in a creamy sauce under a topping of crisp breadcrumbs.

SERVES 4
12 cannelloni tubes or fresh pasta
    sheets
salt
1 onion, chopped
2 tbsp (25g) butter or olive oil, plus
    extra for greasing
12oz (350g) mushrooms, chopped
1 garlic clove, crushed
2oz (50g) fine fresh breadcrumbs
2 tbsp chopped fresh flat-leaf
    parsley
freshly ground black pepper
11fl oz (300ml) sour cream
1 tsp of cornstarch

Cook the pasta as described in the previous recipe, drain, spread out on a clean cloth and leave to one side.

Preheat the oven to 400°F (200°C).

Fry the onion in the butter or olive oil for 5 minutes; add the mushrooms and garlic and fry for 5 minutes more. If the mushrooms give off much liquid, increase the heat and boil hard until this has evaporated.

Remove from the heat, add the breadcrumbs, parsley and seasoning.

Spoon the mushroom mixture into the cannelloni, or on top of the lasagna sheets, then make into rolls.

Place them in a greased shallow ovenproof dish. Mix the sour cream with the cornstarch, then pour evenly over the cannelloni to cover. Bake for 45 minutes.

Ricotta-stuffed cannelloni in tomato sauce

You can use cannelloni or homemade pasta for this recipe, which is impressive-looking but easy to do and popular with everyone. Serve with a arugula or other green salad.

SERVES 4 ❄
12 cannelloni tubes or fresh pasta
salt
8oz (225g) ricotta
1 garlic clove, crushed
2 tbsp milk
freshly ground black pepper
tomato sauce (see page 71)
olive oil, for greasing

Plunge the pasta into boiling salted water. Cook the cannelloni for 4–5 minutes only or until pliable but not collapsed, the pasta sheets until just tender.

Drain the pasta well and spread out on a clean cloth.

Preheat the oven to 400°F (200°C).

Mix the ricotta with the garlic, milk and seasoning.

Spoon the ricotta mixture into the cannelloni, or spoon on top of the pasta sheets, then make into rolls.

Place in a greased shallow ovenproof dish, cover with sauce and bake for 45 minutes.

Cannelloni with walnuts, tomatoes and red wine

Dried basil is used in the stuffing mix rather than fresh because of the delicious intense flavor it gives when cooked.

SERVES 4 ❄
12 cannelloni tubes or fresh pasta
    sheets
salt
1 onion, chopped
2 tbsp olive oil, plus extra for greasing
1 garlic clove, crushed
8oz (225g) tomatoes, skinned (see
    page 40) and chopped
6oz (175g) shelled walnuts, chopped
6oz (175g) fine fresh wholegrain
    breadcrumbs
1 tsp dried basil
5fl oz (150ml) red wine
freshly ground black pepper
2 cups (575ml) cheese sauce
    (see page 65)

Plunge the pasta into boiling salted water. Cook the cannelloni for 4–5 minutes only, so that it's pliable but not collapsed, the pasta sheets until just tender.

Preheat the oven to 400°F (200°C).

Fry the onion in the oil for about 8 minutes, with a lid on the pan, then add the garlic and fry for a further minute or two.

Remove from the heat, add the tomatoes, walnuts, breadcrumbs, basil, wine and seasoning.

Spoon the mixture into the cannelloni or put on top of the pasta sheets, then make into rolls.

Place the plump rolls in a greased shallow ovenproof dish and cover with the cheese sauce.

Bake for 45 minutes or until golden brown and bubbling.

Hot conchiglie with avocado and mozzarella cheese

Excellent as a hot first course or a light supper dish.

SERVES 4–6

8–12oz (225–350g) conchiglie
    (pasta shells)
salt
2 large avocados
2 tbsp freshly squeezed lemon juice
6oz (175g) mozzarella cheese
2 tbsp olive oil
2 garlic cloves, crushed
2 tbsp chopped fresh flat-leaf
    parsley
freshly ground black pepper
grated Parmesan-style cheese, to
    serve

Cook the pasta in plenty of boiling salted water until just tender, then drain thoroughly.

While the pasta is cooking, halve each avocado, remove the stone and skin, dice the flesh and sprinkle with lemon juice. Dice the mozzarella.

Add the olive oil, garlic, parsley, avocado and cheese to the hot drained pasta, stirring gently over the heat to distribute the ingredients and warm the avocado and cheese slightly, but being careful not to get it too hot; it doesn't need to cook at all.

Grind in some black pepper to taste, then serve immediately.

It's good with some grated Parmesan-style cheese over the top.

Conchiglie with red and white beans in parsley butter

This is an attractive dish with the contrasting beans and fresh green parsley butter.

SERVES 4–6

8–12oz (225–350g) conchiglie
    (pasta shells)
salt
14oz can red kidney beans
14oz can cannellini beans
3 tbsp (40g) butter, softened
3 tbsp chopped fresh flat-leaf
    parsley
2 tbsp freshly squeezed lemon juice
freshly ground black pepper

Cook the pasta in plenty of boiling salted water until just tender, then drain thoroughly.

Put the beans, together with their liquid, into a saucepan, and heat through gently while the pasta cooks.

Meanwhile, beat the butter with the parsley and lemon juice until well blended; leave to one side.

Drain the beans. Add the parsley butter and beans to the hot drained pasta and season.

Stir gently then serve immediately.

Farfalle with zucchini, peas and mint

Fresh flavors and pretty colors are combined in this summery dish.

SERVES 4–6

8–12oz (225–350g) farfalle
salt
2 tbsp (25g) butter
1 tbsp olive oil
1lb (450g) zucchini, thinly sliced
6oz (175g) shelled peas
2 tbsp chopped fresh mint
freshly ground black pepper
grated Parmesan-style cheese

Cook the pasta in plenty of boiling salted water until just tender, then drain thoroughly.

While the pasta is cooking, melt the butter and oil in a large saucepan and cook the zucchini and peas over a gentle heat until tender (about 5–8 minutes).

Add the zucchini and peas to the hot drained pasta, together with the remaining oil and butter from the pan and the chopped mint.

Stir gently, adding salt and pepper to taste. Spoon onto a hot dish, sprinkle with grated cheese and serve at once.

Farfalle with mushrooms and parsley

Serve with a tomato and watercress salad for a light supper dish.

SERVES 4–6

8–12oz (225–350g) farfalle
salt
2 tbsp (25g) butter
1 tbsp olive oil
12oz (350g) button mushrooms, sliced
1 garlic clove, crushed
2 tbsp chopped fresh flat-leaf parsley
1 tbsp freshly squeezed lemon juice
freshly ground black pepper
grated Parmesan-style cheese (optional)

Cook the pasta in plenty of boiling salted water until just tender, then drain well.

Meanwhile, heat the butter and oil in a large saucepan and fry the mushrooms and garlic for 4–5 minutes or until the mushrooms are just tender.

Remove from the heat, stir in the parsley, lemon juice and seasoning, then add this mixture to the hot drained pasta. Stir gently to distribute the ingredients and check the seasoning.

Serve at once, sprinkled with grated Parmesan cheese (if using).

Quick lasagna bake

A quick and easy lasagna that's excellent with a green salad.

SERVES 4

6oz (175g) dried or "no cook" lasagna noodles
salt
5fl oz (150ml) milk
11fl oz (300ml) sour cream, natural yogurt or cheese sauce (see page 65)
1lb (450g) onions, sliced
2 tbsp olive oil, plus extra for greasing
14oz can chopped tomatoes
freshly ground black pepper
4oz (125g) grated cheese

Cook the traditional dried lasagna noodles in plenty of boiling salted water until tender, then drape the pasta pieces over the sides of the colander to prevent them from sticking together. Or use the "no cook" type of lasagna and add the milk to the sour cream.

Preheat the oven to 400°F (200°C).

Fry the onions in the oil, with a lid on the pan, until tender (about 10 minutes).

Put a layer of noodles in the base of a greased shallow ovenproof dish.

Top with half the onions and tomatoes, season with salt and pepper, then sprinkle with a third of the grated cheese.

Repeat these layers, then cover with lasagna noodles.

Spread the sour cream, yogurt or cheese sauce over the top, so the lasagna is completely covered, sprinkle with the remaining cheese and bake for 45 minutes or until bubbling and golden.

Lasagna baked with eggplant, onions and tomatoes

A delicious, colorful and welcoming dish that can be prepared in advance, then baked and served with a green salad or lightly cooked purple sprouting broccoli. If you have time to do the pre-cooking salting process with the eggplant, they will absorb less oil; if not, cook them right away, using a bit more oil than given. Eggplant will absorb all the oil you throw at it, so the trick is to cook it slowly over a gentle heat and it will soften.

SERVES 4 ✤

12oz (350g) eggplant
salt
4–6 tbsp olive oil, plus extra for greasing
2 onions, sliced
6oz (175g) lasagna noodles, traditional or "no cook"
12oz (350g) tomatoes, peeled and sliced
4oz (125g) grated cheese
2 cups (575ml) cheese sauce (see page 65)

Peel the eggplant, cut into thin discs, place in a colander and sprinkle with salt. Leave for 30 minutes, then rinse, pat dry and fry in the oil until tender and lightly browned on both sides. Drain well on paper towels and set aside.

Fry the onions in the remaining oil for 10 minutes.

Cook the traditional lasagna noodles in plenty of boiling salted water until just tender. Drain well, and drape pieces over the sides of the colander to prevent them from sticking together.

Lasagna and brown lentil bake

Alternatively, use "no cook" noodles and make the cheese sauce using the usual quantity of butter and flour but with an extra 5fl oz (150ml) milk.

Preheat the oven to 400°F (200°C).

Cover the base of a greased shallow ovenproof dish with noodles, top with half the eggplant, onions and tomatoes, some grated cheese and cheese sauce.

Repeat the layers, then cover with lasagna noodles, the rest of the cheese sauce and grated cheese.

Bake for 45 minutes or until bubbling and golden.

This dish is tasty, filling and very cheap to make.

SERVES 4 ❄

6oz (175g) lasagna noodles, traditional or "no cook"
salt
2 onions, chopped
1 stalk of celery, chopped
1 carrot, finely chopped
2 tbsp olive oil, plus extra for greasing
2 tsp ground coriander
7oz (200g) dried brown lentils, soaked and cooked (see pages 176–7), or 2 x 14oz cans
freshly ground black pepper
2 cups (575ml) cheese sauce (see page 65)
2oz (50g) grated cheese (optional)

Cook the traditional lasagna noodles in plenty of boiling water until just tender. Drain thoroughly, then drape the pieces over the sides of the colander to prevent them from sticking together.

Or use "no cook" lasagna noodles and make the cheese sauce with the usual amount of butter and flour and an extra 5fl oz (150ml) of milk.

Preheat the oven to 400°F (200°C).

Fry the onions, celery and carrot in the oil for 10–15 minutes or until tender and lightly browned, then stir in the ground coriander and cook for a minute or two longer.

Drain the lentils and add to the vegetables, together with salt and pepper to taste.

Put a layer of noodles in a greased shallow ovenproof dish, cover with half the lentils and a quarter of the sauce. Repeat the layers, then cover with noodles, the remaining sauce and cheese (if using). Bake for 45 minutes or until bubbling and golden.

Lasagna, red kidney bean and wine bake

Cheap to make, yet tasty enough for an informal supper party served with the remaining wine.

SERVES 4 ❄
6oz (175g) lasagna noodles, traditional or "no cook"
salt
2 onions, chopped
2 tbsp olive oil, plus extra for greasing
7oz (200g) dried red kidney beans, soaked and cooked (see pages 176–7), or 2 x 14oz cans
14 oz can chopped tomatoes
2 tbsp tomato purée
½–1 tsp ground cinnamon
2 tbsp red wine
freshly ground black pepper
2 cups (575ml) cheese sauce (see page 65)

Cook the traditional lasagna noodles in plenty of boiling salted water until just tender. Drain thoroughly, then drape the pieces over the edges of the colander to prevent them from sticking together.

Alternatively, use "no cook" lasagna noodles and make the cheese sauce adding an extra 5fl oz (150ml) milk to the usual quantity of butter and flour.

Preheat the oven to 400°F (200°C).

Fry the onions in the oil for 10 minutes, with a lid on the pan.

Drain the kidney beans (rinsing the canned ones) and add to the onions, along with the tomatoes. Mix well, mashing the beans.

Add the tomato purée, cinnamon, wine and seasoning.

Put a layer of noodles in a greased shallow ovenproof dish, cover with half the red bean mixture and a quarter of the sauce.

Repeat the layers, then top with noodles and remaining sauce.

Bake for 45 minutes or until it's golden brown, bubbling and smells wonderful.

Lentil, tomato and red wine lasagna

This dish consists of layers of lasagna and a tasty mixture of lentils, tomatoes and wine, topped with cheese sauce. The lasagna can be made in advance and is wonderful with a crisp green salad and a glass of red wine.

SERVES 4–6
2 tbsp olive oil, plus extra for greasing
1 onion, chopped
2 garlic cloves, crushed
1 medium–large red or green pepper, seeded and chopped
6oz (175g) split red lentils
14oz can chopped tomatoes
1 bay leaf
1¼ cups (275ml) vegetable stock or water
2 tbsp tomato purée
5fl oz (150ml) red wine
¼ tsp each of dried oregano, thyme and basil
½ tsp ground cinnamon
1 tbsp chopped fresh flat-leaf parsley
salt and freshly ground black pepper
sugar
6oz (175g) lasagna noodles, traditional or "no cook"

FOR THE TOPPING
2 eggs
5fl oz (150ml) milk
8oz (225g) fromage frais
4oz (125g) grated cheese

Heat the oil in a medium-sized saucepan and fry the onion for 10 minutes, then add the garlic, pepper, lentils, tomatoes, bay leaf, stock or water and tomato purée.

Bring to a boil and simmer gently for 20–30 minutes or until the lentils are tender and most of the water absorbed.

Remove the bay leaf and stir in the wine, herbs, cinnamon and chopped parsley. Mix well, then add salt, pepper and a little sugar to taste.

While the lentil mixture is cooking, prepare the pasta.

Half fill a large saucepan with lightly salted water and bring to the boil. Ease the pieces of traditional lasagna noodles into the boiling water and cook them for about 8 minutes or until they are just tender, then drain and drape the pieces of lasagna round the edge of the colander so they don't stick together.

Or use "no cook" lasagna noodles but soak it briefly in cold water so that it's wet when you put it in the dish.

Preheat the oven to 400°F (200°C).

Put a layer of lasagna noodles in the base of a greased shallow ovenproof dish and cover with half the lentil mixture; follow this with another layer of noodles, followed by the rest of the lentils, finishing with a layer of noodles.

To make the topping, whisk together the eggs, milk and fromage frais, season lightly and pour this over the top of the lasagna. Sprinkle with the grated cheese.

Bake for about 45 minutes or until golden brown and bubbling.

Vegetable lasagna with basil

Lasagna layered with a tender, basil-flavored mixture of vegetables and cheese sauce: easy to make, great to eat.

SERVES 4 ❄

6oz (175g) lasagna noodles, traditional or "no cook"
salt
8oz (225g) onions, chopped
8oz (225g) carrots, finely diced
8oz (225g) leeks, shredded
8oz (225g) zucchini, thinly sliced
2 tbsp olive oil, plus extra for greasing
3 tomatoes, skinned (see page 40) and chopped
4oz (125g) button mushrooms, sliced
1 tbsp chopped fresh basil
freshly ground black pepper
2 cups (575ml) cheese sauce (see page 65)
1oz (25g) grated Parmesan-style cheese

Cook the traditional lasagna noodles in plenty of boiling water until just tender, then drain. Drape the pieces over the sides of the colander to prevent them from sticking together.

Alternatively, use "no cook" lasagna noodles and make the cheese sauce adding 5fl oz (150ml) extra milk to the usual quantity of butter and flour.

Preheat the oven to 400°F (200°C).

Fry the onions, carrots, leeks and zucchini very gently in the oil, covered, for 20 minutes, stirring occasionally.

Add the tomatoes, mushrooms and basil, and cook for 5 minutes. Season to taste.

Put a layer of lasagna noodles in a greased shallow ovenproof dish, top with half the vegetable mixture and a quarter of the sauce.

Repeat, then cover with noodles, the rest of the sauce and the cheese.

Bake for 45 minutes or until golden and bubbling.

Quick spinach and ricotta lasagna

This is one of those dishes you can put together in moments, using frozen spinach (which needs to thaw first) and the kind of lasagna noodle that doesn't need pre-cooking. The result is very tasty. A tomato salad goes well with it.

SERVES 4
3 tbsp (40g) butter
3 tbsp (40g) all-purpose flour
1 pint (575ml) milk
4oz (125g) grated cheese
salt and freshly ground black pepper
1lb (450g) frozen spinach, thawed
9oz (250g) ricotta cheese
a pinch or two of freshly grated nutmeg
4–6oz (125–175g) "no-cook" lasagna noodles

Preheat the oven to 400°F (200°C).

Firstly, make a thin cheese sauce by melting the butter in a saucepan and stirring in the flour, then adding the milk and stirring over the heat until the mixture thickens. Add half the grated cheese and salt and pepper to taste. Remove from the heat.

Put the thawed spinach into a bowl, add the ricotta cheese and mix well; season with salt, pepper and nutmeg. Put a layer of half this mixture into the base of a shallow ovenproof dish; cover with pieces of lasagna noodles, breaking them to fit if necessary. Pour some sauce over, to cover.

Repeat the layers, ending with all the sauce. Sprinkle with the rest of the cheese.

Bake for 30–40 minutes or until golden and bubbling.

Macaroni with butter beans, tomatoes and black olives v

Simple, colorful and delicious.

SERVES 4–6
8–12oz (225–350g) macaroni
salt
8oz (225g) dried Lima beans, soaked and cooked or 2 x 14oz cans
2 tbsp olive oil
2 tbsp freshly squeezed lemon juice
12oz (350g) tomatoes, sliced
8–12 black olives
freshly ground black pepper
a small handful of basil leaves, torn, to garnish
grated Parmesan-style cheese, to serve (optional)

Cook the pasta in plenty of boiling salted water until just tender, then drain thoroughly.

While the pasta is cooking, heat the Lima beans in their liquid.

Drain the beans, add to the hot drained pasta together with the olive oil, lemon juice, tomatoes, olives and salt and pepper to taste.

Stir gently over the heat until the ingredients are well distributed and piping hot, then serve immediately with some torn basil leaves over the top.

Serve with the grated cheese (if using).

Macaroni and cheese

The ultimate in comfort food! Light, tasty and delicious, tender macaroni with plenty of sauce and a crisp crumb topping. A cooked green vegetable such as broccoli or spinach is the perfect accompaniment.

SERVES 4 ❄
4oz (125g) short macaroni
salt
3 tbsp (40g) butter, plus extra for greasing
3 tbsp (40g) flour
2 cups (575ml) milk
6oz (175g) Cheddar cheese, grated
freshly ground black pepper
2oz (50g) fresh breadcrumbs

Preheat the oven to 400°F (200°C).

Cook the macaroni in boiling, salted water until just tender, then drain.

Make the sauce: melt the butter in a saucepan, stir in the flour, cook for a few seconds, then stir in a third of the milk. Bring to a boil, stirring, then add another third of the milk and repeat until all the milk has been added.

Remove from the heat, add the macaroni, two-thirds of the grated cheese and some seasoning.

Spoon into a greased shallow ovenproof dish, top with breadcrumbs and the remaining cheese and bake for 40 minutes or until crisp and golden brown.

Macaroni with four cheeses

A classic dish that's really just a sophisticated version of macaroni and cheese. The four different cheeses each bring a distinctive flavor and texture. Make sure the cheeses are suitable for vegetarians.

SERVES 4
4oz (125g) short macaroni
salt
1 tbsp (15g) butter
1¼ (275ml) ½ and ½
2oz (50g) Parmesan-style cheese, grated
3oz (75g) Emmental cheese, cubed
3oz (75g) provolone cheese, cubed
3oz (75g) mozzarella cheese, cubed
freshly ground black pepper

Cook the macaroni in boiling salted water until just tender.

Drain the macaroni, return to saucepan and add the butter and cream.

Stir gently over the heat, then add half the Parmesan-style cheese and all the other cheeses, season, and stir gently until the cheeses are heated through and beginning to melt.

Sprinkle with the remaining Parmesan-style cheese and serve at once.

Macaroni with peppers v

Full of color and warm, Mediterranean flavors.

SERVES 4
2 large onions, chopped
1 large yellow pepper, seeded and sliced
1 large red pepper, seeded and sliced
1 tbsp olive oil
4 tomatoes, sliced
1 garlic clove, crushed
8oz (225g) short macaroni
salt and freshly ground black pepper
a handful of black or green olives
a small handful of basil, torn
grated Parmesan-style cheese, to serve (optional)

Cook the onions and peppers gently in the oil in a large saucepan with the lid on the pan for 10–15 minutes or until they are tender, then add the tomatoes and garlic and cook for a few minutes more.

Meanwhile, cook the macaroni in plenty of fast-boiling salted water until just tender.

Drain the macaroni, add to the vegetable mixture, season and heat through.

Serve topped with a few black olives and scattered with torn basil leaves.

Pass the grated cheese (if using) at the table.

Pappardelle with wild mushrooms

Lovely wide ribbons of pasta coated in buttery, garlicky juices and mixed with tender wild mushrooms are just so delicious! If you can find a bag of mixed mushrooms, these are ideal, or you can make your own mixture – oyster mushrooms, shiitake, cremini, whatever you prefer.

SERVES 2
salt
7oz (200g) pappardelle
1 tbsp olive oil
3 tbsp (40g) butter
9oz (250g) mixed wild mushrooms, sliced
1 garlic clove, crushed
freshly ground black pepper
¼ cup chopped fresh flat-leaf parsley

Bring a large saucepan of salted water to a boil, add the pasta and cook until it is tender but with some bite.

Meanwhile, heat the oil and butter in a large saucepan. Add the mushrooms and cook gently for 4–5 minutes or until tender. Stir in the garlic, cook for a few seconds longer, then season to taste with salt and pepper.

Drain the pasta, put it back in the still-hot pan and add in the mushrooms and all their liquid. Stir in the parsley, then taste and adjust the seasoning if necessary. Serve in warm dishes and eat at once.

Pasta with lentils and tomatoes v

You can use either spaghetti or tagliatelle for this, or a short pasta like penne rigate if you prefer. It's good with a crisp leafy salad and some hot garlic bread (see page 55).

SERVES 4

1 large onion, chopped
4 tbsp olive oil
1 small red pepper, seeded and
    finely chopped
2 garlic cloves, crushed
7oz (200g) brown or Puy lentils,
    drained
14oz can chopped tomatoes
1 tbsp tomato ketchup
1 tbsp chopped fresh flat-leaf parsley
½ tsp ground cinnamon
salt and freshly ground black pepper
8oz (225g) tagliatelle, spaghetti or
    penne rigate

Cook the onion and the red pepper in the oil in a large saucepan for 8 minutes, with a lid on the pan.

Stir in the garlic and cook for another couple of minutes.

Add the lentils, tomatoes and tomato ketchup. Cook gently, uncovered, for a few minutes or until the tomatoes have thickened to a sauce. Season with salt and pepper to taste.

Meanwhile, cook the pasta in plenty of fast-boiling salted water until just tender.

Drain the pasta, put back in the pan and add the sauce. Stir gently to mix, then serve.

Penne with asparagus and morels

Fresh morel mushrooms, which are in season at the same time as asparagus, are a wonderful treat, though undeniably expensive. A cheaper way to enjoy them is to use dried morels, which you can buy at large supermarkets. Soak them in boiling water to reconstitute them, then drain and use as described in the recipe. Just make sure you have rinsed away any grit that sometimes clings to them.

SERVES 4

14oz (400g) penne

FOR THE SAUCE

9oz (250g) tender asparagus,
    cut into 1in (2.5cm) pieces
2 tbsp (25g) butter
2 tbsp olive oil
7oz (200g) morel mushrooms, sliced
2 garlic cloves, crushed
2 cups (575ml) cream (½ and ½ or
    heavy cream)
salt and freshly ground black pepper

First make the sauce. Cook the asparagus in a pan of boiling water until it is just tender (about 4–7 minutes, depending on the thickness of the stems). Drain and set aside.

Heat the butter in a saucepan with 1 tablespoon of the oil. Add the morels and garlic and cook gently for 5–10 minutes or until any liquid has boiled away. Pour in the cream and simmer until reduced by half. Add the asparagus and season to taste with salt and pepper. Set aside.

Bring a large saucepan of salted water to a boil, add the pasta and cook until tender. Just before the pasta is done, gently reheat the sauce. Drain the pasta and return to the hot saucepan with the remaining olive oil. Add the sauce to the pasta and mix gently. Serve in warm dishes and eat at once.

Opposite: Ravioli with ricotta and hazelnut filling in green herb sauce (see page 222)

Ravioli with cheese filling in tomato sauce

SERVES 4 ❄

double quantity homemade pasta
    dough (see page 210)
8oz (225g) ricotta
3oz (75g) grated cheese
1oz (25g) Parmesan-style cheese,
    grated
salt and freshly ground black pepper
1 egg, beaten
tomato sauce (see page 71)

Make the pasta dough as described
on page 210, then roll it out as
thinly as you can into long pieces
(or use a pasta machine). Place the
sheets on lightly floured surface to
prevent them from sticking.

Mix together the ricotta and
grated cheeses and season to taste.

Place small mounds of the cheese
mixture about 1¼in (3cm) apart on
half the pieces of pasta, brushing
around each mound with beaten egg.

Cover with the rest of the pasta,
pressing it down around the edges
and trying to exclude as much air
as possible.

Cut between the mounds with
a pastry wheel or sharp knife.

Put the ravioli on a lightly floured
surface and leave to dry for 30
minutes. Then drop them into a
large saucepan of boiling salted
water and cook for 4–6 minutes.

Meanwhile, heat the tomato
sauce in small pan, then pour over
the drained ravioli and serve.

Ravioli with ricotta and hazelnut filling in green herb sauce

The cooked ravioli will freeze, but
add the cream and herbs later.

SERVES 4

double quantity homemade pasta
    dough (see page 210)
8oz (225g) ricotta cheese
1 garlic clove, crushed
4oz (125g) skinned hazelnuts (see
    page 140), grated
salt and freshly ground black pepper
1 egg, beaten
5fl oz (150ml) ½ and ½
2 tbsp chopped mixed fresh herbs

Make the pasta dough as described
on page 210, then roll out as thinly
as you can into long pieces, as in
the previous recipe, and place on
lightly floured surface.

Mix together the ricotta, garlic,
nuts and seasoning to taste.

Place small mounds of ricotta
mixture about 1½in (3cm) apart on
half the pieces of pasta, brushing
around each mound with beaten
egg.

Cover with the rest of the pasta,
pressing down around the edges to
try and exclude as much air as
possible.

Cut between the mounds with
a sharp knife or a pastry wheel.

Put the ravioli on a lightly floured
surface and leave to dry for 30
minutes. Then drop them into a
large saucepan of boiling salted
water and cook for 4–6 minutes.

Meanwhile heat the ½ and ½ and
herbs in small pan, then pour over
the drained ravioli and serve.

VARIATION

Ravioli with ricotta and spinach

Make the filling as described in the
main recipe, using spinach instead
of the hazelnuts. Place 7oz (200g)
washed spinach leaves in
a saucepan, with just the water
clinging to them, and cook for 3–4
minutes or until tender. Drain very
well, then chop and mix with the
ricotta cheese, garlic and salt and
pepper to taste. Cook as described,
and serve with garlic butter and
grated Parmesan-style cheese if
desired.

Spaghetti with eggplant and wine sauce v

A delicious quick supper dish. I like to make it with an inexpensive Italian red wine and drink the remaining wine with the meal. The sauce will freeze.

SERVES 4 ❄

3 tbsp olive oil
1 onion, chopped
1 garlic clove, crushed
1 eggplant, diced
1 green or red pepper, seeded and chopped
1 tsp dried basil
14oz can chopped tomatoes
¼ cup red wine
salt and freshly ground black pepper
8–12oz (225–350g) spaghetti
grated Parmesan-style cheese, to serve (optional)

Heat 2 tablespoons of the oil in a large saucepan, add the onion and cook, covered, for 5 minutes, browning lightly.

Add the garlic, eggplant, green or red pepper, dried basil, tomatoes and wine and cook gently for 25 minutes; season with salt and pepper.

Cook the spaghetti in plenty of boiling, salted water until just tender, then drain thoroughly into a colander.

Return the drained spaghetti back into the still-hot saucepan and add the remaining oil and some freshly ground black pepper.

Add the sauce to the spaghetti, mix gently and serve. Or, if you prefer, serve the spaghetti on warm plates and top with the sauce. Sprinkle with the grated cheese (if using).

Spaghetti with brown lentil Bolognese v

A very tasty vegetarian version of this classic meat dish. The sauce freezes well.

SERVES 4 ❄

7oz (200g) diced brown lentils or 2 x 14oz cans
2 onions, chopped
3 tbsp olive oil
2 garlic cloves, crushed
2 stalks of celery, finely chopped
2 carrots, finely diced
2 tbsp tomato purée
salt and freshly ground black pepper
8–12oz (225–350g) spaghetti
grated Parmesan-style cheese, to serve (optional)

Cook the dried lentils in plenty of water until tender (about 45–60 minutes), then drain. If using canned lentils, simply drain. In either case, keep the liquid.

Brown the onions in 2 tablespoons of the oil, add the garlic, celery and carrots. Cover and cook gently for about 15 minutes or until tender.

Add the lentils, tomato purée, seasoning and a little reserved liquid to make a thick, soft consistency.

Cook the spaghetti in plenty of boiling, salted water until just tender, then drain thoroughly into a colander.

Return the spaghetti to the pan and stir in the remaining oil, and salt and pepper to taste.

Add the sauce to the spaghetti, mix gently and serve. Or, if you prefer, serve the spaghetti on warm plates and top with the sauce. Sprinkle with the grated cheese (if using).

Spaghetti with lentil and tomato sauce v

This dish is useful for those times when you suddenly find yourself having to produce a meal quickly, out of practically nothing. The split red lentils cook in under 30 minutes without soaking and the other ingredients are basic store-cupboard fare. If there's sauce left over, or you make extra, it freezes well. A fresh, crisp green salad goes well with this.

SERVES 4 ❄
3 tbsp olive oil
1 large onion, chopped
1 large garlic clove, crushed
14oz (400g) can chopped tomatoes
½ tsp dried basil or oregano
½ tsp powdered cinnamon
8oz (225g) split red lentils, washed
15fl oz (425ml) water
2 tbsp red wine (optional)
salt and freshly ground black pepper
8oz (225g) spaghetti
grated Parmesan-style cheese,
    to serve (optional)

Heat 2 tablespoons of the oil in a large saucepan and cook the onion, with a lid on the pan, until tender (about 10 minutes).

Stir in the garlic, then add the tomatoes, herbs, cinnamon, lentils, water and wine (if using) and bring to a boil.

Simmer the mixture with a lid on the saucepan for about 25 minutes or until the lentils are tender. Taste and season with salt and pepper.

Shortly before the lentils are done, cook the spaghetti in plenty of boiling, salted water until just tender, then drain thoroughly in a colander.

Return the drained spaghetti back into the still-hot saucepan, and add the remaining oil and some freshly ground black pepper.

Add the sauce to the spaghetti, mix gently and serve. Or, if you prefer, serve the spaghetti on warm plates and top with the sauce. Sprinkle with the grated cheese (if using).

Spaghetti with lentil and wine sauce v

This is a delicious spaghetti dish with a rich-tasting lentil, wine and tomato sauce. The sauce can be made in advance, if convenient, and reheated when you need it. Serve with a green salad with a good garlicky dressing and some robust red wine. The sauce will freeze.

SERVES 2–3 ❄
1 tbsp olive oil
1 onion, chopped
1 large garlic clove, crushed
1 tsp dried basil
14oz can chopped tomatoes
4oz (125g) dried green lentils,
    washed
1 tbsp tomato purée
1¼ cups (275ml) red wine or dry
    cider
1¼ cups (275ml) vegetable stock
salt and freshly ground black pepper
8oz (225g) spaghetti
butter
grated Parmesan-style cheese,
    to serve (optional)

Heat the oil in a medium-sized saucepan and cook the onion for 10 minutes, with a lid on the pan, until softened and lightly browned.

Add the garlic, basil, tomatoes, lentils, tomato purée, wine or cider and stock. Bring to a boil, then put a lid on the saucepan, turn down the heat and leave to cook gently for about 45 minutes, stirring from time to time, until the lentils are tender and the mixture is reduced to a thick purée. Season with salt and plenty of pepper.

Shortly before the lentils are done, cook the spaghetti in plenty of boiling, salted water until just tender, then drain thoroughly in a colander.

Spaghetti with pesto

Return the drained spaghetti back into the still-hot saucepan, and add the remaining oil and some freshly ground black pepper.

Add the sauce to the spaghetti, mix gently and serve. Or, if you prefer, serve the spaghetti on warm plates and top with the sauce. Sprinkle with the grated cheese (if using).

There aren't many foods more satisfying than a bowl of steaming spaghetti coated in green pesto. Pesto is easy to find — but look for a vegetarian one as some are made with Parmesan cheese, which isn't vegetarian. It's also easy and worthwhile making your own pesto when you have time. This is fragrant and wonderful.

SERVES 4–6

12–14oz (350g–400g) spaghetti
grated Parmesan-style cheese, to
    serve

FOR THE PESTO

1 garlic clove, peeled
1 cup (50g) packed basil leaves
¼ cup (25g) grated Parmesan-style
    cheese
1oz (25g) pine nuts
4–6 tbsp extra-virgin olive oil
small squeeze of lemon juice
salt and freshly ground black pepper

The easiest way to make the pesto is to blend all the ingredients to a purée in a food processor or blender, or by using an electric hand blender.

Otherwise, crush the garlic to a paste with a little salt, using a pestle and mortar, then gradually add the rest of the ingredients, crushing and mixing to make a thick, smooth sauce. The lemon juice helps to preserve the color.

Cook the spaghetti in plenty of fast-boiling, salted water until just tender, then drain and place back in the still-hot saucepan.

Add 2 tablespoons of boiling water to the pesto, to loosen it, then add it to the spaghetti, stirring gently until the pasta is green and glossy. Season with salt to taste.

Serve at once with more Parmesan-style cheese.

Spaghetti alla puttanesca v

This is a wonderfully punchy, classic pasta dish. You can vary the heat by adding more or less chili. It's worth buying good-quality canned tomatoes for this as they are richer and quickly reduce to a delicious sauce.

SERVES 4 ❄

14oz (400g) spaghetti or spaghettini
salt
2–3 tbsp olive oil
1 onion, chopped
2 garlic cloves, finely sliced
2 x 14oz cans chopped tomatoes
1 tsp dried oregano
1 dried red chili, crumbled
2oz (50g) pitted black olives, sliced
2 tbsp salted capers, rinsed
1 tbsp sun-dried tomato purée or
    ordinary tomato purée
freshly ground black pepper
a little chopped fresh flat-leaf
    parsley, to serve

Fill a large saucepan with plenty of water and put it on the stove to heat up for the pasta. When the water boils, add the spaghetti along with 1 tablespoon of salt and give the pasta a quick stir. Briefly put the lid on until it starts to lift, showing that the water has come back to a boil, then let the pasta bubble away, uncovered, for about 8 minutes or until it is tender but still has some bite to it.

To make the sauce, heat 2 tablespoons of the oil in a large saucepan. Add the onion, cover and cook gently for 10 minutes or until soft but not brown. Add the garlic, stir well and cook for a further 1–2 minutes. Stir in the tomatoes, together with their juice, breaking them up with a wooden spoon, and the oregano, chili, olives, capers and a seasoning of black pepper. Bring to a boil, then turn the heat down and leave to simmer for 10–15 minutes or until the liquid has evaporated and the sauce is thick.

Add the tomato purée to the tomato sauce and heat through gently, stirring from time to time. Check the seasoning, adding salt and pepper to taste if it needs it.

Drain the pasta, then put it back into the still-warm pan. Either add 1 tablespoon of olive oil to the spaghetti, serve it on warm plates and spoon the sauce on top, or add the sauce directly to the pasta, toss gently and serve. Scatter with chopped parsley in either case.

Spaghetti with fresh tomato sauce and basil

A delicious summer supper dish made with well-flavored tomatoes and fresh basil. Serve with grated cheese and a green salad with a good olive oil dressing. The sauce will freeze.

SERVES 4 ❄

1 onion, chopped
2 tbsp (25g) butter
2 tbsp olive oil
1 garlic clove, crushed
1½lb (700g) tomatoes, skinned
    and chopped
salt and freshly ground black pepper
8–12oz (225–350g) spaghetti
1 tbsp (15g) butter
a few fresh basil leaves, torn,
    to garnish

First make the sauce: cook the onion gently in the butter and 1 tablespoon of the oil until softened (about 10 minutes).

Add the garlic and tomatoes and cook gently for 10–15 minutes or until pulpy. Season with salt and pepper.

Cook the spaghetti in plenty of boiling salted water for 7–10 minutes or until just tender.

Drain well, put back into the pan with the remaining oil, and salt and pepper to taste.

Add the sauce to the spaghetti, mix gently and serve. Or, if you prefer, serve the spaghetti on warm plates and top with the sauce. Scatter with the torn basil leaves.

Tagliatelle with easy cheese sauce

Another delicious pasta dish that you can rustle up in a moment. Serve it with a tomato and black olive side salad. When buying the blue cheese, check it's vegetarian.

SERVES 4–6
12oz (350g) tagliatelle
salt
1 tbsp (15g) butter
5fl oz (150ml) ½ and ½
6–8oz (175–225g) creamy blue cheese, cut into rough dice
freshly ground black pepper
grated Parmesan-style cheese, to serve

Cook the tagliatelle until just tender in plenty of boiling salted water; drain well and put back into the saucepan.

Add the butter, ½ and ½, cheese and a grinding of black pepper to the tagliatelle and stir over a gentle heat until the cheese has melted.

Spoon onto hot plates, sprinkle with Parmesan-style cheese and serve at once.

Tagliatelle with mushroom and sour cream sauce

Creamy and delicious, this pasta dish goes well with a lettuce, tomato and basil salad.

SERVES 4
1 onion, chopped
2 tbsp olive oil
2 tbsp (25g) butter
1 garlic clove, crushed
12oz (350g) button mushrooms, sliced
1 tsp cornstarch
10fl oz (275ml) sour cream
salt and freshly ground black pepper
freshly grated nutmeg
8–12oz (225–350g) tagliatelle
1–2 tbsp chopped flat-leaf parsley, to garnish

Cook the onion gently in 1 table-spoon of the oil and the butter in a lidded pan until softened (10 minutes).

Add the garlic and mushrooms and cook gently for 4–5 minutes. Stir in the cornstarch, then add the sour cream and stir for a minute or two until thickened. Remove from the heat, season with salt, pepper and nutmeg, then set aside.

Cook the tagliatelle in plenty of fast-boiling salted water until just tender, then drain, put back in the still-hot saucepan, add the remaining oil and some freshly ground black pepper.

Keep the tagliatelle warm while you reheat the sauce gently, stirring often.

Add the sauce to the tagliatelle, mix gently and serve. Or, if you prefer, serve the pasta on warm plates and top with the sauce. Sprinkle with chopped parsley.

Tagliatelle verde with sweet pepper sauce

A pretty blend of colors: green tagliatelle with a vivid orange-red sauce. Serve with a watercress or arugula salad to complete the color scheme. The sauce will freeze.

SERVES 4–6 ❄
1 onion, chopped
3 tbsp olive oil
1 garlic clove, crushed
3 large red peppers, seeded and chopped
14oz can chopped tomatoes in juice
2 tbsp tomato purée
¼ cup fino sherry
salt and freshly ground black pepper
12oz (350g) spinach tagliatelle
grated Parmesan-style cheese, to serve

First make the sauce: fry the onion gently in 2 tablespoons of the oil for 5 minutes, then add the garlic and red peppers and cook for 10 minutes.

Add the tomatoes, tomato purée, sherry and seasoning and cook for another 10–15 minutes. Season with salt and pepper.

Cook the tagliatelle in plenty of boiling salted water until tender. Drain well, return the tagliatelle to the still-hot pan and swirl in the remaining oil.

Add the sauce to the tagliatelle, mix gently and serve. Or, if you prefer, serve the pasta on warm plates and top with the sauce. Serve with grated Parmesan-style cheese.

Tortiglioni with garlic, olive oil and fresh herbs v

Pasta tubes cook quickly and are excellent served simply as a first course or as a quick supper with extra grated cheese and a juicy tomato and watercress salad.

SERVES 4–6
12oz (350g) tortiglioni
salt
¼ cup olive oil
2 garlic cloves, crushed
freshly ground black pepper
3 tbsp chopped fresh herbs
grated Parmesan-style cheese, to serve (optional)

Cook the tortiglioni in plenty of boiling salted water until just tender, then drain.

Put the olive oil into the pan in which the pasta was cooked, add the garlic and stir over the heat for a few seconds.

Add the drained pasta and stir gently until the pasta is piping hot and the garlic and oil well distributed. Season to taste.

Finally, add the herbs, stir again, and serve immediately on hot plates. Sprinkle with grated Parmesan-style cheese (if using).

Vermicelli with young carrots, broad beans and mint

A delectable and pretty summer pasta dish. If savory isn't available, use other chopped fresh herbs such as mint, parsley or tarragon.

SERVES 4–6
1 onion, chopped
3 tbsp (40g) butter
1 tbsp olive oil
8oz (225g) young carrots, finely diced
12oz (350g) shelled fava beans
salt and freshly ground black pepper
8–12oz (225–350g) vermicelli
2 tbsp chopped savory
grated Parmesan-style cheese, to serve (optional)

Cook the onion in the butter and oil in a large saucepan, covered, for 5 minutes, then add the carrots and beans and cook gently, with the lid on again, for 10–15 minutes or until the vegetables are tender. Season with salt and pepper.

Cook the pasta in plenty of boiling salted water until just tender, then drain thoroughly.

Add the cooked vegetables to the pasta, together with the chopped savory. Mix gently and check the seasoning.

Serve at once, sprinkled with grated Parmesan-style cheese (if using).

Vermicelli with chickpeas and garlic v

This traditional Italian dish is called *tuoni e lampo*, or "thunder and lightning", to describe the different textures of the pasta (soft) and the chickpeas (firm). It's also good made with wholegrain pasta spirals.

SERVES 4–6
8–12oz (225–350g) vermicelli
salt
7oz (200g) chickpeas, soaked and cooked (see pages 176–7), or 2 x 14oz cans
3 tbsp olive oil
2 garlic cloves, crushed
freshly ground black pepper
grated Parmesan-style cheese, to serve (optional)

Cook the pasta in plenty of boiling salted water until just tender, then drain thoroughly.

While the pasta is cooking, heat the chickpeas in their liquid.

When the pasta is ready, drain the chickpeas and add to the pasta, together with the oil and garlic.

Stir gently over the heat until the ingredients are well mixed.

Check the seasoning, grinding in some black pepper, then spoon onto warm plates, sprinkle with grated cheese (if using) and serve immediately.

Wholewheat pasta savory bake

A quick, cheap and tasty dish that's good served with a cooked green vegetable.

SERVES 4 ❄

4oz (125g) wholewheat or
    wholegrain fusilli
salt
2 onions, chopped
2 tbsp olive oil, plus extra for
    greasing
4oz (125g) mushrooms, chopped
8oz (225g) tomatoes, skinned (see
    page 40) and chopped
1 egg, beaten
4oz (125g) Cheddar cheese, grated
freshly ground black pepper
fresh wholegrain breadcrumbs,
    for topping

Preheat the oven to 375°F (190°C).

Cook the pasta in plenty of boiling salted water until just tender, then drain and leave to one side.

Cook the onions in the oil for 7 minutes, in a covered pan. Add the mushrooms and tomatoes and cook for 3 minutes more.

Add the egg and stir for a moment or two longer. Then remove from the heat.

Stir in the pasta spirals, two-thirds of the grated cheese and season to taste.

Put the mixture into a lightly greased shallow ovenproof dish, sprinkle with breadcrumbs and the rest of the cheese and bake for 25–30 minutes or until bubbling and golden.

Wholewheat pasta and eggplant bake

A wonderful first course, light lunch or supper dish.

SERVES 4 ❄
2 onions, chopped
6–8 tbsp olive oil
1lb (450g) eggplant
3oz (75g) wholegrain auelli
3 tomatoes, skinned (see page 40)
    and chopped, or 8oz can
1 tbsp tomato ketchup
1 tsp dried oregano
1 egg, beaten (optional)
freshly ground black pepper

FOR THE TOPPING
2oz (50g) fresh breadcrumbs
2oz (50g) Cheddar cheese, grated

Cook the onions in 2 tablespoons of the oil in a lidded pan for 10 minutes.

Slice the eggplant into thin rounds (about ¼in (6mm)) and fry in the remaining oil for a few minutes on each side until tender and golden. Try not to let them absorb too much oil; they will soften if you're patient. Blot them on paper towels when they're done.

Cook the pasta in plenty of boiling salted water until just tender, drain and mix with the cooked onions, the tomatoes, ketchup, oregano, egg (if using) and some seasoning. Preheat the oven to 400°F (200°C).

Put the eggplant slices in the base of a greased shallow ovenproof dish. Spoon the pasta mixture on top, cover with the rest of the eggplant slices and sprinkle with the breadcrumbs and grated cheese. Bake for 30 minutes or until golden brown.

Wholewheat pasta with tomato sauce v

This is not only quick and tasty, but virtuous too. Serve with a arugula or watercress salad. The sauce freezes well.

SERVES 4 ❄
1 onion, chopped
3 tbsp olive oil
14oz can chopped tomatoes
salt and freshly ground black pepper
12oz (350g) wholegain auelli
grated Parmesan-style cheese,
    to serve (optional)

Cook the onion in 2 tablespoon of the oil in a medium-sized saucepan, covered, for 10 minutes until softened but not browned.

Add the tomatoes, blend with an electric hand blender or in a food processor, or leave it chunky, if you prefer. Season and set aside.

Meanwhile cook the pasta in a large saucepan half filled with boiling salted water, until it is the tenderness that you like.

Drain the pasta and return it to the still-warm saucepan with the remaining oil and some seasoning.

Quickly reheat the sauce and add to the pasta; mix gently and serve, or, if you prefer, serve the pasta on warm plates and top with the sauce. Serve with grated Parmesan-style cheese (if using).

Grains
and rice

Grains — buckwheat, bulgur wheat, millet, polenta, quinoa, couscous, wild rice, barley, oats and rice — are great for adding variety and nutrients to vegetarian and vegan dishes. Although often thought of as just starchy carbohydrates, they also contain valuable protein, vitamins and minerals.

Grains are cheap to buy, easy to cook and perfect for bulking out a meal. They are a natural accompaniment to stews and curries, the sweet starchiness absorbing the juices and creating a lovely balance of textures and flavors. They're also delicious in their own right, such as for a salad, paella or risotto. In this chapter you'll find a guide to cooking grains to perfection as well as recipes for all occasions — try the quinoa tabbouleh for a summer al fresco meal, warming squash risotto in winter and millet and zucchini pilaf for a simple, nourishing midweek supper (see pages 245, 251 and 241). Whatever you enjoy eating, it's worth making plenty as grains freeze very well.

Guide to using rice and grains

Amaranth Tiny grains, about the size of couscous. Contains complete protein and calcium, like quinoa, but has a very sticky texture when cooked. Best added to baked dishes in small quantities if you want to increase the nutritional value, or buy it 'popped' (like baby puffed wheat) or cracked and add to muesli or granola.

Barley A modest, unassuming grain, with a sweet flavor. Has been eaten for centuries and often added to stews and casseroles. It makes an interesting, chewy risotto or salad with hazelnuts and scallions, but I love the flour best for its sweet, gentle flavor.

Buckwheat This isn't really a grain at all, though it's always classified as one. It's actually the seed of a plant which belongs to the sorrel family. The grains are larger than rice and are triangular-shaped. It has an unusual taste which goes well with strongly flavored vegetables. You can buy it either toasted or untoasted. I prefer to buy untoasted and toast before cooking: rinse the buckwheat in a sieve under the cold tap. Put it into a dry saucepan and cook over a moderate heat for 5 minutes, stirring, until toasty and looking a bit more golden. To cook: add the water and bring to a boil. Cover with a lid, and leave it to stand, off the heat, for 15 minutes, for al dente, or over a gentle heat for 5–15 minutes if you want it softer.

Bulgur wheat Sometimes called "burghul" wheat, or referred to as "cracked wheat" in Middle Eastern recipes, this is wheat which has been cracked and steamed. It consists of little golden-brown grains and, in the packet, looks a bit like demerara sugar! You soak it in water for 15–20 minutes, then use it as the basis of salads (see page 102); or you cook it like rice, except that it will take only 15–20 minutes.

Couscous This is made from semolina and looks golden and granular in the packet, rather similar to bulgur wheat. It has a delicious flavor. To use couscous, just follow the packet directions, which usually involve covering the couscous with boiling water and adding a little salt and olive oil.

Millet This has small, round pale golden grains. It's got a pleasant flavor and makes a nice change from rice. You cook it as described for rice, except that it takes only 15–20 minutes to cook.

Oats I love the creamy texture of oats when you add water and indeed you can now buy "milk" and "cream" made from oats, along with the soy milks in the health-food store. Oats are most useful as oatmeal (for porridge, oatcakes, etc.) or in their "rolled" form. Buy real oats with nothing added, not mucked-around "instant" ones.

Polenta Golden meal made from ground corn, widely used in Italy to make a kind of porridge, or allowed to become cool and firm, then fried. Quick-cook or instant polenta is widely available and easy to use following the packet directions.

Quinoa Confusingly pronounced "keen-wa", this little pearly grain contains complete protein and is rich in calcium. It looks slightly translucent with a little "Saturn" ring around each grain when cooked, and has an unusual, slightly "squeaky" texture. Boil quinoa in double its volume of water for 12–15 minutes or until tender. Leave it still covered for another 10 minutes or so, then fluff it gently with a fork.

Rice Types of rice that I use regularly and that appear in this book are risotto rice (Arborio or Carnaroli), paella rice (Calasparra) (see recipes on pages 243 and 249), basmati rice, both white and brown, and short-grain organic brown rice. For all these, I prefer the infusion method; putting the rice into a pan with enough water to be absorbed during cooking, bringing to a boil, then cooking over a low heat with the lid on the pan. The basic proportions are 1 cup of rice to 2 cups of water, though you can reduce the water for white basmati rice to 1¼–1½ cups of water. This gives an excellent result, but you have to take extra care. Put the rice and water into a heavy-based saucepan, bring to the boil, give it a quick stir, then cover with a lid and turn the heat right down to low and set the timer for 14 minutes. Take the rice off the heat immediately but don't remove the lid — just leave the pan to stand for 15 minutes. Then lift the lid and enjoy the smell and sight of perfect rice!

To cook brown rice perfectly, put 1 cup of rice into a saucepan with 2 cups of water (or 8oz (225g) rice to 1 pint (575ml) water.) Add a little salt if you want. (Personally, I never salt the water when I'm cooking rice, vegetables or anything else;

I much prefer to add it once food is cooked.) Bring to a boil, then put a lid on the pan, turn down the heat and leave to cook very gently for 40–45 minutes, when rice will be tender and have absorbed all the water. Then remove from the heat and let it stand, still covered, for a further 10–15 minutes. Cook brown basmati rice in the same way for 25–30 minutes.

You can save time by using a pressure cooker, which will cook brown rice in about 15 minutes from start to finish. Put the rice into the pressure cooker pan using the same proportions of rice to water as above. Bring up to pressure and cook for 10 minutes at full pressure. Then allow the pressure to reduce naturally, open the pressure cooker, and there is your perfectly cooked rice. This is a particularly good method for short-grain organic brown rice, which I find a beautifully soothing, healing grain.

Seitan This is wheat gluten — the protein part of wheat — that has been extracted and simmered in stock. The result is a tasty, chewy, "mock" meat. Like tofu, it has been made for centuries in the East and is completely natural. It adds an extra texture to vegetarian cooking. You can buy it in a jar or sometimes fresh in the refrigerator case from really good health-food stores. There are various meat-flavored (but vegetarian, of course) varieties although I much prefer to buy the natural type and add my own flavorings or make my own, which is very easy (see page 251).

Wild rice Technically a seed, although treated as a grain. The long black seeds look attractive when cooked with white or brown rice, and add a smoky flavor and chewy texture. Cook it like brown rice; it takes 45–50 minutes and is done when its sides peel back, making it look as though it's flecked with white.

Warm barley salad v

Cooked barley is tender, juicy, chewy and sweet. It makes a pleasant change from rice. Try it in this piquant salad, which is wonderful with a dollop of smooth hummus on the side and some crunchy lettuce leaves, such as Little Gem or Romaine.

SERVES 4

9oz (250g) pearl barley
2 cups (575ml) water
2 tbsp pine nuts, toasted (see page 140)
a pinch of salt
1 tsp Dijon mustard
1 tbsp red wine vinegar
1 tbsp olive oil
a bunch of scallions, finely chopped
a handful of fresh basil leaves, roughly chopped
2 tbsp small capers, drained and rinsed
2 handfuls of pitted black olives

Put the barley into a heavy-based saucepan with the water, bring to a boil, then cover, turn the heat down and cook over a very gentle heat for 50 minutes or until the barley is tender and all the water absorbed.

While the barley is cooking, toast the pine nuts by stirring them over the heat in a dry saucepan for a few minutes until they brown very lightly and smell toasted. Remove from the heat.

Mix the barley grains with a fork to separate and fluff them, then stir in the salt, mustard, vinegar, oil, scallions, basil, capers, olives and toasted pine nuts and serve.

VARIATION
Warm barley salad with sun-blush tomatoes v

Stir in a handful of sun-dried or sun-blush (semi-dried) tomatoes from the deli, drained and blotted of excess oil, along with the other ingredients; their bright color and sweet chewiness make a pleasant addition.

Mediterranean barley risotto v

Barley doesn't become creamy like risotto rice, so there is no need to stir it, as this won't make any difference to the result. Here, the barley is combined with roasted Mediterranean vegetables to produce a glorious, juicy, colorful mixture. It is equally good eaten hot, warm or cold.

SERVES 4–6

9oz (250g) pearl barley
2½ cups (700ml) water
1 large red onion, cut into chunks
1 large zucchini, cut into chunky pieces
1 large eggplant, cut into chunky pieces
2 red and 2 yellow peppers, seeded and cut into chunks
8 garlic cloves, chopped
juice of ½ lemon
3–4 tbsp olive oil
salt and freshly ground black pepper
14oz can plum tomatoes (organic if possible)

Set the oven to 350°F (180°C).

Put the barley into a saucepan with the water, bring to a boil, cover, turn the heat down and leave to cook over a very gentle heat for 40–50 minutes, or until all the water has been absorbed and the barley is swollen and tender. Remove from the heat and leave to stand, still covered, for a further 5 minutes or so.

While the barley is cooking, place the vegetables and garlic into a large roasting pan. Sprinkle with the lemon juice, oil and some salt

continued next page

and pepper, then mix with your hands so that they are all coated in the mixture. Roast for 20 minutes, giving the vegetables a stir after about 10 minutes. Add the tomatoes and cook for 15–20 minutes more or until the vegetables are tender. Season with more salt and pepper if necessary.

Stir the barley with a fork, and add some salt and pepper to taste, then gently mix the barley with all the vegetables. You can reheat it a little, if you wish, before serving.

VARIATION

Barley and red onion risotto with goat cheese

Make as for the main recipe, using red onions instead of the vegetables. Peel and slice 2lb (900g) red onions and place in a roasting pan with 3–4 tablespoons of olive oil, 2 tablespoons of honey or maple syrup and 2 tablespoons of balsamic vinegar. Mix well, then roast for 25–30 minutes or until tender. Mix with the barley along with 8oz (225g) goat cheese, cut into small cubes, and a handful of toasted pine nuts too, if you like.

Buckwheat and mushrooms v

The flavor of buckwheat goes really well with strongly flavored dark mushrooms — field mushrooms, if you can get them — and garlic and onions. A garlicky tomato sauce complements with this.

SERVES 4

9oz (250g) untoasted buckwheat
2 cups (575ml) water
2 large onions, chopped
2 stalks of celery, finely chopped
1 tbsp olive oil
4 garlic cloves, crushed
12oz (350g) dark, open mushrooms, sliced
1 tbsp tomato purée
2 tbsp dark soy sauce
salt and freshly ground black pepper
2 tbsp chopped fresh flat-leaf parsley, to garnish

Rinse the buckwheat in a sieve under the cold tap. Put it into a dry saucepan and cook over a moderate heat for 5 minutes, stirring from time to time, until it smells gorgeously toasty and looks a bit more golden.

Add the water and bring to a boil. Cover with a lid, and leave it to stand, off the heat, for 15 minutes, for an al dente texture, or over a gentle heat for 5–15 minutes if you want it softer.

Meanwhile fry the onions and celery in the oil in another saucepan, covered, for 10 minutes or until soft, then add the garlic and mushrooms and fry for a further 3–4 minutes.

Drain any excess water from the buckwheat. Using a fork, gently mix in first the tomato purée and soy sauce, then the mushroom mixture.

Season with salt and pepper and scatter some chopped parsley over.

VARIATION

Buckwheat, mushrooms and tomatoes v

Make as described, mixing in a handful of sun-dried tomatoes, drained of excess oil, and 2 tablespoons of chopped fresh basil, when you add the mushroom mixture to the buckwheat. Omit the parsley.

Bulgur wheat pilaf v

This pilaf is delicious as the basis of a Middle Eastern-style meal, starting with hummus or chilled cucumber soup and ending with fresh orange salad with honey and orange flower water. You can make the pilaf in advance and heat it through in a covered dish in a moderate oven for about 30 minutes, but it's best to add the nuts just before serving so that they retain their crispness. Serve with a juicy tomato and basil salad, perhaps with some olives thrown in too.

SERVES 3–4 ❄

8oz (225g) bulgur wheat
2 cups (575ml) boiling water
2 tbsp olive oil
2 large onions, chopped
2 garlic cloves, crushed
1 red pepper, seeded and chopped
2oz (50g) raisins
salt and freshly ground black pepper
2–4oz (50–125g) cashew nuts, almonds or pine nuts, roasted on a dry baking sheet in a moderate oven, to serve

Put the bulgur wheat and boiling water into a large bowl or saucepan, cover and leave on one side for 15 minutes; it will absorb the water and swell up.

Heat the oil in a large saucepan and fry the onions for 5 minutes, covered, without browning them, then add the garlic and pepper and fry gently for another 5 minutes.

Add the bulgur wheat together with the raisins, stirring over the heat until they're well coated with oil. Season with salt and pepper to taste.

Cook over a low heat for 5–10 minutes to heat through. Serve sprinkled with nuts.

VARIATIONS

Bulgur wheat pilaf with carrots, nuts and raisins v

Make as descibed, frying 8oz (225g) diced carrots with the onions, and 1 teaspoon of ground cinnamon. Increase the quantity of raisins to 4oz (125g) and use the full quantity 4oz (125g)) of nuts.

Bulgur wheat and feta cheese pilaf

This mixture of chewy, garlic-flavored bulgur wheat and soft melted cheese is delicious. Make as described, with or without the raisins. When the pilaf is cooked, stir in 7oz (200g) feta cheese, drained and diced. Let is stand over the heat for a minute or two, to melt the cheese a little, then scatter with toasted pine nuts and serve at once, with a tomato salad.

Brown rice with tomatoes and cashew nuts

This recipe appeared in my first book and is a family one that I was brought up on. The mixture of ingredients, with the hint of lemon, and the crunchy topping, is delicious. For a vegan version, omit the eggs and use olive oil.

SERVES 3–4 ❄

4oz (125g) brown rice, short or long grain
14oz can chopped tomatoes
4oz (125g) cashew nuts, grated
2 hardboiled eggs, chopped
2 tbsp chopped fresh parsley
1 tsp grated lemon rind
1–2 tbsp freshly squeezed lemon juice
salt and freshly ground black pepper
1¼ cups water

FOR THE TOPPING

a handful of dried breadcrumbs or cornflakes
a pat of butter
a scattering of grated cheese

Put the rice into a pan with 1¼ cups (275ml) cold water. Bring to a boil, then cover and cook very gently for 40 minutes or until tender and the water absorbed.

Preheat oven to 350°F (180°C).

Fork through the rice, then add the tomatoes, cashew nuts, hardboiled eggs, chopped parsley, lemon rind and juice.

Season, then put into an ovenproof dish, cover the top with breadcrumbs, or, what my mother used, cornflakes, a little butter and a scattering of grated cheese.

Bake for 20–30 minutes or until heated through and golden. Serve with a green salad or lightly cooked vegetables.

Carrot, potato and pea curry v

A simple, lightly spiced curry that's delicious with fluffy basmati rice, some mango chutney and crunchy golden poppadums or chapattis.

SERVES 4

1oz (25g) ghee or 2 tbsp olive oil
1 large onion, chopped
2 garlic cloves, crushed
2 tsp grated fresh root ginger
1 bay leaf
3 tsp ground coriander
3 tsp ground cumin
1 tsp turmeric
½ tsp chili powder
8oz can tomatoes
1 tsp salt
freshly ground black pepper
2 cups (575m) water
12oz (350g) carrots
12oz (350g) potatoes
4oz (125g) peas

Heat the ghee or oil in a large saucepan and fry the onion for 7–8 minutes, then add the garlic, ginger, bay leaf and spices and stir over the heat for 2–3 minutes.

Mix in the tomatoes, salt, a grinding of pepper and the water. Simmer for 5–10 minutes while you prepare the vegetables.

Peel and slice the carrots, peel the potatoes and cut them into even-sized chunks.

Add the potatoes and carrots to the tomato mixture and simmer gently for 15–25 minutes or until the vegetables are almost tender, then put in the peas and simmer for a further 5 minutes.

Check the seasoning before serving.

Leek and cauliflower curry v

Although this is not an authentic Goan curry, its slightly sweet flavor is delicious. Enjoy it with some brown basmati rice and any of the following: mango chutney, salted almonds or cashew nuts, sliced, skinned tomatoes, sliced bananas, dried coconut and onion rings.

SERVES 4

8oz (225g) leeks
1 small cauliflower
8oz (225g) potatoes, peeled
2 tbsp all-purpose flour
1 level tbsp turmeric
8oz (225g) tomatoes, chopped
2 small onions, sliced
1 small cooking apple, peeled, cored
   and chopped
¼ cup olive oil or ghee
2 tsp curry powder
1¼ cups (275ml) water
1 tbsp crushed coriander seeds
3 rounded tbsp mango chutney
salt and freshly ground black pepper

Trim the roots and woody ends off the leeks and discard. Clean the leeks thoroughly by slitting lengthways down one side and washing under running water. Cut into pieces. Wash the cauliflower and divide into florets. Cut the potatoes into equal pieces. Mix the flour and turmeric in a large bowl, add all the vegetables and the apple and turn them gently until coated.

Heat the oil or ghee in a large pan, add the vegetables and fry lightly. Add the curry powder, water, coriander seeds and chutney. Cook for 30 minutes, then season to taste. Serve with boiled rice.

Celery rice v

A tasty way of using up those outer stalks of celery! You'll need a large saucepan for this recipe. It makes quite a lot, but if there's any left over, it's excellent as a filling for red peppers (just halve, seed, fill with the mixture, cover with foil and bake in a moderate oven for about 40 minutes or until the peppers are tender); or cold, as a salad, perhaps decorated with black olives.

SERVES 5–6 ❄

2 large onions, chopped
2 tbsp olive oil
8 stalks of celery, sliced
2 red peppers, seeded and chopped
2 garlic cloves, crushed
8oz can chopped tomatoes
12oz (350g) brown rice
1 quart (1.2 liters) water
salt and freshly ground black pepper
2 tbsp chopped fresh flat-leaf
   parsley

Fry the onions gently in the oil, with a lid on the pan, for 5 minutes, without browning them.

Put in the celery and peppers, and cook for an additional 5 minutes.

Add the garlic, tomatoes, rice, water and some salt. Bring to a boil, then let mixture simmer away, uncovered, for 40 minutes, until the rice is just about tender and nearly all the water has been absorbed.

Take the pan off the heat, cover, and leave to stand, so that the rice can finish cooking in its own steam, for a further 10–15 minutes.

Fluff up the mixture with a fork, season to taste, and serve sprinkled with the chopped parsley.

Chinese-style fried rice v

If you plan ahead with this dish, by cooking the rice in advance, it's very quick and easy to make.

SERVES 3
1 large onion, chopped
1 green pepper, seeded and chopped
1 garlic clove, crushed
1 tbsp grated fresh root ginger
2 tbsp ground nut or olive oil
8oz (225g) can pineapple chunks in natural juice, drained and chopped
8oz (225g) mushrooms
8oz (225g) beansprouts
12oz (350g) cooked rice (about 4oz (125g) uncooked rice)
1 tbsp dark soy sauce
salt and freshly ground black pepper
4–6oz (125–175g) blanched almonds, to garnish

Fry the onion, pepper, garlic and ginger in the oil for 5 minutes, then add the pineapple, mushrooms, beansprouts and rice.

Cook over a high heat for 3–4 minutes, stirring all the time, then add the soy sauce, and salt and pepper to taste. Pile the rice mixture on a heated serving dish, scatter with the almonds and serve.

Zucchini rice v

A lovely recipe for the summer, when zucchini are plentiful. You can get this dish started, then go and enjoy the sunshine while the rice cooks! Serve it with a green salad and some crunchy bread. If any of the rice is left over, it's also delicious cold, as a salad.

SERVES 4 ❄
2 onions, chopped
2 tbsp olive oil
1 large red pepper, seeded and chopped
1½lb (700g) zucchini, washed and fairly thickly sliced
1 large garlic clove, crushed
6oz (175g) brown rice
14oz (400g) and 8oz (230g) can tomatoes
salt and freshly ground black pepper
2 tbsp chopped fresh flat-leaf parsley, to garnish

Fry the onions in the oil in a large saucepan, covered, for 5 minutes, without browning them, then add the pepper and cook for a further 3–4 minutes. Add the zucchini, garlic and rice and stir well.

Add the tomatoes and a little salt and pepper. Bring the mixture to a boil, then cover, turn the heat right down, and leave to cook gently for 40 minutes. (The rice cooks in the liquid produced by the vegetables; no extra water is added.)

After this, take the pan off the heat, give the mixture a stir with a fork, then leave the pan to stand, covered, for 10–15 minutes, so that the rice can go on cooking in its own steam. Check the seasoning, sprinkle with parsley and serve.

Spicy couscous v

When we say couscous we generally mean just the grain, but here it refers to the complete dish: the grain served with a warmly spiced vegetable stew containing raisins, chickpeas and pine nuts.

SERVES 3–4
1 large onion, chopped
3 tbsp olive oil
2 large carrots, diced
2 tomatoes, chopped
4oz (125g) dried chickpeas, soaked and cooked (see pages 176–7), or 14oz can
1 tsp ground cinnamon
1 tsp ground cumin
1 tsp ground coriander
2 tbsp tomato purée
3oz (75g) raisins
15fl oz (425ml) water
8oz (225g) couscous
2 tsp freshly squeezed lemon juice
salt and freshly ground black pepper

TO GARNISH
2 tbsp chopped fresh flat-leaf parsley
2 tbsp pine nuts, toasted (see page 140)

Fry the onion in the oil in a large saucepan, with a lid on the pan, for 10 minutes or until they're tender.

Peel and dice the carrots and add them to the onions together with the tomatoes, chickpeas, spices, tomato purée, raisins and water. Bring the mixture to a boil, then simmer gently for about 30 minutes or until the vegetables are cooked.

About 10 minutes before the stew is done, prepare the couscous grain according to the packet directions.

continued next page

Add some more water to the stew if it needs to be a bit thinner, then stir in the lemon juice, season with and salt and pepper to taste, scatter with the chopped parsley and toasted pine nuts, and serve with the couscous grain.

Spicy couscous with harissa v

Make as described and serve with harissa, a hot Moroccan paste, for people to add themselves. You can buy this from large supermarkets, or you can make it yourself by mixing together ¼ cup of olive oil, 2 tablespoons of tomato purée, the juice of 1 lime and 1 teaspoon of cayenne pepper.

Fifteen-minute rice

There's a bit of poetic license here, because the rice does have to be already cooked when you start making this dish, but provided you plan ahead, perhaps cooking double the amount of rice for a meal earlier in the week, supper can be on the table pronto.

SERVES 4–6
6 eggs
12oz–1lb (350–450g) leftover cooked rice
½ stick (50g) butter
2 heaped tbsp all-purpose flour
2 cups (575ml) milk
1–2 tsp curry powder
salt and freshly ground black pepper
a drop or two of Tabasco sauce
a pinch or two of paprika, to garnish

Put the eggs into a saucepan, cover with boiling water and cook for 10 minutes, then cool under cold water, peel off the shells and slice the eggs.

Make a sauce by melting the butter in a saucepan and stirring in the flour. When it froths, stir in a third of the milk, beat well until smooth, and repeat the process twice more, until all the milk has been added and you have a smooth sauce. Flavor with the curry powder, salt, pepper and Tabasco. Keep warm over a low heat.

Reheat the rice in the microwave, or in a saucepan with just a small amount of water in the pan to prevent sticking.

Put the rice into a warmed serving dish, top with the eggs, pour the sauce over the top, scatter a pinch or two of paprika over, and serve.

Millet, cauliflower and parsley mash v

Cooked millet and cauliflower can be puréed together to make a pleasant replacement for mashed potatoes, which are not eaten in the macrobiotic diet. They are also delicious, I think, in their own right, especially when mixed with plenty of garlic and parsley, and swirled with some lovely golden-green olive oil. Try them with a red bean salad (see page 96), for a tasty light meal.

SERVES 6
8oz (225g) millet
1¾ cups (400ml) water
1 cauliflower, trimmed and divided into florets
a large bunch of flat-leaf parsley
4 garlic cloves, crushed
salt and freshly ground black pepper
3–4 tbsp extra-virgin olive oil

Put the millet into a dry saucepan and set over a medium heat for about 4 minutes, stirring often, until it smells toasted. Pour in the water, being careful because it will bubble up and produce steam. Bring back to a boil, cover and leave to cook for 15 minutes or until it has absorbed all the water and looks fluffy and pale.

Meanwhile, bring 1in (2.5cm) water to a boil in another saucepan, add the cauliflower, cover with a lid and cook until tender (about 6–7 minutes, depending on the size of the florets). Drain well.

Reserve a good sprig of the parsley for garnishing, then remove the stems from the rest and discard these.

Blend the cauliflower, millet,

garlic and parsley leaves in a food processor or using an electric hand blender, until smooth and creamy. Season well with salt and pepper. Smooth the mixture into a warm, shallow serving dish, swirl the top with the olive oil, coarsely grind some pepper over the top and garnish with the reserved parsley.

Millet, cauliflower and parsley cakes v

Make the mixture as described and leave to cool completely, then form into flat cakes — not more than ½in (1cm) thick is best — and coat in a little wholewheat flour. Fry the cakes in hot olive oil for at least 3–4 minutes on each side or until nicely browned and crisp. Garnish with parsley, and serve with tartar sauce (see page 70).

Millet and zucchini pilaf v

Millet cooks in 20 minutes and has an attractive pale golden color and a pleasant flavor that makes a change from rice.

SERVES 4

8oz (225g) millet
2 onions, chopped
1 red pepper, deseeded and chopped
2 garlic cloves, crushed
1 tbsp olive oil
2 cups (575ml) water
1lb (450g) zucchini, sliced into fairly chunky pieces
2 tbsp chopped fresh flat-leaf parsley
salt and freshly ground black pepper

First toast the millet by stirring it in a dry saucepan over a moderate heat for about 5 minutes or until the grains are lightly browned, smell toasted and some start to "pop". Set aside.

Fry the onions, pepper and garlic in the oil in a medium-sized saucepan, covered, for 10 minutes.

Add the millet, water and zucchini, and bring to a boil. Cover, turn the heat down and leave to cook for 20 minutes or until the millet is fluffy and the water absorbed. Stir in the chopped parsley, season to taste and serve.

Mushroom rice with almonds and red peppers v

The secret of this recipe is to use plenty of mushrooms and to cook them thoroughly, separately from the rice, so that you get a really rich flavor and a tender, moist texture. This is a nice easy-going dish because if necessary you can cover it with foil and keep it warm for a while in a low oven. Serve with a green salad; and I must admit I also like it with rich Béarnaise sauce (see page 63)!

SERVES 4–6

8oz (225g) long-grain brown rice
2 cups (575ml) dry cider or good vegetable stock or a mixture
salt
¼ cup olive oil
1 large onion, chopped
2lb (900g) button mushrooms, sliced
2 large garlic cloves, crushed
2oz (50g) blanched almonds, slivered
1 red pepper, seeded and chopped
freshly ground black pepper
2 tbsp chopped fresh flat-leaf parsley, to garnish
grated Parmesan-style cheese, to serve (optional)

Put the rice into a medium-sized, heavy-based saucepan and add the cider, stock or cider and stock and a level teaspoon of salt.

Bring to a boil, give the rice a quick stir, then cover the saucepan, turn the heat right down and leave the rice to cook very gently for 45 minutes.

Take the saucepan off the heat and leave to stand, still covered, for a further 15 minutes.

continued next page

Nutty brown rice with vegetables v

Heat 2 tablespoons of the oil in a large saucepan and fry the onion for 5 minutes or until beginning to soften, then add the mushrooms and garlic and cook for a further 20–25 minutes, stirring from time to time, until all the liquid has disappeared and the mushrooms are dark and glossy-looking.

Heat the rest of the oil in another small saucepan or frying pan and fry the almonds until golden, then take them out and place on a piece of paper towel. Quickly fry the red pepper, for 10 minutes or until just tender.

Add the mushrooms, red pepper and almonds to the cooked rice, stirring gently with a fork. Season with salt and plenty of pepper.

Spoon the mixture onto a large, warmed plate or shallow ovenproof dish, heaping it up well, and sprinkle with freshly chopped parsley. Serve with the Parmesan-style cheese.

VARIATION
Mushroom rice with artichoke hearts v

Make as described, adding the drained contents of a 7oz pack of marinated artichoke hearts (from the deli) to the mushrooms a few minutes before they're done, to give the artichokes a chance to warm through, before adding to the rice.

A dish of brown rice mixed with colorful vegetables and topped with shiny golden nuts always looks mouth-watering and inviting, and isn't difficult to prepare. Serve the rice with a crisp salad and a sauce, if you like — tangy cheese sauce, sharp-tasting horseradish or lemon and mustard go well.

SERVES 4

10oz (275g) long-grain brown rice
2¼ cups (500ml) water
salt
2 tbsp olive oil
2 large onions, chopped
3–4 garlic cloves, crushed
2 tsp grated fresh root ginger
1 tsp coriander seeds, lightly crushed
1 eggplant, cut into small dice
1 red pepper, seeded and chopped
½–1 green chili, seeded and finely sliced
12oz (350g) button mushrooms, whole or halved
2 tomatoes, roughly chopped
4oz (125g) hazelnuts, roasted (see page 139)
freshly ground black pepper

Put the rice into a medium-sized saucepan with the water and a teaspoon of salt. Bring to a boil, then cover and cook very gently for 40–45 minutes or until the rice is tender and all the water absorbed.

Heat the oil in a large saucepan, add the onions and fry, with a lid on the pan, for 5 minutes.

Add the garlic, ginger and coriander seed, stir over the heat for a few seconds, then add the eggplant, red pepper and chili and fry for a further 10 minutes.

Add the mushrooms and cook for 5–10 minutes more or until all the vegetables are done.

When the rice is cooked, stir it gently with a fork to fluff it, then mix it lightly with the vegetables. Add the tomatoes and half the nuts and season well with salt and freshly ground black pepper. Serve with the rest of the nuts on top.

Vegetarian paella v

I think a big pan of paella, straight from the stove, is a perfect dish for informal entertaining. It looks stunning — golden rice studded with red peppers, tomatoes, green peas, pale artichoke hearts and lemon slices — and everyone loves it, plus it needs no accompaniments.

If you've got a large paella pan, that's ideal, but a wok or a large frying pan will do fine. I use a frying pan measuring 11–12in (28–30cm) across and it works perfectly. This recipe makes a lot, enough to feed a happy crowd, but if there's any left over it reheats well, can be made into croquettes, used to stuff peppers or, my favorite, simply eaten cold as a salad with a handful of olives and some chopped parsley sprinkled over the top.

SERVES 6–8

¼ cup olive oil

2 onions, sliced

2 large red peppers, seeded and sliced

5 cups (1.5 liters) vegetable stock

2 large garlic cloves, crushed

1 heaped tsp paprika

a good pinch of cayenne pepper

½ tsp saffron strands

salt and freshly ground black pepper

1lb (450g) paella or risotto rice

a few drops of yellow vegetable coloring (optional)

4 tomatoes, quartered

4oz (125g) frozen peas

2 x 7oz marinated artichoke hearts

1 lemon, cut into wedges, to garnish

Heat the oil in a large saucepan and fry the onions and peppers for 10 minutes, letting them brown a bit round the edges.

Meanwhile make up some vegetable stock using good-quality bouillon powder or cubes, if not using homemade (see page 11), and bring to a boil in another pan.

Stir the garlic, paprika, cayenne and saffron into the pan with the onions and peppers and season with salt and pepper.

Add the rice, stirring well so that it gets coated with the oil and spices.

Pour in the hot vegetable stock, and, if you like, stir in a drop or two of yellow vegetable coloring to intensify the color of the saffron. Bring to a boil and leave to simmer, uncovered, for 10 minutes.

Add the tomatoes and peas and mix, bringing the rice from the sides of the pan into the center for even cooking. Arrange the tomatoes and artichoke hearts attractively on top of the rice.

Cover and cook without stirring for an additional 15–20 minutes or until the rice is cooked (test it from around the edges of the pan where it cooks more slowly) and all the stock has been absorbed.

Remove the pan from the heat and cover the top with a thick clean tea towel. Then serve, garnished with lemon wedges round the edge.

VARIATIONS

Paella with brown rice v

If you use normal long- or short-grain brown rice to make this, the vegetables tend to get rather over-cooked by the time the rice is done. I find the answer is to use brown basmati rice. Make the paella as described, using brown basmati rice instead of white paella rice, but after the 10 minutes of fast boiling it will need another 25–30 minutes to cook completely. This doesn't give quite the same consistency as paella rice, but it still makes a very pleasant dish.

Paella with beans v

Make as described, adding the contents of a 14oz can of red kidney beans, drained and rinsed, and 2 heaped tablespoons of chopped flat-leaf parsley, when you add in the tomatoes. Leave out the peas; the artichoke hearts are optional.

Oven-baked paella v

This is a useful dish because after you've finished the preparation, you can put it in the oven and forget about it! After you've done the initial cooking of the onions, peppers and spices, stir in the rice as described; cook over the heat for a minute or two. Add the stock and bring to a boil, then, unless you're using a pan that can go from the stove to the oven, transfer this mixture into a large, shallow ovenproof dish.

continued next page

Arrange the tomatoes and artichoke hearts on top. Cover with a piece of foil and bake in the oven, preheated to 350°F (180°C) for 45 minutes or until the rice is cooked and all the water absorbed.

Oven-baked paella with salted almonds v

Make the oven-baked paella as described. While it is baking, prepare some salted almonds to serve with it. Put 8oz (225g) blanched almonds (bought ones or, for perfection, home-blanched, see page 139) in an even layer in a lightly oiled baking pan. Place in the oven, below the paella, for about 10 minutes or until light golden brown — don't let them get too dark. Immediately pour them out onto a piece of baking parchment sprinkled with sea salt and a pinch of cayenne pepper, shake them in the paper so that they all get coated, then keep them wrapped in the paper until you're ready to serve them. Serve scattered over the paella, along with some green olives and a glass of chilled fino sherry.

Seared polenta with tartare sauce

Serve with a juicy tomato salad for a lovely, relaxed summer dish that is good any time of the year!

SERVES 4

8oz (225g) instant polenta
3½ cups (1 liter) boiling water
a bunch of parsley, finely chopped
4oz (125g) Parmesan-style cheese, finely grated
salt and freshly ground black pepper
a few drops of Tabasco sauce
olive oil, for greasing and shallow-frying
4oz (120g) mixed salad leaves
a little vinaigrette (optional)
tartare sauce, (see page 70), to serve

Add the polenta to the water, in a thin steady stream, whisking all the time. Reduce the heat and let it simmer for 5–10 minutes, or until it's very thick and leaves the sides of the pan, stirring from time to time. Remove from the heat and stir in the parsley, cheese, salt, pepper and Tabasco.

Turn the mixture onto a lightly oiled baking sheet or large plate and spread and press it out to a depth of ¼–⅓in (6–8mm). Leave to cool completely and become firm. Just before serving, put the salad into a bowl and toss in a little vinaigrette, if you like.

Cut the polenta into manageable pieces and shallow-fry for 2–3 minutes on each side or until crisp and lightly browned.

Put a pile of the salad on four plates and arrange the fried polenta next to it, then add a spoonful of the tartar sauce and serve.

Soft polenta with wild mushrooms

Creamy polenta with rich, juicy mushrooms is wonderful comfort food. You can use any type of mushrooms; the bags of wild mushrooms supermarkets sell are good value, or you can make up your own selection, using cremini mushrooms and any of the more exotic ones that you can find. Some dried mushrooms in the mixture deepens the flavor.

SERVES 4

3 cups (850ml) water
2 cups (575ml) milk
3 tbsp (40g) butter
2oz (50g) Parmesan-style cheese, finely grated

FOR THE MUSHROOMS

½oz (15g) dried porcini mushrooms
7fl oz (200ml) boiling water
2 tbsp olive oil
2 tbsp (25g) butter
1lb 2oz (500g) mixed cremini and wild mushrooms, sliced
2 garlic cloves, crushed
2 tbsp chopped fresh flat-leaf parsley, plus extra to garnish
salt and freshly ground black pepper

Start with the mushrooms: put the dried mushrooms in a small bowl and cover with the boiling water. Leave to soak for 10 minutes or so, to soften.

Heat the oil and butter together in a large saucepan, add the sliced mushrooms and fry for 3–4 minutes or until tender. Add the garlic and dried mushrooms, along with their soaking water. Turn up the heat and let it bubble away gently for about 10 minutes or until the mushrooms are beautifully tender and all the liquid has been absorbed. Add the parsley and salt and pepper to taste.

For the polenta, bring the milk and water to a boil in a large saucepan. Add the polenta to the water in a thin steady stream, whisking all the time to prevent lumps. Reduce the heat and let it simmer for about 6 minutes or until thick and smooth, stirring from time to time. Add the butter, cheese and salt and pepper to taste.

Spoon the polenta onto warm plates and top with the mushrooms and some chopped parsley. Serve at once.

VARIATION
Vegan soft polenta with wild mushrooms v

Use soy milk and pure vegetable margarine instead of the butter. Replace the Parmesan-style cheese with a hard vegan cheese, such as Cheezly.

Quinoa tabbouleh v

Quinoa is a wonderful grain, one of the few to contain all the amino acids essential for a complete protein. Mixing it with lots of fresh herbs, as in this recipe, is a lovely way to serve it, and you can eat this hot, warm or cold. You could add other ingredients too, such as olives, cherry tomatoes or diced cucumber — it's very versatile and delicious served with some Little Gem or Romaine lettuce leaves, for scooping it up.

SERVES 4
200g (7oz) quinoa
1¾ cups (14fl oz) water
1 tsp vegetable bouillon powder or a stock cube
a bunch of flat-leaf parsley, chopped
a bunch of mint, chopped
4 scallions, chopped
1½ tbsp freshly squeezed lemon juice
1 tbsp olive oil
salt and freshly ground black pepper

Put the quinoa into a sieve and rinse under the cold tap , then put it into a dry saucepan and stir over the heat for 3–4 minutes, until it is lightly toasted; the moisture clinging to it will prevent it from burning.

Add the water and bouillon powder or stock cube to the quinoa, bring to a boil, then cover, reduce the heat and leave to cook gently for 20 minutes or until the liquid has been absorbed and the quinoa is tender. Remove the pan from the heat and leave to stand, still covered, for a further 10 minutes.

Let the quinoa cool slightly, or completely, then stir in the chopped herbs and scallions, lemon juice and oil. Mix well, then season.

Quick and easy Thai-flavored quinoa v

This is so easy to make and tastes creamy, spicy and delicious. Serve it with bok choy with toasted sesame oil (see page 124), or purple sprouting broccoli with sesame and lime.

SERVES 4
2 heaped tbsp Thai red curry paste (make sure it is vegetarian – see page 70)
1 onion, chopped
7oz (200g) quinoa, rinsed
1½lb (700g) frozen mixed vegetables
2 x 14oz cans coconut milk, full fat or reduced fat
9fl oz (250ml) water
salt
chopped fresh coriander, to garnish

Put the Thai curry paste and onion into a large saucepan over a moderate heat and stir for a few seconds to release the flavors. Add the quinoa, along with the frozen vegetables, coconut milk and water. Bring to a boil, then turn the heat down and leave to simmer for 15 minutes or until the quinoa is cooked. Add salt to taste, then garnish with chopped coriander and serve.

Red beans with brown rice and vegetables v

Golden rice flecked with red kidney beans and green, red and orange vegetables. Serve with a green salad.

SERVES 4 ❄

2 onions, chopped
¼ cup olive oil
2 garlic cloves, crushed
12oz (350g) long-grain brown rice
1 tsp turmeric
3 cups (850ml) vegetable stock
salt and freshly ground black pepper
4 carrots, diced
2 zucchini, sliced
1 red pepper, deseeded and chopped
4 tomatoes, skinned and chopped
4oz (125g) dried red kidney beans, cooked and drained (see pages 176–7) or 14oz can, drained and rinsed
2 tbsp chopped fresh flat-leaf parsley, to garnish

Fry the onion in the oil for 10 minutes, covered.

Stir in the garlic, rice and turmeric.

Pour in the stock and season with salt and pepper. Bring to a boil, cover and simmer for 20 minutes.

Add the carrots to the pot but don't stir it in. Cover, and continue to cook for 10 minutes.

Add the rest of the vegetables and the beans; again, don't stir them in. Cook for a further 10 minutes (40 minutes in all).

Remove from the heat and leave to stand for 15 minutes. Mix gently with a fork, then check the seasoning, sprinkle some chopped parsley over and serve.

Mediterranean rice with chickpeas and tomatoes v

This is an unusual rice and chickpea dish, with warm, sunshine flavors. A crisp salad of chicory and lettuce hearts with a balsamic vinaigrette (see page 78) goes well with it.

SERVES 4

8oz (225g) dried chickpeas or 2 x 14oz cans
8oz (225g) basmati rice
1½ cups (350ml) water
salt
1 large onion, chopped
2 tbsp olive oil
1 tsp dried oregano
2 garlic cloves, crushed
4oz (125g) sun-dried tomatoes, drained of oil and roughly chopped
a few sprigs of thyme
2 tbsp (25g) butter (optional)
freshly ground black pepper
2–3 tbsp torn basil leaves
grated Parmesan-style cheese, to serve (optional)

If you're using dried chickpeas, soak and cook them as usual (see pages 176–7), then drain them. Drain and rinse the canned chickpeas.

Put the rice into a medium-sized saucepan with the water and a little salt. Bring to a boil, then immediately lower the heat to just a thread, put a lid on the saucepan, and leave to cook very gently for 14–15 minutes, then remove from the heat at once and leave to stand for 8–10 minutes.

Meanwhile, fry the onion in the olive oil in a large saucepan for 8 minutes, then stir in the oregano and garlic, and cook for a couple of minutes more.

Add the chickpeas and tomatoes to the onion mixture, along with the cooked rice, thyme and butter (if using).

Mix gently with a fork, seasoning to taste, and lastly forking through the fresh basil.

Serve at once, with Parmesan-style cheese (if using).

VARIATION

Rice and chickpeas with spices and pine nuts v

Cook the rice as described. Omit the oregano when you fry the onion; instead, add 1 teaspoon each of ground cumin and ground coriander, and a good pinch each of turmeric and cayenne pepper. Leave out the sun-dried tomatoes, butter, thyme and fresh basil, and instead add a small bunch each of chopped fresh coriander and parsley, and 1½oz (40g) toasted pine nuts. Omit the cheese and serve with a cucumber salad and a bowl of hummus.

Opposite: Quinoa tabbouleh (see page 245)

Jamaican "rice and peas" v

The "peas" in this dish are actually red kidney beans, but this recipe was given to me by a friend who lives in the Caribbean and I've kept the original name. It's an appealing mix of creamy, coconut-flavored rice with thyme, red pepper and red beans. You can use either brown or white rice for this; brown rice takes 15–20 minutes longer to cook. Serve with a crisp green salad with a herby dressing.

SERVES 4
2 tbsp olive oil
1 onion, chopped
1 red pepper, seeded and chopped
350g (12oz) long-grain rice, brown or white
14oz can coconut milk
1¼ cups (10fl oz) water
½ tsp dried thyme
salt and freshly ground black pepper
200g (7oz) dried red kidney beans, soaked, cooked (see pages 176–7) and drained, or 2 x 14oz cans, drained and rinsed

Heat the oil in a large saucepan and fry the onion and pepper for 10 minutes, letting them brown a bit round the edges.

Add the rice, stirring well so that it gets coated with the oil.

Pour in the coconut milk and water, and add the thyme and some salt and pepper.

Bring to a boil, cover the saucepan, turn the heat right down and leave to cook very slowly for 25–30 minutes for white rice, 45 minutes for brown, or until the rice is tender and all the liquid absorbed.

If your saucepan is big enough, about 10 minutes before the rice is done, pop the beans in on top of the rice, without stirring, cover and finish cooking the rice. Let the pan stand, off the heat, for 5 minutes before serving.

If the beans won't fit in your pan, let the rice finish cooking completely, then, using a fork so that you don't mash the rice, mix the beans in, and cook for another few minutes, covered, to heat the beans through.

Rice and spinach tian

This Provençal dish is named after the earthenware casserole dish in which it is traditionally cooked. It can be made from any green vegetable, although spinach or chard are the most usual, with zucchini sometimes added too. It can be served hot or cold. I like to make it with brown rice, which seems in keeping with its rustic wholesomeness, but by all means use white if you'd prefer (cooking according to the packet directions).

SERVES 4 ❉
175g (6oz) brown rice
scant 2 cups (575ml) water
salt
2 tbsp olive oil
1lb (450g) washed leaf spinach
2–3 garlic cloves, crushed
1 tbsp chopped fresh flat-leaf parsley
4oz (125g) Cheddar cheese, grated
2 eggs (optional)
freshly ground black pepper
2–3 tbsp dried breadcrumbs (see page 183)
2–3 tbsp grated Parmesan-style cheese
2 tbsp olive oil

Rinse the rice then put it into a saucepan with the water and a teaspoon of salt, bring to a boil, then turn the heat down. Leave the rice to cook very slowly, with a lid on the saucepan, for 40–45 minutes or until it's tender and all the liquid has been absorbed. (If there's still some water left in the pan, take it off the heat and leave covered for 10–15 minutes, after which you should find the water has been absorbed.)

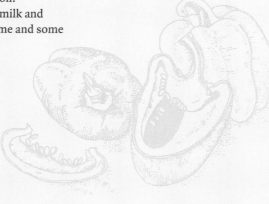

Favorite risotto

Preheat the oven to 400°F (200°C).

Heat the olive oil in a large saucepan and add the spinach; turn it in the hot oil for 2–3 minutes until it has softened slightly and is glossy-looking from the oil.

Remove from the heat and mix in the cooked rice, garlic, parsley and grated Cheddar cheese. If you're using the eggs, beat them and add. Season to taste with salt and a good grinding of pepper.

Spoon the mixture into a shallow ovenproof dish and top with the breadcrumbs and grated Parmesan-style cheese, then drizzle the olive oil over.

Bake uncovered for 30–40 minutes or until its puffed up and golden brown and crisp on top.

I've made many risottos in my time but this is my family's all-time favorite. The celery gives a lovely background flavor that I find enhances any risotto. You can use a little dry white wine to start the risotto off, but I find Vermouth really good for this; I love the herby flavor, and the fact that I can keep a bottle of it handy in the cupboard.

SERVES 4

1 quart (1.2 liters) vegetable stock (good-quality bouillon powder or stock cubes are fine)
¾ stick (75g) butter
2 tbsp olive oil
1 large onion, finely chopped
2 garlic cloves, crushed or finely chopped
½ head of celery, finely chopped
12oz (350g) risotto rice — Arborio or Carnaroli
4fl oz (125ml) dry Vermouth
salt and freshly ground black pepper
4oz (125g) Parmesan-style cheese, grated

Pour the stock up into a saucepan and set over a gentle heat.

In another, large saucepan, heat 2 tbsp (25g) of the butter and the olive oil, add the onion, garlic and celery, stir, and fry very gently, with a lid on the pan, for 15 minutes or until they are tender but not browned. Stir often.

Add the rice to the vegetables, stirring over the heat for 1–2 minutes or until the rice looks glossy, then pour in the Vermouth: it will bubble up and smell divine.

Once all the liquid has bubbled away, turn the heat down and start adding the hot stock, a ladleful at a time. Allow each ladleful to be absorbed by the rice before adding the next, stirring well all the time to bring out the creaminess of the rice.

Continue like this until all the stock has been added and the rice is soft and creamy but still has a slight bite (about 15 minutes). If all the stock is absorbed before the rice is quite done, add a bit more hot water.

Season to taste, then remove from the heat, add the remaining butter and the cheese, and stir well. Cover with a thick clean tea towel and leave to stand for 2 minutes. Then serve and eat as soon as possible, while it's still creamy and oozy.

The basic risotto can be varied in many ways by adding different vegetables.

VARIATIONS

Asparagus risotto

A pretty, fresh-looking risotto with the wonderful flavor of asparagus. Prepare 1lb (450g) asparagus by bending the stems and discarding the tough ends where the stems break. Cut the tips into 1½in (3cm) lengths. While the risotto is cooking, steam or boil the asparagus until just tender and set aside. Add the cooked asparagus along with the butter and grated cheese at the end; mix gently, and leave to stand as described.

continued next page

Seitan v

Red beet risotto

If you love beets, this is such a treat; it's worth making for its amazing color alone! You need 14oz–1lb (400–450g) raw beets. Peel the beets and chop into tiny dice. Fry the beets along with the onion, garlic and celery. You can use the Vermouth as usual, or you could use vodka instead. When the risotto is done, stir in a tablespoon or two of freshly squeezed lemon juice along with the butter. You don't necessarily need the cheese with this variation: see what you think; maybe offer it separately, so people can choose for themselves at the table.

Butternut squash and sage risotto

Another favorite of mine. You need about 1lb (450g) of butternut squash (weighed with the skin on), and it has to be roasted first, halve lenthwise. Brush it all over with olive oil (no need to peel) and roast at 400°F (200°C) for about 30 minutes or until the squash is tender. Cut it into cubes, removing the skin and any seeds as you go.

Make the risotto as described, add the roasted squash along with the butter and grated cheese at the end, and 1–2 tablespoons of chopped fresh sage (it has quite a strong flavor, so add it sparingly the first time you make this dish). Or fry some sage leaves in olive oil until they're crisp, and scatter them on top of the risotto, perhaps with a swirl of pumpkin seed oil, too.

Arancini

Thrifty Italians have always turned leftover risotto into crisp croquettes and they're gorgeous! In fact, I sometimes make an extra-large risotto especially with these in mind. You simply form the risotto into little rounds and coat them in beaten egg and dried breadcrumbs or, as I like to do, in cornstarch paste (6 tablespoons of cornstarch mixed to a paste with 6–7 table-spoons of cold water) and bread-crumbs for an extra-crisp result. Then fry in olive oil until crisp and golden brown on both sides. I like them with a tomato and basil salad.

Seitan has been made and eaten in Japan for centuries; like tofu, it's one of the natural "mock" meats, a chewy, natural protein made from wheat gluten. You can make it yourself from gluten flour, or you can buy it from good specialty health-food stores in a jar preserved in tamari. Seitan is delicious just fried with some garlic, or it be used in any of the ways you'd use meat.

MAKES ABOUT 9OZ (250G), TO SERVE 2

3½oz (100g) gluten powder
1 tbsp tamari or shoyu soy sauce
4–5 tbsp water

FOR THE STOCK

15 fl oz (425ml) water
1 tsp vegetable bouillon powder

Put the gluten powder into a bowl. Add the soy sauce and water and mix; it will become springy and bouncy almost immediately. Knead for a minute or two, then stretch it flat with your hands, fold and roll it. Flatten it again, then with a sharp knife slice it into small pieces — they will swell as they cook.

Bring the water and bouillon powder to a boil in a saucepan. Add the seitan pieces, cover and leave to simmer for 30 minutes. Drain.

The seitan is now ready for use. It can be eaten as it is; fried crisp in oil, or added to a tasty sauce, such as seitan with mushroom and Marsala sauce overleaf.

Seitan with mushroom and Marsala sauce

Here, seitan is coated with flour, fried in olive oil and covered in a mushroom and Marsala sauce. Serve with creamy mashed potatoes (see page 131) and thin green beans.

SERVES 2

12oz jar seitan in tamari sauce, drained, to yield about 8oz (225g)
2 tbsp all-purpose flour
2 tbsp olive oil
1 onion, sliced
4oz (125g) cremini mushrooms, halved
¼ cup Marsala
3½fl oz (100ml) crème fraîche
salt and freshly ground black pepper

Rinse the seitan to reduce the saltiness. Put on a plate, sprinkle with the flour and turn the pieces of seitan in the flour to coat.

Heat the oil in a large saucepan or frying pan, add the seitan and fry for a few minutes until crisp and golden, turning the pieces to cook on all sides. Remove the seitan from the pan with a slotted spoon and set aside.

Add the onion to the pan, cover and cook, gently, for 5 minutes. Don't let the onion brown. Add the mushrooms and cook for 4–5 minutes or until they are tender.

Put the seitan back in the pan and pour in the Marsala. Let the mixture bubble over the heat for a minute or two to reduce slightly, then stir in the crème fraîche and salt and pepper to taste. Cook for a further 1–2 minutes, just to heat the cream, then serve.

Spiced rice v

This is delicious with vegetable curries, simple stews or vegetable mixtures. I must admit, this is a dish that I like best made with white basmati rice, though it does work very well with the brown rice too (see variations).

SERVES 4

8oz (225g) white basmati rice
11fl oz (300ml) boiling water
1 tbsp olive oil
1 onion, chopped
2 garlic cloves, finely chopped
2–3 tsp cumin seeds
salt and freshly ground black pepper

Put the rice into a heavy-based saucepan with the water. Immediately it comes back to a boil, turn the heat right down; put a lid on the pan and set your timer for 14 minutes. Then remove the pan from the heat and leave it to stand, with the lid still on, for a further 10–15 minutes.

This gives you plenty of time to prepare the remaining ingredients. Heat the oil in a small saucepan, add the onion and cook for about 7 minutes or until browned at the edges, then add the garlic and cumin seeds, and cook for a further 2–3 minutes. Remove from the heat.

When the rice is ready, fluff it gently with a fork, and stir in the onion mixture from the pan.

Season with a little salt and pepper to taste and serve.

Spiced brown basmati rice v

Make this exactly as described in the main recipe but use 15fl oz (425ml) water and cook for 25–30 minutes.

Golden spiced rice v

This is a very pretty variation. Add ½ teaspoon of turmeric to the onion mixture along with the cumin. Stir this into the rice as described, along with 1–2 tablespoons of freshly squeezed lemon juice. As you add the turmeric, the rice will turn yellow, and when you stir in the lemon, the color will lighten and brighten. This is lovely with some chopped fresh coriander scattered over the top.

Spiced rice with raisins and pine nuts v

You can make the rice exactly as in the main recipe, simply stirring 1½oz (40g) each of raisins and pine nuts in at the end, along with the onions. You could add a piece of cinnamon stick and a couple of crushed cardamom pods to the onions, along with, or instead of, the cumin. Sometimes I add a bay leaf too. It's rewarding and fun to try different spices and combinations — that's the joy of cooking.

Too-tired-to-cook rice v

This is very simple, very healing; one of the things I make when the last thing I feel like doing is cooking! Put the rice on to cook, then go away and do something else for about 40 minutes. Then, quickly finish the dish off and enjoy. Shoyu and tamari soy sauces are available from health-food and Asian stores.

SERVES 4
8oz (225g) short- or long-grain brown rice
2 cups (575ml) water
1 tsp shoyu or tamari soy sauce, plus extra to serve (optional)
2oz (50g) sunflower or pumpkin seeds
sea salt

Put the rice, water and soy sauce into a heavy-based saucepan and bring to a boil. Boil hard for 5 minutes, then put a lid on the pan and turn the heat right down.

Leave for 40 minutes, then remove the pan from the heat and allow to stand for 10–15 minutes.

Meanwhile, put the seeds into a small pan and toss them over the heat until, after a minute or two, they start to smell wonderful and to sizzle and pop.

Fluff the rice with a fork, spoon it into deep, warm bowls, and tip the sizzling seeds on top. Serve with extra soy sauce, if liked.

VARIATIONS
Too-tired-to-cook rice with sesame v

This is lovely with sesame seeds instead of, or indeed as well as, the sunflower or pumpkin seeds. Toast them in a pan as described; they will start to jump out of the pan when they're ready — it only takes a minute or two. You could continue the sesame theme by serving with some tahini, thinned with water and lemon juice, as a sauce.

Too-tired-to-cook rice with tofu v

Cook the rice as described, then fork through some cubes of tofu just before serving. You could use a really light fresh tofu from a Chinese store; just slice it and toss in shoyu or tamari soy sauce and add, along with some chopped scallions and toasted sesame seeds; or you could add bought, marinated tofu cubes.

A lovely condiment to have with this is gomasio. In a dry saucepan stir 1 teaspoon of sea salt with 3 tablespoons of sesame seeds until the seeds smell toasty and start to jump out of the pan. Cool a little, then crush to a powder with a pestle and mortar or grind them in an electric coffee grinder. This is wonderful sprinkled over any of these variations or indeed any bowl of plainly cooked rice.

Vegetable pilaf v

Spicy golden rice, garnished with slices of tomato, hardboiled egg and fresh coriander. Serve with curry sauce (see page 238) and some naan bread or chapattis.

SERVES 4
1 onion, chopped
1 tbsp olive oil
1 large garlic clove, crushed
1 bay leaf
2 tsp turmeric
4–5 cardamom pods
piece of cinnamon stick
pinch of ground cloves
1–2 tsp salt
10oz (275g) brown basmati rice
2¼ cups (500ml) water
4oz (125g) frozen peas

TO GARNISH
2 tomatoes, sliced
1 hardboiled egg, sliced (optional)
a small bunch of coriander, roughly chopped

Fry the onion in the oil for 10 minutes, browning it a bit, then stir in the garlic, bay leaf, spices and salt.

Add the rice and water and bring to a boil. Put a lid on the saucepan, turn the heat right down and leave to cook very gently for 25–30 minutes. Allow it to stand off the heat, still covered, for 10 minutes.

Cook the peas in boiling water or in the microwave. Fork the rice through, adding the peas.

Serve garnished with the slices of tomato and egg (if using), and the fresh coriander.

Tarts and pies

A glorious golden pastry roll or pie always makes a fantastic centerpiece dish and provokes the kind of "oohs" and "ahs" that are music to the ears of any cook. Everyone loves a pie. They can be warming and satisfying for a winter's meal — try the walnut pâté en croûte for a delicious Christmas dinner — or light and summery, such as the carrot, zucchini and parsley quiche and individual asparagus tarts (see pages 283, 261 and 270).

Naturally, pastry features in all these recipes, crisp shortcrust for tarts and some pies, flaky puff for other pies and "en croûtes" and filo for others. Nothing beats homemade shortcrust pastry and I encourage you to try making it yourself (see the recipe opposite); it's really easy. Homemade puff pastry (see page 259), with all its flaky layers and buttery flavor, is fun to make when you've got the time. I always use store-bought filo, though. This gives excellent results and is really simple to use.

Basic pastry recipes
Shortcrust pastry

Making pastry isn't difficult and it's very rewarding to do. I like making my own because I know exactly what's going into it and can choose the type of flour and, even more importantly, use the best fat for health and flavor. That means butter if you're vegetarian and a pure, non-hydrogenated vegetable margarine if you're vegan.

I used to use only 100 per cent wholewheat flour, which is undeniably the healthiest flour, for everything except puff pastry. However, as I've grown older I've lightened up a bit and I will use a half-and-half mixture of 100 per cent wholewheat and unbleached white flour. Recently I've discovered wholewheat spelt flour which makes the most beautiful, light wholegrain pastry with a deliciously sweet flavor. I also like finely milled wholewheat flour.

The only occasion when I use just white flour is to make my own puff pastry; I enjoy doing it and it's well worth the effort, but it doesn't happen very often. You can buy some excellent ready-made puff pastry. I would always recommend the all-butter variety; or pure vegetable if you're vegan. The same applies to shortcrust pastry, although I do urge you to have a go at making your own; it's an easy skill to learn and results in delicious pastry.

Here are the basic pastry recipes:

This is the easiest pastry to make and the most useful. Use the type of flour you like; all plain white, all wholewheat or a half-and-half mix of white and wholewheat.

MAKES ENOUGH FOR ONE 8–9IN (20–23CM) TART SHELL
1½ cups (200g) all-purpose flour
½ tsp salt
7 tbsp (100g) butter, softened
2–3 tbsp water

You can make this in a food processor. Just blend the flour, salt and butter together until combined, then add water and briefly blend again to make a pliable dough.

Or, do it by hand. Sift the flour and salt into a bowl. If you're using wholewheat flour, sift through as much flour as you can, then add the residue of bran from the sieve (the purpose of the sifting is to aerate the flour, not to remove the bran).

Add the butter then rub it into the flour with your fingertips, lifting the mixture high out of the bowl to incorporate as much air as possible and make the pastry light.

Continue until the mixture looks like fine breadcrumbs, then add the water a little at a time and use your fingertips to press the mixture together and form a dough.

Put the dough on a lightly floured surface and knead lightly for a minute or two until smooth.

At this point it's really best to let the dough rest in the fridge for 30 minutes, covered in cling film or greaseproof paper — if you've got time.

Before rolling out the dough, use your hands to press it roughly into whatever shape you want — a round, oval or rectangle — then roll out on a well-dusted work surface or board using light, even strokes and use as required.

VARIATION
Cheese shortcrust

Make this in the same way as shortcrust above, sifting ½ teaspoon mustard powder with the flour and adding 2–5oz (50–150g) grated cheese after rubbing the fat into the flour.

How to make a tart shell

Easy wholegrain spelt flour pastry

I discovered this by accident; it's richer than a normal shortcrust, really easy to make and comes out very light and crumbly, just how I like wholegrain pastry to be. Spelt flour — flour milled from the original, oldest variety of wheat — has a lovely sweet, nutty flavor and is becoming more widely available from health-food stores and supermarkets.

MAKES ENOUGH FOR ONE 8–9IN (20–23CM) TART SHELL 1¼IN (3CM) DEEP
Heaping 1½ cups (200g) plain wholegrain spelt flour
1¼ sticks (150g) salted butter, softened

Put the flour and butter into a bowl then, using a fork, lightly blend them together until a dough forms. Gather it up into a ball, knead lightly on a floured board and roll out — not too thinly.

It's a bit delicate, so you might find it easiest to slide it straight from your board into the tart pan or pie dish (see right), rather than try and pick it up.

The previous quantities are right for a medium-sized, round tart shells; for larger or deeper tart shells, or other shapes, just increase the quantity of pastry as necessary. If you have pastry left over, it will keep in the fridge. Alternatively make jam tarts (see page 361) or re-roll it with some grated cheese and make cheese straws.

1 QUANTITY OF SHORTCRUST OR EASY WHOLEMEAL SPELT FLOUR PASTRY (SEE PAGES 257 AND 258)

Preheat the oven to 400°F (200°C). Put a baking sheet on the shelf to heat up; this will give a good boost of heat to the bottom of the tart, helping it to crisp up.

On a floured surface or board roll out the pastry fairly thinly so that it is 1½in (4cm) wider all round than the diameter of the tin.

Lift the pastry into the pan, using either the rolling pin or, and this is easier with crumbly wholemeal pastry, sliding it straight off a pastry board into the pan. Press the pastry into the pan, trim the edges and prick the base lightly all over.

Put a piece of baking parchment into the pastry shell and weigh it down with porcelain baking beans, dried beans or rice. This "baking blind" prevents the pastry from bubbling up as it cooks.

Bake for 10–15 minutes, then remove the paper and beans and put the pan back in the oven. Bake for a further 5–10 minutes or until pastry is set and feels crisp and firm when lightly touched.

Keeping tarts crisp

If you want to ensure that your tart has a lovely crisp base, there are a couple of things you can do. Firstly, I find the thinner the pastry, the crisper it's likely to remain, so it's worth taking extra care on the rolling out.

In addition, some people brush the base of the tart shell with egg white when they take it out of the oven, then put it back in for a few more minutes to set the egg white and "waterproof" the base.

My preferred method is to heat 2 tablespoons of oil in a small saucepan just before taking the pastry shell out of the oven. Pour the oil into the pastry shell as soon as it comes out of the oven to cover the base (you may not need all the oil). Or, if the recipe includes something like fried onion, you could fry this in the oil and add it at this point, too. You can then put the filling straight in on top or leave the pastry shell to get cold before proceeding.

Freezing pastry dishes

Pastry shells freeze well. I think it's best to bake them first, so that they're ready to use when they come out of the freezer; I always try to have a few in my freezer at Christmas time. They will also keep for a few days in an airtight container. You can also freeze tarts after filling and baking. Recipes that are suitable for the freezer are shown by the symbol ❄ .

Flaky pastries
Cream cheese pastry

This is the easiest way I know of making a pastry with a flaky texture; it also works well when made with a half-and-half mixture of white and wholewheat flour. It's suitable for pie crusts, savory rolls and tartlets.

MAKES ABOUT 14OZ (14OZ)
1½ cups (200g) all-purpose flour
½ tsp salt
7 tbsp (100g) butter
3½oz (100g) full-fat cream cheese
1 tsp freshly squeezed lemon juice

Make as for shortcrust pastry (see page 257): either put all the ingredients into a food processor and blend to a pliable dough or sift the flour and salt, rub the butter in, then mix in the cream cheese and lemon juice.

Chill for 1 hour before using.

Puff pastry

I've tried lots of different ways to make puff pastry and this is the best and easiest. The result is golden, flaky and buttery.

MAKES JUST OVER 1LB 2OZ (500G)
2 cups (250g) plain flour
½ tsp salt
2¼ sticks (250g) cold butter
about 5fl oz (150ml) cold water
a squeeze of lemon juice

An hour or so before you want to make the pastry, put the flour and salt into a bowl and chill in the fridge, along with the butter. Add a squeeze of lemon juice to the water and put that into the fridge to chill too.

Cut the butter into $^{1}/_{3}$in (7mm) dice and add to the bowl of chilled flour and salt. Lightly mix the dice with the flour; don't rub in at all.

Pour in the water and gently mix with the flour, taking the flour from the sides of the bowl into the center, until it all holds together in a soft, lumpy ball.

Put the ball of dough onto a well-floured board or work surface and pat it into a rough rectangular lump (short sides as top and bottom edges). Then start rolling it away from you, with a rolling pin and using short strokes.

Once you've flattened it out a bit, fold the top two corners down to within a third of the bottom edge and fold the bottom edge up. Turn the pastry to the right, so that you now have the two folded edges on the left and right.

Roll it out again as you did before, fold and turn it again.

Do this a minimum of four times, ideally 7–8. If it starts to get sticky with the butter, you need to stop and pop it into the fridge for a bit.

Once you've done your last rolling and folding, wrap the pastry in some plastic wrap or greaseproof paper and put into the fridge to chill for at least an hour before using.

Making a single-crust pie

First prepare the filling, then leave it to cool completely.

To make the pastry lid, pat the pastry out to roughly the shape of the dish, then roll it out ¼in (6mm) thick and about 5/8in (1.5cm) wider all round than the top of the dish.

Cut a strip from the outer edge of pastry, dampen and place on the rim of the dish.

Put the filling into the dish and, if it's moist and soft, stand an egg cup in the center of the dish to help support the pastry. Brush the pastry strip on the rim with cold water, then place the pastry sheet on top and press the edges together.

Using the back of a small knife, make small marks along the edges of the pastry join, like flaky layers of pastry, then flute the edges using your fingers and a knife, or press the prongs of a fork all round the edge to make a pretty effect.

Insert the blade of a knife under the pastry at the sides of the pie to make a gap for the steam to escape; or make a couple of steam-holes in the top of the pie. Decorate with pastry trimmings as desired and brush the top of the pie with beaten egg or milk to glaze, if you wish.

Using filo pastry

Making a double-crust pie

Prepare and cool the filling. Take just over half the pastry, pat into the shape of the dish and roll out to about ⅛in (2mm) thick and about 1–1½in (2.5–4cm) larger than the dish. Lift the pastry into the dish, press into place, then spoon the filling in on top: it needs to fill the dish generously, piled up to the center.

Roll out the remaining pastry so that it is ½in (1cm) larger than the dish, then place on top of the dish to cover the filling. Press the pastry edges together, then trim, finish the edges, decorate and glaze as described for a single-crust pie (see previous page).

There's no need to be nervous about using filo pastry. It's probably the easiest pastry of all to cook with and always gives good results. The sheets of pastry may look fragile when you open the packet, but they're quite resilient and if you do tear one or two, who cares! You can always patch them up.

The only thing you need to remember is that filo pastry does dry out quickly and can become brittle. As long as you keep your pile of pastry covered with a clean damp cloth while you're working, you'll have no problem, and once you get the hang of it you'll probably find you work so fast that you won't even need the damp cloth.

Some packs of filo contain large sheets, others are smaller; it varies from brand to brand. If the sheets are too big for you, just cut them with scissors or a sharp knife, then simply position a sheet of filo pastry in your pie dish, tart pan or whatever container you're using, leaving the edges untrimmed as you work.

Brush the sheet of filo with olive oil or melted butter, then put another on top of it, overlapping them as necessary. Keep repeating this, building up the layers of pastry. When you've got enough layers, or have used half the packet, put your filling on top, and start covering with more layers of filo to make the upper crust of the pie.

When all the filo is in place, you can tidy up the edges, rolling them up neatly to make a rim and cutting away any bits you don't need. Pieces that are left over can be cut into ribbons or scrunched up and brushed with olive oil to decorate, if you wish. You can have fun here and make it it look very pretty if you're in the mood.

Tarts and quiches

Asparagus quiche

This is a creamy, delicious tart with a crisp pastry shell. Serve with buttered new potatoes for an early summer lunch.

SERVES 6 ❄

8in (20cm) cooked shortcrust pastry tart shell (see pages 257–8)
1lb (450g) asparagus, trimmed (see page 109)
salt and freshly ground black pepper
1 small onion, chopped
1 tbsp olive oil
4oz (125g) Gruyère cheese, grated
1¼ cups (275ml) ½ and ½
2 eggs
1 tbsp chopped fresh flat-leaf parsley

Preheat the oven to 350°F (180°C).

Cook the asparagus for about 10 minutes or until it is just tender when pierced with a sharp knife. Season with salt and pepper.

Fry the onion gently in the olive oil, covered, for 10 minutes or until tender but not browned.

Put the onion into the base of the tart, sprinkle with half the cheese and arrange the cooked asparagus over the top.

Whisk the ½ and ½ and eggs together until smooth; stir in the parsley and season with salt and pepper.

Pour the liquid mixture over the asparagus and cheese and sprinkle with the remaining cheese.

Bake the tart for 30 minutes until the filling is puffed up, golden and set.

Eggplant, red pepper and cheese quiche

This is a pretty quiche with a chunky, eggplant filling set in a light custard.

SERVES 4–6 ❄

8in (20cm) cooked shortcrust pastry tart shell (see pages 257–8)
2 tbsp olive oil
2 large onions, chopped
1 eggplant (about 8oz (225g)), cut into ½in (1cm) chunks
1 red pepper (about 6oz (175g)), seeded and chopped
1 fat garlic clove, crushed
salt and freshly ground black pepper
4oz (125g) Cheddar cheese, grated
2 eggs
5fl oz (150ml) milk or ½ and ½

Preheat the oven to 350°F (180°C).

Heat the olive oil in a medium-sized saucepan and fry the onions, covered, for 5 minutes or until beginning to soften.

Add the eggplant, red pepper and garlic, cover and cook gently for about 10 minutes until they are tender. Season with salt and pepper.

Put two-thirds of the grated cheese in the base of the pastry shell, then spoon the eggplant mixture on top and sprinkle with the rest of the cheese.

Whisk together the eggs and milk or ½ and ½ and pour evenly over the top of the tart.

Bake for 50–60 minutes or until the filling is set and golden.

Carrot, zucchini and parsley quiche

This summery tart looks as good as it tastes.

SERVES 4–6 ❄

8in (20cm) cooked shortcrust pastry tart shells (see pages 257–8)
1 onion, chopped
6oz (175g) carrots, diced
1 tbsp olive oil
1 tbsp (15g) butter
6oz (175g) zucchini, sliced
5fl oz (150ml) ½ and ½ or milk
1 egg
2 tbsp chopped fresh flat-leaf parsley
salt and freshly ground black pepper

Preheat the oven to 350°F (180°C).

Fry the onion and carrots in the olive oil and butter, with a lid on the pan, for 10 minutes, without browning. Add the zucchini and cook gently for a further 5–7 minutes or until the vegetables are tender. Spoon into the pastry shell.

Whisk the ½ and ½ or milk with the egg, parsley and seasoning. Pour into the pastry shell.

Bake for 30–35 minutes or until the filling is set and golden. Serve hot or at room temperature.

Cauliflower, Stilton and walnut tart

Tender cauliflower with the salty tang of Stilton and the crunch of walnuts make a tasty tart, which is delicious with a crisp leafy salad including some endive and a balsamic dressing.

SERVES 4–6
8in (20cm) cooked shortcrust pastry
    tart shell (see pages 257–8)
1 small cauliflower
2 tbsp (25g) butter
2 tbsp (25g) flour
1¼ cups (275ml) milk
4oz (125g) Stilton cheese, grated
salt and freshly ground black pepper
2oz (50g) chopped walnuts

Preheat the oven to 350°F (180°C).
    Break the cauliflower into florets, boil or steam for 5–7 minutes or until just tender, then drain.
    Melt the butter in a saucepan, add the flour, cook for a few seconds, then gradually pour in the milk and stir over the heat to make a smooth sauce. Simmer gently for 5–10 minutes, to cook the flour, then remove from the heat, mix in 3oz (75g) of the cheese and season.
    Add the cauliflower to the sauce, stirring gently to coat.
    Spoon the mixture into the pastry shell, sprinkle with the rest of the cheese and the walnuts. Return the tart to the oven for 30 minutes or until golden brown. Don't let the walnuts burn; cover lightly with foil after 20 minutes if necessary.

VARIATION

Cauliflower, Cheddar and walnut tart

This is a lovely variation, made this time with Cheddar cheese and using eggs instead of the sauce. Put the cooked cauliflower into the pastry shell with the grated cheese and walnuts. Whisk together two eggs and 5fl oz (150ml) milk, season and pour evenly over the top. Bake at 375°F (190°C) for about 50 minutes or until the filling is set. Serve at once.

Swiss cheese and onion tart

This tart has a layer of little cubes of cheese in the base, which helps keep the pastry crisp. Vegetarian Gruyère is available or you could use all Emmental instead. Serve with a juicy tomato and basil salad.

SERVES 4–6 ❄
8in (20cm) cooked shortcrust pastry
    tart shell (see pages 257–8)
1 onion, chopped
1 tbsp (15g) butter
1 tbsp olive oil
3oz (75g) each Gruyère and
    Emmental cheese
2 eggs
5fl oz (150ml) ½ and ½ or milk
salt and freshly ground black pepper
a pinch of freshly grated nutmeg

Preheat the oven to 350°F (180°C).
    Fry the onion gently in the butter and oil for 10 minutes or until it's soft but not browned.
    Cut the cheese into 6mm (¼in) dice and scatter half of it over the base of the pastry shell. Put the onions on top, and then the rest of the cheese.
    Whisk together the eggs and ½ and ½ or milk, season with salt, pepper and nutmeg, and pour into the pastry shell.
    Bake the tart for 30–35 minutes until it's puffed up and golden.

VARIATION
Edam cheese and onion tart

Make this in the same way but use 6oz (175g) Edam cheese instead of the Gruyère and Emmental. This is more economical but still delicious.

Quick cheese and tomato tart

If you put a simple filling straight into an unbaked pastry shell, the tart can be on the table in an hour. Although the pastry may not be quite as crisp as when it's pre-baked (or "blind baked"), if you use my easy wholegrain spelt flour pastry (see page 258) you'll find that what it lacks in crispness it more than makes up for in tenderness. This is delicious with a simple salad or steamed fine green beans.

SERVES 4–6 ❄

butter or oil, for greasing
1 quantity easy wholegrain spelt
   flour pastry (see page 258)
2oz (50g) grated cheese
6 scallions, chopped, or
   ½ onion, finely chopped
2 tomatoes, sliced
salt and freshly ground black pepper
1 egg
5fl oz (150ml) ½ and ½ or heavy
cream

Preheat the oven to 375°F (190°C).
   Put a baking sheet into the oven to heat up (baking the tart on this helps the shell to cook crisply).
   Grease a 8in (20cm) round tart pan or dish.

Put the pastry dough onto a lightly floured work surface or board and knead lightly into a round, then roll out into a circle to fit your tart pan or dish.
   Ease the pastry in, press down and trim the edges. Don't prick the base.
   Sprinkle the cheese and scallions or onion over the pastry, then arrange the tomatoes on top and season with salt and pepper.
   Whisk the egg and cream in a bowl with a little seasoning. Pour over the tomatoes.
   Put the tart into the oven and bake for 40 minutes or until the pastry is crisp and golden brown and the center is set and puffed up.

Chickpea and mushroom tart

This tart is delicious served hot with a crisp salad or cooked green vegetable. The variation (see next page), using hummus and a crunchy topping of sesame seeds instead of the egg, milk and cheese, is lovely too.

SERVES 4–6 ❄

8in (20cm) cooked shortcrust pastry
   tart shell (see pages 257–8)
1 tbsp olive oil
1 onion, sliced
1 large garlic clove, crushed
4oz (125g) button mushrooms,
   sliced
14oz can chickpeas, drained and
   rinsed
1 tbsp chopped fresh flat-leaf parsley
salt and freshly ground black pepper
1 egg
5fl oz (150ml) milk or ½ and ½
3oz (75g) grated cheese

Preheat the oven to 180°C (350°F).
   Heat the olive oil in a saucepan and fry the onion for about 7 minutes or until it is nearly tender but not browned. Add the garlic and mushrooms and cook for a further 3–4 minutes.
   Stir in the chickpeas and the chopped parsley. Season with salt and pepper and put the mixture into the pastry shell.
   Beat together the egg and milk or ½ and ½. Season with salt and pepper and pour into the pastry shell. Scatter the grated cheese over the top.
   Bake the tart for 40–50 minutes or until it is set and golden brown.

continued next page

VARIATION

Chickpea, mushroom and hummus tart v

This variation is vegan if you use pure vegetable margarine to make the tart shell. Omit the egg, milk or cream and grated cheese. Instead, mix the onion, mushrooms, chickpeas and parsley with 8oz (225g) hummus. Spoon into the pastry shell, level the top and scatter with 1 tablespoonful of sesame seeds. Bake as described.

Leek lattice tart

If you're making your own pastry shell for this, save the pastry trimmings to roll out and cut into strips for the lattice over the top; if you're using a ready-made pastry shell, just make it a lovely leek tart and don't worry about the lattice! Either way, this mixture of sweet leeks, sour cream and parsley is delicious.

SERVES 4–6 ❄

8in (20cm) cooked square or round shortcrust tart shell (see page 257–8) and any pastry trimmings (optional)
8 thin leeks, trimmed
salt and freshly ground black pepper
10fl oz (275ml) sour cream
2 egg yolks or 1 whole egg
1 tbsp chopped fresh flat-leaf parsley

Preheat the oven to 375°F (190°C).

Trim the leeks to fit the pan; if they're really small, they're lovely left whole, but if the leeks are larger or your tart shell smaller, slice them as necessary.

Cook the leeks in boiling water until tender: this might take 15–20 minutes for whole leeks, less time if they're cut. In either shell, drain them very well.

Arrange the leeks in the pastry shell, sprinkle with salt and pepper.

Whisk the cream with the egg yolks or egg, parsley and some seasoning, and pour over the leeks.

If you have pastry trimmings, re-roll these and cut into long, narrow strips. Criss-cross these in a lattice over the top.

Bake for 35–40 minutes or until golden brown and set.

Lettuce, pea and spring onion tart

Summery flavors in a light and delicious tart. Serve with new potatoes and fine green beans for a summer lunch.

SERVES 4–6 ❄

8in (20cm) cooked shortcrust pastry tart shell (see pages 257–8)
2 tbsp (25g) butter
6 scallions, chopped
½ lettuce, shredded
4oz (125g) shelled fresh peas or frozen baby peas
2 tbsp chopped fresh mint
5fl oz (150ml) ½ and ½
1 egg yolk
salt and freshly ground black pepper

Preheat the oven to 350°F (180°C).

Melt the butter in a saucepan over a gentle heat, add the scallions, lettuce and peas and gently sauté together in the butter for 2–3 minutes.

Remove from the heat, mix in the mint, ½ and ½, egg yolk and seasoning; pour into the pastry shell and bake for 30–35 minutes or until the filling is set and golden.

Wild mushroom quiche

Creamy, light and delicately flavored, this is a delightful tart. You can sometimes buy bags of wild mushrooms in supermarkets and these are great for this dish, but it is delicious made with any type of mushroom. If you haven't got enough wild mushrooms, make up the quantity with ordinary ones.

SERVES 4–6 ❄
8in (20cm) cooked shortcrust pastry
    tart shell (see pages 257–8)
3 tbsp (40g) butter
1 tbsp olive oil
1 onion, finely chopped
1 garlic clove, crushed
8oz (225g) wild mushrooms, sliced
1 heaped tbsp chopped fresh flat-
    leaf parsley
3 egg yolks
5fl oz (150ml) ½ and ½
salt and freshly ground black pepper
a pinch of freshly grated nutmeg

Preheat the oven to 350°F (180°C).

Heat the butter and olive oil in a large saucepan, add the onion and cook gently, without browning and with a lid on the pan, for 10 minutes or until the onion is soft but not browned.

Add the garlic and wild mush-rooms to the onion and fry for a further 3 minutes or so without a lid on the saucepan.

If the mushrooms produce a lot of liquid, strain it off (save for stock), put them back in the pan with a little more butter and fry for a further minute or two. Add the chopped parsley.

Put the egg yolks into a medium-sized bowl and whisk them with the ½ and ½. Season with salt, pepper and nutmeg to taste and pour into the pastry shell.

Bake in the oven for about 30 minutes or until set and golden. Serve the quiche hot or warm.

Creamy vegan mushroom tart v

I promise you that unless you tell someone this is vegan, they'll never guess that it's not made with lots of cream. It tastes smooth, rich and delicious. The quantities given make a filling about ½in (1cm) deep; if you want it deeper, just double everything and allow 10 minutes or so longer for it to cook.

SERVES 4
8in (20cm) cooked shortcrust pastry
    tart shell (see pages 257–8),
    made with pure vegetable fat
1 onion, finely chopped
1 tbsp olive oil
1 garlic clove, crushed (optional)
8oz (225g) button mushrooms,
    thinly sliced
8oz creamy garlic and herb-flavored
    vegan cheese
1 tbsp finely chopped fresh flat-leaf
    parsley
salt and freshly ground black pepper

Preheat the oven to 350°F (180°C).

In a large saucepan, fry the onion gently in the olive oil for 7 minutes, then add the garlic and mushrooms and cook for another 3–5 minutes, without a lid on the pan. If the mushrooms made a lot of liquid, boil vigorously until it disappears, leaving them tender and glossy.

Remove from the heat, then stir in the cheese, parsley and salt and pepper to taste.

Spoon the mixture into the pastry shell, spreading it level.

Bake for 25–30 minutes or until the filling is set. Serve hot, warm or cold.

Onion quiche

Quick pastry pizza

Creamy vegan asparagus tart v

Make as described, using 8oz (225g) cooked and chopped asparagus instead of the mushrooms.

Creamy vegan leek tart v

Omit the onion, garlic and mushrooms. Use 12oz (350g) chopped, cooked leeks. Mix with the creamy vegan cheese as described, adding a pinch of freshly grated nutmeg with the parsley.

Creamy vegan onion tart v

Increase the amount of onion from 1 onion to 12oz (350g) and use 2 tablespoons of olive oil to fry them in a large saucepan, covered, for 10–15 minutes or until tender. Add the garlic for the last couple of minutes of cooking, then remove from the heat and continue as described, stirring in the cheese and seasoning. The chopped parsley is optional in this.

Crisp pastry with a creamy onion filling. Serve it with new potatoes and fine green beans or a wonderful mixed leaf salad.

SERVES 4–6 ❋
8in (20cm) cooked shortcrust pastry tart shell (see pages 257–8)
1lb (450g) onions, thinly sliced
1 tbsp (15g) butter
1 tbsp olive oil
2oz (50g) Gruyère-style cheese, grated
4 egg yolks or 2 whole eggs
5fl oz (150ml) ½ and ½
½ tsp mustard powder
salt and freshly ground black pepper

Preheat the oven to 350°F (180°C).

Heat the oil and butter in a large saucepan, add the onions, cover and cook gently until they're soft and golden (about 10 minutes).

Put the onions into the pastry shell and sprinkle the grated cheese on top.

Whisk together the egg yolks or eggs and the ½ and ½, mustard and seasoning. Pour this mixture into the pastry shell.

Bake for about 30 minutes or until golden and set. Serve hot or warm.

A very useful recipe for those emergencies when you find yourself having to rustle up food unexpectedly. It's quick to make, very tasty and uses basic store-cupboard ingredients. People always seem to eat more of this than you're expecting, so if in doubt, make extra. Serve with a green salad, which you can prepare while the pizza is cooking.

SERVES 2–3 ❋
8oz (225g) half-and-half mix of wholewheat and all-purpose flour
4 tsp baking powder
6 tbsp olive oil
4oz (125g) Cheddar cheese, grated
½ cup water
2 onions, chopped
1 garlic clove, crushed
2 tbsp tomato purée
1 tsp dried oregano
salt and freshly ground black pepper

Preheat the oven to 425°F (220°C).

Put the flour and baking powder into a bowl, add 4 tablespoons of the oil, a quarter of the grated cheese and all the water, and mix to a thick, soft, slightly lumpy dough with a fork.

Knead the dough lightly on a floured work surface or board then leave it to rest for a minute or two while you make the pizza topping.

In a large covered saucepan, fry the onions in the remaining oil for 10 minutes or until soft and lightly browned.

continued next page

Remove from the heat and stir in the garlic, tomato purée and oregano. This won't need much (if any) seasoning because of the saltiness of the cheese.

Roll the dough into a piece to fit a 12in (30cm) round pizza pan or a 9in x 13in (23cm x 33cm) jelly roll pan. Press down well.

Spread the tomato mixture over the pizza, right to the edges. Sprinkle with salt and pepper and the remaining cheese. Bake for 10–15 minutes or until the base is cooked right through, the cheese topping is golden brown and the pizza smells wonderful.

VARIATIONS

Quick pastry pizza with olives

Any toppings you put on this pizza are best added before you put on the cheese, which helps to hold them in place. Olives are good; distribute a small handful of whatever type you like over the top of the pizza. I think little black olives go particularly well on this.

Quick pastry pizza with artichokes

A handful of marinated artichoke hearts in oil (from a jar or from the deli) are excellent; drain the artichokes and cut into slices. Arrange on top of the pizza, then scatter with the grated cheese.

Quick pastry pizza with red peppers

One or two red peppers, from a jar of preserved peppers, drained, blotted dry, thinly sliced and put on top of the pizza before the grated cheese make an excellent topping. I find jars of peppers keep very well in the fridge once opened as long as the liquid in the jar covers the peppers and the lid is screwed on firmly.

Quick vegan pastry pizza v

This recipe also works with vegan instead of dairy cheese. Simply replace the grated dairy cheese with the same quantity of vegan, whatever flavor you fancy, and bake at a slightly lower temperature, 400°F (200°C) for 15 minutes. The cheese doesn't melt in quite the same way, but this is still good when eaten straight from the oven.

Ratatouille tart

A quickly made ratatouille, with added sour cream and an egg to set it, makes a moist and tasty filling for a tart. Delicious served with new potatoes and a leafy salad.

SERVES 4–6 ❄

8in (20cm) cooked shortcrust pastry tart shell (see pages 257–8)
2 tbsp olive oil
1 onion, chopped
4oz (125g) eggplant (about ½ medium-sized one), diced
4oz (125g) zucchini (about 1 medium-sized one), diced
1 small red pepper, seeded and chopped
1 garlic clove, crushed
2 tbsp tomato purée
5fl oz (150ml) sour cream
1 egg
salt and freshly ground black pepper
2oz (50g) grated cheese (optional)

Preheat the oven to 350°F (180°C).

Heat the olive oil in a large saucepan, add the onion, eggplant and red pepper and fry gently for 10–15 minutes or until they're nearly soft. Add the zucchini and garlic and fry for a further 5 minutes or so until all the vegetables are tender.

Whisk the eggs and cream. Remove from the heat and stir in the tomato purée, cream, egg and seasoning.

Spoon the mixture into the pastry shell and scatter the grated cheese over the top (if using).

Bake for 25–30 minutes or until the filling is set and the cheese on top is golden brown and crisp.

Spinach tart

Chopped green spinach, cream cheese and Parmesan-style cheese make a lovely filling for a tart. It's best served hot and is good with a tomato and onion salad.

SERVES 4–6 ✸

8in (20cm) cooked shortcrust pastry tart shell (see pages 257–8)
8oz (225g) tender spinach leaves or frozen chopped spinach, thawed
3oz (75g) low-fat, soft white cheese
1 egg, beaten
grated nutmeg
salt and freshly ground black pepper
1oz (25g) Parmesan-style cheese, finely grated

Preheat the oven to 350°F (180°C).

If you're using fresh spinach, rinse it and cook it in a dry saucepan, with just the water clinging to it, for a few minutes or until tender and wilted. Drain well. Frozen spinach just needs to be dried by pressing it against the sides of a sieve to squeeze out any extra water.

Put the spinach in a bowl and stir in the soft white cheese, the egg, a good grating of nutmeg and some salt and pepper. Mix well.

Spoon the spinach mixture into the shell and smooth the surface; finish with the grated Parmesan-style cheese.

Bake for about 30 minutes or until the filling is set and the cheese melted and golden brown.

Quick scallion quiche

Here is another speedily made tart. It uses scallions, which are quick to prepare and need no pre-cooking. If you've time to bake the pastry shell before adding the filling, it's crisper, but either way this tart is delicious served hot.
Try making with easy spelt flour wholegrain pastry (see page 258).

SERVES 4–6

8in (20cm) cooked shortcrust pastry tart shell (see pages 257–8)
large bunch of scallions
11fl oz (300ml) sour cream
2 egg yolks
salt and freshly ground black pepper

Preheat the oven to 350°F (180°C). Put a baking sheet into the oven to heat up (this helps the quiche cook crisply).

Wash, trim and chop the scallions and put them in the pastry shell.

Whisk the sour cream and egg yolks and season to taste. Pour over the scallions.

Place the quiche on the pre-heated baking sheet and bake in the center of the oven for 45–50 minutes or until set.

Sweetcorn soufflé tart

This is an unusual tart with a soufflé filling. Don't be nervous of it because it is a type of soufflé: it's easy to make and delicious eaten as soon as it comes out of the oven, all golden brown and puffy.

SERVES 4–6

8in (20cm) cooked shortcrust pastry tart shell (see pages 257–8)
10oz can sweetcorn without added sugar
1¼ cups (275ml) milk
2 tbsp (25g) butter
2 tbsp (25g) all-purpose flour
2 eggs, separated
salt and freshly ground black pepper
a pinch of paprika
1–2oz (25–50g) grated cheese

Preheat the oven to 375°F (190°C).

Drain the sweetcorn and transfer the liquid to a glass measuring cup, then fill with milk to equal 1¼ cups.

Make a roux by melting the butter and stirring in the flour to make a smooth paste.

Remove from the heat to gradually stir in the milk, then stir over a gentle heat until thickened.

Beat in the egg yolks and sweetcorn, and salt, pepper and a pinch of paprika to taste.

Whisk the egg whites until they are standing in stiff peaks and fold into the mixture.

Spoon the mixture into the pastry shell, scatter with the grated cheese and bake for 25 minutes or until risen and golden. Serve immediately.

Tartlets and small pastries

Vegetable tart

Individual asparagus tarts

This tart consists of a crisp pastry shell filled with a mixture of tender vegetables in a tasty cheese sauce, heated and browned in the oven. You can use frozen vegetables instead of fresh ones, for speed.

SERVES 4–6 ❄

8in (20cm) cooked shortcrust pastry tart shell (see pages 257–8)
1¼lb (600g) mixed vegetables (e.g. carrot, zucchini, onion, cauliflower, leek), sliced
2 tbsp (25g) butter
2 tbsp (25g) all-purpose flour
10fl oz (275ml) skimmed milk
1¼ cups (125g) grated cheese
½ tsp mustard powder
4oz (125g) button mushrooms, sliced
salt and freshly ground black pepper

Preheat the oven to 350°F (180°C).

Cook the vegetables in boiling water until just tender, then drain.

To make the sauce, melt the butter in a saucepan, add the flour, cook for 1–2 minutes, then gradually pour in the milk and stir over the heat until thickened.

Add half the grated cheese and the mustard, then stir in the vegetables and mushrooms, and season with salt and pepper.

Pile the mixture into the pastry shell and sprinkle with the rest of the cheese. Bake for 20–25 minutes, until golden brown.

These light, creamy little tarts make a very good starter for a dinner party; they're also nice with salad for lunch. They are lovely made in individual tart pans if you've got them. Otherwise any small oven-proof dishes.

MAKES 6 TARTS ❄

1 quantity of shortcrust pastry, easy wholegrain spelt flour pastry (see pages 257 and 258) or 1lb packet ready-rolled shortcrust pastry
2 tbsp olive oil
1 onion, finely chopped
1 small garlic clove, crushed
2 tbsp (25g) butter
2 eggs
1¼ cups (275ml) milk or ½ and ½
salt and freshly ground black pepper
pinch of freshly grated nutmeg
8oz (225g) fresh or frozen asparagus, cooked (see page 109) and cut into 1in (2cm) lengths.

Place a baking sheet in the center of the oven and preheat to 400°F (200°C).

If you're using homemade pastry, roll it out on a lightly floured work surface or board.

Use the pastry to line six individual tart pans. Prick the bases all over and place the pans on the baking sheet in the oven.

Bake blind (see page 258) for 10–15 minutes or until crisp and golden brown.

To "waterproof" the tartlet shells and prevent any possibility of soggy bottoms, heat the oil until it is very hot and brush over the tarts as soon as you take them out of the oven.

Turn the oven setting down to 180°C (350°F).

Fry the onion and garlic in the butter over a gentle heat for 10 minutes, but don't let them brown.

Take the pan off the heat and add the whisked together eggs and milk or ½ and ½. Season with salt and pepper and add some grated nutmeg to taste.

Arrange the asparagus in the tart shells and then pour in the egg mixture, dividing it equally between them.

Bake the tarts for about 20 minutes or until the filling is set. Serve them hot or warm.

Opposite: Individual asparagus tarts

Hot avocado tartlets

These crisp little tartlets have a topping of tender, buttery avocado bathed in a sharp cheese sauce, with a hint of cayenne. The combination of flavors and textures is excellent; just don't overcook them — avocado is delightful when just warmed but spoils if overheated.

MAKES 6 TARTLETS

1 quantity of shortcrust pastry, easy wholegrain spelt flour pastry (see pages 257 and 258) or 1lb packet ready-rolled shortcrust pastry
2 tbsp rapeseed or ground nut oil
2 tbsp (25g) butter
2 tbsp (25g) flour
1¼ cups (275ml) milk
1 tsp Dijon mustard
4oz (125g) Parmesan-style cheese, grated
salt and freshly ground black pepper
2 avocados
1 tbsp freshly squeezed lemon juice

Preheat the oven to 400°F (200°C).

Roll out the pastry (spread it out if ready-rolled) and line six 4in (10cm) tartlet pans.

Bake blind (see page 258) for 15 minutes.

To ensure crisp tartlet shells, heat the oil and brush the interior of the tartlets with it as soon as they come out of the oven. Set aside.

Melt the butter in a saucepan, add the flour, cook for a moment then gradually pour in the milk, stirring until thick. Add the mustard and three-quarters of the cheese; season to taste.

Peel the avocados, cut into bite-sized chunks and sprinkle with lemon juice.

Gently stir the avocado into the sauce. Divide between the tarts, sprinkle with the rest of the cheese. Bake for about 15 minutes or until heated through and lightly browned on top.

Vatruski

In Russia these light, delicious curd cheese tartlets are traditionally served either on their own as a first course or as an accompaniment to red beet soup (see page 12). Alternatively, just serve them hot from the oven and offer a bowl of sour cream and chopped dill for people to spoon over the top.

MAKES 16 TARTLETS ✽

8oz (225g) cottage cheese, ricotta cheese or quark
1 egg
salt and freshly ground black pepper
1 quantity of shortcrust pastry, easy wholegrain spelt flour pastry (see pages 257 and 258) or 1lb packet ready-rolled shortcrust pastry
1 egg beaten with ½ tsp salt, to glaze

Preheat the oven to 425°F (220°C).

Make the filling by mixing the cottage cheese, ricotta or quark with the egg, and seasoning with salt and pepper.

If you're using homemade pastry, roll it out on a lightly floured work surface or board or just spread out the bought pastry.

Cut the pastry into 3in (16 x 7.5cm) rounds.

Put 1 heaped teaspoon of the cheese mixture on each round. Press the edges of the rounds up towards the centre to make a rim.

Brush the beaten egg glaze over the pastry, then bake for about 20 minutes or until set, puffed up and golden brown. Serve straight from the oven.

Tyropita

Instant nostalgia for anyone who has holidayed in Greece, these little "pies" — really triangular pastries — are very easy to make. You need a large packet of filo pastry. Serve hot with some tzatziki for dipping (see page 49) or, for a light meal, with a Greek salad of cucumber, tomato and kalamata olives dressed with olive oil and lemon juice.

MAKES ABOUT 30 PASTRIES ❊
14oz (140z) feta cheese, crumbled
2 eggs, beaten
freshly ground black pepper
1lb packet filo pastry, completely
    thawed if frozen
½cup olive oil, to glaze
2–3 tsp sesame seeds

Preheat the oven to 400°F (200°C).
    Mash the feta with a fork, then mix in the eggs, to make a creamy consistency. Add a drop or two of water as well if it seems a bit stiff. Season with pepper.
    Open the packet of filo pastry and cut the sheets in half vertically, making 24 strips, each about 9in x 5in (23cm x 12.5cm). Keep the sheets covered with a clean damp cloth to prevent them drying out as you work.
    Brush a strip with oil, then place 1 heaped teaspoon of the feta mixture at the top of the long strip at the left-hand corner. Fold this corner over, making a triangle shape, then fold that over and over, until all the strip has been used up and you have a nice neat triangular-shaped pastry. Make sure it's completely but lightly coated with oil and place on a baking sheet.
    Continue in this way until all the

filling has been used up and you have about 30 "pies". Scatter them with the sesame seeds.
    Bake for 10–15 minutes or until the pies are firm and golden brown. Serve hot, while they're light and flaky.

VARIATION
Tyropita with fresh herbs

This is also lovely with 1–2 tablespoons of chopped fresh herbs added. Dill is especially good; or fresh oregano or thyme. Chop the herbs and add to the cheese mixture.

Little ricotta cheese pies with chilli tomato sauce

These little pies with their creamy white filling, crisp wholegrain pastry and tangy tomato sauce, make a wonderful first course.

MAKES 12 PIES ❊
1 quantity of shortcrust pastry or
    easy wholegrain spelt flour pastry
    (see pages 257 and 258) or 1lb
    packet ready-rolled shortcrust
    pastry
9oz (250g) ricotta cheese
1 garlic clove, crushed
salt and freshly ground black pepper
1 onion, chopped
2 tbsp olive oil
14oz can chopped tomatoes
¼–½ tsp chili powder

Preheat the oven to 425°F (220°C).
    Roll out the pastry (spread it out if ready-rolled) on a lightly floured work surface or board.
    Using a pastry cutter, cut the pastry into 2½in (24 x 6cm) rounds. Place half of them in a 12-hole muffin tin.
    Mix the ricotta cheese with the garlic and seasoning, then divide between the tartlets. Place the remaining circles on top, press together.
    Make a steam-hole in the top of each pie, then bake for 15 minutes or until crisp and golden brown.
    Meanwhile make the sauce; fry the onion in the oil for 10 minutes, add the tomatoes and chili powder, cook for a further 10 minutes or so until reduced. Blend, season and reheat. Serve with the hot pies.

Spiced chickpea and potato pasties v

These are popular with children and are delicious hot or cold.

MAKES 4 PASTIES ❄

1 onion, chopped
2 tbsp olive oil
8oz (225g) potato, peeled and cut into ¼in (6mm) dice
1 tbsp ground coriander
1 tsp ground cumin
14oz can chickpeas
salt and freshly ground black pepper
1 quantity of shortcrust pastry, easy wholegrain spelt flour pastry (see pages 257 and 258) or 1lb packet ready-rolled shortcrust pastry
beaten egg or soy milk, to glaze

Fry the onion in the oil for 5 minutes, then add the potato and spices. Cook gently, covered, for 10–15 minutes or until the potatoes are just tender. Stir often.

Drain and rinse the chickpeas and add to the potato mixture, then season to taste. Leave to one side until cool.

Preheat the oven to 400°F (200°C).

Roll out the pastry (spread it out if ready-rolled) and divide it into four pieces; roll each into a circle 6in (15cm) across.

Spoon a quarter of the chickpea mixture into the center of each circle. Fold up the pastry and press the edges together. Brush with the glaze, then place on a baking sheet. Bake for 20–25 minutes, then serve at once or leave to cool.

Leek and tarragon parcels

These creamy and delicious parcels make a lovely starter. The vegan version is excellent, too.

SERVES 6–8

1 tbsp olive oil
1 tbsp (15g) butter
2 onions, sliced
1lb 2oz (500g) leeks, thinly sliced
1 tbsp (20g) fresh tarragon, lightly chopped
5fl oz (150ml) heavy cream
5oz (150g) low-fat cream cheese
¼ cup capers, rinsed and halved
salt and freshly ground black pepper
9oz packet filo pastry (6 sheets, each approximately 20in x 9½in (500mm x 240mm)
olive oil, for brushing

Preheat the oven to 400°F (200°C).

Heat the oil and butter in a large saucepan until the butter melts. Add the onions, cover with a lid and cook gently for 5 minutes.

Add the leeks and tarragon, stir, cover and cook for 15–20 minutes or until the leeks are very tender.

Add the cream and bubble over the heat for about 10 minutes or until thickened slightly.

Remove from the heat and add the cream cheese, capers and salt and pepper to taste. Leave to cool.

Make triangular parcels: cut the filo pastry in half right down the middle, and across, making 24 strips, each about 9in x 5in (23cm x 12.5cm). Take one of the strips of filo, place a good spoonful of the leek mixture at the top of the strip then fold the strip over on itself to make a triangle, brush with oil, and keep folding and brushing with oil until you get to the end of the strip

of filo. Place on a baking sheet and repeat with the rest of the mixture and filo until all the filling has been used up and you have about 30 pastries.

Bake for 20 minutes or until crisp and golden brown. Serve at once.

VARIATION

Vegan leek and tarragon parcels v

Make as described, but omit the butter and use 2 tablespoons of olive oil to fry the onions. Replace the cream with vegan single cream (such as "Soya Dream") and the dairy cream cheese with vegan cheese.

Mushroom and egg pasties

The wholegrain pastry used for these pasties has a nutty flavor and texture that contrasts well with the creamy filling.

MAKES 8 PASTIES
½ stick (50g) butter
4oz (125g) mushrooms, sliced
¼ (50g) all-purpose flour
15 fl oz (425ml) milk
4 hardboiled eggs, finely chopped
salt and freshly ground black pepper
a pinch of mace or freshly grated nutmeg
1 tbsp chopped fresh flat-leaf parsley
1½ x quantity of shortcrust pastry, easy wholegrain spelt flour pastry (see pages 257 and 258) or 2 x 1lb packets ready-rolled shortcrust pastry
beaten egg, to glaze

Melt the butter and fry the mushrooms until tender, then add the flour. When the mixture froths, draw off the heat and gradually add the milk.

Return the mixture to the heat and stir until thickened, then leave to simmer very gently for 10 minutes to cook the flour.

Stir in the hardboiled eggs and salt, pepper, mace or nutmeg to taste, plus the parsley. Leave to get completely cold.

Preheat the oven to 400°F (200°C).

Divide the pastry into eight pieces, rolling each into a circle 6in (15cm) across. Place a good heap of the filling on each, damp the edges and gather up the sides to the center, Cornish pasty-style. Brush with the beaten egg and bake for 20–25 minutes or until golden and crisp.

Little mushroom pies with yogurt and scallion sauce

I make these in bun tins — the kind with shallow indentations for making jam tarts or mince pies in. They are lovely as a starter, served warm with the chilled creamy sauce, or for a party but without the sauce.

MAKES 12 PIES ❋
1 tbsp (15g) butter
1 tbsp olive oil, plus extra for greasing
1 onion, chopped
1 large garlic clove, crushed
1lb (450g) button mushrooms, sliced
1 tbsp chopped fresh flat-leaf parsley
salt and freshly ground black pepper
1 quantity of cheese shortcrust pastry, easy wholegrain spelt flour pastry (see pages 257 and 258) or 1lb packet ready-rolled shortcrust pastry

FOR THE SAUCE
10fl oz (275ml) natural yogurt
3 tbsp ½ and ½
3 tbsp finely chopped scallions

First prepare the filling. Heat the butter and oil in a large saucepan and fry the onion for about 5 minutes or until it is beginning to soften, then add the garlic and mushrooms and fry for a further 20–25 minutes or until the mushrooms are very tender and all the liquid has boiled away, leaving them dry. Add the parsley and salt and pepper to taste. Set aside to cool.

If you're using homemade pastry, roll it out on a lightly floured work surface or board; spread it out if using ready-rolled. Use a round cutter to stamp out 24 circles. Grease the tin very well. Use half the pastry circles to line the holes.

Preheat the oven to 400°F (200°C).

Put 1 heaped teaspoon of the mushrooms into each pastry shell and put one of the remaining pastry circles on top, pressing down lightly; make a hole in the top of each pie to let the steam out.

Bake the pies for about 15 minutes or until they are golden brown.

While they are cooking, make the sauce by mixing the yogurt with the ½ and ½ and scallions, seasoning with salt and pepper.

When the pies are done, carefully remove them from the tin and serve hot, with the sauce.

The pies will freeze, but not the sauce.

Mushroom vol au vents

Serve these as a first course or light lunch, or for supper with ratatouille and a green salad.

MAKES 8 VOL AU VENTS
1 quantity of puff pastry (see page 259) or 18oz packet frozen puff pastry or a packet frozen ready-made vol au vent shells
1lb (450g) button mushrooms, chopped
2 tbsp (25g) butter
2 tsp cornstarch
1¼ cups (275ml) ½ and ½
salt and freshly ground black pepper
a pinch of freshly grated nutmeg

Preheat the oven to 400°F (200°C).

If you are using a block of puff pastry, roll it out, in one direction only, using short strokes, so that it is ½in (1cm) thick. Cut into rounds with a lightly floured 2in (5cm) cutter. With a cutter one size smaller, mark each circle with another, inner circle without pressing all the way through. Alternatively, use ready-made vol au vent shells.

Place the vol au vents on a damp baking sheet, then bake at the top of the oven for 30 minutes.

Meanwhile fry the mushrooms in the butter for 5 minutes. Add the cornstarch and gradually mix in the ½ and ½, stiring until thickened.

Remove from the heat and season with salt, pepper and grated nutmeg.

Using a small sharp knife, gently ease out the tops of the vol au vent shells. Scoop out and discard the inner pastry layer. Fill the vol au vents with the mushroom mixture.

Reheat for 10–15 minutes before eating, but do not fill in advance or the shells will go soggy.

VARIATIONS
Asparagus vol au vents

This is a lovely variation. Use 1lb (450g) chopped, cooked asparagus instead of the mushrooms. Melt the butter in a saucepan, stir in the cornstarch until smooth, then gradually stir in the ½ and ½. Stir over the heat for 3 minutes or so, until it has thickened, then remove from the heat and stir in the asparagus. Season with salt and pepper.

Leek vol au vents

Make these as described for the asparagus variation, using 1lb (450g) chopped, cooked leeks.

Samosas v

These little Indian pasties with their spicy vegetable filling are delicious as a first course or any time as a snack. Some mango chutney or tzatziki (see page 49) goes well with them. When I've got time I love to make them the traditional way (as here), with a thin, wholewheat casing; it's easy and satisfying to do and the result is excellent. Chapatti flour (available from Indian stores), fine wholegrain or wholegrain spelt flour will give the best results, though any wholegrain flour will do.

MAKES 32 SAMOSAS
2 large potatoes
2 tbsp olive oil
1 tsp cumin seeds
1 green chili, seeded and thinly sliced
1 tsp grated fresh root ginger
a good pinch of chili powder, or more to taste
½–1 tsp garam masala
4oz (125g) frozen peas
2 tbsp chopped fresh coriander
1–2 tsp freshly squeezed lemon juice
salt and freshly ground black pepper

FOR THE PASTRY
Scant 2 cups (225g) wholewheat flour
½ tsp salt
1 tsp baking powder
2 tbsp olive oil
6–7 tbsp cold water
oil, for deep- or shallow-frying

First make the filling. Peel the potatoes and cut them into ½in (1cm) dice.

Heat the oil in a large saucepan; stir in the cumin seeds, chili and ginger; cook for a few seconds until the cumin seeds start to "pop", then add the potatoes and stir so that they all get coated with the spicy oil. Cover and cook over a low heat for about 10 minutes or until the potatoes are tender, stirring often. If they start to stick, add a splash or two of water.

Remove from the heat and stir in the chili powder, garam masala, peas and chopped coriander. Season with lemon juice, salt and pepper then let the mixture cool.

To make the samosa pastry, put the flour, salt and baking powder into a bowl. Stir in the oil and enough water to make a soft but not sticky dough. Cover with a clean damp cloth and leave to rest for 15 minutes if possible.

Divide the dough into 16 pieces. Roll each piece into a ball then use a rolling pin to roll each into a circle about 6in (15cm) in diameter. Cut the circles in half to get 32 half circles.

To make a samosa, dampen the cut edge of one of the half circles with cold water and press together to form a cone shape. Put 1 heaped teaspoon of the filling in the cone, then dampen the top with cold water and fold the corners over to make a little triangle-shaped packet, pressing the edges well together.

When all the samosas are ready, deep-fry them a few at a time until they are golden and crisp. Drain them well and serve hot or cold. You can also shallow-fry them (provided the oil in the frying pan is deep enough), turning them over to cook both sides.

VARIATIONS
Filo samosas v

Make the filling mixture exactly as described. Cut sheets of filo pastry into long strips: you will get two or four of these to a sheet of filo depending on its size; if the filo comes in a pack of six large sheets, you will get four strips to each sheet; if there are 12 pieces in the pack, you will get two strips per sheet. Take a strip of filo pastry, place a good spoonful of the potato mixture at the top of the strip then fold the strip over on itself to make a triangle, brush with olive oil, and keep folding and brushing with olive oil until you get to the end of the strip of filo. Fry the samosas as described or brush them with oil, place on a baking sheet and bake for 20 minutes at 400°F (200°C). Serve at once.

Sausage rolls

This recipe, one of my earliest inventions, consists of a simple "sausage" mixture encased in a very rich cheese pastry. These are always very popular.

SERVES 4 ❄
4oz (125g) ground nuts (hazelnuts, almonds, walnuts or a mixture)
2oz (50g) cooked, mashed potato (see page 131)
2 onions, finely chopped and fried
1 tsp yeast extract
1 tsp dried basil
1 egg, beaten
salt and freshly ground black pepper

FOR THE SPECIAL CHEESE PASTRY
5oz (175g) plain wholewheat flour
1 tsp baking powder
1 stick (125g) butter, diced
3oz (75g) grated cheese
1–2 tbsp sweet chutney or tamarind paste

To make the sausages, mix all the ingredients to a fairly stiff consistency.

Place small rolls of the mixture on a greased baking sheet and bake in the oven at 325°F (160°C) for 20 minutes.

Meanwhile make the pastry: mix together the flour, baking powder butter and cheese to form a dough.

Roll the pastry out carefully on a lightly floured work surface or board or between two pieces of baking parchment (it will be rather tacky) and brush with sweet chutney.

Put the sausages on the pastry and wrap it round each to form rolls.

Increase the oven setting to 450°F (230°C), and bake the rolls for 10 minutes. Serve hot or cold.

Pies and rolls

Little tomato tarts with sour cream

These creamy tarts are quick and easy to make and full of the flavors of summer. A salad of mixed summer leaves and herbs goes perfectly with it.

MAKES 6 TARTS

1 quantity of shortcrust pastry, easy wholegrain spelt flour pastry (see pages 257 and 258) or 1lb packet ready-rolled shortcrust pastry
2 tbsp olive oil (optional)
1lb (450g) tomatoes, skinned (see page 40), seeded and sliced
salt and freshly ground black pepper
1–2 tbsp torn or chopped fresh basil
11fl oz (300ml) sour cream
2 egg yolks

Place a baking sheet in the center of the oven and preheat to 400°F (200°C).

Use the pastry to make six individual tart shells as described for individual asparagus tarts (see page 270), brushing the bases with hot oil when the tarts come out of the oven, as described, to "waterproof", if you wish.

While the tart shells are cooking, put the tomatoes into a sieve or colander, sprinkle with salt and pepper and leave to one side.

Pat the tomato slices dry with paper towels or a clean cloth, then put them in the pastry shells. Sprinkle the basil leaves over.

Whisk together the sour cream and egg yolks, add some seasoning, then pour over the tomatoes.

Bake the tarts in the oven for about 20 minutes or until the filling is set. Serve hot or warm.

Lima bean and chutney roll v

Melt-in-the-mouth wholegrain pastry, onions, Lima beans and sweet chutney make a tasty savory roll that's good hot or cold, and ideal for packed lunches.

SERVES 4 ❄

2 onions, sliced
2 tbsp olive oil
4oz (125g) dried Lima beans, soaked and cooked (see pages 176–7), or a 14oz can
salt and freshly ground black pepper
1 quantity of shortcrust pastry, easy wholegrain spelt flour pastry (see pages 257 and 258) or 1lb packet ready-rolled shortcrust pastry
2–3 tbsp sweet chutney or tamarind paste
beaten egg or soy milk, to glaze

Fry the onions in the oil for 10 minutes or until soft.

Drain the butter beans (rinsing the canned ones), then add to the onions, and season with salt and pepper to taste. Leave on one side to cool.

Preheat the oven to 400°F (200°C).

If you're using homemade pastry, roll it out into two rectangles, each 10in x 9in (25cm x 23cm).

Place one rectangle on a baking sheet, spread with the chutney and spoon the bean mixture on top.

Dampen the edges with water, cover with the second rectangle and press the edges together.

Brush with beaten egg or soy milk and prick with a fork.

Bake for 25–30 minutes or until the pastry is set and golden.

Lima bean and tomato pie v

The wholegrain crust gives this pie a lovely country look, but it's also good made with the puff pastry instead.

SERVES 4 ❄

1 large onion, chopped
1 tbsp olive oil
1 tbsp tomato purée
14oz can chopped tomatoes
½ tsp dried basil
salt and freshly ground black pepper
a little sugar
7oz (200g) dried Lima beans, soaked, cooked (see pages 176–7) or 2 x 14oz cans, drained and rinsed
1 quantity shortcrust pastry, easy wholegrain spelt flour pastry (see pages 257 and 258) or 1lb packet ready-rolled shortcrust pastry
beaten egg or soy milk, to glaze (optional)

Preheat the oven to 400°F (200°C).

Fry the onion in the oil for 10 minutes, then add the tomato purée, tomatoes, basil and salt and pepper to taste and simmer gently for 10 minutes.

Mix in the Lima beans, check the seasoning and pour into a 1 quart (1.2 liter) pie dish.

Roll out the pastry if you're using homemade; use the pastry to cover the top of the pie. Crimp the edges and decorate the top as you fancy.

Glaze with the egg or soy milk (if using) and bake for 20 minutes, then turn the heat down to 375°F (190°C) and cook for a further 10–15 minutes until the pie is golden brown and crisp.

Coulibiac

This Russian roll, with its flaky golden crust and filling of tender cabbage, rice and hardboiled egg, is delicious served with a soured cream and herb sauce (see page 44), made with dill.

SERVES 6
1 onion, chopped
1 tbsp (15g) butter
12oz (350g) cabbage, shredded
4oz (125g) button mushrooms, sliced
12oz (350g) cooked rice
¼ cup chopped fresh flat-leaf parsley
2 hardboiled eggs, chopped
salt and freshly ground black pepper
1 quantity of puff or cream cheese pastry (see page 259) or 1lb packet ready-rolled puff pastry
beaten egg or milk, to glaze

Fry the onion in the butter for 5 minutes; add the cabbage and mushrooms, and cook for a further 10 minutes or until cabbage is tender.

Add the rice, parsley, hardboiled eggs and seasoning. Allow to cool. Preheat the oven to 425°F (220°C).

If you're using homemade pastry, roll it out into two rectangles, each 10in x 9in (25cm x 23cm); divide ready-rolled pastry into two equal pieces.

Spoon the rice mixture on top of one of the pieces of pastry; dampen the edges with water.

Fold the second piece of pastry in half lengthways. Make diagonal slashes about ½in (1cm) apart to within ½in (1cm) of the fold; open out and place on top of the mixture, pressing the edges together. Brush with the glaze. Bake for 35 minutes or until puffed up, crisp and golden.

Whole Brie baked in filo

This is a wonderful dish for a party — hot, oozing Brie wrapped in crisp golden filo pastry. If you can't buy large sheets of filo pastry, use smaller sheets and put them together, overlapping them slightly to get big enough pieces to wrap the Brie in. Serve with warm apricot jam and a green salad.

SERVES 8–10
9oz packet filo pastry – one with large sheets is best (6 sheets, about 20 x 9½in (500 x 240mm)
olive oil, for brushing
about 2¼lb (1kg) under-ripe whole Brie
1lb (450g) jar apricot jam

Spread out a sheet of filo pastry on a baking sheet that's large enough to hold the Brie. Brush the filo with oil, put another sheet on top, brush with oil and repeat until they are all done.

Unwrap the Brie and put it in the middle of the filo pastry. Pull up all the sides of the filo and press or scrunch them together over the top of the pastry. Brush with oil. Keep in a cool place until you are ready.

Preheat the oven to 375°F (190°C) and bake for 30 minutes or until the filo is crisp and golden brown. If it gets too brown on top, cover with foil — it's important to bake it long enough for the pastry underneath to cook.

Leave to cool for about 10 minutes before serving. While this is happening, heat the jam gently in a saucepan. Transfer the Brie to a large serving dish and serve with the apricot sauce.

Cheese and onion pie

This traditional English pie makes a warming family meal, served with a homemade tomato sauce (see page 71) and vegetables. As the pastry is rich, and so is the cheese, I prefer to cook the onions in water rather than in oil, for a better-balanced dish.

SERVES 6 ❄
salt
1lb (450g) onions, sliced
1 quantity of shortcrust, puff or cream cheese pastry (see pages 257 and 259), or 1lb packet ready-rolled puff pastry
8oz (225g) grated cheese
freshly ground black pepper
beaten egg or milk, to glaze

Cook the onions in boiling salted water until just tender (about 10 minutes). Drain well, then leave to cool.

Preheat the oven to 425°F (220°C).

Divide the pastry in half. If you're using homemade pastry, roll one half out on a lightly floured work surface or board. Place in a 9-inch (1 liter) pie dish.

Mix the onions with the cheese and seasoning, then spoon on top of the pastry. Moisten the edges of the pastry with cold water.

Use the rest of the pastry to cover the pie (rolling out the homemade pastry), pressing the edges together and trimming if you like.

Brush with the beaten egg or milk if you want a shiny finish, then bake for 30–35 minutes or until the pastry is crisp and golden brown.

continued next page

Cheese and onion turnover

My mother always used to make this in the form of a crescent-shaped turnover and it was a great favorite with me and my sister. To make this variation, roll the pastry into a large oval and transfer to a large baking sheet, put the onions and grated cheese on one half and fold over. Press the edges together, prick the top, glaze with the milk or beaten egg, if you like, and bake for 25–30 minutes.

Goat cheese puff pastry pies

These little flaky pies, all golden and oozing with melted goat cheese and which you can put together in moments, are excellent with some cranberry sauce, creamy mashed potatoes and thin green beans. Put the potatoes on to cook before you pop the pastries in the oven, then you can mash them and cook the beans while the pastries are cooking. Bon appétit!

SERVES 4
13oz packet ready-rolled puff pastry
2 x 3½oz goat cheeses (with a soft rind)
cranberry sauce, to serve

Preheat the oven to 400°F (200°C).

Roll the pastry slightly on a floured surface: you need to be able to get 4in (8 x 10cm) rounds from it. If you have a cutter that size, that's perfect; otherwise cut round a small saucer or a template made from a piece of card.

Cut the goat cheeses in half horizontally. Put half a goat cheese, cut side uppermost, on a pastry round. Place another piece of pastry of top and press the two pieces of pastry together all round with your fingers. Make a hole for the steam in the top.

Put the pastries onto a baking sheet and bake for 12–15 minutes or until puffed up and golden brown. Serve with the cranberry sauce.

Leek pie

Thick cream is traditionally used for this delicious Cornish pie. Thinking of all those calories, I have included a lighter version using single cream, though for a treat, use clotted cream.

SERVES 4 ❄
2¼lb (1kg) leeks
1oz (25g) extra-mature Cheddar cheese, grated
5fl oz (150ml) ½ and ½
2 eggs, beaten
salt and freshly ground black pepper
1 quantity of shortcrust, puff or cream cheese pastry (see pages 257 and 259), or 1lb packet ready-rolled puff pastry
beaten egg or soya milk, to glaze

Wash the leeks and cut them into 1in (2.5 cm) pieces. Put them into a large saucepan, cover with cold water and bring to a boil. Simmer the leeks gently for about 10 minutes or until they're tender, then drain them very well in a colander, using a spoon to press out all the water.

If you're using homemade pastry, roll it out on a lightly floured work surface or board, so that it is big enough to fit on top of your pie dish. Preheat the oven to 400°F (200°C).

Mix the leeks with the grated cheese, ½ and ½, eggs, and salt and pepper to taste. Put the mixture into the pie dish and cover with the pastry, trimming it to fit and decorating it as you fancy.

Brush the top with a little beaten egg. Bake the pie for 20–25 minutes or until the pastry is golden and cooked. Serve immediately.

Mushroom pudding

This is a steamed pudding, rather like a vegetarian steak and kidney one. It's very easy to do and makes a warming meal in winter. I like to serve it with mashed potatoes and red cabbage.

SERVES 4 ❄

1 quantity of cheese shortcrust pastry (see page 257) or 1lb packet ready-rolled shortcrust pastry
12oz (350g) dark mushrooms, sliced
1 onion, chopped
1 tsp tomato purée
1 small garlic clove, crushed
salt and freshly ground black pepper
1 tsp yeast extract
2 tbsp hot water

If you're making your own pastry, follow the directions on page 257. Leave the pastry to chill while you grease an 3 cup pudding basin and make the filling.

Put the mushrooms into a bowl and mix with the remaining ingredients, softening the yeast extract in the hot water.

Roll out two-thirds of the pastry and use to line the pudding basin; spoon the mushroom mixture into this, then cover with the rest of the pastry, rolled out to fit the top. Trim the edges and prick the top with a fork.

Cover with a piece of foil, secured with string. Steam the pudding for 2½ hours (or 1 hour in a pressure cooker).

When the pudding is done, slip a knife down the sides of the bowl to loosen the pudding, then turn out onto a warmed serving dish.

Flaky mushroom roll v

This has always been a popular dish in my family. I like it with light and creamy celeriac mash and some cranberry sauce (see pages 119 and 65).

SERVES 4 ❄

4oz (125g) couscous
1¾ cups (400ml) boiling water
½oz (15g) dried porcini mushrooms
2 tbsp olive oil
2 onions, chopped
1 garlic clove, crushed
8oz (225g) white mushrooms, chopped
¼ cup chopped fresh flat-leaf parsley
1 tbsp freshly squeezed lemon juice
2 tsp dark soy sauce
salt and freshly ground black pepper
1 quantity puff or cream cheese pastry (see page 259), or 1lb packet ready-rolled puff pastry
beaten egg or soya milk, to glaze

Put the couscous into a bowl and cover with 1¼ cups (300ml) of the boiling water. Set aside.

In another small bowl, or an old cup, put the porcini mushrooms and cover with the rest of the boiling water. Set aside to steep.

Heat the oil in a large saucepan, add the onions and cook, covered, for 10 minutes. Add the garlic and white mushrooms and cook, uncovered, until all liquid has boiled away. Remove from the heat.

Drain the porcini; check that they're not gritty — if they are, give them a quick rinse — and chop finely. Add them to the mushrooms in the saucepan.

Drain any excess liquid from the couscous and add to the mushroom mixture, along with the parsley, lemon juice, soy sauce and a good seasoning of salt and pepper. Leave to cool.

Preheat the oven to 425°F (220°C).

Divide the pastry in half, rolling each into a rectangle 12in x 10in (30cm x 25cm).

Place one half on a baking sheet. Spoon the mushroom mixture on top, leaving the edges clear. Dampen the pastry edges.

Fold the second piece of pastry in half lengthways. Make diagonal slashes about ½in (1cm) apart to within ½in (1cm) of the fold; open out and place on top of mixture, pressing down the edges.

Brush with the glaze. Put the roll into the oven and bake for 10 minutes, then turn the setting down to 325°F (160°C) and bake for a further 30–40 minutes or until the roll is crisp and golden brown.

VARIATION

Flaky eggplant roll v

Omit the porcini mushrooms and the white mushrooms. Cut an eggplant into ¼in (6mm) dice and seed and chop a small red pepper. Cook these in the oil with the onions. Add 1 tablespoon each of ground cumin and coriander to the pan along with the garlic. Use just 2 table-spoons of the parsley and 1 table-spoonful of chopped fresh mint, and throw a small handful of raisins into the mixture, along with 2 chopped tomatoes and a small handful of toasted sliced almonds. Wrap with pastry and bake as described.

Spanakopita

This is very easy to make and always popular. I love it with a juicy tomato salad.

SERVES 4
1lb 2oz (500g) fresh or frozen
    spinach
a bunch of scallions, chopped
7oz (200g) feta cheese, crumbled
salt and freshly ground black pepper
9oz packet filo pastry
olive oil, for brushing

Preheat the oven to 400°F (200°C).

Wash and cook the fresh spinach in a large saucepan for about 5 minutes, or until wilted and tender; drain well and chop. Cook frozen spinach according to the directions on the packet. Drain well.

Add the scallions, feta and seasoning to the spinach.

Brush a pie dish or jelly roll pan with olive oil, lay a piece of filo pastry in it and brush with oil; put another piece on top and continue in this way until half the filo has been used and the dish is lined — don't trim the filo, leave the edges hanging. (Some packs of filo contain six large sheets of filo — cut these in half if they're too big for your tin and overlap them as necessary.)

Put the spinach mixture on top.

Brush a piece of filo on both sides with oil and place on top of the spinach, then cover with another piece of filo, brush with oil and continue until all the filo has been used.

Tidy up the ends of the filo, rolling them together at the edges to make it neat. With a sharp knife score the top diagonally both ways to make the traditional diamond shapes. Brush with oil, make 2–3 steam holes and bake for 30–40 minutes or until crisp and golden.

Vegetable and butter bean pie with flaky crust v

Serve this pie with mashed potatoes and a cooked green vegetable for an economical and delicious family meal.

SERVES 4–6 ❄
1 onion, chopped
2 tbsp olive oil
14oz (14oz) can chopped tomatoes
8oz (225g) carrots, sliced
12oz (350g) leeks, trimmed and
    sliced
4oz (125g) mushrooms
14oz can butter beans
salt and freshly ground black pepper
1 quantity of puff or cream cheese
    pastry (see page 259), or 1lb
    packet ready-rolled puff pastry

Fry the onion in the oil for 5 minutes, covered, then add the tomatoes, carrots, leeks and mushrooms and cook gently for about 30 minutes or until the vegetables are tender, stirring often.

Drain and rinse the beans and add to the mixture, together with salt and pepper to taste. Spoon into a 9-inch pie dish, then leave to cool.

Preheat the oven to 425°F (220°C). If you're using homemade pastry, roll it out on a lightly floured work surface or board.

Cut strips from the pastry, brush with water and stick round the rim of the pie dish. Then ease the pastry onto the top of the pie, pressing the edges together around the rim. Press the prongs of a fork around the edge of the pie. Make 2–3 steam holes in the top of the pastry, then bake for 30 minutes.

Walnut pâté en croûte

I think of this dish as my *Woman's Hour* one; it's the one I made in the studio for Christmas and which provoked a record number of requests for a recipe! It makes a gorgeous main course for a special meal: a moist wine-flavored pâté in a crisp crust of golden pastry. Serve with all the festive trimmings: gravy, cranberry sauce, bread or horseradish sauce, roast potatoes and vegetables. This can be made in advance (but don't brush with beaten egg) and frozen for up to 4 weeks. It's best to allow it to defrost completely, then brush with the beaten egg just before baking.

SERVES 8–10

1 tbsp (15g) butter
1 onion, chopped
1 small stalk of celery, chopped
1 large garlic clove, crushed
1 tomato, skinned (see page 40) and chopped
4oz (125g) button mushrooms, chopped
8oz (225g) unsweetened chestnut purée
6oz (175g) cashew nuts, grated
2oz (50g) shelled walnuts, grated
1 tbsp brandy
½ tsp each paprika, dried thyme and dried basil
1 egg or 2 egg yolks, beaten
salt and freshly ground black pepper
1 quantity of puff or cream cheese pastry (see page 259), or 1lb packet ready-rolled puff pastry
beaten egg, to glaze

Preheat the oven to 425°F (220°C).

To make the filling, melt the butter in a large saucepan and fry the onion, celery and garlic for 7 minutes or until nearly soft, then add the tomato and mushrooms and cook for an additional 3 minutes or so.

Remove from the heat and add the chestnut purée, grated nuts, brandy, paprika, dried herbs and egg or egg yolks. Mix well, then season with salt and pepper and leave to cool.

If you're using homemade pastry, roll out one-third to a rectangle 6in x 12 in (15cm x 30cm); roll ready-rolled pastry to the same size.

Put the filling on top of the pastry strip, piling it up into a loaf shape and leaving the edges clear. Moisten the edges with cold water.

Roll out the rest of the pastry to cover the top of the chestnut mixture, encasing it completely. Trim the edges, decorate with pastry trimmings and brush with beaten egg.

Bake for 30 minutes or until puffed up, golden and crisp.

VARIATION

Vegan walnut pâté en croûte V

You can make an excellent vegan version of this delicious recipe. Use 1 tablespoon of olive oil to fry the vegetables at the beginning, instead of the butter, and omit the eggs — the mixture will still hold together, but you will just need a little extra care when slicing it. Make sure that the puff pastry you use is a pure vegetable one and, for the glaze, brush with soy milk instead of beaten egg.

Cheese
and eggs

Some of the tastiest, easiest and most popular vegetarian dishes contain cheese and eggs. These great protein-rich ingredients can make all the difference for new vegetarians.

In this chapter you'll find many quick, simple dishes, such as Welsh rarebit, pipérade and the ultimate "fast food" — omelettes (see pages 301, 299 and 295). You'll also find filling, versatile and delicious crêpes (see pages 296–8); become adept at making these and not only will you be able to knock out a hot and popular snack in no time, but you will also open the door to a whole range of wonderful main courses.

The same can be said about soufflés, which really are easy (see pages 301–4)! And there's no doubting their impressiveness; I love dishes that have the "wow" factor! Another such dish is a gougère — a puffy, golden ring of savory choux pastry with a mushroom, onion and red wine sauce (see page 293).

When choosing ingredients for these recipes, make sure you buy free-range (preferably organic) eggs and look for cheeses marked as suitable for vegetarians. There's a vegetarian replacement of some kind for every type of cheese even though it may have a different name. I find the staff at cheese counters to be a very helpful source of information on this, as is the internet.

Sformati di asparigi

This Italian savory pudding is a cross between a soufflé and a savory loaf.

SERVES 4 AS A MAIN DISH, 6 AS A STARTER

1lb (450g) asparagus, trimmed and cut into 1in (2.5cm) pieces
4 tbsp (50g) butter
¼ cup (50g) all-purpose flour
1¼ cups (275ml) milk
2–3 tbsp Parmesan-style cheese, grated
salt and freshly ground black pepper
3 eggs
1 tbsp chopped fresh flat-leaf parsley
a few flat-leaf parsley sprigs, to garnish

Preheat the oven to 350°F (180°C).

Cook the asparagus in 2in (5cm) fast-boiling water until tender, then drain.

Make the sauce by melting the butter and stirring in the flour; when it's blended add the milk in three batches, keeping the heat high and stirring well each time. (Wait until the mixture thickens before adding any more milk.) Take off the heat and add the Parmesan-style cheese and salt and pepper.

Whisk the eggs and mix into the sauce; gently stir in the drained asparagus and chopped parsley. Check the seasoning and pour the mixture into a lightly greased shallow ovenproof dish.

Put the dish into a baking pan containing about 1in (2.5cm) of very hot water and place it in the center of the oven. Bake for about 1 hour or until the mixture is set. Top with some parsley sprigs and serve.

Cauliflower, egg and potato bake

This is a filling dish that's like a substantial cauliflower cheese. If you don't like eggs you could put in a layer of sliced mushrooms instead — you'll need about 8oz (225g). Serve with some lightly cooked greens.

SERVES 4–6

1½lb (700g) even-sized small–medium potatoes
1 head cauliflower
salt and freshly ground black pepper
3 cups (850ml) cheese sauce (see page 65)
6 hardboiled eggs, sliced
dried breadcrumbs (see page 183)
a little butter, for greasing and topping

Scrub the potatoes then cook them in their skins in boiling water until they're tender; drain and cool them, then slip off the skins with a sharp knife. Cut the potatoes into slices.

Wash the cauliflower and break it into even-sized florets. Cook these in a little boiling water for about 7 minutes or until they're just tender, then drain well.

Preheat the oven to 375°F (190°C).

Grease a large shallow ovenproof dish with butter, then place a layer of the potato slices in the base, and season lightly. Follow this with some of the sauce, then the cauliflower, some more seasoning, the egg slices, then some more sauce. Continue like this until everything has been used, ending, if possible, with layers of potato and sauce.

Sprinkle the top with breadcrumbs, dot with a little butter and bake for about 30 minutes or until heated through and brown on top.

Cheese, pepper and tomato bake

This is an economical family bake that's quick to make and low in calories. I like it best with a tomato sauce and Bircher potatoes (see pages 71 and 128) and cauliflower or a lightly cooked green vegetable. This dish freezes well, either cooked or par-cooked.

SERVES 4 ❋

1 large onion, chopped
1 small–medium green pepper, seeded and chopped
8oz (225g) can chopped tomatoes
4oz (125g) wholegrain bread
6oz (175g) grated cheese
2 tbsp chopped fresh flat-leaf parsley
1 egg, beaten
½–1 tsp Tabasco sauce
salt and freshly ground black pepper

Preheat the oven to 400°F (200°C).

Put the onion, green pepper and tomatoes into a bowl and crumble in the bread with your fingers. Mix well to break up the bread.

Add most of the grated cheese, the parsley, beaten egg and enough Tabasco sauce to give a pleasant "lift". Season with salt and pepper.

Spoon the mixture into a shallow, lightly greased ovenproof dish, sprinkle with the remaining cheese and bake for about 30 minutes, or until set and golden brown.

Baked soufflé pudding

This quick dish is a bit like a substantial soufflé but much easier and less stressful to make, and very tasty. It's good served with a tomato sauce.

SERVES 4

6oz (175g) aged Cheddar cheese, grated
1 garlic clove, crushed
4oz (125g) fresh brown breadcrumbs
a pinch of cayenne pepper
salt and freshly ground black pepper
3 eggs, separated
1¼ cups (275ml) milk
2 tbsp (25g) butter, melted

Preheat the oven to 425°F (220°C).

Mix together the cheese, garlic, breadcrumbs, cayenne and some salt and pepper. Beat the egg yolks and add the milk and melted butter.

Whisk the egg whites until they stand in stiff peaks. Fold these into the other ingredients, then put the mixture into a greased soufflé dish and bake in the oven for 30 minutes or until well risen and golden. Serve at once.

Cheese and egg pie

This is a family recipe, which my mother evolved as a vegetarian replacement for fish pie. It's a very soothing dish. Broiled or roasted vine tomatoes and a lightly cooked green vegetable go well with this.

SERVES 4

2 tbsp cornstarch
2 cups (575ml) milk
1 bay leaf or a pinch of mace
1 tbsp (15g) butter
2oz (50g) cheese, grated
salt and freshly ground black pepper
6 hardboiled eggs
1½lb (700g) creamy mashed potatoes (see page 131)

Preheat the oven to 375°F (190°C).

Mix the cornstarch with a little of the milk to a thin creamy consistency.

Put the rest of the milk in a saucepan with the bay leaf or mace and bring to a boil, then remove the bay leaf and pour the milk over the cornstarch mixture, stirring all the time. Pour back into the pan, add the butter and cook gently till thickened, still stirring, then beat in the cheese and remove from the heat. Season to taste.

Chop the eggs and stir into the sauce. Pour the mixture into a shallow ovenproof dish and top with the creamy mashed potatoes. Run the prongs of a fork over the top.

Bake for 30–40 minutes or until bubbling hot.

Cheese fondue

There's something very convivial and celebratory about a fondue and this is perfect for those occasions when you want to make something delicious and a bit special.

SERVES 4–6

1 garlic clove
1¼ cups (275ml) dry white wine
8oz (225g) Gruyère cheese, grated
8oz (225g) Emmental cheese, grated
2 tbsp cornstarch
1–2 tbsp kirsch (optional but good)
salt and freshly ground black pepper
a pinch or two of freshly grated nutmeg
1–2 large French loaves, cut into bite-sized chunks and warmed in the oven

Halve the garlic and rub the cut surfaces over the inside of a medium-sized saucepan or special fondue pan (if you have one).

Put the wine and cheese into the saucepan and heat gently, stirring all the time, until the cheese has melted.

Mix the cornstarch to a paste with the kirsch (if using) or use a drop more wine. Pour this paste into the cheese mixture, stirring all the time until you have a lovely creamy consistency.

Occasionally, the cheese goes all lumpy and stringy at this point. Don't worry; if you beat it vigorously for a moment or two with a whisk, all will be well.

Season the fondue with salt, pepper and nutmeg, then place the saucepan over the lighted burner and let everyone start dipping their bread into the delicious mixture.

Cheese fritters

Baked eggs

This is another all-time favorite recipe. It's a fried version of gnocchi and may sound unpromising, but the crisp, tasty fritters are loved by everyone who tries them. I serve them with lemon slices and a parsley or tartar sauce (see pages 64 and 70). They freeze excellently; I do this after coating them in breadcrumbs and they can then be fried from frozen as required.

SERVES 4 ❄

2 cups (575ml) milk
1 small whole onion, peeled
1 bay leaf
1 clove
4oz (125g) polenta
4oz (125g) Cheddar cheese, finely grated
½ level tsp mustard powder
salt and freshly ground black pepper
olive oil, for shallow-frying

FOR THE COATING
½ cup cornstarch
8–9 tbsp cold water
packet of dried breadcrumbs

Put the milk, onion, bay leaf and clove into a saucepan and bring to a boil. Then remove from heat, cover and leave for 10–15 minutes.

Remove and discard the onion, bay leaf and clove. Re-boil the milk and sprinkle in the polenta, stirring all the time. Simmer until very thick (about 5 minutes).

Remove from the heat and beat in the cheese, mustard and some salt and pepper.

Spread the mixture onto a piece of baking parchment to a depth of about ½in (1cm). Smooth the top and leave until completely cold. Once set, cut the mixture into pieces.

To make the coating, mix the cornstarch and water together to a thick, coating consistency. Dip each fritter first in the cornstarch mixture then into the dried bread-crumbs, so that it is completely coated in crumbs. Press it gently back into shape if necessary.

Fry on both sides in hot oil until crisp and golden. Drain well.

One of the quickest and simplest suppers that you can enjoy.

SERVES 4

4oz (125g) mushrooms or tomatoes
4 eggs
a little butter
¼ cup ½ and ½
salt and freshly ground black pepper
4 pieces of toast, to serve

Preheat the oven to 350°F (180°C).

Chop the mushrooms or tomatoes and fry lightly in the butter.

Put a little of the mushroom mixture into the bottom of four ramekin dishes, then break in an egg and pour 1 tablespoon of cream into each.

Sprinkle the tops with salt and a grinding of black pepper, place the dishes in a roasting pan containing some boiling water, cover with foil, and bake in the oven for 20–30 minutes or until the eggs are set.

Serve at once, with hot toast.

Quick and easy egg croquettes

This was my aunt's invention: crisp little egg croquettes that can be rustled up in a moment. Try them with broiled tomatoes.

SERVES 2–4
½ stick (50g) butter
1 heaped tbsp cornstarch
1¼ cups (275ml) milk
salt and freshly ground black pepper
a pinch of mace or freshly grated nutmeg
2 tbsp grated cheese
4 hardboiled eggs, finely chopped
2 tbsp chopped fresh flat-leaf parsley
all-purpose flour, for coating
olive oil, for shallow-frying

Melt the butter in a pan and blend in the cornstarch. Remove from the heat and add the milk slowly, stirring. Bring to a boil, stirring all the time until the mixture thickens considerably.

Add salt, pepper and a pinch of mace or nutmeg and the grated cheese and allow the cheese to melt before adding the eggs and parsley.

When the mixture has cooled a little, shape into croquettes.

Coat with flour and shallow-fry both sides in very hot oil until golden brown. Serve at once.

Egg croquettes

These are quite substantial croquettes with a hint of the savory flavor of yeast extract and a crisp crumb coating. Make a quick tomato sauce at the same time (see page 71) for a tasty meal in moments.

SERVES 2–4
4 hardboiled eggs
1 tbsp (15g) butter, softened
4oz (125g) fresh wholegrain breadcrumbs
½ tsp yeast extract (e.g. Marmite)
1 tbsp chopped fresh flat-leaf parsley
salt and freshly ground black pepper
1 egg, beaten
dried breadcrumbs (see page 183)
olive oil, for shallow-frying
flat-leaf parsley sprigs, to garnish

Chop the eggs finely and mix with the butter.

Add the breadcrumbs, yeast extract, chopped parsley, salt and pepper and half the beaten egg to make a stiff paste.

Mold into eight small balls, dip in the remaining egg, coat with dried breadcrumbs and fry on both sides in the oil.

Drain and serve garnished with parsley sprigs.

Quick egg curry

Easy to make and gently spiced, this is great with fluffy basmati rice, either brown or white, your choice, and some lime pickle.

SERVES 4
6 eggs
1 large onion
½ cup olive oil
2 tsp white mustard seeds
2 tsp ground coriander
2 tsp ground cumin
2 tsp turmeric
2 tbsp all-purpose flour
1½ cups (1 pint) water
¼ cup tomato purée
½ cup (15g) canned coconut cream and reduce water to 1½ cups
salt and freshly ground black pepper
cooked basmati rice, to serve

Hardboil the eggs, shell and slice them, and keep warm and covered in the ovenproof serving dish you will be using for the curry.

Peel and chop the onion and fry gently in the oil, in a covered pan, for about 10 minutes or until tender.

Add the spices and cook for a further 1–2 minutes or until the mustard seeds start to "pop".

Stir in the flour, add the water and tomato purée and simmer gently for 10 minutes, then add the coconut cream, and some salt and pepper. Pour over the hardboiled eggs. Serve with the cooked rice.

Eggs Florentine

A real classic: just poached eggs on a bed of tender spinach topped with a smooth creamy cheese sauce and crunchy breadcrumbs.

SERVES 4

4 eggs
1lb (450g) spinach leaves
salt and freshly ground black pepper
a pinch of freshly grated nutmeg
1 tbsp (15g) butter
1¼ cups (275ml) cheese sauce (see page 69)
2oz (50g) grated cheese
1oz (25g) fresh breadcrumbs

Poach the eggs until just cooked. You can do this by breaking them into a saucepan or deep frying pan containing simmering water to cover and a tablespoonful of vinegar, or you can drop them into greased cups and stand these in simmering water until the eggs have set; 3–4 minutes in each case.

Meanwhile, wash the spinach and cook in a pan without any water until wilted and tender. Drain very well and add salt, pepper, the nutmeg and almost half the butter.

Butter a shallow ovenproof dish, or four individual ramekins, and spread a layer of spinach in the base.

Place the eggs on top and cover with the cheese sauce.

Sprinkle with the grated cheese and breadcrumbs, and dot with the rest of the butter.

Put under a moderately hot broiler for a few minutes or until golden brown and crisp. Serve at once.

Baked stuffed eggs

These stuffed eggs are good as a first course baked in individual dishes and served with hot toast, or as a main course with fluffy boiled rice and perhaps a buttery spinach purée.

SERVES 4 AS A MAIN DISH,
8 AS A STARTER

8 hardboiled eggs
2 large onions
½ stick (50g) butter
1 tbsp chopped fresh flat-leaf parsley
salt and freshly ground black pepper

Preheat the oven to 350°F (180°C).

Cut the hardboiled eggs in half and take out the yolks; put the whites to one side.

Peel and finely chop the onions. Melt the butter in a medium-sized saucepan and use some of it to brush a shallow ovenproof dish that is big enough to hold all the egg whites in a single layer.

Add the onions to the rest of the butter in the saucepan and fry it gently, with a lid on the pan, for 10 minutes, without letting it brown: stir often.

Take the saucepan off the heat and add the egg yolks, mashing them into the onions until they're fairly creamy and smooth, then stir in the parsley and season.

Spoon the mixture into the egg white cavities, piling it up neatly, then put the egg whites into the greased dish.

Cover the dish with foil and bake in the oven for about 30 minutes or until the eggs are heated through.

Glamorgan sausages

These little cheesy "sausages" are delicious with salad and some chutney. If you make the sausages tiny they're good as a nibble with drinks. Here I've used a traditional egg and breadcrumb coating but you could equally well use the cornstarch and breadcrumb coating given for cheese fritters (see page 289).

SERVES 4

12oz (350g) Caerphilly cheese or mild Cheddar, grated
4oz (125g) fresh wholegrain breadcrumbs
1 tsp mustard powder
6 tbsp cold water
freshly ground black pepper
all-purpose flour, for dusting
1 egg, beaten with 1 tbsp of cold water
dried breadcrumbs (see page 183)
oil, for shallow-frying

Mix together the cheese, fresh breadcrumbs, mustard, cold water and some pepper to taste.

Gather the mixture into a ball then divide it into eight pieces and roll each into a sausage shape on a floured board.

Dip each little sausage into the beaten egg and then into the dried breadcrumbs. Heat a little oil in a frying pan and fry the sausages quickly all over until they're crisp, then drain them and serve immediately.

continued next page

Gnocchi alla Romana

Nutty Glamorgan sausages

You can also make a delicious nut version of the previous recipe which isn't authentic but still delicious. Use 8oz (225g) grated cheese and 4oz (125g) grated cashew nuts or hazel nuts with the breadcrumbs, mustard and water, as above. It's also nice flavored with a little chopped rosemary.

Glamorgan sausage bake

Both the Glamorgan sausage mixtures are good baked instead of fried — press the mixture into a greased ovenproof dish and bake it at 400°F (200°C) for about 45 minutes. The result is rather a crisp savory cake that can be cut up and served with a parsley or tomato sauce (see pages 64 and 71); it's also delicious cold with chutney and salad.

When this is brought to the table, sizzling and golden brown, people find it difficult to believe it's made from polenta, which they associate with dull school puddings. It's delicious and though you've got to allow time for the polenta mixture to get completely cold, it's easy to make and can be prepared in advance. It also freezes well. A juicy tomato, onion and olive salad goes well with this — or some peas.

SERVES 4

6oz (175g) polenta
1½ tsp salt
freshly ground black pepper
nutmeg
3 cups (850ml) milk
6oz (175g) grated cheese (including some Parmesan-style)
2 eggs, beaten
olive oil

Put the polenta into a large bowl with the salt, a good grinding of pepper and some nutmeg and mix it to a cream with some of the milk.

Bring the rest of the milk to the boil, then pour it into the polenta mixture, stirring all the time.

Pour the polenta and milk mixture back into the saucepan and stir over a fairly high heat until it thickens. Then let the mixture simmer gently until it's very thick and has lost its very granular appearance, stirring from time to time. In Italy they say that the mixture is ready when a spoon will stand up in it unsupported. In practice I find you can only achieve this if you've happened to use a small, deep saucepan, and that 10 minutes simmering is about right.

Remove the saucepan from the heat and stir in two-thirds of the cheese and the eggs, which will cook in the heat of the mixture. Taste and add more seasoning if necessary.

Lightly oil a large plate, tray or other suitable flat surface and turn out the polenta mixture onto this, spreading it to a thickness of about 6mm (¼in). Leave it to get completely cold – overnight if possible.

When the mixture is cold it will be firm enough to cut into shapes. Traditionally it is cut into small circles with a pastry cutter, which makes the finished dish look very attractive, but squares will do fine too.

Brush a large flat ovenproof dish with oil — I use a 12in (30cm) pizza pan, which is ideal — and arrange the gnocchi in slightly overlapping circles, like roof tiles.

Brush the top of the gnocchi with some oil and sprinkle with the remaining grated cheese, then either bake for about 15 minutes in a fairly hot oven, 400°F (200°C) or put the whole dish under a hot broiler for about 20 minutes. Get the gnocchi really crisp and golden, then serve at once.

Gougère with mushrooms, onions and red wine sauce

This is an impressive and delicious dish, a big puffed-up ring of golden choux pastry, the center filled with button mushrooms and onions in a red wine sauce. It's lovely served with baby Brussels sprouts and creamy mashed potatoes.

SERVES 6

FOR THE GOUGÈRE
1 stick (125g) butter
1¼ cups (275ml) water
1¼ cups (150g) all-purpose flour
1 tsp salt
4 eggs, beaten
6oz (175g) grated cheese
a good pinch of cayenne pepper
red wine sauce (see page 69),
    to serve

FOR THE FILLING
3 onions, sliced
1 tbsp (15g) butter
8oz (225g) baby button mushrooms,
    left whole
salt and freshly ground black pepper

You can make the main preparations for the various parts of this dish in advance if that is most convenient for you.

To make the gougère, put the butter and water into a medium-sized saucepan and heat gently until the butter has melted, then turn up the heat and bring the mixture to a boil.

Mix the flour with the salt and quickly pour into the saucepan all at once. Stir over the heat with a wooden spoon for 1 minute, by which time the mixture will have formed a glossy ball of dough, then take the saucepan off the heat and transfer the dough into a clean bowl.

Add about a quarter of the beaten egg and beat vigorously with a wooden spoon until the dough has absorbed the egg and become smooth and glossy again, then add another quarter and beat again. Repeat until all the egg has been used and the mixture holds its shape softly.

Stir in about two-thirds of the grated cheese and add the cayenne pepper. Cover and set aside.

To make the filling, fry the onions in the butter for 10 minutes or until they're soft, then add the mushrooms and fry for an additional 3–4 minutes or until they too are tender. Season with salt and pepper and leave on one side.

To finish the gougère, preheat the oven to 400°F (200°C). Oil a large ovenproof dish — a pizza pan is ideal if you have one, but any large shallow ovenproof dish will do — and spoon the gougère mixture all round the edge, heaping it up into as neat a ring as possible but leaving the center open.

Sprinkle the top of the ring with the rest of the grated cheese, then bake the gougère for 40 minutes or until it is puffed up and golden brown.

When the gougère is nearly done reheat the onions and mushrooms gently, as well as the sauce.

Take the gougère out of the oven, spoon the mushroom mixture into the center and pour a little sauce over the mushrooms and onions — serve the rest of the sauce separately in a pitcher. Serve the gougère immediately.

Tip
You can put other things into the center of a gougère — try a buttery purée of spinach in the middle and cheese sauce (see page 65) served separately.

Omelette

A perfect omelette is one of the very fastest of fast foods and yet, when well made, a gourmet treat — light and golden brown on the outside, creamy and moist within. Just be ready to eat it immediately, while it's still at its best. If you want a change, there are lots of ways you can vary the basic omelette (see right). The important thing is to have the filling all ready to pop into the omelette before you start to cook it because speed is essential.

SERVES 1
3 eggs
salt and freshly ground black pepper
1½ tbsp (20g) butter, cut into small
 dice

Beat the eggs with a fork to break them up and combine. Season with salt and a grinding of pepper, and stir in half the diced butter.

Put the frying pan — a 6–7in (15–18cm) one is best if you've got one as it makes a nice thick omelette — over a high heat for about 1 minute, then turn the heat down and put in the rest of the butter.

When the butter foams and begins to brown, pour the egg mixture into the center of the pan. Swirl the pan so that the egg spreads all over the base. Then use a rubber spatula to draw the set egg from the sides to the center, swirling the pan as you do so to make the liquid egg in the middle run to the edges — keep the heat up high. All this happens very quickly — the omelette will be done in under a minute.

Loosen the edges of the omelette quickly with the spatula, fold the omelette over and turn it out on to a warmed plate. Eat immediately.

VARIATIONS
Cheese omelette

As soon as the omelette is as set as you want it in the middle — remember it will go on cooking a bit in its own heat — sprinkle 1oz (25g) finely grated Gruyère cheese onto it, fold it over and serve. Or you could use a mixture of Gruyère and Parmesan-style cheese, for extra flavor.

Mushroom omelette

Before you cook the omelette, sauté 2oz (50g) washed, sliced mushrooms — button mushrooms, cremini mushrooms, wild mushrooms, your choice — in a little butter until tender. Keep them warm while you make the omelette, then put them on top, fold the omelette over and serve. A little chopped fresh parsley is nice scattered over the mushrooms. This is a wonderful way to eat a few really precious mushrooms such as St George's mushrooms or morels in the late spring, or chanterelles in the autumn.

All mushrooms release a lot of water; one way of dealing with it is to drain the water off (saving it for soups, etc.), blot the mushrooms on paper towel or a clean cloth, then re-fry them in some more butter or olive oil for a minute or two further until they are cooked.

Asparagus omelette

A few spears of tender cooked asparagus, about 2oz (50g) after trimming, make a delicious filling. Have the asparagus hot and ready so that you can put it on the omelette as soon as the egg has set enough for your taste. A little finely grated Parmesan-style cheese is good in this, too.

Artichoke heart omelette

Add 2oz (50g) of sliced artichoke hearts (from a can or the deli counter of a supermarket) to the omelette just before you fold it over.

Herb omelette

Easy and appealing; just snip or sprinkle 1 tablespoon of chopped fresh green herbs — parsley, chives, chervil, tarragon — over the omelette when it's ready to fold, flip it over and serve.

Watercress omelette

An omelette and a salad in one! Put a handful of watercress on top of the just-setting omelette and fold it over. The watercress will wilt a bit in the heat but will add a crunchy peppery freshness to the golden silky omelette.

New potato, pea and mint frittata with lemon mayonnaise

This is a lovely frittata, with layers of firm, delicately flavored new potatoes, sweet and tender peas and fragrant mint. The mayonnaise is the final touch — make it yourself as described on page 76 or use a good-quality bought one for speed. Accompany with a lovely leafy salad or platter of tender, new-season vegetables.

SERVES 4

1½lb (700g) new potatoes
2 tbsp olive oil
1 onion, sliced
4oz (125g) frozen baby peas
2 tbsp chopped fresh mint
salt and freshly ground black pepper
8 eggs
2oz (50g) Parmesan-style cheese, finely grated
lemon mayonnaise (see page 76), to serve

Cut the potatoes into ¼in (6mm) slices and cook in a pan of boiling water for 7–10 minutes or until just tender. Drain.

Meanwhile, heat the oil in a large oven proof frying pan suitable for putting under your broiler. Add the onion to the pan and cook gently, without browning, for 5–10 minutes.

Mix the potato slices with the peas and mint, and season to taste with salt and pepper. Put the potato mixture into the frying pan, making sure that all the ingredients are evenly distributed and the potatoes slices are nicely layered.

Whisk the eggs lightly, season with salt and pepper, and pour into the pan, over the potato slices, moving them a little as necessary so that the egg runs right down to the bottom of the pan. Sprinkle the grated cheese on top.

Cook over a low–moderate heat for about 5 minutes or until the sides and base seem to be set. Preheat the broiler to high.

Put the pan under the broiler, Broil for about 5 minutes, or until the frittata is set all over and the top is golden brown.

Loosen the sides and base of the frittata with a flexible spatula, then invert a large plate over the frying pan and turn out the frittata. You can then invert another large plate over that and turn it over, so that the frittata has its lovely golden brown cheesy side up. Serve in wedges with a spoonful of lemon mayonnaise on each plate.

Basic crêpe batter

I usually make this batter in a blender, which is very labor-saving, but you can equally well mix it by hand. Some people say it's necessary to let a batter stand for at least 30 minutes before using it, but I must say, I rarely if ever do this, and the crêpes are fine. For best results you do need a small frying pan, about 7in (18cm) across. Having been brought up on wholewheat crêpes, I can't bear the blandness of white ones, but these days I compromise and will always use a half-and-half mix of wholewheat and white flour, at least when I'm making them for other people!

MAKES ABOUT 12 CRÊPES
1 cup (125g) half wholewheat and
   half all-purpose flour
¼ tsp salt
2 eggs
2 tbsp melted butter
1¼ cups (275mm) skimmed milk
butter or olive oil, for frying

If you're using the quick blender method to make the batter, simply put the flour, salt, eggs, melted butter and 7fl oz (200ml) milk into the blender jar and blend at medium speed for 1–2 minutes, to make a smooth, creamy batter. You could use an electric hand blender to do this, putting the ingredients in a pitcher or narrow deep container for the blending .

Or, for the traditional method, sift the flour and salt into a bowl, make a well in the center and add the eggs, melted butter and about a third of the milk. Mix to a smooth consistency, gradually adding the remaining milk, then beat well for 1–2 minutes.

Either way, the batter needs to be the consistency of thin cream.

To fry the crêpes, set a small frying pan over a low heat and add a teaspoon or two of butter or oil.

When the pan is hot and the butter melted, pour any excess oil into an old cup; the frying pan needs to be just "greased", with no excess fat.

Pour in about 2 tablespoons of batter — enough to coat the bottom of the frying pan thinly — and swirl it round so that the base of the pan is covered.

Fry for a minute or two, until the base is set, then, using a spatula, quickly flip the crêpe over to cook the other side for a second or two.

Lift out the crêpe and put it on a plate while you make the rest. Brush the frying pan with butter or oil before making each crêpe.

Tips
1 Don't be deterred if your first crêpe breaks or isn't quite perfect; this is normal with crêpe making.
2 Pile the crêpes up on top of each other on the plate as they're done — there's no need to put pieces of greaseproof paper between the crêpes.
3 It is a good idea to keep an old pastry brush specially for oiling the frying pan, as the heat of the pan makes the bristles curl; alternatively, use a pad of paper towels.

4 Crêpes freeze very well: simply wrap the pile of cooled crêpes in foil and put them in the freezer. When you want to use them, loosen the foil and let them thaw out naturally, or put the foil parcel in a low oven if you want to speed up the process. They will also keep for several days in the fridge.

VARIATIONS
Buckwheat crêpe batter

Make as in the main recipe but replace half the flour with buckwheat flour, for dark, nutty-tasting crêpes. Try them filled with flat mushrooms, ricotta and some fried onion mixed in, or with tomato-based mixtures such as ratatouille (see page 132).

Mixed vegetable batter

Add 2 tablespoons of finely chopped scallion or leek and 2 tablespoons of finely diced raw carrot to the basic batter mixture for interesting flecked crêpes with a slightly chewy texture.

Spinach crêpe batter

Stir 3 tablespoons of drained cooked spinach into the batter for green crêpes. Try these with a creamy mushroom filling.

Crêpes stuffed with asparagus

One for the asparagus season. An alternative to the sauce topping is to use two large cartons of sour cream.

SERVES 6
basic crêpe batter (see opposite)
2¼lb (1kg) asparagus
2 tbsp chopped fresh flat-leaf parsley
½ stick (50g) butter
½ cup (50g) all-purpose flour
2 cups (575ml) milk
1 bay leaf
1 tsp mustard powder
6oz (175g) grated cheese, preferably Double Gloucester
salt and freshly ground black pepper

First make the crêpe batter and cook 12–15 thin crêpes.

To make the filling, break off the hard stems at the base of the asparagus — these ends are too tough to eat, though they could be used to make stock. Wash the asparagus gently to remove any grit.

Cook the asparagus in a steamer, or by laying it flat in a large frying pan and covering with water, or by roasting or grilling it (see page 109). It will take around 10 minutes to cook; get it to the degree of tenderness that you like. Add the chopped parsley.

While the asparagus is cooking, make the sauce. Melt the butter in a large saucepan and stir in the flour, cook for a moment or two then add about a fifth of the milk and the bay leaf and stir over a high heat until the mixture is smooth and very thick. Then add another lot of milk and repeat the process until it has

all been incorporated and you've got a smooth sauce.

Take the saucepan off the heat, stir in the mustard and 4oz (125g) of the grated cheese and season the sauce carefully. If you're having some white wine with the meal, a couple of tablespoons of it will make a delicious addition.

To assemble the dish, put a heaped tablespoon of asparagus on each crêpe, roll the crêpe neatly and place it in a large shallow, greased ovenproof dish. These crêpes look best arranged in a single layer but you will need a big dish to accommodate them.

When the crêpes are all in the dish, pour the sauce evenly over them, removing the bay leaf. Sprinkle the remaining cheese over the top and cover the dish with a piece of foil.

When you're ready to bake the crêpes, set the oven to 350°F (180°C). Bake them for about 1 hour, removing the foil about 15 minutes before the end of that cooking time to brown the cheese on top.

VARIATIONS

Buckwheat crêpes stuffed with ratatouille

Use buckwheat batter (see opposite) to make crêpes. Fill with ratatouille made according to the recipe on page 132. Top with cheese sauce and bake as above.

Crêpes stuffed with leeks

For this variation, make crêpes as opposite, then for the filling wash and slice 2lb (900g) leeks and cook them in a little fast-boiling salted water for about 10 minutes, until just tender. Drain well and add ½oz (15g) butter, 1 tablespoon of chopped fresh parsley, and salt and pepper to taste. Fill the crêpes with the leek mixture, then top with the sauce and cheese and bake as described.

Crêpes stuffed with lentil and mushroom filling

For this variation use the basic crêpe batter (see opposite) to make 10–12 thin crêpes, then leave them on one side to cool while you make the filling. Fry a large onion and garlic clove in 1 tbsp (15g) butter in a medium-sized saucepan for 5 minutes, then stir in 6oz (175g) split red lentils, 1¼ cups (275ml) water or stock, 14oz can chopped tomatoes, ½ teaspoon cumin and 2 tablespoons of wine. Let the mixture simmer gently, uncovered, for 30 minutes. Add 8oz (225g) washed and sliced mushrooms and cook for a further 5–6 minutes, then season with salt and freshly ground black pepper. Spread a little of the lentil mixture on each crêpe; roll the crêpes up neatly and arrange them side by side in a well-greased, shallow ovenproof dish. Pour the sauce over the crêpe rolls, sprinkle with grated cheese and bake as described.

continued next page

Crêpes stuffed with mushrooms and artichoke hearts

First make the basic crêpe batter (see page 296) and cook 12–15 thin crêpes. To make the filling, fry 1 finely chopped onion in 2 tbsp (25g) butter for 10 minutes without letting it brown. Add 1½lb (700g) halved or quartered button mushrooms and cook for a further 5 minutes. If the mushrooms produce lots of water, let them boil vigorously until the mixture is fairly dry. Take the saucepan off the heat and stir in the 2 crushed garlic cloves, 2 x 7oz tubs marinated artichoke hearts, drained and sliced, and 2 tbsp chopped parsley. Sharpen the mixture with a little lemon juice and add salt and freshly ground black pepper to taste. Divide the filling between the crêpes, roll up neatly and place them side by side in the shallow ovenproof dish. Cover with the sauce and cheese and bake as described.

Crêpes stuffed with spinach and ricotta cheese

Make the basic crêpe batter (see page 296) and cook 12–15 thin crêpes. Cook 2lb (900g) fresh spinach, or use 2 x 11oz (300g) packets frozen spinach. Add 8oz (225g) ricotta cheese. Season with salt, freshly ground black pepper and grated nutmeg. Fill the crêpes with this mixture, cover with the sauce and cheese and bake as described.

Chili red bean crêpes

Warming, Mexican flavors in this dish, which is delicious served with a lettuce and avocado salad and a bowl of sour cream.

SERVES 4
basic crêpe batter (see page 296)
butter, for frying
7oz (200g) dried red kidney beans, soaked and cooked until tender (see pages 176–7), or 2 x 14oz cans
2 tbsp olive oil
2 onions, chopped
2 garlic cloves, crushed
1 bay leaf
½ tsp oregano
14oz can chopped tomatoes
1 tbsp tomato purée
¼–1 tsp chili powder
salt and freshly ground black pepper
5fl oz (150ml) vegetable stock
4oz (125g) grated cheese

Use the crêpe batter to make 10–12 thin crêpes (see page 296); these can be made in advance if it's more convenient.

Preheat the oven to 180°C (350°F), gas mark 4. Drain the beans (rinsing the canned ones).

Heat the oil in a medium-sized saucepan and fry the onions for 10 minutes, without browning, then add the garlic, bay leaf, oregano, tomatoes, tomato purée and chili powder and let it all simmer gently, uncovered, for about 10–15 minutes or until thick.

Add half of this tomato mixture to the cooked beans, mashing them roughly and seasoning with salt, pepper and, if necessary, more chili powder to taste.

Spread about 2 tablespoons of this bean mixture on each crêpe, roll them up and place them side by side in a well-greased shallow ovenproof dish.

Thin the rest of the tomato mixture with the stock and blend it to make it smooth if you like. Season to taste, pour over the crêpes and sprinkle the top with grated cheese.

Bake for about 30 minutes or until heated through and browned on the top.

Cheese and asparagus roulade

A rich and delicious dish for a special occasion and not that difficult to make, honestly!

SERVES 4
¼ cup grated Parmesan-style cheese
2oz (50g) fresh white breadcrumbs
5fl oz (150ml) milk
4 eggs, separated
6oz (175g) Emmental cheese, grated
a good pinch or two of cayenne pepper
salt and freshly ground black pepper

FOR THE FILLING
12oz (350g) cooked asparagus, chopped into ¾in (2cm) pieces
2 tsp cornstarch
1¼ cups (300ml) heavy cream
2 tbsp chopped fresh flat-leaf parsley
2 tbsp freshly squeezed lemon juice
flat-leaf parsley sprigs, to garnish

Preheat the oven to 400°F (200°C). Line a 9in x 13in (23cm x 33cm) jelly roll pan with baking parchment; sprinkle evenly with half the grated Parmesan-style cheese.

In a large bowl mix together the breadcrumbs, milk, egg yolks, grated Emmental cheese, cayenne and plenty of salt and pepper to taste. Set aside.

Whisk the egg whites until stiff and fold into the cheese mixture.

Spread the mixture into the jelly roll pan and bake for 10–15 minutes or until the mixture springs back when touched lightly in the center.

Invert the roulade out onto a piece of baking parchment that has been sprinkled with the remaining Parmesan-style cheese. You can allow the roulade to get cold at this point if you wish and reheat it later, or proceed, peeling away the baking parchment.

To make the filling, which you could do while the roulade is baking, melt the butter in a medium-sized saucepan, add the asparagus and stir over a gentle heat.

Mix the cornstarch to a paste with a little of the cream, then add the rest of the cream. Pour this cornstarch-and-cream mixture into the pan with the asparagus and stir over the heat for 4–5 minutes or until thickened. Remove from the heat and stir in the parsley, lemon juice and seasoning to taste.

Spread the roulade with the asparagus filling, and using the baking parchment underneath to help, roll it up, starting with one of the short sides, and slide it onto an ovenproof serving dish. Pop it back into the oven for 10–15 minutes to reheat, puff up and brown a bit more. Garnish with a sprig or two of parsley and serve immediately. It's also lovely cold.

Pipérade

Full of the flavors of the south of France, this tasty mixture of tomatoes, peppers and onions in creamy, lightly set scrambled egg makes a good quick supper dish, served with warm crisp French bread or wholewheat rolls.

SERVES 4
2 onions
2 garlic cloves
1 green pepper
1 red pepper
4 tomatoes
½ stick (50g) butter
6 eggs
salt and freshly ground black pepper
chopped fresh flat-leaf parsley, to garnish

Peel and chop the onions and peel and crush the garlic; wash, seed and chop the peppers and skin (see page 40) and chop the tomatoes.

Melt the butter in a large saucepan, put in the onion and fry it for about 5 minutes without letting it brown, then mix in the garlic, peppers and tomatoes and cook for a further 5 minutes over a low heat with the lid on the saucepan.

Meanwhile beat the eggs in a small bowl with some salt and pepper.

When the vegetables are tender pour the eggs into the saucepan and stir gently over a low heat until they are lightly scrambled, but don't let them get too dry — it's best to keep the heat low all the time and take the pan off the stove while the mixture is still slightly runny.

Check the seasoning, then serve at once, sprinkled with chopped parsley and accompanied with some warm bread.

Quick soufflé omelette

Another almost-instant supper recipe. Serve with a green or tomato salad.

SERVES 4
6 eggs, separated
2 tbsp (25g) all-purpose flour
2oz (50g) Gruyère or Cheddar
    cheese, grated
salt and freshly ground black pepper
1 tbsp (15g) butter

Preheat the broiler to high.

Whisk the egg whites until stiff and reserve while you beat the yolks with the flour until smooth and creamy. Mix in the grated cheese.

Fold the egg whites into the egg yolk mixture, along with some seasoning.

Melt the butter in a frying pan with an oven-proof handle, or a shallow ovenproof dish suitable for putting under your broiler.

Pour the egg mixture into the piping hot butter and fry quickly until the underneath is cooked; then place under the hot broiler to cook the top and finish the soufflé. Serve immediately.

Vegetarian Scotch eggs

Scotch eggs look attractive when they're sliced, and are useful for picnics and buffets. The secret of getting the outside to stick to the eggs is to dip the hardboiled egg into beaten egg before putting the coating on. The protein content of these Scotch eggs is excellent and they're good for lunch boxes, with some nice crisp salad. You can use other combinations of nuts — pecans are a tasty addition.

MAKES 4 SCOTCH EGGS
1 onion, grated
2oz (50g) hazelnuts, roasted (see
    page 139) and grated
2oz (50g) almonds, grated
2oz (50g) grated cheese
2 rounded tsp tomato purée
1 egg
1 tbsp chopped fresh thyme or
    1 tsp dried
salt and freshly ground black pepper
4 hardboiled eggs
beaten egg and crisp wholewheat
    breadcrumbs (see page 183),
    to coat
oil, for deep-frying

First make the outside coating for the Scotch eggs; simply mix the onion, nuts, cheese, tomato purée, egg and thyme into a fairly firm paste and season, adding a tablespoon of stock, water or cider to soften the consistency a little, if necessary.

Dip the hardboiled eggs in the beaten egg and then press the nut mixture round to cover them completely.

Coat the Scotch eggs in egg and breadcrumbs, or you could use the cornstarch and breadcrumb coating described for cheese fritters (see page 289).

Heat the oil in a deep frying pan to a temperature of 375°F (190°C), or when a ½in (1cm) cube of bread dropped into the oil turns golden brown in 1 minute. Deep-fry the Scotch eggs for 2–3 minutes or until golden brown and crisp, and drain on crumpled paper towels. Leave the Scotch eggs until they are cool, then cut each in half or into quarters and serve with salad.

VARIATION

Lentil Scotch eggs

Use a mixture of well-drained green lentils from a 14oz can, mashed with a fried onion, 1 teaspoon of dried thyme or 1 tablespoon of chopped fresh thyme, 4oz (125g) walnuts, finely grated, 1 tablespoon of tomato purée or ketchup and salt and pepper to taste. Add a spoonful or two of beaten egg to hold it together and use the rest to dip the hardboiled eggs in before molding the mixture around them. Coat and deep-fry them as described. This shows that very successful partnership of lentils and hardboiled eggs in a particularly attractive form.

Welsh rarebit with grilled vine tomatoes

Some say "rarebit", some say "rabbit"; either way it's quick and tasty. The broiled tomatoes provide the finishing touch.

SERVES 2–4

4 bunches of cherry tomatoes on the vine
4 large slices of wholewheat bread
8oz (225g) Cheddar or Caerphilly cheese, grated
3 tbsp milk or beer
cayenne pepper
freshly ground black pepper

Heat the broiler to high.

Put the tomatoes onto a small baking tray that will fit under the broiler and place them under the heat for a few minutes or until they cook and soften.

Meanwhile toast the bread: arrange the slices on a baking sheet that will fit under the broiler.

Put the grated cheese and milk or beer into a saucepan and heat them together, stirring all the time, until the cheese has melted. Remove from the heat and add a pinch of cayenne pepper and a grating of black pepper.

Pour this cheese mixture over the toast and pop it under a moderately hot broiler for about 5 minutes or until the cheese is bubbly and lightly browned.

Serve immediately, with a bunch of broiled vine tomatoes on each piece.

Cheese soufflé

I think this is perhaps the best soufflé of all with it's satisfying savory flavor and lovely golden color. I like a mixture of Gruyère or Emmental and Parmesan-style cheese for this; but a strongly flavored Cheddar is good too for everyday cooking while a red cheese, such as Leicestershire or Double Gloucester, makes the soufflé a beautiful rich golden color. Cheese soufflé is lovely with a leafy green salad with a balsamic dressing (see pages 75).

SERVES 4

3 tbsp (40g) butter
2 tbsp (25g) flour
7fl oz (200ml) milk
6oz (175g) Gruyère cheese, grated
2oz (50g) Parmesan-style cheese, finely grated
4 egg yolks
1–3 tsp Dijon mustard
salt and freshly ground black pepper
6 egg whites

Grease a 6 cups (1.7 liter) soufflé dish with a little butter or oil.

Melt the butter in a large saucepan and stir in the flour; cook for a few seconds then add the milk. Stir the mixture over a high heat until it first goes lumpy then smooth and very thick.

Stir in the grated Gruyère and half of the Parmesan-style cheese, transfer the mixture to a large bowl and leave until it's cool, then stir in the egg yolks, mustard and a good seasoning of salt and pepper. (You can cover the mixture and leave it for several hours at this stage if necessary.)

Set the oven to 375°F (190°C). Place a baking sheet on the top shelf — it will get hot and when you put your soufflé dish on it there will be a nice blast of heat from the base to get things off to a good start.

Whisk the egg whites. They need to be stiff enough for you to be able to turn the bowl over without them coming out, but not so stiff that you could almost slice them with a knife, so stop in time.

Mix a rounded tablespoon of egg white into the cheese mixture to soften it, then transfer the rest of the egg whites on top of the mixture and using the side of a flattish metal spoon or a spatula, fold the egg whites into the cheese mixture until the whites are pretty much incorporated and you have a very light airy mixture.

Pour the soufflé gently into the prepared dish — ideally the mixture needs to come up almost level with the rim; it doesn't matter if it's lower but don't pile it up above the rim or it will ooze all over the place as it cooks. Scatter the remaining Parmesan-style cheese on top.

Bake the soufflé for 30–35 minutes or until it looks firm when you shake it slightly — you can test it if you like with a fine skewer; it's done when the skewer comes out clean.

Individual cheese soufflés

Puffy, golden, individual cheese soufflés look impressive and make a marvelous first course or lunch dish. They're also very practical because they take only 15–20 minutes to cook so you can get the initial preparation done in advance, then add the egg whites and pop the soufflés in the oven 15 or 20 minutes before you want to eat. As a starter these soufflés are ideal before one of the low-protein vegetable dishes. Or for an easy-going lunch with a friend, serve them after avocados, with a tasty green salad and fruity pudding.

MAKES 3 INDIVIDUAL SOUFFLÉS
2 tbsp (25g) butter
2 tbsp (25g) flour
5fl oz (150ml) milk
pinch each of mustard powder and
    cayenne pepper
4oz (125g) grated cheese
2 eggs, separated

Prepare three individual soufflé dishes or ramekins — by greasing lightly with oil or butter. Place a baking sheet in the center of the oven.

Melt the butter in a medium-sized saucepan and stir in the flour; when it froths add the milk, mixing well over a gentle heat for a few minutes until smooth and thick.

Remove from the heat, cool slightly then add the seasoning, grated cheese and the egg yolks. (The mixture can be prepared in advance up to this stage.)

Preheat the oven to 375°F (190°C).

Whisk the egg whites until they are very stiff and able to hold their shape but not dry.

Mix a heaped tablespoon of egg white into the cheese mixture to loosen it, then add the rest and carefully incorporate it by folding the cheese mixture gently over it with a metal spoon, so that you don't flatten the egg white.

Divide the mixture between the little dishes and place them in the oven on the hot baking sheet. Bake for 15–20 minutes or until risen and golden brown.

Serve immediately; they will keep in the oven for a further few minutes if you turn off the heat but the sooner they are served the better they are.

Tip
These quantities will double satisfactorily to serve 6. To serve 4 use the basic mixture with an extra egg.

Leek soufflé

The chunky pieces of leek in this soufflé give it a delicate flavor and interesting texture. Try to find really thin leeks if you can, then they can be sliced into nice neat pieces that will stay firm when they're cooked. I think this soufflé is best served with just one well-cooked vegetable such as buttered baby carrots, sprouts or peas.

SERVES 4
3–4 thin leeks (weighing 12oz (350g)
    before you trim them)
3 tbsp (40g) butter
3 tbsp (40g) flour
1¼ cups (275ml) milk
4 egg yolks
salt and freshly ground black pepper
a pinch of freshly grated nutmeg
6 egg whites

Prepare a 6 cups (1.7 liter) soufflé dish by greasing generously.

Trim and clean the leeks and cut into 1in (2.5cm) lengths. Cook in ½in (1cm) boiling water until they're just tender (about 7–10 minutes). Drain and set aside.

Melt the butter in a medium-sized saucepan and put in the flour; cook for a few seconds then add the milk. Stir the mixture over a high heat until it first goes lumpy then smooth and very thick.

Transfer the sauce to a large bowl — this cools it slightly ready for adding the egg yolks and is more convenient later when you want to fold in the egg whites. Beat in the egg yolks one by one then gently

continued next page

Opposite: Leek soufflé

Mushroom soufflé

stir in the leeks. Season the mixture with salt, pepper and nutmeg — be fairly generous because the egg whites will "dilute" the flavor. You can now leave this mixture until just before you want to cook the soufflé — I have kept it for several hours in the fridge and it has been perfect.

When you're ready to cook the soufflé place a baking sheet on the middle shelf of the oven.

Preheat the oven to 375°F (190°).

Whisk the egg whites until they're thick and standing in soft peaks but don't let them get hard and dry.

Stir a generous heaped tablespoon of egg white into the leek sauce mixture to loosen it, then add all the egg white on top of it and gently fold it in with a metal spoon. When it has pretty well all been incorporated, pour the mixture gently into your prepared dish — it needs to come up almost to the rim, but no higher; if it is lower it will still taste good even though it won't look so impressively high and puffy, but if it is piled above the rim it will overflow.

Put the soufflé on the baking sheet and bake for 30–35 minutes or until it looks firm when you move the dish slightly and a knife or skewer pushed gently down into the soufflé comes out clean. If it's done before you're quite ready, turn off the oven and the soufflé will keep for 4–5 minutes longer although it won't be quite so puffy.

This is a delicious soufflé — when you cut it open the chunks of mushroom look very appetizing. It's nicest made with firm white button mushrooms. Serve with some cooked fine green beans.

SERVES 4
6oz (175g) button mushrooms
½ stick (50g) butter
1 garlic clove, crushed
3 tbsp (40g) flour
1¼ cups (275ml) milk
4 egg yolks
salt and freshly ground black pepper
6 egg whites

Prepare a 6 cup (1.7 liter) soufflé dish by greasing with a little butter.

Wash the mushrooms then cut them into halves or quarters so that the pieces are all roughly the same size. Melt a quarter of the butter in a medium-sized saucepan and put in the mushrooms. Cook them gently without a lid on the pan for about 5 minutes, then stir in the garlic. If the mushrooms make a lot of liquid, drain it off (it can be saved for stock).

Melt the rest of the butter in another medium-sized saucepan and stir in the flour, cook for a few seconds then add the milk. Stir the mixture over a high heat until it first goes lumpy then smooth and very thick.

Take the saucepan off the heat and pour the sauce into a large bowl. Let it cool a bit then mix in the mushrooms (drain off any excess liquid), egg yolks and seasoning to taste. Set aside (for several hours or overnight in the fridge if necessary) until you're ready to cook the soufflé.

Put a baking sheet on the top shelf and preheat to 375°F (190°C). Whisk the egg whites until they're stiff but not dry and fold them carefully into the mushroom mixture. Spoon the soufflé into the prepared dish — ideally it needs to come just to the top but no higher — and bake it for 30–35 minutes or until it's golden brown, well risen and it looks firm when moved slightly. A knife or skewer inserted will come out clean. Serve at once.

Tip

If you want to expand this soufflé to serve six people, here are the quantities. Use a 7 cup (2 liter) dish and 5 tbsp (60g) butter, 8oz (225g) mushrooms, 3 tbsp (40g) flour, 11fl oz (300ml) milk, 5 egg yolks and 7 egg whites. You will need to cook it for few minutes longer, too; test it with a knife or skewer, as described.

Toad-in-the-hole

My father, a Dalesman born and bred, used to make Yorkshire pudding every Sunday when I was growing up. We used to eat it with lashings of my mother's onion gravy, roast potatoes and greens he had grown in the garden. My father was very creative in the kitchen and would sometimes add other ingredients and create a toad-in-the hole, like this. Use your own favorite vegetarian sausages in this recipe.

SERVES 4
¼ cup rapeseed or ground nut oil
1 cup (125g) all-purpose flour
½ tsp salt
2 eggs
5fl oz (150ml) milk
5fl oz (150ml) water
8 vegetarian sausages, lightly fried
    according to packet directions
salt and freshly ground black pepper

Preheat the oven to 425°F (220°C).
    Put the oil into a 8in (20cm) square roasting pan or large shallow ovenproof dish, and heat in the oven.
    Next, make the batter. Sift the flour into a bowl with the salt. Make a well in the center and break the eggs into it. Mix to a paste, gradually drawing in the flour, then stir in the milk, but don't overbeat.
    Transfer the batter to a pitcher, so that it will be easy to pour into the pan.
    Have the sausages cooked and hot. When the oil in the pan is smoking hot, quickly pour the batter into it and pop the hot sausages on top.

Close the oven door immediately and leave to cook for about 25 minutes or until well risen, crisp and golden brown. Serve at once.

VARIATION
Yorkshire pudding

You can follow the recipe above, without the addition of the sausages, to make a Yorkshire pudding. Or you might like to make individual puddings. I use muffin tins for this. Just put 1 teaspoon of rapeseed or ground nut oil into each cup and heat as described. Pour the mixture in, almost to the top, and cook for about 15 minutes. The number you get will depend on the size and depth of your muffin tins, but this recipe makes enough for four people.

Desserts

"Afters", sweets or desserts — call them what you like — really round off a meal and add that perfect sweet finishing touch. They don't have to be an everyday event, but at the weekend or for a special meal or a treat, they're definitely among life's pleasures.

In this chapter you will find hot and cold desserts. The "hot" section includes indulgent tarts and desserts, such as pear and cardamom tarte Tatin, classic bakewell tart and mini sticky toffee puddings (see pages 319, 313 and 321). I've also included ever-popular crumbles, such as plum and rhubarb (see page 320), which you can easily adjust to almost any fruit you fancy.

In the "cold" section of this chapter you'll find some delicious, easy desserts. There are healthier options, such as fresh orange salad with honey and orange flower water and blackcurrant and cassis sorbet (see pages 330 and 337) as well as mouth-watering cheesecakes — the uncooked lemon cheesecake (see page 326) can be rustled up in moments. If you are looking for something special, try the meringues and pavlova, and for an everyday dessert that keeps for ages, nothing beats homemade ice cream.

Guide to preparing fruit

Apple Use dessert apples with or without the skin; slice, core and add to salads or fruit salad mixtures or grate to make a real fruit muesli. Stew apples as described on page 313, serve with cream and shortbread cookies or as a sauce with savory dishes, or make into a crumble (see page 320) or ice cream (see page 336). For baked apples, see page 312, and for apple pie, see page 314 using uncooked apples in place of the fruits given.

Apricot Ripe apricots are delicious raw; less perfect apricots are best cooked. Poach in a vanilla-flavored sugar syrup or put into an oven-proof dish with 3 tablespoons of sugar and 1–2 tablespoons water to 1lb (450g) apricots and bake for 30–60 minutes at 350°F (180°C). Cooked apricots can be made into a crumble, served on a crisp pastry crust or puréed and made into sorbets.

Banana Top sliced banana with a dollop of yogurt or fromage frais and some maple syrup or honey and chopped nuts; or, for a treat, peel and cut lengthways, put a scoop of vanilla ice cream between the halves and top with melted chocolate and chopped nuts. Also good cooked in a crumble (see page 320). Or make a slit down the top of a banana and bake whole in the oven, at 375°C (190°F) for about 20 minutes or until soft, then serve with cream, yogurt or rum butter. For extra indulgence, insert squares of chocolate into the slit, wrap in foil and bake.

Blackberry Wash, pick over and serve with sugar and cream; or poach as described on page 312 and eat with cream or yogurt, topped with crumble (see page 320), or puréed and made into sorbets and sauces . For blackberry ice cream follow the recipe on page 337 using cooked blackberries instead of strawberries and cashew nuts.

Blackcurrant Wash and remove the stems or, for a purée, leave the stems on. Poach as described on page 312. Blackcurrant purée is delicious with ice cream or made into a sorbet (see page 337).

Blueberry Widely available from supermarkets. Delicious eaten raw, by the handful, or mixed with yogurt; lovely in pies and all the dishes described for blackberries.

Cherry Wash sweet cherries and serve them as they are or remove stems and pits and add to a fruit salad. Also delicious made into a compôte. Stew cherries with a little water until tender, add sugar to taste and perhaps a splash of kirsch, if you have some handy.

Custard apple Lumpy green or greenish-yellow fruit. They're ripe when they feel soft to the touch; if you buy them when hard, they will ripen at room temperature. To eat, simply cut in half and scoop out the white flesh, which tastes, not surprisingly, of custard. Discard the skin.

Date Delicious, shiny plump fresh dates are available from larger supermarkets and groceries. Serve as they are or slice and stone and add to fruit salads; or remove the pits and fill the centers with nuts or almond paste. If you can't get fresh dates, try Medjool dates; they're dried, but still plump and juicy.

Fig Serve ripe figs Greek-style with a bowl of thick creamy yogurt and honey, or slice and add to fruit salads.

Gooseberry Wash and leave gooseberries as they are if you're going to purée them, otherwise "top and tail", then cook in a sugar syrup as described on page 312. Add a few sprigs of elderflowers for a delicious flavor. Can be puréed and made into sauce or pie.

Grape Just wash grapes gently and arrange in a fruit bowl or on a cheese-board; or halve, remove seeds and add to a fruit salad or arrange on top of a sponge cake and glaze with jam.

Grapefruit Halve horizontally, loosen sections with a sharp knife, carefully easing out the white skin and membranes. Can be sprinkled with sweet sherry and a little sugar or topped with soft brown sugar and dots of butter and broiled for a retro starter. Or cut out the segments as described for oranges (next page).

Greengage Prepare as for plums.

Kiwi Ready when it feels just soft to the touch. Use raw, peeled and sliced in fruit salads and to decorate cheesecakes and creams.

Lemon To use the skin, preferably buy unwaxed organic lemons or scrub well in warm water to remove residue of chemical sprays, then grate finely or pare off thinly. Use both the juice and the rind to flavor ice creams, fools and sorbets as well as cakes and pastries.

Lime Gives a delicious flavor to creams and a lovely garnish for fruit fritters or crêpes.

Loganberry Prepare and use as for

blackberries.

Lychee Looks like a small horse chestnut, with a reddish prickly shell. Inside it has translucent white fragrant flesh and a large shiny brown pit. Serve raw, or peel, pit and add to an exotic fruit salad.

Mango These large, oval fruits range in color from green to gold, often splashed with red. They are ripe when just soft to the touch and, hopefully, with a delicious fragrance. To prepare, first cut in half and remove the stone: make two downward cuts, each about ¼in (6mm) from the stalk at the top. As you cut down, you will feel the large flat pit and the two halves will fall apart. Serve the halves as they are and scoop out the juicy golden flesh with a teaspoon; or cut off the skin, slice the flesh and add to fruit salads. Mango also makes an excellent sorbet or ice cream.

Melon Cantaloupe has a rough, warty skin and deep grooves, as if ready for slicing; the flesh is orange, fragrant and juicy. Charéntais are similar but smaller. Muskmelons have a netted skin and green or yellow aromatic flesh; delicious little Ogen melons belong to this group, as do winter melons, which have smooth, green, yellow or white skins but very little flavor. Honeydew have ridged green or yellow skins and sweet white or pale green flesh. Watermelons have smooth green skin, scarlet flesh and shiny brown seeds. Melons are best when they feel heavy and yield to slight pressure at the stem end. Serve large melons cut in slices, the smaller ones halved and filled with sweet sherry or port, ripe

strawberries or a scoop of ice cream. They can also be made into a sorbet (see page 338).

Nectarine Prepare these delicious, juicy fruits as for peaches.

Orange Scrub skins, if using, to remove residue of chemical sprays, or use unsprayed organic oranges where possible. Use the rind, either grated or thinly pared, for flavoring; the juice is good instead of sugar syrup in fruit salads. Oranges can be peeled and divided into segments; but the best way is to cut round with a sharp knife and a sawing action, removing both the peel and the white skin. Then insert the knife and cut each segment away from the inner skin. Hold the orange over a bowl to catch the juice. Good in fruit salads or served on their own.

Passion fruit Granadilla or passion fruit has a wrinkled brown skin, sweet fragrant greenish flesh and quite a number of seeds. Halve the fruits, scoop out the flesh and add to fruit salads or use to top ice cream.

Pawpaw From the same family as the custard apple. Large, pear-shaped fruits that smell fragrant and feel soft when ripe; the flesh inside is pink with tiny black seeds. Halve the fruits, scoop out the seeds and eat the flesh with a teaspoon; or peel, slice and add to fruit salads (see page 328).

Peach Delicious, fragrant, juicy summer fruit; some varieties have golden flesh, others white, which is a real delicacy. To skin peaches, put them into a bowl, cover with boiling water and leave for 2 minutes; drain and slip off the

skins with a sharp knife. Slice and cover with sweet white wine, add to fruit salads or make into peach brûlée (see page 331).

Pear Wash thin-skinned dessert pears and serve simply, or peel, core and slice and serve with cream, a raspberry purée or as part of a fruit salad. Buy them in advance and allow them to ripen for several days at room temperature. If they're unripe, try poaching them.

Persimmon of which Sharon Fruit is a type, looks like a ripe tomato and is ready for eating when it feels very soft. The flesh is delicious, very sweet and tastes like fresh dates. Peel, slice and eat just as it is or add to fruit salads.

Pineapple Dark golden brown in color with a pronounced sweet smell when it's ripe and sweet. Can be served in wedges or peeled and sliced and added to fruit salads, compôtes, smoothies and sorbets. Try a carpaccio of pineapple: very thinly slice some pineapple, then drizzle honey, sugar syrup or raspberry coulis over (see opposite).

Plum Slice and pit sweet plums and add to fruit salads; poach sharper plums in syrup as described on pg 312, make into pies or crumble.

Pomegranate Halve, scoop out the scarlet flesh, add to fruit salads (or leafy salads) or use as a topping for a pale creamy pudding or coleslaw.

Quince Peel, core and slice, then stew or add to pies. The fruits of the scarlet-flowered Japanese quince, or *Chaenomeles japonica*, are edible and, like cultivated quinces, make an excellent jelly preserve that is fragrant and delicious.

Raspberry Eat raw with cream and sugar, or make into ice cream (see page 337), sorbets or a fresh purée for serving with ice cream or other fruits. Raspberry coulis is useful for pouring over fruit salads, ice cream and so on. Make this by blending then straining fresh or frozen raspberries, sweeten with sugar. You can use it uncooked, or bring it to a boil then cool, which makes it extra glossy.

Redcurrant Prepare as described for blackcurrants; mix with raspberries and strawberries to make traditional dishes, summer pudding or raspberry and redcurrant tart (see pages 335 and 321).

Rhubarb Cut off the leaves (don't eat, they're poisonous) and pull off any strings from the sides of the rhubarb. Cut rhubarb into even-sized pieces, poach as described overleaf; make into a fool or crumble (see pages 323 and 320). It's best not to serve rhubarb more than once a week because, like spinach, its high oxalic content hinders the absorption of magnesium and calcium.

Strawberry Wash strawberries gently, removing the stems, and serve with sugar and cream or use in a variety of recipes, such as tarts, cheesecakes or ice cream (see pages 321, 325 and 337). Strawberry coulis or purée (see overleaf) makes a delicious accompaniment for ice cream, yogurt or fromage frais or for pouring over ripe peaches (see page 331).

Tangerine, satsuma, clementine and mandarin Peel and eat these as they are or divide into segments and add to fruit salads.

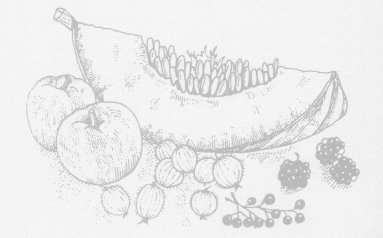

Basic preparation and cooking

Buy ripe, firm fruit and prepare quickly, cutting with a sharp stainless steel knife. Always eat as soon as possible. Coat cut surfaces of fruit that you're going to serve raw with lemon or orange juice to prevent discoloration.

The method of cooking fruit most frequently used, and one that is suitable for almost all types, is poaching.

To poach fruit, first make a sugar syrup. For 1–1½lb (450–700g) fruit you need 1¼ cups (275ml) water (or other liquid, such as wine or cider) and ⅓ cup (75g) granulated sugar or mild honey. Put the sugar or honey and water into a heavy-based saucepan and heat gently until dissolved. Then turn up the heat and boil rapidly for 2 minutes. Add the prepared fruit, bring back to a boil, then leave to simmer gently until the fruit feels tender when pierced with the point of a sharp knife.

It's important to give large fruits like whole or halved pears and peaches time to cook right through to the center or they may discolor. Allow at least 20–30 minutes for whole pears and 15–20 minutes for halved fruit.

The syrup can be flavored with thin slices of lemon or orange peel, a cinnamon stick, a stalk of lemon grass, a vanilla pod or a few heads of fresh elderflowers; add when making the syrup and remove before serving the fruit. (The vanilla pod can be rinsed, dried and used several times.)

Let the fruits cool in the syrup or remove with a slotted spoon and thicken the syrup by boiling rapidly until reduced in quantity.

Soft, juicy fruits are best poached in the minimum of water or none at all. Put redcurrants and blackcurrants, blueberries, cranberries and blackberries into a heavy-based saucepan with 2 tablespoons of water to 1–1½lb (450–700g) fruit and heat gently until the juices run and the fruit is tender. Instead of the water use butter for apples, redcurrant or other mild jelly for rhubarb. When the fruit has softened, add sugar or mild honey to taste; do not add this sooner or the outside of the fruits may toughen.

Cooked fruit, as well as uncooked soft fruits such as raspberries and strawberries, can be puréed. Simply use a food processor, blender or electric hand blender. If you want the mixture really smooth, push it through a sieve after that. Serve as a sauce or make into ice cream, fools or sorbets.

If you want vegan cream that resembles dairy cream, you can buy single cream (called Soy Dream Topping) in health-food stores and some supermarkets, as well as a delicious, thick, soured-type cream made from soy. This can be used as you might use crème fraîche; and you can sweeten it to taste. If you want a thick, fluffy cream, sweetened soy creams, sold in aerosol cans, are available from large health-food stores.

Hot desserts

Baked apples with raisins v

It's easy to forget about this quick, simple and delicious pudding. Baked apples are lovely served just as they are, or with a spoonful of cream or yogurt. Other fillings can be used instead of the raisins; dates are good, as is a spoonful of the healthy mincemeat (see page 316).

SERVES 4
4 large cooking apples
2oz (50g) raisins

Wash the apples and remove the cores using an apple corer or by cutting them out neatly with a sharp pointed knife.

Score around the middle of the apples, just cutting the skin. Place in a shallow ovenproof dish. Fill the cavities of the apples with the raisins, pressing them down well.

Bake the apples, uncovered, at 350°F (180°C) for 45–60 minutes or until the apples are tender but not collapsed.

French apple tart

This is mouth-watering with its topping of glazed apple slices, moist filling of apple purée and crisp pastry shell.

SERVES 4–6
8in (20cm) cooked pastry tart shell (see pages 257–8)
2lb (900g) cooking apples, peeled, cored and sliced
2 tbsp (25g) butter
⅓ cup (75g) sugar
2 large Cox or Granny Smith apples
3 tbsp sieved apricot jam, warmed

Preheat the cooking apples, butter and sugar into a heavy-based saucepan and cook gently, uncovered, for about 15 minutes.

Preheat the oven to 400°F (200°C).

Spoon the apple purée into the tart shell. Peel the Cox apples and slice them thinly. Arrange the slices on top of the purée, then spoon the jam over them.

Bake for 20–30 minutes or until the apple slices are tender. Serve warm or cold.

Bakewell tart

Everyone loves this traditional tart with its crisp pastry covered with jam and a light almond sponge, and it's very easy to make.

SERVES 6
1 quantity of shortcrust pastry or easy wholegrain spelt flour pastry (see pages 257 and 258)
7 tbsp ((100g) butter
3 tbsp raspberry jam
1¾ stick (25g) butter, softened
½ cup (125g) superfine sugar
2 eggs
¼ (25g) all-purpose flour
2oz (50g) ground almonds
a few sliced almonds, to decorate
½ and ½, to serve (optional)

Preheat the oven to 425°F (220°C), and place a heavy baking sheet on the top shelf to heat up with the oven.

Roll out the pastry and ease it into a 8in (20cm) lightly greased tart pan; prick the base and trim the edges. Spoon the jam into the tart shell and spread.

Put the butter, sugar, eggs, flour and ground almonds into a bowl and beat for 2 minutes or until light and creamy. Spoon this mixture over the jam and decorate with a few sliced almonds.

Place the tart on the heated baking sheet and bake for 5 minutes, then turn the oven down to 350°F (180°C) and bake for a further 30–35 minutes or until golden and firm to the touch.

Serve hot or cold with ½ and ½, if liked.

Blueberry plate pie

I use wholewheat flour as I like its flavor and wholesome appearance but white flour or a half-and-half mixture could be used instead.

SERVES 4–6
1½ quantity of shortcrust pastry or easy wholegain spelt flour pastry (see pages 257 and 258)
2 tbsp (25g) superfine sugar
3–4 tbsp cold water
1lb (450g) blueberries
2oz (50g) sugar
1 tbsp (15g) butter
milk, to glaze

Preheat the oven to 400°F (200°C).

Roll out a third of the pastry and use to line a 20–23m (8–9in) pie plate. Put the blueberries on top, sprinkle with sugar, then dot with butter.

Roll out the rest of the pastry and place over the top of the fruit. Trim around the edges, decorate with leftover pastry and make two or three steam holes. Brush with milk, bake for about 30 minutes or until golden on top.

Blackberry and apple pie v

This is a deep pie with a lovely pastry top.

SERVES 4–6
1 quantity of shortcrust pastry or easy wholegrain spelt flour pastry (see pages 257 and 258)
1lb (450g) blackberries
1lb (450g) apples, peeled, cored and sliced
⅓-½ cup (75–125g) sugar
2–3 tbsp water
milk, to glaze
superfine sugar, to decorate

Preheat the oven to 400°F (200°C).

Roll out the pastry quite thickly and cut out so that it is about 1in (2.5cm) wider all round than the pie dish. Cut ½in (1 cm) strips of pastry from the trimmings, brush with cold water and press round the rim of the pie dish.

Mix the fruit with the sugar and put in the dish; sprinkle with the water.

Ease the pastry on top of the fruit, molding it over. Trim around the edge of the pie, decorate with any leftover pastry and make 2–3 steam holes. Brush with milk, bake for 15 minutes, then reduce the heat to 350°F (180°C) for 15–20 minutes. Sprinkle a little caster sugar over before serving.

Blackcurrant lattice tart with lemon pastry v

You could use a good-quality blackcurrant jam or one of the lovely no-added-sugar jams from health stores instead of the fruit, if you prefer. You'll need less sugar if you use jam.

SERVES 6
1 quantity of shortcrust pastry or easy wholegrain spelt flour pastry (see pages 257 and 258), in either case adding the grated rind of 1 lemon to the flour before mixing with the fat
1½ tbsp cold water
2 x 12oz jars bottled blackcurrants or about 12oz (350g) fresh ones
2–4oz(50–125g) sugar
1 tbsp cornstarch
milk and extra sugar, to glaze
crème fraîche or cream, to serve (optional)

Preheat the oven to 425°F (220°C) and place a heavy baking sheet on the top shelf to heat up with the oven.

Roll out the pastry and ease it into a 8in (20cm) lightly greased tart pan; trim the edges.

Put the blackcurrants into a bowl and sprinkle with the sugar and cornstarch. You will probably need the full amount of sugar for fresh blackcurrants but less for ones which have been bottled in a light syrup. Gently turn the black-currants so that they all get coated with the sugar and cornstarch.

Spread the blackcurrants evenly in the tart shell. Gather up and re-roll the pastry trimmings, cut into thin strips and arrange in a lattice on top of the fruit.

Brush the strips with milk and sprinkle with a little extra sugar.

Place the tart on the heated baking sheet and bake for 5 minutes, then turn the oven down to 350°F (180°C) and bake for a further 30–35 minutes or until the pastry is golden brown.

Serve hot or cold, with crème fraîche or pouring cream, if you like.

Traditional Christmas pudding

When I was growing up my father always made our Christmas pudding; this is his delicious recipe. Vegetable suet is available from health-food stores and larger supermarkets, although you could use cold butter or a block of vegetable margarine instead.

SERVES 8–12

8oz (225g) currants
4oz (125g) golden raisins
4oz (125g) large raisins
4oz (125g) candied orange peel
1oz (25g) blanched almonds
1 cup (125g) all-purpose flour
½ tsp salt
½ tsp freshly grated nutmeg
½ tsp ground ginger
1½ tsp mixed pie spice or cinnamon
8oz (225g) muscovado sugar
4oz (125g) fresh wholegrain
　　breadcrumbs
8oz (225g) vegetable suet, shredded
rind and juice of 1 lemon
2 eggs
1 tbsp molasses
about ¼ cup milk or milk and rum

Wash and dry the fruits; stone and chop the raisins (if necessary), finely chop the peel and blanched almonds.

Sift the flour with the salt and spices and mix with the sugar, breadcrumbs and suet. Next add the fruits, almonds and candied peel, along with the lemon rind and strained juice.

Beat the eggs and stir into the mixture, then mix in the molasses.

Add sufficient milk or mixed milk and the rum, to make a soft mixture which will fall heavily from the spoon when shaken. Stir it all well together and don't forget to make a wish.

Put the mixture into a well-greased 1 quart basin, or two 2 cup basins, and fill to 1in (2.5cm) from the top. Cover with baking parchment and tie on a pudding cloth, or cover with greased foil, or use a plastic pudding basin with a clip-on lid.

Steam for 4 hours. Cool and store in a dry place; steam for another 3 hours before serving.

Linzertorte

This light, crumbly Austrian tart is delicately flavored with spices and lemon rind and melts in your mouth.

SERVES 6 ❄

6oz (175g) plain wholewheat flour or wholegrain spelt flour
1 tsp ground cinnamon
a pinch of ground cloves
6oz (175g) ground almonds (or whole unblanched almonds pulverised in a blender)
3 tbsp (40g) sugar
1½ sticks (175g) butter
1 egg yolk
6–8oz (175–225g) raspberry, cherry or blackcurrant jam
a little confectioner's sugar, for dusting
½ and ½, to serve

Sift the flour, cinnamon and cloves into a bowl or food processor; add also the residue of bran left in the sieve. Add the ground almonds, lemon rind and sugar. Add the butter and blitz briefly, or rub the butter into the dry ingredients until they look like breadcrumbs. Gently mix in the egg yolk to make a soft dough.

If possible wrap the dough in a piece of foil or cling film and chill it in the fridge for 30 minutes or so. If you have time for this the dough will be easier to roll out but it isn't essential if you're in a hurry.

Set the oven to 400°F (200°C) and place a heavy baking sheet on the top shelf to heat up with the oven.

On a lightly floured work surface or board roll out three-quarters of the dough to fit a 8–9in (20–23cm) lightly greased fluted tart pan. Spread the jam evenly over the pastry.

Roll out the rest of the pastry and cut into long strips; arrange these strips in a lattice over the jam, then fold the edges of the pastry down and press them in to make a sort of rim round the edge of the tart.

Place the tart on the heated baking sheet and bake for 25–30 minutes until it's slightly risen and golden brown.

You can serve the tart hot, cold or, my choice, warm. Sift a little confectioner's sugar on top before taking it to the table. It's nice with ½ and ½.

Fresh and spicy mincemeat v

Why add extra sugar and fat to mincemeat? The fat is only a hang-over from the days when it was made with minced meat, and the sugar isn't necessary because the dried fruit is very sweet. So I make this lighter version, which is delicious and can be made fresh just before you want to use it.

ENOUGH 24 MINCE PIES

4oz (125g) dried fruit mix, from health-food stores, including apricots and apple rings
6oz (175g) mixed dried small fruits, including raisins, golden raisins and dried blueberries
2oz (50g) apple-juice-infused or plain dried cranberries
¼ cup Marsala or fresh orange juice
2 tbsp maple syrup
½ tsp ground ginger
½ tsp pie spice
½ tsp ground cinnamon
1 small banana, peeled

Chop the fruit mix using a knife or snip it with scissors. Put into a bowl with the raisins and blueberries, dried cranberries, Marsala or orange juice, maple syrup and spices. Mix well, then cover and leave for 12–24 hours.

Put the mixture into a food processor along with the banana and pulse until the fruit is chopped and tender, but still has some texture.

This mincemeat will keep for a week in a covered bowl in the fridge.

Traditional mincemeat v

This is my mother's recipe and I can never make it without seeing her in my mind's eye with her apron on, the big kitchen table strewn with flour, pie pan and jars of mincemeat and the air full of the wonderful aroma of mince pies baking in the oven as batch after batch of beautiful wholemeal mince pies were produced. Well, we had big Christmases in those days: usually 16 or more of us sitting down to nut roast on Christmas Day.

MAKES ABOUT 7LB (3KG)
1lb (450g) currants
1lb (450g) golden raisins
1lb (450g) raisins
1lb (450g) cooking apples
6oz (175g) candied orange peel
2oz (50g) glacé cherries
2oz (50g) pitted dates
2oz (50g) blanched almonds
1lb (450g) vegetable suet, shredded
1⅓ cups (350g) muscovado sugar
½ tsp freshly grated nutmeg
½ tsp ground ginger
1 tsp pie spice
½ tsp salt
2 lemons
2 tangerines
5fl oz (150ml) rum or brandy

Wash the dried fruit and pat dry in a clean cloth. Peel, core and chop or grate the apples. Chop the peel, cherries, dates and blanched almonds. Mix them all together in a large bowl and add the vegetable suet.

Stir in the sugar, spices and salt. Grate in the rind of 1 lemon and 1 tangerine, and add the juice of both lemons and both tangerines; finally, pour in the rum or brandy. Mix thoroughly with a wooden spoon.

Put into clean, sterilized jars and store in a cool, dry place. Make into mince pies (see next recipe).

To sterilize the jars, either run them through a complete dishwasher cycle, or wash them well in soapy water, rinse thoroughly and put them, upside down, on the rack in a low oven, 275°F, 140°C and leave for 30 minutes to dry.

Mince pies v

Mince pies are fun to make. The secret is to stock up on bun or muffin tins, non-stick if possible. That way you can leave the mince pies in the tins until you want them; I sometimes get them all ready then freeze them, uncooked, in the tins, ready to finish off in the oven later. I'd encourage you to try making your own pastry, but you could use good-quality store-bought instead.

MAKES 12 PIES ❉
1½ quantities of easy wholegrain spelt flour pastry (see page 258)
10–12oz (300–350g) traditional mincemeat or ½ quantity of fresh and spicy mincemeat (see previous recipe and opposite)
2–3 tbsp milk or soy milk, for brushing
a little superfine sugar, for sprinkling

Preheat the oven to 425°F (220°C).

Roll the pastry out fairly thinly, but be gentle with it: it is not intended to be rolled out extra thin.

Cut circles to fit a 12-hole bun or muffin tin; for my tins I use a 2¾in (7cm) round cutter for the base of the tins and a 2½in (6cm) cutter for the top.

Ease the larger circles of pastry into the tins and fill with a good spoonful of mincemeat. Cover with a smaller pastry circle to fit the top, pressing down lightly.

Brush the tops of the pies with milk or soy milk and sprinkle quite thickly with superfine sugar. With a skewer make a steam hole in the center of each pie.

Bake for about 10 minutes. Cool slightly, then carefully remove from tin using a spatula.

Crêpes Suzette

Contrary to their reputation, crêpes Suzette aren't difficult to make — you do all the preparation well in advance — and are delicious for a treat, especially after a light main course.

MAKES ABOUT 12 CRÊPES
basic crêpe batter (see page 296)
a little butter, for frying

FOR THE SAUCE
1 stick (125g) butter
heaping ½ cup (150g) superfine sugar
grated rind and juice of 3 small–medium oranges
grated rind and juice of 1 lemon
2 tbsp orange liqueur such as Grand Marnier
¼ cup brandy

Make about 12 thin crêpes, using about 2 tablespoons of batter for each one and frying them in the butter. As the crêpes are done, pile them up on a plate and keep them in a cool place until needed.

When you're ready to serve the crêpes, put the butter, sugar, grated orange and lemon rind and juice, and the orange liqueur (if using), into a large frying pan or shallow flameproof dish that you can take to the table, and heat gently to melt the butter and sugar.

Turn off the heat, then dip the crêpes in this mixture, one by one, coating each side then folding it in half and in half again, so that it's a triangular shape. As each crêpe is done, push it to the side of the frying pan.

When all the crepes have been dipped, leave them in the frying pan or dish until you're almost ready to eat them, then put the frying pan or dish over the heat to warm through the sauce and the crêpes.

When the crêpes are heated through, turn up the heat high for about 1 minute to make the sauce very hot, quickly pour in the brandy and set it alight with a lighter or by tilting the frying pan down towards the gas flame.

You can take it to the table at this point, burning away. The flame will die out in a few seconds, when all the alcohol has been burnt off. Serve immediately.

VARIATIONS
Crêpes with maple syrup

Make the crêpes as described and serve warm with maple syrup and a dollop of crème fraîche.

Chocolate crêpes with black cherries

You can also make chocolate or carob crêpes by replacing 1 tablespoon of the flour in the batter with 1 tablespoon of cocoa or carob powder. Add 1 teaspoon of sugar to this batter and serve the crêpes with black cherries (fresh or frozen) which have been simmered with a little water and sugar until they are sweet and bathed in a glossy syrup. Serve with crème fraîche or whipped cream.

Crêpes with apples and raisins

Crêpes are also delicious filled with the apple and raisin compôte mixture on page 323 and served with thick natural yogurt.

Crêpes with ricotta and glacé fruits

Another delicious filling for crêpes is a mixture of ricotta cheese, chopped dried and glacé fruits and a little grated orange or lemon rind and sugar to taste.

Easy pear tarte Tatin with cardamom

A variation on a classic dish that has survived the test of time, this is a wonderful combination of tender caramelized pears and crisp pastry. It's easiest to make using a tarte Tatin pan (a small ovenproof cast iron frying pan — about 10in (25cm) in diameter), but you can improvise, using a normal frying pan to caramelize the pears, then putting them into cake pans for the baking. Cardamom, one of my favorite spices, gives this a beautiful flavor.

SERVES 6

5 ripe firm pears, Comice if possible
6 cardamom pods
scant ½ cup (100g) superfine sugar
½ stick (50g) butter
11oz (375g) ready-rolled puff pastry
crème fraîche, to serve

Peel the pears then cut them into quarters and remove the cores.

Crush the cardamom pods and extract the seeds; set the seeds to one side and discard the pods.

Put the sugar into a tarte Tatin pan or frying pan. Cook over a high heat for a few minutes or until it is golden brown, then add the pears and turn them so they are coated with the sugar. Leave to cook over a high heat for 2–3 minutes, to "roast" them.

Add the butter and cardamom seeds and cook for a further 10–15 minutes or until the pears are tender and any water they have produced has boiled down with the sugar into a thick caramel sauce; that's the secret of a good tarte Tatin.

Preheat the oven to 400°F (200°C).

Roll the pastry briefly on a floured surface or board to make it slightly thinner, then cut a round about ½in (1cm) wider than the top of the tarte Tatin pan or the pan you are using.

If you're using a cake pan for the next stage, transfer the pears and their sticky sauce to this, pouring some of the sauce in first, then adding the pears, rounded side down; scrape in all the gooey juice from the pan, too.

If you're using the pan, move the pears as necessary so that they are rounded side down, as that is the side you will see when the tarte is turned out later. Put the pastry on top, tucking it down the inside the edges of the pan, to form the crust of the tart when it's turned out. Prick the pastry, then bake the tarte for 15–20 minutes or until crisp and golden brown.

Remove the tarte from the oven and leave to stand for about 5 minutes, then loosen it with a spatula. Put a plate over the top of the pan, and holding the pan in a cloth to protect your hands and arms, turn it over, so that the tarte comes out on the plate. Be very careful: the caramel is hot! The beautiful rounded caramelised pears will be on top, with crisp pastry around them. Serve with crème fraîche.

VARIATIONS

Easy pear tarte Tatin with vanilla

Leave out the cardamom. Slit a vanilla pod down its length, then, using the point of a sharp knife, scoop out the seeds without damaging the pod. Add the pod and seeds to the pan along with the pears. When you arrange the pears in the pan before putting on the pastry, make sure the vanilla pod is underneath the pears, so that when the tarte is turned out, it will be on top. For a luxurious touch, serve with lightly sweetened whipped cream with a tablespoonful or so of eau de vie de poire stirred into it: very expensive to buy, but great with pear dishes for a treat and keeps for years.

Easy apple tarte Tatin

Make as described, omitting the cardamom and using apples instead of pears. Granny Smith or Cox apples are particularly suitable.

Easy plum tarte Tatin

Use enough sweet ripe but firm plums to cover the base of your pan; halve the plums and remove the stones.

Vegan tarte Tatin v

Use pure vegetable margarine instead of butter and make sure that the puff pastry you use is vegan. Serve with vegan sour cream, such as Sour Supreme, from health-food stores.

Wholewheat plum crumble

A fruit crumble is the perfect dessert for entertaining. Not only is it really easy to make but everyone loves it! I use wholewheat flour but do feel free to use white flour or a mixture. It's nice with some oats added (see variation below).

SERVES 4–6
1½lb (700g) plums
about 1 cup (75–125g) sugar
1¾ cups (225g) plain wholewheat
   flour
1 tsp baking powder
1 tsp allspice
4oz (125g) demerara sugar
6 tbsp (75g) butter

Preheat the oven to 350°F (180°C).
   Halve the plums and take out the stones.
   Put the plums into a shallow pie dish and sprinkle with the sugar.
   To make the topping, sift the flour, baking powder and allspice into a bowl, adding the bran left in the sieve too.
   Mix in the sugar and then rub in the butter until the mixture looks like fine breadcrumbs.
   Sprinkle your crumbly mixture over the top of the plums in an even layer and press down lightly.
   Bake for 40 minutes or until the crumble is crisp and the plums tender. Serve hot or warm.

VARIATIONS

Wholewheat rhubarb crumble

Make this as described, using 1½lb (700g) trimmed rhubarb cut into ½in (1cm) pieces instead of the plums.

Wholewheat apple and raisin crumble

For this, first make the apple and raisin compôte (see page 323). Top with crumble and bake for 25–30 minutes.

Oaty crumble

This is a lovely variation. Simply replace a proportion of the flour with the same quantity of rolled (not "jumbo") oats; 2oz (50g) oats and 6oz (175g) wholewheat flour is a good combination. Mix them together then proceed according to the main recipe, adding the sugar and rubbing in the butter.

Banana crumble with almonds

For this unusual but speedy variation, replace 2oz (50g) of the flour with ground almonds. Slice 4–6 large bananas into a shallow, greased baking dish. Cover with the crumble, sprinkle with 1oz (25g) sliced almonds and bake for 25–30 minutes.

Pumpkin pie

An American friend gave me this recipe, which I've adapted to give the right quantity for a 8–9in (20–23cm) tart pan. It makes a lovely autumn pudding, sweet and warmly spiced. Serve warm with cream. Try scattering some roughly chopped walnuts over the top of the pie.

SERVES 6
8in (20cm) cooked shortcrust pastry
   tart shell (see pages 257–8)
2¼lb (1kg) sugar pumpkin, weighed
   in the store with skin and seeds
¼ cup water
Packed ½ cup (125g) soft dark brown
   sugar
½ tsp ground ginger
½ tsp ground cinnamon
a little freshly grated nutmeg
a pinch of ground cloves
5fl oz (150ml) ½ and ½
2 eggs

Preheat the oven to 350°C (180°F).
   Peel the pumpkin and remove the seeds. Cut the pumpkin into even-sized pieces, put them into a heavy-based saucepan with the water and cook gently, with a lid on the pan, until the pumpkin is tender (about 10 minutes).
   Drain the pumpkin into a colander and press gently with a spoon to extract as much water as possible.
   Put the pumpkin into a bowl and add the sugar, spices, cream and eggs. Mix well, then pour into the tart shell and bake for about 50 minutes or until it's set.

Raspberry and redcurrant tart

A pretty, jeweled tart that's perfect in the summer when soft fruits are in season.

SERVES 16

1 cup (125g) plain wholewheat flour
½ stick (50g) butter
1oz (25g) caster sugar
1 egg yolk
12oz (350g) raspberries
4oz (125g) redcurrants, stems removed
8oz (225g) redcurrant jelly, warmed

Sift the flour into a bowl (adding back the bran in the sieve) and rub in the butter until the mixture looks like breadcrumbs. Add the sugar and egg yolk; mix to form a dough. Cover with cling film and chill for 30 minutes.

Preheat the oven to 400°F (200°C).

Roll out the pastry and line a 8in (20cm) tart pan with a removable bottom. Prick the base of the pastry and trim the edges. Bake for 15 minutes, then allow to cool.

Arrange circles of raspberries and redcurrants in the flan case. Pour the redcurrant jelly over the fruit; then cool before serving.

Strawberry tartlets

Delicious summer tartlets that melt in your mouth. Serve them as they are or with heavy cream.

SERVES 4

6oz (175g) plain wholewheat flour
4oz (125g) butter
2 tsp superfine sugar
1–2 tbsp cold water
Heaping ¼ cup redcurrant jelly, warmed
8oz (225g) small strawberries, hulled

Sift the flour into a food processor or mixing bowl, adding back any bran left behind in the sieve. Add the butter and sugar, and either whisk in the processor or rub together with your fingertips until the mixture looks like fine breadcrumbs.

Add cold water to make the mixture hold together to form a dough. If there's time, leave the dough to chill, covered in cling wrap in the fridge, for 30 minutes.

Roll out the pastry thinly and use a cutter to stamp out circles to fit small tartlet tins. Prick very lightly, bake for about 8 minutes, then cool.

Brush a little redcurrant jelly over each tartlet shell, then arrange 3–4 strawberries in each and spoon some redcurrant jelly over them so that they glisten. Cool before serving.

Mini sticky toffee puddings

Everyone loves sticky toffee puddings and these couldn't be easier to make. You will need eight 6fl oz (175ml) mini pudding basins or an eight-hole muffin tin with the same capacity.

MAKES 8 DESSERTS ❅

3oz (75g) pitted dates
5fl oz (150ml) boiling water
6 tbsp (75g) butter
¾ cup (150g) light brown sugar
2 eggs
1 tsp vanilla extract
1⅓ (175g) self-raising flour
½ tsp baking soda

FOR THE TOFFEE SAUCE

½ stick (50g) butter
¾ cup (175g) light soft brown sugar
1¼ cups (275ml) heavy cream

Preheat the oven to 350°F (180°C).

Grease the pudding basins or tins generously with butter and sprinkle the insides with flour, tapping out the excess.

Put the dates into a bowl, cover with the boiling water and leave to cool until tepid and the dates are softened. Put the dates into a food processor along with the butter, sugar, eggs, vanilla extract, flour and baking soda and whiz until the mixture is smooth and thick, then pour into the pudding basins or muffin tin, dividing it equally between them. Bake for about 20 minutes or until the puddings have risen and spring back when touched lightly in the center.

continued next page

Treacle tart v

While the desserts are cooking, make the sauce: put the butter, sugar and half the cream into a saucepan and stir over the heat until melted and combined. Let it bubble over the heat for a further minute or two, stirring all the time, then remove from the heat and stir in the rest of the cream.

Slip a knife around the desserts to loosen, then turn them out and serve with the sauce drizzled over them. Alternatively, turn the desserts out into a shallow heatproof dish. Pour the toffee sauce over and around them, cover and leave until you are ready to eat them

Reheat the desserts in the oven, heated to 350°F (180°C) for 15–20 minutes, or pop them under a hot broiler for 8–10 minutes or until the sauce is bubbling. They also freeze very well.

This is a very popular pudding in my family and it's something I often make for family celebrations, including Christmas. I always use wholewheat pastry; the easy wholegrain spelt flour pastry on page 258 gives a melt-in-the-mouth result.

SERVES 4–6

1 quantity of easy wholegrain spelt flour pastry (see page 258) or 13oz (375g) ready-rolled shortcrust pastry
1lb (450g) golden syrup
4oz (125g) fresh breadcrumbs

Preheat the oven to 375°F (190°C).

Use the pastry to line a greased 8in (20cm) tart pan, trimming the edges of the dough and pricking the base of the tart. Put the syrup into a large saucepan and warm gently until liquid. Stir in the breadcrumbs and leave to cool slightly.

Pour the syrup mixture into the pastry shell. Bake for 20–25 minutes or until the pastry is crisp and the filling golden brown and set but not dry. Serve warm.

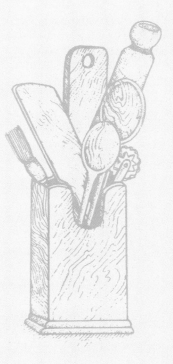

Cold desserts

Apple and raisin compôte with orange v

I am particularly fond of this compôte because it relies on the natural sweetness of the apples and raisins without added sugar. It's at its best and most luscious when made with Cox or other sweet apples, though it also works well with cooking apples.

SERVES 4–6
2lb (900g) apples
2 tbsp (25g) butter
8oz (225g) raisins
juice and grated rind of 1 orange

TO SERVE
crème fraîche, thick natural yogurt
   or whipped cream
shortbread cookies

Peel, core and slice the apples and place in a heavy-based saucepan with the butter, raisins and orange juice and rind.

Cook gently, with a lid on the pan, for about 10 minutes, stirring frequently, until the apples look pulpy.

Serve hot or cold — with crème fraîche, thick natural yogurt or whipped cream. Some crunchy shortbread cookies go well with it.

Apricot fool

This smooth, golden cream looks and tastes too rich and luxurious to be good for you — but it is! The best dried apricots are those that have been dried without sulphur dioxide to preserve their color, so they look unappetisingly brown, but their flavor is excellent. The same applies to the little Hunza apricots, which are wonderful but need to be stoned. This freezes well for 4–6 weeks.

SERVES 4 ❄
6oz (175g) dried apricots (8oz (225g)
   if using Hunza apricots with
   stones)
12oz (350g) low-fat cream cheese
1 tbsp honey (optional)
a few toasted (see pages 139–40)
   sliced almonds or sesame seeds

Wash the apricots well in hot water. Put them into a medium-sized saucepan and cover with cold water. Leave to soak for an hour or so if possible, then simmer them over a low heat for 20–30 minutes or until they're very tender and the water is reduced to just a little syrupy glaze. (It's best to let them soak first, but I have found that you can get away with just simmering them if you're rushed for time.) Leave to cool. If you're using Hunza apricots, remove and discard the stones.

Blend the apricots in a food processor or blender to a thick purée. Mix the apricot purée with the cheese, beating well until smooth and creamy, and add the honey (if using).

Spoon the mixture into four dishes — it looks lovely in glass ones — and chill. Serve sprinkled with a few toasted sliced almonds or sesame seeds.

VARIATION
Vegan apricot fool v

Make as described, using 1½ tubs of plain Tofutti cream cheese from the health-food store, and sweeten with agave or maple syrup for a delicious creamy non-dairy fool.

Chocolate and orange mousse

A tempting rich and velvety chocolate mousse.

SERVES 6

8oz (225g) dark chocolate
2 tbsp fresh orange juice
grated rind of 1 orange
1 tbsp orange liqueur such as Triple sec — or use brandy
4 eggs, separated
a little whipped cream (optional)
a few toasted almonds, chocolate curls or thin strands of orange peel (optional)

Break up the chocolate and place in a bowl. Set over a saucepan of boiling water, or microwave it for a minute or two, until the chocolate has melted. Don't let it overheat.

Stir the orange juice and rind into the melted chocolate, then the liqueur or brandy and the egg yolks.

Whisk the egg whites until they're standing in soft peaks then gently fold them into the chocolate mixture using a metal spoon and a cutting and folding motion.

Spoon the mixture into six little dishes — tiny ramekins or wine glasses work well. Chill in the fridge, ideally overnight.

Tip

It's lovely served just as it is or you can decorate it with some whipped cream and toasted sliced almonds, chocolate curls or long thin strands of orange peel. To make the chocolate curls just run a potato peeler down the flat side of a bar of chocolate; for the orange strands, use a zester or peel off very thin pieces of rind and cut into thin lengths.

Vegan chocolate mousse

This tastes just like a conventional chocolate mousse made with eggs and cream and yet it's completely vegan! I don't think anyone will guess the main ingredient is avocado, unless you tell them. You can buy a tub of coconut oil, sometimes called coconut butter, from good health-food stores. It keeps well for months.

SERVES 6

10oz (300g) ripe avocado, weighed without skin and pit (about 2 really large ones)
4oz (125g) good-quality cocoa powder
2 tbsp coconut oil, such as Essential Organic Virgin Coconut Oil
7fl oz (200ml) agave or maple syrup
2 tsp vanilla extract
a pinch of salt

TO DECORATE

1–2 tbsp cacao nibs
a few fresh strawberries with their stems still attached

This recipe is made really quickly and easily with the aid of a food processor. Simply put all the ingredients into the machine and process until thick and smooth. You will need to open the food processor and push down the mixture from the sides a couple of times.

Spoon the mixture into small bowls and chill in the fridge until required: it will keep for several hours. Serve decorated with the cacao nibs and strawberries, whole or sliced into a fan with the stem still attached.

Refrigerator chocolate cake

Sweet, chocolatey, easy to make and even easier to eat.

SERVES 6–8

2 sticks (225g) unsalted butter, at room temperature
1 tbsp dark soft brown sugar
2 eggs, separated
8oz (225g) plain chocolate
2 tbsp sherry or rum (optional)
8oz (225g) semi-sweet (preferably wholewheat) cookies, lightly crushed

TO SERVE

5fl oz (150ml) whipped cream
2oz (50g) sliced almonds, toasted (see page 139)

Cream together the butter and sugar; when light and fluffy beat in the egg yolks.

Melt the chocolate as in the recipe for chocolate and orange mousse (see left), then add it to the butter and sugar mixture, along with the sherry or rum (if using) and beat well. Stir in the crushed cookies.

Whip the egg whites until stiff but not dry and gently fold into the chocolate mixture.

Line a square cake pan with baking parchment and spoon in the mixture. Smooth the top and chill in the fridge until firm.

To serve, turn out of the pan and spread with whipped cream. Scatter the nuts over the top.

Cheesecake on a chocolate crust

A delicious smooth cheesecake swirled with a sharp-tasting blackcurrant purée on a crisp crust of chocolate and nuts. It's easy to make and requires no baking.

SERVES 6

4oz (125g) graham crackers, crushed (see next recipe)
4oz (125g) dark chocolate, melted
2oz (50g) chopped mixed nuts
8oz (225g) smooth low-fat cream cheese
1¼ cups (275ml) heavy cream
1oz (25g) sugar
3 tbsp thick blackcurrant purée (made by blending then straining the drained contents of a 12oz jar of blackcurrants or 8oz (225g) fresh or frozen blackcurrants, cooked and sweetened to taste)
a little grated chocolate, to decorate

Put the crackers, chocolate and nuts into a bowl and mix together, then spread evenly in a 8in (20cm) spring-form cake pan with a removable bottom. Leave in a cool place while you make the filling.

Whip the cheese, cream and sugar together. Lightly mix in the blackcurrant purée, just swirling it rather than mixing it in too much.

Pour the topping over the crust. Chill in the fridge for at least 2 hours, preferably overnight.

Remove the sides of the pan and sprinkle with grated chocolate to decorate.

Strawberry cheesecake

This recipe makes a big, luscious cheesecake with a shiny strawberry topping. A wonderful pudding for a summer party.

SERVES 8–10

6oz (175g) graham crackers
6 tbsp (75g) butter, melted
12oz (350g) ricotta cheese
3 eggs
1 tsp vanilla essence
½ cup (125g) superfine sugar
5fl oz (150ml) sour cream

TOPPING

5fl oz (150ml) sour cream
1lb (450g) small ripe strawberries, hulled
6–8 tbsp redcurrant jelly

Preheat the oven to 300°F (150°C).

Put the graham crackers in a plastic bag on a board and crush them with a rolling pin, then mix them with the butter. Press the crumb mixture evenly into the base of a 8in (20cm) spring-form cake pan with a removable bottom. Leave in a cool place while you make the filling.

Blend or whisk together the ricotta, eggs, vanilla essence, sugar and sour cream until they are smooth and creamy. Pour the mixture into the pan on top of the crust.

Bake the cheesecake for 1½ hours or until it looks set and feels firm to a very light touch. Cool, then lightly beat the sour cream and spread over the top of the cheesecake. Chill in the fridge for 2–3 hours.

To finish the cheesecake, arrange the strawberries evenly over the top. Melt the redcurrant jelly in a small, heavy-based saucepan over a gentle heat, then pour over the strawberries in a thin layer to glaze.

Leave to cool, then carefully remove the cheesecake from the pan to serve.

Quick lemon curd cheesecake

This recipe, which I devised to use up some lemon curd, is fast and easy to make and has a wonderful creamy lemony flavor.

SERVES 6

6oz (175g) graham crackers
6 tbsp (75g) butter
8oz (225g) smooth low-fat cream cheese
6 tbsp good-quality lemon curd
5fl oz (150ml) heavy cream, whipped

Crush the crackers in a plastic bag with a rolling pin. Melt the butter and mix with the crumbs. Press the crumb mixture into a 8in (20cm) spring-form cake pan, or tart pan on a flat dish; leave in the fridge to become firm.

Mix the cream cheese with 4 tablespoons of the lemon curd and fold in the cream.

Spoon into the prepared pan, smooth the top and leave to set in the fridge. Glaze the top by spreading with the rest of the lemon curd, slightly warmed if necessary, before serving.

VARIATION

Uncooked strawberry cheesecake

Leave out the lemon curd and use ¼ cup (50g) superfine sugar instead. Top with 8oz (225g) ripe hulled strawberries, halved if necessary.

Quick strawberry cheesecake

Another fast cheesecake, flavored with lemon and topped with strawberries. It's the lemon juice that makes this dish work, because the acidity firms up the cream that holds it all together.

SERVES 6

6oz (175g) graham crackers
6 tbsp (75g) butter, melted
14oz (400g) smooth low-fat cream cheese
finely grated rind of 2 lemons
2 tbsp (25g) superfine sugar
5fl oz (150ml) heavy cream
¼ cup freshly squeezed lemon juice
8oz (225g) strawberries
confectioner's sugar, to sift
fresh mint leaves, to decorate

Put the crackers into a plastic bag, secure lightly then crush with a rolling pin. Transfer the crumbs to a bowl, add the melted butter and mix to combine.

Press the mixture into a 8–9in (20–23cm) spring-form cake pan with a removable bottom; don't attempt to go up the sides of the pan. Place in the freezer or fridge while you prepare the topping.

If there is a little liquid on top of the cream cheese, pour it away, then put the cheese into a bowl and add the lemon rind and sugar. Stir to make a creamy mixture, then add the cream and whisk until thick.

Add the lemon juice and stir with a spoon — the acid in the juice will make the mixture even thicker.

Spoon the cream cheese mixture into the pan. Take it to the edges but don't try to smooth the surface. Put it into the fridge until required.

To finish, top the cheesecake with strawberries, garnish with confectioner's sugar and transfer the cheesecake from the pan onto a pretty serving dish. Serve as soon as possible, decorated with mint leaves.

VARIATIONS

Quick lime cheesecake

This is delicious, too. Make as described, using the rind and juice of limes instead of lemons. I like this one served plain, without any fruit topping, just the flavor of the limes, the creamy cheese and the crunchy biscuits. If you wanted to make it a little special, you could melt some dark chocolate, put it into a plastic bag, snip a small piece off the corner and drizzle the chocolate in zigzags across the top.

Quick vegan cheesecake v

You can make a lovely vegan version of this cheesecake using pure vegetable margarine for the crust, vegan cream cheese, from a health-food store, and leaving out the double cream. The lemon juice isn't needed for "setting" this, so just add a teaspoonful or two for sharpness, and flavor it with the grated lemon rind, as described. Make sure the graham crackers you use for the base are vegan; there are many on the market from which to choose.

Coffee banoffi

This is rather a grown-up version of banoffi pie; the coffee balances the sweetness of the toffee and the Tia Maria gives it a warming kick. You can buy condensed milk that has already been caramelized (or *dulce de leche*) or you can make your own by boiling an unopened can of sweetened condensed milk in water to cover, for 2–4 hours: the longer you simmer it, the thicker it will be, but don't let it burn dry. Once done, this will keep for ages in your store cupboard.

SERVES 6–8
8oz (225g) graham crackers
1 stick (125g) butter, melted
1 tbsp strong instant coffee powder
   or granules
1 tbsp boiling water
1¼ cups (275ml) heavy cream
1 tbsp superfine sugar
6 tbsp Tia Maria
2–3 large bananas
14.5 can caramelised condensed
   milk, a jar of *dulce de leche* or
   normal condensed milk boiled as
   described above and cooled
chocolate-coated coffee beans, if
   available, or 2–3 tbsp grated dark
   chocolate, to decorate

Grease a 8–9in (20–23cm) tart pan with butter. Put the crackers into a plastic bag and crush with a rolling pin or in a food processor, then mix the crumbs with the melted butter. Press into the prepared pan and put into the fridge or freezer to chill for a minute or two while you prepare the rest of the ingredients.

Dissolve the instant coffee in the boiling water and set aside.

Whip the cream into soft peaks with the sugar, Tia Maria and dissolved instant coffee.

Remove the crust from the fridge or freezer. Peel the bananas and cut them into even-sized slices to fit your pan; lay them in position, covering the base. Spoon the caramel condensed milk or *dulce de leche* over the top of the bananas, then spoon the whipped coffee cream on top to cover everything. Keep in the fridge until required, then decorate with chocolate-coated coffee beans or grated dark chocolate and serve. If there's any left over, it will keep for several days in the fridge.

Dried fruit compôte in ginger wine v

You can buy dried fruit mixtures at health-food stores and in some supermarkets and they make a lovely dessert, especially if you stew the fruit and then marinate it in ginger wine, as in this recipe. (An alternative, if you don't want to use the wine, is to add some ground ginger or chopped stem ginger to the water.) Top it with a generous dollop of sharp-tasting thick natural yogurt, vegan sour cream or crème fraîche for a delicious blend of flavors and textures.

SERVES 4–6
1lb (450g) mixed dried fruit —
   apricots, peaches, pears, prunes
   and apple rings
5fl oz (150ml) ginger wine
thick Greek yogurt, vegan sour
   cream or crème fraîche, to serve
   (optional)

Put the dried fruit into a medium-sized saucepan, cover generously with cold water and, if possible, leave to soak for a couple of hours or so.

Simmer the fruit over a gentle heat, without a lid on the saucepan, for about 30 minutes or until it is very tender and the liquid has reduced to just a little glossy-looking syrup.

Remove from the heat and pour in the wine. Leave to cool, then chill in the fridge before serving.

It looks good in a glass bowl, or in individual glasses, topped with a swirl of cream or thick yogurt.

Fruit platter v

Perfect fresh fruits, served on a base of smoothly puréed ripe mango.

SERVES 4
1 ripe mango
5fl oz (150ml) water
2 kiwi fruit
2 ripe figs
4oz (125g) strawberries
4 sprigs of fresh mint, to decorate

To make the sauce, first remove the stone from the mango. The easiest way to do this is to stand the mango up with the stem end at the top. Then, using a sharp knife, cut down, right through the mango, about ¼in (6mm) away from the stem. The piece of mango will fall away, revealing the pit. Make another similar cut the other side. Then peel off the skin and cut the extra pieces of mango flesh away from the pit. Put all the mango flesh into a blender with the water and whip to a smooth purée. Add a little more water if necessary to get the right consistency. Chill in the fridge.

To assemble the dish, peel the kiwi fruit and slice into thin rings; cut the figs lengthways into quarters or eighths; hull the strawberries and halve if necessary.

Pour some of the mango sauce over the base of four flat serving plates. Arrange the kiwi slices, figs and strawberries on top. Decorate with a sprig of fresh mint and serve as soon as possible.

Easy exotic fruit salad v

In this fruit salad, orange juice is used instead of sugar syrup for a lighter, fresher result.

SERVES 4–6
1 small ripe pineapple
1 ripe mango
4 kiwi fruit
1 pawpaw
5fl oz (150ml) fresh orange juice

Cut the leafy top and prickly skin from the pineapple and remove the "eyes" with a sharp pointed knife.

Cut the pineapple into even-sized pieces and put into a bowl.

Halve the mango and remove the stone (see page 310) and peel. Cut the flesh into dice and add to the bowl.

Peel and slice the kiwi fruit, peel, seed, and slice the pawpaw. Add these to the bowl, together with the orange juice. Chill in the fridge before serving.

Easy summer fruit salad v

Apricots, peaches and strawberries soaked in orange juice, with or without a dash of orange liqueur, and chilled to make a luscious fruit salad. Just right for a hot summer's day.

SERVES 4
8oz (225g) ripe apricots
2–3 ripe peaches
8oz (225g) strawberries
5fl oz (150ml) fresh orange juice
thinly pared rind from ½ orange
1–2 tbsp Cointreau or other orange liqueur (optional)

Wash the apricots and peaches, halve the fruit and remove the stones. Slice the flesh fairly thinly.

Wash and hull the strawberries; halve or quarter any large ones so that they are all about the same size.

Put all the fruits into a pretty bowl and pour in the orange juice.

Snip the orange rind into thin slivers and add these to the fruit, together with the liqueur (if using). Chill in the fridge for 1 hour or so before serving, if possible.

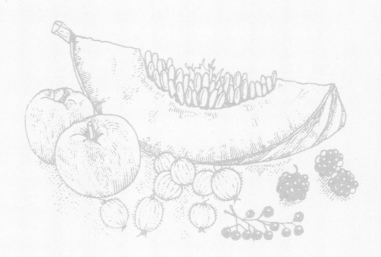

Easy winter fruit salad v

Winter is, surprisingly, a very good time for making a fruit salad: excellent apples such as Cox and Russet are easy to come by and there are plenty of good citrus fruits, and grapes. This is a simple refreshing salad, made with fruit juice instead of sugar syrup and is very good after you've eaten too many rich things at Christmas.

SERVES 4–6
2 large oranges
4 tangerines
2 large apples, preferably Cox
8oz (225g) black or green grapes
5fl oz (150ml) fresh orange juice

Cut the peel and pith off the oranges, cutting right into the flesh and holding them over a bowl to catch the juice. Then cut the segments away from the inner white skin. Put the segments into the bowl.

Peel the tangerines and divide into segments; peel, core and slice the apples; wash, halve and deseed the grapes. Add all these to the bowl, together with the orange juice and mix well. Chill in the fridge before serving.

Raspberry jelly v

Normal jelly and gelatine are unsuitable for vegetarians and vegans; we use a jelling agent made from agar, a type of seaweed. You can buy this in flake form from larger health-food stores; you can also buy vegetarian gelatine from the baking section of supermarkets. Vegetarian jelly crystals, in a variety of different fruit flavors, are available from any health-food store. They all set quickly and make a good jelly, though they tend to get cloudy if you put them in the fridge; and they're best eaten within a few hours of being made.

SERVES 4–6
1lb (450g) fresh or frozen raspberries
10oz carton raspberry and cranberry juice
¼ cup superfine sugar
¼oz packet vegetarian gelatine powder or 3–4 tsp agar flakes

TO DECORATE
whipped cream (optional)
shelled pistachio nuts, coarsely chopped

Divide the raspberries between four or six dishes.

Put the fruit juice and sugar into a large saucepan. Sprinkle the gelatine powder or flakes over the top of the cold liquid. Don't stir the flakes, but do stir the powder into the liquid.

Heat gently, until the powder or flakes have dissolved; don't rush this, it's best to do it slowly and may take 5 minutes if you're using flakes. Once it has dissolved, bring to the boil, boil for a few seconds, then remove from the heat.

Pour the jelly over the raspberries. Leave to cool, but do not refrigerate. Top the jellies with whipped cream (if using) and a scattering of pistachio nuts.

Tip
If you're using flavored jelly crystals, omit the fruit juice and sugar and just use 1¾ (400ml) boiling water and follow the packet directions, much like making a normal jelly. You will only need 5–6oz (150–175g) of raspberries for this version.

VARIATION
Apricot jelly with fresh apricots and strawberries v

For this jelly, use a type of apricot juice called "apricot nectar", which is available in a carton from large supermarkets, instead of the raspberry and cranberry juice. Replace the raspberries with six ripe apricots, halved and sliced, and a handful of sweet, ripe strawberries, hulled and sliced. Decorate with whipped cream and a small strawberry, or slice of strawberry, with its green leafy top still attached.

Fresh mango compôte v

If you can find some really ripe medium-sized mangoes, they make a wonderful dessert that's very simple to do. If you can find the fragrant little Alfonso mangoes, these are the best of all; they're tiny, so you'll need about ten of them. The mangoes need to feel soft to the touch; like avocados they will ripen if put into a paper bag and left for 2–3 days.

SERVES 4–6
5 medium-sized ripe mangoes

Wash the mangoes then stand them on a board with the stem end at the top. Slice each mango down from the top, cutting about ¼in (6mm) each side of the stem. Cut the skin from the two halves and from the flesh around the stones. Cut as much of the flesh away from around the stones as you can.

Dice all the flesh. Put a cupful of mango pieces into a blender or food processor with 1–2 cups of water or orange juice and whip to a purée. Add this to the rest of the mango pieces. Chill in the fridge before serving in glass bowls.

Fresh orange salad with honey and orange flower water v

One of the most refreshing desserts I know, this is delicious served well chilled. The orange flower water is optional; it can be bought at Middle Eastern stores and gives a fragrant, honeyed flavor to this dish.

SERVES 4–6
1 tbsp honey, preferably orange blossom, or use agave syrup, for a vegan version
2 tbsp boiling water
6 large oranges
5fl oz (150ml) fresh orange juice
2 tbsp orange flower water (optional)

Put the honey into a large bowl and mix with the boiling water until dissolved.

Scrub one of the oranges in warm water and pare off the peel with a potato peeler. Cut the peel into fine shreds and add to the honey and water.

Cut the peel and pith from the oranges, holding them over the bowl as you do so, to catch any juice. Cut the segments away from the inner skin and put them into the bowl. Squeeze the remaining skin over the bowl to extract any extra juice.

Add the 5fl oz (150ml) orange juice to the oranges in the bowl, together with the orange flower water (if using). Stir well, then chill in the fridge before serving.

Pashka

A traditional Easter dish from Russia where it's made in a special tall pyramid-shaped mould and decorated with the initials "XB" for "Christ is Risen." I use a 6in (15cm) clay flower pot that I scrubbed and baked in a hot oven to sterilize. Pashka needs to be prepared several hours before you want to eat it to allow time for the liquid to drain away through the hole in the flower pot, leaving the mixture firm enough to turn out. It's delicious served with macaroons or slices of Madeira cake.

SERVES 6
2 egg yolks
3oz (75g) vanilla sugar — or superfine sugar and a drop or two of vanilla essence
¼ cup ½ and ½ or whole milk
1½lb (700g) ricotta cheese
1 stick (125g) unsalted butter, softened
2oz (50g) chopped candied fruits
2oz (50g) blanched almonds, chopped
a little chopped glacé fruit and edible spring flowers, to decorate

Beat the egg yolks and sugar together until they're pale and foamy. Put the cream or creamy milk into a small saucepan and bring it just to a boil, then pour it over the egg yolks and sugar. Pour the whole lot back into the saucepan and stir over a gentle heat until it has thickened — this won't take a moment, so watch it carefully. Leave on one side to cool.

Beat together the cheese and butter; add the candied fruits and nuts and finally the cooled custard.

Line your 6in (15cm) flower pot with a double layer of dampened muslin or cheesecloth, spoon in the pashka mixture and smooth the top. Fold the ends of the muslin over the top, cover with a saucer and a weight and leave in a cool place or the fridge for several hours, preferably overnight. Some moisture will seep out of the hole in the base of the flower pot so stand it on a plate.

To serve the dessert, invert the flower pot onto a serving dish, turn out the pashka and carefully peel off the muslin. Decorate with the glacé fruit and edible spring flowers such as primroses and violets.

Peach brûlée

A very popular dessert that's quick and simple to prepare, and convenient because it is best made in advance.

SERVES 6

6 large ripe peaches
2–3 tbsp orange, peach or apricot liqueur (optional)
1¼ cups (275ml) heavy cream
demerara sugar

Put the peaches into a bowl and cover with boiling water. Leave for 2 minutes, then drain the peaches and slip off the skins with a sharp knife.

Halve, pit and thinly slice the peaches. Put the slices into a flameproof shallow dish and sprinkle with the liqueur (if using).

Whip the cream until it stands in soft peaks, then spoon this on top of the peaches, smoothing it evenly over them.

Cover with an even layer of demerara sugar. Heat the broiler to high, then put the peach mixture under the broiler until the sugar melts. Or use a kitchen blow torch if you have one.

Remove from the heat; cool, then chill in the fridge for several hours before serving.

VARIATION
Vegan peach brûlée v

Make as described, using a 8oz tub of Sour Supreme vegan sour cream instead of the cream. Chill thoroughly in the fridge after broiling or blasting the sugar.

Peaches in strawberry purée v

This dish consists of juicy, ripe peach slices bathed in a pink strawberry purée — a perfect way of using frozen strawberries.

SERVES 6

6 large, ripe peaches — white ones are best if they're available
2 tbsp freshly squeezed lemon juice
1lb (450g) ripe strawberries
2oz (50g) sugar

Cover the peaches with boiling water; leave for 2 minutes, then drain. Slip the skins off using a sharp knife.

Halve the peaches and remove the pits, then slice the flesh. Put the slices into a pretty glass bowl or six individual ones and sprinkle with half the lemon juice to preserve the color.

Wash and hull the strawberries. Put into a blender with the rest of the lemon juice and reduce to a purée. Press the mixture through a sieve, to make it really smooth, then add the sugar gradually — taste the mixture as you may not need it all.

Pour the strawberry purée over the peaches or pour a pool of purée onto individual serving plates and arrange the peach slices on top.

VARIATION
Pears in raspberry purée v

Peel whole pears — really ripe Comice ones, if you can get them. If you can't find perfect pears, suitable for serving raw, then poach them as described for vanilla poached pears next page. Make the sauce as described but use raspberries instead of strawberries.

Peaches in white wine

This is a simple yet very delicious pudding. Make it in the summer when peaches are cheap and good. You can also make this using red grape juice instead of wine.

SERVES 6

6 ripe peaches
1¼ cups (275ml) sweet white wine
2 tsp sugar

Put the peaches into a bowl and cover with boiling water. Leave for 2 minutes, then drain. Remove the skins with a sharp knife and cut the peaches into thin slices, discarding the stones.

Put the peach slices into a glass serving bowl. Mix the wine with the sugar and pour over the peaches. Chill in the fridge before serving.

Pears in red wine v

These pears, cooked whole and deeply stained by the red wine, make a gorgeous pudding. Serve them hot or cold, with whipped cream that's been lightly flavored with cinnamon and the almond tuiles on page 356.

SERVES 6

½ cup (125g) sugar
1¼ cups (275ml) water
1¼ cups (275ml) red wine
a few drops of red vegetable food
   coloring (optional)
6 ripe pears
whipped cream flavored with a little
   sugar and ground cinnamon
   (optional)

Put the sugar, water and wine into a heavy-based saucepan and heat gently until the sugar has dissolved. Then boil rapidly for 2 minutes. Add a drop or two of red vegetable food coloring: this is optional, but gives such a pretty result.

Peel the pears, keeping them whole and leaving the stems on. Put them into the syrup and let them cook gently, with a lid on the pan, for 30 minutes (or longer if necessary) — they must be really tender right through. You can intensify the color of the pears by adding a drop or two more food coloring as necessary.

Remove the pears to a shallow serving dish. Thicken the cooking liquid if necessary by boiling rapidly without a lid until reduced to 3–4 tablespoons; spoon over the pears.

Vanilla poached pears v

Make as described, using double the amount of water and omitting the red wine and food coloring. Add a vanilla pod to the water in the pan, for delicious, meltingly tender pears delicately flavored with vanilla.

Pineapple and grape compôte v

1 large ripe pineapple
4oz (125g) green grapes
4oz (125g) black grapes
2 tbsp honey or agave syrup
2 tbsp orange juice or Grand Marnier
   orange liqueur

Remove the prickly skin and spiky top from the pineapple. Cut the flesh into neat dice, removing and discarding the hard core.

Halve the grapes and remove any pips.

Arrange the fruit in a large glass bowl, pour over the honey or agave syrup and orange juice or Grand Marnier, and turn once or twice to mix.

Leave for at least 2 hours in the fridge. Serve as it is or with cream or thick yogurt.

Mocha meringue gâteau

This recipe appeared in my first book, *Simply Delicious*, and people still ask me for it! It's lovely for a party and the great joy is that, unlike most meringue gâteaux, you can make it well in advance; in fact, it's best made the day before.

SERVES 4

2 egg whites
½ cup (4oz) superfine sugar
2 tsp instant coffee

FOR THE FILLING
3oz (75g) plain chocolate
1 stick (125g) butter, softened
2 egg yolks
½ cup (125g) granulated sugar
5fl oz (150ml) water
1oz (25g) grated chocolate

Preheat the oven to 225°F (110°C).

Draw three 6in (15cm) circles on baking parchment and place on one or more baking sheets.

To make the meringue, whisk the egg whites until they are standing in stiff peaks, then whisk in the sugar and coffee.

Spread the mixture over the circles on the parchment paper and bake in the very cool oven for 3 hours or until they are thoroughly dried out. Allow to cool, then carefully remove the meringue circles from the paper.

Meanwhile make the chocolate cream filling. Break the 3oz (15cm) chocolate into pieces and put into a bowl over a pan of boiling water to melt, or melt it in the microwave if you prefer.

Beat the butter until very light, then beat in the egg yolks and melted chocolate.

Put the granulated sugar and water into a saucepan and heat until the thread stage is reached — 215-235°F (108-118°C); that is, when a drop of the mixture forms thread when you put it between two teaspoons and pull them apart.

Allow the syrup to cool slightly, then very gradually add it, drop by drop at first, to the butter cream, beating all the time.

Place one meringue circle on a serving plate and cover with half the chocolate cream. Place the second meringue circle on top, and cover with the rest of the chocolate cream. Finally, place the third meringue circle on top and scatter with the grated chocolate.

This is best made the day before it is required and kept in the fridge.

Raspberry meringue gâteau

This is a superbly rich and indulgent pudding that's ideal for a special occasion. It's also delicious made with sweet ripe blackberries, either freshly picked or frozen.

SERVES 6

3 egg whites
¾ cup (175g) superfine sugar
1¼ cups (275ml) double cream
12oz (350g) raspberries, fresh or
    frozen and thawed
confectioner's sugar, to sift

Preheat the oven to 250°F (120°C). First make the meringue. Whisk the egg whites until they stand in stiff peaks, then whisk in half the sugar to make a smooth, glossy mixture. Fold in the rest of the sugar using a metal spoon.

Draw two circles, 8in (20cm) in diameter (use a plate as a template), on baking parchment placed on top of two baking sheets.

Spoon the meringue to cover the circles in an even layer and bake in a very cool oven for 2–3 hours or until crisp and dry but not brown.

Leave the meringue circles to cool completely, then peel off the paper. Store in an airtight container until required for filling. They will keep for a week or more.

To fill the meringue, put one of the layers on a flat serving dish. Whip the cream until standing in soft peaks.

Spread half of the cream mixture over the meringue and top with half the raspberries.

Cover with the other meringue circle and the rest of the cream and raspberries and sift a little confectioner's sugar over the top. Serve as soon as possible.

VARIATION
Raspberry pavlova

For this lovely variation with its crisp outside and marshmallowy center, preheat the oven to 350°F (180°C). Whisk 4 egg whites until they stand in stiff peaks. Use 1 cup (225g) superfine sugar mixed with 2 teaspoons of cornstarch, and whisk into the egg whites in 2–3 batches, resulting in a beautiful, glossy meringue mixture. Finally stir in 1 teaspoon of red or white wine vinegar and 1 teaspoon of vanilla extract. Spoon the whole of the mixture onto baking parchment in a 8–9in (20–23cm) circle. Put into the preheated oven then turn the setting down to 300°F (150°C) and bake for 1¼ hours or until crisp. Leave the pavlova to cool in the oven if possible. Heap the whipped cream and raspberries on top and sift confectioner's sugar over the top.

Stawberries with coeurs à la crème

Hearts of cream cheese surrounded by shiny red strawberries is a classic and beautiful French summery pudding. You need to start making the hearts the night before you want to serve them. The quantities I've given are right for six white heart-shaped china dishes with small holes in the base. Alternatively, you can make some holes in the base of cream, yogurt or small cottage cheese cartons and use these; I've also used a colander successfully. And if you can't get muslin or cheesecloth to line the molds, paper towels or pieces of gauze from the drug store make good substitutes.

SERVES 6

1lb 10oz (750g) ricotta cheese
6fl oz (175ml) heavy cream
3 tbsp superfine sugar, plus extra for
    sprinkling
1lb 2oz (500g) strawberries

Put the cheese into a large bowl, mix it with the cream and sugar and beat with a wooden spoon until the mixture thickens and holds its shape.

Line your white china dishes, yogurt, cream or cottage cheese pots, or colander, with muslin or cheesecloth, then spoon in the creamy mixture and smooth the surface.

Stand the containers or the colander on a plate to catch the liquid that will drain off and place them in the fridge overnight.

Summer pudding v

Next day wash and hull the strawberries, halving or quartering any larger ones as necessary. Then sprinkle them lightly with sugar and leave on one side.

To serve, turn the creamy cheese mixture out onto a large plate and carefully peel off the muslin. Arrange the strawberries round the cheese or cheeses.

Don't assemble this dish until just before you need it or the juice from the strawberries can spoil the look of it. It's a good way of making a few strawberries go further.

This is one of those dishes that is easy to make, and best done well ahead of time. It looks beautiful and is always popular. Try and use an assortment of fruits, with some, but not too many, blackberries, so you end up with a pretty ruby color.

SERVES 4–6
1½lb (700g) red fruit — raspberries, redcurrants, blackcurrants and strawberries, as available
4oz (125g) superfine sugar or honey
8–10 thin slices of thin white bread, crusts removed

Wash the fruit, removing stems and stalks as necessary.

Put the fruit into a large heavy-based saucepan with the sugar or honey and heat gently until the sugar has dissolved and the juices are running. Remove from the heat.

Lightly grease a 3½ cups (1 litre) pudding basin or bowl. Soak pieces of bread in the juice from the fruit, then arrange in the basin or bowl to completely cover the base and sides.

Spoon the fruit in on top of the bread and cover with more bread to make a lid. Place a saucer and a weight on top and leave in the fridge for several hours, or overnight if possible.

To serve, dip the basin in very hot water, slip a knife around the edge of the pudding, then invert over a plate. Serve with whipped cream (if desired).

VARIATION
Individual summer puddings v

You can make this in 4–6 individual dishes, in which case you'll need more slices of bread and they need to be really thin — best to cut them yourself from a 2–3-day-old loaf of bread — as the proportion of bread to fruit will be higher and you want to end up with a generous amount of sweet and juicy fruit.

Trifle

A traditional trifle is a delicious, light dessert that's well worth the effort.

SERVES 6–8

1 small sponge cake or 6–8 soft ladyfingers
3 tbsp raspberry jam
¼ cup fino sherry (optional)
3 eggs
¼ cup (2oz) superfine sugar — vanilla sugar if you have it, otherwise add a few drops of vanilla essence
2 cups (575ml) milk
9fl oz (250ml) heavy cream
1oz (25g) toasted sliced almonds

Split the sponge cake and sandwich with the jam, then cut into smaller pieces. Put the pieces of sponge into the base of a glass serving dish and pour the sherry over. Leave to one side. Whisk the eggs and sugar together in a bowl; put the milk into a saucepan and bring it just to a boil, then pour it over the egg mixture and whisk again.

Strain the mixture back into the saucepan and stir over a gentle heat for just a minute or two until it thickens. Don't let it overcook or it will separate. If this does happen I've found if I whip in the blender or with an electric hand blender at a high speed, amazingly, it seems to be all right again.

Pour the custard over the sponge pieces and leave on one side to cool.

To finish the trifle, whip the cream until it's softly thickened, then spoon it over the top of the trifle. Chill the trifle in the fridge, then sprinkle the almonds over the top just before you serve it, so that they're still crisp.

Apple and honey ice cream with blackberry sauce

Apples and blackberries are one of those classic pairings and this is a different way of putting them together. The pale green ice looks pretty with the vivid deep red sauce.

SERVES 4

8oz (225g) cooking apples, peeled, cored and sliced
3 tbsp honey
1 tsp grated lemon rind
11fl oz (300ml) heavy cream
8oz (225g) blackberries
1 tbsp sugar

Put the apples and honey into a heavy-based saucepan and cook gently until pulpy. Then stir in the lemon rind, purée in a food processor, blender or with an electric hand blender and cool.

Whip the cream until it forms soft peaks, then fold into the cooled purée.

Pour the mixture into a suitable container and freeze until firm, beating once or twice during freezing, or freeze in an ice cream maker according to the manufacturer's instructions.

To make the sauce, put the blackberries into a heavy-based saucepan, cook gently for 10 minutes until pulpy, then add the sugar, blend and sieve. Chill in the fridge.

Remove the ice cream from the freezer 30 minutes before serving; spoon into individual glasses and pour the sauce on top.

Easiest-ever ice cream

This is ridiculously easy to make, very smooth and creamy, loved by everyone and freezes perfectly without stirring. What's not to like?

SERVES 4

2 cups (575ml) heavy cream
14oz can low-fat sweetened condensed milk

Whisk the cream, with an electric whisk for speed and ease, though you can do it by hand, until soft peaks form.

Add the condensed milk to the cream and whisk again until combined.

Pour into a suitable container — a rigid plastic box is ideal — and freeze until firm.

Remove the ice cream from the freezer for 15 minutes or so before you want to serve it.

VARIATION

Easiest-ever chocolate ice cream

This is a beautiful rich chocolate ice cream. Make as described, adding 11oz (300g) plain dark chocolate, melted, to the mixture when you add the cream. I sometimes use this chocolate ice cream as the basis for an iced "Christmas Pudding", by adding some raisins and chopped candied fruit which have been soaked in fino sherry, along with some sliced almonds, and freezing it in a plastic container.

Strawberry and cashew nut ice cream v

This tastes rich and creamy, yet is totally non-dairy.

SERVES 4–6
8oz (225g) cashew nuts
11fl oz (300ml) water
8oz (225g) strawberries, hulled
1 tbsp agave syrup, or to taste

Put the cashew nuts and water in a food processor or blender and whip to a cream.

Add the strawberries and agave syrup and whip again.

Freeze in an ice cream maker, following the manufacturer's instructions. Alternatively, pour into a plastic container and freeze until solid.

Remove from the deep freeze a good 30 minutes before you want to eat it.

Blackcurrant sorbet with cassis v

It's the cassis that gives this recipe a pleasant "kick", but you could leave it out!

SERVES 4–6
1lb (450g) fresh or frozen blackcurrants
5fl oz (150ml) water
½ cup (125g) sugar
1 egg white (optional)
6 tbsp cassis
a little lightly whipped cream, to serve (optional)

Put the blackcurrants and water into a saucepan, cook gently for 10–15 minutes until soft, then add the sugar. Blend, then sieve. Reserve 3 tablespoons of the purée.

Pour the rest of the mixture into a suitable container and freeze until solid around the edges or put it into an ice cream maker and follow the manufacturer's instructions.

If you're making the sorbet without an ice cream maker, you can make it lighter by adding egg white before the mixture freezes completely. Whisk the egg white until stiff and whisk into the semi-frozen blackcurrant purée to make a fluffy mixture. Pour the mixture back into the container and freeze again until solid.

Make a simple sauce by mixing the reserved purée with the cassis.

Take the sorbet out of the freezer 30 minutes before eating. Serve in individual glasses with sauce on top and cream (if using).

VARIATION
Strawberry sorbet v

I think this sorbet is one way of making the best of the frozen strawberries, because for this their mushiness is actually an advantage. Make as described, using fresh or frozen strawberries instead of the blackcurrants and without the cassis; you could use an orange liqueur instead if you wished.

Melon sorbet with crystallized mint leaves v

This is prettiest if you can find two small melons with flesh of contrasting colors, orange and pale green. Make the sorbet in two separate containers and put a spoonful of both in each bowl. Leave out the mint leaves if you haven't time to do them; but they are pretty for a special occasion and can be made in advance and stored in an airtight tin.

SERVES 6

2 small ripe melons, if possible one with orange flesh and one with green, each weighing about 1½lb (700g)
2 tbsp freshly squeezed lemon juice
¼ cup (50g) sugar
2 egg whites (optional)

FOR THE MINT LEAVES
20 fresh mint leaves
1 egg white
granulated sugar

Halve the melons, take out the seeds and then scoop all the flesh from the skins, keeping the two colors separate.

Blend each batch of scooped-out melon flesh, add half the lemon juice and half the sugar to each, then taste and add a little more sugar if necessary.

Pour the two mixtures into separate containers, then freeze as described for the blackcurrant sorbet (see page 337). Whisk the egg whites until stiff and add half to each container to lighten the mixture if you're not using an ice cream maker.

About an hour before you want to eat the sorbets, take them out of the freezer and put them in the fridge to give them time to soften a little.

Put alternate spoonfuls of each color in individual glasses and decorate with the mint leaves.

To make the mint leaves, brush them all over with egg white then dip them into the sugar, coating them on both sides. Lay them on baking parchment and put them into a very cool oven, 250°F (120°C) for about 2 hours to dry out, until they are crisp and brittle. Cool, then store in an airtight tin until needed.

Pineapple sorbet v

Here a pineapple is halved and the flesh made into a sorbet, served in the skin and decorated with fresh strawberries.

SERVES 6

1 large ripe pineapple
½ cup (125g) sugar
2 cups (575ml) water
1 egg white (optional)
8oz (225g) small, ripe strawberries, hulled

Halve the pineapple from top to bottom, cutting right through the leaves. Scoop out the flesh, discarding the hard core.

Heat the sugar and water gently in a pan until the sugar has dissolved, then boil for 2 minutes.

Blend the pineapple with this sugar syrup. Leave to cool.

Freeze the mixture in an ice cream maker, following the manufacturer's directions.

Alternatively, pour it into a shallow container and freeze until solid around the edges. Whisk the egg white, then add the pineapple mixture, and whisk until well blended. Put the sorbet back into the freezer until it is solid.

About 30 minutes before you want to eat the sorbet, take it out of the freezer to soften. I often give it a good whisking at this point or even whip it in the food processor to make it really light and smooth.

Spoon the sorbet into the pineapple skins, decorate with strawberries and serve at once.

Opposite: Blackcurrant sorbet with cassis
(see page 337)

Yogurt

Making yogurt is easy once you get organised, and if you eat a lot of it, you can certainly save money. You'll probably find you need to buy a fresh pot every three or four times you make it, otherwise just save a little from the previous batch to start the next. When you're making yogurt you can make a very simple dessert by putting some of the mixture into little individual ramekins; it will set beautifully and get firm as it chills. Then all you have to do is top it with some maple syrup, honey, chopped nuts, granola, preserved ginger or sugar-free jam before serving. Make sure your yogurt "starter" really is live; most of the yogurt sold in supermarkets isn't. Read the carton carefully or go to your health-food store.

MAKES 575ML (1 PINT)
2 cups (575ml) skimmed milk
2 rounded tbsp skimmed milk
    powder
1 tsp fresh natural yogurt — from a
    carton or from your last batch

Put the milk into a saucepan and bring up to a boil, then leave to simmer gently without a lid for 10 minutes. This reduces the milk slightly and helps to make the yogurt thick and creamy.

Remove the saucepan from the heat and leave until the milk is lukewarm. Meanwhile, wash a couple of jars and sterilize them as described on page 317.

Whisk the skimmed milk powder and the yogurt into the milk then pour it into your clean jars, cover with foil and leave in a warm place for a few hours or overnight until it's firm. Near a radiator is a good place, or in an airing cupboard.

Allow the yogurt to cool, then put it into the fridge to chill and firm up.

Vegan yogurt v

MAKES 575ML (1 PINT)
2 cups (575ml) soy milk
yogurt starter culture (from health-
    food stores)

Any yogurt culture will work as well on soy milk as it does on dairy milk.

Put the soy milk into a saucepan and bring to a boil, then cool to lukewarm.

Add the starter as directed on the packet and stir well.

Pour the mixture into a thermos flask or large jar or bowl which has been sterilized by being rinsed out with boiling water.

Cover the jar or bowl with cling film or foil and wrap in a warm towel. Leave in a warm place for 5–8 hours or until set, then chill in the fridge.

This first batch will not be 100 per cent vegan, but a tablespoon of this can be used to start the next batch, which will be. The yogurt gets thicker and better each time.

Yogurt glory

Vanilla fudge

If you like yogurt, this is a mouth-watering way of serving it, in a tall glass to look like a pink and white-striped candy cane. It looks far more calorific than it really is and is a treat for dieters.

A lovely fudge, which is easy to make and popular with everyone.

SERVES 2
1 banana
4fl oz (125ml) raspberry,
    blackcurrant or strawberry yogurt
    (preferably without artificial
    flavoring or coloring)
4fl oz (125ml) low-fat natural yogurt
5oz (15g) hazelnuts, roasted
    (see page 139) and chopped

MAKES 600G (1¼LB)
1 stick (4oz) butter
14oz can sweetened condensed milk
1lb 2oz (500g) superfine sugar
a few drops of vanilla essence

Peel the banana and slice thinly.

Spoon a little of the flavored yogurt into the base of two tall glasses, then add some banana slices.

Top with a layer of natural yogurt followed by more of the fruit yogurt. Continue in this way until all the ingredients are used up.

Sprinkle the nuts on top and serve at once.

Line a 8in (20cm) square pan with baking parchment.

Put the butter into a large, heavy-based saucepan. Add the condensed milk and sugar and heat gently, stirring until the sugar has dissolved. Raise the heat and boil for 5 minutes, stirring all the time, until the fudge starts to come away from the sides of the pan and a little dropped into a cup of cold water forms a soft ball. During this time brown specks will rise to the top, gradually dispersing to create a caramel color.

Remove the fudge from the heat, add a few drops of vanilla essence, beat with a wooden spoon until it becomes grainy and begins to set, then pour into the pan. When cool, mark it into squares. Cut into squares when it is completely cold.

Baking

Is there anything more satisfying than time spent baking? I love being in my warm kitchen with the radio on, a mug of tea by my side and the air full of the scent of warm sugar, spices, and vanilla. It's soothing to the soul and nurturing to the spirit and at the end of
it you've got something delicious to share with others.

The recipes I like the best are those that are easy and undemanding yet give excellent results every time. The ones in this chapter range from light springy sponges, little buns, and cupcakes to Christmas cake (see page 348). There are lots of favorites, such as flapjacks, chocolate chip cookies, fast and wonderful chocolate brownies, and millionaire's shortbread (see pages 360, 358, 347, and 362).

Whenever I can I use wholegrain flour; I particularly like wholegrain spelt flour. For lighter results, I'll use light brown flour (available from some supermarkets) or mix wholegrain with unbleached organic white flour. My favorite sugars are treacly unrefined muscovado or golden superfine sugar when a lighter one is needed; and for fats, butter (salted is fine for baking, unsalted for icings) or mild-flavored olive oil.

Icing, fillings, and toppings

Traditional almond paste

It's very easy to make your own almond paste and it tastes far better than any you can buy.

ENOUGH TO COVER ONE 8–9IN (20–23CM) ROUND CAKE ❋
1lb (450g) ground almonds
8oz (225g) superfine sugar
8oz (225g) confectioner's sugar
1 tsp freshly squeezed lemon juice
a few drops of almond extract
2 eggs, beaten

Put the ground almonds and superfine sugar into a bowl, then sift in the confectioner's sugar and mix together.

Add the lemon juice, almond extract, and enough egg (you may not need it all) to make a smooth, firm paste. Knead lightly; use immediately.

Cream cheese icing

You can use honey instead of the confectioner's sugar; this will make a creamy icing, whereas the confectioner's sugar version will firm up a little more. I sometimes make it without the butter and this, too, gives a softer result.

ENOUGH TO FILL AND TOP ONE 7IN (18CM) ROUND CAKE
4oz (125g) low-fat cream cheese
1oz (25g) confectioner's sugar
a few drops of vanilla extract
2 tbsp (25g) unsalted butter, softened

Beat all the ingredients together until smooth and creamy.

Maple almond paste v

Although this doesn't contain sugar, it tastes like conventional almond paste and can be used similarly. It's also vegan.

MAKES 12OZ (350G) ❋
4 tbsp (50g) unsalted pure vegetable margarine
1 tbsp maple syrup
2 tsp freshly squeezed lemon juice
4oz (125g) rice flour
4oz (125g) ground almonds
a few drops of almond extract

Mix all the ingredients together, flavoring with a little almond essence. Handle the mixture lightly to prevent the almonds becoming oily.

Fudge icing

A delicious icing with a fudgy consistency, and it's very easy to make.

ENOUGH TO TOP AND FILL ONE 7IN (18CM) ROUND CAKE
3 tbsp (40g) butter, softened
2 tbsp water
6oz (175g) confectioner's sugar
a few drops of vanilla extract

Heat the butter and water gently until the butter melts. Remove from the heat and sift in the confectioner's sugar. Add the vanilla extract and beat well. The icing will thicken up as it cools.

The flavor can be varied as for simple buttercream (see next page).

Glacé icing

ENOUGH TO COAT THE TOP OF ONE 7IN (18CM) ROUND CAKE
4oz (125g) confectioner's sugar
1–2 tbsp warm water

Sift the confectioner's sugar into a bowl, then add the water and beat until smooth and glossy. Use at once.

Simple buttercream

ENOUGH TO TOP AND FILL ONE
7IN (18CM) ROUND CAKE
½ stick (50g) butter, softened
4oz (125g) confectioner's sugar,
    sifted, or soft dark brown sugar
1–2 tbsp hot water

Beat the butter until light, then add
the confectioner's sugar or soft
dark brown sugar and beat again,
adding enough water to make a
light consistency.

VARIATIONS

Chocolate buttercream

Add 2oz (50g) of melted chocolate
or 1 tablespoon cocoa dissolved in
the hot water.

Coffee buttercream

Add 2 teaspoons of instant coffee
dissolved in the hot water.

Orange or lemon
buttercream

Add the grated rind of an orange
or lemon and mix with orange or
lemon juice instead of water.

Reduced sugar buttercream

Replace 2oz (50g) of the sugar with
2oz (50g) dried skimmed milk
powder or granules; beat well until
smooth.

Royal icing

Traditional royal icing is very easy
to make. A little glycerine, which
can be found in drug stores or cake
decorating and craft shops, is
usually added to prevent it from
setting too hard. If you want to use
this, you'll need to check the
particular brand to make sure it is
vegetarian. The icing is perfectly all
right without glycerine as long as
you eat it fairly soon so that it
doesn't have a chance to get hard.
Alternatively, you could spread
bought fondant icing onto your
cake instead.

ENOUGH TO ICE TOP AND SIDES
OF ONE 8–9IN (20–23CM)
ROUND CAKE
2lb (900g) confectioner's sugar
4 egg whites
1 tbsp freshly squeezed lemon juice
2 tsp glycerine (optional)

Sift the confectioner's sugar. Put
the egg whites into a bowl and
whisk until just frothy, then add the
confectioner's sugar a little at a
time, beating well after each
addition. When about half has been
added, beat in the lemon juice.
When all the confectioner's sugar
has been added, beat in the
glycerine (if using).

Cakes

Almond and cherry ring

A pretty ring-shaped cake that is easy to make.

MAKES ONE 8IN (20CM) ROUND CAKE ✽
1¼ cups (150g) self-raising flour
5oz (150g) glacé cherries
1½ sticks (175g) butter
¾ cup (175g) superfine sugar
3 eggs, beaten
5oz (150g) ground almonds
a few drops of almond extract
1 quantity of glacé icing (see page 345)
1oz (25g) toasted sliced almonds

Preheat the oven to 350°F (180°C). Line a 8in (20cm) ring pan using strips of baking parchment.

Sift the flour. Rinse the cherries; slice half of them and keep to one side. Chop the remainder.

Cream the butter and sugar until light, then gradually beat in the eggs.

Fold in the flour, ground almonds, chopped cherries, and extract.

Spoon into the pan, smooth the top and bake for 55–60 minutes.

Remove from the pan, strip off the paper and leave to cool. Spoon the icing over the top of the cake and decorate with the reserved sliced cherries and toasted almonds.

VARIATION
Rose ring

This makes a very pretty cake and is easy to do. Cook as above, but leave out the cherries. Make the glacé icing using triple-distilled rose water instead of water or a few drops of rose extract, and color it pink. Spoon the icing over the cake and arrange a bunch of tiny pink garnet roses in the center.

Fast and wonderful chocolate brownies

Measuring, melting, and stirring are all that's required to make these brownies. Put them into the oven before you sit down to eat and they'll be ready for dessert, all warm and gooey. Serve with cream, ice cream, or thick natural yogurt.

MAKES ABOUT 15 BROWNIES
7 tbsp (100g) butter, in rough pieces
3½oz (100g) plain chocolate, broken into pieces
1 cup (225g) packed light soft brown sugar
2 eggs, beaten
1¼ cups (150g) self-raising flour
1 tsp vanilla extract
3½oz (100g) walnut pieces or roughly chopped pecans
3½oz (100g) milk or plain chocolate chips or chocolate cut into small chips

Preheat the oven to 350°F (180°C). Line the base and sides of a 8in (20cm) square pan with baking parchment.

Melt the butter and chocolate in a saucepan over a gentle heat. Remove from the heat and stir in the sugar, eggs, flour, and vanilla extract. Beat together until smooth, then stir in the nuts and chocolate chips or chocolate.

Pour into the pan and bake for about 30 minutes — the brownies will be firm at the edges and still soft in the middle. If you want them a bit firmer, bake for 5 minutes longer.

Leave to cool for a few minutes, then cut into slices. Remove from the pan with a spatula.

Little buns

MAKES 15 BUNS ✽
1⅓ cups (175g) self-raising flour
1 tsp baking powder
1 stick (125g) butter, softened
½ cup (125g) superfine or dark soft brown sugar
2 eggs
1–2 tbsp water

Preheat the oven to 375°F (190°C). Fill a muffin tin with paper liners.

Make an all-in-one sponge mix as described on page 353 and divide the mixture between the cake liners, half-filling them.
Bake for 10–15 minutes or until golden brown. Cool on a wire rack.

VARIATIONS
Cupcakes

Ice the little buns thickly with a double quantity of buttercream (see opposite) and make them really pretty with whatever decorations you fancy — chocolate drops, little sweets, sugar flowers.

Butterfly cakes

Make buns as above. When they are cold, cut a thin slice from the top of each, then cut each slice in half and leave to one side. Spoon or pipe a dollop of buttercream on top of each cake, then press the two cut pieces on top like butterfly wings. Pipe or spoon any remaining buttercream decoratively between the "wings." Dredge with confectioner's sugar.

Christmas cake

This is our traditional family Christmas cake recipe.

MAKES ONE 8IN (20CM) ROUND CAKE ❄

1½ cups (175g) plain wholewheat flour
1 tsp pie spice
1½ sticks (175g) butter, softened
¾ cup (175g) packed soft dark brown sugar
5 eggs, beaten
1 tbsp molasses
juice and grated rind of 1 lemon
1½lb (700g) mixed dried fruit
3oz (75g) glacé pineapple, chopped
4oz)125g) glacé cherries, halved
3oz (75g) ground almonds
1½oz (40g) blanched almonds, chopped
1 tbsp brandy

FOR THE TOPPING
3 tbsp apricot jam
1 quantity of almond paste (see page 345)
1 quantity of royal icing (see page 346) or pack fondant icing (optional)
silver balls and other items or glacé fruit, to decorate

Preheat the oven to 275°F (140°C). Line a 8in (20cm) round cake pan with baking parchment and tie a piece of brown paper around the outside, securing it with string. That will prevent the cake from overcooking at the edges before the center is done.

Sift the flour and spice into a bowl, adding also the residue of bran left in the sieve.

Cream the butter and sugar until light and fluffy; then gradually beat in the eggs. If the mixture shows signs of curdling, add a spoonful of flour. Stir in the molasses, then fold in the flour.

Gently mix in the lemon juice and rind, the dried and glacé fruit and nuts.

Put the mixture into the pan, hollowing the center slightly.

Bake for 4½–5 hours, then cool on a wire rack.

Prick the top of the cake and sprinkle with brandy. Wrap in greaseproof paper, store in a pan until you want to ice it. This cake improves with keeping, and you can "feed" it with another spoonful or so of brandy after a week or so.

Put on the almond paste 7–10 days before Christmas. First, make sure the cake is level: trim with a bread knife if necessary.

Sieve the apricot jam and melt gently in a small saucepan.

Use a piece of string to measure all around the outside of the cake, and another to measure its depth.

Roll two-thirds of the almond paste into a rectangle half the perimeter of the cake and twice the depth, then cut in half lengthways. Brush each piece with melted apricot jam.

Roll the cake onto the strips to cover the sides and press the seams together.

Roll out the remaining almond paste to fit the top. Brush with jam, place on top of the cake, and roll gently with a rolling pin. Roll a straight-sided jam jar around the outside of the cake to help the almond paste to stick.

Leave in a cool airy place to dry before applying the icing: ideally 2–3 days if you're going to eat the cake soon, 6–7 days for one you're going to keep longer.

To "rough ice" the cake, simply put all the icing on top of the cake and roll it backwards and forwards with a palette knife a few times to remove air bubbles. Then spread evenly over the cake. Finally, use the blade of the knife to rough up the icing into peaks. The cake can be decorated with silver balls, bought decorations or shapes cut or molded from colored almond paste — or whatever you fancy.

An alternative is to decorate the top of the cake with glacé fruit either with or without almond paste. Use melted apricot jam to stick the fruit on, then brush jam over the top.

Or use bought fondant icing, which you simply roll out into a circle large enough to cover the top and sides of the cake and press it into position, cutting away the excess icing.

Wholewheat Dundee cake

This is a delicious, crumbly fruity cake.

MAKES ONE 8IN (20CM) ROUND CAKE ❄

2⅓ cups (300g) plain wholewheat flour
1 tsp baking powder
1½ sticks (175g) butter
¾ cup (175g) packed soft brown sugar
3 large eggs, beaten
8oz (225g) golden raisins
6oz (175g) currants
2oz (50g) candied citrus peel, chopped
2oz (50g) glacé cherries, halved
1 tsp grated orange rind
2oz (50g) ground almonds
about 6 tbsp cold water
1oz (25g) blanched slivered almonds

Preheat the oven to 325°F (160°C). Line a 8in (20cm) pan with two layers of baking parchment.

Sift the flour with the baking powder and mix in any bran left in the sieve.

Cream the butter and sugar until light and fluffy, then add the beaten eggs, a little at a time, beating constantly and adding a little flour if the mixture starts to curdle. (It curdles if the egg is added too quickly.)

Fold in the flour, dried fruit, orange rind, and ground almonds, adding the water to give a soft mixture that drops easily from the spoon.

Put the mixture into the lined pan and arrange the slivered almonds on top. Bake for 2–2½ hours or until a toothpick inserted into the cake comes out clean. Cool the cake in the pan. Turn out, remove the paper, and serve.

Vegan fruit cake v

A fruit cake for vegans and non-egg-eating vegetarians like my daughter Meg. The cake is light and delicious.

MAKES ONE 7IN (18CM) ROUND CAKE ❄

1¾ cups (225g) all-purpose flour, wholemeal or half and half
2 tsp baking powder
1 tsp pie spice
¾ cup (175g) packed soft brown sugar
6 tbsp olive oil
1lb (450g) mixed dried fruit
2oz (50g) glacé cherries, quartered (optional)
1oz (25g) soy flour
1oz (25g) ground almonds
1 cup (225ml) water
1oz (25g) sliced almonds

Preheat the oven to 325°F (160°C). Line an 7in (18cm) cake pan with baking parchment.

Sift the flour, baking powder, and spice into a large bowl, tipping in the bran from the sieve too.

Add all the remaining ingredients to the bowl except for the sliced almonds. Beat together with a wooden spoon (or in a food processor) for 2 minutes, then spoon the mixture into the pan and sprinkle with the sliced almonds.

Bake for about 2¼ hours or until a toothpick inserted in the center comes out clean.

Let the cake cool for 15 minutes in the pan, then turn it out onto a wire rack, strip off the paper, and leave until completely cold. Store in an airtight tin. This cake will keep for 3 months in the freezer.

Everything-less fruit cake v

This is my amazing eggless, sugarless, fatless cake. It certainly isn't conventional, but all my friends, like it (and have asked for the recipe!) and it has always been popular with readers. It comes out just like a moist, rich fruit cake. You could also make it gluten-free by using gluten-free flour instead of wholemeal.

MAKES ONE 2LB (900G) LOAF-SIZE CAKE ❄

8oz (225g) cooking dates (not sugar-rolled)
1¼ cups (275ml) water
1lb (450g) mixed dried fruit
175g (6oz) plain wholewheat flour or gluten-free flour, sifted
1 tbsp carob powder (optional)
3 tsp baking powder
1 tsp pie spice
grated rind of 1 orange or lemon
1½oz (40g) ground almonds
¼ cup fresh orange juice
a few sliced almonds

Preheat the oven to 325°F (160°C). Line a 2lb (900g) loaf pan with baking parchment.

Put the dates and water into a saucepan and heat gently until the dates are soft, then remove the pan from the heat and mash the dates to break them up.

Add the dried fruit, flour, carob powder (if using), baking powder, spice, grated rind, ground almonds, and orange juice.

Spoon the mixture into the pan, leveling the top. Sprinkle with the almonds and bake for about 1½ hours or until a toothpick inserted into the center comes out clean. Allow to cool slightly in the pan, then turn out and finish cooling on a wire rack.

My mother's gingerbread

This is my mother's recipe, which she made when I was a child, and it's lovely. When she was well organized, my mother would make a double batch and let one get sticky in a pan; mostly, though, she'd rustle one up quickly for visitors.

MAKES 20 PIECES

1 stick (125g) butter, plus extra for greasing
2oz (50g) golden syrup or honey
6oz (175g) black molasses
1¾ cups (225g) plain wholewheat flour
2 level tsp baking powder
½ tsp ground ginger
scant ½ cup (75g) soft brown sugar
2 eggs, beaten
2oz (50g)) chopped walnuts, candied citrus peel or stem ginger
5fl oz (150ml) milk
½ tsp baking soda

Preheat the oven to 325°F (160°C). Line a square pan with two layers of baking parchment or greased greaseproof paper.

Melt the syrup, molasses, and butter in a pan over a moderate heat, stirring occasionally. Let it get cool enough for you to put your hand against the pan.

Sift the flour with the ginger and baking powder into a mixing bowl, tipping in any bran from the sieve. Add the sugar and nuts, peel or stem ginger. Make a well in the center and pour in the warmed molasses mixture and the beaten eggs. Quickly beat in the milk with the baking soda dissolved in it, and pour the mixture into the pan.

Bake for 1½ hours or until well risen and firm to the touch.

Lemon drizzle cake

Light, moist, and tangy with lemon, this cake is very easy to make and always popular.

MAKES ONE 2LB (900G) LOAF-SIZE CAKE

2 sticks (225g) butter, softened
1 cup (225g) superfine sugar
finely grated rind of 2 lemons
1¾ cups (225g) self-raising flour, sifted
2 tsp baking powder
4 eggs

FOR THE DRIZZLE TOPPING

juice of 2 lemons
3½oz (100g) superfine sugar

Preheat the oven to 350°F (180°C). Line a 2lb (900g) loaf pan with a strip of non-stick baking paper to cover the base and narrow sides. Put the butter, sugar, lemon rind, and flour into a bowl or a food processor and sprinkle in the baking powder. Break in the eggs, then beat or process for 2–3 minutes or until everything has combined and the mixture is thick, smooth, and creamy.

Spoon the mixture into the pan and gently level the top. Bake for about 45 minutes or until the cake has risen, shrunk away from the sides of the pan, feels firm to a light touch and a toothpick inserted into the center comes out clean.

While the cake is cooking, mix the lemon juice and sugar in a small bowl and set aside.

As soon as the cake comes out of the oven, prick the top thoroughly all over and pour the sugar mixture over the top. Set aside to cool, then remove the cake from the pan and strip off the paper.

Lemon and poppy seed muffins v

These are light and delicious. You can enjoy them just as they are or top with lemon glacé icing (see variation opposite).

MAKES 16 MUFFINS

2 cups (250g) all-purpose flour
2 tsp baking powder
a pinch of salt
2 tbsp poppy seeds
heaping ¾ cup (200g) superfine sugar
6 tbsp mild-flavored olive oil
6 tbsp soy milk
½ tsp vanilla extract
2 tbsp freshly squeezed lemon juice
grated zest from 1 lemon

Preheat the oven to 350°F (180°C). Line two muffin tins with paper liners.

Sift the flour, baking powder, and salt into a large bowl, then mix in the poppy seeds and sugar.

In a separate small bowl or pitcher, mix together the oil, soy milk, vanilla extract, lemon juice, and rind.

Pour the oil mixture into the bowl with the flour and mix quickly with a fork until just combined; don't overmix, as a few little lumps of flour don't matter. Spoon the mixture into the paper liners, filling them to the top.

Bake for about 15 minutes or until the muffins feel firm and springy to a light touch. Leave to cool on a wire rack.

VARIATIONS

Iced lemon and poppy seed muffins v

Make exactly as described and leave to cool. Ice with a double quantity of lemon glacé icing (see page 345) and top with some strands of lemon rind.

Orange, spice, and cranberry muffins v

For this warm and spicy variation, use grated orange rind and orange juice instead of the lemon rind and juice. Omit the poppy seeds and vanilla extract. Add 1 teaspoon of pie spice to the flour mix, and stir in 3½oz (100g) dried cranberries. These can also be iced, as described above, using orange glacé icing.

Madeira cake

This traditional golden cake — a favorite of my daughter Kate and the base for many of her childhood birthday cakes — has a deliciously tender texture and buttery flavor.

MAKES ONE 7IN (18CM) ROUND CAKE ❄

1 cup (125g) plain wholewheat flour
1 cup (125g) self-raising flour
1½ sticks (175g) butter, softened
¾ cup (175g) superfine sugar
4 eggs, beaten
2 thin slices of citrus peel

Preheat the oven to 325°F (160°C). Line an 7in (18cm) round deep cake pan with baking parchment.

Sift the flours together, adding the bran from the sieve, too.

Cream the butter and sugar until very light and fluffy, then gradually add the beaten egg, 2 tablespoonfuls at a time, beating well after each addition; it's worth being patient with this.

Fold in the sifted flour using a strong spatula or metal spoon. Spoon the mixture into the pan, smoothing the top. Bake for 30 minutes, then carefully open the oven and place the peel on top of the cake, without removing the cake from the oven. Bake for a further 25-40 minutes or until a toothpick inserted into the center comes out clean.

Let the cake rest in the pan for 15 minutes, then turn it out of the pan and place on a wire rack to cool completely.

Never-fail meringues

Meringues are very easy to make. The only slightly tricky bit is deciding when to stop whisking the egg whites, but once you've got the hang of that, you'll be able to turn out perfect batches every time. They can be made in advance and keep well in an airtight container for at least a week.

MAKES ABOUT 16 MERINGUE HALVES

2 egg whites
½ cup (125g) superfine sugar
whipped cream to sandwich the meringues (optional)

Preheat the oven to 250°F (120°C). Line a baking sheet with baking parchment.

Make sure your bowl and whisk are very clean and free from grease. Put the egg whites into the bowl and whisk until they are standing in stiff peaks and you can turn the bowl upside down without them falling out. Whisk in the sugar a tablespoonful at a time until the mixture is thick and glossy.

Put heaped tablespoonfuls of the mixture onto the lined baking tray, leaving a little room around them, though they won't spread much.

Bake for 2 hours or until they are pale golden in color and completely dried out: pick one up and tap it on the base to check. The exact timing will depend on the size of the meringues.

Leave them to cool, then either store in an airtight tin or sandwich them together in pairs with whipped cream and serve.

Vegan orange sponge slices v

This is a beautiful light orange sponge, yet it contains no eggs or dairy products.

MAKES ONE 8IN X 12IN (20CM X 30CM) RECTANGLE, CUTTING INTO 14–16 PIECES

1½ cups (175g) plain wholewheat flour or half wholewheat, half white
1 tsp baking powder
4oz (125g) pure vegetable margarine
½ cup (125g) packed light soft brown sugar
rind and juice of ½ orange
5fl oz (150ml) soy milk

FOR THE ICING

2 cups (250g) confectioner's sugar, sifted
grated rind and juice of ½ orange
1–2 tbsp warm water (optional)

Preheat the oven to 350°F (180°C). Line a 8in x 12in (20cm x 30cm) Swiss roll pan with baking parchment.

Sift together the flour and baking powder, adding the residue of bran from the sieve too.

Cream the margarine and sugar, then gently fold in the sifted ingredients and orange rind alternately with the soy milk and orange juice. If the mixture looks a bit lumpy, beat it well and it will smooth out again.

Spread the mixture in the prepared pan and bake for 20 minutes or until it springs back when touched. Cool in the pan. Put the confectioner's sugar into a bowl with the grated rind, and add enough of the juice, and a little water if necessary, to make a thick but pouring consistency. Pour over the cake, spreading it gently to the sides and into the corners. Cut into fingers when the icing has set.

Parkin

A simple recipe for a sticky, well-flavored oatmeal cake. It gets stickier if wrapped in foil and stored for 2–7 days. This recipe is naturally egg-free.

MAKES ONE 8IN (20CM) SQUARE, CUTTING INTO 12 PIECES ❄

1 cup (125g) plain wholewheat flour
2 tsp baking powder
2 tsp ground ginger
1¼ cups (125g) medium oatmeal
scant ½ cup (75g) soft dark brown sugar
½ cup (125g) black molasses
½ cup (125g) golden syrup or honey
1 stick (125g) butter
¾ cup (175ml) milk

Preheat the oven to 350°F (180°C). Line a 8in (20cm) square pan with baking parchment.

Sift the flour, baking powder, and ginger into a bowl, adding any residue of bran from the sieve, too. Mix in the oatmeal.

Put the sugar, molasses, syrup, and butter into a pan and heat gently until melted. Cool until you can comfortably place your hand against the pan, then stir in the milk.

Add the molasses mixture to the dry ingredients and mix well.

Pour into the pan, bake for 50–60 minutes or until firm to the touch. Cool on a wire rack and cut into squares when cold.

VARIATION

Vegan parkin v

Use pure vegetable margarine instead of butter and soy milk instead of dairy milk.

Rock cakes

We don't make rock cakes much these days but my mother was always rustling them up and we'd eat them all warm and spicy from the oven. They're so quick to make and good to eat; I think they're due to make a comeback! A lovely variation is to replace the dried fruit with chocolate chips.

MAKES 8 CAKES ❄

1 stick (125g) butter, diced, plus extra for greasing
1¾ cups (225g) all-purpose flour, wholewheat or half and half
2 tsp baking powder
1 tsp pie spice
scant ½ cup (75g) soft dark brown sugar
4oz (125g) mixed dried fruit
1 egg, beaten
1–2 tbsp milk

Preheat the oven to 425°F (220°C). Grease a baking sheet or cover it with a piece of baking parchment.

Sift the flour, baking powder, and spice into a large bowl.

Add the butter and rub in with your fingertips until the mixture looks like fine breadcrumbs, then use a fork to stir in the sugar, dried fruit, and egg. The mixture needs to be fairly stiff and just hold together; only add a little milk if necessary.

Place tablespoons of the mixture about 1½in (4cm) apart on the baking sheet.

Bake for 15 minutes or until golden brown and firm. Cool on the baking sheet for 5 minutes then transfer to a wire rack.

All-in-one sponge

The quick, modern version of the traditional Victoria sponge. I find it works just as well with butter as with soft margarine, as long as the butter is soft.

MAKES ONE 7IN (18CM) CAKE ❄

1 stick (125g) margarine or butter, softened, plus extra for greasing
scant 1 cup (125g) self-raising wholewheat, white or wholewheat flour (or half and half)
1 tsp baking powder
½ cup (125g) superfine sugar or dark soft brown sugar
2 eggs
1–2 tbsp water (optional)
3 tbsp jam
superfine sugar or confectioner's sugar, for dusting

Preheat the oven to 350°F *180°C). Grease two 7in (18cm) sandwich pans and line the bases with baking parchment.

Sift the flour and baking powder into a large mixing bowl, adding the residue from the sieve. Add the margarine or butter, sugar, and eggs. Beat for 2–3 minutes or until the mixture is light and glossy.

Add the water if necessary, a little at a time, to make a soft, dropping consistency. Divide the mixture between the two pans and smooth the tops.

Bake for 35 minutes or until the center of each cake springs back when touched lightly. Cool for 30 seconds, then turn the cakes out onto a wire rack, strip off the paper, and leave to cool.

Sandwich the cakes with jam and sift a little confectioner's sugar on top or sprinkle with superfine sugar.

VARIATIONS
Chocolate cake

Sift 1 tablespoon of cocoa with the flour. You may need to add a little extra water to make a soft dropping consistency. When the cake is cool it can be sandwiched and iced with one of the fillings/toppings on pages 345–6.

Coffee and walnut cake

Make the cake as described, adding 1 tablespoon of good-quality instant coffee, dissolved in 1 tablespoon warm water, along with the eggs. Bake and cool. Make up a double quantity of buttercream (see page 346). Put 2 tablespoons of buttercream into a piping bag fitted with a medium-sized tip. Sandwich the cake with a third of the remaining buttercream. Spread the sides of the cake with the rest of the buttercream, then coat the sides in chopped walnuts by putting the walnuts on a piece of baking parchment, holding the cake like a wheel, and rolling it over the chopped nuts. Cover the top of the cake with the rest of the buttercream, decorate with swirls of piping and walnut halves.

Lemon daisy cake

Make the cake as described, adding the grated rind of a lemon before the eggs. Bake and cool. Fill and ice with a lemon-flavored buttercream (see page 346), then decorate with mimosa balls and sliced blanched almonds on top to resemble daisies.

Rose cake

For a pretty pink, rose-flavored cake, make as described, using triple-distilled rose water or a few drops of rose extract. Sandwich the cooled cake with a red jam and/or a little whipped cream. Cover the top with glacé icing (see page 345), made with triple-distilled rose water instead of water. Then decorate with some crystallized rose petals.

Vegan sponge cake v

It is surprising what a light and delicious cake you can create without using eggs. I make this cake a lot; in fact I would say it's the sponge cake of choice in my family, and sometimes I like to make a larger one, in two 9in (23cm) pans, so below I've given the quantities for this, and there's also a chocolate version (see variations), which is very popular.

MAKES ONE 7IN (18CM) ROUND CAKE ❄

6 tbsp mild-flavored olive oil or grapeseed oil, plus extra for greasing
1¾ cups (225g) self-raising flour (half wholewheat, half white)
2 tsp baking powder
¾ cup (175g) superfine sugar or soft dark brown sugar
1 cup (225ml) water
1 tsp vanilla extract
2 heaped tbsp jam and superfine sugar, for dusting, or 1 quantity of fudge icing or buttercream (see pages 345 and 346)

Preheat the oven to 350°F (180°C). Grease and line the bases of two 7in (18cm) sandwich pans.

Sift the flour and baking powder into a bowl. Add the superfine sugar, then stir in the oil, water and vanilla extract. Mix to a smooth batter-like consistency and pour into the pans.

Bake for 25–30 minutes or until the center springs back to a light touch.

Turn the cakes out onto a wire rack and leave them to cool, then strip off the paper.

Sandwich the cakes together with the jam and sprinkle with superfine sugar, or fill and top with fudge icing or buttercream.

VARIATIONS
Large vegan sponge cake v

For enough mixture to fill two 9in (23cm) sandwich pans, increase the ingredients as follows:
2¼ cups (275g) self-raising flour, 2½ teaspoons of baking powder, heaping ¾ cup (200g) superfine sugar or soft brown sugar, 9 tablespoons of olive or grapeseed oil, 1¼ cups(300ml) water and 1½ teaspoons of vanilla extract. Make as described, and bake for 35–40 minutes or until the cake springs back when pressed lightly in the center.

Vegan chocolate cake v

Make exactly as described but replace ½ cup (75g) of the flour with cocoa powder.

Opposite: Rose cake (see page 353)

Swiss roll

Classic, simple, fun to make and eat, but you do need a food processor or electric beater unless you're feeling patient and energetic.

MAKES ONE SWISS ROLL, CUTTING INTO 8 SLICES ❄

½ cup (60g) all-purpose flour, plus extra for dusting
3 eggs
½ cup (125g) superfine sugar
4oz (125g) raspberry jam, warmed
superfine sugar, to decorate

Preheat the oven to 400°F (200°C). Line a 13in x 9in (33cm x 23cm) Swiss roll pan with baking parchment. Sift the flour.

Break the eggs into a large bowl or the bowl of a food procesor, and whisk lightly. Add the sugar.

Whisk the eggs and sugar until the mixture is very thick and fluffy and able to hold the trail of the whisk for 3 seconds; this will take 5 minutes.

If you are going to whisk this by hand, half fill a large saucepan with water and bring to the boil. Set your bowl over the pan of steaming water and whisk for 10–15 minutes until the mixture is as described above.

Gently fold in a quarter of the flour; repeat with the remainder.

Pour into the pan, bake for 8–10 minutes or until the mixture is firm in the center and springs back when pressed lightly.

Turn out onto a piece of greaseproof or baking paper that has been sprinkled with flour. Leave until completely cold, then trim the edges and spread with jam. Turn the roll so that the long side is toward you and gently roll up. Sprinkle with superfine sugar.

Traditional Victoria sandwich cake

The all-in-one method of making a cake is great (see page 353), but real connoisseurs say you can't beat the traditional method. It is soothing and satisfying to make, I must admit, and the light and buttery result does justify the time spent.

MAKES ONE 7IN (18CM) ROUND CAKE ❄

1½ sticks (175g) butter, softened, plus extra for greasing
1⅓ cups (175g) self-raising flour (half wholewheat, half white)
¾ cup (175g) superfine sugar
3 eggs, beaten
1–2 tbsp water

FOR THE FILLING AND TOPPING

a few strawberries or raspberries and 5fl oz (150m) heavy cream, whipped, or 3 tbsp raspberry jam
superfine or confectioner's sugar, for dusting

Preheat the oven to 350°F (180°C). Grease two 7in (18cm) sandwich pans and line the bases with baking parchment circles.

Sift the flour onto a plate, adding also the residue of bran from the sieve.

Cream the butter and sugar until very light and fluffy — you can do this by hand, or with an electric beater.

Whisk the eggs, then add to the creamed mixture gradually, a teaspoonful at a time, beating well after each addition to ensure that the mixture doesn't curdle, whisking in a tablespoon of the flour if it does.

Gently fold in the flour and divide the mixture between the pans, smoothing the tops.

Bake for 25–30 minutes or until the cake springs back when pressed lightly.

Cool on a wire rack, then fill with whipped cream and sliced strawberries in the summer. Alternatively, use jam or any of the fillings on pages 345–6, or the suggestions given for varying the basic all-in-one sponge on page 353. Dredge the top with superfine or confectioner's sugar.

Cookies
Crisp almond tuiles

These are lovely for serving with fruit salads and creams; impressive, yet not difficult to make.

MAKES 18 TUILES

6 tbsp (75g) butter, softened
⅓ cup (75g) superfine sugar
a few drops of almond extract
scant ½ cup (50g) all-purpose flour, sifted
2oz (50g) sliced almonds

Preheat the oven to 400°F (200°C). Cover a baking sheet with baking parchment.

Beat the butter and sugar until light, then stir in the almond extract, flour, and sliced almonds.

Put teaspoonfuls onto the baking parchment and flatten with a fork, allowing plenty of room for the biscuits to spread.

Bake until they are browned at the edges (6–8 minutes).

Leave to stand for 1–2 minutes or until firm enough to lift from the pan, but not brittle, then place over a rolling pin, tall glass or jam jar to curl as they cool. Store in an airtight container.

Brandy snaps

Crisp brandy snaps are delicious with or without the filling of whipped cream. They're easy to make and lovely for a special occasion.

MAKES ABOUT 14 BRANDY SNAPS
½ stick (50g) butter
¼ cup (50g) muscovado sugar
¼ cup (50g) golden syrup or honey
scant ½ cup (50g) all-purpose flour
½ tsp ground ginger
a little grated lemon rind

TO SERVE
5fl oz (150ml) heavy cream, whipped
a few drops of brandy (optional)

Preheat the oven to 325°F (160°C). Cover 1–2 baking sheets with baking parchment.

Put the butter, sugar, and golden syrup into a saucepan and stir over a gentle heat until melted.

Remove from the heat and sift in the flour and ground ginger, adding a little grated lemon rind to taste.

Drop teaspoonfuls of the mixture onto the lined baking sheets leaving plenty of room for them to spread, flatten lightly with a palette knife.

Bake for 8–10 minutes or until golden. Cool for 1–2 minutes or until just firm enough to handle, then loosen with a knife and quickly roll a brandy snap around the greased handle of a wooden spoon or small rolling pin, then slide off and leave to cool.

This process must be done quickly or the brandy snaps will harden. If this happens, pop them back into the oven for a few seconds to soften.

When the brandy snaps are completely cold, spoon or pipe the whipped cream (flavored with a touch of brandy, if you like) into them.

Brandy snaps can be made a day or two in advance and stored in a tin ready for filling with cream later.

Butter cookies v

Lovely crisp cookies that you can eat as they are or decorate with icing and colored sugar, or whatever you fancy.

MAKES ABOUT 28 COOKIES
1¼ sticks (150g) butter or pure vegetable margarine, softened
⅓ cup (75g) superfine sugar
1¾ cups (225g) all-purpose flour, sifted

TO DECORATE
glacé Icing (see page 345)
hundreds and thousands, sugar strands, silver balls, and anything else you fancy

Preheat the oven to 350°F (180°C). Line two baking sheets with baking parchment.

Put all the ingredients into a food processor and blitz until a dough forms. Alternatively, cream the butter or margarine and sugar in a bowl, then add the flour and gradually work it in using your fingertips to make a dough.

Roll the dough out on a lightly floured work surface or board to about ⅛in (2mm), cut into shapes and put on the baking sheets.

Bake for about 10–15 minutes or until the cookies are golden brown and set. Leave them to cool on the baking sheets, then transfer to a wire rack. When they are cold, ice with glacé icing — an easy way to do this is to put the icing in a small plastic bag and snip off one of the lower corners, just enough to be able to squeeze out a nice ribbon of icing — and decorate as desired.

Cheese cookies

These crisp homemade cheese cookies always disappear fast. It's fun to experiment with different flours — they're lovely made with half wholewheat, half barley, rye, or buckwheat flour, and sometimes I add some dried herbs, chopped nuts, sesame, cumin, or caraway seeds, too.

MAKES ABOUT 32 COOKIES ❄

1¾ cups (225g) plain wholewheat flour or half wholewheat and half white
1½ sticks (175g) butter, softened
6oz (175g) Cheddar cheese, grated
a good pinch each of mustard powder and cayenne pepper

Preheat the oven to 450°F (230°C).
Sift the flour into a bowl, adding any bran residue from the sieve, and mix in the butter with a fork. Add the grated cheese, cayenne pepper, and mustard.

Form into a dough, roll out ¼in (6mm) thick, cut into 2in (5cm) rounds, prick each several times with a fork, and bake for 15–20 minutes, or until golden brown.

The cookies will get crisp as they cool. Store in an airtight tin.

Tip
These cookies will freeze. Cool them then place in a rigid container and freeze. To use, spread them out on a wire rack to defrost at room temperature — this will only take about 40 minutes.

Chocolate chip cookies v

These cookies are very popular with children, both to make and eat. They can be completely vegan if you use pure vegetable margarine and vegan chocolate.

MAKES 18 COOKIES

1 stick (125g) butter or pure vegetable margarine, softened
½ cup (125g) superfine sugar
1 tsp vanilla extract
1½ cups (200g) self-raising flour, sifted
1 tsp baking powder
7oz (200g) milk chocolate chips or milk chocolate cut into chips
1 tbsp water

Preheat the oven to 350°F (180°C).
Cream the butter and sugar in a large bowl until light and fluffy. Stir in the vanilla extract, flour, baking powder, and chocolate chips, and add the water to make a dough. Put tablespoonfuls of the mixture onto two greased, lined baking sheets, spacing well apart. Flatten each gently with your fingers.

Bake for about 12 minutes or until golden brown. Leave on the baking sheets for 5 minutes, then transfer to a wire rack to cool. Store in an airtight tin for up to a week.

Chocolate shortbread

This chocolate-topped shortbread is so easy to make and always popular. It freezes well; see cheese cookies opposite.

MAKES 15 PIECES ❄

1 stick (125g) butter, softened, plus extra for greasing
¼ cup (50g) packed dark soft brown sugar
heaping ¾ cup (100g) plain wholewheat flour, sifted
2½oz (60g) dried coconut, unsweetened
2 tbsp cocoa powder
2oz (50g) plain chocolate, for the topping

Preheat the oven to 350°F (180°C).
Cream together the butter and sugar until well blended, then add the flour, coconut, and cocoa and mix well.

Press the mixture firmly into the Swiss roll pan (a palette knife helps here) and bake for 30 minutes.

While the shortbread is cooking, break the chocolate into small pieces or grate coarsely.

When the shortbread is cooked, scatter the chocolate over the top, and return to the oven for a minute or two, until the chocolate has melted. Remove the shortbread from the oven and spread the chocolate evenly over top. Cool in the pan, then cut into slices.

Crunchy cookies

These are quick to make, sweet and crunchy to eat.

MAKES 18 COOKIES ❄
½ stick (50g) butter
¼ cup (50g) demerara sugar
¼ cup (50g) golden syrup or
    molasses
½ tsp baking soda
1 cup (75g) rolled oats
½ cup (50g) plain wholewheat flour

Preheat the oven to 350°F (180°C). Cover 1–2 large baking sheets with baking parchment.

Melt the butter, sugar, and syrup together in a saucepan over a gentle heat. Remove from the heat and cool slightly.

Stir in the baking soda and mix well. Add the oats and sift in the flour, adding also the residue of bran from the sieve.

Put heaped teaspoons of the mixture in little heaps on the baking parchment.

Bake for 10–15 minutes or until golden brown. Cool on the baking sheets; lift off carefully with a spatula. These cookies freeze well and thaw quickly.

Date slices

These oaty shortbreads sandwiched with sweet date and vanilla purée and have always been one of my favorite healthy cookies. They also make a good dessert, eaten warm from the oven with a dollop of thick yogurt or some cream.

MAKES 16 SLICES ❄
8oz (225g) chopped dates — not
    the "sugar-rolled" type
5fl oz (150ml) water
1 tsp vanilla extract (optional)
1½ cups (175g) plain wholewheat
    flour
1¾ cups (175g) porridge oats
1½ sticks (175g) butter
⅓ cup (75g) demerara sugar
2 tbsp cold water

Preheat the oven to 375°F (190°C). Line a 8in x 12in (20cm x 30cm) Swiss roll pan with baking parchment.

Put the dates into a saucepan with the water and heat gently for 5–10 minutes or until the dates are mushy. Remove from the heat and mash with a spoon to make a thick purée, looking out for and removing any stray pits as you do so. Stir in the vanilla extract (if using). Set aside to cool.

Sift the flour into a bowl, adding also the residue of bran from the sieve and the oats.

Rub in the butter with your fingertips or a fork, then add the sugar and water, and press the mixture together to form a dough.

Press half this mixture into the lined pan, spread the cooled date purée on top, then cover evenly with the remaining oat mixture and press down gently but firmly.

Bake for 30 minutes. Cool in the pan, then cut into sections and remove with a spatula. Date slices freeze well and defrost very quickly; so can be eaten almost immediately.

I think this is the best version of these, though for a sugarless recipe, make as usual, just omitting the sugar. Handle carefully, as the mixture is rather crumbly.

Flapjacks v

If you use ordinary rolled oats for these, the flapjacks will be crisp; if you use jumbo oats or muesli base, they come out gooey and toffee-like.

MAKES 15 FLAPJACKS ❄

scant ½ cup (125g) muscovado sugar
1 stick (125g) butter or margarine
1 slightly rounded tbsp golden syrup or honey
1¾ cups (175g) rolled oats

Preheat the oven to 375°F (190°C). Line a 8in x 12in (20cm x 30cm) Swiss roll pan with baking parchment.

Melt together the sugar, butter, and golden syrup, then stir in the oats.

Spread into the Swiss roll pan, and bake for 10–15 minutes or until golden brown.

Cool a little, then cut into slices. Generally, it's best to remove the flapjacks from the pan when they are quite cold. With the jumbo oat version, however, it's a good idea to get them out of the pan before they are completely cold because they're inclined to stick, though the lining of baking parchment certainly helps.

Gingerbread men v

All my children (and now grand-children) have loved cooking with me, gingerbread men (hearts, bears, stars, etc.) being one of their favorite things to make. We usually decorate the cookies with white glacé icing after baking, giving them faces, buttons, patterns and any other details.

MAKES 10–12 COOKIES ❄

⅓ cup (75g) superfine sugar
2 tbsp golden syrup
1 tbsp black molasses
7 tbsp (100g) butter or pure vegetable margarine
½ tsp baking soda
1–2 tsp ground ginger
1¾ cups (225g) all-purpose flour (white, wholewheat or a mixture)
a few tbsp extra flour for rolling

TO DECORATE

glacé icing (see page 345)
hundreds and thousands, silver balls and anything else you fancy

Preheat the oven to 350°F (180°C). Line two large baking sheets with baking parchment.

Put the sugar, syrup, molasses, and butter or margarine into a large saucepan and heat gently, until melted, stirring often. Remove from the heat and leave until it's cool enough for you to put your hand against the pan.

Stir in the baking soda, ginger, and flour to make a dough. It will be quite soft; if it's too soft to roll out, leave it on one side to cool for 20–30 minutes or so, until it's ready.

Roll the dough out quite thinly (about the thickness of a quarter) in plenty of flour, and cut into gingerbread men or whatever shapes take your fancy.

Put them on the baking sheets and bake for 10–15 minutes or until they feel firm. They won't change color, so you'll need to go by feel. It's better to undercook them rather than overcook — the dough is edible uncooked in any case, and I dare say quite a bit of it will get eaten during the rolling and cutting process!

Put the biscuits on a wire rack to cool. Decorate them with glacé icing. An easy way to do this is to put the icing in a small plastic bag and snip off one of the lower corners, just enough to be able to squeeze out a nice ribbon of icing. Then let your imagination take over.

Hazel nut shortbread

This shortbread has a rich caramely, nutty flavor.

3oz (75g) hazel nuts
1 stick (125g) butter, softened, plus
    extra for greasing
¼ cup (50g) muscovado sugar
scant 1½ cups (175g) plain
    wheatwheat flour (see page 369)

Preheat the oven to 350°F (180°C).

If the nuts are the kind still in their brown outer skins, spread them out on a dry baking sheet and bake in the oven for about 20 minutes or until the nuts under the skins are a golden brown. Then either rub off the outer skins or leave them on.

If the nuts have already had their outer skins removed, you could just roast them for a few minutes in the oven to improve the flavor or use them as they are.

In either case, grind them quite finely in a nutmill, blender, or food processor.

Turn the oven setting down to 325°F (160°C).

Cream the butter and sugar until they're light and fluffy, then beat in the flour and hazel nuts, to make a dough.

Press the dough into a lightly greased 7in x 11in (18cm x 28cm) Swiss roll pan. Prick the top thoroughly with a fork.

Bake for 1 hour. Cut into slices while still hot, then leave to cool in the pan before removing. This shortbread freezes well.

Jam tarts v

These are so easy to make and children love them, Use their favorite flavor of jam, or lemon curd. If you want to cut down on sugar, you could use a sugar-reduced jam, or one of the no-sugar-added ones that health-food stores sell.

MAKES 12 TARTS ❄
1 quantity easy wholegrain spelt
    flour pastry (see page 258), made
    with pure vegetable margarine
4oz (125g) jam

Preheat the oven to 400°F (200°C).

On a lightly floured work surface or board roll out the pastry and cut circles to fit a 12-hole bun tin: for the tin I use that's a 2¾in (7cm) cutter.

Put the pastry circles gently into the cavities in the bun tin, then drop a teaspoonful of jam into each. Don't make the spoonfuls too big or they'll bubble over the edges of the tarts as they cook.

Bake for about 10 minutes or until the pastry has set and is very lightly browned. Allow to cool in the tin, then lift them out carefully with a palette knife.

Macaroons

Easy to make and lovely with cold, creamy desserts for a special occasion.

MAKES 12 MACAROONS
1 egg white
4oz (125g) ground almonds
½ cup (125g) superfine sugar
rice paper
12 whole blanched almonds

Put the egg white into a good-sized bowl and whisk lightly, just to break it up.

Stir in the ground almonds and superfine sugar and mix to a paste.

Lay the rice paper on a baking sheet and put spoonfuls of the macaroon mixture on it, leaving room for them to spread a little.

Smooth the macaroons with the back of a spoon dipped in cold water and place an almond in the center of each. Bake for 15–25 minutes.

Transfer to a wire rack, tearing the rice paper to separate the macaroons; trim off the remaining paper when thy have cooled.

Oatcakes v

Crispy, nutty oatcakes are easy to make and easier to eat. Try them for breakfast or tea with butter and clear honey or serve them with a creamy dip or cream cheese.

MAKES 24–28 OATCAKES ❄

2½ cups (225g) medium oatmeal, plus extra for dusting and finishing
½ tsp baking powder
½ tsp salt
2 tbsp (25g) butter or pure vegetable margarine, melted
6 tsp hot water

Preheat the oven to 400°F (200°C).

Put the oatmeal into a bowl with the baking powder, salt, and butter or margarine. Mix them together lightly, then stir in enough warm water to make a dough.

Sprinkle some oatmeal on a work surface or board and turn the dough out onto this, kneading lightly, then roll it out to a thickness of about ⅛in (2mm), sprinkling the surface with a little extra oatmeal, if necessary, to prevent it from sticking. You can either roll the mixture into a circle and then cut it into wedges, or stamp it into rounds using a pastry cutter.

Transfer the oatcakes to a lined baking sheet and bake them for about 15 minutes or until firm and lightly colored. Let them cool on the sheet for a few minutes, then transfer them to a wire cooling rack. Or serve them straight from the oven, all warm and crumbly.

Shortbread

Crisp, buttery, and very easy to make, this can be whipped up in no time at all. I use light brown flour or a mixture of half white flour and half wholewheat. They're also gorgeous made with wholegrain spelt flour.

MAKES 20 PIECES

1 stick (125g) butter, softened
¼ cup (50g) superfine sugar
scant 1 cup (125g) all-purpose flour
2 tbsp (50g) cornstarch
a little superfine sugar, for sprinkling

Preheat the oven to 300°F (150°C). Lightly grease a 7in x 11in (18cm x 28cm) Swiss roll pan.

Put the butter and sugar into a bowl and beat together with a wooden spoon until light and creamy. Sift in the flour and cornstarch and mix to make a dough. Alternatively, put all the ingredients into a food processor and blitz for a minute or two until a dough forms. Press the dough into the pan to cover it evenly — it will be quite thin — then prick all over.

Bake for 20–25 minutes or until set and golden. Leave to cool slightly, then cut into slices with a sharp knife. Sprinkle with a little superfine sugar. Remove the pieces from the pan when completely cold.

VARIATION
Millionaire's shortbread

For this rich and delicious treat, crunchy shortbread topped with caramel and chocolate, bake the shortbread as described and leave to cool completely (don't cut it). Then make a caramel by melting 1½ sticks (175g) butter, ¾ cup (175g) superfine sugar, ¼ cup of golden syrup, and a 14oz can of condensed milk over a gentle heat. Allow to bubble over the heat for about 8 minutes, until thick, golden, and fudge-like, stirring all the time. Pour this over the short-bread and leave until completely cold. Melt an 8oz bar of milk or plain chocolate and spread it over the top of the caramel. When it's set, cut into small pieces with a sharp knife.

Scones and teabreads

Easy wholewheat scones

These scones freeze well after baking.

MAKES 12 SCONES ❄
just under 5fl oz (150ml) tbsp milk
1 tbsp freshly squeezed lemon juice
1¾ cups (225g) self-raising flour — I
    like light brown self-raising, or a
    half-and-half mixture of
    wholewheat and white flour
¼ tsp baking powder
½ stick (50g) butter, softened
¼ cup (50g) light muscovado sugar

Preheat the oven to 400°F (200°C).
    Mix the milk with the lemon juice and set aside.
    Sift the flour and baking powder into a bowl, adding any bran left in the sieve, too.
    Rub in the butter, so that it resembles breadcrumbs, add the sugar and then pour in the milk mixture and mix to a soft dough.
    Press the dough out with your hand until it is ¾in (2cm) thick, then cut into rounds using a 2in (5cm) round cutter.
    Place on a floured baking sheet and bake for about 12–15 minutes or until risen and firm. Cool on a wire rack.

VARIATIONS

Cheese scones

Leave out the sugar. Sift ½ teaspoon of mustard powder with the flour, and add 4oz (125g) grated cheese to the mixture after rubbing in the butter.
    Some chopped walnuts, say 2oz (50g), are also good in this, or try a cheese, mustard, and sesame variation: make as for cheese scones, but roll the mixture out on a board which has been sprinkled with sesame seeds.

Sultana scones

Add 2oz (50g) golden raisins to the mixture along with the milk.

Baby scones

The scones can be made from the same basic mixture cut out with a tiny round cutter measuring ½in (1cm) across. They are a bit fussy to make but perfect for a tea party, topped with jam and clotted cream. Using a small cutter will give about 30 scones and they will take about 10 minutes to cook.

Easy wholewheat scone circle

One large scone that can be cut into wedges and served like normal scones.

MAKES ONE CIRCLE, CUTTING INTO 8 PIECES ❄
2 tsp fine oatmeal
scant 1 cup (125g) plain wholewheat
    flour, plus extra for dusting
1 heaped tsp baking powder
2 tbsp (25g) soft dark brown sugar
a pinch of salt
2 tbsp (25g) butter
6 tbsp milk

Preheat the oven to 350°F (180°C).
    Sift together the oatmeal, flour, and baking powder, adding any bran left in the sieve, then add the sugar and salt.
    Rub in the butter with your fingertips or a fork until the mixture resembles breadcrumbs.
    Mix in enough milk to make a soft, pliable consistency.
    Shape into a round on a floured baking pan and cut across and across into eight sections. Bake for 15 minutes or until risen and firm.

VARIATION

Molasses scone circle

Use 1 tablespoon of black molasses and only ¼ cup of milk, stirring the two together before adding.

Banana bread

An old favorite.

MAKES ONE 1LB (450G) LOAF,
CUTTING INTO 10 SLICES ❄

1¾ cups (225g) wholemeal flour
2 level tsp baking powder
a pinch of salt
½ stick (50g) butter, plus extra for
    greasing
¼ cup (50g) dark muscovado sugar
3oz (75g) golden syrup or clear
    honey
1 egg, beaten
2 bananas, peeled and mashed
2oz (50g) shelled walnuts, chopped

Preheat the oven to 350°F (180°C).
Grease a 1lb (450g) loaf pan and
line with a long strip of baking
parchment.

Sift together the flour, baking
powder and salt, adding any bran
left in the sieve.

Put the butter, sugar, and syrup
into a pan and heat gently to melt.

Make a well in the center of the
flour and pour in the syrup mixture;
mix quickly, then add beaten egg,
mashed bananas, and chopped
walnuts.

Mix well; pour into the pan and
bake for 1 hour until firm to touch.
Cool on a wire rack.

VARIATION

Date and walnut loaf

Make this in the same way, using
4oz (125g) chopped dates and a
little milk to make a soft, dropping
consistency, instead of the bananas.

Soda bread

Very quick to make and delicious
eaten warm with butter and runny
honey. It's best eaten the same day,
though it does make good toast if
there's any left over.

MAKES ONE ROUND LOAF ❄

scant 2¼ cups (250g) plain
    wholewheat flour, plus extra for
    dusting
1 tsp baking powder
1 tsp salt
2 tsp sugar
1 cup (225ml) buttermilk or live
    natural yogurt

Preheat the oven to 450°F (230°C).

Sift the flour, baking powder, and
salt into a large bowl, adding any
bran left in the sieve, and stir in the
sugar.

Pour in the buttermilk or yogurt
and mix quickly to a soft dough.

Knead the dough lightly in the
bowl for a few seconds until it is
smooth, soft and firm, but not
sticky.

Shape the dough into a tall round
with your hands — make it as high
as you can because it will spread out
as it cooks — and place it on a
floured baking sheet.

Cut a deep cross in the top to
help it to open out and spread as it
cooks.

Bake for 10 minutes, then turn
the oven setting down to 400°F
(200°C) and cook for a further
15–20 minutes or until the base of
the loaf sounds hollow, like a drum,
when you tap it with your knuckles.
Let it cool a bit, then eat
it while it's still warm.

VARIATION

Vegan soda bread v

Use a live, unsweetened natural soy
yogurt instead of the dairy yogurt.

Spelt flour wraps v

These wraps are delicious hot, crisp, and puffy from the pan with a curry or vegetable dish, or cold, rolled around a salad filling. The spelt flour gives them a wonderful lightness and sweet flavor.

MAKES 6 WRAPS
5oz (150g) wholegrain spelt flour
¼ tsp salt
2 tbsp olive oil
about 4 tbsp water
a little olive oil, for frying

Sift the spelt flour into a bowl. Add the salt and oil, and enough water to make a soft dough — the consistency of soft modeling clay. Divide the dough into six even-sized pieces. Roll each piece into a ball and flatten it with the palm of your hand, then roll each piece out into a thin round, about 6in (15cm) across.

Heat a little oil, about 1 table-spoon, in a frying pan. Add one of the circles of dough and fry until set and flecked with brown on one side, then flip it over and fry the other side. Remove the wrap from the frying pan and fry the rest in the same way. Add a little more oil if necessary, but the wraps don't need much oil; the pan really only needs to be "oiled."

Quick-and-easy date tea bread v

You can whip this tea bread up very quickly and it tastes delicious sliced and buttered.

MAKES ONE LOAF, CUTTING INTO 10 SLICES ❄
6oz (175g) chopped dates
7fl oz (200ml) water
1¾ cup (225g) self-raising wholewheat or light brown flour
1 tsp baking powder
¼ cup mild-flavored olive oil, plus extra for greasing
1 tsp vanilla extract

Put the dates into a large saucepan with the water, bring to the boil, then remove from the heat and leave until the water is tepid and the dates mushy. Mash the dates a little with a wooden spoon to break them up a bit, but leave them quite chunky.

Preheat the oven to 350°F (180°C). Line the base and narrow sides of a 2lb (900g) loaf pan with a long strip of baking parchment and grease the sides.

Sift the flour and baking powder into the pan on top of the dates, adding any bran left in the sieve.

Add the olive oil and vanilla extract and stir well.

Spoon the mixture into the pan, bake for about 40 minutes or until the center feels springy and a toothpick inserted into the center comes out clean.

Cool on a wire rack. Serve cut into thick slices, and buttered if you like.

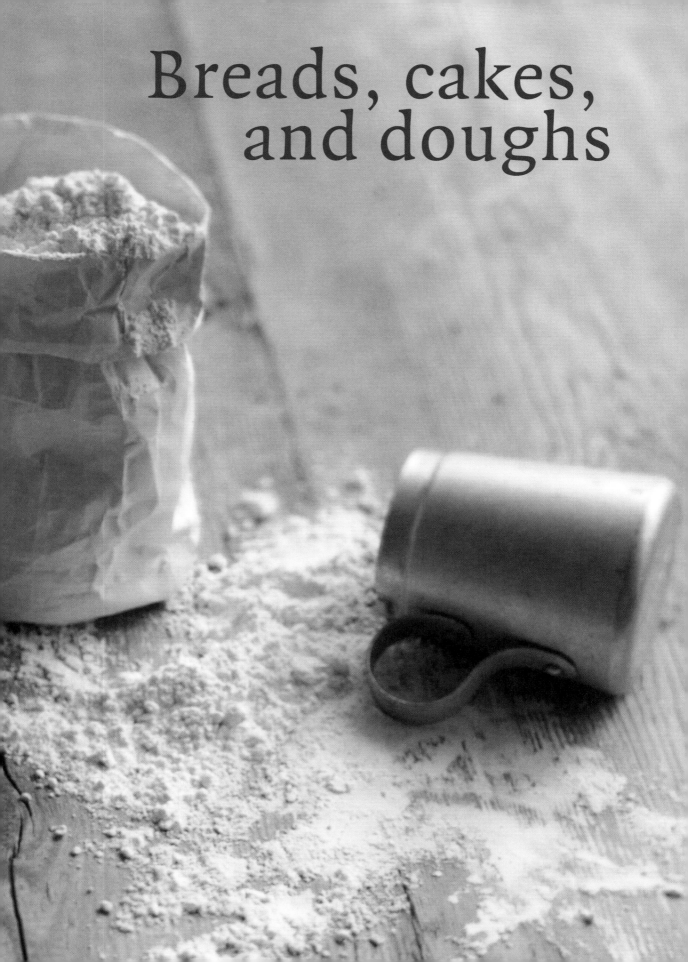

Breads, cakes, and doughs

"Breadmaking is easy," we cookery writers say. However, what we might add is "if you do it often". If you make bread only occasionally or are attempting it for the first time, it's more intimidating. That's mainly because you're not quite sure what the yeast is going to do; but there are only really three things that can go wrong: using stale yeast, which won't rise; getting the mixture too hot, which kills the yeast (though it doesn't mind the cold); and adding too much sugar or salt, which also kills the yeast.

You can easily avoid these pitfalls, produce wonderful results every time and fill your home with the smell of freshly baked bread by following these easy recipes and instructions. Once you've got a bit of confidence, try some of the other lovely things you can make with yeast such as fruit bread, pizzas, crumpets and hot cross buns (see pages 378, 383, 374 and 377). If you've got a breadmaker, you can adapt some of the recipes in this chapter following the manufacturer's directions.

How to make perfect wholegrain bread

If you're baking for a family or have a freezer, I think it's worth making a good batch at a time, using a 3lb 5oz (1.5kg) bag of flour, or even double this. You can use all wholegrain flour, or if your family isn't used to wholegrain flour, you might use wheatmeal flour, which is flour that has been sieved once by the millers to remove the coarsest part of the grain and contains 85–90 per cent of the grain, whereas wholegrain or wholewheat (the two names are interchangeable) flour consists of 100 per cent. Or you might find it best to use wheatmeal flour or wholewheat flour with a proportion of strong white bread flour (preferably unbleached) — half and half is a good mixture to start with.

I advise using dried yeast for your first attempt, because it's more predictable and, I think, easier when you're learning. But it's important that the dried yeast is fresh, so buy it from a store which has a quick turnover and, unless you know you're going to do a lot of breadmaking, it's best to buy a small quantity to start with. The "easy-blend" yeast which you can buy is also excellent and even easier to use.

If you're converting a recipe, remember that 1oz (25g) fresh yeast equals ½oz (15g) dried yeast or one ¼oz sachet of easy-blend yeast.

If you want to use fresh yeast, or to use it for some of the recipes in this section, you can usually buy it by the 1oz (25g) weight from bakers and some supermarkets. It needs to be creamy beige in color, moist, crumbly and sweet-smelling.

A dark, mottled color, sticky or very dry texture and an "off" smell mean that the yeast is stale and will not work. Fresh yeast will keep for up to a week in a screw-top jar in the fridge. To use it, just crumble it into the liquid given for the recipe and stir to blend. There's no need to add any sugar to this liquid.

A warm place, like an airing cupboard, is ideal for encouraging the dough to rise. The bread will rise just as well standing on the kitchen work surface or in the fridge, it'll just take longer — see the guide on page 370. Don't let it get too hot.

MAKES FIVE X 1LB (450G) LOAVES

1¼ cups (275ml) hand-hot water
½ tsp sugar (not needed for easy-blend yeast)
2 tbsp dried yeast or 2 x ¼oz sachets easy-blend yeast
3lb 5oz (1.5kg) bag of plain wheatmeal or wholewheat flour, or a mixture of wholewheat flour and strong white bread flour
2 tbsp muscovado sugar
4 tsp fine sea salt
¼ stick (50g) butter
2–2½ cups (575–700ml) hand-hot water (if you're using easy-blend yeast, you can add this to the smaller quantity of water to make 3–3½ cups (850ml–1 liter))

If you're using easy-blend yeast, skip this paragraph. If you're using ordinary dried yeast, put 1¼ cups (275ml) of the warm water into a small bowl and stir in the ½ tsp of sugar and the dried yeast. Leave to one side for 5–10 minutes to froth up.

Prepare your loaf pans by greasing them thoroughly with butter or oil, then leave them to one side in a warm place if there's one handy, but this isn't essential. If you're buying pans, get traditional ones with high slanting sides. But if you're making bread for the first time, or haven't got any, you can use any sort of deepish pan — even a round cake tin; just remember to fill it half full of dough.

Put your flour into a large bowl — the bowl of an electric mixer if this has a dough hook attachment, or you might be able to use a food processor, in which case follow the manufacture's instructions.

Add the 2 tablespoons of sugar and the salt and the easy-blend yeast (if using). Rub in the butter with your fingers.

If you're using ordinary dried yeast, by this time you will find that it has frothed up quite dramatically into a lovely volcanic mass and you can add 2 cups (575ml) of the warm water.

If you're using easy-blend yeast, add 3 cups (850ml) of the water.

Mix everything together until the dough forms — add more warm water if the dough seems too stiff. It needs to be firm, but soft enough to handle pleasantly.

If you've got a dough hook on your mixer (a worthwhile investment) you can now leave it to knead the dough for 5 minutes. Or if you're doing it in a food processor, the processing time is much faster than that; follow the manufacturer's instructions.

Otherwise, turn the dough out and knead it by hand, pushing and pummelling, folding and refolding it, for 5–10 minutes. As you knead the dough you'll feel it change from a course, lumpy and slightly sticky texture to a smooth, supple, silky one.

Put the dough back in its bowl, cover it with a clean damp cloth then place the bowl in a large plastic bag and leave it to double in size. This takes 1 hour in a warm place, slightly longer if the bowl is just standing on the working surface and up to 2 hours if the kitchen is cold (see guide opposite).

Punch the risen dough down with your fist and knead it a little — just 1–2 minutes this time, to wake the yeast up again.

Cut the dough into five equal-sized pieces and shape them to fit the pans. I find the best way to do this is to flatten each piece with the palm of my hand, then gently roll it up and pop it into the pan with the fold underneath. Then I press the sides and corners down so that the center of the loaf is higher, coming up into a nice dome shape.

Put the loaves in a warm place with the damp cloth again and preheat the oven to 475°F (240°C).

They'll take about 30 minutes to rise: as soon as the dough is just peeping over the tops of the pans, put them into the oven. Don't let them over-rise or they'll collapse in the oven, but if there is still some rise left in them the heat will give them a final boost and they'll have a lovely domed crust.

Once it has risen, the bread can be baked as it is, or it can be finished by being brushed and

sprinkled with various ingredients. For a crusty loaf, brush with salted water (1 part salt to 3 parts water); if you want a shiny golden finish, use creamy milk, soy milk or beaten egg; or melted butter or margarine for a crisp, crunchy crust. After being brushed, the loaves or rolls can be sprinkled with cracked wheat, poppy seeds, sesame seeds or other seeds such as caraway or cumin.

After the loaves have been in the oven for 10 minutes, turn the heat down to 400°F (200°C) and bake for a further 25 minutes.

Turn the loaves out of their pans straight away — if they're done, they will sound hollow when you tap them on the bottom with your knuckles — and leave them on a wire rack to cool. If they don't sound hollow, pop them back in the oven, without their pans, for a few more minutes.

Tip
You can make two large loaves and one small loaf if you'd prefer; large loaves take about 10 minutes longer to bake.

Granary Cob
Granary flour (a brand name) only available in the UK, is a malted flour made up by mixing 3 cups of extra strong wholemeal flour with ½ cup of wheat bran and ½ cup of cracked wheat. Cracked wehat is wholegrain that has been crushed or cut into small pieces to give a nice chewy texture. 1-3 teaspoons of malt extract can be added too, but is not essential.

Guide to bread rising times

First rising times

IN A WARM PLACE 74°F (23°C)
45–60 minutes
e.g. an airing cupboard, by a radiator

AT ROOM TEMPERATURE 65–70°F (18–21°C)
1½–2 hours

IN A COOL ROOM OR LARDER
8–12 hours

IN THE FRIDGE
up to 24 hours
(brush the dough with oil and cover the bowl with cling film to prevent a hard crust forming)

Second rising (proving) times

IN A WARM PLACE 74°F (23°C)
30 minutes
e.g. an airing cupboard, by a radiator

AT ROOM TEMPERATURE 65–70°F (18–21°C)
40–50 minutes

IN A COOL ROOM OR LARDER
2–3 hours

IN THE FRIDGE
up to 12 hours
(brush the dough with oil and cover with cling wrap; leave at room temperature for 15 minutes before baking)

Almond braid

This is a beautiful, flaky braid with a moist filling of almond paste, a sticky apricot glaze and topped with crunchy sliced almonds. It's fun to make and worth the effort.

MAKES ONE LARGE PASTRY ❄

½ quantity of croissant dough (see page 374)
8oz (225g) almond paste (see page 345)
2 tbsp apricot jam, strained and warmed
2 tbsp sliced almonds
a little confectioner's sugar, for dusting

Roll out the dough to a rectangle about 14in x 10in (35cm x 25cm).

Roll the almond paste into a strip 13in (33cm) long and 3in (7.5cm) wide and place down the center of the dough, so that there is about 3½in (9cm) of dough either side of it.

Make diagonal cuts in the pieces of dough either side of the almond paste, about ½in (1cm) apart, then fold alternate strips over to make a braid effect, tucking in the top and bottom ends neatly.

Place the braid on a baking sheet, cover and leave to rise for about 30 minutes or until puffy.

Preheat the oven to 425°F (220°C). Bake the braid for 25–30 minutes until crisp and golden.

When it comes out the oven, brush it with apricot jam and sprinkle sliced almonds down center. Cool on a wire rack, then dust with confectioner's sugar.

Bran bread v

This high-fiber bread tastes good and has a pleasantly light texture.

MAKES TWO 1LB (450G) LOAVES ❄

½oz (15g) fresh yeast or 2 tsp dried yeast and ½ tsp sugar or ¼oz sachet easy-blend yeast
17fl oz (475ml) warm water
1½lb (700g) plain wholewheat flour
2oz (50g) bran
1 tbsp sugar
2 tsp salt
1 tbsp oil

Dissolve the fresh or dried yeast in a cup of the measured water; if you're using dried yeast add the ½ teaspoon of sugar too. Leave for 10–15 minutes until frothed up.

Mix the flour, bran, sugar, salt and oil in a large bowl, also the easy-blend yeast (if using). If you're using other types of yeast, add them now.

Add the water and mix to a dough. Knead for 5–10 minutes, cover and leave until doubled in bulk: about 1 hour in a warm place.

Knock back, knead lightly, shape and put into greased loaf pans. Cover and leave until the dough has doubled in size again; about 30 minutes.

Preheat the oven to 450°F (230°C).

Bake the bread for 10 minutes, turn the setting down to 400°F (200°C) and bake for 25 minutes more, then turn the bread out onto a wire rack to cool.

Easy baps v

Quick and simple to make using easy-blend yeast, these are delicious warm for breakfast or with a savory filling.

MAKES 8 BAPS ❄

5fl oz (150ml) milk or soy milk
5fl oz (150ml) water
½ stick (50g) butter or pure vegetable margarine
8oz (225g) plain wholewheat flour
8oz (225g) strong white bread flour, plus extra for dusting
1 tsp salt
1 tsp sugar
¼oz sachet of easy-blend yeast

Heat the milk, water and butter gently until the butter melts; cool to lukewarm.

Mix the flours, salt, sugar and yeast in large bowl, add the milk mixture and mix to a dough.

Knead for 5 minutes, put into a bowl, cover and leave in a warm place for about 1 hour or until doubled in bulk.

Preheat the oven to 425°F (220°C).

Knock back the dough and knead briefly. Divide it into eight pieces, form into smooth rounds, dust with flour and place well apart on a floured baking sheet.

Cover and leave in a warm place for 15–20 minutes or until well risen. Bake for 15–20 minutes. Cool on a wire rack.

Bread rolls

Warm homemade rolls are wonderful for serving with so many dishes and they're really not difficult to make. This recipe is based on half a 3lb 5oz (1.5kg) bag of flour. If you don't like egg, you can replace this with a little extra milk.

MAKES 24 ROLLS ❄

7fl oz (200ml) hand-hot water
1 tbsp dried yeast and ½ tsp sugar
    or ¼oz sachet easy-blend yeast
1lb 10oz (750g) wholewheat flour,
    plus extra for dusting
2 tsp salt
1 tbsp sugar
½ stick (50g) butter, plus extra for
    greasing
7fl oz (200ml) milk
1 egg, beaten

If you're using ordinary dried yeast, put the water into a small bowl and stir in the yeast and the ½ tsp of sugar. Leave to one side for 10 minutes to froth up.

Meanwhile put the flour (and the yeast if using easy-blend), salt and the 1 tablespoon of sugar into a bowl and rub in the butter.

Pour the frothed-up yeast (or the water if using easy-blend yeast) into the center of the flour and add the milk and egg; mix together to make a firm but pliable dough.

Turn the dough out and knead it for 10 minutes, then put it back into the bowl, cover with a clean damp cloth, stand the bowl inside a large plastic bag and leave until it's doubled in size.

This takes about 1 hour in a warm place or 1–2 hours just standing on a work surface, depending on how warm the room is.

When the dough has risen, preheat the oven to 425°F (220°C).

Punch down the dough, knead it again lightly then divide it into 24 pieces.

Form the pieces into rounds then flatten them with the palm of your hand and place them on greased baking sheets, 1in (2.5cm) apart, to allow room for them to spread. Cover them with a clean damp cloth and leave in a warm place for 20–30 minutes to double in size.

Sprinkle the rolls with a little flour then bake them for 15 minutes. Cool on a wire rack.

It's easy to vary these rolls: roll them in flour and place them closer together, ½in (1cm) apart, for soft rolls you pull apart or brush with melted butter or beaten egg for a crisp crust.

VARIATION
Freezer rolls

It's very convenient to be able to take a batch of partly cooked rolls from the freezer, finish them off in the oven and serve them fresh and warm. You can do this if you bake them first at a low temperature, then freeze them, defrost them as needed then bake them at a higher temperature. Follow the previous recipe but bake the rolls at 300°F (150°C) for 20 minutes, just to "set" the rolls. Cool them completely, then pack in plastic bags and freeze. To use, let the rolls thaw out at room temperature for 45–60 minutes, then bake at 450°F (230°C) for 10 minutes. They can be cooked while still frozen, but will take a bit longer — about 15 minutes.

Brioches

These classic French rolls make a delicious breakfast treat.

MAKES 12 BRIOCHES ❄

½oz (15g) fresh yeast or 2 tsp dried yeast plus ½ tsp sugar or ¼oz sachet easy-blend yeast
2 tbsp warm water
8oz (225g) strong white bread flour
½ tsp salt
1 tbsp sugar
½ stick (50g) butter, softened, plus extra for greasing
3 eggs, beaten

Dissolve the fresh or dried yeast in the warm water; if using dried yeast add the sugar too. Leave for 10–15 minutes or until frothy.

Mix the flour, the easy-blend yeast (if using), salt and sugar; if you're using dried or fresh yeast, add that, then mix in the butter and eggs to make a sticky dough.

Knead the dough for 5 minutes, adding a little more flour if necessary.

Put the dough into a bowl, cover and leave for 1–1½ hours or until doubled.

Punch down and divide into 12 pieces. Remove a quarter of each piece, then roll the rest into a ball and place in a greased 12-hole bun tin. Make hole in the center with your finger. Roll the remaining piece of dough into a small ball and place on top.

Cover and leave to rise for 1 hour until puffed up. Preheat the oven to 450°F (230°C). Bake the brioches for 10 minutes and serve warm.

Cheddar and walnut bread

Serve this crusty, richly flavored bread warm from the oven with homemade soup, pâté or cheese and salad.

MAKES ONE ROUND LOAF ❄

½oz (15g) fresh yeast or 2 tsp dried yeast and ½ tsp sugar or ¼oz sachet easy-blend yeast
7fl oz (200ml) hand-hot water
10oz (275g) plain wholewheat flour
1 tsp salt
1 tbsp (15g) butter, plus extra for greasing
3oz (75g) Cheddar cheese, grated
2oz (50g) shelled walnuts, chopped

Dissolve the fresh or dried yeast in the water; for dried yeast, add the sugar too. Leave for 10–15 minutes or until frothy.

Mix the flour and salt in a bowl, plus the easy-blend yeast (if using); rub in the butter.

Add the yeast liquid, if you're using fresh or dried yeast, or the water if you're using easy-blend yeast, and mix to a fairly soft dough.

Knead for 5–10 minutes, put the dough into a bowl, cover with a clean damp cloth and leave until doubled in size — about 1 hour in a warm place.

Knock back the dough and knead in the cheese and nuts. Form into a round loaf and place on a greased baking sheet. Cover and leave until well risen (about 20–30 minutes).

Bake the loaf at 450°F (230°C) for 10 minutes, then turn the setting down to 400°F (200°C) and bake for a further 15–20 minutes. Cool on a wire rack.

Christmas fruit loaf

The candied fruits make this a pretty, jewelled loaf. It's nice for Christmas because it's festive without being too rich. The best way to get the crushed cardamom is to buy some cardamom pods at a health-food or Indian store and crush them using a pestle and mortar or with the back of a spoon — then keep the seeds and discard the pods. You can leave it out, but cardamom does give a beautiful flavor and is a useful flavoring for curries and spicy rice dishes, too.

MAKES ONE LARGE LOAF ❄

1 stick (125g) butter, softened, plus extra for greasing
3½fl oz (100ml) lukewarm milk
½ tsp superfine sugar
2 tsp dried yeast or ¼oz sachet easy-blend yeast
1lb (450g) wheatmeal flour
a pinch of salt
¼ cup (50g) soft dark brown sugar
½ tsp crushed cardamom
2 tsp vanilla essence
rind of ½ lemon
8oz (225g) mixed candied fruits, chopped
2 eggs, beaten

First grease a 2lb (900g) loaf pan with butter.

If you're using dried yeast, put the milk into a small bowl, stir in the sugar and leave to one side to froth up.

continued next page

Mix together the flour, the easy-blend yeast (if using), salt and soft brown sugar, and rub in the butter; add the cardamom, vanilla essence, lemon rind, candied fruit and eggs.

Make a well in the center and pour in the yeast mixture, or the milk if using easy-blend yeast. Mix to a soft dough, adding a little more flour if necessary, then knead for 10 minutes.

Put the dough into an oiled bowl, cover with a clean damp cloth then with a plastic bag and leave it in a warm place until doubled in bulk — about 1 hour.

Punch the dough down, knead it again lightly, form into a loaf shape and put into the prepared pan.

Cover the loaf with the cloth and plastic bag again and leave in a warm place for about 30 minutes to rise.

Preheat the oven to 350°F (180°C).

When the loaf has come up to the top of the pan, bake it until it's golden and crisp. If it's done, the loaf will sound hollow when turned out of its tin and tapped on the base; if not, pop it back into the oven for a few more minutes.

Leave on a wire rack to cool. It's nice served with a rich pudding, like pashka (see page 330), or sliced and buttered for brunch or tea.

Croissants

These are really satisfying and fun to make.

MAKES 12 CROISSANTS ❄

1lb (450g) strong white bread flour
¼oz sachet easy-blend yeast
1 tsp sugar
1¾ sticks (200g) butter
1¼ cups (275ml) warm water
beaten egg, to glaze

Put the flour into a bowl or electric mixer along with the yeast, sugar and 1oz (25g) of the butter. Rub in the butter, then pour in the water and mix to a dough. Knead for 5 minutes, then roll it out to a long rectangle about ½in (1cm) thick.

Dot one-third of the remaining butter over the top two-thirds of the dough, leaving a ½in (1cm) border. Fold the bottom third of the dough up over the center, then fold the top third down.

Turn the dough so the fold is on the right-hand side; press the edges with the rolling pin to seal.

Repeat the rolling and folding twice, using the rest of the butter.

Put the dough in a plastic bag in the fridge for 1 hour, then roll it into a rectangle 22in x 14in (54cm x 35cm) and cut in half lengthways.

Cut each strip into six triangles with a 6in (15cm) base. Roll the triangles up from the base, brush with egg, curve into crescents and place on two greased baking sheets. Prove for 30 minutes.

Preheat the oven to 425°F (220°C).

Bake the croissants for 15–20 minutes or until puffed up, flaky and golden brown.

Crumpets v

Crumpets are fun to make and surprisingly quick and easy. If you haven't got crumpet rings, you can use egg-poaching rings. I have also successfully used an 7in (18cm) tart ring, cutting the crumpet into quarters for serving!

MAKES ABOUT 12 CRUMPETS ❄

½oz (15g) fresh yeast or 2 tsp dried yeast and ½ tsp sugar or ¼oz sachet easy-blend yeast
11fl oz (300ml) hand-hot milk, or soy milk, and water, mixed
8oz (225g) strong white bread flour
1 tsp superfine sugar
1 tsp salt
butter or margarine, for greasing

Dissolve the fresh or dried yeast in the milk and water; if using dried yeast, add the ½ teaspoon of sugar too. Leave for 10–15 minutes to froth up.

Combine the flour, easy-blend yeast if using, sugar and salt in a bowl. Add the yeast liquid (or just the milk and water if using easy-blend yeast) and mix to a smooth batter.

Cover with a clean damp cloth and leave in a warm place for 45 minutes or until frothy.

Grease a frying pan and crumpet rings with butter.

Place the rings in the frying pan, set over a low heat. Half fill the rings with the batter.

Cook gently for about 5 minutes until the tops are set and covered with little holes.

Remove the rings, turn the crumpets over to cook for 1–2 minutes. Serve immediately or allow to cool, then toast them.

Danish pastries

Light, crisp and not too sweet, Danish pastries are ideal for serving with coffee on a special occasion. They take time to make, but are not difficult; I found it particularly satisfying to produce a wholewheat version that was light and delicious. They freeze well, but leave the final icing until just before serving.

MAKES 18 PASTRIES (SIX OF EACH VARIETY) ❄

1 quantity of croissant dough (see opposite)
2oz (50g) mixed dried fruit
3 tbsp (40g) superfine sugar
1 tsp pie spice
4oz (125g) marzipan
beaten egg, to glaze
glacé icing (see page 345)
sliced almonds, to decorate

Roll the dough out ½in (1cm) thick and divide into three equal pieces.

Roll out one of these pieces into an oblong 12in x 8in (30cm x 20cm), sprinkle with the dried fruit, sugar and spice and roll up like a jelly roll. Cut into six pieces, make two deep cuts in each and open out slightly.

Cut both remaining pieces of dough into six and roll each into a square 4in (10cm).

Cut the marzipan into 12 pieces. Make six of these into 1in x 4in (2.5cm x 10cm) strips.

Place a strip of marzipan down the middle of six squares of dough, fold the pastry over and press the edges to seal. Make 4–5 gashes along the edge.

Form the rest of the marzipan into rounds, place one in the center of each remaining square of dough and fold the corners to the center.

Brush all the pastries with beaten egg.

Preheat the oven to 425°F (220°C).

Leave the pastries for 20 minutes, until puffy, then bake for 20 minutes. Cool, then ice and sprinkle with sliced almonds.

Easy rosemary focaccia v

This is such a quick and easy recipe for a beautifully light and fragrant loaf.

SERVES 4–6

5oz (150g) plain wholewheat flour
5oz (150g) strong white bread flour
5 tsp salt
¼oz sachet easy-blend yeast
2 tbsp olive oil, plus extra for greasing
about 7fl oz (200ml) warm water

FOR THE TOPPING

leaves from 2–3 rosemary sprigs
1 tsp good-quality sea salt
2 tbsp olive oil

Put both the flours into a food processor with the salt, yeast and oil and process for half a minute. Add the water through the feeder tube of the food processor to make a soft dough. Leave in the food processor, with the top on, for about 45 minutes, until the dough has doubled in size.

Preheat the oven to 425°F (220°C).

Put the dough into a well-oiled 8in (20cm) square pan, pressing it well into the corners.

Make several indentations all over with your fingers, scatter the rosemary and sea salt over the top, drizzle with the oil and bake for 25 minutes or until the dough is risen and cooked right through. Serve warm.

French bread v

It's fun to make your own baguettes; they are delicious, have a crispy crust and the smell in the house when they're baking is mouth-watering.

MAKES TWO BAGUETTES ❄
1oz (25g) fresh yeast or ½oz (15g) dried yeast and ½ tsp sugar or ¼oz sachet easy-blend yeast
1¼ cups (275ml) hand-hot water
1½lb (700g) strong white bread flour
2 tsp salt
2 tsp sugar
2 tbsp (25g) butter or pure vegetable margarine, softened, plus extra for greasing
yellow cornmeal or extra flour, for coating

If you're using fresh or dried yeast, dissolve the yeast in the water; if using dried yeast, add the ½ teaspoon of sugar too. Leave for 10–15 minutes until frothy.

Combine the flour, salt and remaining sugar in a large bowl, plus the easy-blend yeast (if using). Rub in the butter.

Add the yeast and water (or just the water if using easy-blend yeast), and mix to a dough, adding a little more water if necessary.

Knead for 10 minutes, then put the dough into a clean bowl, cover with a clean damp cloth and leave until doubled in size — about 1 hour in a warm place.

Knock back the dough, knead briefly, put the dough back into the bowl, cover and leave to rise again: 40–45 minutes.

Knock back, divide the dough in two, then sprinkle the work surface with cornmeal and roll the dough into two long thin baguettes.

Place the baguettes on a greased baking sheet, cover and leave to prove for 30 minutes.

Brush with cold water, then bake at 400°F (200°C) for 1 hour, brushing the crust with cold water every 10–15 minutes.

Granary cob v

This crusty round loaf is delicious with butter and honey.

MAKES ONE 2LB (900G) LOAF ❄
1oz (25g) fresh yeast or ½oz (15g) dried yeast and ½ tsp sugar or ¼oz sachet easy-blend yeast
15fl oz (425ml) hand-hot water
1½lb (700g) granary flour (see pg 370)
1 tbsp sugar
1½ tsp salt
2 tbsp (25g) butter or pure vegetable margarine, softened, plus extra for greasing
cracked wheat, for topping

Dissolve the fresh or dried yeast in a cup of the measured water; if using dried yeast add the ½ teaspoon of sugar. Leave for 10–15 minutes until frothed up.

Put the flour, 1 tablespoon of sugar and the salt into a large bowl and add the easy-blend yeast (if using). Rub in the butter or margarine, then pour in the yeast and water (or just the water if using easy-blend yeast) and mix to a dough. Knead for 5–10 minutes, put back in the bowl, cover with a clean damp cloth and leave until doubled in bulk: 1 hour in a warm place.

Knock back, knead lightly and shape into a round. Sprinkle with cracked wheat. Place on a greased baking sheet, then cut a deep cross in the top. Cover and leave in a warm place for 30 minutes or until well risen.

Preheat the oven to 425°F (220°C). Bake for 40–45 minutes, then cool on a wire rack before serving.

Herb bread v

Served warm from the oven, fragrant herb bread is delicious with soup. This bread takes just 2 hours to make from start to finish.

MAKES ONE 1LB (450G) LOAF
6 tbsp milk or soy milk
6 tbsp hot water
½oz (15g) fresh yeast or 2 tsp dried yeast and ½ tsp sugar or ¼oz sachet easy-blend yeast
10oz (275g) wholewheat flour
4 tsp sugar
1 tsp salt
2 tbsp (25g) butter or margarine, softened, plus extra for greasing
1 small onion, grated
½ tsp each oregano and rosemary

Mix the milk and water; if you're using fresh or dried yeast, blend it with the milk and water. If using dried yeast add the ½ teaspoon of sugar too; in either case, leave for 10–15 minutes to froth.

Combine the flour, easy-blend yeast (if using), sugar and salt in a large bowl. Rub in the butter or margarine and add the onion and herbs. Pour in the liquid and yeast (or just the liquid if using easy-blend yeast) and mix to a dough.

Knead for 5–10 minutes. Put the dough back into the mixing bowl, cover with a clean damp cloth and leave until doubled — 45 minutes in a warm place.

Preheat the oven to 450°F (230°C). Knock back the dough, shape and place in a greased 1lb (450g) loaf pan. Cover and leave for 20–30 minutes to rise.

Bake for 10 minutes, then reduce the oven setting to 400°F (200°C) for 25 minutes. Serve warm.

Hot cross buns v

Fragrantly spiced buns, fun to make and delicious served warm.

MAKES 12 BUNS ❄
1 quantity of bread roll dough (see page 372), kneaded and risen once
½ tsp each pie spice, ground cinnamon and freshly grated nutmeg
3oz (75g) currants
1½oz (40g) chopped mixed citrus peel
2oz (50g) sugar
3oz (75g) shortcrust pastry (see page 257)
2 tbsp milk or soy milk

Knock back the dough, then add the spices, currants, chopped mixed peel and half the sugar. Knead the dough until they're mixed in.

Divide the dough into 12 pieces, form into rounds and place 1in (2.5cm) apart on a greased baking sheet.

Cover with a clean damp cloth and put in a warm place for 30 minutes or until well puffed up.

Preheat the oven to 425°F (220°C).

To make the crosses, roll out the pastry thinly, cut into strips and arrange a cross on top of each bun. Bake for 20 minutes.

Heat the milk and remaining sugar until the sugar is dissolved, then brush over the buns. Cool on a wire rack.

Mixed grain bread v

This bread has a delicious flavor and chewy texture and it was a great favorite with my youngest daughter, Claire, when she was little.

MAKES ONE 1LB (450G) LOAF ❄
½oz (15g) fresh yeast or 2 tsp dried yeast and ½ tsp sugar or ¼oz sachet easy-blend yeast
7fl oz (200ml) hand-hot water
6oz (175g) wholewheat flour
3oz (75g) rye flour
1oz (25g) cracked wheat
3oz (75g) medium oatmeal
1 tsp salt
1 tbsp oil, plus extra for greasing

If you're using fresh or dried yeast, dissolve it in the water; if you're using dried yeast, stir in the sugar too. Leave in a warm place for 10–15 minutes or until frothy.

Combine the flours, the easy-blend yeast (if using), the cracked wheat, oatmeal, salt and oil in a large bowl.

Pour in the yeast and water (or just the water if you're using easy-blend yeast and mix to a dough).

Knead the dough for 10 minutes, place in a bowl, cover with a samp cloth and leave until doubled in bulk — about 1 hour in a warm place.

Knock back the dough, knead briefly, shape and put into a greased 1lb (450g) loaf pan. Cover with a clean damp cloth and leave in a warm place until doubled in size.

Bake the loaf at 425°F (220°C) for 10 minutes, then turn the oven setting down to 400°F (200°C) for a further 20 minutes. Cool on a wire rack.

Nut, raisin and honey bread

A slightly sweet bread that's delicious sliced and buttered.

MAKES ONE 1LB (450G) LOAF ❄

½oz (15g) fresh yeast or 2 tsp dried
   yeast and ½ tsp sugar or ¼oz
   sachet easy-blend yeast
5fl oz (150ml) warm water
8oz (225g) plain wholewheat flour
1 tsp salt
1 tbsp (15g) butter, plus extra for
   greasing
2oz (50g) each sliced almonds,
   raisins and honey

If you're using fresh or dried yeast, dissolve it in the water; for dried yeast add sugar too and leave it for 10–15 minutes or until frothy.

Mix the flour, the easy-blend yeast (if using) and the salt in a bowl. Rub in the butter.

Mix to a dough with the yeast and water (or just the water if using easy-blend yeast), then knead for 5–10 minutes.

Put the dough into the bowl, cover with a clean damp cloth and leave until doubled in size — about 1 hour in a warm place.

Knock back the dough, then knead in the almonds, raisins and honey.

Shape the dough and place in a greased 1lb (450g) loaf pan. Cover and leave until the center of the bread has risen 1in (2.5cm) above top of pan.

Bake at 450°F (230°C) for 10 minutes, then turn down to 400°F (200°C) for a further 20–25 minutes. Turn out onto a wire rack to cool.

Opposite: Nut, raisin and honey bread

Pear bread

Serve slices of this Swiss pear bread warm with coffee or hot with cream for a delicious dessert. You can leave out the kirsch and wine but they do give a beautiful flavor for a special occasion. You can buy dried pears from health-food stores.

MAKES ONE LARGE LOAF ❄

2oz (50g) butter, plus extra for
   greasing
5 tbsp lukewarm milk
1 tsp dried yeast or ¼oz sachet easy-
   blend yeast
¼ tsp superfine sugar
5oz (150g) plain wholewheat flour
5oz (150g) strong white bread flour
a pinch of salt
½ cup (125g) soft brown sugar
1 egg, beaten
1 cup (275ml) water
4oz (125g) dried pitted prunes
8oz (225g) dried pears
2oz (50g) seedless raisins
rind and juice of ½ lemon
¼ tsp ground cinnamon
¼ tsp freshly grated nutmeg
1 tbsp each of dry red wine and
   kirsch (optional)
Milk or beaten egg, to glaze

Grease a large baking sheet with butter; leave to one side.

If you're using dried yeast, put it into a small bowl with the milk, stir in the sugar and yeast. Leave in a warm place for the yeast to froth up.

Put the flours and salt into a large bowl and stir in the easy-blend yeast (if using) and rub in the butter and add half the soft brown sugar.

Make a well in the center and pour in the yeast and milk (or just the milk if using easy-blend yeast),

then add the beaten egg. Mix everything together to make a smooth, soft dough, adding a little more flour if necessary.

Turn the dough onto a floured work surface or board and knead it for 10 minutes, then place in a clean, oiled bowl, cover it with a clean damp cloth then put the bowl inside a large plastic bag and leave it in a warm place for about 1 hour or until it has doubled in bulk.

Meanwhile put the water, prunes, pears and raisins into a small pan and heat gently until soft, thick and dry. Strain, finely chop or blend the mixture, then add the lemon rind and juice, the remaining sugar, the cinnamon and nutmeg, plus the wine and kirsch (if using). Don't make the mixture too liquid — it needs to hold its shape.

To assemble the pear bread, take the risen dough and knead it for a minute or two, then put it onto a lightly floured work surface or board and roll out into a large square, about 15in x 15in (38cm x 38cm) and not more than ¼in (6mm) thick.

Spread the fruity filling over the square to within about 1in (2.5cm) of the edges. Fold the edges over to enclose the filling, then roll it firmly like a jelly roll and put it onto the prepared baking sheet. Prick the pear bread all over, cover with a clean damp cloth and put it into a warm place for 20 minutes to rise.

About 15 minutes before the pear bread is ready, preheat the oven to 350°F (180°C). Brush the milk or beaten egg over and bake it in the center of the oven for about 35 minutes or until it's golden brown and crisp. Serve warm.

Poppy seed braid v

Delicious white bread with crunchy poppy seeds.

MAKES ONE LARGE BRAID ❄
1oz (25g) fresh yeast or ½oz (15g)
    dried yeast and ½ tsp sugar or
    ¼oz sachet easy-blend yeast
15fl oz (425ml) warm dairy or soy milk
1½lb (700g) strong white bread flour
1½ tsp salt
1½ tsp sugar
½ stick (50g) butter or margarine
beaten egg, or soy milk, to glaze
poppy seeds, to decorate

Blend fresh or dried yeast with the milk; for dried yeast add the ½ teaspoon of sugar too. Leave for 10–15 minutes or until frothy.

Put the flour, easy-blend yeast (if using), salt and 1½ teaspoons of sugar into a large bowl, then rub in the butter or margarine.

Add the yeast and milk, or just the milk if you're using easy-blend yeast, and mix to a dough.

Knead for 10 minutes, put into a bowl, cover with a clean damp cloth and leave until doubled in bulk — about 1 hour in a warm place.

Knock back the dough, knead briefly, then make a braid: divide the dough into three equal pieces, roll each into a sausage about 12in (30cm) long, fat in the middle and tapering at the ends. Start braiding from the center, finishing the ends off to a neat point. Place on a greased baking sheet, cover and leave to prove for 30 minutes or until puffy.

Preheat the oven to 450°F (230°C). Brush the braid with beaten egg or with soy milk, sprinkle with poppy seeds and bake for about 35 minutes. Cool on wire rack.

Fast-and-easy bread v

If you've never made bread before, this is the one to start with. It doesn't need kneading and it really is as quick as making a simple cake. The texture is a little different from ordinary bread, being moister, which means that the bread keeps well and the flavor is very good. You can bake one 2lb (900g) loaf, but I think it comes out better in two smaller pans. You do need to use 100 per cent wholewheat flour for this recipe to work.

MAKES TWO 1LB (450G) LOAVES ❄
15fl oz (425ml) hand-hot water
1 tbsp dried yeast and ½ tsp sugar or
    ¼oz sachet easy-blend yeast
butter, for greasing
1lb 2oz (500g) plain wholewheat
    flour
1½ tsp sugar
1½ tsp salt
cracked wheat, to decorate

If you're using dried yeast, put the water into a jug or bowl and stir in the yeast and ½ teaspoon of sugar. Leave to one side for 10 minutes — it will froth up like a glass of beer.

Thoroughly grease two 1lb (450g) loaf pans or one 2lb (900g) pan.

Put the flour, 1½ teaspoons of sugar and salt and the easy-blend yeast (if using), into a large bowl, or the bowl of your electric mixer.

Pour in the frothy yeast mixture or just water (for easy-blend yeast) and mix well to a smooth but sticky dough — it won't be firm enough to knead.

Spoon the dough into the pans or pan — it needs to come halfway up the sides. Sprinkle with some cracked wheat, pressing it down lightly with the back of a spoon.

Cover the bread lightly with cling film and leave it to rise. It needs to come to within ½in (1cm) of the top of the pan and this takes approximately 30 minutes at room temperature. (The bread will rise a bit more when it gets into the oven.)

Preheat the oven to 400°F (200°C) after the bread has been rising for 15 minutes. Bake the bread for 30 minutes for two small loaves, 40 minutes for one large.

Turn out the bread and cool on a wire rack.

Tip
If you like this bread you might like to make a larger batch. Use a whole 3lb 5oz (1.5kg) bag of flour and treble all the ingredients except the yeast: 4½ cups (1.3 litres) water, 2 level tablespoons of sugar, 1 slightly rounded tablespoon of salt and 2 tablespoons (or one sachet) of dried yeast or 2 x ¼oz sachets easy-blend yeast. These quantities make six small or three large loaves.

Rye bread with molasses and cumin v

This loaf has lovely deep flavors and is wonderful with homemade red beet soup (see page 12) or spread with butter or soft goat cheese.

MAKES TWO ROUND LOAVES ❅
1oz (25g) fresh yeast or ½oz (15g) dried yeast plus ½ tsp sugar or ¼oz sachet easy-blend yeast
13fl oz (375ml) warm water
12oz (350g) rye flour
12oz (350g) wholewheat flour
1 tbsp salt
1 tbsp (15g) butter or pure vegetable margarine, plus extra for greasing
½ cup (125g) black molasses
2 tsp cumin seeds

Dissolve the fresh or dried yeast in the water; if you're using dried yeast, add the sugar too. Leave 10–15 minutes to froth.

Mix the flours, the easy-blend yeast (if using) and the salt; rub in the butter or margarine, then add the molasses, cumin and yeast liquid (or just the water if using easy-blend yeast).

Mix to a dough and knead for 5–10 minutes.

Place the dough in a bowl, cover and leave until doubled in size — about 1 hour in a warm place.

Knock back the dough and knead again briefly. Form into two round loaves, place on greased baking sheets, cover and leave for 30 minutes or until well risen.

Preheat the oven to 450°F (230°C). Bake the loaves for 10 minutes, then reduce the oven setting to 400°F (200°C) and bake for 25 minutes. Leave to cool.

Swedish tea ring v

A pretty semi-sweet yeast cake that is made in the form of a ring and decorated with icing, cherries and almonds.

SERVES 8–10 ❅
1 quantity of dough as given for poppy seed braid (see opposite), kneaded and risen once
½ stick (50g) butter or pure vegetable margarine, melted
¼ cup (50g) soft dark brown sugar
1 tsp ground cinnamon

TO DECORATE
1 quantity white glacé icing (see page 345)
a small handful of glacé cherries
1–2 tbsp sliced almonds

Knock back the dough, then roll into a rectangle 9in x 12in (23cm x 30cm).

Brush the rectangle of dough with melted butter or margarine, then sprinkle with the sugar and cinnamon.

Roll the dough up like a jelly roll then form into a ring.

Place the ring of dough on a greased baking sheet and, with scissors, make slashes at an angle, 1in (2.5cm) apart, and pull out the cut sections.

Cover and leave in a warm place until puffy: about 30 minutes.

Preheat the oven to 375°F (190°C). Bake the ring for 30–35 minutes. Decorate with glacé cherries and nuts.

Savarin

A light and spongy savarin, made in a ring mold, glossy with syrup glaze, filled with poached or fresh fruit — perhaps red wine-poached pears (see page 332), or fresh figs — and decorated with crystallized fruits, sugared flowers and mint leaves (see page 338), makes a colorful and spectacular dessert for a special occasion.

SERVES 8–10 ❅
1 level tbsp dried yeast or ¼oz sachet easy-blend yeast
6 tbsp lukewarm milk
2 tbsp (25g) superfine sugar
8oz (225g) strong white bread flour
1 tsp salt
4 eggs, beaten
1 stick (125g) butter, softened, plus extra for greasing

FOR THE SYRUP AND GLAZE
½ cup (125g) superfine sugar
¼ cup water
¼ cup rum
¼ cup apricot jam, sieved and warmed

TO DECORATE
fresh, poached or glacé fruit
crystallized mint leaves or flowers
whipped cream

Put the dried or easy-blend yeast, milk, sugar and 2oz (50g) of the flour into a bowl and mix. Cover and leave in a warm place until frothy — about 60 minutes.

continued next page

Add the rest of the flour, the salt, eggs and butter. Beat vigorously for 4–5 minutes, then pour the mixture into a greased 8–9in (20–23cm) ring mold to half fill it.

Cover with a clean damp cloth and leave in a warm place for 30–40 minutes or until it has risen to about ½in (1cm) from the top.

Bake at 375°F (190°C) for about 20 minutes or until a skewer inserted into the center comes out clean.

Turn out onto a wire rack, cool, then prick with a skewer.

Heat the ½ cup (125g) sugar in the water until dissolved; add the rum, pour over the cake, then brush with the apricot jam.

Place the cake on a serving plate and fill the center with fresh or poached fruit, and decorate as desired with crystallized mint leaves and flowers to make it look gorgeous. Serve with whipped cream.

Wholewheat stick v

MAKES ONE LOAF ❊
½oz (15g) fresh yeast or 2 tsp dried yeast and ½ tsp sugar or ¼oz sachet easy-blend yeast
1¼ cups (275ml) warm water
1lb (450g) plain wholewheat flour
1 tsp salt
1 tbsp (15g) butter or pure vegetable margarine, plus extra for greasing
cracked wheat, to decorate

Blend fresh or dried yeast with water; if using dried yeast add the sugar. Leave for 10–15 minutes to froth up.

Combine the flour, easy-blend yeast (if using) and salt in a large bowl. Rub in the butter or margarine. Add the yeast and water (or the warm water if you're using easy-blend yeast) and mix to a dough.

Knead for 5–10 minutes or until smooth, then put the dough into a bowl, cover and leave until doubled in bulk: 1 hour in a warm place.

Knock back the dough. Knead briefly, then roll into a long stick, sprinkle with cracked wheat and place on a greased baking tray.

Slash the top of the stick several times with a sharp knife, then cover with cling film and leave in a warm place for 30–45 minutes or until puffy.

Preheat the oven to 425°F (220°C). Bake the stick for 25–30 minutes or until it sounds hollow when tapped. Cool on a wire rack.

Yeasted fruit cake

This light, semi-sweet cake is easy to make and great with a cup of coffee.

MAKES ONE 8IN (20CM) ROUND CAKE ❊
1 level tbsp dried yeast or ¼oz sachet easy-blend yeast
6 tbsp lukewarm milk
2 tbsp (25g) sugar
8oz (225g) strong white bread flour
1 tsp salt
2 eggs, beaten
1 stick (125g) butter, softened, plus extra for greasing
grated rind of 1 orange
8oz (225g) mixed dried fruit
3 tbsp demerara sugar

Put the dried or easy-blend yeast, milk, sugar and 2oz (50g) of the flour into a bowl and mix together. Cover with a clean damp cloth and leave in a warm place until sponge-like — about 30–40 minutes.

Add the rest of the flour, the salt, beaten eggs, butter, grated orange rind and mixed dried fruit. Beat vigorously for 4–5 minutes.

Pour into a greased 8in (20cm) deep-sided cake pan. Cover, leave for 30–40 minutes or until doubled in size.

Sprinkle with demerara sugar. Bake at 400°F (200°C) for 30–35 minutes. Cool on a wire rack.

Easy homemade pizza

This homemade pizza recipe couldn't be easier

SERVES 4 ❄
5oz (150g) plain wholewheat flour
5oz (150g) all-purpose flour
½ tsp salt
¼oz sachet easy-blend yeast
2 tbsp olive oil
about 7fl oz (200ml) warm water

FOR THE SAUCE AND TOPPING
1 onion, chopped
1 tbsp olive oil
2 garlic cloves, crushed
14oz can chopped tomatoes
1 tsp dried mixed herbs
salt and freshly ground black pepper
4–6oz (125–175g) mozzarella cheese, grated
8–12 black olives, pitted

For the quick dough, put both the flours into a food processor with the salt, yeast and olive oil and process for half a minute.

Add the water through the tube of the food processor, to make a soft dough. Leave in the machine, with the top on, for about 45 minutes or until doubled in size.

Meanwhile make the sauce. Fry the onion in the oil, with a lid on the pan, for 10 minutes or until tender. Add the garlic, tomatoes and herbs and simmer for 10 minutes or until thick. Remove from the heat and season with salt and pepper.

Heat the oven to 425°F (220°C). Put a large baking sheet into the oven to heat up.

Roll the dough out as thinly as you can and place on a baking sheet. Cover with the tomato sauce, scatter with the grated cheese and arrange the olives on top.

Slide into the oven on top of the hot large baking sheet — this will give heat from underneath, which will help the pizza to be crisp.

Bake for about 15 minutes or until the dough is crisp and the cheese melted and golden brown.

Tip
If you find that there is a bit more dough base than there is topping to cover it, you can make this into garlic bread. Roll it out thinly, then make some shallow cuts in the top. Cover with olive oil mixed with crushed garlic. Bake alongside the pizza.

VARIATIONS
Mushroom pizza

Make this as described, but omit the olives and top the pizza with 4oz (125g) washed and finely sliced button mushrooms, brushed lightly with olive oil.

Herby pizza

Sprinkle the top of the tomato pizza with plenty of dried oregano or marjoram; drizzle a little olive oil over the top to moisten the herbs.

Pepper pizza

Wash and seed a large green or red pepper. Cut into strips and arrange on top of the pizza with or without olives.

Artichoke pizza

Finely slice 3–4 marinated artichoke hearts; arrange the slices on top of the tomato mixture, along with the olives.

Index

Acknowledgements

I'm so grateful to HarperCollins – and especially my commissioning editor Lizzy Gray – for inviting me to write this beautiful *New Complete Vegetarian* and for masterminding the whole project and assembling such a brilliant team: Kate Whitaker, who worked with food stylist Joss Herd and prop stylist Penny Markham to produce the beautiful photographs; Kathy Steer and Kate Parker who edited it with such care and attention to detail; Andrew Barron who designed the layout and made it all look so good; and James Annal, who designed the amazing jacket. My warm thanks go to them all, and also to my own support team: my agent Barbara Levy, and my dear family, especially my husband, Robert.

About the author

Photograph courtesy of Ant Jones for *Cook Vegetarian!* magazine

Rose Elliot is Britain's foremost vegetarian cookbook author and her books have won her popular acclaim all over the world. Rose has written over 60 vegetarian or vegan books, with total sales of over three million copies.

During the period in which Rose has been writing, the number of people who are vegetarian, or partially vegetarian, has surged from a few hundred thousand to over four million in the UK, and many have said it was Rose's books that inspired them to change.

Rose contributes to a variety of magazines and newspapers. She successfully pioneered the popular vegetarian column in the *Guardian Weekend* magazine and writes a regular column in the monthly magazine *Cook Vegetarian!* Rose has appeared many times on radio and television; one of her broadcasts on Radio 4's "Woman's Hour" led to the largest number of requests for recipes ever known. Rose is patron of the Vegetarian Society in the UK, VIVA! (Vegetarian International Voice for Animals) and The Vegetarian and Vegan Foundation. In 1999 Rose received the MBE from the Queen "for services to vegetarian cookery."

For more about Rose, information on her books, vegetarian foods and the vegetarian lifestyle, visit www.roseelliot.com.